DATE DUE

AM. H.C.
LIBRARY

M. H. C.
LIBRARY DEC 11 '72

GAYLORD — PRINTED IN U.S.A.

CITY AND REGION

INTERNATIONAL LIBRARY OF SOCIOLOGY AND SOCIAL RECONSTRUCTION

Founded by Karl Mannheim

Editor: W. J. H. Sprott

A catalogue of the books available in the INTERNATIONAL LIBRARY OF SOCIOLOGY AND SOCIAL RECONSTRUCTION, and new books in preparation for the Library, will be found at the end of this volume

CITY AND REGION

A GEOGRAPHICAL INTERPRETATION

by
ROBERT E. DICKINSON
Professor of Geography, University of Leeds

Andrew S. Thomas Memorial Library
MORRIS HARVEY COLLEGE, CHARLESTON, W. VA.

LONDON
ROUTLEDGE & KEGAN PAUL LTD
60677

*First published 1964
by Routledge & Kegan Paul Ltd
Broadway House, 68–74 Carter Lane
London, E.C.4*

*Printed in Great Britain
by Butler & Tanner Ltd
Frome and London*

© *Robert E. Dickinson 1964*

*No part of this book may be reproduced
in any form without permission from
the publisher, except for the quotation
of brief passages in criticism*

301.36
D56 c

CONTENTS

PREFACE   *page* xv

PART I. THE URBAN SETTLEMENT AS REGIONAL CENTRE

1. THE REGION AS A SOCIAL UNIT   3
1. THE SOCIAL UNIT
2. THE REGIONAL CAPITAL
3. THE METROPOLITAN CONCEPT
4. CITIES AND SIZE
5. THE URBAN REGION

2. THE NATURE OF THE CITY   19
1. THE HISTORICAL ASPECT
2. THE DYNAMICS OF URBAN GROWTH
3. THE CHANGING STRUCTURE OF THE CITY
4. THE GROWTH OF THE URBAN AREA: CENTRALIZATION
5. CONCENTRATION
6. DECONCENTRATION
7. DECENTRALIZATION
8. RECENTRALIZATION
9. RESIDENTIAL SEGREGATION
10. DOMINANCE, INVASION, AND SUCCESSION

3. THE CITY AS A REGIONAL CENTRE   49
1. THE URBAN CENTRE
2. THE SERVICE FACTOR
3. THE ADMINISTRATIVE FACTOR
4. THE INDUSTRIAL FACTOR: THE ECONOMIC BASE
5. THE BASIC *v.* NON-BASIC RATIO
6. THE HIERARCHY OF CENTRES

4. TOWN–COUNTRY RELATIONS   87
1. GERMANY
2. FRANCE
3. UNITED STATES
4. ENGLAND

CONTENTS

PART II. THE STRUCTURE OF THE CITY

5. THE STRUCTURE OF THE CITY page 125
1. Theories of Urban Growth
2. Examples of Urban Growth: Chicago
3. Examples of Urban Growth: Paris
4. Examples of Urban Growth: Stockholm

6. THE CITY AS A WHOLE 163
1. The General Build of the City
2. The Urban Plan
3. The Rural–Urban Fringe
4. The Location of Industry
5. The Distribution of Population
6. Areas of Social Disorganization and Blight
7. The Journey to Work
8. Traffic Flows
9. Sequent Occupance: The Case of New York

7. REGIONS WITHIN THE CITY: THE NATURAL AREA 199
1. The Natural Area
2. Ecological Studies of Natural Areas
3. The Neighbourhood Unit: A British Study
4. The Natural Area as a Planned Unit
5. Institutions and Service Areas
6. Commercial Centres in the Urban Area
7. Commercial Centres in the San Francisco Area
8. The Structure of the Central Business District

PART III. THE CITY-REGION

8. THE REGIONAL RELATIONS OF THE CITY 227
1. The Concept of the City-Region
2. The Town–Country Symbiosis
3. The Structure of the City-Region
4. The Urban Tract
5. Zurich: An Example
6. The Regional Impact of the City on Rural Economy
7. The Regional Impact of the City on Industrial Location
8. The Regional Impact of the City on Social and Economic Conditions

CONTENTS

9. THE REGIONAL RELATIONS OF THE CITY: CASE STUDIES page 257
1. Lyon
2. Cologne
3. Leeds and Bradford
4. Salt Lake City

10. THE CITY-REGION IN THE UNITED STATES: I 284
1. Development of the Metropolitan Region
2. Growth of Urban Population
3. Urban Regions
4. The Changing Structure of the Central City
5. The Urban Impact on the Countryside: The Highway
   Appendix to Chapter 10: The Metropolitan District of the United States Census Bureau

11. THE CITY-REGION IN THE UNITED STATES: II 311
1. The Functional Classification of Cities
2. The Definition of Metropolis and Region
3. The Regions and Their Capitals: The Manufacturing Belt
4. Centres of the Middle South
5. The Cotton Belt (The South)
6. The West-Centre
7. The West
   Appendix to Chapter 11: Standard Metropolitan Areas, 1940–60

12. THE CITY-REGION IN WESTERN EUROPE 336
1. Urban Agglomerations
2. Urbanized Regions
3. The Areas of City-Access
4. The Functions of the Cities
5. Commuting Patterns
6. Capitals and Their Regions: France
7. Capitals and Their Regions: Germany
8. A Theoretical Hierarchy of Cities

13. THE CITY-REGION IN BRITAIN 394
1. Definition of the Conurbations
2. The Build of the Major Conurbations
3. Recent Growth Trends: Greater London
4. The Growth of the Central Business Districts
5. The Major Cities and their Regions: Food Supplies

vii

CONTENTS

6. BUSINESS AND FINANCE
7. THE MAJOR CITIES AS CULTURAL CENTRES
8. THE URBAN HIERARCHY AND URBAN FIELDS
9. COMMUTING AREAS
10. STRUCTURE OF A CITY-REGION: METROPOLITAN LANCASHIRE

PART IV. REGIONALISM AND THE CITY-REGION

14. THE CASE FOR THE REGION page 435
1. THE REGION AS AN INTERMEDIATE AREA BETWEEN LOCAL UNIT AND STATE
2. CULTURAL AND POLITICAL REGIONALISM
3. REGIONAL TOWN PLANNING
4. PRACTICAL OR *AD HOC* REGIONS
5. PROBLEMS OF REGIONAL DEVELOPMENT

15. REGIONALISM IN FRANCE 447
1. THE REGIONAL MOVEMENT
2. THE HISTORICAL PROVINCES
3. THE MODERN REGIONS AND THEIR CAPITALS
4. POST-WAR PLANNING REGIONS

16. REGIONALISM IN BRITAIN 467
1. THE DEMAND FOR NEW REGIONS
2. THE TOWN-PLANNING REGION
3. REGIONAL SCHEMES IN THEORY AND PRACTICE
4. LOCAL GOVERNMENT AREAS
5. METROPOLITAN ORGANIZATION
6. POST-WAR TOWN AND COUNTRY PLANNING IN ITS REGIONAL ASPECTS
7. REALISM AND THE NEW REGIONS

17. REGIONALISM IN THE UNITED STATES 505
1. THE DEMAND FOR NEW REGIONS
2. STATE PLANNING
3. REGIONAL PLANNING
4. GEOGRAPHICAL REGIONS
5. PLANNING AND DEVELOPMENT REGIONS
6. METROPOLITAN REGIONALISM

18. REGIONALISM IN GERMANY 529
1. THE PROBLEM OF *NEUGLIEDERUNG*
2. INTER-WAR PROPOSALS
3. INVESTIGATION AND ACTION IN THE THIRTIES
4. POST-WAR DEVELOPMENTS
5. POST-WAR SITUATION

CONTENTS

19. INTERNATIONAL ASPECTS OF REGIONALISM: CONCLUSION   page 554
1. CITY-REGION AND STATE
2. FRONTIER ZONES
3. THE CITY-REGION IN THE STATE
4. PROBLEMS OF REGIONAL ECONOMIC DEVELOPMENT
5. THE CITY AND ITS REGION
6. THE VIABILITY OF THE LOCAL GOVERNMENT UNIT
7. THE MONSTER-CITY AND THE NOTION OF MEGALOPOLIS
8. CONCLUSION

INDEX   577

LIST OF FIGURES

1a. The theoretical distribution of Regional Service Centres (after Christaller) *page* 53
1b. The hexagonal pattern of Regional Service Areas (after Christaller) 53
2. System of Central Places (after Christaller and Berry) 55
2a. Scania, South Sweden. Urban Settlements and their Hinterlands (after Godlund). 73
3. The Distribution of Towns as Regional Service Centres in South Germany (after Christaller) 75
4. The Urban Hierarchy in England and Wales (after Smailes) 78
5. The Sevenfold Hierarchy of Nested Functions (after Philbrick) 82
6. Areal Functional Organization in the Chicago Region (after Philbrick) 84
7. Medieval Towns and Routes in South Germany (after Gradmann) 88
8. Central Places and their Fields in Bavaria (after Boustedt) 93
9. The Urban Field of Siegen (after Schöller) 96
10. Central Places and Service Areas of the Siegerland, Germany (after Schöller) 97
11. Central Places in Southern France (after Coppolani) 99
12. Central Places in Southwestern Wisconsin (after Brush) 108
13. Central Places in Southern England (after Bracey) 113
14. Markets in East Anglia in the Sixteenth Century 116
15. Markets in East Anglia in the Early Nineteenth Century 117
16. Bus centres and their Hinterlands in East Anglia (after Green) 118
17. Concentric Theory of Urban Growth (after Park and Burgess) 126
18a. The Sector Theory of Urban Growth (after Hoyt) 128
18b. The Multiple Nuclei Theory of Urban Growth (after Harris and Ullman) 128
19. Chicago: Layout and Land Use 132
20. Paris: Layout and Land Use 133
21. The main highways of Chicago and Paris 137
22. Population Changes in the City of Chicago, 1950-60 (after Chicago Plan Commission) 138

LIST OF FIGURES

23. Density of Population in Chicago (after Chicago Plan Commission) page 140
24. Community Areas of Chicago, 1959 (Department of City Planning, Chicago) 142
25. The Topographical Formation of Paris (after Demangeon) 144
26. Population Changes in Greater Paris, 1936–54 (after Bastié) 146
27. The Urban Zones of Paris, 1951 (after Chombart de Lauwe) 147
28. The Urban Zones of Paris, 1960 (after Bastié) 149
29. The Distribution of Population in Inner Stockholm, 1950 (after William-Olsson) 153
30. The Differentiation of Inner Stockholm, 1960 (after William-Olsson) 154
31. The Structure of Greater Stockholm (after William-Olsson) 159
32. Summer Cottages around Stockholm, 1953–54 (after William-Olsson) 161
33. Cities of the United States: Percentage of Downtown Travel by Public Transport in early 1950's (after W. Owen) 191
34. Cities of the United States: Mass Transport and Economic Growth (after W. Owen) 191
35. The City-Region of Zurich (after Carol) 245
36. Lyon Region: Distribution of the Silk and Artificial Fibre Industries (after Labasse) 259
37. Lyon Region: Telephone Connections between towns (after Labasse) 260
38. Lyon Region: Commuting Traffic (after Labasse) 263
39. Lyon Region: Secondary residences in the Region (after Labasse) 264
40. Cologne Region: Land Use 267
41. Cologne Region: Growth Trends (after Meynen) 270
42. The Zones of Influence of Leeds and Bradford 276
43. Yorkshire Marketing Areas (after *Geographia*) 278
44. Salt Lake City: Tributary Areas 281
45. United States: Population Distribution, 1960 (from U.S. Census) 286
46. United States: Standard Metropolitan Statistical Areas, 1960 (from U.S. Census) 291
47. United States: Areas of City Access 294
48. Suburbanization in the United States: Percentage of rural non-farm to total population in rural territory by counties (from U.S. Census) 305
49. United States: Metropolitan Regions (by the author, 1932) 313

LIST OF FIGURES

50. United States: Metropolitan Regions (after Bogue, 1949) page 314
51. United States: Major Trade Areas (after Thomas and Crisler) 314
52. United States: Newspaper Circulation Areas 315
53. United States: Federal Reserve Districts and Branch Territories, 1954 (after Duncan et al.) 316
54. The Competitive Hinterlands of New York and Boston (after H. L. Green) 322
55. Western Europe: Growth of Metropolitan Areas, 1950–60 338
56. Urbanized Areas in Western Europe 340
57. Western Europe: Population Changes, 1950–60 342
58. Urbanized Regions of West Germany (after Isenberg) 346
59. Conurbations of the 'Randstad Holland' (after Winsemius) 348
60. France: Location of Decentralized Industries, 1950–58 (after Faucheux) 351
61. Areas of City Access in Western Europe 353
62. Functional Classification of Towns in Western Europe (after W. William-Olsson, *Economic Map of Europe*) 355
63. Commuting in West Germany (by *Kreise*) 360
64. Commuting in Belgium: Percentage of resident-employed to total employed in each commune (after O. Tulippe) 361
65. Spheres of Influence of French Cities (after G. Chabot) 368
66. Road Traffic Flows in France (after Boudeville) 370
67. Occupational Structures in West Germany (after *Die Erwerbspersonen nach Vorherrschenden Wirtschaftsbereichen*, 1950) 372
68. Urbanized Regions of West Germany (after Boustedt) 374
69. Traffic Flows in Württemberg (after R. Hoffmann) 375
70. Zones of Influence of Frankfurt-am-Main (after Schrepfer) 376
71. The City-Region of Frankfurt: Commuting to Selected Cities in Hessen, 1950 (after Hessen, Einzugsbereiche, 1950) 377
72. The City-Region of Frankfurt: Newspaper Circulations of the Central Places (after Hartke) 378
73. Historical Provinces of West Germany (after *Die Neugliederung des Bundesgebietes*, 1955) 379
74. Metropolitan Cities and their Regions in West Germany (according to the author) 381
75. Commuting in Rhineland-Westphalia (after *Landesplanungsstelle*, Düsseldorf) 383
76. Commuting areas in Rhineland-Westphalia 384
77. The Service and Supply Areas of the Ruhr (after Pounds) 385
78. Commuters to Volkswagen Plant, Wolfsburg, June 1955 (data from the Wolfsburg plant) 386

LIST OF FIGURES

79. Commuters to B.A.S.F. (Badische Analin- und Sodafabrik, Ludwigshafen), June 1955 (data from the B.A.S.F.) *page* 387
80. The Hierarchy of Capitals and their Regions in Western Europe (after Christaller) 388
81. Urbanized Areas in Britain, 1951 395
82. The Conurbations of England and Wales (after Freeman) 397
83. The Growth of Population in Britain, 1951–61 398
84. England and Wales: Marketing Regions (after *Geographia*) 423
85. England and Wales: Second-order Centres and their Hinterlands (after Carruthers) 424
86. England and Wales: Daily Out-movement of Workers in 1951 (after Lawton) 426
87. England and Wales: Daily Out-movement to Selected Towns, 1951 (after Lawton) 427
88a. South-east Lancashire and North-east Cheshire: Built-up areas in 1951 (after L. P. Green) 430
88b. Journey to Work to Manchester, Salford, Stockport, Stretford and Urmston, 1951 (after L. P. Green) 430
88c. South-east Lancashire and North-east Cheshire: Bus Service Areas of towns with Populations of 3,000 and over in 1946–47 (after L. P. Green) 430
88d. Metropolitan Lancashire: Proposed Two-tier Reform of Local Government Areas (after L. P. Green) 430
88e. The South-east Lancashire Conurbation, 1951 (after the Census) 431
88f. The South-east Lancashire Conurbation: Density of Population, 1951 (after L. P. Green) 431
89. France: Economic Regions (after Coppolani) 449
90. France: Historical Provinces 454
91. France: Regions proposed by Charles-Brun (1911) 457
92. France: Regions proposed by Vidal de la Blache (1910) 459
93. France: National Planning Regions 463
94. France: Regions proposed by Gravier 466
95. England and Wales: Civil Defence Regions and twelve other Administrative Divisions 471
96. England and Wales: Divisions proposed by C. B. Fawcett, 1917, revised in 1942 476
97. England and Wales: Regions proposed by G. D. H. Cole, 1921 477
98. England and Wales: Regions proposed by E. G. R. Taylor, 1941 480
99. England and Wales: Regions proposed by E. W. Gilbert, 1941 481
100. England and Wales: Standard Regions of the Census 482

LIST OF FIGURES

101. England and Wales: Regions of Electricity Boards, 1947 *page* 483
102. England and Wales: Regions of Hospital Boards, 1945   484
103. England and Wales: Regional Planning Organization of the Ministry of Town and Country Planning in 1946   485
104. England and Wales: Green Belts and New Towns (after Ministry of Housing and Local Government, *The Green Belts*, 1962)   498
105. Great Britain: Development districts in Britain (after Manners)   500
106. United States: Agricultural Regions (after Baker)   511
107. United States: Regions of Manufacturing Intensity (after Strong)   511
108. United States: Possible Planning Regions based upon major Metropolitan Influence (after National Resources Board)   512
109. United States: Possible Planning Regions based upon composite Planning Problems   512
110. United States: Economic Provinces and Economic Regions (after Bogue)   513
111. United States: National Resources Board Planning Districts, based upon Group-of-States arrangements   516
112. United States: National Resources Board Water Resources Districts, based upon a single function   516
113. United States: Population Regions (after U.S. Census)   522
114. United States: Socio-economic Regions (after Odum and Wooster)   522
115. Germany: Regions proposed by Preuss in 1918 (after Vogel)   532
116. Germany: Regions proposed by Luther in 1928 (after Vogel)   534
117. Germany: Economic Regions in 1927 (after Scheu)   538
118. Germany: Regions proposed by Weitzel in 1928 (after Vogel)   539
119. Germany: Regions proposed by Baumann in 1928 (after Vogel)   540
120. Germany: Regional Planning Districts in 1936   540
121. Germany: Regions proposed by Münchheimer in 1949   543
122. West Germany: Regions proposed by Christaller in 1949   545
123. West Germany: Regions of Planning Authorities, based on administrative regions, 1952 (after Institut für Raumforschung)   546
124. West Germany: Changes in State areas as expressed by popular vote (after Schöller)   548
125. Socio-economic Units in Baden-Württemberg (after *Landesplanungstelle*, Stuttgart)   565

PREFACE

This book, like its predecessor in this series (*City Region and Regionalism*, 1947), is not about planning. It is concerned with the inherent geographical structure of society upon which planning must be based, and it insists that knowledge of the spatial anatomy of society must precede the treatment of its defects. The study is limited to the countries of the United States and western Europe, though its procedures and generalizations can be extended to other lands.

A basic feature of the life and organization of advanced societies is the cohesion of socio-geographic groups at various levels. There are many aspects to this field of study. We select for examination the role of the central place—be it hamlet, village, town, city, or metropolis—as a focus of human activity and organization and leadership in the service of a surrounding tributary area. This space-group is being subjected to profound changes under the influence of the forces of the twentieth century—notably ease of circulation, increased complexity of societal organization, and the increasing impact of urbanization. These changes present new problems to the societies of North America and western Europe, to say nothing of other parts of the world. We need to develop concepts and devise techniques for the study of the structure of these groupings, with respect to their areas and their centres, in order more fully to understand and provide for the planning of land and its use and the government and welfare of its occupants.

This field of study has been called 'human ecology' in the United States and 'social morphology' in France. It began in the United States with the work of Park, Burgess, and McKenzie at the University of Chicago in the twenties. It has undergone changes in scope among the human ecologists themselves, who now tend to discard the essentially geographic aspects of community structure. The more important theoretical statements and many substantive studies by sociologists and geographers are contained in a volume of articles collected and edited by Theodorson.[1] Other collections are by Mayer

[1] G. A. Theodorson, *Studies in Human Ecology*, Row, Peterson, Evanston, Ill., 1961.

PREFACE

and Kohn[1] and Hatt and Reiss.[2] The general scope of the field of study is dealt with in a book by Amos Hawley.[3] Among continental workers, particular attention is drawn to M. Halbwachs' little book on *Morphologie Sociale* (Collection Armand Colin, 1938), recently published in an English translation.[4] Some of the most significant work during the past twenty years has been concerned with the analysis of distributions and areal correlations with a mathematical approach. These quantitative aspects can be studied in the appropriate books and there is no need to repeat them here.[5] Finally attention is drawn to the work of Jean Gottmann on *Megalopolis: The Urbanized Northeastern Seaboard of the United States* (New York, 1961). This is a geographic study of this urbanized area that deals specifically with the problems handled in this book. It is an indispensable work, though unfortunately it appeared after this manuscript was complete. On various aspects of this field, see also *Regional Planning*, Seminar, Tokyo, 28 July to 8 August, 1958, United Nations, Department of Economic and Social Affairs, New York, 1959.

The nature, causes, and consequences of spatial factors are underestimated by social scientists and by planners, presumably because these factors are supposed to be obvious or beneath the serious consideration of the scientist, who is far more concerned with basic trends and laws. The geographer looks at particular places and the way in which spatial phenomena interact one on the other. He must classify his data on this basis and formulate general trends and laws. But he must also use these data to see, when other things are not equal, as in point of fact they never are, how they operate to account for the siting of particular places and the way in which they hang together in area. The explosion of the city and the range of association of the city over a still wider area, and the areal differences within the urban area are all concerned with just such problems.

[1] H. M. Mayer and C. F. Kohn, *Readings in Urban Geography*, University of Chicago Press, 1959.
[2] P. K. Hatt and A. J. Reiss, *Cities and Society. The Revised Reader in Urban Sociology*, Free Press, Glencoe, Ill., 1957.
[3] Amos Hawley, *Human Ecology. A Theory of Community Structure*, New York, 1950.
[4] M. Halbwachs, *Population and Society: Introduction to Social Morphology*, translated by Ottis Dudley Duncan and Harold W. Pfautz, Free Press, Glencoe, Ill., 1960.
[5] W. Isard, *Location and Space Economy*, Wiley, New York, and Chapman and Hall, London, 1956; and *Methods of Regional Analysis: An Introduction to Regional Science*, Wiley, New York and London, 1960. A Lösch, *Die räumliche Ordnung der Wirtschaft*, Fischer, Jena, 1940. C. Ponsard, *Economie et Espace: Essai d'intégration du facteur spatial dans l'analyse économique*, Sedes, Paris, 1955. O. Boustedt and H. Ranz, *Regionale Struktur- und Wirtschaftsforschung*, W. Dorn, Bremen, 1957. Attention is also drawn to the *Proceedings of the I.G.U. Symposium on Urban Geography Lund 1960*, edited by Knut Norborg, Lund, 1962, 602 pages.

PREFACE

The book falls into four parts. Chapters 1, 2, and 3 deal with the concept of the region as a social unit in terms of centre and field. It examines the role of the town as a regional centre and the dynamics of urban growth. Chapter 4 illustrates the nature of town–country relations in selected areas in the United States and western Europe. Chapter 5 contains several studies of particular cities. Then follow two chapters on the structure of the city as a whole (Chapter 6) and on the functional areas that make up the whole (Chapter 7). The next chapters deal with the nature of the relationships between the city and its environs (Chapter 8) and this is illustrated by several examples (Chapter 9). There follows, in terms of the foregoing concepts, a survey of the nature of the city-region in the United States (Chapters 10 and 11), in western Europe (Chapter 12) and, for more special consideration, in England and Wales (Chapter 13). The city and its explosion present fundamental problems in contemporary society—the re-organization of local government areas and major political units, regional and national planning, etc. This theme, under the general rubric of 'regionalism', is covered in the last chapters. The case for the region is briefly covered in Chapter 14. This is followed by chapters on regionalism in France (Chapter 15), England and Wales (Chapter 16), and the United States (Chapter 17). In view of its great importance we have added a chapter on Germany. This is on the assumption that our book on the *Regions of Germany* in this series is not likely to be reprinted and the treatment is brought up-to-date (Chapter 18). The concluding Chapter 19 considers certain international aspects of the whole problem of the city-region.

We have endeavoured to bring population data up-to-date but this is not always possible since the latest census data are not available for each country and in any case these will have to be thoroughly worked out and their implications examined before one can reach presentable conclusions. The vocabulary may oscillate between English and American usage. We are so divided in our allegiance that we prefer the difference to stand as between tram and street car, truck and lorry, and the like. Most of the maps have been redrawn. I am glad to acknowledge the assistance of my cartographer, Mr. John Collier, research assistant, Mr. John Louis Smith, and secretary, Mrs. Sybil Whiteley. I am especially indebted to my young colleague Dr. Barry J. Garner for giving much time to criticism and suggestions for Chapters 1, 2, 3, 8, 10, and 11.

ROBERT E. DICKINSON

ACKNOWLEDGEMENTS

Figs. 1a and 1b, 3, 14, 15, 17, 25, 42, 70, 89, 90, 91, 92, 95, 96, 97, 98, 99, 100, 101, 102, 103, 106, 107, 108, 109, 111, 112, 113, and 114 are reproduced from *City Region and Regionalism*, Kegan Paul, London, 1947.
Figs. 115, 116, 117, 118, 119, and 120 are reproduced from *The Regions of Germany*, Kegan Paul, London, 1944.

Acknowledgements are made to the authors and publishers for permissions to redraw, modify, or reproduce the following maps and diagrams:
Fig. 2 to W. Christaller (Das Grundgerüst Europas, *Frankfurter Geog. Hefte*, 1950). Fig. 4 to A. E. Smailes and the editors of *Geography* (Vol. 29, 1944). Figs. 5 and 6 to Allen Philbrick and the editors of *Economic Geography* (Vol. 33, 1957). Fig. 8 to O. Boustedt from a map presented to the I. G. U. symposium at Lund in 1960. Figs. 9 and 10 to P. Schöller and the Provinzial Institut für Westfälische Landes- und Volkskunde (Reihe I, Heft 8, Münster, 1955). Fig. 11 to J. Coppolani, *Le Réseau urbain de la France*, Paris, 1959. Figs. 12 and 13 to J. E. Brush and H. E. Bracey and the editor of the *Geographical Review* (Vol. 45, 1955). Fig. 16 to F. H. W. Green and the editor of the *Geographical Journal* (Vol. 116, 1950). Figs. 18a and 18b to C. D. Harris and E. Ullman and the editor of *Annals of the American Academy of Political and Social Sciences*, Philadelphia (Vol. 242, 1945). Figs. 22, 23, and 24 to the Chicago Plan Commission. Figs. 26 and 27 to M. Bastié and the editor of the *Annales de Géographie* (January–February 1958). Fig. 28 to M. Chombart de Lauwe and Presses Universitaires de Paris. Figs. 29, 30, 31, and 32 to W. William-Olsson, *Stockholm's Structure and Development*, Stockholm, 1960. Figs. 33 and 34 to W. Owen and the Brookings Institution, *The Metropolitan Transportation Problem*, 1956. Fig. 35 to Hans Carol and the editor of *Raumforschung und Raumordnung*, Heft 2/3, 1956, Bad Godesberg. Figs. 36 to 39 to J. Labasse, *La Région Lyonnaise*, Paris, 1960. Fig. 41 to E. Meynen in the *Festschrift zum Deutschen Geographentag*, Köln, 1960. Figs. 45 and 46 to the United States Bureau of Census, Fig. 50 to D. H. Bogue

ACKNOWLEDGEMENTS

and Fig. 51 to Thomas and Crisler, both taken by permission from O. D. Duncan et al., *Metropolis and Region*, Resources for the Future Inc., Johns Hopkins Press, 1960. Fig. 54 to H. L. Green and the editor of *Economic Geography* (Vol. 31, 1955). Fig. 58 to G. Isenberg and the Institut für Raumforschung (March 1957), Bad Godesberg. Fig. 59 to J. Winsemius and the editor of the *Tijdschrift voor Econ. en Sociale Geog.*, Rotterdam (Vol. 51, July 1960). Figs. 60 and 105 to G. Manners and the editor of *Economic Geography* (Vol. 38, 1962). Fig. 64 to the editor of the *Geographical Review* (Vol. 47, 1957). Fig. 62, based upon W. William-Olsson's Economic Map of Europe (wall map). Figs. 63 and 75 to the editor of the *Annals of the Association of American Geographers* (Vol. 49, December 1959). Fig. 66 to M. Boudeville, *Espaces Economiques*, Que Sais-Je series, 1962. Fig. 67 to map prepared by the Bundesamt für Landeskunde, Bad Godesberg (Director, E. Meynen). Fig. 68 to O. Boustedt and the *Akad. f. Raumforschung und Raumordnung* (Band XIV, 1960), Hanover. Fig. 69 to R. Hoffmann and the editor of *Raumforschung und Raumordnung*. Fig. 72 to W. Hartke and the editor of *Rhein-Mainische Forschungen* (Heft 32, 1952). Fig. 77 to N. J. G. Pounds, *The Ruhr: an historical and economic geography*, Faber and Faber, London, 1952. Figs. 78 and 79 to the B.A.S.F. and Volkswagen authorities for data provided in July 1955. Fig. 80 to W. Christaller and the editor of *Frankfurter Geog. Hefte* (1950). Fig. 81 to the Ordnance Survey and Ministry of Housing and Local Government. Fig. 83 to the Department of Geography, London School of Economics, and the editors of *The Times*, London (November 1962). Fig. 82 to T. W. Freeman, *The Conurbations of Great Britain*, Manchester University Press, 1959. Fig. 84 to *Geographia*, London (*Marketing and Media Survey*). Fig. 85 to I. Carruthers and the editor of the *Geographical Journal* (Vol. 123, September 1957), London. Figs. 86 to 87 to R. Lawton and the editor of *Town Planning Review*, Liverpool (1959), and *Tijdschrift voor Ec. en Soc. Geog.*, Rotterdam (1963). Fig. 88 to L. P. Green, *Provincial Metropolis*, London, 1959. Fig. 104 to *The Green Belts*, published by Ministry of Housing and Local Government, H.M.S.O., 1962. Fig. 110 to D. Bogue and the Glencoe Press (*Population of the United States*, 1959). Figs. 121 and 122 to W. Münchheimer and W. Christaller and the editor of *Frankfurter Geog. Hefte* (1951). Fig. 124 to P. Schöller and Provinzial Inst. f. Westfälisches Landes u. Volkskunde, (Band 12, 1959), Münster. Fig. 125 to Landesplanungsstelle, Stuttgart.

PART I

The Urban Settlement as Regional Centre

Chapter 1

THE REGION AS A SOCIAL UNIT

1. THE SOCIAL UNIT

The terms region and regionalism have been widely used in recent years with reference to a great variety of problems. All demand, in one form or another, the substitution of new geographical units for existing administrative units, which, as a legacy of the past, are quite unsuited to the requirements of modern society. Regional planning deals primarily with the physical planning of town and countryside, and the term is generally used in reference to an extension of town planning; indeed, in France it is often called 'urban regionalism'. It may include the general planning of resources, as in the organization and work of the Tennessee Valley Authority (T.V.A.) in the United States, an aspect which is becoming increasingly prominent in the planning programmes of other countries. Regionalism is also identified with the movement for the re-organization of local government and the devolution of administrative and legislative powers. The outstanding instance of all such aims being put into practice is in the total reconstruction of the economy and social structure of the U.S.S.R.

The term 'region' is undoubtedly one of the catchwords of our day among both popular and scientific writers. To the practical man of affairs a region is simply an area with certain characteristics (often mere size), in virtue of which it is a suitable unit for some particular purpose of business or administration. To the scientist, and above all to the geographer, a region is an area which is homogeneous in respect of some particular set of associated conditions, whether of the land or of the people, such as industry, farming, the distribution of population, commerce, or the general sphere of influence of a city. Such an association is discovered to exist in terms of a single common factor or in terms of a variety of interdependent areal factors. Regional investigation seeks to discover in what degree and over what areas selected phenomena are found to be homogeneous or 'regionalized'. The main problems of regional study, therefore, lie in the selection of suitable criteria for the recognition of such regional homogeneities, their representation, and the elucidation of the forces that shape them.

Some writers conceive of 'natural administrative units', that is, units suitable, in virtue of their being social and economic entities, to be used as administrative units. In this sense, a region is thought of as a 'natural' areal unit, natural in the sense that it is a real, existing unit, arising spontaneously from the very structure of society, in contrast to the 'artificial' administrative units, which have been imposed in the past and are often ill-adjusted to modern needs. Such a natural unit, it is argued, is the rational one to use as the basis for the organization of modern communities for any particular purpose—be it for planning town and countryside, developing resources, organizing a new system of local government, collecting statistical and census data, or for the regionalization of such public services as health, water supply, and housing. In all these respects new unit areas are required, differing certainly in character and extent for particular purposes, but better adapted to these purposes than the existing outmoded administrative units. Moreover, assuming that different areas are used, it is essential that there should be as close geographical co-ordination between them as is practicable.

In brief, many of the most vital problems of modern society find their common ground in the basic concept of the region—what kind of area it shall be, what purpose it shall serve, how it should work. Regionalization as a fact, if not regionalism as a movement in the French sense, is a fundamental feature of the organization of our national life. Business has long recognized its indispensability. Each of the countries of western Europe and North America is faced with the need for a new hierarchy of local government areas and new areas for purposes of planning and development within a nation-wide framework. It is upon these two aspects of regionalism that public attention has been concentrated in recent years.

All these varied problems have a common denominator, namely, the demand for a new socio-geographical unit in the place of the existing administrative unit. This idea is found in the notion of the 'social unit' indicated some years ago by the late Mr. Frank Pick as the essential basis of physical planning. In order to plan for the future, he wrote, it is essential to arrive at 'some understanding of the social unit upon which democracy is to be built'. For this purpose

'the integration of society demands a special study. . . . A *social unit* must be devised—rather must come to birth—not too large to destroy personal contact and not too small to fail to afford variety and diversity. And the social unit must involve all classes and carry within it no class distinction. How much preliminary thought is needed here,

THE REGION AS A SOCIAL UNIT

for if the unit is not rightly and naturally conceived, the social structure will never be securely built up. The town, the city, the metropolis itself, and finally the region will be aggregates of social units differentiated and combined to fulfil ever higher and broader conceptions of the good life.'[1]

This is, in effect, a restatement of the concept of regionalism, which has been elaborated on broad philosophical lines by such scholars as the late Patrick Geddes and, in more recent years, by Lewis Mumford, but which still requires much attention from the social scientist. In the words of Lewis Mumford in his *Culture of Cities* (London, 1938): 'The re-animation and re-building of regions as deliberate works of collective art is the grand task of politics for the coming generation.' It is essential to realize that in this sense a region is a geographical area with a considerable measure of unity in its activities, services, and organization. It is, in other words, *an area of common living*.

Much has been written in elaboration of this concept of a region. The idea has been associated particularly with geographers. It is still widely assumed that the geographer's prime concern is to examine similarities in social structure only in so far as they are attributable to a uniformity in the character of the land and its physical features. This limitation is now clearly admitted to be scientifically unsound. An area of common living can be defined only in terms of the key traits of that common living, that is, in terms of social considerations, not of a particular set of physical factors which condition only in part that pattern of living. This mode of approach throws emphasis on the study of regional associations, and recognizes that with a marked degree of regionalization there emerges a homogeneous area, clearly defined in its core, vaguely defined towards its borders, usually where it merges into adjacent regions of similar definition. Thus 'the culture economy of regionalism' takes into account 'the whole phenomenon of the new mobility of people, the migrations to and from cities', and it differs from 'the pure geographical area in that it is characterized not so much by boundary lines and actual limits as it is by flexibility of limits, by extension from a centre, and by fringe or border margins which separate one area from another'.[2] There is no need, however, to emphasize unduly this matter of the vagueness of the territorial limits of regions. In practice, there are many occasions when a

[1] Frank Pick, *Britain Must Rebuild*, Kegan Paul, London, 1941.
[2] H. W. Odum and H. E. Moore, *American Regionalism, A Cultural-Historical approach to National Integration*, New York, 1938. See also *Regionalism in America*, 20 essays ed. by M. Jensen, Madison, 1951.

regional limit is clearly defined, as, for instance, when it corresponds with a political frontier of old standing or with a marked physical divide. Changes in population density and economic structure or the keen competition of two adjacent cities may also give rise to a clearly marked cultural divide or what may be called a steep cultural gradient. The application of this concept was made very clear years ago by cultural anthropologists such as Wissler and Kroeber. It is basic to the numerous studies of this kind made by geographers and others in the areas of occidental society. The procedure rests essentially on the selection of a number of key criteria and the precise determination of the degree of their correlation place by place and the exact range of their distribution. Thus, such an entity has a core in which all traits occur, and outer areas of lower correlation, with breaks or gradients that may be very gradual or extremely sharp.

The region as a social unit must be examined in terms of those phenomena which provide the key to the social structure. This is a search for diagnostic criteria. These may well include such criteria as the intensity of economic intercourse, as reflected by the interchange of goods between one district and another, banking and credit relations, communications and accessibility; as well as common cultural elements—religious ties, traditions, the influence, past and present, of a dominant city, similarities of habits, standards, knowledge and skills.[1] Tests of regional homogeneity, states an American authority, may be applied 'by examining a few factors which would give a clue to the economic similarities and dissimilarities, to political cleavages or cohesion, and to the general cultural likenesses and differences'.[2] In addition to the basic considerations of agriculture and industry, three particular measurable criteria are suggested by the same authority—the volume of movement of vehicles, the more important banking ties, and the service areas of large mail-order houses. Other possible tests are the sphere of influence of educational institutions, as measured by the distribution of students' homes, religious affiliations, long-distance telephone communications, and the circulation of newspapers.[3] In this sense, the fullest measure of regional homogeneity is to be discovered not by considering each of these regional associations *per se*, but through the analysis of the ways in which they are interlocked with each other in space. Clearly, this approach demands a central regionalizing principle. This is undoubtedly to be found in the functions of the nucleated settlement as a regional centre.

[1] E. A. Gutkind, *Creative Demobilization*, Vol. 1, 1943, pp. 234–5.
[2] *Ibid.*, p. 235, quoted from the Report of the Pacific Northwest Regional Planning Commission to the National Resources Committee.
[3] *Ibid.*, p. 235.

THE REGION AS A SOCIAL UNIT

The ideal hierarchy of community associations, centred in village, town, city, or city sub-centre, is not to be thought of as something drawn out of the blue by the planner or the architect. It exists in the fabric of our society, and the geographical structure of this society must be thoroughly understood if we are to discover and rectify its maladjustments and to elaborate principles of planning in accordance with its needs. Consequently, we need to know the geographical web of existing space relations. These relations are complicated and their areas overlap widely, but they are integrated into what may be called socio-economic units through the medium of the central service centre, be it neighbourhood, town, or metropolis.

This conception of the integration of human circulations at successive levels as the potent regionalizing principle in the life and organization of society is basic to the whole framework of this book. While it involves, above all, what are commonly regarded as economic circulations, it also embraces social, cultural, and political associations viewed in the light of their historical development. A region conceived on this basis is an area of interrelated activities, kindred interests and common organization, brought into being through the medium of the routes which bind it to the settlement centres in which its institutions, services, and organizations are segregated.

Various objections have been made to the idea of the geographical continuity of the sphere of influence of a city and the arbitrary nature of any generalized line that may be drawn to embrace it. Indeed, the regional concept itself has recently been attacked.[1] Geographers have been demonstrating for a generation that no single area enjoys what O. D. Duncan has recently called 'a complete spectrum of relations' with a central city. Many studies recognize the tendency for common sets of relations to develop in sectors or zones around the city, but that generalized linear boundaries are obviously arbitrary. Moreover, it has long been apparent that the webs of relationships of a city, as also the area of collection and distribution of a port, involve close relations with certain areas and less intimate relationships with widely scattered places. But the fact remains that every city, as a centre of attraction and repulsion, is a dominating focus for a surrounding area.

Duncan's approach is that of a statistician rather than that of a geographer. We agree entirely on the point, with which he apparently takes issue, that 'there is no such thing as a single, uniquely defined "region" which manifests a full spectrum of city-regional

[1] O. D. Duncan and Associates, *Metropolis and Region, Resources for the Future*, Baltimore, 1960.

relationships'. Duncan should be aware from the literature (notably in languages other than English) that geographers have long since ceased to make such naïve assumptions. A 'hinterland' may indeed, as Duncan (by no means for the first time) points out, have 'holes in it'. Such an area is not a geographical continuity. These are what Duncan calls new refinements. But they are accepted and demonstrated in many studies by geographers. The 'geometry of city-region relationships' is certainly complex, but the fact that this author is approaching it from the angle of quantitative or statistical analysis obscures the realities of the relations between the city and its environs which historically is the most essential feature of the growth of cities. It is not true, as Duncan asserts, that 'the most worthy attempt to conceptualize city-region relationships—is Isard's inter-regional input-output model'. This statistical approach assumes that a region merely provides a framework for investigation. The problem of defining the spatial structure of the web of relationships of a city is a *terminus ad quem* not an *origo a qua*. Regionalization and the discovery of principles of regionalization are research objectives in themselves. They are based on empirical research from particular cases. The city is a human phenomenon, not simply a bundle of statistics. Its complex relations with its surroundings are as much cultural and administrative in nature as they are economic. They have developed and changed within the same area for many centuries in western Europe. The relations between the city and its surroundings—the role of the 'regional' factor in its development and present functions—cannot be adequately determined through statistical analysis. What is needed in addition is historical evaluation.

2. The Regional Capital

The idea of a regional capital or *chef-lieu* was first defined by the French advocates of regionalism. Such *chefs-lieux* were, in fact, regarded as the capitals of the geographical regions proposed as new administrative units. The great French geographer, Vidal de la Blache, defined the regions which exist in modern France on the basis of their history, culture, and, above all, orientation towards a central capital city, the regional capital. He wrote: 'It is not the number of its inhabitants, still less the number of its functionaries; it is not even the type of occupation which constitutes the regional capital. It is a superior element which enters into all aspects of its activity.' [1] Such a city is often termed by French writers a 'natural capital', which grows to importance without the intervention of high authority, by virtue of its favourable geographical position, and the enter-

[1] Vidal de la Blache, 'Les Régions Françaises', *Revue de Paris*, December 1910.

prise of its people. It is the *chef-lieu* of a large surrounding area, which, in the same sense, may be regarded as a 'natural' area, cutting across, and bearing little relation to the administrative divisions. For this region the city functions as a capital, despite its lack of political status.

Let us examine further this idea of a regional capital. Professor Raoul Blanchard, the distinguished dean of French geographers, wrote in 1910 as follows:

'It applies to a city, which owes its importance to its population and its prosperity, to its antiquity and its historical reputation (and generally both causes together), and which is, as it were, the head of the region. In it is established the central (state) authority; from it are issued orders and decisions; in it are centred administrative and judicial affairs, and the seats of tribunals and major administrative functions. Thus, it is a political capital. But the capital can have, and should have, other roles. As the head of a region, it must be guarded and defended, for it cannot fall with impunity into the hands of an enemy; it should, moreover, possess the authority to execute the will of the central State. The capital, then, has a military role. Intellectual influence, moreover, is almost an indispensable function on behalf of the region, whether it be through the medium of newspapers and other publications, or through educational institutions. Finally, the capital has an economic role, especially as it is almost always this economic importance which has brought in its train political pre-eminence. It is a centre of supply of foodstuffs for the surrounding regions; it is also their market; it directs their expansion; and these influences make themselves felt over a more or less wide area, the extent of which depends at once upon the commercial facilities presented by the country and on the degree of economic activity of the city, compared with that of neighbouring cities.[1]

In its economic role, Blanchard continues: 'It is, for a more or less extensive region, the city from whence come directions, in which there is the financial capital, and through which transactions are effected.'[2] Its commercial role takes various forms:

'In it are effected the buying and selling for the region which it commands. On the one hand, the capital serves as intermediary between the production of the region and its demands from the exterior; on the other hand, it sells to the region and supplies it with what it cannot produce, whether the city produces these goods itself, or

[1] R. Blanchard, *Grenoble: Étude de Géographie Urbaine*, 1911, augmented Grenoble, 1935, pp. 205-6.
[2] *Ibid.*, p. 221.

whether it has them brought from outside the region. Finally, on the routes which cross in the capital there pass in transit both the products going from one part of the region to another, and goods coming from or going to places outside the region.[1]

It is good to quote this conceptual framework as expressed by Professor Blanchard since it indicates the very early start of this kind of study, and it has inspired many other studies in France by his successors, particularly in cities such as Lyon and Grenoble, the last being for so many years the seat of Blanchard's work.

3. THE METROPOLITAN CONCEPT

This concept of a regional capital is practically identical with that of the city as an economic metropolis, which was elaborated by the American economic historian, N. S. B. Gras, forty years ago.[2]

The highest grade of city which serves as an outstanding centre of human affairs is termed an economic metropolis; the area which is dependent on it, its metropolitan area; and the type of organization which sustains it, metropolitan economy. Accepting the definition of Gras, metropolitan economy is 'the organization of producers and consumers mutually dependent for goods and service wherein their wants are supplied by a system of exchange concentrated in a large city, which is the focus of local trade and the centre through which normal economic relations with the outside are established and maintained'.[3] A city becomes metropolitan 'when most kinds of products of the district concentrate in it for trade as well as transit; when these products are paid for by wares that radiate from it; and when the necessary financial transactions involved in this exchange are provided by it'.[4] Such a city will have a population considerably larger than that of surrounding towns; it will be an independent centre of trade, with a large variety of regional industries and a large wholesale business; it will be a financial centre; and finally, a cultural and administrative centre. The structure of the metropolitan community, in terms of its distinctive functions and of the range of its web of activities and associations has been the subject of a vast amount of work during the past generation. Particularly important in the States was the work of the 'human ecologist', R. D. McKenzie, and, in the fifties, the work of Donald Bogue

[1] *Ibid.*, p. 222.
[2] N. S. B. Gras, *An Introduction to Economic History*, Harper, New York, 1922, and R. D. McKenzie, *The Metropolitan Community, Recent Social Trends Monographs*, McGraw-Hill, New York, 1933.
[3] Gras, *op. cit.*, p. 186.
[4] *Ibid.*, p. 294.

THE REGION AS A SOCIAL UNIT

of the Scripps Foundation. Many scholars have made contributions to various aspects of this field of study in the last twenty years.

The dominance of the economic metropolis is a basic feature of the organization of modern society, since it arises from that geographical specialization of function which is rooted in cheap and rapid transport. Moreover, the great complexity of our modern civilization brings to the city a further variety of functions which it performs for farms, factories, and people around it. Metropolitan economy is a universal feature of modern civilization. It *is* modern civilization. In the past, metropolitanism was confined to a few cities. Today many cities formerly tributary to the older metropolises are becoming increasingly independent of them. Several cities of Britain, such as Manchester, Birmingham, and Glasgow, have acquired a large measure of independence of London, as centres of organization, business, and opinion. They have become metropolitan in function and structure. Similarly in the United States, the cities of the Middle West and the Far West have passed rapidly through the phases of commerce and industry in serving their regional markets, and are now in large measure independent financial and cultural centres. It is true, however, that the status of such cities is not equal to that of New York or London, each of which not only serves its region, but is the central economic focus of the State, and at a still higher level, is an international economic and cultural entrepot. In Germany the case is different, for the historic metropolitan cities have in many cases long been the capitals of independent states, and have developed and maintained the functions of fully-fledged metropolitan cities without relation to Berlin. Examples are Munich, Hanover, and Stuttgart. Others have never enjoyed such political status, but they are outstanding economic centres. Examples are Cologne and Frankfurt. So strong and constant are the controls of location that the structure of modern metropolitan economy has been superposed upon the pattern of distribution of cities and towns which existed long before the modern era. It is true that the great growth of industrial population has added to their importance as industrial and commercial centres, but, without exception, all the large European cities that now rank as metropolitan centres enjoyed 'capital status' for centuries both as regional centres and as centres for specialized trade and industry.

The structure of the modern city shows two fundamental differences from the city of the past. In the first place, there has been a radical change in the character and complexity of city functions which is commensurate with the change in the structure of civilization itself. Secondly, the absence of rapid transport in the past necessitated the concentration of population in small areas within

THE URBAN SETTLEMENT AS REGIONAL CENTRE

which all needs could be satisfied and within which all the institutions of urban society were concentrated. In a word, centripetal forces have determined the structure and spatial distribution of towns. The most fundamental change today is the *specialization of function by place*, made possible by cheap mechanized transport, so that activities and institutions that were formerly concentrated within one town are now spread over a wide area. 'The modern metropolitan community, unlike the pre-motor city, obtains its unity through territorial differentiation of specialized functions rather than through mass participation in centrally located institutions.'[1] Centripetal forces still determine the character of both 'town' and 'city', but centrifugal forces have changed the structure of the urban community. One speaks currently of the 'exploding metropolis' and 'the dispersed city'. The modern city is consequently no longer a compact settlement unit. It is becoming the headquarters of a group of interrelated towns and satellite settlements, yet forming one community centred upon the city. This close interrelationship between widely scattered places, forming an integrated functional unit with subordinate centres in the towns but with its nerve centre in the city, is the essential characteristic of modern society.

The general spatial structure of the metropolitan or city-region was described as follows by the American sociologist, R. D. McKenzie, thirty years ago.

'The metropolitan (or city) region thus considered is primarily a functional entity. Geographically it extends as far as the city exerts a dominant influence. It is essentially an extended pattern of local communal life based upon motor transportation. Structurally, this new metropolitan regionalism is axiate in form. The basic elements of its patterns are centres, routes and rims. The metropolitan region represents a constellation of centres, the interrelations of which are characterized by dominance and subordination. Every region is organized around a central city or focal point of dominance in which are located the institutions and services that cater to the region as a whole and integrate it with other regions. The business sub-centres are rarely complete in their institutional or service structure. They depend upon the main centre for the more specialized and integrating functions.'[2]

This city or metropolitan region is not to be regarded as a clearly defined geographical unit with sharply defined limits. It is rather a constellation or cluster of centres around the capital. The influence of the latter is effected in its environs by a radiating system of

---
[1] R. D. McKenzie, *The Metropolitan Community*, 1933, p. 71.
[2] *Ibid.*, p. 70.

THE REGION AS A SOCIAL UNIT

traffic routes, and, further afield, by isolated single strands running to separate towns, each of which, in its turn, is a local centre of radiating routes through which it, rather than the metropolis, becomes the dominant centre for local affairs. It is in the 'suburban' area that the most potent influence is exercised by the metropolitan community. But this influence extends much further over a more vaguely defined 'trade area', which, though having little contact with the local institutions and life of the city, provides a wide penumbra to the inner area, and may be included in the general concept of the city-region.

'By reducing the scale of local distance, the motor-vehicle extended the horizon of the community and introduced a territorial division of labour among local institutions and neighbouring centres which is unique in the history of settlement. The large centre has been able to extend the radius of its influence; its population and many of its institutions, freed from the dominance of rail transportation, have become widely dispersed throughout surrounding territory. Moreover, formerly independent towns and villages and also rural territory have become part of this enlarged city complex. This new type of super-community organized around a dominant focal point and comprising a multiple of differentiated centres of activity differs from the metropolitanism established by rail transportation in the complexity of its institutional division of labour and the mobility of its population. Its territorial scope is defined in terms of motor transportation and competition with other regions. Nor is this new type of metropolitan community confined to the great centres. It has become the communal unit of local relations throughout the entire nation. Its development has introduced a vast amount of rearrangement of populations and institutions, a process which is still far from having attained an equilibrium.'[1]

4. CITIES AND SIZE

When does a city qualify for the title of metropolis? The population aggregates employed by statisticians and others are of limited use to designate city character generally, and the status of a city as a regional capital cannot be measured from the number of its inhabitants. The 100,000 and million figures are often used to indicate respectively 'large cities' and 'super-cities', or what have been facetiously called 'millionaire cities'. There is no doubt about recognizing the super-city which usually has over a quarter of a million inhabitants and often well over a million. It is normally a political capital,

[1] *Ibid.*, pp. 6-7.

though New York is a great exception, far larger in population than any other city in the country. Apart from mere size, one must look for the head offices of business, banks, stockbrokers, services, and for independent institutions for art and education, and for leadership in ideas. There is a grading in the importance of cities as regional centres of this kind and only a few come into the top category as fully-fledged metropolitan centres. On the other hand, the larger the city agglomeration and the greater the density of population in its environs the more effective will be its impact on the surrounding area and the closer the integration of the city and its environs.

Among the large European cities with over 100,000 inhabitants there is a clear distinction in the level of leadership as between the small regional capitals and the 'super-city', the true 'metropolis', or the 'primate city', with over 250,000 or usually well over a million people. Small though they are, with well under 250,000 people, such cities as Grenoble, Nancy, Dijon, Freiburg, or Münster each play the role of a regional capital. Each serves as the leader of the countryside and towns in an extensive tributary region. Each is an historic centre of economy and culture. Some in the past have been political capitals and cultural centres with ancient Universities. Today, each has a leading Press, a University, and is a pre-eminent centre of wholesaling, retailing, finance, and administration. They represent all that a majority of the townsmen and countryfolk ever see of city life. Yet cities of this small size can scarcely support such activities in very great number or quality, since they serve dominantly rural areas.

In a very different category are the super-cities which, in virtue of their very great size, enjoy all the functions of leadership. 'All over the world', writes Mark Jefferson, 'it is the law of the capitals that the largest city shall be super-eminent, and not merely in size, but in national influence.' This is the 'primate city'. Indeed, the same writer goes on to declare a law that 'a country's leading city is always disproportionately large and exceptionally expressive of national capacity and feeling'.[1] Probably the main distinction between one of these super-cities and the smaller cities is that the former is an independent 'head office', a heart to a national body. They are financial centres and headquarters of banks, exchanges, and big business. In Europe, all the political capitals of the present States fall into this category. In addition, however, there are many cities of the same order in the provinces, such as Manchester, Cologne, Munich, Lyon, Lille, and Milan. There are at least a dozen such metropolitan cities in the United States.

[1] Mark Jefferson, 'The Law of the Primate City', *Geographical Review*, Vol. XXIX, 1939, pp. 226–32.

THE REGION AS A SOCIAL UNIT

Thus, the idea of the regional metropolis is that of leadership over neighbouring tributary towns. Hence functions of leadership are graded in towns which fall into a series, based on their importance as regional centres. Recognition has long been given, as a matter of common observation and record, to this phenomenon. It is above all evident in our common usage of the terms village, town, city, capital, and metropolis, that reflect the graded series of such a hierarchy of regional centres.

5. THE URBAN REGION

We have described in general terms the nature of the city as a regional centre. In point of fact, however, adjacent city-regions frequently overlap and, indeed, even their urbanized areas may coalesce to form much more extensive urban regions.

The concept of an aggregate of closely spaced and functionally interrelated towns, extending far beyond the boundaries of their constituent administrative divisions, was first put forward by Sir Patrick Geddes in his book *Cities in Evolution* published in 1915 (though written, as he tells in the preface, before the outbreak of war in 1914). The population map, he writes, reveals London as a sprawling 'polypus' (rather than an 'octopus'), that like a coral reef has a stony skeleton and living polyps—a 'man-reef'. This 'province covered with houses' extends far beyond the limits of brick-and-mortar of Greater London proper, ranging for certain purposes to include outlying cities such as Brighton on the south coast. In the provinces we find 'great and growing masses', each essentially like another London. Turning his eye to Lancashire as a starting point, Geddes declared that Manchester and Liverpool are 'historic expressions' and 'we have here another vast province almost covered with house-groups, swiftly spreading into one, and already connected up at many points, and sometimes by more than sufficient density of population along the main lines of communication'. 'Here, far more than even Lancashire commonly realizes, is growing up again another Greater London as it were—a city-region of which Liverpool is the seaport and Manchester the market, now with its canal port also; while Oldham and the many other factory towns, more accurately called "factory districts", are the workshops.'

Geddes continues:

'To focus these developments, indeed transformations, of the geographical traditions of town and country in which we were brought up, and express them more sharply, we need some little extension of our vocabulary; for each new idea for which we have not yet a

THE URBAN SETTLEMENT AS REGIONAL CENTRE

word deserves one. Some name for these city-regions, these town aggregates, is wanted. Constellations we cannot call them; conglomerations is, alas, nearer the mark at present, but may sound unappreciative; what of "conurbations"? That perhaps may serve as the necessary word, as an expression of this new form of population-grouping, which is already, as it were, subconsciously, developing new forms of social grouping, and of definite government and administration by and by also.'

He goes on then to name these conurbations outside Greater London. Lancashire has been noted. The 'dark galaxy of towns' in the West Riding is divided into two groups, the West Riding woollen textile towns, and 'South Riding' round the steel and coal of Sheffield. Around Birmingham is the 'larger city-region of Midlandton'. The coal-mining valleys and the major cities of Swansea and Cardiff together form one unit described as South Waleston. The Tyneside towns 'with which we must plainly also take those of Wear and Tees, as constituting a new regional community a natural province—Tyne-Wear-Tees we may perhaps call it'. In Scotland, Greater Glasgow and Greater Edinburgh, each with its neighbouring towns, showed signs of rapidly merging to form one new conurbation—a bi-polar city-region, that may be tentatively called Clyde-Forth. These six conurbations, each upon its coalfield, together with the great metropolis of Greater London form the country's 'New Heptarchy'.

Such groupings, continues Geddes, are also to be found abroad. France has its Greater Paris, and the Riviera is picked out as a potential conurbation when its rapidly growing centres merge with each other. In Germany, Berlin and the Ruhr are singled out for special mention. It is vaguely suggested that the latter, together with Düsseldorf and Cologne, form one vast entity. In the United States, growth is taking place with great rapidity and can go much further. Pittsburgh is cited as a conspicuous example of a Black Country comparable with the Midlands. Chicago and New York are also noted.

'Greater New York, now linked up, on both sides, by colossal systems of communications above and below its divided waters, is also rapidly increasing its links with Philadelphia—itself no mean city—and with minor ones without number in every possible direction. For many years past it has paid to have tramway lines continuously along the roads all the way from New York to Boston, so that, taking these growths altogether the expectation is not absurd that the not very distant future will see practically one vast city-line along the Atlantic coast for five hundred miles, and stretching back

THE REGION AS A SOCIAL UNIT

at many points; with a total of, it may be, as many millions of population.'

The 'Great Lakes' and 'Texas' are also vaguely referred to as the sites of future agglomerations of similar proportions. Such is the general notation of a city-region or conurbation as put forward in vague but suggestive terms by Sir Patrick Geddes.

The urbanized areas have expanded with alarming rapidity in the last fifty years, especially in the years since World War II, a period which has witnessed the tremendous revolutionary impact of the automobile and the truck. The anticipations of Patrick Geddes and H. G. Wells of fifty years ago have in large measure been realized. They envisaged the time when the big cities would merge with each other to produce much larger, sprawling and interdigitating aggregates. This process has been referred to as regional urbanization. A single urbanized area, with a compact core and a wide periphery, can be likened to the yoke and the white of a fried egg. Urban sprawl outside the cities is causing them to coalesce so as to form a cluster of fried eggs or even a 'gargantuan scramble'.

These urbanized areas and their dependent regions are the outstanding realities of population distribution today. Examples are the so-called 'Megalopolis' of the urban belt on the Atlantic seaboard of the United States, the so-called 'coffin belt' of central England, the ring (*Randstad*) of Holland, and the extensive urbanized regions of the German Rhinelands. The range of impact of cities extends still further beyond the limits of their built-up areas to a wide penumbra in the countryside. Cities are becoming increasingly inter-dependent. The life and activities of cities and towns are making an ever deeper imprint on the countryside, so that the distinction between urban areas and countryside is becoming increasingly vague.

These regions of urbanization call for precise definition and they will be examined later. These are the areas which are growing most rapidly, a fact that is hidden by the slow rate of growth of individual major cities that have been over-spilling their administrative boundaries for nearly fifty years. Geddes urged half a century ago that such areas call for common treatment in order to solve their problems of sanitation, transport, and government. These problems, still unresolved, are far more urgent today than they were half a century ago. They are greatly aggravated by the fact that any one area includes literally hundreds of administrative and *ad hoc* divisions. Their problems of spatial organization call for reorganization at the local, regional, and national levels. They cut across the boundaries of cities and even of State frontiers. All authorities, from the city planning department to the national ministry, must base their plans for action on a thorough diagnosis of the character and trends of growth in these areas. Authorities must, above all else, have standards of planning that are acceptable for the social and well being of the whole community. They must find avenues of action, beyond the level of the individual city and even beyond that of the extended city, so as effectively to cope with undesirable trends at the national level.

Chapter 2

THE NATURE OF THE CITY

1. THE HISTORICAL ASPECT

The city is not merely an aggregate of economic functions. Throughout history it has been above all else a seat of institutions in the service of the people of the countryside. In the words of Lewis Mumford, 'it is art, culture, and political purposes, not numbers, that define a city'.[1] These activities—economic, cultural, and political —are segregated at fixed points in space to serve the society that calls them into being. This is the most essential phenomenon of the growth and structure of the urban community, upon which all other generalizations or hypotheses must be based.

The city has the characteristics of what Mumford calls both a container and a magnet. The container is the physical and permanent assembly of physical structures in which the functions, processes, and purposes of the city are developed and transmitted through time. The idea of the magnet refers to the force of attraction (and repulsion) of people and institutions. It is a spatial force. With this must be associated, writes Mumford, 'the existence of a "field" and the possibility of action at a distance, visible in the "lines" of social force, which draw to the centre particles of a different nature'.[2] This is the field of association or catchment area of the city. This is its region. Though written with reference to the origin of ancient cities, this basic generalization is equally true of the modern metropolis.

The urban settlement, in the broadest sense, arises through the combination at a fixed place of a variety of the special functions which are needed in the service of a civilized society. These functions may be, and are, carried out individually and separately in widely scattered places. This was true of the beginnings of urban life in Europe. It is true today in that there are widely scattered clusters of miners' houses around a mine, of residences on a lake or sea-front,

---

[1] Lewis Mumford, *The City in History*, London, 1961, p. 125.
[2] *Ibid.*, pp. 82–3.

THE URBAN SETTLEMENT AS REGIONAL CENTRE

of scattered or clustered suburban residences, and of other urban components, all of which are essentially *unifunctional* in character. It is the coagulation of varied functions, and particularly those of service and socio-economic cohesion, that give rise to a 'balanced' settlement structure which begins to assume the traits of a town. Such settlements vary in character and status from one place to another, from one area to another, and from one cultural realm to another, as well as at different periods of cultural development. This is notably the case in western Europe. Here various names are used in different languages to characterize urban centres at different periods. The term *town* has most general use. It designates a place with a minimum number of distinct functions, and in consequence a distinct type and grouping of building structures, which distinguish it from a cluster of farmsteads in a village settlement. However, it should be emphasized that the historical and actual distinction between town and village is not always a sharp one.

The Latin term *civitas* is the common etymological root of civilization and city. It was originally used to describe the district of organization under the Roman Empire. It was later transferred to the centre of a district or diocese in which the Christian bishopric was sited. In France this nucleus became the *cité*. It is still so called and the term city is still popularly (though inaccurately) used in Britain to denote a town with a cathedral, though there is no corresponding name, as an alternative to *Stadt* (town) in German. The term *civitas* was used in the documents of the early Middle Ages to describe a confused variety of urban settlements, but by the middle of the twelfth century it began to be used with a more precise meaning. It referred to a compact settlement having a special law (in German, *Stadtrecht*) with rights of self-government for its freemen or burgesses. It was normally walled, and usually had a market that was held at a place or places in the centre of the settlement (market rights were a normal privilege accorded to the settlement early in its development). Such a settlement was also a seat of industry and commerce, carried on, and in large part controlled, by the guilds. *Civitas* has its equivalent in *ville* in French, *Stadt* in German, and *town* in English. But it did not cover all settlements that were urban, as conditions of growth differed between different areas. There were numerous places that had only some of the above-mentioned characteristics, and these were often intermingled with agricultural activities or functions of lower status. Many had more elementary forms of self government; others were unwalled; most had market rights, though these were not essential. The type, number, and frequency of these smaller settlements vary from one area to another. They are called *Flecken* in German, *bourgs* in French, and *market*

THE NATURE OF THE CITY

towns in English. But there was, and there still is, no essential difference in the functions of these numerous urban settlements in the countryside, be they dwarf towns or thriving market towns, or great cities.

There is thus no consistent definition of a city. It is a town that enjoys a measure of leadership among towns. One may call the change from small to large town a continuum, but popular usage in all languages recognizes a difference in function and size between the hamlet, through the town, to the metropolis.

In modern times, the great growth of urban population has created new centres, but it has more usually caused historic cities to expand greatly in population and area. Over the last hundred years, economic functions have become increasingly important and dominant in the growth of cities. Commerce, in particular, has caused centralized functions to become increasingly concentrated in the centres of the cities on the site of their historic cores. The term *city* as used in Europe designates the business core that has grown as a distinctive element of the urban structure in the last seventy-five years. The functional importance of an urban centre can be gauged from the physical size of its central business district.

It will be apparent that there are three aspects to the nature of a city. It has distinctive functions, it has distinctive forms or physical structures, and it has, in varying ways and degrees, distinctive modes of areal arrangement and organization. Let us glance briefly at each of these as keystones to our interpretation of the character of the contemporary city as a regional centre.

First, the functions of the city throughout its history have been threefold—cultural, administrative, and economic. It is a serious error to regard the economic functions as exclusive criteria of the character of a city, important as these may be in our time. The earliest cities in south-western Asia, north-western India and north-western China, as well as in western Europe, were in the first place permanent seats of cultural institutions. The temple and the palace, the precincts of the gods and the earthly rulers, were their nuclei of settlement. This was equally true of the central place of the Roman and Greek cities (*forum* and *agora*). The secular or the ecclesiastical stronghold, walled in the early Middle Ages, was the point of origin of the earliest towns in western Europe. Around and outside them grew the settlements that during the eleventh and twelfth centuries eventually became fully-fledged towns. Not until the early twelfth century, as at Freiburg-in-Breisgau and Lübeck, were urban settlements established anew, without reference to a preceding stronghold. Market place, through-route, ecclesiastical stronghold, and the castle of the territorial lord, became the generating forces in both

THE URBAN SETTLEMENT AS REGIONAL CENTRE

the functions and forms of the medieval town. In the Renaissance and after, towns were sought and many were built by the nobility and the rulers as places of residence. Territorial lords in western Europe generally lived in castles outside the town, though they often founded walled towns or located fortresses within existing towns.

The administrative function refers to the activities that are located in a town in order to govern the area round it. The independent medieval town sought to be the centre of a territory as extensive as it could effectively wrest from its neighbouring competitors or from the territorial lords. This was notably the case in western Germany and northern Italy. Such functions were increased in the nineteenth century and after with the added complexities of government in the organization of space for defence, food supply, and service.

The role of industry and commerce needs no special emphasis. Commerce includes regular retail trade as carried on during the Middle Ages in the central market place and other places that emerged for special sales around it. Wholesale trade seems to have been begun by merchants clustering outside the earliest of the medieval strongholds. One hears of such settlements outside the strongholds of northern France and Flanders (Latin, *portus*), while in western Germany a special law (*jus mercatorum*) was granted in favour of these merchants' settlements. The merchants became the leading group in the towns of the medieval period and in the following centuries. The commercial activities became increasingly important after the industrial and commercial revolutions. This will be examined more fully later.

These functions have varied in importance in the origins and development of every town. Classification of towns based upon the relative importance of these functions leads to the recognition of variations among towns from one area to another. Large-scale industry was a primary determinant of urban growth in the nineteenth century, but in the last fifty years, in both western Europe and America, it has been outstripped by the numbers engaged in commerce, service, and the professions.

The second distinctive feature of the urban centre, and thus especially of the city, is that its functions are reflected in its distinctive building forms. These comprise both the individual buildings and the way in which they are grouped together to give a distinct ground-plan and build to the city. Ecclesiastical nucleus, secular stronghold, market place, main thoroughfare, and the great public monument (especially in the Renaissance and Baroque periods) have all played important roles in the build of the city. The terrain on which the city is sited is also an integral part of its build, be it a naturally defended site—on a high river meander, a hill-top, or an island in a former marsh—or a site favourably situated at a convergence of natural routeways, river, river-crossing, or overland route. The institution and the residence, whether the humble home or the noble's mansion, contribute at each phase of cultural growth to the total build and plan of the city. The morphology of the town is a reflection of its functions and of the ideas of planning and building at each phase of its development. In the words of F. Ratzel 'like functions beget like forms'. But the nature of both depends on the cultural realm in which they develop. The temple and palace of the clerics and kings in the ancient city are followed by the church and castle in the medieval epoch, the palace of bishop and king in the Baroque period, and the public building, factory, bank, and store in the contemporary city.

The third aspect of the city that calls for special emphasis may be called its organization. By this we refer to the fact that every agglomeration of institutions and people needs some degree of spatial organization both as a whole and in its parts. There is a natural tendency for institutions and residences to arrange themselves in separate districts, be they segregations of crafts on streets or adjacent to water, or of guilds around the market centre, or of ethnic groups in separate sectors (walled off, as in the Ghetto). The town is also divided into parishes, each with its own church as the centre of its religious and social life. Towns expanded outside their walls *in suburbio* and these areas usually fell into separate parishes. Many small towns in Germany expanded by the deliberate foundation of a new town twinned on to the existing town, with separate wall, plan, government, and organization.

The modern industrial town was essentially compact but grew out of scale, unlike the historic city, and modern planners are still searching for substitutes for the local district organizations of the historic city. The spatial organization of the town involves some measure of public control or responsibility that may affect the whole or the parts of the town. There is the role of protection from disease, fire, and flood; the maintenance of law and order; the provision of public utilities—water, sewerage, refuse disposal, gas, and electricity. One of the greatest problems of the modern city is the establishment of new forms of organization to cope with the problems of living in vast numbers over extensive urbanized areas. This is a problem of organization both for the smaller districts and for the whole of the urbanized area, far beyond the limits of the administrative boundaries of the constituent units. Municipal organization, zoning legislation, and city and regional planning, which must be evolved in opposition to the traditional attitudes of lesser municipalities are the major kinds of spatial organization of the city.

THE URBAN SETTLEMENT AS REGIONAL CENTRE

Transport is essential to the growth, functioning, and organization of cities. All their activities are essentially dependent on the movement of food and materials into the city and the export of its goods (normally manufactured and smaller in bulk than the imports) and its services. It is thus clear that a productive hinterland and access to it, as well as long-distance communications with a wider area (for the development of specialized services and markets), are literally vital to the functioning of a city. Without these the population of a city would die within a matter of weeks, and the laying in of supplies would only postpone the evil day. Only the advent of the improved road and canal in the eighteenth century, followed by the railroad and the steamship in the mid-nineteenth century, have made it possible for the city to draw regularly on a wider area, and indeed even to have the world as its market.

Access to water transport was a *sine qua non* if the city was to grow to anything of more than local importance, restricted to an immediate hinterland, that could be reached only by road, on foot, horse, or pack wagon. The size of a city was dependent upon both the productivity and access of its hinterland, as well as on its contacts with the wider world by river and sea communications. And these conditions, though modified by the advent of the canal and the road and the improved conditions of sea navigation in the eighteenth century, continued in their essentials until the mid-nineteenth century.

The improved macadamized roads, the railroad, and the steamship heralded a new epoch of transport upon which the growth of modern urbanism is based. Revolutionary advances have taken place in the last seventy-five years or more by the advent of electricity and the internal combustion engine. Most railroad nets were completed in the 1860's and remained the chief means of transport for fifty years. The last generation has witnessed the phenomenal expansion of a close network of first-class, hard-surfaced roads. Throughout all western Europe and North America almost every dwelling is within a few miles of a highway. These advances have permitted the expansion over large areas of greatly extended means of access with reduced time and cost in getting from one place to another.

These circumstances are reflected in the expansion of the city and in the development of urban sprawl. In London in 1801 only the wealthiest, travelling by private horse and carriage, could live up to three or four miles from their work in the city. The overwhelming majority of people walked to their place of work or pleasure. The same was still essentially true at mid-century. The same, incidentally, is still true in the cities of the pre-industrial areas of the world. By

1871 London already had some horse buses and horse tramways. The rail net had developed and cheap fares for workers were enforced by Parliament on the railroad companies. In the last years of the century the electric railroad and the underground, the tram and the bus were in operation. The electric tram became the main cause of the expansion of the city area beyond the confines of the Victorian city. The so-called inter-urban lines played an important part for some thirty years in the United States, and are still prosperously maintained on the continent, though the inter-urban electric track and the street-car have now virtually disappeared in the United States. It is no longer necessary for the urban functions to be centralized in the city centre. Workplace, shopping place, and residence can be built, and are being built, outside the central city. This is based upon the universality of the automobile in the States and this condition will undoubtedly extend to western Europe increasingly during the next fifty years. We are thus witnessing not only *urban sprawl* but also what can be literally described as the disintegration of the city, an *urban explosion* whereby urban land uses are being dispersed over wide areas.

2. THE DYNAMICS OF URBAN GROWTH

The face of the land and the way of life of the people in North America and western Europe are being radically transformed by the growth and expansion of urban areas. In the latter half of the nineteenth century the railroad facilitated the clustering of urban population in narrowly confined areas. During the past fifty years, and especially since the end of World War II, electric power and the internal combustion engine have made it possible for urban land uses and urban ways of life to expand widely into the countryside. New industries have contributed substantially to this expansion. Moreover, the rapid tempo of economic growth, coupled with the increasing level of living, have promoted the increasing competition for building space in the heart of the cities, from which they and their tributary areas can be most effectively served. Urban sprawl and the skyscraper are the two major antitheses of this growth and they have made a varying impact in intensity and range both in different countries and different sections of the same country.

Economic development is clearly reflected in shifts in occupational structure. It is customary to recognize three rather ill-defined groups of occupation—the primary activities, concerned with the production of earth-bound materials, mainly agriculture and mining; the secondary activities, concerned with the production of manufactured goods; and the tertiary activities, that are concerned with the provision of services of all kinds. The distribution of these groups in the occupational structure of the countries of North America and western Europe is shown on the table on p. 27. A main feature is the small proportion of the working population dependent on agriculture which has been decreasing steadily in the twentieth century. It has fallen in the United States from about 30 per cent. in 1900, to 12·5 per cent. in 1950, and 8·6 per cent. in 1960. In Britain the figure has remained at about 5 per cent., but during the fifties the numbers of agricultural workers have been decreasing. The percentage of agricultural workers has fallen in Belgium and the Netherlands from about 30 per cent. in 1900 to 7 and 10 per cent. respectively in 1960. In France, there were 22 per cent. in agriculture in 1960 as compared with 45 per cent. in 1900 and it is expected to fall to 15 per cent. by 1975. In the Germany of 1939 there were 18 per cent. in agriculture as compared with 27 per cent. in 1907 and 40 per cent. in 1880. West Germany had only 14 per cent. so employed in 1960. In Italy the percentage fell from 59 in 1900 to 29 in 1961. These low proportions stand in marked contrast to the predominantly peasant societies to the south and east, as, for example, Spain and Poland.

The rural exodus continued rapidly in the fifties. From 1950 to 1960 Italy lost 29 per cent. of its agricultural workers, West Germany 30 per cent., Belgium and the Netherlands, one-third, and Great Britain, one-quarter. The United States lost a quarter and Canada one-third of their farm workers over the same period.

There has long been a surplus of agricultural workers in both the United States and western Europe, and substantial and increasing numbers of the cultivators are moving from the land or are engaging in part-time work off their holdings. The steady transfer of workers from village to town during the fifties will continue in the coming decades. The continuing tempo of economic growth will mean the transfer of more people from agriculture to industry and service and thus the continued growth of the urban population.

The non-agricultural activities fall into the two major divisions of manufacturing industries and services. The proportion in manufacturing industries (secondary occupations), as classed in the national censuses, seldom passes above 45 per cent., not only in countries as a whole, but also in their constituent administrative divisions.

The tertiary occupations embrace 'trades and services'. They are generally defined in the national censuses as including transport, commerce, finance, utilities, professional and domestic services. The table indicates that, with an increasing standard of living and a higher proportion of non-agricultural workers living in urban areas, the proportion in services increases. In the United States in 1950

THE NATURE OF THE CITY

OCCUPATIONAL STRUCTURE OF SELECTED COUNTRIES

Country	Agriculture	Industry	Trades, Services
Canada, 1951	19·3	36·0	44·7
United States, 1950	12·5	37·0	50·5
Austria, 1951	32·6	37·6	29·8
Belgium, 1947	12·5	50·2	37·3
France, 1954	27·5	37·2	35·3
Germany (West), 1954	20·6	46·4	33·0
Italy, 1954	41·2	31·4	27·4
Netherlands, 1947	19·8	34·2	46·0
Spain, 1950	49·6	25·5	24·9
Sweden, 1950	20·5	41·1	38·4
United Kingdom, 1951	5·3	49·2	45·5

SOURCE: *Report on the World Social Situation*, United Nations, New York, 1957, p. 92.

NOTE: 'Trades, Services', in column 4, include commerce, transport, storage, communications, public and private services. Industry, in column 3, includes mining and quarrying, construction and utilities.

the latter comprised about one half of the total employment. In Canada, the Netherlands, and the United Kingdom the proportion is slightly lower; it ranges from 30 to 40 per cent. in other areas of western Europe. In all these countries, there is every indication that the tertiary services have constituted the most rapidly increasing section of the employment structure during this century. Moreover, today in the United States the gross personal income of tertiary workers far exceeds that of industrial workers. It is of interest to note by way of comparison that predominantly agricultural countries have only 10 to 20 per cent. of their workers in the tertiary occupations (e.g. Yugoslavia 10·8, Turkey 6·9, India 16·2), and other agricultural countries with a substantial industrial component have 20 to 30 per cent. in tertiary occupations (e.g. Japan 32·5, Italy 27·4).[1]

The growth of population and of standards of living have recently been observed in the case of Sweden, where they are having profound effects on the rate of growth of cities, especially Stockholm.

'The growth of Stockholm's population, as that of other cities, is partly accounted for by a shift in the balance of Sweden's economy over the past 20 years. The total population of the country has increased from 6,000,000 to 7,500,000, while the proportion engaged in agriculture has declined from 36 per cent. to 13 per cent. and the

[1] See P. George, *Introduction à l'Étude Gèographique de la population du Monde*, Paris, 1951, pp. 105–12.

proportion engaged in industry, trade, general administration, and the professions has moved up from 56 per cent. to 84 per cent. In 10 years the gross national product has more than doubled, and the percentage of population of working age is increasing in relation to the total population. Three-tenths of the gross national product go to investment, seven-tenths to consumption, and the current tendency favours investment.'[1]

A similar statement in the French Press highlights the great importance of these changes. Attention is drawn to the pressing need for a greatly extended system of education to cope with the needs of a rapidly changing society. It is pointed out that by 1975 only 15 per cent. of the French workers will be engaged in agriculture. The greater part of the new jobs will be in the tertiary occupations rather than in industry. Indeed, over the past fifteen years, the Peugeot plant has employed a constant number of workers, but the number of employees in white-collar jobs (as opposed to manual blue-collar workers) has increased by 40 per cent. and the number of engineers has doubled. At the beginning of the century 80 per cent. of the country's workers were in manual jobs (industry and agriculture), and only 20 per cent. in services and clerical jobs. In A.D. 2000 this situation will be reversed. Hence the need for a rapidly extended and improved system of education.[2]

These changes are rooted in technological developments. Geddes, fifty years ago, and Lewis Mumford, in our time, speak of the paleotechnic and the neotechnic eras. The paleotechnic era was based on the use of coal and iron, the railroad, and the steamship. It began with the Industrial Revolution in England and spread sporadically in the early nineteenth century to the continent—to small surface coal-fields like Le Creusot and St. Etienne in central France and Liège in Belgium. It did not gather momentum on the continent until the last decades of the century. This was the period of most rapid growth of urban populations, when the countryside was drained of large numbers of workers to work in the 'insensate industrial towns'. Industry was rigidly tied to the coal-fields in the first half of the century, especially in England. On the Continent, the full impact of industrial growth came after 1870, when the railroad net was almost complete. Great regional capitals, like Cologne, were able to share in the industrial growth. This industrial growth was concerned above all with the output of producer goods (notably railroad stock and ships) and only to a limited degree with that of consumer goods (mainly textiles and metal goods). It was also essentially an era

[1] Leader in *The Times*, 11 June 1962.
[2] Jean Grandmougin in *L'Aurore*, 7 September 1962.

THE NATURE OF THE CITY

of rugged individualism. This epoch was considered by Geddes to be nearing its end at the turn of the century.

New techniques became available to man with a chain of inventions between 1870 and 1930. They have resulted in an increasing change of tempo in the structure of human societies. Electrification, based on the use of the turbine, has facilitated the widespread distribution of power from both thermal and hydraulic sources. The advent of the internal combustion engine has meant a revolution in means of transport, and the construction of a universal net of first-class hard-surfaced highways throughout these lands. New sources of power have come into use, brown coal (especially in Germany), hydro-electricity, and oil. New kinds of industry have also developed —automobiles, aircraft, artificial fibres, plastics, the distillation of coal and (notably since the war) the petro-chemical industries. Communications have been revolutionized by the automobile, telephone, radio, and television. Together with these changes has come about a raising of the standard of living and a growing social conscience which has been responsible for the steady increase of social welfare facilities undertaken by the State. If the Industrial (or Paleotechnic) Revolution is justified as a descriptive term, we surely have here another revolution covering a similar period of time about one hundred years later. This may be called the Neotechnic Revolution. It forms the basis of the urban dynamics of the twentieth century.

All these changes have come about at different tempos in different States and in different sections of the same State. The changes we have given above in the first half of this century reflect, in fact, growth under the impact of the techniques of paleotechnic society. The years of prosperity in the twenties were still based on late nineteenth-century foundations, while the thirties were marked by stagnation. But in the inter-war years there were many indications of changes to come. In Britain, there occurred a great growth of new industries in north-west London and the Midlands at a time when the provincial industrial areas were hit by appalling unemployment. There was also the great growth of new thermal electric and chemical plants on the brown coal-fields of Germany, while changes were taking place on a bigger scale in the United States. But the great impetus has come during and since the last war—within the last twenty years. The contributions of the new techniques, born in the preceding generation, have now gained full momentum. America experienced unprecedented growth as the Allied 'arsenal' during the war years. The rates of growth of national product for the period 1950–60 are shown in the table on p. 30.

THE URBAN SETTLEMENT AS REGIONAL CENTRE

AVERAGE ANNUAL GROWTH RATES OF GROSS NATIONAL PRODUCTS

Country	1950–55	1955–60	1950–60
France	4·4	4·2	4·3
Belgium	3·3	2·4	2·9
Netherlands	5·6	4·2	4·9
Germany	9·0	6·1	7·6
Italy	6·0	5·9	5·9
United Kingdom	2·4	2·4	2·4
Norway	3·5	3·3	3·5
Sweden	3·1	3·3	3·2
Denmark	2·1	4·6	3·3
Switzerland	5·7	4·4	5·0
Austria	7·0	5·2	6·1
Portugal	4·2	3·7	3·0
U.S.A.	4·3	2·3	3·3
Canada	4·6	3·2	3·9

SOURCE: Statistical Office of the European Community, November 1961.

Rates of economic growth have been high on the Continent in the 'fifties' (see above). The 'miracle' of American wartime production has been followed in the 'fifties' by a slowing down in the tempo of growth but a tremendous upsurge of consumer buying. Germany has had its 'miracle' and it would now seem to be Italy's turn, since the latter's rate of industrial growth is currently the highest in Europe. France has achieved wonders of reconstruction despite its crippling overseas commitments in money and men. Britain remains sluggish, if not stagnant, overburdened by the weight of its overseas economic and military commitments. New highways, and the prodigious increase in the number of trucks and cars, are putting the railroads out of business. The consumption of oil and electricity has rocketed since the war. Western Europe must import most of its oil from abroad, and mammoth tankers are feeding refineries built since the war at the great port entrances for distribution by truck and pipe line to the interior. Coal, instead of being a basic British export, is now reduced in production owing to high costs and the export surplus has virtually disappeared. Big advances have been made in the production of electricity, and transmission lines carry power to most parts of every land and, other things being equal, industry can be widely dispersed. Full employment means an ever-rising standard of living. This means an increasing demand for consumer goods, homes, and automobiles. Every country is trying to cope with these demands. The United States with the aid of thousands of miles of super-highways hopes to keep its vehicles on the move. The European

THE NATURE OF THE CITY

countries—especially Britain—are being choked by the increase of vehicular traffic on medieval highways.

The increasing amount of business of all kinds results in the ever-growing number of persons engaged in the tertiary occupations. With this higher standard of living and the expansion of education and research, there is an ever larger number of young people in what Jean Gottmann calls the quaternary occupations. America aims at 50 per cent. of its youth at Universities, and this means the growth of many large new communities catering for the student populations. Great Britain is aiming at 10 per cent. and its programme of university expansion is modest and exclusive. The continental universities have opened wide their doors, irrespective of the lack of accommodation. These vie in size with the American universities. The growth of all kinds of services is a white-collar revolution, an expression of the neotechnic era now in full flood. It is as fanciful to talk about the 'biotechnic era' now as it was of the neotechnic era fifty years ago. We may be on the threshold of such a new era, but atomic power and space travel are harbingers of the future and as yet have made a negligible impact on society.

A higher standard of living means such things as the eight-hour day, five-day week, holidays with pay, substantial retirement pensions (especially in the States), and more education. People wish to live in new homes out of the cities in clean air with plenty of space around them. They like to spend their vacations in the country. Recreation and tourism are manifestations of the affluent society and are producing widespread effects in man's relation to the land. The senior citizens of America seek to retire and enjoy life in congenial physical and social surroundings. At present the heart of the desert is the vogue. The urbanization of the desert in the south-western States is one of the most phenomenal new features of the American scene.

What effects are these changes having on the process and character of urban growth? These we may put in the broadest terms and examine them more closely in subsequent chapters.

First, the highway. The advent of a universal system of motor roads over the last fifty years has greatly reduced the friction of distance. The great bulk of freight and passengers in most countries is today carried by road. The fact that the motor vehicle is a free agent and an economical short distance and small load carrier, has greatly increased, and made virtually ubiquitous, the intimate contact between the city and its hinterland. 'Rural and urban have truly met and . . . field and centre are almost fusing.'[1] The spatial expression

[1] Firey, Loomis, and Beegle, 'The fusion of urban and rural' in J. Labatut and W. J. Lane, *Highways in our National Life*, Princeton, 1950.

THE URBAN SETTLEMENT AS REGIONAL CENTRE

of this centrifugal trend is fourfold. First, there is a developing and expanding fringe on the outskirts of the cities that is partly urban and partly rural. Second, there is ribbon development, or string-along-the-road settlement, along the highways radiating from the cities. Third, there is the development around towns and cities of service areas which are generally greater in extent than the fringe areas. Fourth, there is the formation of satellite sub-centres beyond the city, each with its own fringe, ribbons, and service areas. Thus 'villages serve as centres for little fields; towns are centres for large fields; and cities function as centres for the largest fields. Each field, with its centre is successivly subsumed into the next larger one, in hierarchical fashion.'[1]

This urban expansion has hitherto been mainly in the form of compact private or municipal real estate developments. But individuals are now living in houses scattered far and wide. We have a new kind of area in which residences are scattered in the midst of farmland or woodland, a kind of semi-urban landscape that in America Gottmann has described as having a 'nebulous or quasi-colloidal structure'. It is closely akin to what Tunnard has called 'interurbia', in which houses and urban amenities are widely dispersed but easily reached by car. Furthermore, such houses frequently extend far beyond the limits of water or sewage facilities.

Second, while much of this dispersion is indeed caused by those who work in the city, it is due also to the establishment of factories out in the country to which residential areas have access by automobile or bus. The 'suburbanization of industry'—establishment of plants on the urban periphery—began effectively in the inter-war period and has continued to increase since 1945. Such plants are associated with the road rather than with the railway. The day of the exclusive pull of the railroad has gone. Highway and truck are the principal determinants except for the heavy industries, such as oil refineries, chemical plants, thermal electric plants, etc., that of necessity must be accessible to the raw materials that they use.

Third, the growth of services, on the other hand, is having various repercussions. The chief of these is the increasing growth of the central business district and, in recent years in the United States, the loss of some of its activities to suburban shopping centres. Many 'communication-oriented pursuits' need proximity to a host of other occupations and services. They seek such sites for convenience or prestige. Many can move out from the cities. This is eminently true of the retail services that naturally tend to follow the population. The change goes on freely in the States; in Britain it has been retarded by various factors, one of which is sheer inertia. The central

[1] *Ibid.*, p. 157.

business district is a vast and expanding nest of skyscrapers or 'high-rise buildings'. It is on the increase in post-war Europe and is marked since 1950 by the advent of the skyscraper—even in Britain. But the rate of metabolism is conditioned by the varying dynamics of economic growth between different areas and countries.

Fourth, in the central cities there is need for the replacement of obsolescent buildings, which date mainly from the period of 1850 to 1914 and lie around the central commercial district. Slum clearance has been prompted in the industrial towns of Britain by the unsuitability of houses for human occupation. But in these same British cities, the cleared or derelict areas lie in waste; and ironically the demand for land appears to be far behind the rate at which the buildings can be demolished. Moreover, the process of demolition is held up by the relatively slow tempo with which new homes can be built. On the other hand, in the United States private house-building is booming and city centres expanding, but the blighted residential areas are being removed at a very slow rate. On the Continent, of course, and especially in Germany, the war-time destruction of cities necessitated speedy reconstruction, and indeed, through the fifties, Germany, with the same population as Britain, was building twice as many houses year by year.

Fifth, there is the rapid increase of housing and the spread outwards of the urban area along the main lines of communication. Residential buildings and open spaces (including streets) make up about three-quarters of all urban land uses. They are obviously the main contributors to the urban explosion: where they go, eventually services and industries will go. Stores will go to service the housewife, plants to tap the local labour supply, both male and female.

Sixth, there is the fantastic increase in tourism of all kinds. In the later nineteenth century this was limited to the spas for the wealthy. The seaside resort grew in the last decades of the nineteenth century and became popular over short distances, mainly in Britain. These new ways of living have given rise to a new kind of industry—tourism. Far and wide are to be found places in which the source of income is derived from the feeding and entertaining of urbanites, not only the wealthy or the professional middle class, as was the case fifty years ago, but also the so-called 'working class' or the 'blue-collar' workers (as they are called in the United States), as well as the 'white-collar' workers. The highway is frequented by pulsating streams of automobiles. The motel is one of the remarkable additions to the American landscape and often forms continuous ribbons, miles in length, along main transcontinental highways on the outskirts of towns. This kind of development has been restricted in

THE URBAN SETTLEMENT AS REGIONAL CENTRE

Europe owing to shorter distance between towns; but the holiday camp is one of its manifestations.

Finally, all these developments are reflected in the increasing daily movements of urban populations. These are the daily waves of movement to and from work, to and from the central or other business districts, and the factory. There are also the daily movements to school, to entertainment, and to shopping. These are not all focused on the centre; they intercross in bewilderingly complex patterns. There are also the seasonal movements to and from places of recreation and along frequented 'scenic' routes. A State such as California is having to give serious attention to the prospects of increased tourism with a rapidly growing population, which, more than any other in the world, is dedicated to the outdoor life. Around every city there is developing a circle of temporary summer homes, numerous retreats, and frequented beauty spots. The national park movement is an attempt to provide such facilities and at the same time to preserve natural amenities from vandalism.

It has become almost customary to regard these changes in society, together with the increased rapidity and range of communications, as conducive to uniformity. In fact, standards of living, cultures, and aspirations vary immensely not only from one country to another, but also from one locality to another within the same country, whether in western Europe or the United States, or in Africa or India. The spectrum of 'economic health', as it has recently been called, varies enormously with local natural resources, the number and condition of the people, and the degree of their access to the poles of economic impetus in the great urban areas. The degrees of urbanization and the economic status associated with them vary from place to place. We need measures to locate them with precision before we can start to explain or remedy them.

These are the features of the urban explosion. The explosion brings new trends in the location of urban land uses and in the spatial impact of urban ways. It brings new features and forces in the patterns of spatial relations, new problems in the organization of space. It is to the character and forces of spatial cohesion of urban groups that we turn in the following pages.

3. THE CHANGING STRUCTURE OF THE CITY

The city of the Industrial Society occupies a dominant position in the economy of its country. In terms of the whole metropolitan areas in which they are situated, '... the cities dominate their hinterlands in such activities as wholesale trade, finance and business services, while accounting for lesser proportions of retail trade and manu-

facturing'.[1] Their relative dominance, however, is changing and will continue to change in the second half of this century.
This statement is made of the city in the United States. The same trends are found in the west European city, but their relative importance depends on the rate of growth of each urban area. The reader in Leeds or Birmingham must bear in mind the enormous differences between the English conurbation and most continental or American cities.

The *conurbation* of west Yorkshire, where we write, with an area of nearly 500 square miles, had a population of 1·5 millions in 1900 as compared with 1·7 millions in 1950. The numbers living in Leeds and other west Yorkshire towns are virtually the same as fifty years ago. The urban landscapes with their heavy Victorian imprint have not essentially changed in this period, except for some demolition of the slums, reconstruction in the city centres, and the extension of suburban areas. The main streets of the central cities were in existence long before the automobile era that began in the 1900's. This is an area of stagnation, in which there are virtually no new manufacturing plants and most of the plants, like the tens of thousands of pre-1914 houses, are obsolescent.

At the other extreme of urban growth is Los Angeles in California. The contiguous *cities* of Los Angeles–Long Beach, with 500 square miles—almost the same as the whole of west Yorkshire—increased from about 100,000 in 1900 to 2·8 millions in 1960. The whole *urbanized area* with an area of 1,370 square miles, increased from about 200,000 in 1900 to 6·5 millions in 1960. The whole area has experienced a prodigious growth of manufacturing industries (oil, motion pictures, aircraft, automobiles, etc.), especially during and since World War II. Almost the entire area has been built since 1920 and now spreads widely over southern California. Nearly all the dwellings of Los Angeles (85 per cent.) have been built since 1920 and two-thirds of them are detached houses. Los Angeles is, above all other cities, the creation of the automobile. Here, are two extremes of urban growth that must be borne in mind by the reader, whether he lives in an agglomeration of the paleotechnic era or a city of the automobile era.[2] They express enormous differences in the whole process of urban metabolism.

There would appear to be little, apart from accessibility, to favour the central cities for the concentration of economic activities as

[1] R. Vernon, *The Changing Economic Functions of the Central City*, A Committee of Economic Development (C.E.D.) report, New York and London, 1959.
[2] Howard J. Nelson, 'Spread of an Artificial Landscape over Southern California', *Annals of the Ass. of Am. Geog.*, Supplement, Vol. 49, No. 3, Part 2, September 1959.

compared with their suburban fringes. They have no edge in labour costs. Though space costs are high in terms of acreage, they are not disadvantageous in cubic space for small manufacturing units and office space as compared with the suburbs. Transport costs favour the localization in the central city of activities such as wholesale food and newspaper distribution, but increasing congestion is causing many distributors to shift to the edge of the congested centres to points from which they have easier access to their consumers in the surrounding areas. This trend accounts for the fact that in the States 'a ring of warehouses and terminals is commonly to be found at the edges of the central cities, oriented to the servicing of local consumers'.[1] Bakeries and bottling plants are showing the same kind of shift. However, the provision of special federal freight rates for certain commodities inside a city and not to areas beyond it, persuades smaller producers to stay within city boundaries. This helps particularly to keep diverse manufacturing enterprises within the central cities. Retail trades move out so as to cut the time and costs of the transport of the customers. Tax levels tend to be generally higher in the central city than outside it and this is often decisive in the location of an activity.

In fact, high concentration within the city arises from the clustering of thousands of small manufacturing units that need speedy transport facilities to each other and to their market. In six major metropolitan areas in the States in 1947, for example, clothing, printing, toys, and jewellery were almost entirely concentrated in the city as against the rest of their metropolitan areas, and they were almost all in small units with less than fifty employees. These are predominantly concerned with unstandardized products which rely on intimate and immediate interlinkages with other producers so as to enjoy the benefits of 'external economies of scale'. They contract for outside services or goods which they cannot economically provide or use themselves. Interlinkage is one of the major reasons for the concentration of manufactures in major cities.

From these general observations, we now turn to some of the current new trends that are changing this dominant economic role of the central cities. These trends are again especially characteristic of the American city, but, though less pronounced, they are also taking place in the European city. Population growth has spread to the suburban areas which are growing much more rapidly than the central cities. In the States this trend began in general after 1910. In the 1910–20 decade the maximum growth took place in a five-mile ring beyond the edges of the central cities, and since 1920 it has extended to a five- to ten-mile ring. The central cities in the fifties

[1] *Ibid.*, p. 21.

were commanding a decreasing proportion of the retail trade as compared with their suburbs. The same is true of wholesale trades, a trend due to the factors of high transportation costs in the heart of the city (especially with the shift from rail to truck) and the obsolescence of its building structures. Manufacturing shows a relative decline in the central cities of all metropolitan districts and in some cities, such as Boston, Chicago, Detroit, Pittsburg, St. Louis, and San Francisco, there has been an absolute decrease in the fifties of the number of jobs in manufacturing. The dependence of plants in the nineteenth century on rail and water transport and also on accessible labour within walking distance, tied industry rigidly to the cities. Obnoxious industries began to move out first, as in the stock yards of Chicago, though they were usually quickly engulfed in the rapid spread of urban buildings. The main shifts have taken place owing to various factors, such as the obsolescence of buildings, the replacement of the old multi-storey mills by the one-storey buildings on large sites, and zoning regulations since the twenties, which often inhibited further growth of existing plant in the same site or district. Further, the problem of assembling bits of land in a city for an extended site is legally expensive and financially prohibitive. The car and the truck give new mobility in the choice of sites in relation to the assembly and distribution of both goods and workers. Moreover, by the extension of factory space, small concerns can often enjoy the external economies of scale in peripheral areas now that many other interdependent concerns are established there. Office jobs cling hard to the central cities and especially to the central business district, and they have elbowed out many other less competitive uses. They have also attracted a great variety of parasitic activities, such as advertising agencies, and services, such as barber shops, beauty parlours, etc. Yet even these latter are growing in the American suburbs on a big scale, for such services might just as well be located near the homes of the workers, and their families. This is true of stores, services, banks, movies. Offices too are moving out. As Negroes and other outside groups at low income levels settle in the central cities, original white population moves out. The number of young women in the cities is thus reduced and the market can be more effectively tapped by putting the plants near the labour supply on the suburban periphery. This is an incipient, but a real trend in American cities. Many firms evacuated in Britain during the war have stayed put in their wartime sites in smaller towns.

These trends in the central cities—the spread of obsolescence and congestion, the changes in population, and the centrifugal shift of activities to the suburbs—are affecting the physical structure of the central city. There is already apparent a decline in the intensity of

THE URBAN SETTLEMENT AS REGIONAL CENTRE

use of land in the middle zones of the city for residence, business and manufacturing, and it is expected that this will increase during the coming decades.

There remain then two possibilities in this process of urban growth. Low income housing or open space projects may occupy the land that is cleared of obsolescent buildings, or the middle class may come back to be housed in multi-storeyed medium or high income apartments from which they may enjoy the full amenities of metropolitan life without long journeys to them. The latter is unlikely on a large scale, though there is evidence of it in American cities. To count on such a trend in the industrial cities of Britain would be entirely unrealistic. The first is the expected trend and it will cost money. It raises problems of compulsory purchase, demolition and redevelopment by private or municipal enterprise. And all such projects cost fabulous sums of money which are beyond the resources of most municipalities. Herein lies the core of the problem of city planning for the coming decades.

4. THE GROWTH OF THE URBAN AREA: CENTRALIZATION

We shall now turn to a brief enumeration of the various forces that contribute to the location of uses and activities in the city, and their distribution within the urban area.

The tendency for people and their activities to cluster in cities to overcome the 'friction of space' has been described as the essence of the process of urban growth.[1] Services demanded can most efficiently be carried out at central locations within clustered communities. This holds true for industry, commerce, or administration. This process of centralization is the primary cause of the past origins and modern growth of the city. The nucleus of most modern urban growth is the historic core. Today this normally comprises the hub of the city, from which the built-up area has spread steadily outwards both concentrically and radially, or by the growth of physically separate centres that gradually merge with the main urban area.

Centripetal forces have played a dominant role in all historical phases of urban growth. Throughout each period of town development in the western world, towns have emerged by the coagulation of structures as institutions, together with the dwelling places of their dependents. The earliest institutions to take permanent form in western Europe were the strongholds of the church and the secular

---

[1] R. M. Haigh and M. C. McCrea, 'Major Economic Factors in Metropolitan Growth and Arrangement', in *Regional Survey of New York and Environs*, Vol. I, New York, 1927, pp. 38-9.

rulers. The market place as a permanent architectural form (as opposed to the institutional arrangement for temporary assembly, that long preceded it) seems to have been a later development, certainly in the case of the oldest towns. Every early medieval town in western Europe has evidence of several separate nuclei in its vicinity before the appearance of the permanent urban settlement in the early Middle Ages. In Gaul and West Germany, hill-top earthwork, riverside Roman camp, early Christian abbeys, manorial nuclei of diverse kinds, pre-Roman evidences of meetings for buying and selling (documentary evidence and archeological finds), all point to the use of a particular locality before the settlement had its embryonic but permanent medieval beginnings.

Not all places of temporary assembly became sites of market trades and crafts. Urban development took place only at a few of those places which enjoyed superior nodal positions for the exercise of their regional functions. Once the idea of the medieval town was fully developed in the mid-twelfth century, new settlements were often established as market centres, and these were laid out as the focal institutions of the new town. Examples are Lübeck, Munich, and Freiburg. This process of coagulation is described by Lewis Mumford as 'the urban implosion' with reference to the ancient city. Centripetal forces drew these institutions to one place in the service of a dependent area. The concept is equally appropriate to urban development in western Europe in the early Middle Ages, when the overwhelming majority of the towns had their beginnings. It is also appropriate to the development of modern urbanism in so far as growth tends to cluster around focal points.

Prior to the advent of the modern highway and the railroad, the city was necessarily extremely compact and dominated by centripetal forces, because of the slowness of getting from one place to another on foot, on a beast of burden, or by a wheeled cart, on earthen and difficult tracks. Baedeker plans of towns in western Europe, reveal that even as late as 1900 the larger cities were still compact, clustered around their walled cores, and sharply demarcated from the surrounding countryside.

During the last fifty years, with the advent of ever faster and cheaper transport by the electric railway and latterly by the automobile, centrifugal forces have become increasingly important in addition to the continued operation of centripetal forces. The latter are clearly evidenced in the continued growth of nearly all (extended) urban areas at rates above the average for their countries as a whole. Within the urban areas, these forces are particularly evident in the continued, and indeed accelerated, competition of commercial activities for sites in the central business district, and in the appalling increase of vehicular traffic to and from the centre, presenting urban society with a well-nigh insuperable problem.

5. CONCENTRATION

Concentration denotes the tendency for similar uses, both non-residential and residential, to concentrate in distinct areas within the city. The process causes the clustering of homes, services, and institutions. It manifests itself in the emergence of a central business district, commercial sub-centres, and in the concentration of factories in distinct areas. It is the basis of the daily rhythm of movement of workers between homes and workplaces.

The location of the different kinds of urban land use is determined by three sets of conditions—economic forces, social attitudes and values, and public legislation. The operation of economic forces assumes the free operation of the law of supply and demand and that the use of any portion of land is determined by the factors of maximum economic efficiency—i.e. maximizing returns from a transaction involved in the purchase of the land for a particular purpose.

'Each parcel of land occupies a unique physical relationship with every other parcel of land. Because in every community there exists a variety of land uses, each parcel is the focus of a complex but singular set of space relationships with the social and economic activities that are centred on all other parcels. To each combination of space relationships, the market attaches a special evaluation, which largely determines the amount of the bid for the site which is the focus of the combination. Thus certain locations are more highly valued for residential use than other sites because of the greater convenience to shops, centres of employment, and recreational facilities. Corner locations command a higher price for certain types of retail use because of greater convenience to streams of pedestrian traffic.'[1]

In considering the 'dynamics of efficiency' in the location of urban activities, the same author, following the interpretation of R. M. Haigh,[2] gives key emphasis to the effort to minimize the 'friction of space', that is, the costs and time involved in overcoming the factor of distance. Thus, each activity seeks a site at which the costs of distance are reduced to a minimum. Through a process of bidding in the real estate market, the activity which can best exploit the locational attributes of a given site will probably occupy it.

[1] R. U. Ratcliff, *Urban Land Economics*, New York, 1949, pp. 283-4.
[2] *Op. cit.*

The economic forces, however, are offset by other conditions. Among these are social values and attitudes. These are the forces that have been investigated above all by human ecologists. It has been shown that such group attitudes can effectively maintain the uniqueness of status of a particular area of a city, such as Beacon Hill in Boston or Chelsea in London. The public interest also determines land uses through the development of legislation to promote socially desirable objectives, such as the protection of the health, welfare, morals, and safety of the people. It is reflected in bye-laws pertaining to sanitation, housing, building-codes, controls of the location of non-residential uses in residential areas, protection against atmospheric pollution, accidents, noise, smell and smoke, and even against building proposals considered to be offensive to public taste. One of the widest regular controls is exercised through the control of densities of residential population.

Many of these measures are embodied in the zoning laws which have been generally adopted in the last fifty years in the countries of western Europe and the United States. Such laws have been in general permissive, applying to areas that are already built-up, and usually with greater stringency the better the class of the residential property. We still await an organized body of planning legislation to apply to areas that are likely to become urban. The countries of western Europe are now seeking this end, but in many cases (e.g. western Germany) the natural processes of growth are so fast that public legislation and action cannot keep pace with them. The ideas of the green belt, the optimum size for cities, the new town, etc., are such new positive ideas. The United States, in the face of the unprecedented rate of expansion of its cities, is still searching for legislation to provide curbs on the disposition of land uses. It has been recently stated that land use controls in the public interest have five objectives—to guide the use of land, curb the misuse of land, prevent the abuse of land, regulate non-use or disuse of land, and guide the re-use of land (urban redevelopment, slum clearance, and rehousing).[1]

In regard to the segregation of functions in different sectors of the urban area, an outstanding feature, common to every city in the western world (and note carefully the reservation since other principles operate in the pre-industrial cities of other cultural realms), is the high degree of concentration of business and services in its centre, the '100 per cent. locations'. This central district is very small—often facing on to a market-place or a single street in the case of a small town—but it becomes larger and more compact in larger cities. Not

---

[1] Charles Abrams, *Urban Land Problems and Policies, Housing and Town and Country Planning Bulletin*, No. 7, United Nations. 1953, p. 34.

only is there a general concentration of business and services—shops, hotels, offices, restaurants, public buildings—but the different services are also segregated in districts within it. Owing to the great demand for space in this centre, land values are always here the highest in the city. The great demand for space in the centre has a twofold effect on its structure. First, there is the trend of vertical expansion, that is, the construction of multi-storeyed buildings, and, second, the trend of horizontal expansion, that is, the expansion of the business area to the adjoining streets and districts. This horizontal expansion usually involves the conversion of residential properties, which are quite unsuited for business uses. Ultimately such properties are destroyed and make way for a modern hotel, office, or civic building. This extension may be caused by private enterprise or by municipal slum clearance. The effect of the expansion of the city centre, with its high land values, is to raise values of the land around it. Since the city expands normally from its centre outwards, buildings become progressively older towards the centre. Thus, the combination of high land values and obsolescent buildings, ripe for demolition, explains the dingy-looking 'zone of deterioration' that surrounds the central business centre of almost every city. In the American city in particular, where 'real estate' is fluid, old buildings are let at high rentals and the sites (plus buildings) eventually sold at high profits. The expansion of the centre—especially of its high-class shopping and hotel quarter—is normally in the direction of the high-class residential district, as in the shift towards Kensington in London and northward in Manhattan to Central Park in New York City.

On the other hand, many commercial activities do not require a central location. Just as there develops a system of central places over a permanently settled countryside, so commercial and other services tend to segregate at strategic points within the urban complex to serve their clientele. These commercial sub-centres vary in size, depending on the types of goods and services offered, and range from the most complex (i.e. a regional shopping centre) right down to the ubiquitous individual shops that serve the immediate neighbourhood. Similarly, public buildings, such as government offices, museums, fire-stations, church, chapel, school, club, and places of entertainment are governed by their own particular requirements of turnover and access as to the best location. Some of these perform general services and require a central location, removed however from the congestion of the central business district. At the other extreme are the fire-station, church, pub and club that obviously need to be placed in the midst of the local community which they serve (through government provision, through the voluntary group choice of the community, or the enterprise of an individual).

The parish church served for centuries as a primary focus for the local community. The market place served as its general focus and was accessible to all its parts in some ten or fifteen minutes. This was in fact a primary determinant of the layout of the planned forms of the medieval town. Expansion of the historic town, however, was reflected in particular in the development of a number of separate market places for separate purposes and the fairs were often held just outside the walls or, in the nineteenth century, alongside the railroad or the highway. In Germany during the Middle Ages as towns grew in size, several towns, each with a central market, wall, and its own system of government, were literally 'twinned' on to each other. All these processes of segregation and location are involved in the concept of concentration.

6. Deconcentration

This term refers to the tendency for people and institutions to migrate from the existing concentrations within the urban area to the open land on its outskirts. It is the result of centrifugal as opposed to centripetal forces. It arises in part from the availability of cheap transport services to the city centre and to all parts of the urban complex; in part from the congestion in the central business district; and especially from the obsolescence of the old, often condemned, living areas clustered around it. This is the most remarkable and fundamental feature in the development of the modern city during the past thirty or forty years. In the United States it is often referred to as the 'urban explosion', which stands in expressive contrast to Mumford's 'urban implosion'. It is resulting in the diffusion of urban land uses to extensive areas of the immediately surrounding countryside. The external attractive factors contributing to this trend are the availability of ample land for extensive one-storey plants, loading yards, recreation grounds, and parking space. Low prices for land and probably lower tax rates than in the city, coupled with access to a ring road or new arterial highways are other attractions. Above all else residential developments are attracted by the availability of space for individual houses with large gardens, and by the prospect of lower tax rates (that often proves eventually to be a false investment as the area is built up and has to provide and finance its own services).

This process of deconcentration is intimately associated with the extension of the urban area through accretion at its periphery. Together with the centralization of new activities and people from other parts of the country, it leads to the development of suburban communities, whether they be dormitories for city workers or industrial communities in which the working population works in nearby places of employment. The external growth takes various forms. Where compact growth takes place on the suburban outskirts, it may be associated with the growth of large built-up residential sectors, or it may take place around pre-existing nuclei, be they villages, small towns, or newly established industrial sites.

In its explosion the city has developed a fringe of mixed urban and rural uses. The range of seasonal residence has extended widely to distances of 50 miles or more—a journey time of one or two hours, notably for those who do not require to be at the bench or the office each day. This occurs especially around cities that offer special scenic amenities—such as the islands around Stockholm or Seattle, or many lakes that lie around Milwaukee or Zurich. With faster means of travel many of the summer residences have now become permanent homes.

7. Decentralization

Deconcentration implies simply the diffusion of the brick and mortar of the urban complex. Decentralization, on the other hand, implies the shedding of certain of the city's activities—such as industry or commerce or administration—and their dispersal to a distinct and separate town that itself functions as an independent local and regional centre. The dispersal of administrative functions was particularly important during the 1939–45 war. This process has been going on for a considerable period both around the big cities and over the wider countryside. It is evident in the development of existing small towns and the establishment of 'garden cities' and 'satellites' (in the proper sense of these terms). Policies of planning in Britain seek to establish new self-contained towns and encourage industry to locate in small towns in the countryside, though such trends are far exceeded by the abnormally rapid growth of many American and continental cities.

Communities that for centuries have had an agricultural base are now oriented predominantly, in terms of their employment structure, to non-agricultural occupations. Workers living in the countryside are now able to travel long distances to work—by bicycle, rail, or bus in Europe, and by automobile in the States. The phenomenal increase in the number and complexity of city services in recent years has extended the range and especially the intensity of urban influence. As a result many rural areas have become in a real sense a part of an urban association and the old distinction between rural and urban is now well nigh meaningless.

8. Recentralization

Recentralization is a term that is considerably more meaningful than decentralization in expressing the process of urban growth. Decentralization would simply mean, if taken literally, the scattering of functions from the urban area to less congested places elsewhere. Recentralization more specifically refers to the regrouping of decentralized activities with other activities. The decentralized factory may be located in relation to an integrated community with a central place as its focus. Such a process, writes Gaston Bardet,[1] can take place in four ways: first by the grouping of giant establishments complementary to each other; second, by the transfer of smaller industrial establishments to regional cities; third, by the dispersion of small establishments into important villages; and fourth, by the dispersion of tiny establishments into small family concerns with a few employees. All four features are to be found in all countries, either as natural trends or as objectives of planned development. Each involves a different kind of spatial structure in which the central places will assume different forms in both size and distribution.

The large industrial complex consisting of one or more vast individual units is an important growing feature of modern times. Such complexes cannot, to advantage, be added to an existing city or to a small town. They need to be made the nucleus of new cities. Since one such plant may occupy up to 40,000 to 50,000 workers, as at the Badisch Analin and Soda Fabrik at Ludwigshafen, or the Volkswagen Plant at Wolfsburg, these pose real planning problems which may be solved in different ways. Firstly, the large plant, be it the iron and steel works, the oil refinery, the chemical works, or the new coal-mine (as in the Ruhr) employing 10,000 to 50,000 workers, may comprise the nucleus and the basis of growth of new communities. Adequate economic and social provisions should be available, but the size should not exceed around 50,000 and a maximum of 100,000. The township should be planned so that workers are within two kilometres of their work and also of the facilities offered by the central business district.

The second mode of growth occurs when smaller units of different sizes and categories are transferred into existing towns of some 10,000 to 20,000 inhabitants. Here, the number of employees and the services required should in aggregate be less than the existing population of the town so as not to destroy its character and equilibrium. The optimum of 10,000 families (say 35,000 people) should also not be exceeded. New industries should be linked as far as

---

[1] Gaston Bardet, *L'Urbanisme*, 1955, in the *Que Sais-Je?* series.

possible to the skills of the artisan who is so typical of the small towns of France and Germany.

Third, the small establishments may be dispersed in the countryside, near to existing villages and small towns. This does not necessarily involve the immigration of new workers, but rather involves the absorption of workers in the villages and in the countryside. Unlike the two previous modes of growth the immigration of population plays no part. This growth is excellently illustrated in many of the growing villages and small towns of Württemberg in Germany. Such industries are normally related to the established skills and interests of the local population as is evidenced by the manufacture of watches and clocks, weighing machines, textiles, and musical instruments in Württemberg.

Fourth, the dispersion of small family workshops means that the same worker is both a peasant cultivator and a domestic artisan. This is generally considered from a social point of view to be an extremely desirable element in the structure of the rural population. It survives on the continent because of the survival of small holdings (associated particularly with those areas in which the custom of divided inheritance is practised) and where also the handicrafts and skilled manual crafts have not disappeared. Such a worker has a divided livelihood, holding a little land at home in his native village, and working elsewhere in a factory.

These features of industrial localization and their associated residential and secondary growth are normal trends in the location of activities in the organization of space. They vary greatly in their relative importance from one country and one area to another, for they are largely related to local economic and social conditions and traditions. Moreover, they have developed and are continuously developing, both by natural growth and also by the attempts at planned growth through either the large employer or State policy.

9. Residential Segregation

This refers primarily to the concentration of residents into districts, similar to the concentration of distinct economic uses. Individuals tend to gravitate not only to areas in which they can compete for a livelihood more efficiently, but to areas populated by others of similar race, interests, culture, or economic status. The principle of residential segregation is, in a measure, inherent in building practice, for houses are built in groups or in large estates, usually nowadays of exactly the same type, so that they automatically cater for people of the same economic and social level. Consequently, areas of residential segregation are normally clearly defined by the type of housing, and the geographical extent of that type may be blocked out as a district. This does not mean, of course, that houses are necessarily tenanted in the way originally intended, for with time they become old-fashioned or dilapidated and their status may completely change preparatory to demolition.

The segregation of similar groups is also paralleled by the tendency in the more compact urban areas for locality groups to develop and patronize their own kinds of institutions. The church (and its parish) is the oldest kind of local grouping in the town and served for many centuries as the nexus of a separate community. Institutions in the modern city serve the same purpose, though most of them in the inner areas have lost contact with their original geographical base. The concept of local neighbourhood, usually associated with the old and often poorest districts, is another form of locality grouping. The tendency for groups to localize in this manner has caused the sociologists to speak of such homogeneous areas as 'natural areas' and 'natural associations', which may often be more or less clearly defined and demarcated.

10. Dominance, Invasion, and Succession

These terms have actually been devised by the urban ecologists. They indicate the process of change in the use and occupants of buildings. These changes usually occur together in one area and thus demarcate such an area from its neighbours by a more or less sharp gradient of transition. A building is erected as a *form* to fulfil a particular *function*. With the passage of time, obsolescence sets in, and new economic factors come into play with new demands for land. The old occupants move out and new ones come in. This process of change, when characterized not only as to kind but as to its precise areal texture and extent, is referred to by geographers as 'sequent occupance'.

Dominance refers to the tendency for a given use to be established in an area, so that competition from other uses is not very effective, invasion being obstructed and even obsolescence checked. Under such circumstances the gradient to adjacent areas may be very sharp. Developing as a normal expression of the economic process, it is strengthened and prolonged by the conscious policy of the group living in the area—an ethnic group or a strongly conscious social group that gives prestige value to the area (Beacon Hill in Boston, Chelsea in London). The zone may also be maintained by public action through zoning laws.

With the passage of time change in residential character and obsolescence of buildings are bound to come. A dominant land use or population group is slowly displaced by another. The history of a housing district in the inner zone of any big city or of houses near the business district of a town illustrate the process. The buildings are let in floors and single rooms as residences, offices, or workshops. The building appears dilapidated and the social and economic status of such a district changes, usually for the worse. Landlords hold off on improvements, since they anticipate the sale of the land, but rentals are exorbitantly high. In consequence, disreputable uses paying high rentals creep in, and, moreover, quarters are let under appalling conditions of congestion. One population group often displaces another, fine old properties being subdivided into one-room dwellings for the new occupants.

This process of change—of metabolism—is particularly marked in the large American city, where not only is the process of urban growth rapid, but where there is also a large immigration, since the war, of new people, mostly coloured, who seek immediate living quarters in areas such as this. The process is most marked—this certainly can be considered as a basic law—on the margins of the city centre and along the grand highways radiating from it. The root causes are to be found in the increase of land values in districts of old property. The phenomenon of deterioration occurs, in various stages and degrees, in a large part of the inner and middle zones of our cities and constitutes one of the greatest problems. In all major cities there will be found areas of 'mixed uses', as the planners like to call them, that normally correspond with the areas described above. A major headache for every planner is to locate these areas, to determine who lives in them and how far their grouping should be preserved when the area is demolished and its people transferred elsewhere. Indeed, refurbishing, demolition, and renewal are the culmination of this process. Rebuilding on the same sites demands new architectural forms designed to fulfil new functions. The problem is to know, from the standpoint of what is economically and socially desirable, not only what to put on the cleared sites, but how to design new groups of physical structures and the best location for them in order to meet the social needs of the people who are displaced.

Chapter 3

THE CITY AS A REGIONAL CENTRE

1. The Urban Centre

Every urban settlement, large or small, is in some degree a headquarters of trades and institutions, for the very essence of urban character is the provision of goods and services for a tributary area. 'Cities do not grow up of themselves, countrysides set them up to do tasks that must be performed in central places.'[1] Thus wrote the late Mark Jefferson, one of the most stimulating geographers of the last generation, using for the first time, we believe, the term 'central place' to mean a focus of manifold human activities serving a surrounding area.

Every place acts as a focus, located at the confluence of routes and traffic flows, by means of which it associates with a surrounding area, its field of association. The status of a central place may be evaluated in a variety of ways as a measure of what Sir Halford Mackinder called, many years ago, its nodality, or to use the term of current parlance, centrality.

The theory of centrality, as developed in recent years, is exclusively concerned with the localization of trade and institutions. It occupies a key point throughout this book. But the geographic view, as presented in these pages, embraces *all* those activities that contribute to the growth and structure of the city as a focus, be they classified as manufacturing industries, on the one hand, or services, effected through trade and institutions, on the other hand. Centrality of services, in this more limited circumscription, is only one aspect of the geographic interpretation of the city. However, it seems logical to apply the theory of centralization to both services and industry, and this is how we propose to interpret it in this work.

From this point of view, the activities of an urban centre fall into two broad categories, basic and non-basic. The basic activities are

---

[1] Mark Jefferson, 'The Distribution of the World's City Folk', *Geographical Review*, Vol. XXI, 1931, p. 453.

those which bring income to the place from outside its limits. They are mainly industrial in character, though they may well include other activities, such as commerce, finance, administration, recreation (tourism), and education. These basic activities can be subdivided according to the geographical origin of their income. On the one hand, the range of these activities (e.g. the sales of industrial products or clientele of a tourist resort) are nationwide or even international. On the other hand, there are those activities which mainly serve and draw from a more or less extended and continuous area around the urban centre, the range of the association depending on the nature of the goods or service and on the competition of neighbouring centres. The terms trade area, sphere of influence, hinterland (German, 'the land behind'), umland (German, 'the land around'), and urban field are variously used to define this area. These associations may be described as regional. Virtually all basic activities are both regionally and extra-regionally oriented, in varying proportions, depending upon the nature of the good provided. Non-basic activities are those which exist to service the basic workers and their dependents. These are primarily the services and public utilities, etc., which are needed by the whole population. They may be described as the local services. Though it is difficult to separate local, regional, and extra-regional activities one from the other, and indeed to measure the proportion of any activity which falls into the three categories, the distinction is valid and essential to understanding the nature of cities. Our main purpose here is to examine the significance of the regional functions in urban growth. We commence with the role of the urban settlement as a seat of central activities.

Various factors are responsible for the growth of urban settlements. The most important of these throughout history have been the central services of trade and institutions. The places in which they segregate are popularly referred to, according to their broad status, as hamlet, village, market town, city, and metropolis. These are distributed in repetitive spatial patterns and in more or less close relationship and interaction with their environs. Three sets of forces affect at all times, in the past as well as in the present, the functions, size, and distribution of the central places. These have been described as the market principle—that is, the principle of association with a surrounding complementary area; the traffic or transport principle—that is, the principle of growth and distribution based on the movements of through traffic on main routes; and, third, the administrative principle, whereby the organization of occupied land demands the erection of places with the appropriate institutions to carry out the functions of defence, administration, and public service.

THE CITY AS A REGIONAL CENTRE

2. The Service Factor

Services depend upon direct contact with the consumer. If the service is rendered frequently to individuals of all classes in the community, then it will be located in the midst of its clientele in immediate contact with it. This fact determines primarily the location of services such as doctors, barbers, tobacconists, and small general shopkeepers. These are the local services that are proportional to the distribution of population in both the countryside and in urban areas.

Attraction to the consumer market is the ruling force in the location of all types of service, but the services tend to be localized at more widely spaced intervals in accordance with three sets of circumstances. First, the most efficient size of a specialized establishment such, for example, as a department store or a technical institute, demands a location in a town where it can draw both on the population in the whole town and also on that of its environs. Second, the difference in the intensity of demand for various types of service is also instrumental in removing such services away from the village and smaller towns to the larger towns, or from urban neighbourhoods within the big urban areas to the central business district. Thus, the general practitioner may be located in a country town or village, but the brain surgeon is established in the big city. The same fact conditions the location of dealers in high-class goods, such as furniture and jewellery, or specialized retail shops. Third, the increased ease and speed of transport also tend to reduce the attractiveness of the local market for various types of service. Indeed, every development that permits the service to establish contact with its customers more cheaply and more quickly makes it possible for it to choose locations further away, without diminishing the quality of the service. These conditions account for much of the migration of services from village to town and from smaller to larger towns and cities. These considerations are principal determinants not only of the character and distribution of towns over the land, but also of the character and distribution of service institutions within the urban complex.

The degree of segregation of the centralized services, placed so as to reach a dispersed clientele, is based on two factors, namely, the range of the service from the centre, and the population that is required for its efficient provision. The range of service of a commodity—that is, the geographic limit of its collection or delivery—depends on the degree of its specialization and the frequency with which it has to be provided or purchased and the money involved in buying it. In England, for example, tobacco and sweets may be purchased in a nearby village or small town up to three miles distant.

THE URBAN SETTLEMENT AS REGIONAL CENTRE

Regular, but not daily, food items, such as groceries, meat, and bread, may be bought from a store in a town up to eight miles away. Household equipment, purchased more rarely from a few better stocked stores, may be purchased in the latter or a larger town that is more distant. Working clothes may be bought in small towns and adults' clothes and the rarer purchases of furniture, jewellery, boots and shoes, or better clothing, are more likely to be bought on the occasion of a less frequent visit to a big city.

The threshold of a service is the minimum demand (usually expressed by the total population) which is required to support the concern providing the service. For example, a store will require a certain threshold of demand in terms of its income in order to be able to operate at a profit. Similarly, a school requires a certain population, to provide the minimum number of pupils, its threshold, for its effective support. In the same way, a small hospital, library, or any other centralized service is associated with a particular threshold of demand. The area required to provide this threshold will depend on the density of the population, availability of income, needs, and preferences. Spatial competition between similar services also tends to restrict the area available to reach this threshold.

Centralized services will also tend to segregate at particular places. It also follows that there will be a tendency around any one centre for service areas of a variety of trades and institutions to have common general limits, so as to form a zonal boundary. Smaller centres tend to have one such zone around them. Larger centres with a greater variety of services have a more complex structure, which comprises a series of zones at varying distances from the centre. The degree to which service boundaries of trades and institutions coincide is indicative of the degree of geographic cohesion of the area they enclose. It would seem that areas will correspond where there are distinct breaks in the transfer cost pattern. This arrangement is largely conditioned by the spacing and functional structure of the other urban centres in the system.

The outer range of distribution and collection of goods and services around a centre constitutes its trade area.[1] But social institutions also tend to coalesce with this area, at all levels, from the local neighbourhood to the region of the large city. Local government areas are more rigid and often do not correspond with the trading and community areas. Political boundaries and natural boundaries may also cause the coincidence of many trade boundaries.

On the basis of the preceding principles, there emerges a hierarchy of centres, graded according to the degree of concentration of centralized services, which, in considerable measure, may be reflected in

[1] E. M. Hoover, *The Location of Economic Activity*, New York, 1948.

the size of their population. A German scholar, Walther Christaller, has developed this theme.[1] Working on a theoretical basis, and taking the market town with a service radius of 4 km. (2½ miles) as the fundamental unit area, he has drawn up a scheme of distribution of centralized services which, he shows, is closely borne out by the facts of town size and distribution in south Germany. This system is based on what he calls the market principle. Theoretically, in respect of the centralized services, a central place should be located in the centre of

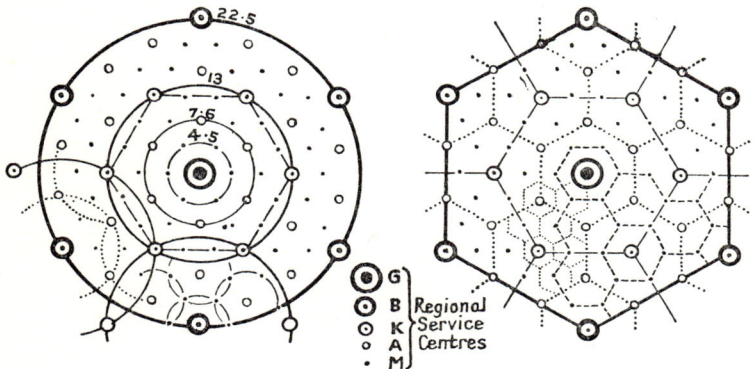

FIG. 1a. The theoretical distribution of Regional Service Centres (after Christaller).

FIG. 1b. The hexagonal pattern of Regional Service Areas (after Christaller).

Compare these diagrams with the table on p. 76. The M centre (market town) is the basis of the whole system. The G centre is equivalent to a county town with about 30,000 to 100,000 inhabitants. The numbers in Fig. 1a give the radius of each circle in miles (after Christaller).

a circular trade area (Fig. 1a). However, circular trade areas overlap, enabling competition between centres in the servicing of intersecting border zones. To resolve this problem, Christaller postulated a system of hexagonal-shaped trade areas in which all places are uniformly spaced from each other. Centres of similar service status are thus equally spaced from each other and serve hexagonal trade areas of the same size. Centres of higher service status will serve larger-sized

[1] Walther Christaller, *Die Zentralen Orte Suddeutschland*, Jena, 1933. For a summary, see Christaller, 'Rapports Fonctionnels entre les Agglomérations Urbaines et les Campagnes', *Comptes Rendus du Congrès International de Géographie*, Amsterdam, 1938, Tome II, Géog. Humaine, 1938, pp. 123–38. See the summary and long bibliography in B. J. L. Berry and A. Pred, *Central Place Studies, a Bibliography of Theory and Applications*, Regional Science Research Institute, Philadelphia, 1961. P. Sargant Florence, 'Economic Efficiency in the Metropolis', in R. M. Fisher (ed.), *The Metropolis in Modern Life*, New York, 1955.

hexagonal trade areas, and accordingly will be uniformly spaced at greater distances from each other. From this geometrical pattern of increasing size of trade areas associated with increased service status, it follows that any centre will be surrounded on the periphery of its trading area by six equally spaced centres of similar lower order, equally spaced from each other and from the dominating central place (Fig. 1*b*). Since there is a gradation of the services with respect to the extent of the areas they serve, there is a corresponding gradation in the degree of their concentration, which in large measure (and especially before the industrial era) is reflected in the settlement size. But this gradation of service concentration is not gradual, nor does the extent of the composite service area of a town vary proportionally with its size. The concentration proceeds in steps, from which there may be recognized a hierarchy of centres. Similarly a town of a particular order will have zonal limits, with sharp gradients, for the services identified with each grade in the hierarchy represented in it.

The grading and distribution of towns, based on the distribution of centralized services, as elaborated by Christaller, are shown on the table on page 76. The population figures are averages for south German towns. Christaller assumes that the smallest complete service centre is the country market town with a market radius of some $3\frac{1}{2}$ to 4 km. and situated about 7 km. from its nearest neighbours. Its hexagonal-shaped market area will then have an area of 45 sq. km. with, according to the average density of population in south Germany, a population of 2,700 persons. Centres of the next higher grade will then be spaced at $\sqrt{3} \times 7$ or 12 km. apart and will serve an area three times as large. The distances between each successive grade will increase by $\sqrt{3}$ and the tributary areas and population served by three times that of the next lower grade. Moreover, lower order centres and their tributary regions 'nest' in the regions of the next higher order centres according to a rule of threes.

This system of central places is based upon the marketing principle, but there are two other centralizing factors at work, transport and administration. Fig. 2 shows the theoretical system of centres based on each of these principles.[1] The diagrams show the arrangement of the centres, the routes and the mode of 'nesting' of service areas, for each of the three principles.

Study of the theoretical system of towns according to the market principle reveals that this distribution is unsuited to the development of an efficient network of communications, linking the places directly

---

[1] As devised by Christaller in 'Das Grundgerüst der räumlichen Ordnung in Europa', *Frankfurter Geog. Hefte*, 1950, and reproduced by Berry and Pred, *Central Place Studies*, 1961.

MARKETING PRINCIPLE

TRANSPORT PRINCIPLE

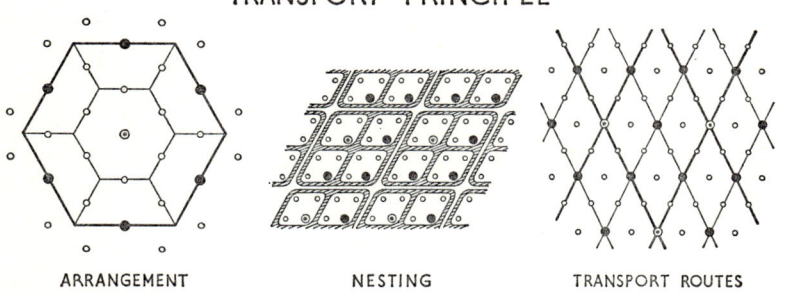

ADMINISTRATIVE PRINCIPLE

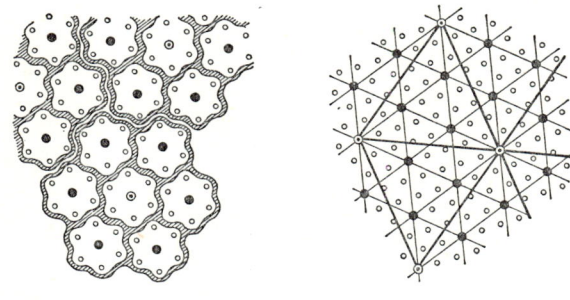

Fig. 2. System of Central Places (after Christaller and Berry).

with each other. A second principle is at work, that may be called the transport principle. Commerce demands routes which shall best serve its needs with the minimum of cost. This involves the maintenance of the route and the actual costs of transport. These demands have been met, not by conscious planning, but by centuries of trial and error. Main military highways and arteries between cities have often persisted since Roman times. Many others emerged in the Middle Ages through linking up short country tracks to form through-routes. From the point of view of commerce, the best theoretical distribution of towns is one which allows the interconnection of the largest number of intermediate places along a direct route between two large cities, leaving the smaller places aside. Moreover, such places should be equally spaced along the route, and the routes should radiate from the central town at equal angular intervals like the spokes of a wheel from the central axle. If the theoretical distribution of towns is based on this principle only, then a considerably larger number of central places of the higher order would be necessary to supply the whole area with the corresponding centralized services. Such a theoretical distribution of towns also reduces the size of the service areas. The latter would lose their theoretical hexagonal shape and be reduced or flattened on the routes. Moreover, if central places were distributed entirely on the basis of the through-traffic principle, the service areas of each centre would be grouped within that of the next higher order centre in accordance with a rule of fours (as opposed to threes for the marketing principle).

Historically, the market factor will dominate in areas where local trade has been more important in the development of the towns than main through-traffic routes. The route factor will be more important where through long-distance traffic has played a more important historical role. The service factor will also be dominant in agricultural areas, whereas densely populated industrial areas can support the larger number of places required when the route factor is more important. The dominance of the route factor may indeed be dictated by the relief of the land which confines routes to single lines along valleys. The basic distinction between the two systems is that one is *areal* in distribution, the other *linear*. The actual distribution and size of places depends largely upon the geographical and historical conditions in the area.

A third factor which affects the functions and distribution of towns is socio-political in character. This arises from the need for administrative areas with administrative centres, as opposed to market areas. This may be called the administrative principle. The ideal administrative unit is one which has a capital in its centre with a group of tributary centres of lower order, and a peripheral area of thinly peopled land separating it from its neighbours. In the past the need for defence has been a primary motive in the use of natural barriers as political frontiers, but the divide between trade and cultural associations, which invariably corresponds with a zone of low population density, is still the ideal boundary between adjacent administrative units, be they of the order of states, or provinces or local districts within the state. The farmer will expect to do his marketing, pay his taxes, and use the institutions—such as the courts of justice—in that town which can be most easily reached and not in a town which can only be reached by devious routes. The local administrative area should be determined primarily on the basis of accessibility to a town, and the divide of local trade associations is the best indicator of this. The natural barrier, such as forest or marsh, was often used as a frontier in the past, but bears little relation to modern associations. The leading idea in the creation of new units, in the past and no less in current planning, is that they should be compact, and roughly equal in area and population.

Ideally, each new unit should have a seat of administration at its centre, and its frontiers should be located in the thinly populated areas which normally are divides between local orientations. This ideal is reached in part by the considerations of the market factor. But a system based on this factor alone would always give to the administrative area imposed upon it several places of the next lower order on its borders, which is in opposition to the principle that an administrative unit should cut across local associations as little as possible. Given the existing pattern of distribution of towns, new principles will have to be used for defining administrative units.

If centres and tributary areas were designed for an area exclusively on the basis of this administrative principle, then the hierarchy would be based on a rule of sevens. As shown on Fig. 2, one centre and its administrative area would have six areas of the same order grouped around it. This would be distinct from the marketing principle in which the hierarchy is based on a rule of three, and the traffic principle which is based on a rule of fours.

We have outlined above the three basic principles that determine the system of distribution of urban centres when regarded as seats of central services. All three normally operate in an area, but the actual mode of their operation depends on the distribution and characteristics of the population and on the circumstances of its historical development. In extreme cases, the marketing principle would apply in an area of uniform economy and population distribution. The traffic principle would apply exclusively to an area in which settlement was confined to narrow belts along the main through routes. The administrative principle would presumably apply exclusively if the administrative divisions and their centres were planned out systematically in an area before the settlement took place. It must, therefore, be very strong in areas of the Middle West where predominantly townships and counties are the rule. Even here, however, the location of the administrative centres does not conform to the theoretical pattern, since they also had to be located with reference to the location of centres on the main rail routes (traffic principle) and the then existing distribution of population (market principle). In any area, then, these strict principles interact according to geographical and historical conditions.

The central place theory as formulated by Christaller has met with a good deal of criticism in Germany, Sweden, and elsewhere. This is based partly on the grounds of the inadequacy of the criteria used to determine centrality (as, for example, his preference for telephone connections rather than retail trade data), and partly on the basis that the principles underlying the theoretical distribution of central places are offset by several others that operate differently through time in different areas. Both of these criticisms are minor and they can easily be met. Central place theory seeks to analyse a single set of determining factors, assuming that other things are equal. The fact is that the Christaller scheme has initiated in the last twenty years many avenues of research that have received fruitful application in many problems of physical and social planning, especially in Germany where the term *Zentralort* or central place is now firmly established among students of cities and planning. The scientific study of geographic patterns of phenomena has been the subject of numerous studies. It is now embodied in substantive works in several countries —by Lösch, Christaller, and Boustedt in Germany, Ponsard in France, Hagerstrand in Sweden, and Isard, Berry, Warntz, and Garrison in the United States. Under the heading of 'regional science' in the United States, such study has drawn recruits from all fields of the social sciences and is becoming of increasing importance as a basis for city, regional, and national planning.[1]

Clearly, the fundamental and universal control exercised by services on the functional character, distribution, and size of towns is only one determining factor. Even in areas not greatly affected by the growth of urban industrial populations, it is modified by such other factors as the relief of the land, the location of routes and river crossings, the distribution of uninhabited land, and the political and economic

---

[1] A. Lösch, *Die Räumliche Ordnung der Wirtschaft*, 2nd ed., Jena, 1944. W. Isard, *Location and Space Economy*, London, 1956, and *Methods of Regional Analysis*, London, 1960. O. Boustedt and H. Ranz, *Regionale Struktur- und Wirtschaftsforschung*, Bremen, 1957. W. Bunge, *Theoretical Geography*, Lund Studies in Geography, Lund, 1962.

circumstances of the early medieval development of the towns. Above all, the distribution of modern industry has determined, far more than any other single factor, the actual *size* of the towns if not their basic distribution. It should be noted, on the other hand, that the varying density of population from one area to another does not appreciably affect the spacing of the towns, nor does the size of the enterprise providing the service, since the need for the service is universal.

The nineteenth century saw the great concentration of industries in special localities, near to raw materials, or at points where these materials could be cheaply assembled. The overwhelming majority of such industrial centres were simply dovetailed into the existing pre-industrial towns which had come into being in the Middle Ages. The old towns were transformed in functional character and size so that industries became dominant, and the centralized services secondary, in their functional structure. Entirely modern urban communities, such as coal-mining, dormitory, and health-resort communities, which have been planted in the countryside, but have no fundamental relations with it, are even more specialized in character. The centralized services, however, together with the predominantly local services such as distributive trades, building trades, transport services, laundering, and confectionery, have increased greatly in the last decades, owing to the rising standard of living of the urban populations as well as to the general increase in the number and complexity of the centralized services. Specialized industrial towns are deficient in many such services, and these must perforce draw from a neighbouring and larger city. There are, however, many towns which possess a 'balance' of all these functions, because they are especially closely integrated with the surrounding countryside. These include, for example, the numerous country market towns in western Europe with a population from 2,500 to 10,000. Especially characteristic is the country town, which has a variety of modern industries, and is the chief centre for the activities and organization of the satellite market towns in its tributary district. The large cities owe their *raison d'être* as great agglomerations primarily to the concentration of industry, but they have also become, in varying degree, outstanding centres of centralized services, proportional to their importance as the capitals of the economic, social, and cultural life of the country and towns around them.

3. The Administrative Factor

The word 'city' is derived from the Latin *civitas*. Its Greek equivalent is *polis*. In ancient Greece and Rome these words embodied the concept of the city-state, that is, the state as a small unit with a central focus of its life and activities, the whole being not too large in area or population to prevent effective government through the assembled body of its citizens. Gallic tribes and the areas they occupied were called *civitates* by the Romans and the Roman civil divisions were based on them, the Roman town centre being usually placed on the site of, or near, the preceding Gallic hill-top *oppidum*. The ecclesiastical dioceses were later adjusted to the same framework with the same centres, the latter being called *civitates* by virtue of their being seats of bishops. But, in general, the word *civitas* acquired a much wider meaning, and after about 1150, when the medieval concept of the town was fully developed, *civitas*, the name given to the town, implied a settlement with industry and commerce, a law of its own, and walled fortifications (see p. 20). The French version, *cité*, was used throughout the Middle Ages as applying more or less strictly to the seat of the bishopric. During the Middle Ages, the town throughout western and central Europe became a centre of defence, administration, industry, and commerce. The medieval town was made *de jure*, or became *de facto*, the centre for its surrounding local territory. The organization of the church demanded a hierarchy of ecclesiastical divisions with central Bishoprics and Archbishoprics. Defence in the early Middle Ages called for the organization of defined territories (though we seldom know their exact extent) around centres which served as places of refuge and administration. In the later Middle Ages feudal lords, in the German lands in particular, established new fortified towns to organize and defend their tattered feudal territories as small compact geographical units. The weekly market was an accompaniment of the medieval town and has remained so until this day, although its function, aspect, and organization have changed. There were laws forbidding the holding of markets within a competitive radius of one already existing—radius of about four to six miles. Other considerations often outweighed this, however, for the basic factor of distance to market and the competition of neighbours eventually sorted out the active centres, while those that were superfluous declined.

In the Middle Ages the town as the centre of civilization was a most important factor in moulding areas of group feeling and organization, as well as in the formation of administrative units. The towns of the early Middle Ages had their origins as centres of secular and ecclesiastical administration, and as such the dioceses had their central bishops' seats, and the counties had their central *burgs*—places of defence and refuge in which the count was installed in order to maintain law and order as the representative of the king or emperor. The establishment of such burgs, each with a tributary area, accounted

THE CITY AS A REGIONAL CENTRE

for the emergence of the administrative units over large areas of Europe. In England we may instance the foundation of the counties of the Midlands which were established as the Danelagh was reconquered by Ethelred and Athelstan of Wessex. The Marches of England against Wales and the similar districts on the eastern borders of the Carolingian Empire were organized in the same way.

The town also emerged as the dominant centre for the trade and administration of justice for a surrounding district; in Germany in particular, independent lords and dukes founded new castle towns as administrative centres for small districts in the later Middle Ages. This association of the countryside with the local market and administrative centre in the past, no less than in the present, is reflected, for instance, in France by the frequent occurrence of a *pays* or province with a name taken from that of the local capital town, e.g. Maconnais, Laonnais, Anjou, Touraine, Poitou.

The seventeenth and eighteenth centuries were the heyday of the provincial political and cultural capital. In Germany each of numerous small states had its own capital, with its own court, and all the apparatus of sovereign government. In France, the traditional capital of each province was the seat of provincial administration, and of the *Parlement*, as well as the seat of the nobility. However, the capitals were robbed of their administrative functions in 1789, when local administration was reorganized and the provinces replaced by the *départements*. In England, the county town became the recognized centre of social and economic life for each county.

'The country gentry with their wives and daughters came to regard a visit to the county-town and indulgence in a round of balls and feasts, visits and functions, in the same light as a season in London is regarded at the present date. . . .'

'The county town was (the countryman's) Metropolis. He was attracted there by business and pleasure, by assizes, quarter sessions, elections, musters of militia, festivals and races. There were the halls in which the judges opened the King's Commission twice a year. There were the markets at which the corn, cattle, the wool and the hops of the surrounding country were exposed to sale. There were the great fairs to which the merchants came from London and where the rural dealer laid in his cutlery and muslin. There were the shops at which the best families of the neighbourhood bought grocery and millinery.'[1]

Many important changes were made at the end of the eighteenth century and in the early nineteenth century in the administrative

---

[1] Edwin A. Pratt, *History in Inland Transport and Communications*, 1912, p. 94.

units of western Europe. These changes were made in the heyday of road transport, just before the development of modern factory industry and the advent of the railway. The most important change was the creation of the *départements* in France in place of the historical provinces. Each *département* was defined so as to have its administrative centre accessible to all parts of the *département* in a day's journey. The *département*, however, often shows a close relation to the earlier province, which was subdivided to form two or three of the new divisions. Each *département* was later divided into *arrondissements* and *cantons* defined on the same principle of accessibility to a central town. In Germany, similar changes took place, partly under the Prussian kings, and partly through the reforms of the Napoleonic regime in the southern states. In Prussia, a fivefold hierarchy of administration units came into being at the beginning of the nineteenth century. The *Provinz* (normally the direct successor of the old historical unit), the *Regierungsbezirk*, the *Landkreis*, and the *Amtgerichtsort*. The last was the successor of the area established in the later Middle Ages around a castle town, and it in turn contained several parishes or *Gemeinden*. The main features of this system are repeated in the other states, although the names of the districts vary. The states (*Länder*) of the Reich are equivalent to the provinces of Prussia in this hierarchy. It may be noted, however, that many of these states are very small, though they enjoyed for centuries the full powers and status of independent sovereignty. In consequence, the small capital city is a very distinctive feature of the towns of Germany.

In Britain at the opening of the nineteenth century, there were only two types of administrative district—the parish and the county. In 1834 new districts were established for the administration of the Poor Law. These 'Unions' were usually defined so as to correspond with the market area of a central town in which the Poor Law Guardians met and the Poor Law Institutions were located. In the 1870's, Rural and Urban Sanitary Districts were established. The Rural Districts normally corresponded with the Poor Law Unions, though the latter have now been abolished. Consequently, the areas of the Rural Districts are today in many ways too small for the requirements of modern organization, function, and transport. The counties have remained without any substantial change since the Middle Ages. Consequently, they are also too small for many purposes of administration and they are grouped to form larger units that fit more closely to modern needs.

It is of interest to note the comparative size of these administrative units. In Prussia the *Landkreis* and its equivalent in Saxony are remarkably equal in area. Each is compact in shape, has an average diameter of 20 to 30 km., and a town at its geometrical centre. This is comparable with the French *canton*. The English Rural District, based on the earlier Poor Law Union, has an average diameter of about 15 km. It is of the same order, although somewhat smaller than, the *canton*. The *Kreis* in Bavaria is the equivalent of the Prussian *Regierungsbezirk* and is roughly equal to a French *département*, with a radius of about 60 to 80 km. from its capital. Each has about fifteen to twenty sub-divisions, with diameters of about 20 km. By way of comparison, Mayenne, a French *département*, has three *arrondissements* and twenty-seven *cantons*, the diameter of the last being about 20 km. The Bavarian *Kreis*, the Prussian *Regierungsbezirk*, and the French *département* are roughly equal in area to a medium-sized English county, such as Leicester or Warwick, which have diameters of about 50 to 60 km.[1]

There is evidently a consistency in the hierarchy of political divisions within states and in the status of the administrative centres associated with them. Where there is a continuous veneer of rural settlement with an even network of urban centres, as in western Europe and in the eastern half of the United States, we may assume, with Christaller,[2] a basic distribution of the smallest clustered settlement—the village—each in the centre of hexagonally arranged parishes, *communes*, or *Gemeinden*. The administrative principle would give a sequence of centres in sevens. The lowest order of administrative centre will be one of the *communes* with jurisdiction over the adjacent six hexagonal-shaped *communes*. This becomes the first order of the hierarchy. The next (second) order of administrative divisions will include the centre exercising authority over six centres of the first order, or a total of $6 \times 7 = 42$ *communes*. The next (third) order will then include one central place of the third order, six of the second order, each of which contains forty-two of the first order, a total of 294 *communes*. (These figures exclude the administrative centre at each level.) This would mean one State capital, six provincial capitals, forty-two second-order capitals and 294 first-order centres. A few states have such an approximate sevenfold division. Examples are Australia, Costa Rica, and Algeria. Many have about forty-nine divisions, e.g. Spain, Greece, Java, the United States, England and Wales.

[1] There is no work that deals with the character and development of politico-geographical divisions and the principles underlying their definition. The reader is referred to G. Montague Harris, *Local Government in many Lands: A Comparative Study*, London, 1933.
[2] A paper delivered to the Seminar on Urban Geography at Lund on the occasion of the meeting of the International Geographical Union, September 1960. 'Die Hierarchie der Städte', *I.G.U. Symposium in Urban Geography, Lund, 1960*, ed. Knut Norborg, Lund, 1962, pp. 3–11. See also his *Das Grundgerüst der räumlichen Ordnung in Europa*, Frankfurter Geog. Hefte, 1950, 96 pp. 3 maps.

The operation of the market principle with a sequence in threes modifies this theoretical administrative system. With such a theoretical system, the first order centres are, in German, the *Amtsorte*. Additional services would tend to segregate at places equidistant from *three* equally spaced centres, i.e. in the centre of a triangle formed by the three equidistant *Amtsorte*. The ratio of the hierarchy and administrative divisions that would develop on this basis would follow a ratio of threes—1–3–9–27–81, with a corresponding number of central places—1–2–6–18–54. That is, for one major city there will be two lesser cities of the next lower order, six of the next lower order, etc. The ninefold (or 8 or 10) division occurs frequently, as in Belgium, the Netherlands, Finland, Yugoslavia, Germany, and New Zealand. A twenty-seven division is rarer but occurs in Ireland, Sweden, and Switzerland. Some ninety divisions occur in France and Italy, and eighteen in Poland and Czechoslovakia. Belgium has nine divisions—Brussels plus six surrounding divisions and two further removed. In France it has been necessary to establish larger and fewer divisions than the ninety *départements*. There are nine to twelve divisions each with about nine *départements* subordinate to it.

The transport principle would have an urban hierarchy based on long-distance commerce, in which the 'nesting' of administrative centres would follow multiples of four. A town will be connected with its six neighbours of the same order by six radiating roads. If an additional centre is required it would be rationally placed half-way between two centres. The system of six radial routes is, of course, an extremely common phenomenon and is well developed in France. An arrangement of administrative divisions on this basis would place the chief centres on the periphery of their areas. The hierarchy of districts would be 1–4–16–64, and of the town hierarchy 1–3–12–48. Some sixteen divisions are found in Paraguay and Nicaragua, and sixty-four in Turkey. Twenty-four divisions occur frequently in Latin America—in Peru, Colombia, Venezuela, Argentina, and Brazil.[1]

4. The Industrial Factor: The Economic Base

The role of the regional market in localizing industry in cities is generally underestimated in studies of urban growth. In Britain, this is probably for the simple reason that the country is so small, that specialization between one city and another in what are essentially regional industries is not possible. Thus a city's products are distributed widely in the tributary areas of other cities. On the Continent

---

[1] The above is according to Christaller, *op. cit.*, and clearly demands further investigation.

and in the United States, on the other hand, many factors have contributed to the growth of both industry and commerce in cities to service the regional market. Of primary importance is the fact that the historic regional capitals on the Continent and the main commercial centres in the United States, which served initially as collecting and distributing centres, have grown to be great modern cities. Moreover, the great distance between such cities, amounting often to hundreds of miles, as compared with tens of miles in Britain, and the system of railway freight rates with 'basing points' as selected towns, have also contributed to the growth of regional functions in the great city.

The industries forming the base of what has been called 'the occupational pyramid' of a community fall into three groups. First, there are material-oriented industries that are tied down to particular sites —mining, shipbuilding and metal smelting, chemicals and other 'heavy industries'. They are located at the source of production of the coal or mineral, on a tideway, or at a convenient place of assembly. Secondly, there are the industries that have origins hidden in the past—located by historical accident, by localizing factors that have long since ceased to be operative. These included the advantages of cheap power, local skilled or cheap labour, or the presence of related industries or services. Typical in this category in Britain, the Continent, and the United States are the textile industries. These two groups make up practically all the immobile industries that are highly concentrated in a few fixed locations. Consequently, they are not oriented primarily to serve regional markets. Thirdly, there are the relatively mobile or 'foot-loose' industries, many of which are of relatively recent development. These are normally concerned with the production of consumer goods for which costs of distribution and the cost of assembling raw materials are small items in the total cost of production. These industries have located at places with good communications, ready access to a market, and near existing sources of labour supply, or the manufacturers' place of residence. On the one hand, these mobile industries are in part highly localized, as in the case of the automobile and electrical engineering industries. On the other hand, there is a vast range of new consumers' industries that are located in all big cities so as to assure effective cover of the regional market.

The second component in the occupational structure of a community is concerned with services. Most of these are essentially local, but some serve a wider or regional clientele. The services in Britain were considered by J. H. Jones to occupy from one-fifth of the total occupied population in a highly industrial area to about two-fifths in others. His definition of services includes 'local industries and services, such as transport, electricity, and gas production, retail distribution, municipal services, hairdressing, tailoring and dressmaking, domestic service, law, education, accountancy and religion'.[1] The local services are the city-fillers of Sombart and the city-supporting or city-serving activities of recent writers. They are generally called the non-basic activities. The proprietor of a newspaper, a retail establishment, a wholesale concern, or an insurance firm could (if willing to do so) state exactly what proportion of his turnover was affected within the city boundaries, in the surrounding towns, and in the wider countryside. He could prepare a detailed analysis of the geographical distribution of his customers from which it would be apparent that many of the services and even of the basic industries have markets covering both 'local' and wider 'regional' needs, as well as serving the outside world, with the products of its basic industries and services.

It will be clear, in fact, that over and above satisfying the needs of a local population, regional industry and service may be so important in a city as to constitute part of the base of the occupational pyramid. The city's function as a regional capital would then be its main *raison d'être*. Manufacturing industries that are regionally oriented may be considered from a twofold viewpoint. On the one hand, they may be concerned with the processing of raw materials drawn from the region—lumber, livestock (slaughtering and meat packing), agricultural products (sugar-beet factories, brewing, flour-milling, canning, etc.), and finishing processes to manufactured products (e.g. dyeing and finishing in the textile industries). On the other hand, both consumers' and producers' goods may be manufactured in a city (or imported wholesale from other cities) for distribution throughout the tributary area—agricultural machinery, fertilizers, hardware. Other industries of this kind that are universally located in big cities are printing, publishing and bookbinding, light engineering, bakeries and bottling plants, clothing, public utility services, and the building trades.[2] Though a few special industries may dominate the industrial structure of a metropolitan city it will invariably be found that commerce, administration, and public service in aggregate employment exceed the industrial occupations of all kinds, which are normally of a diversified character.

Special mention should be made here of the spatial interlinkage of activities, which may or may not be channelled through central cities. Industries agglomerate in order that they may efficiently share and exchange their products and service. Scale economies are derived

[1] J. H. Jones on 'Industry and Planning', in E. A. Gutkind, *Creative Demobilization*, Vol. II, 1945, p. 125.
[2] O. D. Duncan, *Metropolis and Region*, 1960.

from the proximity of blast furnace and steel furnace. Coking, iron smelting, steel making, and rolling mills are normally located together since they are engaged in the various stages of a continuous manufacturing process. Industries using the same materials or producing complementary goods tend to agglomerate. Such is the case with the woollen and worsted industries, and automobile parts and accessories. There is also the interlinkage involved in the use of the same general reservoir of labour. A town dependent on one type of industry has labour that can be used by other industries. Such was the case in the migration of the silk mills of Patterson, N.J. to the Scranton area, where the wives and daughters of coal-miners provided a surplus labour supply. Similarly, light industries employing female labour find prospects in places of primarily male employment—e.g. naval bases and coal-mining centres.

It must again be emphasized that the big cities of Britain, with the possible exception of Edinburgh, had assumed the aspect of industrial agglomerations by the middle of the nineteenth century. They are still primarily industrial agglomerations rather than true metropolitan cities with diversified industry and commerce. On the Continent, the regional capital emerged in the last decades of the nineteenth century primarily as a seat of regional as well as specialized industry by virtue of its already being a focus of railways and roads and a historic capital. It thus had traditions and knowledge in industry and commerce, and large capital reserves that were available for further investment in the city and its hinterland. In the mid-western part of the United States, the cities originated in the middle nineteenth century as commercial centres on rivers and then attracted the railroad, becoming the foci of converging routes. It was not until the last decades of that century that the big cities of the Middle West developed as industrial centres to serve their regional markets, and only since 1900 have they advanced to the final stage of development as seats of diversified industry and independent financial centres.

5. The Basic v. Non-basic Ratio

The nature of the so-called centralized activities and factors involved in their definition and location have been considered. The major problem is one of measuring the importance of these activities in individual centres to enable comparisons between centres in any given area. This requires measurement of the total activities that are oriented to servicing the 'regional market' as opposed to the 'local market', the two market areas being defined with reference to the geographic limits of the 'local' area of the city.

The functions of cities may be interpreted from the standpoint of the relative importance of basic and non-basic activities. As stated above, the basic activities account for the very existence of the city since they bring in income from outside. The non-basic activities service the essential workers and their dependents. This study faces two main problems. First of all, censuses base their data on occupations and if one uses this source the occupational groups must be manipulated in order to separate the proportion of 'basic' occupations from the 'service' occupations and this is, at best, extremely arbitrary. On the other hand, if one seeks to separate the activities on the basis of geographic relationships, then one must distinguish between those activities that bring income into the 'area' and those that support the basic working population within the 'area'. Here there are two difficulties. First, what does one mean by the 'area' or the geographic base; and how can it be kept consistent for comparative study? We have stated that the 'local market' is best considered as the city as a socio-economic unit, though for statistical analysis the administrative area is usually the only one available. In the United States the standard metropolitan district can be used for this purpose for a wide range of census data. Second, how is service or manufacturing output to be measured in terms of the proportion that comes from outside or inside the city area? Direct recourse to the census is the most practicable method. To determine the relation proportions of the 'local', 'regional', and 'extra-regional' markets involves exhaustive analysis in individual cities. Methods and data are not likely to be consistent from place to place and country to country. These are some of the problems presented by the basic–non-basic concept.[1]

Various attempts have been made to measure the importance of service functions in the role of urban centres. The first and most important task is to find measures of the ratio between the basic or 'city-forming' functions and the non-basic or 'city-servicing' functions. This has been arrived at by a variety of statistical methods. Alexandersson[2] in a study of 864 American cities with over 10,000 inhabitants, seeks to separate the 'city-servicing' share of each occupation by a method that calculates the minimum need of an average city so that the surplus in any one occupation is the number of workers above this minimum. This surplus is then regarded as its city-forming or basic element. The minimum figures for each occupation give the numbers of workers that are barely sufficient to meet the

---

[1] See J. W. Alexander on 'The Basic–Non-basic Concept of Urban Economic Functions', reprinted in Mayer and Kohn, *op. cit.*, also the series of articles by R. B. Andrews on 'Mechanics of the Urban Economic Base' in *Land Economics*, XXIX, 1953.

[2] G. Alexandersson, *The Industrial Structure of American Cities. A Geographic Study of Urban Economy in the U.S.*, London, 1956.

needs of the city such as would be found in a unifunctional centre with a weak association with its surrounding area. On this basis it is calculated that the city-serving production employs 37·7 per cent. of all gainfully employed. This gives a ratio of basic to service activities of roughly 100 : 66. While this seems reasonably to fit the facts in small cities, it would probably be too small for the bigger cities.

A similar 'minimum requirements method' for estimating 'internal employment' in a city is used by E. A. Ullman.[1] He found that the gross non-basic employment in fourteen cities with over a million inhabitants reached 56·7 per cent., the remainder being the gross total of basic employment. This gives a B/N ratio of 100 : 140. The percentage for thirty-eight cities with 300,000 to 800,000 people was 48·6 per cent. Following on certain refinements of the method, Ullman found that the larger the city, the larger is the sum of the minima ranging from 24 per cent. for towns of 2,500 to 3,000 to 48·6 per cent. for cities of 300,000 to 800,000 with an approximate B/N ratio ranging from 1 : 0·3 to 1 : 1. The larger the city the larger the number of specialities it can support and the more self-contained the city can be.

Homer Hoyt[2] compared the percentage of total employed in a city to the percentage of total employed for the country as a whole. The difference is the surplus (or deficiency) in each occupation. John Alexander in an exhaustive study of one American town (Madison, Wisconsin) sought to estimate the proportion of custom in each industry or service that was derived from the city clientele and then transferred the percentage figure to the numbers of persons engaged in it. This was an exhaustive study of one city that has also been worked out for others, but this method of analysis is not practicable on the same basis for a large number of cities.

According to Alexander's study of Madison,[3] the ratio of basic to non-basic workers was 100 to 82 (total population 110,000). The ratio in a neighbouring city of Oshkosh was 100 to 160 (total population 47,000). Other basic–non-basic ratios have been worked out for cities such as Detroit 100 to 117 (population 2·9 m.), Cincinnati 100 to 170 (900,000), Albuquerque 100 to 103 (116,000), and New York 100 to 215. The ratio varies widely (even in spite of the probable difference

[1] E. A. Ullman and M. F. Dacey, 'The minimum requirement approach to the urban economic base', *The I.G.U. Symposium in Urban Geography, Lund, 1960*, Lund, 1962, pp. 121–43.

[2] Economic consultant, one of the first exponents of the concept which he has applied and modified in a variety of planning studies. See particularly Homer Hoyt on 'The Development of Economic Base Concept,' *Land Economics*, XXX, 1954, pp. 182–91.

[3] J. W. Alexander, 'An Economic Base Study of Madison, Wisconsin', *Wisconsin Commerce Papers*, Vol. 1, No. 4, Madison, 1953.

due to methods of statistical compilation). The composition of the non-basic element requires special note, since it is not by any means exclusively confined to what are called 'services' in the accepted census classification. Of the total number employed in Madison, the non-basic component included 41 per cent. in services, 30 in trades, 12 in government, 8 in manufacturing, and 9 in others. Oshkosh had essentially the same distribution.

This basic–non-basic ratio does *not* provide an indication of the role of the regional factor in the activities of a city. Such a measure must be derived from the breakdown of the basic activities into their regional and extra-regional components. This presents a real challenge to students of quantitative analysis that would be a signal contribution to the understanding of cities. Statistical methods of this kind have received little attention in Britain. A recent publication is a step in this direction,[1] but contributes little new to this problem. Measures of the regional component can be obtained from the numbers engaged in 'non-local' services, or, more precisely, in the retail trades. Several examples follow.

A broad portrayal of the towns of Britain with over 50,000 inhabitants was attempted in *Ground Plan of Britain*, prepared for the so-called 1940 Council. A map of the 'Wheels of Industry' shows a circle for each city proportional to the population, and each circle is divided into three segments showing the proportion of workers (according to the Census classification) engaged in extractive industries (mainly mining and quarrying), manufacturing industries, and service industries. The last includes transport workers, builders, government servants, professional men, shop-keepers and traders, personal servants, and others. The proportion engaged in services, in this broad sense, is normally between 50 and 75 per cent. of the total employed, although it must be pointed out again that these services include the essentially 'local' services (barbers, local shops, etc.) as well as occupations that have wider regional clientele. It is the latter that is of particular concern to us here. If we exclude those occupations that, on the face of it, are essentially local (utilities, domestic service, construction), this percentage is much less than the swollen total of 50 to 75 per cent., and would probably lie between 40 and 50 per cent. Only in very specialized *industrial* communities does the percentage of services fall below this overall figure, to about a third. The higher proportion is reached in specialized service centres such as ports (e.g. Liverpool, Hull, Southampton), and above all, in London, in each of which over 20 per cent. of all employed are engaged in commerce (including shopping) alone. In the same

[1] C. A. Moser and W. Scott, *British Towns, A Statistical Study of their Social and Economic Differences*, London, 1961.

category are the coastal resorts, like those on the south coast, or inland resorts, like Bath or Harrogate. The high proportion in these resorts is due not to business, finance, or the handling and distribution of goods but to shopping and personal service for the resident population—the holiday-makers, the elderly retired, the invalids, and the residents working in other cities. Other examples of towns in this category are Exeter, Norwich, York, and Gloucester, which are primarily service centres, with a small but significant proportion in manufacturing—25 to 50 per cent. Many of the smaller towns fall into this category. They are clearly concerned not only with service to the town community but also, in greater degree than in the preceding types, to the surrounding countryside. The great cities which are recognized as the provincial capitals, like Birmingham and Manchester, have a proportion of about half and half between service and industry, although in some cases, as in Edinburgh and Newcastle, the proportion in service is much higher. The specialized manufacturing towns, as in Lancashire, the West Riding, Nottinghamshire, and Leicestershire, have up to three-quarters of their workers in manufacturing and extractive industries. These data indicate a wide variation of services in towns of different types, but they still do not give a single measure of the regional status of the towns.

It is generally agreed that the retail trades afford a good overall measure of regional relations in general. A further step in such analysis can be taken by using, for example, the censuses of retail trades that are now available in Great Britain and the United States.

The British census gives figures of turnover in the retail trades for all places with over 2,500 inhabitants. The average trade *per capita* for the country (or a county) indicates the expected level for any one centre. The degree to which such a centre exceeds this figure indicates its level of regional centrality.

In the West Riding of Yorkshire the average trade *per capita* in 1953 was £114 (England and Wales, £122).[1] *Per capita* sales in the large towns are as much as one-third above this average. In contrast, places close to these centres vary from one-third to two-thirds below the average for the whole area. For example, around Leeds (£147 *per capita* sales) the sales in selected small towns are £39, £53, £72 and £74 *per capita*, all clearly subordinate to major centres in their shopping activities. However, small towns a little further from Leeds, and just outside this critical range of commercial influence, have very high *per capita* sales, indicating a high measure of centrality. Examples are Harrogate £207, Ripon £208 and Skipton £223.

In turning to the case of the United States, where similar data

[1] *Census of Distribution and other services*, 1950. Volume I, *Retail and Service Trades*, H.M.S.O., London, 1953.

are available for 1954, we may take a specific illustration in New York State. In Upstate New York the *per capita* sales in Syracuse were one-third above the average *per capita* sales of the whole area ($1,000 *per capita*), so that this proportion must be regarded both as basic and regional in kind. Places in the surrounding area have sales *per capita* that are well below the average, indicating that many of their services are derived from other centres, primarily from Syracuse. Small cities in the countryside, with a high degree of centrality, also have high sales *per capita* due to sales drawn from the environs.

In a study of the retail trade areas of southern Sweden, Sven Godlund classes the urban centres on the basis of a measure of centralization of retail services (Fig. 2a).[1] The index of centralization equals the number of persons engaged in retail trade and service as a percentage of the total population in the settlement. For all Sweden this is 3·9. The centres are graded as follows— regional centres (with an index over 6·5), townlets (5·5 to 6·4), township centres (4·5 to 5·4), market centres (3·5 to 4·4), and special urban settlements (3·5 to 4·4). Regional centres are fully-fledged towns with nineteen selected branches in trade and services. The rest are, in varying degree, small auxiliary centres in the usage of Christaller. The regional centres are the only bus and retail centres of importance. The service areas of the regional centres are determined theoretically simply by fixing points of equidistance along the roads between the centres and then interconnecting them by straight lines. The actual service hinterlands are based on maps of passengers carried per week on buses from 1947 to 1949, and by locating the traffic divides between the centres. There is a remarkable correspondence between the theoretical hinterlands and the actual hinterlands.

6. The Hierarchy of Centres

There are now available numerous studies of the hierarchy of towns as regional centres based on the analysis of the services and institutions offered by them, rather than from the occupational data of the census. These studies have revealed two general principles in the functions and spacing of towns. First, services tend to segregate in ascending order in trait complexes of increasing size and variety of functions, in such a way that the central functions are graded into a recognizable series from the hamlet to the great metropolis. Second, the spacing of such centres follows certain regularities that permit the recognition of systems of distribution which differ from one area

[1] Sven Godlund, 'Bus Services, Hinterland and the Location of Urban Settlements in Sweden, especially Scania', *Lund Studies in Geography*, Series B, Human Geography, No. 3, 1951.

to another according to the circumstances of historical development in the area.

The pioneer work in this connection is Christaller's theory of centrality, which has been briefly outlined above. We now turn to his analysis in the specific area of south Germany. The centralized

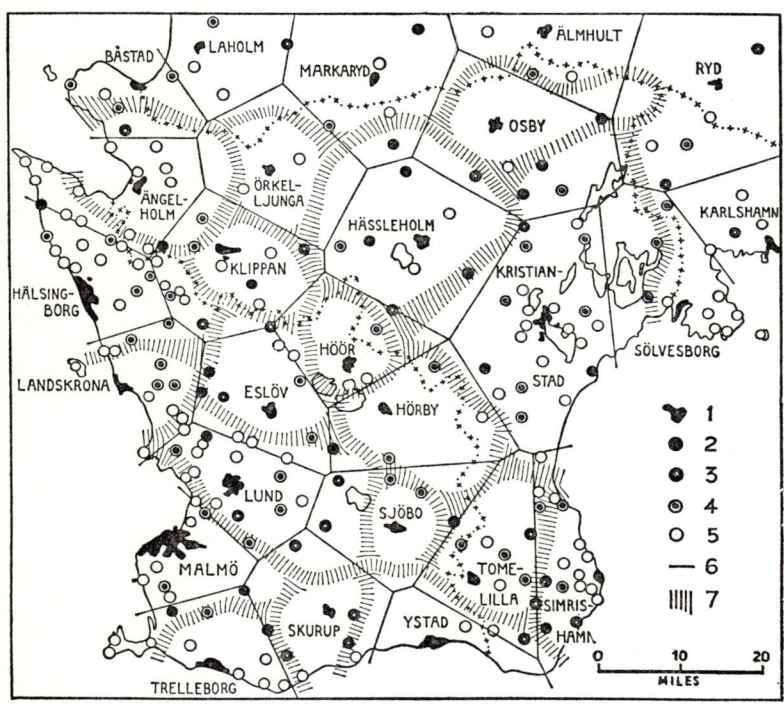

FIG. 2a. Scania, South Sweden. Urban Settlements and their Hinterlands (after Godlund).

1. Regional centre. 2. Townlet centre. 3. Township centre. 4. Market centre. 5. Special Urban Settlement. 6. Boundary of theoretical hinterland. 7. Actual hinterland (defined by bus traffic).

services, as listed by Christaller, are concerned with administration, culture, health, social service, organization of economic and social life, trade, finance, service industries, and the organization of the labour market, and traffic. He lists the specific services and institutions in each category, grouping them, according to grade, into lower, middle, and upper. This empirical method of assessment cannot give an adequate composite measure of the centrality or nodality of a place. Christaller, seeking, like other investigators, a quantitative approach, used the number of telephones as a measure of centrality on the assumption that this was the best measure of general relationships between one place and another.

The centrality of a place (Zz) (that is, the services it provides over and above the local needs of its inhabitants) he measured by the formula $Zz = Tz - \left[Ez \cdot \dfrac{Tg}{Eg} \right]$, where Tz is the number of telephones and Ez the number of inhabitants in the place, Tg and Eg the number of telephones and inhabitants respectively in the area (g = *Gebiet*) served by it. $\left[Ez \cdot \dfrac{Tg}{Eg} \right]$ is what the importance of the centre *ought* to be in proportion to its population, Tz is the *actual* importance, and the difference between them is the centrality. The fraction $\dfrac{Tg}{Eg}$ is the telephone density of the whole area.

From this assessment, there emerged a ranking of urban centres as seats of centralized services. The distribution of these centres in south Germany is shown on Fig. 3 (p. 75). The *market centre* (M) has a normal distance of 7 to 9 km. from its neighbours, and a service radius of 4 to 5 km. It has centralized functions of the lowest grade —registrar's office (*Standesamt*), police station, doctor, dentist, veterinary surgeon (in some centres), a small hotel, a local branch of a district bank, craftsmen, repair shops, breweries and mills, and almost invariably a head post office and telephone and railway station. The *Amtsort* (A) corresponds with the lowest administrative centres, which usually serves three market towns and their parishes. It has a police court, library, elementary school, museum, chemist, veterinary surgeon, bank, cinema, a local newspaper, local trade associations, specialized shops, and almost always it lies on a railway. The *Kreisstadt* (K) is so named from the frequency with which it occurs as the capital of the *Kreis* in Prussia and Hesse, and of the corresponding *Amtsbezirke* in Baden, the *Oberämter* in Württemberg, and *Bezirksämter* in Bavaria. The *Kreis* came into existence as an administrative unit in the early nineteenth century, and has many functions associated with its administrative status that permit its recognition as a well-defined type. The *Bezirk* centre (B) is not so clearly identified administratively, but economically it is very important, and there is a tendency to group *Kreis* districts for administrative purposes into units with centres of a higher order (see below). In Germany, the distinction between the *Kreis* and the *Bezirk* centre is popularly expressed in the terms *Städtchen* (townlet) and *Stadt* (town). The latter has all the main characteristics of a fully-developed town. It has acquired many functions which it can carry out more effectively than the *Kreisstadt* by serving a larger area, which includes

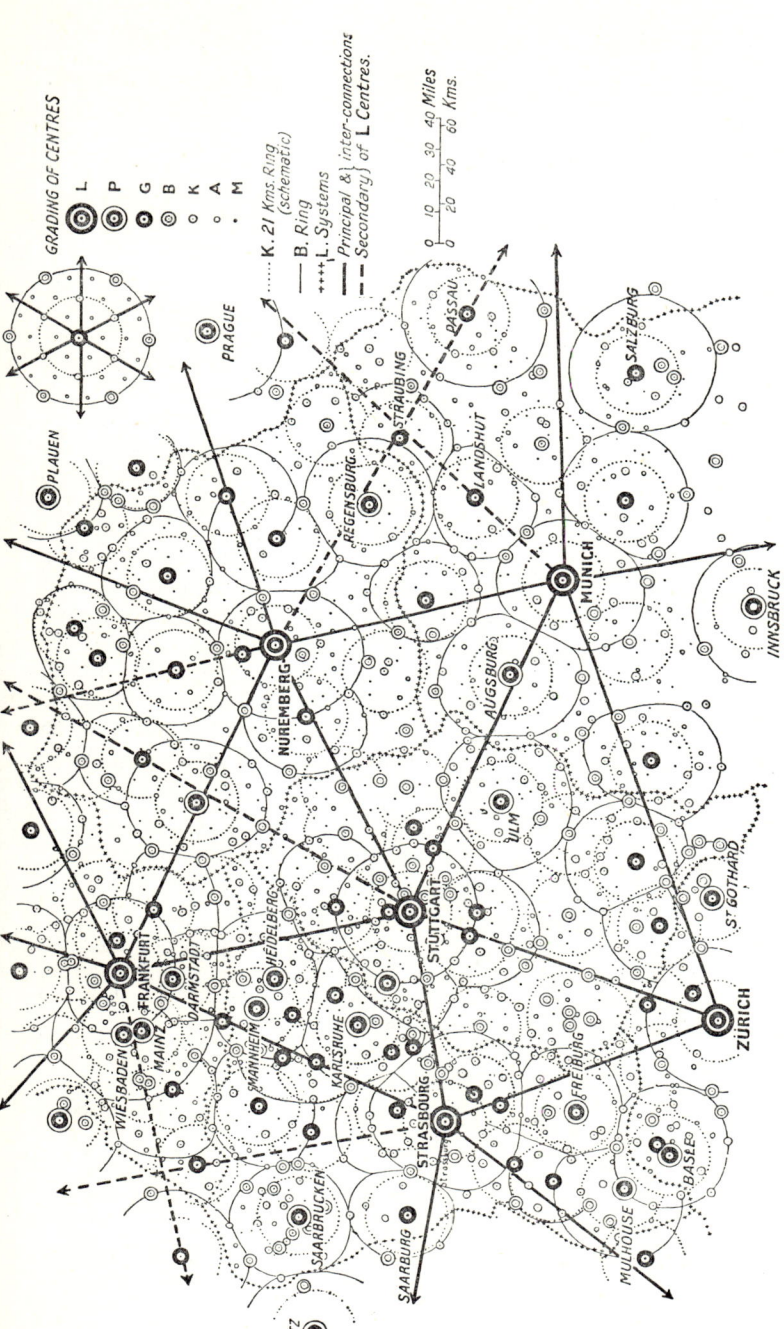

Fig. 3. The Distribution of Towns as Regional Service Centres in South Germany (after Christaller). (Same scale as Fig. 7, p. 88). Service Centres are graded from the *Landeshauptstadt* to the *Marktstadt* (see text). Service Areas are shown as follows: 1. K centres are given a schematic radius of 21 km. 2. B centres are given actual radius of influence (schematically it is 36 km.). 3. Boundaries of the L systems. 4 and 5. Principal and secondary inter-connections of L centres.

several *Kreise*. Thus, in addition to all the functions of the *Kreisstadt*, it also has, for instance, a district labour office, an institute of higher education, specialist doctors, several cinemas, specialist shops and dealers, warehouses, daily papers, several district banks, and post offices. In Britain a corresponding centre would be a country market town such as Bury St. Edmunds. The *Gaustadt* (G) is named after the old German social unit called the *Gau*, comparable with the small French province. The *Mittelstadt* of the statistician includes up to 70,000 inhabitants, and corresponds administratively with the centres of the *Landeskommissariatsbezirk* of the province of Hesse. The *Provinzstadt* (P) corresponds in Prussia with the *Regierungsbezirk* centre and in Bavaria with the groups of *Kreise*. The *Landstadt* (L), with about 500,000 inhabitants, is very prominent in Germany, Italy, and Spain. In southern Germany the *Landstadt* centres are Munich, Frankfurt, Stuttgart, and Nuremberg-Fürth. Similar cities are Strasbourg and Nancy in France and Zurich in Switzerland. Strasbourg, if serving its geographically contiguous districts on the German side of the Rhine, would have a much higher status, whereas, in fact, the centralized services of the upper Rhineland are divided between several major centres that are peripheral to it—Strasbourg, Stuttgart, Mannheim, and Basel. The R or *Reichstadt* is a capital city, but between it and the L centre, Christaller suggests an intermediate type such as Hamburg, Cologne, Düsseldorf, Essen, Munich. He calls these *Reichsteile* centres, since each dominates and serves a large part of the *Reich*. In France, such centres are Bordeaux, Lyon, Marseille, and in Italy, Milan and Naples.

THE STATUS AND DISTRIBUTION OF TOWNS AS BASED ON THE THEORETICAL DISTRIBUTION OF CENTRALIZED SERVICES
(after W. Christaller)
(*Die Zentralen Orte in Süddeutschland*, 1933, p. 72)

This table shows the theoretical distribution of service centres in a predominantly rural area such as south Germany. The figures of average population are broad estimates for this area. The system is regarded as a network of service centres within the service area of the *Landstadt*.

Grades of Town		Approximate Population	Distance Apart (miles)	Service Area (sq. miles)
I. *Marktort*	M	1,000	4·5	18
II. *Amtsort*	A	2,000	7·5	54
III. *Kreisstadt*	K	4,000	13	160
IV. *Bezirkstadt*	B	10,000	22·5	480
V. *Gaustadt*	G	30,000	39	1,500
VI. *Provinzstadt*	P	100,000	67·5	4,500
VII. *Landstadt*	L	500,000	116	13,500

THE CITY AS A REGIONAL CENTRE

The hierarchy of centres may also be determined from an assessment of the number and kind of the central services and institutions, and the degree to which they tend to be associated in one place.

The typically urban institutions in Britain are as follows:

Banks
Specialized retail shops
   General shopkeepers
   Special retailers—draper, chemist, grocer, butcher, footwear
   Department stores
   Chain stores, e.g. Woolworth's
Offices—commercial, administrative, and professional
   Solicitors
   Doctors
   Dentists
   Insurance firms
   Auctioneers
   Other aspects of commerce and finance
   Government Departments—Inland Revenue, Post Office, etc.
Social institutions
   Primary Schools (several in a town)
   Secondary School (one in a small town)
   Cinemas
   Newspaper
   Places of Worship of various denominations
   Assembly Hall
   Hospital

Each of these functions is graded in itself, ranging, for instance, from the retail store in the small country town to the great department stores in the city, or from the local office of a Government department to a regional head office in a central city. They also tend to occur in groups at different levels, so that grades of urban settlement may be recognized. This approach was used by the present writer in a study of the small urban centres of East Anglia that will be summarized in the next chapter. It has been extended by A. E. Smailes to cover all the urban settlements in England and Wales.[1] His map of the 'urban mesh' is shown on Fig. 4 (p. 78).

Smailes points out that a group of three or four banks in one centre is the most reliable indicator of its significance as a shopping and business centre, and that with this economic status there are normally associated a secondary school, a cinema, a weekly newspaper, and a hospital, which express the cultural and social functions of the centre. These five service institutions tend to hang together as

---

[1] A. E. Smailes, 'The Urban Hierarchy in England and Wales', *Geography*, Vol. XXIX, 1944, pp. 41–51. Also Chapter 4, below, for the idea in its application to East Anglia. Reference should also be made to our treatment of English cities in Chapter 10.

a *trait complex*, and they are the key criteria of what may be called a *fully-fledged town*. Other typical features are the professions, branch insurance offices, specialized retail establishments, including multiple

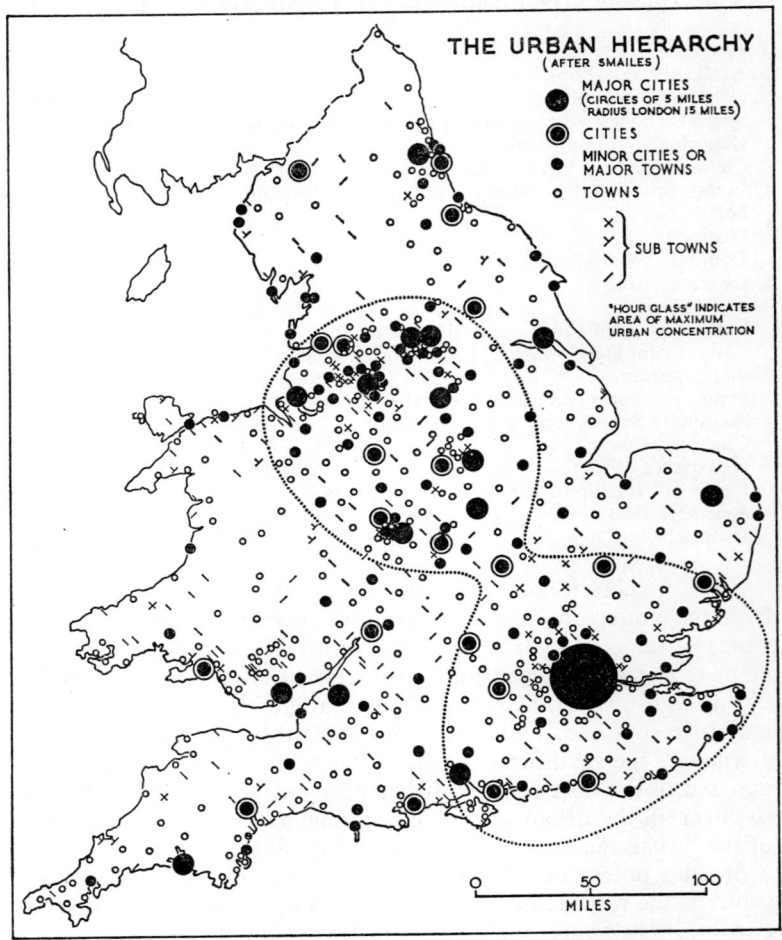

FIG. 4. The Urban Hierarchy in England and Wales (after Smailes).

shops such as Woolworth's in particular, and administrative offices, such as the local Head Post Office, an Employment Exchange, and an Inland Revenue office. Many places that are well equipped in some respects as towns are deficient in others. They may lack one or more of the five minimum key institutions. These Smailes calls *sub-towns*.

Thus, there are many shopping and entertainment centres that lack secondary schools and hospitals; they are usually near larger centres with a full range of services. A few possess the social services but have inferior shopping facilities; these are usually in thinly peopled rural districts beyond the range of influence of fully equipped towns. Most numerous are places with three out of the five key institutions. These are the small service centres, some growing and active, others decadent and inactive. Finally, he recognizes what we have called urban villages, which are intermediate between the rural village and the town proper.

The city is characterized by the greater variety and quality of its services, and it integrates the activities of a number of towns around it. Certain *major cities*, at the head of the hierarchy of urban settlements, have the following distinctive features: they have the regional offices of Government Departments and of private organizations that operate on a national scale, a Stock Exchange, a branch of the Bank of England, the greatest concentration of personnel engaged in wholesale trades, a daily morning newspaper, a University or College, a Medical School, and a large general hospital. Apart from London, outstanding cities, in this sense, are Birmingham, Bristol, Cardiff, Leeds, Liverpool, Manchester, Newcastle, and Nottingham, to which may be added Norwich, Southampton, Plymouth, Hull, Sheffield, Leicester, and Bradford. Small *cities* with a wide range of services but with a more limited sphere of influence bring the total of cities to fewer than forty in all. Between these cities and the towns are what may be called *major towns* or *minor cities*. These form a large and heterogeneous group of about 100, which includes most of the specialized urban centres that are less important as regional centres and are, indeed, in many ways dependent on the latter. These places are grouped into three classes: industrial, county, and resort towns.

Another study of the functional structure of towns is available for Germany.[1] This study, prepared in the thirties, determines the basis of the community structure of towns so as to estimate in what measure they are resistant to economic depression and in what measure they are able to offer opportunities for permanent employment and so fix the demand for new houses—an aim which, in essentials, is similar to that of the P.E.P. report on the location of industry.[2] The approach examined the trade of the town as the seat

---

[1] Gerhard Isenberg, *Erwerbsmöglichkeiten und Krisenfestigkeit als Voraussetzung für die Siedlungstätigkeit. Dargestellt an der Hand der Untersuchung von 10 Mittelstädten im Land Sachsen.* Based on work carried out in 1933–35 in the *Seminar für Stadtebau und Siedlungswesen* at the Technical High School, Dresden (Mimeographed).

[2] P.E.P. (Political and Economic Planning), *Report on the Location of Industry*, London, 1939, Chapter VI, Towns and Industry.

of specialized occupations, producing goods both for an extensive market and for the local service area; and in terms of trade with its service area (described as its 'hinterland'); and the food supplies drawn from its wider hinterland. The living possibilities (*Lebensmöglichkeiten*), or in the more limited sense, *occupational possibilities* (*Erwerbsmöglichkeiten*), are assessed on this threefold basis with the following tentative classification.

The small country town (*Landstadt*) is normally situated in an agricultural area. Until the nineteenth century, it was the seat of the markets and handicrafts serving the surrounding rural parishes. If situated on a main route, it was also a post-station for through coach traffic. In the Middle Ages it was normally the seat of a religious house, or of an *Amtmann*, a count or other great landlord. Some such towns lived almost entirely by agriculture, and were distinct from the *Gemeinde* (parish) only by their wall and special laws. Many of these townlets, usually with less than 2,000 inhabitants, have been unable to take advantage of the modern growth of industry, commerce, and administration. Many which have no railway have declined to the status of villages; they bear the name of towns, but have none of their special functions. In the absence of economic and social opportunity, young people leave such towns. Thus, about 40 per cent. of all the towns of Brandenburg had more inhabitants in 1870 than they had in 1930. Such a town draws about half of its income from the farm products of its own *Gemeinde*, and 20 per cent. from trade with its hinterland—a total of 70 per cent. About one-third of its occupants are engaged in the local services (*Nähererwerbstätigen*).

The *Kreisstadt* is the small administrative centre. It is named from the *Kreis*, the local government district in Prussia of which it is usually the centre. If the administrative area is small, as in south Germany, the town often has under 2,000 inhabitants, but if the area is large, with more than, say, 50,000 inhabitants, the town may have from 2,000 to 5,000 people. Functions other than service accrue to the town by virtue of its being a centre of administration. Those in pleasant surroundings attract retired people or others of independent means. There is little industry. The backbone of the population is its official and professional classes—*Landrat, Finanzamt, Arbeitsamt, Versorgungsamt*, the personnel of the small garrison, the railway station, the post office, the pensioned officials, and retired residents. Special types of *Kreisstadt* arise when one of these classes is dominant —officials, teachers, or retired persons—or when a town is situated at a railway junction. Such towns, though small, are well balanced in their social and economic structure and in the sources from which they draw their income. These are calculated as: agriculture, 15 per cent.; hinterland trade, 22 per cent.; public funds, 25 per cent.; unearned income 20 per cent.; and industry, 16 per cent.

A third type has the same basic features as the *Kreisstadt*, but differs from it in the much greater importance of industry—due to the development of old-established industries or the introduction of new ones. But the economic basis is still sufficiently wide for the town community not to be seriously hit in time of economic depression, for the unemployed, though only temporarily, can be given some other kind of work. The type occurs as small and medium-sized towns, the latter only when there is a group of officials and a garrison. It normally has 10,000 to 40,000 inhabitants. Functions of administration and commerce in relation to the hinterland are not adequate to account for a population of this size, and industry is much more important. In the *Reich* all towns of 20,000 to 50,000 inhabitants are found to average 52 per cent. in industry and handicrafts. Such a town is capable of providing through its local services all the normal requirements of a fully-fledged urban community.

In the industrial town the occupants depend dominantly upon industry, and upon industrial occupations depend in turn the other occupational groups and sources of income. The residential function is of small importance. The industries of the hinterland are identical with those of the industrial town. Industry makes up over four-fifths of the town's income, and this clearly has repercussions on the remaining occupations.

The last type is the metropolitan city, the great centre of business, industry, and culture, serving an extensive area around it, and having nation-wide and international connections. These cities have as a rule about 100,000 inhabitants as a minimum. They are many-sided in their activities and offer a varied range of opportunities for employment.

This is, to our knowledge, the only attempt to measure the local, hinterland, and general trade of towns on the lines of what we have called the local, regional, and extra-regional components.[1]

The principles involved in areal functional organization around central service centres have been formulated and developed in an important article with reference to the United States.[2] Its argument runs as follows.

The hierarchy of nested centres presents six orders. These are illustrated from a thorough study of the Chicago area of the Middle

---

[1] This is further developed by the same author in his 'Tragfähigkeit und Wirtschaftsstruktur', *Veröff. d. Akad. f. Raumforschung u. Landesplanung*, Band 22, 1953.

[2] A. K. Philbrick, 'Areal Functional Organization in Regional Geography', *Economic Geography*, Vol. 33, 1957, pp. 299–326.

West. A seventh order would include the unique case of the 'primate city' of New York.

The six orders of central places increase in degree of specialization, as shown on Fig. 5, in which the nested nature of the hierarchy is shown as a pyramid. Triangles are shown at successive levels of the pyramid so that each function serves as a base for a smaller number

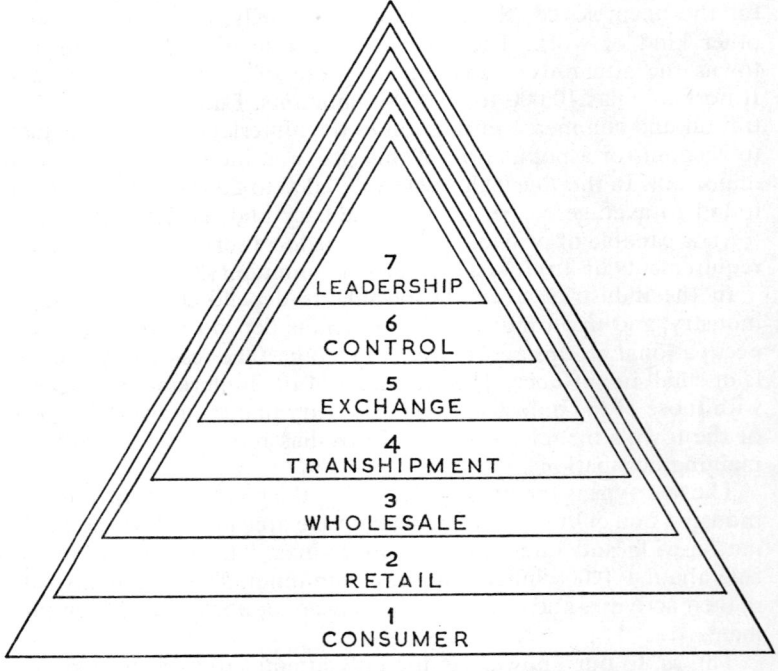

FIG. 5. The Sevenfold Hierarchy of Nested Functions (after Philbrick).

of establishments and locations specializing in the next higher ordered function. The hierarchy of areal units of organization corresponds to the hierarchy of functions. These functions, from the lowest to the highest order, are consumption, retail trade, wholesale trade, transhipment (essentially break of bulk), exchange (i.e. the business of buying and selling), control (i.e. the concentration of economic power for a major regional economy), and leadership (of the primate city). Each of these activities, it is claimed, gives the keynote to each higher category and, the last embracing all the functions characteristic of each of the lower order centres.

The first order is an individual establishment and the area that it organizes. This may be a farmstead, which is the centre of the farm unit with its complex of fields. Or it may be the church or store and its individual service area. The second order emerges as a cluster of commercial and residential establishments, each of which has its individual area of association and which together form the area of organization centred upon the focal place. The configuration of such an area reveals a core, that is, the built-up area with a large share of the total clientele, and a periphery, including the open countryside and other focal places. The area of organization in turn has a double character. It includes the internal area, in which there is a spatially continuous relationship of all places in the area with the focal place; and an external area, in which particular functions of the centre extend to widely diffused and spatially discontinuous places. The focal place of the second order contains one cluster of establishments in its built-up areas.

A place of the third order emerges as functions segregate in such a way that a centre develops as a *cluster of focal places* of the first and second orders. It contains separate embryonic second order areas of organization within a larger compact areal unit. Wholesaling is the clearest indicator of this distinction, and the wholesaler, the retailer, and the consumer typify the essential character of the three orders. Moreover, in the third order centres, there appear within the settlement one or more of these embryonic second order centres, with an emergent aggregation of units in a central business district.

A centre of a fourth order emerges as the focus of *a cluster of clusters of focal places* by specialization in the handling and shipment of goods, people, and information. It becomes, in other words, a centre of transhipment. Philbrick reserves the term *central place* to these centres and those of a higher order, and uses the term *focal place* for the first three orders. In order to classify the central places he lists twenty-five criteria for a large number of cities in the Chicago area and lists twelve of these to detect the distinct character of fourth order status. All these criteria are related to transport and include, for example, the listing of the number of railroad tracks, freight yard capacity, air route connections, number of highway freight carriers, etc. Within 150 miles of Chicago fifteen places were selected as fourth order centres, with a maximum development in Chicago, Milwaukee, Indianapolis, and Grand Rapids. There are an estimated 500 fourth order centres in the entire United States.

The table of criteria indicated above revealed the primacy of Chicago in its area. The system of central places is shown on Fig. 6. Chicago is an outstanding example of a transport centre. It serves as 'the hub of a cluster of central places'. It is the nodal core of a *fifth* order region of areal functional organization. Cities ranking in the

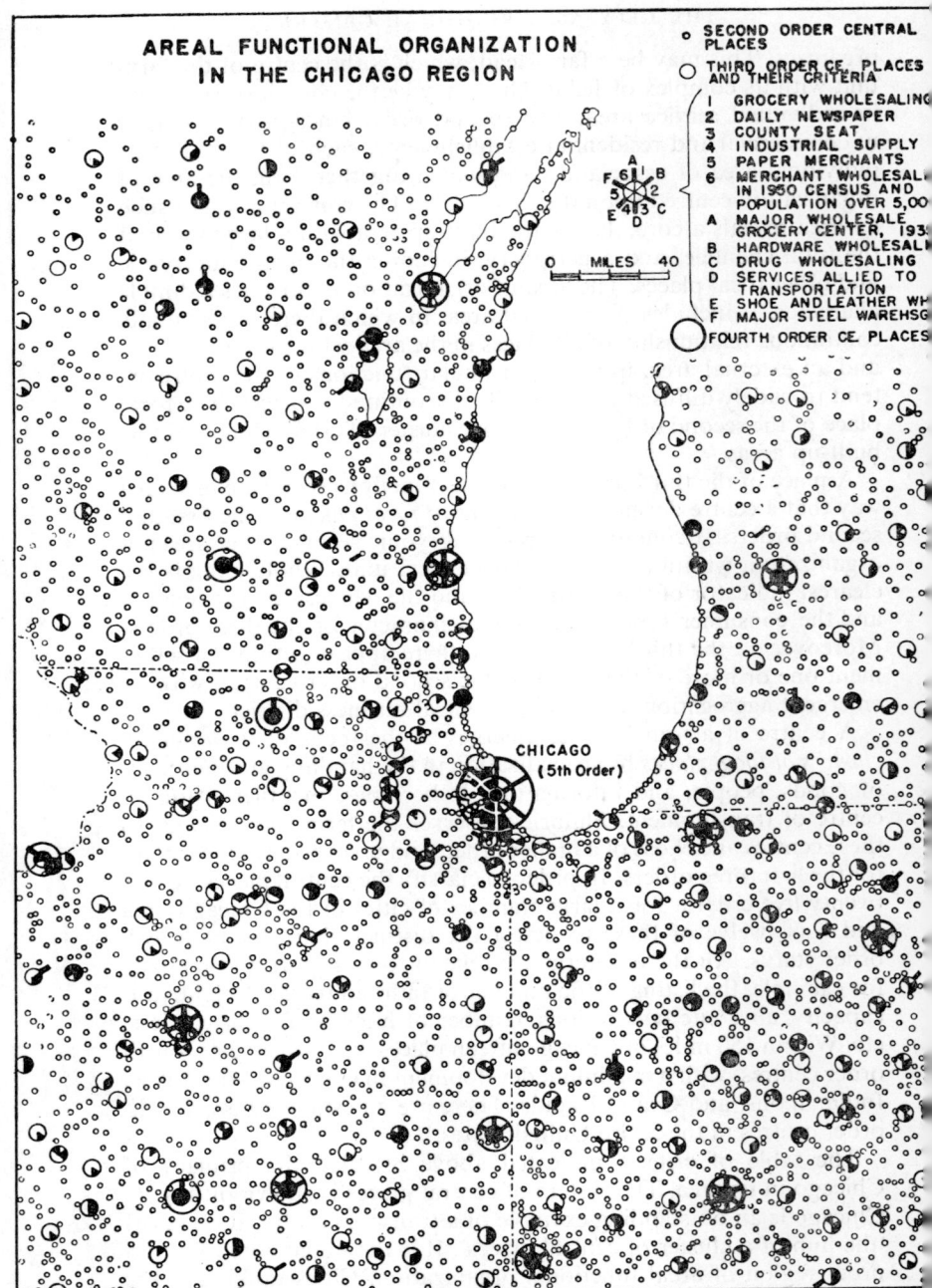

FIG. 6. Areal Functional Organization in the Chicago Region (after Philbrick), showing central places of the second, third, and fourth orders.

fourth and fifth orders in the eastern half of the States are twenty in number. There are some fifty fifth order cities in the States. When given an arbitrary field of influence of 100 miles there is a continuously organized area throughout the north-east of the States, corresponding in general to the manufacturing belt and to the areas with greatest accessibility.

A still higher order of cities emerges through the concentration of all the aforementioned functions in the greatest complexity and by the distributive function of 'control'. These centres are ten in number in the United States. A seventh order status is given to the unique case of New York as the primate city, though Philbrick is in some doubt as to whether Chicago and Los Angeles should also be accorded this status, each giving leadership to east, centre, and west respectively.

An essential principle of this hierarchy is that the functions of each order of place are repeated, together with its distinctive nest of functions, in the centres of the next higher order. Moreover, it is also evident that as the built-up area increases, the activities needed to serve it segregate within it, rather than serving the places outside it. Second and third order centres may exist within the large urban area primarily to serve a section of the population living and working within it. The principles of centrality are clearly applicable to the urbanized area as well as to the open country area, though the density of population in the urban area is much greater than in the countryside and consequently the centres are more closely spaced.

In brief, the main propositions, as discussed in this chapter regarding the theory of centrality, may be briefly summed up as follows.

First, the centralized services are segregated in places in such a way that centres may be graded into some six or seven orders according to the number and magnitude of the functions and their associated population level.

Second, the functions of places of each order are represented in the functions of each successive order.

Third, the central places tend to serve hexagonal, rather than circular, areas and a network of complementary trade areas is arranged like a honeycomb of hexagonal-shaped trade areas, in which, on a purely geometric basis, each centre is in contact with six equal ranking and equidistant centres, and the distance between each successive series increases by $\sqrt{3}$.

Fourth, the number of towns in the different progressive orders from the smallest to the largest form a pyramid in which centres of each order bear a constant mathematical ratio to each other.

Fifth, the location of central places is controlled largely by transport facilities and traffic flows, including both through and radial traffic, the former being served by through routes and the latter by radial routes arranged like the spokes of a wheel and forming the framework of the service areas.

Sixth, the number and spacing of centres of equal size depends on the economic character of the area they serve and especially on the degree of commercialization of its economy and also upon the level of living and the consequent level of demand for access to, and provision of, services.

We shall examine the relevance of these propositions to the character and distribution of services in the relations between town and country, in the structure of the urban area, and in the relations that exist between the big city and the countryside and towns in its surroundings.

Chapter 4

TOWN–COUNTRY RELATIONS

Every nucleated settlement, whether hamlet, village, town, or city, is, in varying degree, a centre of services and organization for a surrounding area. The latter is definable as a variety of catchment areas, that constitute the field of spatial association of the centre. It is common knowledge that the village is normally the centre for the activities of its parish, that the town is the centre for an area within a radius of about five to ten miles, and the great city for a still wider area which it serves in its capacity as a king among towns and a regional centre of economic and social organization. The location of these focal points has been fixed since the time of their origin in the Middle Ages, but, in the last hundred years, industries have caused some to grow as great excrescences upon the countryside without any organic relation to it, and services have tended to concentrate in fewer centres, since in that way the services can be more efficiently rendered.

Thus, fundamental changes in the social structure of the village and in the interrelations of town and village have appeared. The village community has been affected in many ways by the growth and concentration of services in neighbouring villages or small towns. Rural cultures have been profoundly affected by the impact of urban ways of life. In the vicinity of all urban agglomerations there appear changes in the conditions and ways of rural living which upset the balance of rural society. So deeply associated are town and village in their interrelations that in effect no clear-cut distinction can be drawn between the urban and rural ways of life.

In this chapter we shall examine some aspects of these trends, with particular reference to the village community and the smaller towns in rural areas and to the relations between the village and the town. We shall illustrate from particular studies in Germany, France, England, and the United States.

THE URBAN SETTLEMENT AS REGIONAL CENTRE

1. GERMANY

The theory of centrality claims that the laws of the distribution of centralized services in terms of the market principle account primarily for the spacing, size, and functions of urban centres, modified in certain areas by the factors of long-distance trade and administration. In fact, there are here two problems—first, the relative importance of these factors in the development of the medieval town;

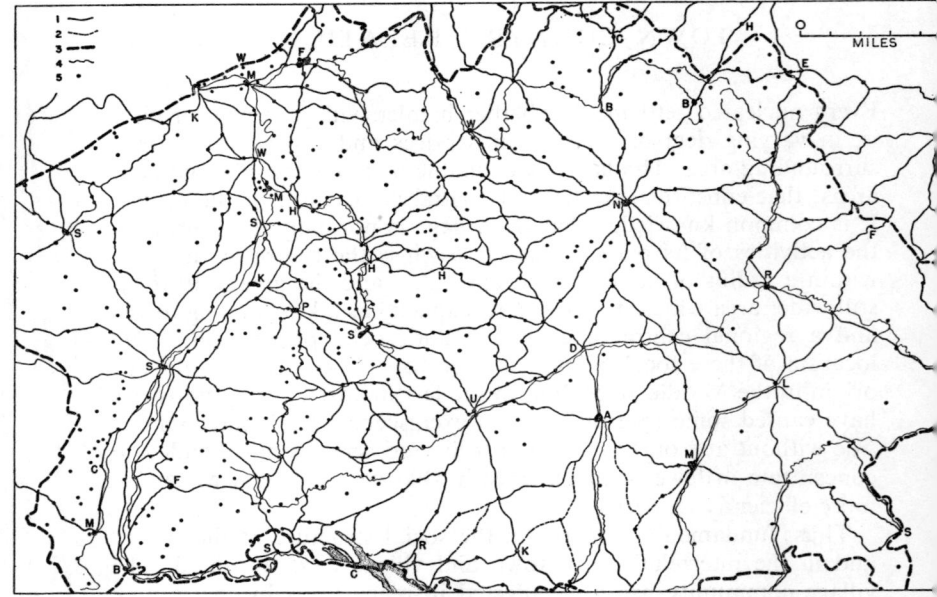

FIG. 7. Medieval Towns and Routes in South Germany (after Gradmann).
1. Medieval Roads. 2. Medieval Roads (probable). 3. Boundary of Area considered. 4. Rivers. 5. Towns (by administrative status). (Same scale as Fig. 3, p. 75.)

and, second, the ranking and distribution of the modern centres, that have been greatly affected by the development of industry and the great increase of centralized functions. We make special reference here to south Germany, the area that was worked on by Christaller.

The pattern of distribution of existing central places, as shown on Fig. 3, p. 75, can only be properly understood by reference to the distribution of the historic towns and the circumstances under which they developed. These towns and the medieval routes are shown on Fig. 7, above, as mapped by the late Robert Gradmann.[1] The vast

[1] Robert Gradmann, *Süd-Deutschland*, Vol. I, 1931.

majority of the present towns and market settlements were in existence by the end of the Middle Ages.[1] The basic *spacing* of urban settlements arose, therefore, in this period. The few towns founded subsequently were court towns and places for religious and political refugees. But these introduce quite minor alterations in the medieval distribution that persisted with little alteration a hundred years ago. Only seventy towns or *civitates* were in existence in south Germany in 1200 and about 500 by the end of the Middle Ages. Possibilities of urban growth were afforded by overland or long-distance trade, local market trade, and defence and administration. Let us consider each of these.

Merchant traffic was confined to the public highway (*via publica* or *regia*) through the regulation of traffic by the Emperor. In considering the importance of long-distance trade in the origin and development of the medieval town, these routes alone come into account. There were very few main routes in south Germany in 1200, the main network developing in the later Middle Ages with the growth, in particular, of trans-Alpine traffic. There were many main routes of early origin in northern Germany, especially on the northern border of the central uplands, and here most of the early medieval towns began as resting-places (*Rastorte*), mainly at river-crossings on these routes. They were used as strongholds or bishops' seats, some of which attracted small settlements of merchants, who ultimately obtained rights of complete self-government. Nearly all the main roads in southern Germany, on the other hand, developed after 1200 and, according to Gradmann, the authority on this area,[2] many of the towns lie *off* the main roads, and long-distance trade cannot have played a decisive part in their growth, whereas in the north the great majority lie *on* the routes. Local market trade played a main part in the development of the town, as is proved not only by their position in relation to the main routes, but also by the fact that the majority were granted the right of holding a weekly market at the time of their foundation. But, against this argument, many were founded without reference to the possibilities of local trade, and, for various reasons, were never able to integrate the trade of their surroundings. The two factors here concerned are long-distance trade and defence and administration.

Numerous towns developed after 1200 on the routes which were then used for through traffic on a big scale with the development of trans-Alpine trade. They were spaced at regular intervals of 25 to 30 km., as, for example, on the roads radiating from Nuremberg and (outside our area) on the skein of routes that ran from north

[1] See the writer's *West European City*, London, 1951, 2nd ed., 1961.
[2] *Ibid.*, pp. 158–69.

to south through the lowland corridor of Hesse across the central uplands. These are comparable in origin and function to the coaching towns that developed in the seventeenth and eighteenth centuries.

One of the chief considerations in the foundation of towns in south Germany in the later Middle Ages was defence and administration. Germany was then plunged into feudal chaos and local territorial lords and bishops, in defending their territories, established towns or walled existing settlements. In organizing their lands on a territorial basis, they erected towns and castles adjacent to them for the administration of fixed districts, to defend frontiers, command routes, and collect revenues. In this way, the *Ämter* districts came into being. Towns appeared, then, adjacent to castles, monasteries, and villages, and markets were raised to town status, to serve as political centres. The grant of a weekly market in such cases often made a tardy appearance. Similarly, rival lords built or acquired towns in rich areas such as the vine-growing districts of Alsace, and along the Rhine gorge, where, in addition, tolls could be levied on traffic using road and river. In the areas of extreme territorial disintegration, such as Alsace and the Neckar basin (in Württemberg) and Switzerland, many towns were established on naturally defended isolated hill sites or on river meanders, very close to each other in different political territories and off the trade routes. On the other hand, in large areas that were under the control of one political authority, as in Bavaria and the Tyrol, there was less demand for fortresses or castles, so that towns are fewer and the unwalled market settlement much more characteristic. Elsewhere in south Germany the unwalled market settlement is rare. Thus, we find that many of these places, through competition with near neighbours, became superfluous. Though enjoying the features of a medieval town, with planned layout, wall, and the machinery of self-government with a town council or *Rat*, they were unable to function as seats of trade and industry. Today, they have a few hundred inhabitants and have dwindled to agricultural villages. Such are the *Zwergstädte* or dwarf towns named by Gradmann, of which Dinkelsbühl is a famous example.

During the mercantilist era in the seventeenth and eighteenth centuries crafts were fostered in town and countryside and to an increasing degree the towns became centres of economic organization. This was especially true of the textile industries that developed during this period. Numerous small towns became seats of specialized industry and seats for the organization of domestic industries carried on in the surrounding countryside. But, in general, very few urban centres in south Germany owe their existence to the appearance of industry, and industry has accrued to the towns in such a way as to be proportional to their size a hundred years ago. The great majority of all the towns in south Germany, as in other countries, have under 10,000 inhabitants. Those with over this figure, which may be safely taken as a broad indicator of real urban character, are fewer in number, but they account for most of the urban population and are the chief seats of industry, commerce, and administration. Towns increased normally in the nineteenth century in proportion to their size and their size was largely proportional to their nodality as route centres. The great bulk of the increase, however, was due to the growth of industry and secondarily to the rendering of services. The towns that are predominantly industrial—taking 50 per cent. of all employed persons as a crude criterion—are markedly concentrated in the south-west, clustered in the Saar coal-field, around Mannheim-Ludwigshafen, around Frankfurt-Mainz-Wiesbaden, in the larger area of the Neckar basin in Württemberg with its focus in Stuttgart, and a group of small towns in the extreme south-west between the Danube and Lake Constance. Munich stands out as a separate great industrial focus. There is a sprinkling of small industrial towns in eastern Bavaria, Nuremberg-Fürth being the chief centre. The distribution and size of these specialized industrial centres are determined by very different factors from those governing the service centres. These, when crudely classified as towns with over 10,000 inhabitants and under 50 per cent. of their workers engaged in industry, are found to be rather evenly spread over the face of the land. In pre-war Germany, only about a fifth of the population, at the maximum a third, were specifically engaged in servicing the market area of the town. The proportions were probably highest in the big cities. Stuttgart, Frankfurt, Munich, and Karlsruhe, for example, had over 40 per cent. of their population engaged in trade, commerce, administration, public service, and the professions.[1]

Fig. 3 (p. 75) shows the distribution of central places. Centrality is measured on the basis of telephone connections in relation to population, and the places are graded into the seven categories discussed on p. 76. The M and the A centres are shown without service areas. The K centres are given a schematic circular area of 21 km. The B centres are shown with their actual service areas, with the equivalent areas for the higher B and G centres. The dotted lines show what are presumably the actual main boundaries between each of the L centres (*Landeshauptstädte*). These are Frankfurt, Nuremberg, Stuttgart, Strasbourg, Munich, and Zurich.

[1] H. Bobek, 'Über Einige Funktionelle Stadttypen und Ihre Beziehungen zum Lande', in *Comptes Rendus du Congrès International de Géographie*, Amsterdam, 1938, Tome II, Géog. Humaine, 1938, pp. 88–102, with maps.

In addition to the towns proper, there are many small centres that serve the countryside.[1] These are small nuclei, which have several centralized services in them, but do not reach the status of an urban centre such as the market (M) town. They are called by Christaller *Hilfszentralen* or auxiliary centres. They fall into several groups.

First, there are places that were formerly towns or market centres. They have lost functions, and even urban character, by the competition of other places. Such has been the fate of many towns on isolated hill tops or within deep river meanders. They were sited originally for reasons of defence, but today lie aloof from the main roads without adequate connection with their surroundings. Some lie so near to bigger towns as to have lost functions to the latter, or even to have been completely absorbed by their expansion. Others have declined through the natural poverty of their surroundings or through changes in political frontiers. All these centres are in the *inactive* order and have been degraded from the status of small towns.

Secondly, some places are definitely in the *active* order. Though small, with an incomplete range of urban services, they fill a useful purpose in servicing their surroundings. They include the small service centres that have often grown around a railway station, or in areas where there is a rising standard of living, or where new industrial establishments and settlements are planted sporadically in an agricultural area. They appear especially in tourist areas such as the Alps and the Black Forest.

Thirdly, there are *permanent*, as opposed to *decadent* and *emergent*, auxiliary centres. Such are the places in mountainous or other sparsely peopled areas that have too thin a veneer of settlement to support towns, however small, at frequent intervals; but must nevertheless be supplied with goods and services and have outlets for the sale of their products.

These auxiliary centres usually lie on the borders of the service areas of the towns where, at points furthest removed from the latter, they are able to supply more effectively some of the local needs. They are also found in isolated and thinly peopled areas, and on the borders of the big cities.

The theory of centrality has been vigorously applied, tested, and refined, especially in Germany, over the last thirty years. A variety of techniques has been employed to put the centres into categories and to define their complementary areas. The term *Zentralort* or central place, as developed by geographers, is now firmly rooted in the terminology and conceptual framework of planners. Two particular studies may be cited as examples—Siegerland and Bavaria.

[1] W. Christaller, *Die Ländliche Siedlungsweise im Deutschen Reich und ihre Beziehungen zur Gemeindeorganisation*, Berlin, 1937.

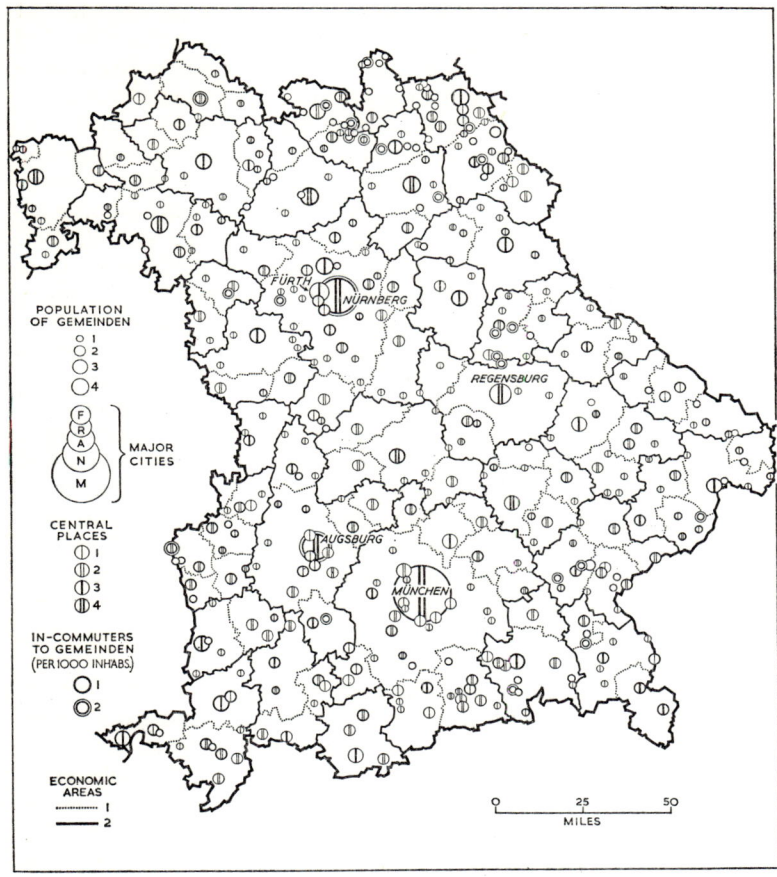

FIG. 8. Central Places and their Fields in Bavaria (after Boustedt).
Population of Gemeinden: 1. Less than 5,000. 2. 5,000 to 20,000. 3. 20,000 to 50,000. 4. 50,000 to 100,000. *Major Cities over 100,000* (Fürth, Regensburg, Augsburg, Nürnberg, München). Places according to degree of centrality: 1. Lower. 2. Middle. 3. High. 4. Highest orders. *Incommuters to Gemeinden* (per 1,000 inhabitants): 1. 65 to 250. 2. Over 250. *Economic Areas:* 1. Functional economic areas. 2. Larger economic areas.

The central places and their orbits in Bavaria have been the subject of a special study by O. Boustedt[1] (Fig. 8). He selects a number of services and determines the percentage of the total of 7,119

[1] O. Boustedt, 'Die Zentralen Orte und ihre Einflussbereiche', *I.G.U. Symposium*, Lund, 1960, pp. 201–26.

THE URBAN SETTLEMENT AS REGIONAL CENTRE

Gemeinden for Bavaria in which each service occurs, irrespective of the number of the same service in one place. This forms the basis of calculation of a *dispersion factor*. The smaller the number of *Gemeinden* in which the service occurs, the greater is the concentration and the higher the centrality. Indices were calculated for nine retail activities and twelve selected central activities, the latter including pharmacies, cinemas, hospitals, chemists, wholesalers, high schools, lawyers, banks, newspapers. Thus, in the retail group, iron, steel, and metal wares, boots and shoes, and bicycles occur in 13·2, 13·1, and 10·5 per cent., and, among the central activities, chemists in 9·1 per cent., but newspapers in only 0·7 per cent. and banks in 0·3 per cent., of all *Gemeinden* (this being the dispersion factor). Similar functions were found to be associated in the same places and this was used as a measure of the centrality of the place.

Some 338 central places were discovered out of the total of 7,119 communities, with 12 (3·6 per cent.) in the highest order, 35 (10·3 per cent.) in the second, and 112 (33·1 per cent.) in the third. Over a half of the total number of places (53·0 per cent.) belonged to the lowest order. Communities with less than 1,000 people were found to have none of the centralized services. When examined in terms of occupational structures and divided into service centres, industrial centres, and agricultural centres, two-thirds were found to be service centres and only one-third industrial centres.

The field of each of these centres was next determined. Different criteria reveal different areas. The area served by one store can be precisely determined by the location of purchasers over a given period of time. But a composite area of all such service areas is, indeed, in its very nature, much less precise. For this reason, the spheres of influence of each of the central services were not adopted as criteria. A large part of the outside relations of places (consumers or producers) is directed to central places. The regular daily needs of the consumer are supplied over a limited area containing probably two-thirds of the total consumer consumption. Transport facilities are the major determinant of the framework of these regional areas and in consequence the following criteria are selected to determine them. First, commuting areas are mapped, based on the census of workers for *Gemeinden* with 100 or more commuters, together with *Gemeinden* with at least ten out-commuters. This is an important indicator since it includes many women who also make their purchases in the places in which they work. Second, the direction and frequency of transport facilities—bus services, train services, and automobile traffic—were used to define areas of accessibility to the nearest centres. There were found to be 108 'primary unit areas' of this kind and 32 larger units. In almost all cases the central places of the highest order are the main traffic centres. Sometimes, however, a traffic area does not fit with *one* centre, but has several lesser centres. Some 16 of the 108 areas are in this class, and they are generally situated where the normal flow of traffic was offset by political frontiers or rugged relief. The places of lowest order are frequently found on the border of the orbits of larger centres of higher order where they serve as auxiliary centres.

We may turn now to another area shown on Figs. 9 and 10.[1] This is situated around the town of Siegen in the eastern portion of the Rhine Plateau. Siegen is the headquarters of an old-established iron mining and iron working area. The plants are concentrated in the so-called *Hüttental* and the town and its environs have a population of close on 200,000. It is the administrative and economic capital of a *Kreis* with which many of its activities are co-extensive. This fact is revealed by many of the circumstances of the historical development of iron mining, iron working, and the communal method of using the woods in the surrounding country for making charcoal and for using the oak bark in the leather industry. This area has its focus in Siegen and extends north and south about 20 km. to north-east and south-west. The outer area around this economic core corresponds with the boundaries of the *Kreis* and extends south-west to include the eastern portion of the *Kreis* of Altenkirchen.

The regional functions of Siegen were subjected to an exhaustive analysis in terms of the historical development of industry and of the administrative and cultural functions. These are shown on Fig. 9. The features may be summed up as follows. Commuting data, examined in detail on the basis of data for each *Gemeinde*, reveal that the main service area of the town of Siegen has a radius of about 10 km. to the north but reaches 15 to 20 km. in the south. Places with bus services with more than ten bus-pairs daily are shown, as well as the railroads to Siegen. In addition there are shown the areas drawn on by the schools of higher and technical education, the circulation of the main newspaper, the areas served by the hospital, and the outer limit of the main retail trade area.

These areas are all based on detailed investigations of places of origin and movement and may be checked in the original work. The boundaries on the map are generalized geographic limits. They are varied in kind and do not have any relation one to the other. They indicate, however, a close association with the central town, an

---

[1] F. Petri, O. Lucas, P. Schöller, 'Das Siegerland: Geschichte, Struktur und Funktionen', *Veröff. d. Provinzial Instituts für Westfälische Landes u. Volkskunde*, Reihe I, Heft 8, Münster, 1955. P. Schöller, 'Stadt und Einzugsgebiet', *Studium Generale*, 10. Jahrg., Heft 10, 1957.

THE URBAN SETTLEMENT AS REGIONAL CENTRE

association that is revealed in the identity of economic activities and interest of the area, focused on its iron working industries, and also in its cultural development and common associations.

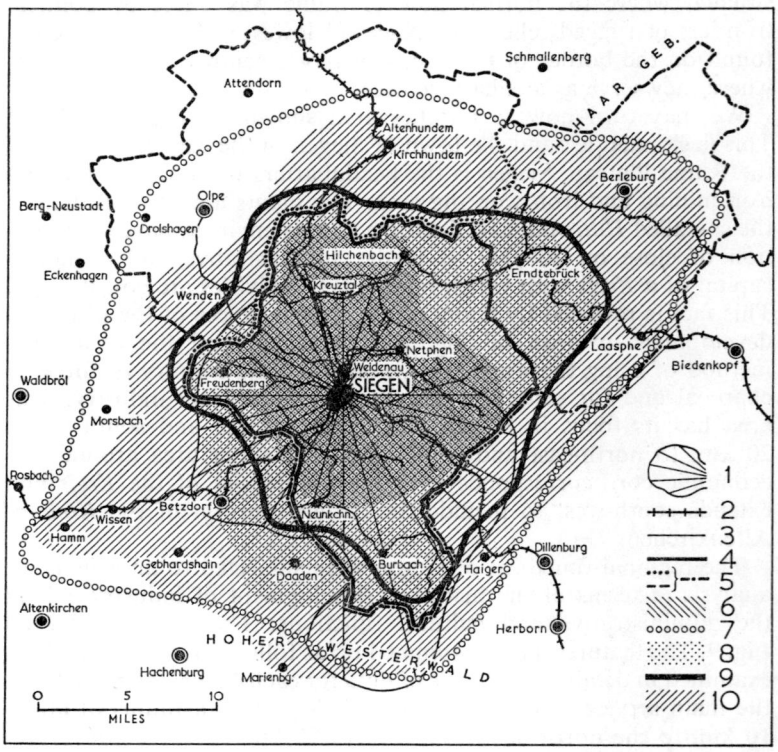

FIG. 9. The Urban Field of Siegen (after Schöller).
1. Main commuting area. 2. Railroads to Siegen. 3. Bus lines to Siegen with more than 10 bus-pairs daily. 4. *Kreis* (administrative) boundary. 5. Administrative areas of (1) Labour and Finance and (2) Chambers of Industry and Commerce. 6. Catchment Area of high schools. 7. Catchment Area of technical schools. 8. Circulation Area of the Siegen newspaper. 9. Catchment Area of hospitals. 10. Retail trade area.

P. Schöller carries his investigation further by examining the functions of the central places and their dependent areas in the surrounding country. The map is shown on Fig. 10. The aggregate of central functions—in the groups of traffic, administration, economy, church, culture, sanitation, and trade—is used as a measure of the centrality of a place. A list of the central functions is given as follows: officials, associations, churches, schools, hospitals, doctors, apothecaries, dentists, lawyers, taxation officers, banks, cinemas, newspapers, printers, retail trade, markets.

The areal spread or the areal attraction of the centres determine,

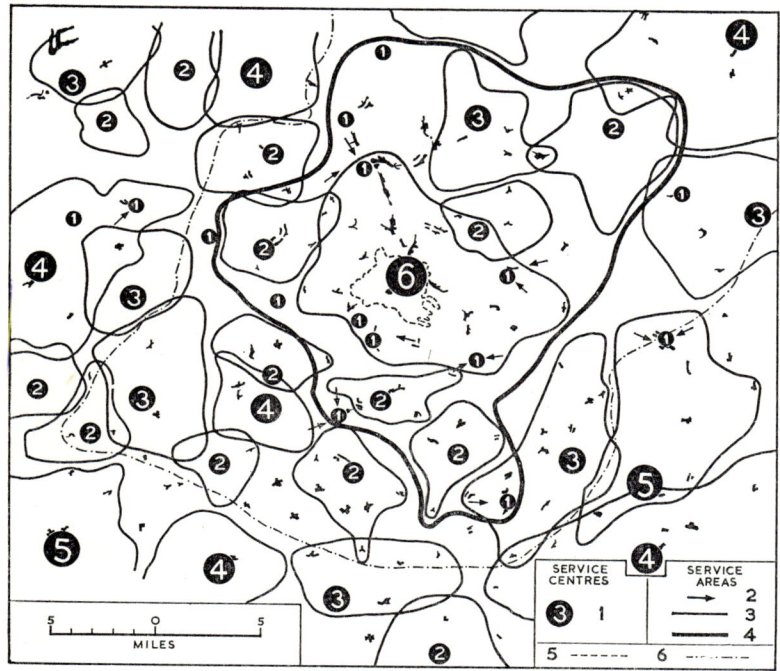

Fig. 10. Central Places and Service Areas of the Siegerland, Germany (after Schöller).

1. Service Centres in six orders, in decreasing order from 6 Siegen. Service Areas: 2. Service Area of auxiliary service centres (Order No. 1). 3. Service Areas for centres No. 2 to 6. 4. The Service Area of Siegen-Weidenau (see also Fig. 9). 5. The boundary of the *Kreis* (admin. dt.) of Siegen. 6. Sphere of Influence of the 6th order centre of Siegen. For further explanation see text.

according to intensity and range, a stepped arrangement of the urban fields. The term *umland* is used for the portion of an urban field that is nearest to the central place up to a distance of about twenty miles, and is intimately associated with the daily life of the centre. The larger centre (and the level at which this takes place still needs investigation) tends to develop a distinct *umland*, beyond which there is a wider area in which more specialized, occasional, functions are exercised. Here most contacts are made direct from the countryside to the smaller towns, while occasional specialized goods and services are derived from the central city. Schöller describes this wider area as the *hinterland*. Beyond it are widely scattered places and towns that have occasional contacts with the central city, as well as with other cities of the same higher order. The umland is thus covered by the lower order of functions, the hinterland by the second order of functions, and the area of influence by the higher order of functions. The map shows this arrangement of centres and their fields.

2. FRANCE[1]

In the urban network of France, the hierarchy of centres falls into four grades, described as *bourgade, centre local, ville maîtresse* and *capitale régionale*, with an occasional intermediate 'supporting' type between the two last that is called a *sous-capitale*. At the bottom of the scale there is a great number of local centres, *les villages centres* whose activities normally reach no further than the boundaries of the commune, though their size and functions vary according to the distribution of the rural settlements. Each category of these lesser centres may be examined here in some detail. The capitals will be considered in a later chapter. The hierarchy of central places in southern France is shown on Fig. 11, to which reference should be made in reading the following.

Le Chef-lieu Communal. Many tiny communal agglomerations are not strictly urban centres; they are the lowest order of the hierarchy of central places. They fall into three types according to differences in the distribution of the rural population.

The first type is a small commune with its farm population clustered in one centre, rather than dispersed in individual farmsteads. Here are to be found the *mairie*, the church, the primary school, and at least one general store, in which are combined the sale of dry goods, haberdashery, tobacco, and even a café. When the population of the centre exceeds some 300 to 350 people, these sales are found in specialized shops, and there is also a butcher, hairdresser, and some kind of mechanic (often a garage as a descendant of the blacksmith or wheelwright). The general store is missing, for lack of clientele, when the commune centre has under about 100 inhabitants, and goods must be purchased from a neighbouring centre. Often the school is located in another village centre, and the *mairie* and the church remain as its only institutions. Bicycle and scooter take the young folk to other and brighter places. This type is found

[1] Source: J. Coppolani, *Le Réseau urbain de la France: Sa Structure et son Aménagement*, Paris, 1959.

characteristically in the areas with a predominantly nucleated form of farming settlement, such as the wheat-growing plains of the north and the valleys and lowlands of the south.

A second type is found in the large communes with a larger centre, often described as a *bourg*. It is frequent in the south-east. These again are seats of local activity confined to the commune. But they are larger, and often have over 1,000 and sometimes 2,000 inhabitants. Instead of a one-class school for pupils of all ages, the *bourg* has a

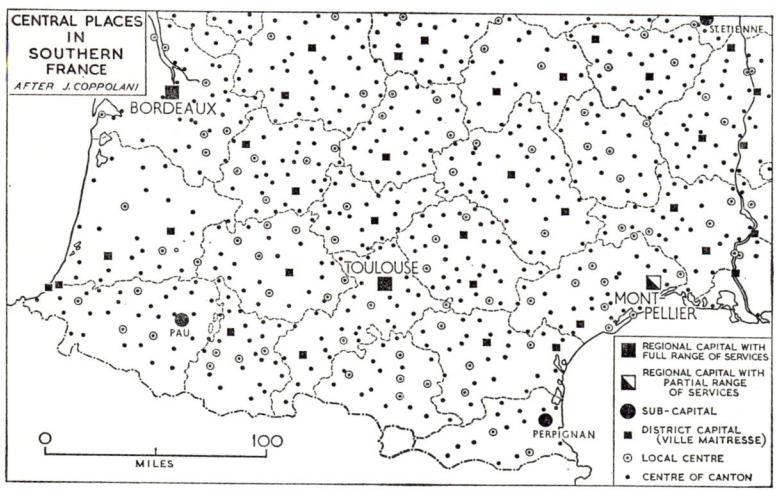

FIG. 11. Central Places in Southern France (after Coppolani).

larger school with classes for different age-groups and several teachers, and there is often a separate school for boys and girls. There is a variety of special shops providing daily requirements—café, haberdasher, and grocer, and more 'occasional' services, such as pastry cook, hosier, pharmacy, woodworker, ropemaker, garagist, and often a doctor. There is usually a village hall, a cinema, and a sports field. All told, the 'tertiary activities' may account for about one-quarter of all the workers. But these places, we repeat, serve the commune, and have no genuine centralized services.

The large commune with dispersed farmsteads presents a different situation. Typical areas are Brittany and the Massif Central. Here occur groups of eight to twelve farmsteads, described as a hamlet or village. Occasionally, alongside the farms will be found the communal church, a mixed school, a *café-tabac-épicerie*, serving the clustered farmsteads and a number of dispersed farmsteads around it. Generally, there is a larger settlement in the middle of the commune, often fortified in the past. Here are the *mairie*, parish church, school, and a number of shops and services as in the *bourg* of the Mediterranean area. Unlike the latter, which houses most of the population, the *bourg* under discussion houses only a quarter to a third of the total population of its commune, and most of its inhabitants are not peasant cultivators but engaged in services. This is a genuine embryonic urban centre.

La Bourgade. The name *bourg* is often used for those settlements that enjoyed a medieval weekly market. In fact, the communes with a total of 4,000 to 5,000 people with a weekly market have an agglomerated population frequently below 2,000, and present an essentially rural aspect. Their people are mainly engaged in agriculture, so that these places can rarely be described as towns on the basis of their market alone. The term *bourg* in this case becomes confused with the genuinely urban settlement of the *bocage* and rather than calling them market towns, as Christaller has suggested, Coppolani suggests *bourgade*. It is the equivalent of the local English term 'market town' and the German *Flecken*. About 900 communes with over 2,000 people have such settlements, but many active *bourgades* have under 2,000 people and are not classified in the French census as urban. The role of markets and fairs has been greatly reduced by the use of the truck for transporting livestock and produce and by the development of creameries, co-operatives, and itinerant merchants. But such centres retain a variety of functions, such as specialized shops (haberdasher, chemist, newsagent and bookstore, shoe and clothing stores, plus various craftsmen), all serving a small surrounding area beyond the commune. Very often the market town was selected in 1789 as the centre of the new administrative area called the *canton* and serves as such today. The advent of the railroad station or a new road, however, has often caused a canton centre to decline at the expense of a near neighbour. On the average, these centres have about 1,000 inhabitants, sometimes over 2,000. They are spaced at an average distance of 15 to 20 km. with an orbit of 8 to 10 km., an area of 150 to 200 sq. km. with a total population of about 5,000 to 8,000. This population becomes somewhat larger in areas of intensive agriculture (e.g. Flanders) and in industrialized areas, such as the coalfields where larger centres serve areas of the same general extent. Such centres merge into the next order in the hierarchy.

Le Centre Local. The centres so far described might quite well be named townlets or rurban centres, since they are not only small but also have a large rural component. We now come to the fully-fledged town. The 'local centre', as it is rather colourlessly named, has always less than one-third of its people engaged in agriculture, but the tertiary component is at least a quarter and can reach one-half. The population sometimes averages 5,000 and can reach 10,000, where there is an industrial component, or where there is tourism. Market and fair are still important attributes. Commerce is no more complex than in the bourgade, but there are furniture stores and hairdressers, and even a small printing establishment and several wholesalers, whose radius of action reaches out to the limits of the influence of the town. But the really distinctive elements are of a cultural kind. There is a local college, one or two seats of *apprentissage*, and a newspaper. There may be a small hospital and a home for old people, a seat of the *Sécurité Sociale*, a local branch of the agricultural syndicates, a branch of an agricultural credit bank, and professional organizations representing the interests of the farming community. The centre may be the seat of a sub-prefecture and of a few administrative services over and above the normal functions of the canton centre. A service of buses links it with the surrounding countryside. These centres are spaced at intervals of 30 to 35 km., a distance that corresponds to the day's journey on horseback before the advent of the railroad. These centres with the bourgades form the basis of the urban network of France. With an orbit of some 15 to 20 km. the population served averages about 40,000 to 50,000.

La Ville Maîtresse. The next category is the typical *chef-lieu* of a *département* with 30,000 to 50,000 inhabitants. The average size of the *département* is about 6,000 sq. km. with some 300,000 inhabitants and its central town has an orbit of about 45 km. radius. Examples are Agen (37,000), Chartres (29,000), and Perigueux (41,000). In the same group are certain towns that serve a part of one or more *départements*. There are quite a number of *départements* with two functionally equal capitals. In sum, there are about 120 of these centres. They have uniform service areas, equivalent to the area of the whole or half of a *département*, and with seldom more than 100,000 people. In the densely peopled areas of the industrial North there are more such cities serving smaller areas. The basic orbit of these centres is the same as was fixed at the time of the formation of the *départements*—namely, areas that could be reached by road to and from the centre in one day. Today, this distance can be covered in about one hour by automobile, a fact that gives to these centres and to the *départements* a very real basis for geographic unity.

As departmental headquarters, these cities are the seats of a variety of administrative functions. They are also important regional economic centres, with the offices of a number of nation-wide concerns—notably a branch of the *Banque de France, Caisse Primaire de Sécurité Sociale, Inspection du Travail*. They are usually the regional headquarters for the chambers of commerce of a number of surrounding towns. There are 158 such centres in France. Each is the centre of a well-developed bus system. Each usually has a diversity of small industries to serve the demands of the surrounding region—printing, clothing, construction. The city may also be a specialized industrial centre, although it is not to this fact that it owes its regional significance. It also has an assortment of educational institutions—lycée, college, library, theatre, learned societies, and frequently a daily paper. Hospital and professional services complete the list of these varied regional activities. Their service areas are usually rather clearly defined with exclusive influence over a radius of 20 to 25 km. Sometimes, when there is more than one centre in a *département*, the administrative and economic functions are divided between them.

Attention is drawn to Fig. 11 which shows the remarkable regularity of the spatial distribution of these centres, plus those of a higher order discussed in Chapter 12.

3. United States

In the United States, local government units, such as townships, villages, and counties, which were created in the pioneer days, in the era of neighbourhood economy, were of necessity small in area and population. With the increasing complexity and multiplying functions of government, hundreds of special districts have been created, each separately administered—for fire protection, library service, lighting, irrigation, schools, and so on. The citizen is also burdened with a bewildering number and variety of elections each year. Thus, the existing units are inadequate to cope with modern needs and there is lack of uniformity among the many local government boundaries. We read over thirty years ago:

'... It is being increasingly recognized that this archaic system is breaking down under the social and economic changes—such as the changes in the mobility and characteristics of population, the increasing interdependence of country, town and city, and the greater emphasis upon education, health, and welfare activities. Local units of government no longer conform to the social and economic relations and functioning of rural society. As a result, discussions and studies looking toward improvement have been initiated and reorganizations have been attempted here and there. The belief that the persistence of these tens of thousands of such local units is a factor in mounting taxation has further stimulated this movement.'

Thus, in such discussions, there arise the questions:

'What criteria should be used to delimit the boundaries of the new units? How many social considerations be given their proper weight along with those of efficiency, economy, or administrative convenience? For it must be emphasized that considerations for the reorganization of local government will need to go far beyond the immediate interests of economy or efficiency.'[1]

The solution of this vast problem lies not only in the reorganization of the system of local government, but also in working out principles for the redefinition of local government areas so that they shall conform to the demands of contemporary social and economic needs.

The first social study of this type to be attempted in rural areas was that of Dr. C. G. Galpin on the *Social Anatomy of an Agricultural Community*, published in 1915.[2] The area examined was Walworth County in the State of Wisconsin, in which twelve service centres were selected for an exhaustive analysis in the period 1911–13. This study revealed the significance of the emergence of 'a rural community', larger than that of the small country neighbourhood. This rural community is made up of the scattered farms and the small town or large village which serves them. Galpin called it the 'rurban community', since it combines the simplest traits and functions of rural and urban life. He showed, by means of large-scale maps (probably the most important innovation of his study), based on detailed farm to farm questionnaires, that surrounding each town there was an area in which the farm-houses depended on the town centres for certain regular services. These services were: general trade, banking, newspaper, milk marketing (the county studied is a commercialized dairy farming area), school, church, and library. Farm families and village or small-town families used the same centre and together form the larger 'rurban' community.

This community area is not static. The rural society of America is rapidly evolving and must adjust its areal organization to new forces. Therefore, in order fully to understand its ecological structure, the centres and their dependent areas must be studied periodically. Literally hundreds of studies on these lines were undertaken in the twenties and thirties by the Agricultural Experiment Stations across the United States. These were summarized, together with other independent researches, by Brunner and Kolb in their monograph on

[1] E. de S. Brunner and J. H. Kolb, *Rural Social Trends, Recent Social Trends Monographs*, McGraw-Hill, New York, 1933, pp. 286 and 287.

[2] Research Bulletin 34, Agricultural Experiment Station of the University of Wisconsin, 1915.

Rural Social Trends in 1933. We shall return to Professor Kolb's latest statement on trends in the last thirty years.

The smallest social unit is termed the *neighbourhood*. This is usually defined as the first grouping beyond the family which has social significance and which is conscious of some local unity. An alternative title is 'rural primary group'. There is a general tendency for the identity of the neighbourhood to be lost owing to the transference of its functions to the village centre, which serves as the first integrating service centre, and to the town. Consequently, except where the neighbourhood still functions actively in more isolated areas, a new rural community grouping is emerging, centred on selected, larger, village centres. After the definition of Dwight Sanderson in his *Rural Community*: 'A rural community consists of the social interaction of the people and their institutions in a local area in which they live on dispersed farmsteads and in a hamlet or village which forms the centre of their common activities'; or again: 'In its geographical aspect, a community is the local area tributary to the centre of the common activities of its people, which centre is normally a village.'[1]

A general grading of the service centres was arrived at by Kolb from studies of three counties in Wisconsin—East and West Dane Counties (by J. H. Kolb) and Walworth County (by Galpin and Kolb).[2] They are described as rural or country centres, rurban or town–country centres, and urban centres. The component services of these various centres were education (the high school), trade (the trade area), religion, social intercourse, commerce, and transport. The composite service areas of towns and village centres had an average of 4·3 miles. The active neighbourhoods continued to be found in the open country between, and well removed from, the village and town service areas. The neighbourhood, which is based on geographical locality, was widening the sphere of its contacts with the town or country centre.

The composite community areas of 140 village centres and the changes in areas from 1924 to 1930 were studied in various parts of the United States for purposes of the monograph on *Rural Social Trends*. 'In every region, and by every method of study, came the report that the high school was the most important single factor

[1] Dwight Sanderson, *The Rural Community: The Natural History of a Sociological Group*, Ginn, New York, 1932, pp. 481 and 484.
[2] See 'Trends in Town–County Relations', Research Bulletin 117, 1933, on Walworth County, Wis.; 'Rural Primary Groups: A Study of Agricultural Neighbourhoods', Research Bulletin 51, 1921; and 'Trends of Country Neighbourhoods: A Re-study of Rural Primary Groups, 1921–1931'. Also J. H. Kolb and D. G. Marshall, 'Neighbourhood–Community Relationships in Rural Society', Research Bulletin, 154, 1944.

gauging village–country relations and areas'[1] and 'there is a growing tendency for such services as trade, education, religion, and recreation to be organized about the village as a centre'.[2]

These studies by Brunner and Kolb were worked over again for the period 1930–36 in the depression years.[3] This revealed that the decrease in the number of neighbourhoods in the twenties was continued in the thirties by almost one quarter. It was found in a series of spot studies that 'those neighbourhoods tended to remain active which were somewhat larger than average, which were at some distance from village centres, and which were characterized by more than single integrating contacts or institutions such as school, church, or store. Larger villages and town centres tended to have a larger number of neighbourhoods within their community areas than the others. Some new neighbourhoods appear (in the period 1930–36) but the maximum had been reached in 1930.'[4]

In the thirties the position in the United States was summed up in the following words.[5]

'From the standpoint of merchandizing, three types of trade centres are developing in rural areas. First, there is the primary service centre, a small town offering goods that are well standardized and frequently demanded. These towns are usually under 1,000 in population. Secondly, there is the shopping centre, a town which, in addition to convenience goods, offers goods in speciality stores. Such places may vary from 1,000 to 5,000 in population. Finally, there is the terminal centre, which is large enough to offer the most specialized kinds of services. These centres are usually the larger cities in a State or other area. A process of integration of service centres is taking place to secure maximum efficiency of the services to the donors of the service and its recipients. The chain store illustrates this point. There is specialization as between shop and shop and the shops of different towns, all being dependent upon the terminal trade centre.'

The same writer pointed out that the country marketing services, such as livestock pens, were dying out in many country places and becoming concentrated in larger centres, facilitated in large measure by the development of road haulage. Only in a few cases, such as

[1] E. de S. Brunner and J. H. Kolb, *op. cit.*, p. 97.
[2] *Ibid.*, p. 92.
[3] E. de S. Brunner and I. Lorge, *Rural Trends in Depression Years. A Survey of Village-centred Agricultural Communities 1930–36*, New York, 1937.
[4] *Ibid.*, p. 108.
[5] C. R. Hoffer, 'Services of Rural Trade Centres', in *Social Forces*, Vol. X, No. 1, October 1931, pp. 66–71.

grain elevators and creameries, does the original distribution of marketing agencies remain. Banks in villages failed during the Great Depression. A bank can exist on an independent basis in a small town with 500 people, but requires support from larger banking centres in times of financial stress. In professional services, the shift to the larger centres is less marked. It is estimated in the States that approximately 1,000 people can support a doctor. About 10,000 people are required to maintain a well-equipped hospital. In social welfare, the county is becoming the unit of support and administration, and there is a vital need for the co-operation of town and country groups. In Michigan, over 50 per cent. of the towns with above 500 in population have cinemas, whereas only a fourth of the towns smaller than this have them, and even in the bigger towns the terminal or metropolitan centre is visited for choice. Newspapers require a town population of at least 1,000. Probably 1,000 people is the requirement to support a church. As for schools,

'assuming 12 to 14 teachers per school and an average of 20 pupils per teacher, there will be needed a minimum of 240 students per high school plus an equal 240 for the elementary schools. This total would require a local population of 2,800 to 3,000 to provide a good local school system, divided half and half between town and country. This figure would permit the effective service of specialized shops, a doctor and dentist, two or three churches, a railroad depot and bus depot, and a library.'[1]

Similar researches have continued into the fifties, though they are much fewer in number.[2] Professor Kolb carried out a third survey of Walworth County in 1947–48 (as in 1911–13 and 1929–30) and a further survey of the Dane Counties in 1950–51. These, and other recent studies, bring out the general trends. First, while earlier studies took the trade area as the best common denominator of the social group, the high school is now regarded as probably a more effective measure of common social ties and group interest. Second, 'village–

[1] D. E. Lindstrom, *American Rural Life: A Textbook in Sociology*, Ronalds Press, New York, 1948, p. 180.
[2] For more recent examples of such studies see the following: A. H. Anderson and C. J. Miller, 'The Changing Role of the Small Town', *Experimental Station of the University of Nebraska, College of Agriculture, Bulletin 419*, May 1953. W. Firey, 'Social Aspects to Land Use Planning in the Country–City Fringe, *Agricultural Experimental Station, Michigan State College, Special Bulletin 339*, June 1946. J. H. Kolb and L. J. Day, 'Interdependence in Town–Country Relations, A Study of Trends in Walworth County, Wis., 1911–13 to 1947–48', *University of Wisconsin, Research Bulletin 172*, December 1950. S. T. Kimball, 'The Fringe, The New Social Frontier', *Agricultural Experimental Station, Michigan State College, Special Bulletin 360*, June 1949.

country and town–country communities are becoming more differentiated and interdependent than increasingly self-sufficient and self-contained'.[1] This is a process of which we are all generally aware, but little is known quantitatively of the spatial patterns that are associated with it.

A noteworthy study of town–country relations has been made in Wisconsin. The field of Brush's study[2] is the six counties of south-western Wisconsin. This is an evenly settled area with a commercial dairy-farming economy. In it there are 234 agglomerated settlements. Three types of central places are recognized.

A hamlet (as defined in an earlier study by Professor G. Trewartha), is considered to have (1) four active residences, at least two of which are non-farm houses; (2) a total of at least six active functional units; and (3) a total of at least five buildings actively used by human beings. It must also have five residential structures or other buildings used for commercial or cultural purposes clustered within one-quarter of a mile. It must contain at least one, but not more than nine, retail and service units. Only grocery stores and elementary schools are generally typical, but taverns, filling stations, and churches are common.

Villages have a larger commercial nucleus with a minimum of ten retail and service units. In addition to the functions of hamlets, there must also be at least four other business units, selling autos, implements, appliances, lumber, hardware, or livestock feed. Three other services such as motor repairs, banking, telephone exchange, or postal delivery must be provided. There are public high schools in more than one-half of these centres, rarely in hamlets, and they are usually incorporated for governmental purposes. Personal and professional services are not well developed.

Towns contain not only all the services represented in the smaller centres, but additional specialized services. There are at least fifty retail units, thirty of which are types other than grocery stores, taverns, and filling stations. High schools and professions (doctor, dentist, veterinarian, and lawyer) are all regularly represented.

The multiplicity of functions of the town is to be attributed to five main causes: first, activities and services catering to the population living within the town; second, service to their larger trade areas plus their own demands permits a wide range of trade and services to smaller centres—specialized stores, financial services, movies,

[1] J. H. Kolb, *Emergent Rural Communities*, Madison, 1959, p. 11. Reference should also be made to *Rural Life in the United States*, New York, 1952, an important symposium sponsored by the Bureau of Agricultural Economics of the U.S. Dept. of Agric. (especially Chapters IV and V).
[2] J. E. Brush, 'The Hierarchy of Central Places in Southern Wisconsin', *Geographical Review*, Vol. 43, 1953, pp. 380–402.

THE URBAN SETTLEMENT AS REGIONAL CENTRE

weekly newspapers, etc.; third, the larger population of the towns can support specialized professional services—medical services, legal services; fourth, the larger market of the town enables it to offer goods and services for farmers which are not available in the smaller centres, e.g. processing plants, wholesaling of farm products, etc.;

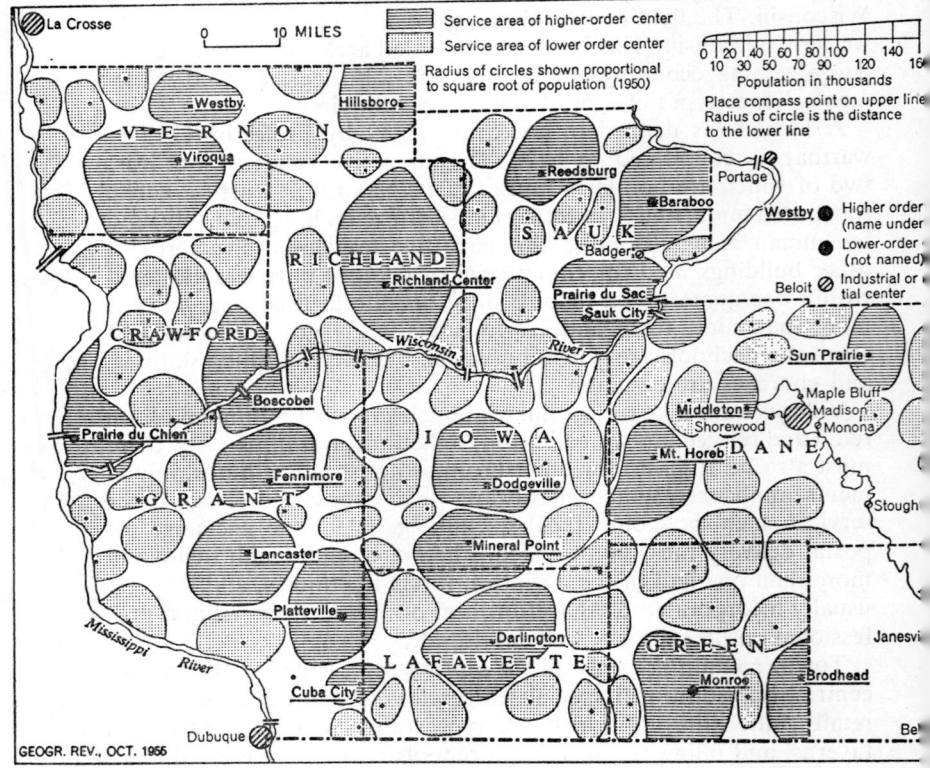

FIG. 12. Central Places in Southwestern Wisconsin (after Brush).

fifth, towns attract salesmen and wholesalers because of their concentration of business and population.

The locational pattern of these centres is shown on Fig. 12, from which the following observations are made by Brush.

'The centres closest to towns are hamlets; villages are further from towns but close to one another. In travelling from villages to towns, one usually passes hamlets. In this respect the locational pattern is in agreement with Christaller's "law of central places". If perfectly spaced in a hexagonal system, in which the distance between centres of each successive class increase by $\sqrt{3}$, the places would be 5·8 miles apart; actually they are spaced at 5·5 miles from each other and from the higher functional class. Villages would be spaced at 10·4 miles apart; whereas actually they are at 9·9 miles from one another and from towns. Towns would be 20·5 miles apart, whereas on the average they are 21·2 miles apart. This, to say nothing else, is a remarkable coincidence of the theoretical with the actual situation. But there are local irregularities of pattern. There is a marked tendency for centres to lie in twos or clusters. Hamlets cluster in areas farthest from the larger centres at a mean distance of 4·8 miles from other hamlets, 5·6 miles from the nearest villages, and 6·9 miles from the nearest towns. Very marked is the crowding together of low-ranking centres in the areas farthest from the larger centres.'

The cause of linear locations is due to the attraction of the railroad—the through traffic principle of Christaller. Several series of villages and towns developed in valleys at dam sites. The occurrence of hamlets in the remoter areas is explainable by the general dispersion of population before 1880 when wagon roads were the main means of transport away from the rivers and railroads were few. A random distribution of small service centres as well as villages and towns developed at a basic spacing of four to six miles throughout the settled area. Since the advent of the truck and car many centres have decreased in size and function, though they have not usually died completely. They cease to function as trade centres but remain as residential units with one or two services. Villages have changed and often added to their functions. The towns alone continue to make marked gains in functions and size.

The trade areas of towns and villages do not fit with the hexagonal system of Christaller. Village areas in particular are only 57 per cent. of their theoretical areas owing to the encroachment of town areas that are four times their theoretical size, reflecting the great attraction of their centralized services. Towns are disproportionately large in relation to their dependent areas. Four or five villages are within the trade area of each town and traffic flows indicate that many villages are linked with two towns.

This study applies to a closely settled area of dispersed farmsteads with a system of commercialized dairy farming. The urban centres in areas of commercialized monoculture in the High Plains present some interesting and important contrasts and trends.[1] Sherman

[1] W. M. Kollmorgen and G. F. Jenks, 'A Geographic Study of Population and Settlement Changes in Sherman County, Kansas, Part I, *Transactions of the Kansas Academy of Science*, December 1951, pp. 449–94, and 'Part II, Goodland', 'Part III, Inventory and Prospect', *ibid.*, March 1952, pp. 1–37.

County in the west of Kansas has under 20 inches of average annual rainfall and was part of the disastrous Dust Bowl of the thirties, as opposed to the more humid lands of eastern Kansas. It is a rectangular area measuring some 35 miles from west to east and 30 miles from north to south. Its county seat and its only urban centre, Goodland, is situated in its exact centre. The total population of the county increased from 6,223 in 1940 to 7,255 in 1950, an increase of 16 per cent. Its county town increased from 3,200 to 4,600 or 44 per cent. The rural population actually decreased by 15 per cent.

Most of the farmed land is under one crop, wheat. Work is concentrated in short periods and for most of the year the land lies idle and untended. Farmsteads are dispersed and were permanently occupied by the farming families. But in recent years, beginning in the thirties, many of the farmers continue to cultivate the land but do not live on it. They now live in the towns. Various reasons are given for this trend. Many farmers move to town to become what are called 'sidewalk farmers'. The absentee ownership of land is increasing and some of the absentees become 'suitcase farmers', living long distances from their farm tracts, generally over 30 miles and outside the boundary of the county. Big landholders operate the land with day labourers, many of whom live in town. Many business men and salaried workers, such as professional men, mail-men, and teachers, buy or rent land and become part-time farmers or side-walk farmers, thus having a second source of livelihood.

The abandonment and removal of farmstead buildings was associated with sales of land, enlargement of operating units, and by the farmers moving into town. The farm homes in the early forties were often crude and makeshift with few utilities. When better times came after the days of drought, especially in the forties, farm buildings—homes, barns, and sheds—were actually moved on wheels to town or they were razed to the ground. According to data collected by Kollmorgen and Jenks, there were about 800 operators of farmed land in the summer of 1950. Of these, 63 per cent. lived in the open country on dispersed farmsteads and may properly be regarded as rural. They operated two-thirds of the farm land. The remaining operators were either 'side-walk' farmers living in nucleated centres, mainly in towns, or 'suitcase farmers', who lived outside the county beyond 30 miles and as the name indicates simply stayed on the land as long as the farm labour required it—for ploughing, seeding, and harvest. The side-walk farmers made up one-third of all the farm operators in the county and farmed a third of the land. These are the operators who are responsible for the new settlement pattern here as well as in other sections of the wheat belt. The city of Goodland has most of these side-walk farmers.

These changes of the settlement structure are associated (in cause and effect) with economic, social, and technological changes. The land was opened to settlement in 1886 and was disposed of under the Homestead Law of 1862, so that the quarter-section holding was imposed although this was manifestly too small for this semi-arid area. The result was catastrophe for many settlers, with a great deal of buying and selling of land, either to consolidate or dispose of land. In 1890 the average size of a holding was 207 acres and in 1950, 1,190 acres. The county was divided by a rectangular net of roads in sections with four quarter sections in each section. In fact, the system was never fully developed and town sites and roads were abandoned or never laid out. Many miles of hard-surfaced roads have been built since the war, some three to eight miles apart. Schools, one of the essential universal requirements, have steadily diminished in numbers. In 1900 there were sixty school districts, presumably all one-room buildings. In 1950 there were only nine one-room schools and four of these had been moved to new locations. Consolidation is going on in the fewer centres. Churches were located in towns years ago, but, with one exception, all churches are now located in the county town of Goodland. Thus, 'Church activities, most school activities, most social activities, and, of course, business activities, are town and city centred. Almost no focal points of strictly rural communities remain.'

Goodland, the only town in the county, is situated in the middle of the county. Its population in 1950 was 4,600, and, though small in numbers, it has all the material essentials of modern living and has virtually no rival within 100 miles. The town site was laid out in 1887 and was reached by the railroad in the following year. The growth of the town was primarily related to its increase of services —such as agricultural supplies, automobiles, building construction— for the agricultural population of the area in a booming period. A quarter of the population received income from farms in 1950. Out of 1,226 farming *land owners* in the county 16 per cent. lived in Goodland and owned 21 per cent. of the farm land in the county. *Operators*, in the county, 808 in number, included 15·7 per cent. who lived in town and operated 19 per cent. of the land, widely spread throughout the county. Many travel 20 to 25 miles to their wheat tracts that may be widely separated. Half of the residences in the town in 1950 had been transferred since 1940. The tiny centres are on the decline and even though they have schools, their teachers often live in Goodland and travel to and from work daily. The service sphere of Goodland extends beyond the county line and to travel 20 to 30 miles for a show or shopping is commonplace.

This is a most interesting new type of 'agrotown' which has developed particularly in the area of wheat cultivation of the Great Plains. The land is not continuously tilled and requires labour only at time of ploughing and harvest. The amenities of modern life can be enjoyed by living in the urban centre. There is no genuine rural centre and no rural life.

4. ENGLAND

It is important to realize that throughout most of the United States the township is an arbitrary geographical unit defined as a rectangle six miles square. With the settlement of the Middle West in the latter half of the nineteenth century, neighbourhood groups had to organize themselves so as to provide the essential social services of all civilized communities—church, school, meeting-places, and general store. The neighbourhood unit is thus comparable in area, population, and function with the parishes of the original thirteen states and with the parish in England; and the tendency for the neighbourhoods to be integrated towards nearby towns and large villages is precisely analogous to the integration of activities in larger centres and to the ever closer service bond between town and country.

The situation in Britain may be illustrated from recent surveys in southern England.[1] Centrality was determined by enquiry in all country villages and hamlets as to where they obtained their services. Four services were selected as diagnostic keys for a number of other services. These were the chemist, as an indicator of medical services, that normally tend to be obtained from the same centre; ordinary shopping facilities; the local bank, that is normally associated with the business professions (auctioneer, accountant, and solicitor); and the cinema, that is a key for general entertainment. For each of these key services, a point is awarded to the towns for which they are visited. If more than one centre is named, the point is divided between them. The aggregate of points in each place is an indicator of its centrality for service to the countryside. Scores range among the seventy centres from 284 to 25 points. Shopping services are concentrated in fewer centres (the upper third) and the medical and business services—for example, the doctor and the auctioneer—are found more frequently in the lesser centres (the lower two-thirds). There is no clear definition of grades, but rather a continuum. But on the basis of the distinction noted above, the first group (major scores as shopping centres) are called 'higher-district

---

[1] H. E. Bracey, 'A Rural Component of Centrality Applied to Six Southern Counties in the United Kingdom', *Economic Geography*, Vol. 32, 1956, pp. 38–50. Also 'Towns as Rural Service Centres', *Trans. Inst. British Geographers*, 1953, and *Social Provision in Rural Wiltshire*, London, 1952.

centres', and the remainder 'lower-district centres'. The former are centres of marked centrality, since clearly, on the basis of their assessment, each is a centre for some twenty-five to thirty villages.

The service areas of each of these central places are mapped out on Fig. 13. These areas include those parishes where the villagers

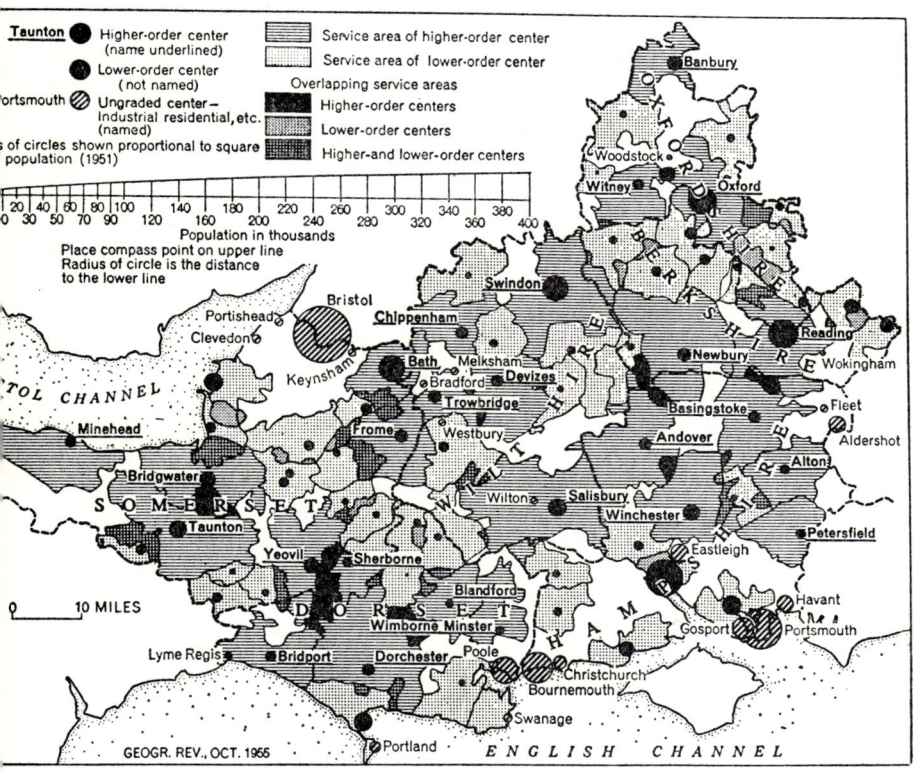

FIG. 13. Central Places in Southern England (after Bracey).
The map is on the same scale as Fig. 12 of Southwestern Wisconsin, with which it should be compared.

obtained at least three of the four selected groups of services. The first five centres serve the major part of the area and its rural population. Note that the new coastal resorts do not make big inroads as general service centres. This function is still overwhelmingly dominated by the country towns where there is a tradition of rural service. In general, entertainment scores keep in step with shopping scores, for the regular visit to town is usually the occasion for 'making a day of it'. Some urban centres give little evidence of rural service components. These have specialized functions, such as the coastal resorts or naval or industrial establishments on the south coast, or a few inland industrial towns.

The map shows clearly the spatial distribution of the service centres. The mean distance apart of all higher-order centres is 21 miles (compare 19 miles apart for the 'towns' of south-western Wisconsin). Shaded areas are served by higher-order centres, stippled areas by lower-order centres, and the unshaded areas obtain their services from various centres that are too low in their scores to be classified as lower-order centres. The majority of the blank areas are in sparsely populated areas served by village centres with a few services.

Further generalizations can be made about this pattern of distribution. The distribution of places is not regular. Each of the six counties has at least one major centre. The centres selected (on the basis of the four criteria) service practically all of the area. Though there is no extensive overlapping, areas overlap slightly owing to the competition of neighbouring centres. Certain areas are served only by lower-district centres. The spacing of centres in the areas served by higher centres is about 15 to 20 miles. One-half of the total survey area is still served by a large number of small country towns. The large centres, though they have been able to increase their range of attraction, are still visited only on rare occasions.

Emphasis should be given (as it is by Bracey) to the tracts of country that are served by closely spaced lower-order centres. This is to be associated with a relatively thin population and the relative inaccessibility to distant large centres. Here the lesser towns retain something of their significance from the pre-bus era. 'The maintenance of the medieval spacing of market towns—four to six miles—into the twentieth century appears to have made it difficult for a single centre to attain a higher status.' These towns suffer from competition with bigger centres but they have served for many centuries as agricultural centres and in the manufacture of woollen cloth. These centres are losing out to the larger centres. But three places acquired some industry and people during the war and their services have increased to serve them. One of the three may become dominant, or they may continue to compete and divide the service for the area between them, or they may all decline through the competition of their larger neighbouring cities. This situation occurs frequently elsewhere throughout the country. This is part of the general trend, greatly accelerated since World War I. The advent of the bus and the lorry has caused services to concentrate in a few larger centres at the expense of a host of smaller old-world country centres. It may well be that these lesser centres will experience a revival, for they still provide a diversity of services, and there is plenty of scope for locating small industrial establishments in such towns.

These observations confirm our own conclusions in East Anglia and are probably generally characteristic for the relatively undisturbed agricultural areas of England. Some towns have grown through the addition of industry and many small country towns have declined to the status of urban (or service) villages, but there is no fundamental alteration of the basic pattern of distribution of all centres. There have, however, been some fundamental changes since the 1920's, that were evident in 1930 and have become more accentuated since. Local government, services and industry have added to the status of the chief centres, and this has been accelerated by the development of bus transport.

These trends as illustrated in East Anglia are shown on Figs. 14, 15 and 16. These show the market towns in the sixteenth century and the early nineteenth century and the third map shows the bus centres (central places) and their hinterlands today.[1]

In conclusion, we note that there are many quite remarkable similarities in the spacing and functions of smaller service centres in the countryside between the United States and western Europe. This is well illustrated in the above cases of southern England and south-western Wisconsin.[2] The maps of these two areas (Figs. 12 and 13) are both on the same scale, so that direct comparisons can be made. The Wisconsin area has about 7,000 square miles, and a rural density of population of thirty persons to the square mile. The English area has the same area, but an average density of rural population of 182 per square mile. The villages in England have several hundred inhabitants and country towns of 2,000 to 15,000 as compared with tiny hamlets and villages and small towns with under 5,000 people in Wisconsin. The total rural population in the six English counties is five times that of the nine Wisconsin counties. The large urban population in the English area may be ignored in this comparison since by and large it has little effect upon town–country relations. Yet the grading and functions and pattern of distribution of the service centres are essentially the same. Little use of the railroad is made in Wisconsin because of the competition offered

---

[1] R. E. Dickinson, 'The Distribution and Functions of the Smaller Urban Settlements of East Anglia', *Geography*, Vol. XVII, 1932, pp. 19–31, and 'The Markets and Market Areas of East Anglia', *Economic Geography*, Vol. X, 1934, pp. 172–82.

[2] J. E. Brush and H. E. Bracey, 'Rural Service Centres in Southwestern Wisconsin and Southern England', *The Geographical Review*, Vol. 45, 1955, pp. 559–69.

in the last thirty years by truck and automobile, though it had a big effect on the growth of centres in the late nineteenth century. In England, this same trend has operated, but the main difference is the ubiquity of the bus on roads that interconnect the towns of the countryside.

Though defined by different methods by Bracey and Brush, the

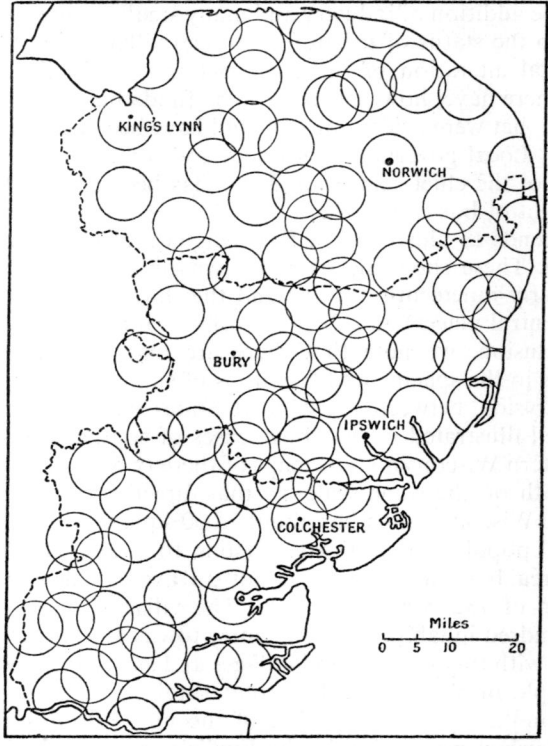

FIG. 14. Markets in East Anglia in the Sixteenth Century.
Each market town is given an arbitrary market area of four miles radius.

service centres in both areas were independently classed and are comparable. 'Higher-order' centres number one in five of all centres and one in three in England. The lower-order centres are recognized in both, but in England they retain many business and medical services, whereas in Wisconsin such services are rarely found in villages, though they retain the schools and entertainment. In the States, the lesser centres have been more effectively deprived of their services at the expense of a few bigger centres than is the case in England.

The similarities in the distribution pattern of the two areas is summarized by the joint authors as follows:

'1. Higher-order centres occur at a mean distance of 20 miles from one another in both areas.

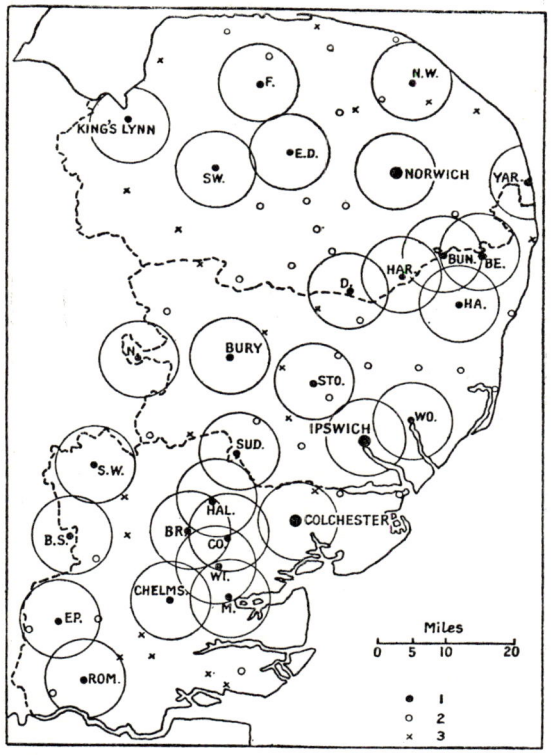

FIG. 15. Markets in East Anglia in the Early Nineteenth Century. Each large market has an arbitrary six miles market radius. 1. Large markets. 2. Small markets. 3. Disused or declining markets.

2. Lower-order centres occur at a mean distance of 10 miles from one another or from centres of a higher order in Wisconsin and mean of 8 miles in England.

3. Higher-order centres have service areas of 129 and 128 square miles in Wisconsin and England respectively; lower-order centres have service areas of 32 and 48 square miles respectively.

4. Higher-order centres tend to form clusters or tiers with few or no centres of lower order close to them.

5. Lower-order centres tend to form rows or belts hemmed in by the service centres of higher-order centres and crowded close to one another with their smaller service areas.'

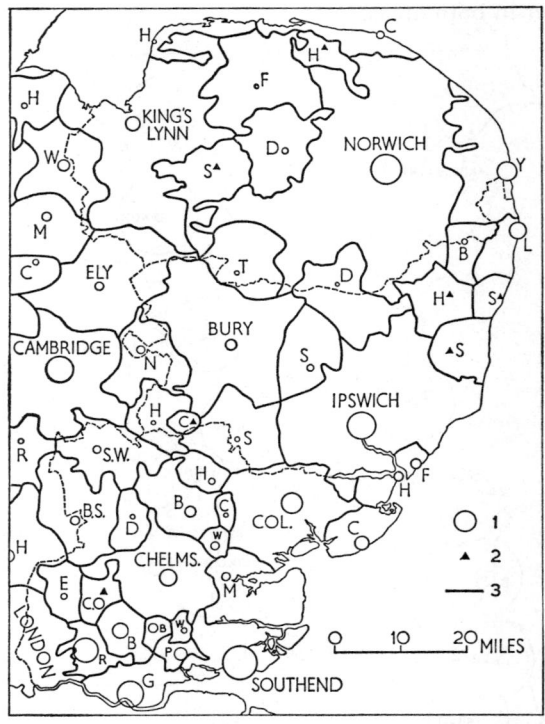

FIG. 16. Bus centres and their Hinterlands in East Anglia (after Green).

1. Main centres; with a population over 3,000 and exceeding the population of the hinterland. 2. Centres with a population less than 3,000 and population smaller than that of the hinterland. 3. Hinterland boundaries.

The blank areas in England are served by small centres with 'incomplete' services (third-order centres). These may be described as 'service villages' in England (actually we described these in 1931 in East Anglia as urban villages) and correspond with what Brush called hamlets in Wisconsin. Centres of this third order occur in England at intervals of four to six miles from one another or from a centre of a higher order. In Wisconsin they occur at intervals of five to nine miles. The hamlets in Wisconsin are mainly found in between the well-defined service areas of the higher-order centres, where services are obtained from lower-order centres or from the nearest village for all but the rudimentary services that are provided by the hamlets.

In England this system has developed from the early medieval pattern of market centres at intervals of four to six miles accessible by cart from the nearest small town in one hour. In the early nineteenth century, before the advent of the railroad, hamlets developed in Wisconsin under essentially the same conditions as in medieval England at intervals of five to six miles as rudimentary service centres for the farmers who lived within one journey hour by wagon roads. Many centres in both areas grew up at staging points along the main through highways, and vestiges of them are still to be found on the highways (e.g. old banks and inns). The railroad stimulated the growth of trade centres. It also caused many an adjacent roadside hamlet to decline. Since 1920 the bus has had much the same effect in England as the automobile in the States. Many more services, however, have been concentrated in the towns in Wisconsin than in England, where the lesser centres still cling to their services though they have lost out in shopping facilities. This is undoubtedly due to the greater mobility of the farming population in the States. But the persistence of service probably reflects the greater conservatism of the English.

At any rate, the basis of the patterns in both areas is a network of centres spaced in general at intervals of about six miles in the days of slow transport by horse and cart from farm to town. A process of selection was put into action by the railroad (more so in Wisconsin than in England). Since 1920, the automobile and truck have become paramount in both areas. Especially in England, the daily bus service, unlike Wisconsin, riddles the countryside to the remotest villages. The development of transport and of marketing organization, and the growth of new social services, have occasioned the concentration of functions in a few centres. This involves considerable extension of the areas which the latter serve, and the diminished viability of the small centres and villages. This maladjustment of present economic, social, and administrative services to the distribution of towns is in the main a medieval legacy. It is reflected in fundamental and general problems of rural activities and organization in both Europe and North America. These are stated with particular reference to England.

Administrative areas, which are based in England upon the parishes and hundreds, established ten centuries past, and the Poor Law Union areas (now abolished), established in 1834 before the advent of modern transport, bear no relation to the existing areas of economic orientation. The present system of administrative areas needs drastic revision, and in its more rational reorganization should be brought into closer geographic alignment with the areas grouped around the urban centres.[1]

In 'social surveys' of rural areas, prior to the formulation of any scheme of reorganization, the distribution and character of all existing social services needs to be thoroughly investigated as a first step. This requires a systematic survey, as far as this is possible from the data available, of the distribution of, and areas served by, hospitals, schools, cinemas, libraries, retail firms, wholesalers, etc. To determine the nature of the necessary reorganization of these services, i.e. to determine whether certain services are redundant or inadequate, selected criteria need to be adopted as a basis. This question has received considerable attention in rural areas in the United States in recent years. It will be evident from the content of this chapter that this has also received attention in England and on the continent in the post-war years and is now accepted as basic to the diagnosis and planning of town and country.[2]

The question arises as to what is the ideal size for the smallest administrative unit. The 'market district' in Germany, as defined by Christaller, has a radius of about three miles and a population of 1,600 to 2,700 inhabitants. He writes: 'We find throughout the Reich that the smallest market district is centred on a place of the lowest grade which is a commercial centre and a seat of administrative and professional services.' The service areas specifically referred to, in addition to those of a commercial kind, are police, telephone and postal districts, professional organizations, and medical services.[3] Its centre is the smallest market town with 1,000 inhabitants. The corresponding feature in East Anglia is the small town with between 1,000 and 2,000 inhabitants, or even the urban village with 750 to 1,000 inhabitants. It is the 'rurban' centre in the States and the *bourgade* in France. This nucleus, together with the half-dozen or more villages served by it, form a district with a total population of about 2,000 to 3,000 in East Anglia. This figure may be taken as typical of other rural areas in Britain with the same density of population. It seems that such a district might serve as a suitable unit area in a new administrative system.

The population of the small country neighbourhood is of necessity

[1] Attention was early drawn to this problem by geographers. See H. J. E. Peake, 'The Regrouping of Rural Population', *Geog. Teacher*, Vol. IX, 1917, pp. 71–7, and 'Geographical Aspects of Administrative Areas', *Geography*, Vol. XV, 1930, pp. 531–46.

[2] An outstanding contribution is H. E. Bracey's study of *Social Provisions in Rural Wiltshire*, London, 1952.

[3] Christaller, *Die Ländliche Siedlungsweise im Deutschen Reich und Ihre Beziehungen zur Gemeindeorganisation*, Berlin, 1937.

very small—200 or 300 people at the outside. The size of the smallest administrative units, which when established in the Middle Ages were units of social life and group organization, varies widely in different countries and districts. The overwhelming majority in Britain have less than 300 inhabitants. This is true also in certain districts on the Continent, but over large areas *communes* and *gemeinden* regularly have several thousand inhabitants. These contrasts lie largely in the circumstances of historical development and in the prevalence of different kinds of rural economy. The nature and distribution of the focal points will thus vary considerably from one pattern of population distribution to another.

An important contribution to this problem is the symposium of the Agricultural Economics Research Institute, Oxford.[1] This is an intensive survey of a particular rural area containing twelve villages covering 24 square miles. Three parishes have just over 1,000 inhabitants each and the remaining twelve have 150 to 350 inhabitants. A main conclusion of this survey is the inadequacy of the small village to function as an active seat of rural activity.

'The village of a few hundred people cannot survive as a healthy organism. It cannot maintain any of the social services; it must send its senior, and sometimes all its children away for their schooling; it must share the services of a district nurse; it cannot bear the overhead costs of water supplies, sewerage, or electric light; it has few shopping facilities; it cannot support the usual recreational organizations, cricket and football clubs, Women's Institutes, Young Farmers' Clubs, Guides and Scouts, and so on, solely because there are not enough men, women, and children of the various age-groups to run them; it cannot give a living or a life to a resident parson or Free Church minister.'

It will be recalled that the late Professor Fawcett, on the basis of the requirements of an elementary school in England, suggested a population of 1,200 to 1,400 as the ideal 'residential unit'. Dr. Orwin, in applying Fawcett's proposal, points out that the three larger villages in this survey area 'approximate to the lower of these figures, and they confirm in many ways that this population can support a vigorous community life'. They are identical with the urban villages of East Anglia. The same writer favours the controlled development of industry in rural areas. 'Dismissing the idea of new industrial towns built round the factories as being anti-social and artificial, the alternative would be to repopulate all the little villages within a certain radius of the factory' instead of establishing

[1] *Country Planning: A Study of Rural Problems*, prepared under the direction of Dr. C. S. Orwin, Oxford, 1944, pp. 274–81.

'housing-estates' in the towns near the factories. 'Villages thus enlarged by the influx of industry should find themselves emancipated from most of the disabilities from which small rural communities . . . are suffering today'. This has been a normal trend in many areas of the Continent and is today being actively encouraged. It has not gone far in Britain, but is today a part of its plan for industrial dispersal.

In all countries of western Europe and in North America the spatial structure of the rural community has been subjected to continuing change by the new space dimension introduced by the truck, the car, and the bus. The establishment of small industries in peasant villages and 'market towns', the dispersion of urban population, whereby villages become dormitories, and the growth of 'new towns', are profoundly changing the countryside, the functions of its centres, and so the web of spatial relations between urban centre and countryside.

PART II
The Structure of the City

Chapter 5

THE STRUCTURE OF THE CITY

In the previous chapters we have examined the structure of both urban and rural settlements as service centres for the areas around them. We shall carry this concept of the region as a social unit a stage further by examining from the same point of view the geographical structure of the large urban complex.

The city, in spite of its great extent and the heterogeneous character of its build and population, is in many ways a unit of social life and organization. It is also an aggregate of small homogeneous units, each having distinctive characteristics and playing a special role in the life of the city as a whole, and all finding their common nerve-centre in the central business district, the site of the original town and the nucleus from which expansion has taken place.

The spatial structure of the city is the product of three basic forces. There are the centripetal forces of attraction and coagulation. There are the centrifugal forces of dispersion and disintegration. There are, thirdly, the forces of spatial differentiation, which result in the segregation of buildings, persons, and activities in distinct areal groupings. Clearly the process of centralization is very much involved in the structure of the city and the areal groups within it.

1. THEORIES OF URBAN GROWTH

Many studies are now available as to the arrangement of land uses and the distribution of population in urban areas, and several hypotheses have been put forward to explain them. These are generally described as the concentric zone theory, the sector theory, and the multiple-nuclei theory. We shall discuss each of these briefly.

A hypothetical pattern of urban growth was described by E. W. Burgess, the Chicago sociologist, in 1923[1] (Fig. 17). The essence of

---

[1] E. W. Burgess, 'The Growth of the City', Chapter II, in *The City*, by R. E. Park, E. W. Burgess, and R. D. McKenzie, Chicago, 1925; originally published as an article in *Proceedings of the American Sociological Society*, Vol. XVIII, 1923, pp. 85–9.

THE STRUCTURE OF THE CITY

this hypothesis is that any town or city tends to expand radially from its centre so as to form a series of concentric zones. These were described in Chicago as follows: (1) the central business zone; (2) a zone of transition and social deterioration, which is being invaded by business and light manufacture; (3) the workers' housing and

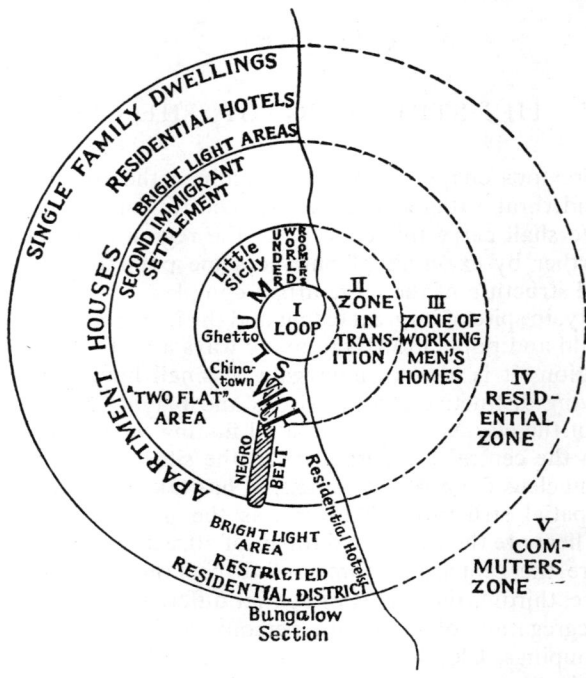

FIG. 17. Concentric Theory of Urban Growth (after Park and Burgess).

This diagram has particular reference to Chicago and should be compared with Fig. 19. The wavy line represents the shore of Lake Michigan.

factory zone; (4) the residential zone of high-class apartment buildings or single-family dwellings; (5) the commuters' zone of suburban areas and satellite cities within a journey of thirty to sixty minutes of the central business district. The main feature is the tendency of each inner zone to extend its area by the invasion of the next outer zone.

This pattern of urban land use is reflected in the social structure. 'In the expansion of the city a process of distribution takes place which sifts and sorts and re-locates individuals and groups by residence and occupation', and 'this differentiation into natural economic and cultural groupings gives form and character to the city' since 'these areas tend to accentuate certain traits, to attract and develop their kind of individual and so to become further differentiated'.[1] Burgess went further and showed that many social phenomena are distributed in a series of gradients outwards from the central business zone. Such phenomena are delinquency rates, sex ratios, percentage of foreign-born individuals, and poverty, each tending to decrease outwards from the centre. As ethnic groups shift out from their first living quarters near the centre, they ultimately become acculturated to the American way of life and tend to disperse in the outer suburban zones.

This concentric zone idea, formulated with special reference to the sociological structure of the urban community of Chicago, has come in for a good deal of criticism as well as support. It takes inadequate account of industrial and railway utilization, of the social disorganization associated with port areas, of the radial extension of commerce and in consequence of high land values on radial thoroughfares. Surface configuration often breaks up the 'ideal' pattern of concentric growth. Land uses and population push out along main thoroughfares to produce a star-like formation, and

'the population and institutions lining the sides of main arterial highways that cut squarely across the various areas of the city are frequently so different from the people and institutions located in the same general area but somewhat removed from the thoroughfares that the principle of concentricity seems to be seriously violated'.[2]

This interpretation is confirmed by Chombart de Lauwe's study of Paris which is discussed below.

A second interpretation of urban growth was put forward by Homer Hoyt (Fig. 18a). He describes it as the 'sector theory', as opposed to the 'concentric theory'. It has particular reference to the shifts of residential neighbourhoods, which Hoyt studied in American cities in great detail. He asserts that residential districts, when defined on the basis of rent levels, tend to shift in definite outward directions in different sectors of the city. Let the city be regarded as a circle divided into a number of sectors by radials from the centre. Hoyt then affirms that in American cities, 'the different types of residential areas tend to grow outward along rather distinct radii,

[1] Burgess, *op. cit.*, p. 56.
[2] Maurice R. Davie, 'The Pattern of Urban Growth', in *Studies in the Science of Society*, edited by G. P. Murdock, New Haven, 1937, pp. 133-61.

THE STRUCTURE OF THE CITY

and new growth on the arc of a given sector tends to take on the character of the initial growth in that sector'.[1] He continues:

'Thus, if one sector of a city first develops as a low rent residential area, it will tend to retain that character for long distances as the sector is extended through the process of the city's growth. On the other hand, if a high rent area becomes established in another sector

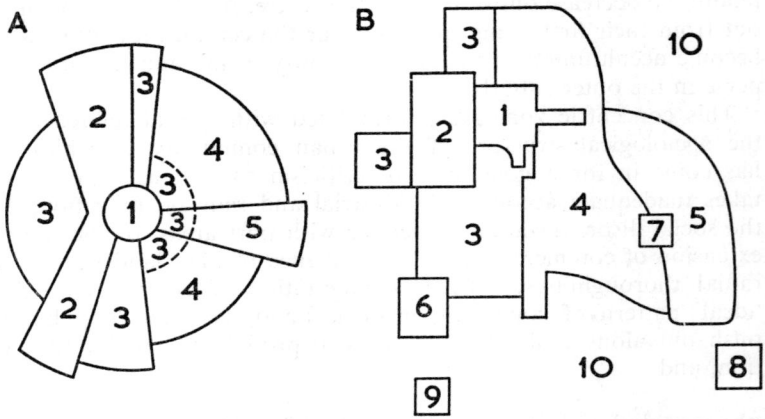

FIG. 18a. The Sector Theory of Urban Growth (after Hoyt).

FIG. 18b. The Multiple Nuclei Theory of Urban Growth (after Harris and Ullman).

Two generalizations of the Internal Structure of Cities. 1. Central Business District. 2. Wholesale Light Manufacturing. 3. Low-class Residential. 4. Medium-class Residential. 5. High-class Residential. 6. Heavy Manufacturing. 7. Outlying Business District. 8. Residential Suburb. 9. Industrial Suburb. 10. Commuters' Zone.

of the city, it will tend to grow or expand within that sector, and new high grade areas will tend to establish themselves in the sector's outward extension.'

The evidence is produced in a series of diagrams of six cities showing the location of fashionable residential areas for 1900, 1915, and 1936. The movement of the high rent area is probably the most important, because it tends to pull the growth of the entire city in the same direction. Hoyt emphasizes, in particular, the tendency for high-rental 'poles' to spread out along a main highway. The new

---

[1] Homer Hoyt, 'The Pattern of Movement of Residential Neighbourhoods', in Mayer and Kohn, *op. cit.*, pp. 499–510. Reprinted from *The Structure and Growth of Residential Neighbourhoods in American Cities*, Federal Housing Administration, 1939.

and better residences are situated on the outward edges of the high rent area to which they are attracted by more attractive sites, the homes of the elite of the community, and the growing first-class commercial centres. As the inner areas are abandoned, lower and intermediate rental groups filter into them. Rentals tend to diminish with increasing distance from the highest rental areas. The low-rental areas are situated furthest from the high rent areas and are normally located on the least desirable land alongside railroad, industrial, or commercial areas.

A third interpretation is the so-called multiple-nuclei theory of urban growth put forward by Harris and Ullman[1] (Fig. 18*b*). According to these authors, cities show a tendency to grow around *several* distinct nuclei rather than from *one* centre of origin. Such nuclei may be the first town settlement, a village cluster, areas of port or railroad facilities, factory, mine, or coastal beach. Each serves as a focus for the local accretion of urban uses. The development of these nuclei as independent 'differentiated districts' reflects a combination of four factors.

'1. Certain activities are tied to particular sites because they have highly specialized needs—such as the retail district (access), the port district (water front locations), the manufacturing district (transport facilities).

2. Certain kindred activities tend to segregate in the same district since they can be more efficiently carried on if in a cohesive unit. This is particularly true of the location of the central business district.

3. Certain unlike activities are detrimental to each other, as for instance the antagonism between factory development and high-class residential development. Retail trade districts, with their heavy traffic congestion, are antagonistic to the means of loading and unloading of the wholesale services.

4. Certain activities are unable to afford the high rents of the most desirable sites, this factor working in conjunction with the foregoing third factor.'

The number of nuclei, reflecting their historical development, varies from one city to another, but in general the larger the city the more its separate nuclei. Districts that serve as nuclei and tend to be located in special locations are the central business district, the wholesale and light manufacturing district, the heavy industrial district, and high-class residential districts. The last tend to be on well-drained higher land away from the area of non-residential uses,

[1] C. D. Harris and E. L. Ullman, 'The Nature of Cities', reprinted by Mayer and Kohn, *op. cit.*, pp. 277–86.

while low-class districts are clustered near to factories and railroad districts. Minor nuclei include cultural centres, parks, outlying business districts, and small industrial centres or even a University.

Most cities, it is claimed by these authors, exhibit some combination of the three trends of development—concentric growth, sector growth and multiple-nuclei growth. The first two assume one dominant centre in the emergence of the urban pattern. The various nuclei listed above may function in the same way as a minor focus of growth. Similarly, dilapidated areas are not merely limited to the environs of the central district. They may be found next to the other nuclei. And, moreover, they may well occur on the fringes of the city.

It should be noted that the latter two interpretations do not refute, but rather modify, the concentric zone hypothesis. Residential areas, according to Hoyt, expand outwards concentrically by sectors. The same forces presumably operate in varying degree from the various lesser nuclei in the urban areas discussed by Harris as well as from a central point of origin.

These interpretations of the internal arrangement of urban land uses have been subjected to appraisal by many workers. Maurice R. Davie[1] in a comparison of land use and other maps of twenty American cities found the following consistent features of arrangement:

'(1) a central business district, irregular in size but more square or rectangular than circular;[2] (2) commercial land use extending along the radial streets and concentrating at certain strategic points to form sub-centres; (3) industry located near the means of transportation by water or rail, wherever in the city this may be—and it may be anywhere; (4) low-grade housing near the industrial and transportation areas, and (5) second- and first-class housing anywhere else. These seem to be the general principles governing the distribution of utilities. Low economic areas are characterized by smaller incomes, fewer radios and telephones, fewer home-owners, fewer one-family dwellings, more two- and multi-family dwellings, more murders, houses of prostitution, juvenile delinquents, dependent families, unemployment, illiterates, and higher birth and infant mortality rates in proportion to population. Such areas, while in general near the centre of the city are by no means confined there, but are found in

---

[1] Maurice R. Davie, *op. cit.*
[2] This is certainly associated with the rectangular street pattern dominant in these cities, a circular shape being more common in European cities, reflecting the circular or oval shape of the old city walls and the modern boulevard that has displaced them.

any zone. They are generally adjacent to industrial and railroad property.'

This refinement of the conception of the 'natural area' of the sociologists and the 'functional area' of the geographers, with which we shall deal later, does not refute the concentric zone hypothesis of Burgess, which is the most comprehensive of these hypotheses and is the one that has received the most critical attention. Studies of European and American cities, from the standpoint of their historical development, the density of built-up land, and the movements of population, substantiate this general theory.[1] It is clear, however, that it has limited validity, for this is only one process of spatial differentiation of land uses and some phenomena in urban areas that must be set against other processes of localization, as well as against the peculiar circumstances of the site and historical development of every individual city.

2. EXAMPLES OF URBAN GROWTH: CHICAGO

Let us begin by comparing the mode of growth of two major cities, Chicago and Paris. Figs. 19 and 20 show their built-up areas and administrative limits on the same scale. For purposes of general comparison it should be noted that there are three kinds of area in each case. In Chicago there are: (1) the central city; (2) the continuously urbanized area containing the central city and its fringes; (3) the standard metropolitan area as of 1950. In Paris the comparative areas are: (1) the central city of Paris; (2) the urbanized area as defined by the census (agglomeration plus suburban fringe); (3) the area of the Paris Region, as defined for planning purposes.

The urban agglomeration of Paris, as defined by Bastié and Brichler (see pp. 148 ff.), has an area of about 580 square miles with 7 million inhabitants. This compares with the urbanized area of Chicago of 960 square miles, on which there live about 6 million inhabitants (1950). The inner urban area of Paris has 300 square miles and 6·3 million inhabitants as compared with 224 square miles in the city of

---

[1] In a thorough study of the changes in the distribution of population in the city of Stockholm between 1880 and 1930, the geographers, whose work is noted below, concluded that 'the growth of the town is practically concentric' and 'distribution changed from high density in the centre and low density on the periphery to the reverse with the formation of a central "city" district'. W. William-Olsson, 'Stockholm: Its Structure and Development', *Geographical Review*, Vol. XXX, 1940, pp. 420–38. Interesting observations on this mode of urban expansion are made by Griffith Taylor with reference to Toronto in 'Environment, Village and City', *Annals of the Association of American Geographers*, Vol. XXXII, 1942, pp. 1–67.

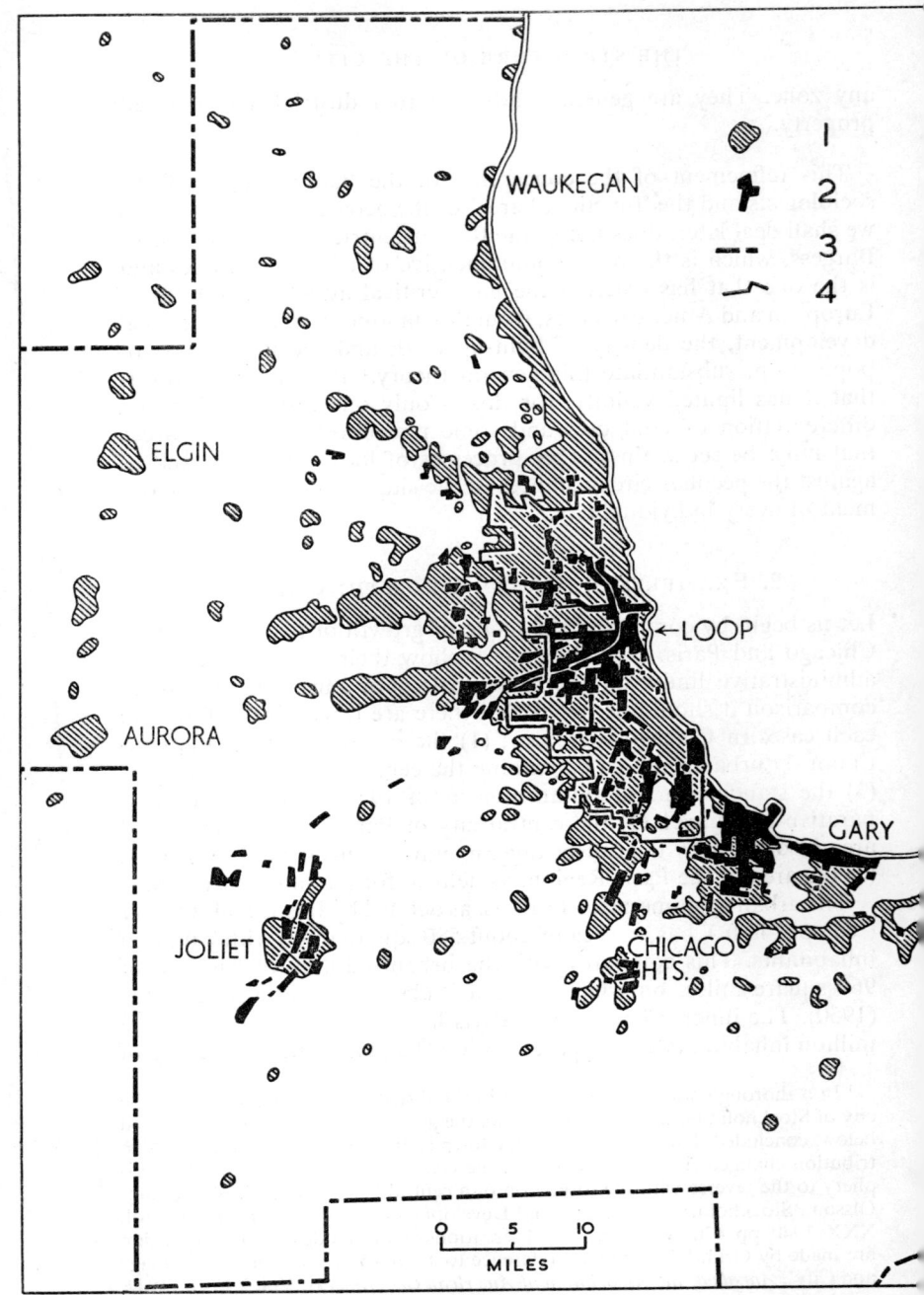

Fig. 19. Chicago: Layout and Land Use.
1. Built-up areas. 2. Industrial areas. 3. Limit of the Standard Metropolitan area (1950). 4. Limit of the City of Chicago. *Note:* Figs. 19 and 20 are on the same scale.

THE STRUCTURE OF THE CITY

Chicago with 3·6 million inhabitants. The standard metropolitan area of Chicago, that reaches far beyond the limits of the continuously urbanized area, covers 3,714 square miles, and has about 6·2 million people, whereas the Paris Region, with less than one-half of this area, has about 7·5 million people. The *département* of the Seine has 5·1 million inhabitants on about 190 square miles—an area roughly comparable to that of the city of Chicago. The two agglomerations

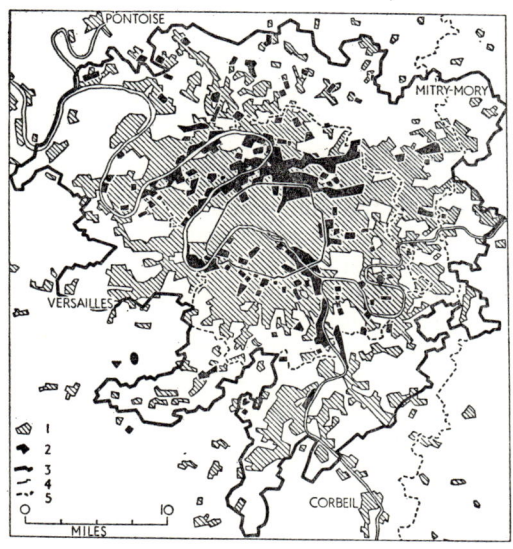

FIG. 20. Paris: Layout and Land Use.

1. Built-up areas. 2. Industrial areas. 3. Limit of Paris Region. Institut National de la Statistique et des Études Économiques (census definition). 4. Limit of the City of Paris. 5. Limits of the Departments.

will now be discussed in more detail since they afford some interesting contrasts in urban growth.

Chicago has grown radially from its original nucleus on the south side of the mouth of the Chicago river, which is now the down-town skyscraper district known as the Loop (so called since it is a rectangle enclosed by an elevated railway). It has a grid plan of streets with radial boulevards and railways. The first railway companies carried their lines to the heart of the city and today over twenty radial lines form a band of steel around the Loop and, together with the river to the north and west, make difficult its lateral expansion, and increase congestion through the concentration here of almost the whole of the passenger traffic in transit. After 1885, decentralization set in, culminating in the opening of three belt lines and marshalling yards that allow the peripheral localization of industry and relieve the centre of some traffic congestion. Industrial areas in the city are situated on the north and south Chicago rivers. The vast complex of the Union Stock Yards, which was sited on the southern outskirts of the city when erected in 1864, is now near the heart of the city and the centre of a great area of squalid slum.

The mode of expansion of the city of Chicago by subdivision of land for sale and building has shown a combination of 'differential attractions' that have been summarized as follows:[1]

'While inter-city transportation lines exerted considerable influence on patterns of initial subdivision, they were ineffective in stimulating individual lot sales. Local mass transit lines, on the other hand, almost always came later than initial subdivision in Chicago, but were closely correlated with the timing and direction of the sales of individual lots. Both municipal parks and outlying settlement nuclei stimulated initial subdivision more than individual lot sales. The great land booms of the nineteenth century interrupted the regular outward expansion of Chicago through gradual initial subdivisions and individual lot sales, and disrupted the close temporal correlations that might otherwise have developed between these growth patterns and transport lines, parks and settlements. Indiscriminate subdivision and lot sales by speculators added areas of prepared land that the growing city was not able to utilize immediately. Since the newly added lands were frequently not related to the existing transportation net or settled areas, a prolonged time lag occurred between initial subdivision, resubdivision and lot sales.'

This commentary serves to remind us that in the development of the urban plan there are to be considered the role of lines of transport (and often urban expansion far exceeds the limits of public transit lines) and the role of boundaries of land ownership and pre-existing field patterns as conditioning factors in the lay-out of the street pattern and of individual plots.[2]

Heavy industry is located on the waterways and on the railroads. The biggest seat of heavy industries, beginning in 1880, is in the Calumet area to the south of the city. Here are located large areas under iron and steel and engineering plants, metal works, oil refineries, etc. There are also several clusters of industrial plants along the Outer Belt railroad 30 to 40 miles outside Chicago. Lesser and

---

[1] J. D. Fellman, 'Pre-Building Growth Patterns of Chicago', *Annals of the Association of American Geographers*, Vol. 47, No. 1, 1957, p. 82.

[2] David Ward, 'The Pre-Urban Cadaster and the Urban Pattern of Leeds', *Annals of the Ass. of Am. Geographers*, Vol. 52, No. 2, June 1962, pp. 150–66.

more diversified industrial clusters are located where the intermediate belt-line railroad intersects the radial trunk lines. Many industries have been located during and since the war in the outer ring along the highways, as shown on Fig. 19, and they have been associated with residential growth.

Suburban settlements extended in the late nineteenth century like beads on a chain along the railways. The arrangement of the concentric residential zones within this framework is shown on Fig. 17 and is summarized on p. 126.

The basic feature of the layout of Chicago is its variety of distinct functional sectors. At the centre is the business district of the Loop. The lake front, with high density apartment houses and parks, stretches north and south from the Loop for eight miles. A semicircular high density inner core surrounds the Loop, and contains on 40 square miles one-half of the industrial establishments of the metropolitan area, a million people, and the greatest ratio of blight and slum, as well as many of the foremost cultural institutions. A medium density ring surrounds this inner core, five miles in width, with good middle-aged apartment duplex and single family houses and a variety of business and manufacturing districts. The North Shore 'prestige' residential area north of Evanston has high-grade residences and low-density development. The South Shore industrial area reaches from South Chicago to Gary with a vast aggregation of heavy industry. Seven distinct sectors of suburban development radiate outwards along the transport lines. A ring of satellite cities reaches to Waukegan to the north, Aurora and Elgin to the west, and Joliet and Chicago Heights to the south. Independent centres lie on or near the Outer Belt lines, and thus connect with each other and with the complex network of metropolitan Chicago. The Fox River valley, even without its satellite cities of Aurora and Elgin, is becoming an integral part of the Chicago complex through its growth as a popular 'prestige' residential area.

Chicago from its inception has had a rectangular grid-iron pattern of major streets at intervals of one mile apart. These streets were originally laid out as section-line roads bounding the square-mile sections of the federal land survey, which was extended right over the site of Chicago in advance of its settlement. These streets carried the network of street railways that finally by 1958 were completely replaced by the motor bus. They are lined by intermittent rows of commercial establishments, while at the intersections are the major shopping centres generally with a cross shape. On the section-streets between the intersections much land was reserved for commercial use (confirmed by the zoning ordinance of 1923) and, since it is in excess of demand, there is haphazard development and many vacant lots, even though the land behind (with a rectilinear pattern) is fully developed for residential purposes. Diagonal streets from the centre follow the routes that lay along low beach lines and morainic ridges, above the level of the surrounding mud land of the lacustrine plain. These also became the earliest plank roads. They facilitate travel to the centre but make very sharp angles with the rectilinear streets that create traffic and building problems.

The expressway system of highways (as shown in Fig. 21) provides a new framework of circulation. Much has been done in and outside the city but the system is not yet complete. It illustrates perfectly what is going on in all the major American cities. The highways provide six or eight lanes, with points of limited access, and no level intersections. The pattern is radial-concentric, centred on the central business district, with two concentric distributor- and by-pass routes and a major concentric belt just outside the main built-up area of the city. A major highway runs along the shore of the lake through the lake-front parks.

These highways are having a great impact on the growth of the metropolitan area. Their construction has involved much demolition in the city. The great increase of suburban population is also largely concentrated along the new expressways. The areas between the older radial routes of suburban growth along radial rail and road routes, that until recently were wedges of rural land, are rapidly being built up for residential development, shopping centres, and factories. Much of this development is taking place in unincorporated areas, not subjected to the regulations of any municipalities. 'The result is a rapidly expanding, almost continuous, unplanned urban mass.'[1] The focus of the whole area is the Loop that is today one of the most congested urban sectors in the world. Nearly one million people pour in daily for employment and pour out in the late afternoon to their homes in Chicago and on its fringes—to say nothing of the flood of people coming in for shopping, entertainment, and business. The automobile has not greatly extended the outer limits of the radial tentacles, but the intermediate areas are being filled up, and, except for a few forest preserves, open spaces are now rare within 50 miles of the centre of Chicago.

The changes of population for 1950 to 1960 are shown on Fig. 22. Decreases have spread from the core to the greater part of the built-up area of the city. The total population increased by about 25 per cent. per decade from 1900 to 1930. It showed no increase from 1930 to 1940, a slight increase of 6·6 per cent. to 1950, and a loss of −1·9 from 1950 to 1960. The population may be calculated in con-

[1] H. M. Mayer, *Chicago: City of Decisions*, Geographic Society of Chicago, 1955, 40 pp.

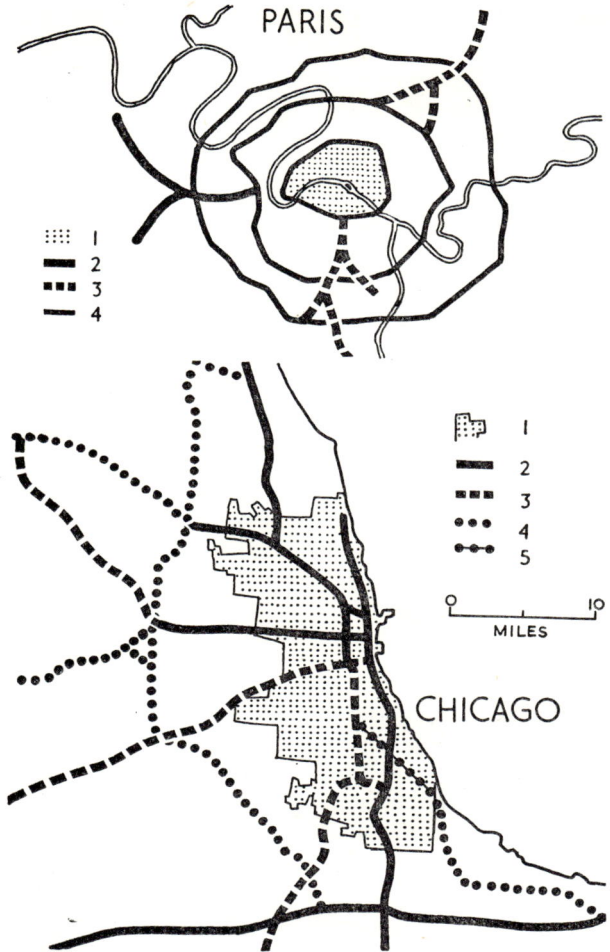

Fig. 21. The main highways of Chicago and Paris.
Paris (1956): 1. The city of Paris. 2. Completed Autoroutes. 3. Proposed Autoroutes. 4. Main ringroads under improvement. Chicago (1960): 1. City of Chicago. 2. Completed Expressways. 3. Proposed Expressways. 4. Toll road. 5. Toll bridge. Note that both maps are on the same scale, as Figs. 19 and 20.

centric zones a mile wide up to a distance of 10 miles from the centre, from 1900 to 1960. From 1910 to 1930 there were substantial losses in the inner zones up to 2 miles, and an accelerated growth in the outer zones. The same pattern is repeated from 1930 to 1940

THE STRUCTURE OF THE CITY

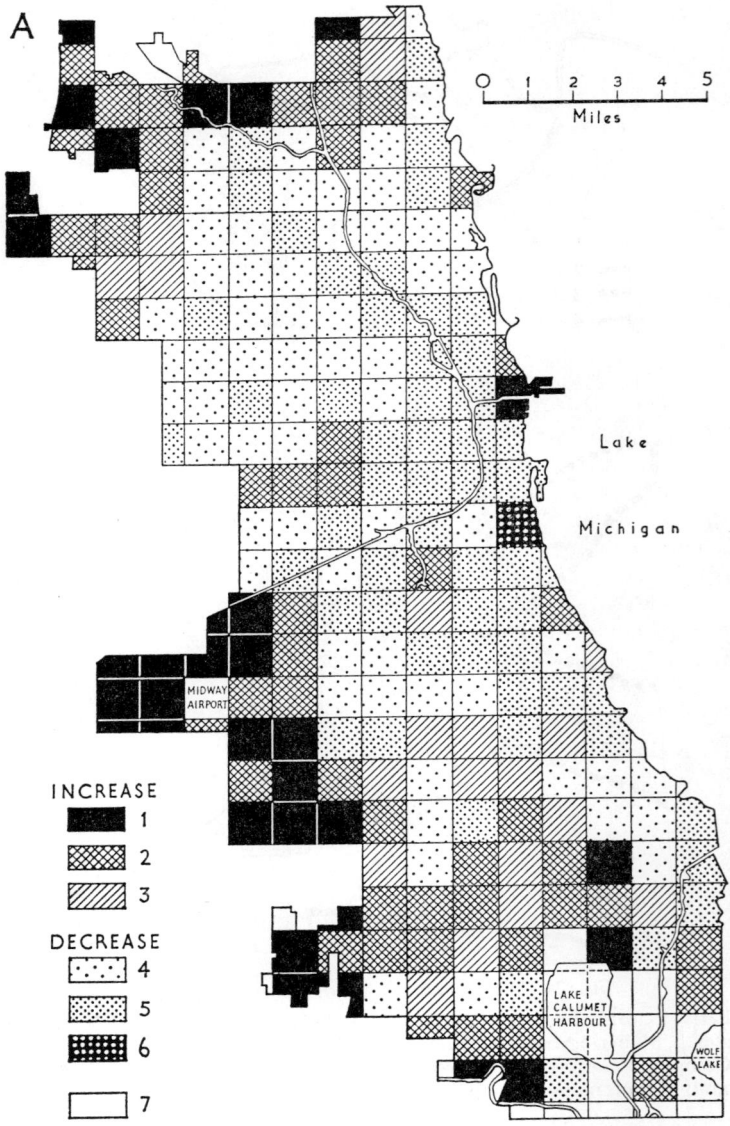

FIG. 22. Population Changes in the City of Chicago, 1950–60 (after Chicago Plan Commission).

Percentage Increase: 1. 50 or more. 2. 10–50. 3. 0–10. Percentage Decrease: 4. 0–10. 5. 10–50. 6. 50 or more. Based on figures per square mile. 7. Square miles with under 1,000 inhabitants.

although decreases have extended to the 4-mile limit. From 1940 to 1950 the process is reversed, for the inner zones increased (due to the slow down in housing) and the 4 to 7-mile zones were stationary. From 1950 to 1960 zones within 7 miles of the centre lost population and there were moderate increases beyond 8 miles. These trends reflect the shift of population from centre to periphery. This is not, however, simply a manifestation of increasing population accretion, but emerges as the spatial expression of metropolitan growth. It reflects the process of centralization, which would more clearly be shown were the 'ring' outside the city and within the metropolitan district included. For it is in the ring that the increase of population has been greatest in recent decades. The urban fringe increased by over 50 per cent. between 1956 and 1960, as compared with a loss of 1·9 per cent. in the city of Chicago.

The gross densities of population per square mile in the city are shown on Fig. 23. The central core is marked by its extremely low residential (night) densities of about 11,000 per square mile with several square miles in which it is below 5,000. This rises abruptly in the congested zones immediately surrounding the Loop, 2 to 3 miles from the centre, to densities of over 30,000 per square mile. Beyond, at distances from 4 to 6 miles, the densities are around 25,000, and in the 8 to 10-mile zones fall to 12,000 per square mile. This distribution has been aptly likened to a volcano with a deep crater.[1] It should be noted, however, that this concentric regularity is markedly broken by the high densities on the lake front. Especially north of the Loop, these are due to the expensive multiple-storey apartments and hotels of the 'Gold Coast'. The core in 1950 had 11,000 resident workers at night, but it employed 275,000 persons in the daytime.

Population movements in Chicago have been the subject of careful examination. The process of outward displacement of population is part and parcel of the whole process of concentric urban growth, and it received special emphasis in studies of the Chicago school. The oldest immigrant stocks are widely distributed throughout the urban area—Germans and Scandinavians in the north and north-west, Irish in the south-west. On the other hand, immigrants of the first generation are more concentrated near the industrial areas and in the zone of transition around the Loop—for example, Italians, Czechs, and Russians. Second-generation immigrants of the same stocks are dispersed in smaller groups throughout the zone of working-class homes. This distribution results from a general process by which recent immigrants first settle in the congested rooming-house

[1] Beverly Duncan, 'Inter-urban population movements', in Hatt and Reiss, *Cities and Society*, 1957, p. 302.

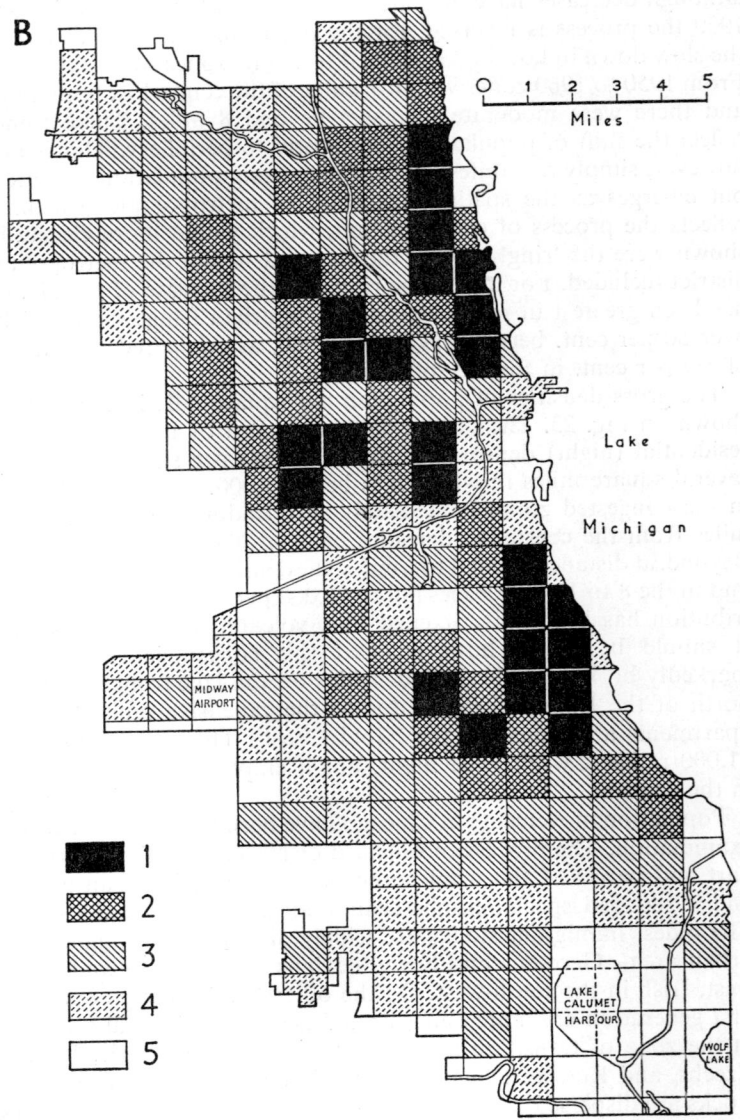

FIG. 23. Density of Population in Chicago (after Chicago Plan Commission). Persons per sq. mile: 1. 30,000 to 70,000. 2. 20,000 to 30,000. 3. 10,000 to 20,000. 4. 5,000 to 10,000. 5. Under 5,000.

districts near the centre. Then, when they have found more or less settled jobs and taken their bearings, they tend to move to better living-quarters farther out from the centre, first segregating into communities of the same stock, and then, finally, after several moves over varying periods, depending on the fortunes of the individual, to the outer periphery, where they are completely dispersed and absorbed into the general 'American' community life. The peripheral zones in particular on the main lines of communication to the north and south along the lake front, to the west of the Loop, and exclusively in the suburban areas, are occupied mainly by people of American origin. Here also are the best-class residential areas. There is thus a gradual decrease in the concentration of each stock outwards from the Loop to a radius of five miles.

The distribution of the Negroes, who have entered Chicago since 1918 and numbered 234,000 in 1930 and 700,000 in 1960, is a notable exception. They are clustered in a narrow north–south belt in south Chicago that cuts across the pattern of concentric zones, and have pushed southwards along Michigan Avenue, ousting the settled white residents, with whom they came into open conflict in the riots of 1918 and 1919. The fine houses of three to five storeys (some formerly the residences of well-to-do and old-established families, like the Armours, the Swifts, and the Rockefellers) have been converted into congested Negro rooming and apartment houses, very overcrowded with a dilapidated external appearance through lack of proper upkeep. The Negro continues to press southwards and has reached the vicinity of the University of Chicago, where he is held at bay by tenants' associations and the like.[1] First-generation immigrants settled first near the Loop in Zone II and, differing greatly in culture and economic status, have moved out along the main avenues of communication, displacing other groups, who in turn have continued the outward trend. P. F. Cressey calculated the distance of specific population groups in zones from the city centre in 1898 and 1930, and was able to demonstrate this centrifugal tendency. It is impossible to say how many moves were made by migrants in the city, but the general result reveals a tendency for the original

---

[1] See P. F. Cressey, *The Succession of Cultural Groups in the City of Chicago*, Ph.D. MS. University of Chicago, 1930, and 'Population Movements in Chicago', *Journal of Social Forces*, Vol. II, 1924. Also C. S. Johnson, *The Negro in Chicago*, Chicago Commission on Race Relations, 1922. P. F. Cressey, 'Population Changes in Chicago, 1898–1930', *American Journal of Sociology*, Vol. XLIV, July 1938, pp. 56–69. The same process has taken place in New York with the spread of the Negro from his Harlem district towards the Central Park and Morningside Heights. It is also found in the outward spread of Jews and foreigners in the districts of north-west London, as well as of the Jews in such cities as Manchester and Leeds.

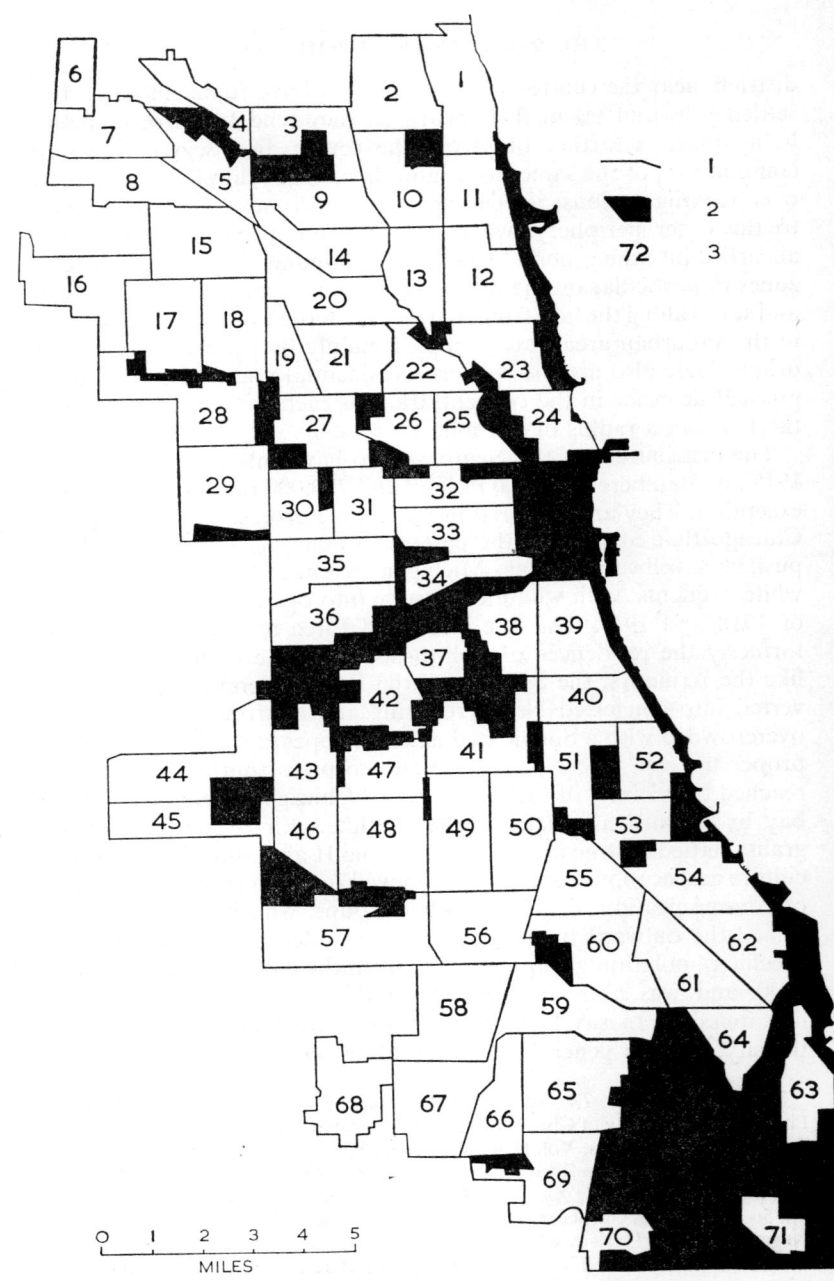

FIG. 24. Community Areas of Chicago, 1959
(Department of City Planning, Chicago).

1. Community area boundary. 2. Non-residential areas (industrial, railroads, cemeteries, and parks). 3. Community area numbers.

THE STRUCTURE OF THE CITY

segregated areas to disappear and their population gradually to be dispersed throughout the city area, except for distinct ethnic communities such as Chinatown and the Black Belt.

Growth extends beyond the city of Chicago throughout the standard metropolitan area, and reaches into north-east Illinois and north-west Indiana. It thus involves tremendous problems of co-ordinated planning for which hitherto there has been little provision. The whole area contains 960 local government authorities, including 6 counties, 108 townships, 192 municipalities, 419 school districts, 235 special function districts (park districts, sanitary districts, drainage districts, etc.). The city of Chicago has had a long tradition of constructive physical planning, beginning with the Burnham plan of 1909, but it was not until 1958 that a single advisory agency was established by the Illinois legislature, the North eastern Illinois Metropolitan Area Planning Commission. But this is an advisory agency only and cannot overrule the authorities of the existing local government. While it includes the whole of the Standard Metropolitan Area (p. 306) plus two adjacent counties, it does not include the heavily urbanized areas to the east beyond the Calumet area in the north-west corner of Indiana.

Neither the municipalities nor the city of Chicago have an adequate tax base to supply an income that will cover their essential expenditure. In the outer areas, writes H. Mayer:

'Suburban schools cannot be built in advance of the need, and constant overcrowding is the result. Sewers, water systems, and other public projects commonly lag behind the need in the suburbs, while in the City of Chicago there may be excess capacity, particularly in the older centrally located areas where population has been reduced by out-migration to the suburbs. Much new development has taken place in unincorporated areas, outside the limits of any municipality, and consequently beyond municipal regulation and beyond the areas served by municipal utilities. Many of the blighted areas and slums of the near future are in such situations.'

The renewal of slum areas costs enormous sums of money. It presents two major problems, as in other American cities. The first is the great cost involved in the acquisition of private land, its clearance and rebuilding. The second is that of relocating the residents and businesses that are displaced in areas of clearance. In Chicago many of the residents are Negroes and there are problems of locating them in the suburbs or elsewhere, since, unfortunately, prejudices are strong. On top of this is the fact that the city's tax base is falling. The new advisory planning agency will take care of water supply, residential, commercial, industrial, public and other uses; and will consider questions of 'urban aesthetics and civic design'. The

THE STRUCTURE OF THE CITY

establishment of this agency has undoubtedly been accelerated by the great and rapid changes in the growth of the whole area since the war.

3. EXAMPLES OF URBAN GROWTH: PARIS

The topographic formation of the historic City of Paris is shown on Fig. 25 and the general layout on Fig. 20. The city has grown from a medieval nucleus that consisted of three parts: the *cité* on the island in the Seine, the site of the Roman and of the early medieval settlement, where are situated today the Palais de Justice and cathedral of

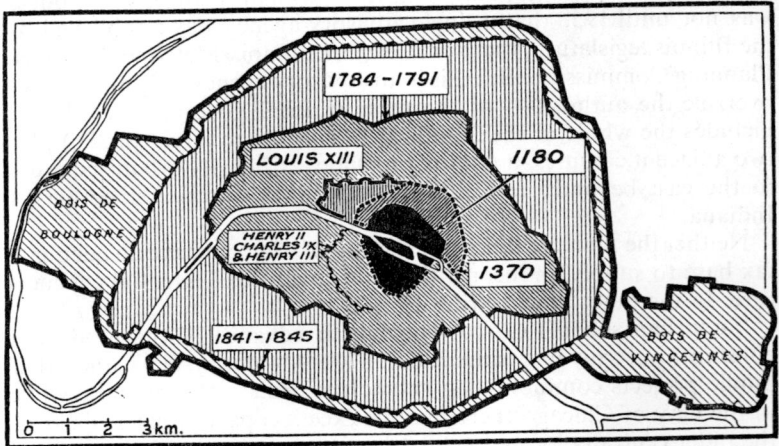

FIG. 25. The Topographic Formation of Paris, showing the dates of fortifications and the present limits of the City of Paris (by a heavy black line) (after Demangeon).

Notre Dame; the *quartier latin* on the rising ground south of the Seine, overlooked by the church of Ste. Geneviève; and the *ville*, the town proper, the medieval seat of commerce and crafts, situated along the river on its north bank. These three quarters were walled in 1210 and the town has been extended at successive stages by fortifications eventually demolished and replaced by boulevards and buildings. The *grands boulevards* lie on the walls built by Charles V and Louis XIII. This is the central district of today. New boulevards have been built, with blocks of flats and public buildings, on the site of the nineteenth-century fortifications that were abolished after 1919, and upon the open zone of 200 metres that lay in front of them. The inner circle of the metropolitan underground runs on the inner side of the latter belt and radial routes run to the old gates through the fortifications. All the chief passenger railway terminals lie just outside the inner *grands boulevards*. This is a compactly built-up area of tenement blocks built for the most part before 1914. Since 1850 the built-up area has extended beyond the city limits, as far as, and beyond, the boundaries of the *département* of Seine. Here are the greatest concentrations of heavy industries, working-class, and suburban housing. Engineering, chemicals, and public utility plants (gas and electricity) lie especially on the flat land adjacent to the Seine westwards, and to the canals on the north and north-east of the city, that have direct contact with the coal-fields of the Nord. Industrial plants, with the usual working-class quarters, appear in the south-east, at the confluence of the Seine and the Marne. South of the city, building is discontinuous and there is little industry, for this is a plateau with deep picturesque valleys forming a residential district that expands westwards in the direction of Versailles.

While the city of Paris lost over 75,000 people between 1921 and 1936 (2,906,000 to 2,830,000), its population in 1954 remained virtually unchanged at 2,850,000. In 1954 the *département* of Seine (less Paris) had 2,304,000 as compared with 2,133,000 in 1936. Areas of rapid growth have shifted to the outer periphery. In the period 1946 to 1954 the portions of the agglomeration outside the *département* of the Seine increased by 10·6 per cent., as opposed to the national average of 5·5 per cent. In comparison, Paris increased by 4·6 per cent. and the Seine *département* by 7·9 per cent. The interesting trend here is the renewed growth of overcrowded Paris itself. Peripheral expansion is typical of other large cities. People move to suburban outskirts. Factories are built on open sites, less expensive than those of the city and with better communications. Old villages and historic small towns are enveloped by the wave of building.

The changes of population over the period 1936 to 1954 are shown on Fig. 26. They reveal the general results of these trends—widespread decreases in the interior and rapid growth on the periphery.

With regard to urban spatial growth, Chombart de Lauwe[1] finds the concentric zone theory, as developed in Chicago, applicable to Paris, with certain modifications. The zones are extended outwards along the main lines of communications. They are also locally offset by social segregations in areas which are superimposed on the zones, without, however, profoundly modifying their arrangement.

Using the criteria of the distribution of residential population, the density of the working population by place of employment, travel time (isochrones), and the distribution of employees of various large

---

[1] See P. H. Chombart de Lauwe, *Paris et l'Agglomération Parisienne, Tome I, L'Espace Social dans une Grande Cité*, Paris, 1952.

industrial establishments, Chombart de Lauwe defines seven concentric zones. These are shown on Fig. 27.

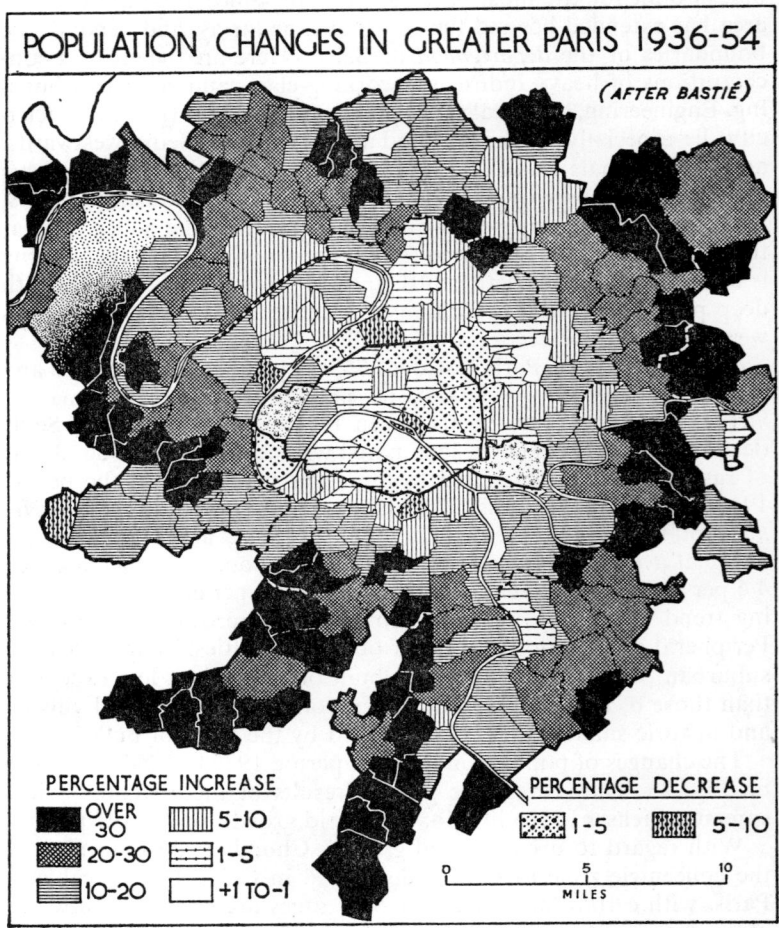

FIG. 26. Population Changes in Greater Paris, 1936–54 (after Bastié).

Zone I is the central business district, characterized by the displacement of residence by non-residential structures, and the consequent outward shift of population and decline in numbers. This district is tending to be displaced to the west.

Zone II is the so-called 'zone of acculturation', and is the equivalent of Burgess' 'zone of transition'. Its buildings are in general deteriorated and it has strong traits of social disorganization. Yet it is a zone of 'contact', experiencing a variety of social and cultural changes. It falls into distinct *quartiers*, such as the *Paris bourgeois* of the west and the *Paris ouvrier* of the east. Between these two areas are Montparnasse and Montmartre, the artist and cabaret quarters of Paris. Similarly, literary and scientific groups are focused on the Latin Quarter and St. Germain des Près. The varied contacts of this

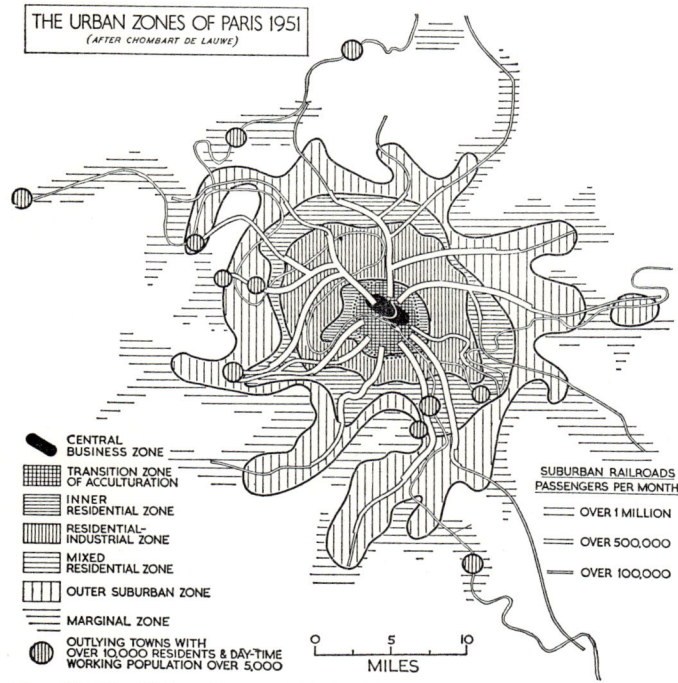

Fig. 27. The Urban Zones of Paris, 1951 (after Chombart de Lauwe). Same scale as Fig. 20, p. 133.

zone are associated with the proximity of the central business district and also of the main railway stations. Distinct ethnic quarters are, for example, the Chinese quarter of the Gare de Nord and the Breton quarters of Montparnasse. 'Nous voyons ici, d'une manière précise, les rapports entre les zones concentriques et les régions sociales.'

Zone III comprises the outlying parts of the peripheral *arrondissements*. It is a mixed zone between the centre and the suburbs. It has both high-class residential areas and a variety of light industries. It is the only part of the city of Paris which has experienced a net increase of population since 1896.

Zone IV is the heavy industrial zone. It is closely associated with a dense residential and mainly 'working class' population (100–500 per hectare) and a very important daytime working population. It includes such vast plants as the Panhard and Citroen automobile plants and many outlying suburban towns.

Zone V is the zone of suburban dormitory communes.

Zone VI embraces large areas of scattered housing and many former villages which have since become towns. The irregular outer limits emphasize the significance of the 'time–distance' factor between place of residence and place of work.

Zone VII comprises the transition zone between the limits of the agglomeration and the surrounding rural area. While not yet integrated with the agglomeration, it is nevertheless slowly undergoing urbanization and definitely comes within the urban sphere of influence of Paris.

This zonal delimitation, based on the use of precise criteria, fails to bring out the localized groups within the city. To define these areas, Chombart de Lauwe uses the terms 'quarter' and 'geographical sector, but he tries also to relate these to the concentric zones. A 'geographical sector' is described as a complex of habitations delimited by such physical obstacles as factory buildings, parks and railroads. It is usually characterized by an economic nucleus or a service centre. Populations vary from 13,000 to 30,000 people. Conditions in these sectors are often conducive to a high degree of social cohesion. They are comparable to the 'social areas' as defined in Chicago and other American cities. A 'quarter' can include a group of streets or houses. It is often distinguished by ethnic or social differences or by proximity of local points of attraction, such as factories and parks. These local areas, that are largely based on social differences, are found to coincide in large measure with the zonal divisions. Around the central business district there are outstanding economic nuclei of production, or service. These component areas occur at the level of a suburban town, a geographical sector, a group of quarters, or of a single quarter.

The limits of the urban agglomeration of Paris as used for the 1954 Census were based primarily on criteria of social participation of communes in the life and social facilities of Paris (schools, shops, entertainment and the like, and not places of work). It *excludes* peripheral areas, such as Versailles, that are, in fact, a part of the built-up area of Paris. In order to arrive at a more realistic definition, Bastié and Brichler[1] used the following criteria—the degree of

[1] J. Bastié et M. Brichler, 'Délimitation de l'Agglomération Parisienne', *Population*, 1960, pp. 433–56. Also J. Bastié, 'La Population de l'Agglomération Parisienne', *Annales de Géographie*, January–February 1958, pp. 12–38.

THE STRUCTURE OF THE CITY

rurality (i.e. the percentage of the workers in a commune engaged in agriculture), the number of inhabitants per commune, density of population per square kilometre less the area with non-urban uses, the rate of growth of population per commune between 1936 and 1959, the daily movement of workers, the proportion of dwellings in collective tenements, the frequency of train and bus services, and

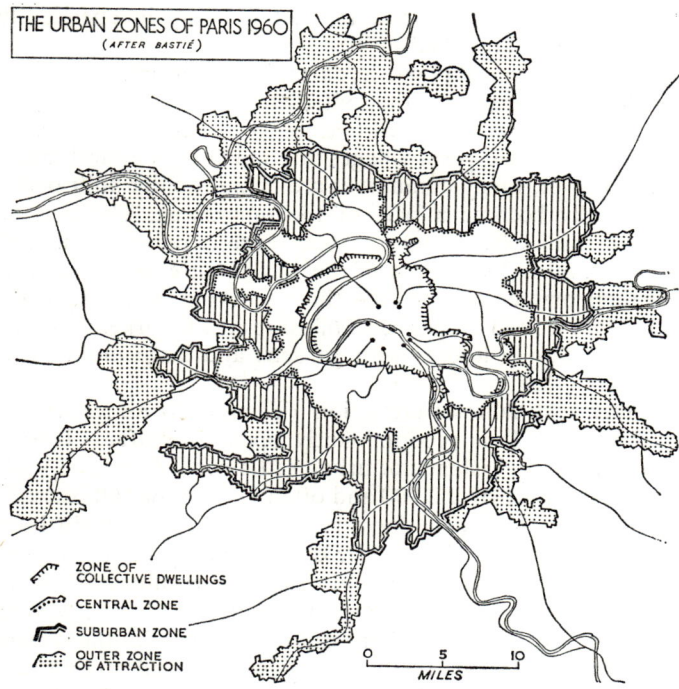

Fig. 28. The Urban Zones of Paris, 1960 (after Bastié).
Compare with Fig. 27, on the same scale.

the continuity of built-up areas. The area so defined is shown on Fig. 28.

Three zones are recognized: the central agglomeration; the suburban zone; and the zone of attraction.

The central area embraces the city of Paris, but it also includes the surrounding communes which have been completely urbanized during this century, so as to be virtually co-extensive with the *département* of Seine. Density of built-up land was the main criterion in defining this area. Density of population generally exceeds 3,000 persons per sq. km. (c. 7,500 per sq. ml.[1]). (Zones I, II, III and IV above.)

An inner area is exclusively occupied by collective tenements with a density in excess of 7,000 per sq. km. (c. 17,500 per sq. ml.). It includes the city of Paris and a border of contiguous communes. The outer area lies around the latter and has mixed habitations with a considerable proportion of single family dwellings. It includes places like Versailles and Saint Germain, that grew up independently of Paris but are now absorbed in it.

The suburban zone V above has a rapid rise of urban population, and its chief work area is in the centre. It contains many 'dormitory' and 'mushroom' communes, with access to the centre by rail. It has many survivals of old rural villages and much agricultural land and woods. However, many communes are being rapidly built over and will eventually become a part of the inner area. The density of population ranges from 100 to 3,000 persons per sq. km. (250 to 7,500 per sq. ml.). Two-thirds of the workers are usually employed outside their own commune, and those working in the *département* of Seine often exceed 50 per cent. of all resident workers. Dwellings include both family houses with gardens and large multi-storeyed tenements.

The outermost 'zone of attraction' (VI and VII above) is a zone of rapid growth. It is predominantly open agricultural land with much woodland and islands of urban settlement. The density of the population is rarely over 2,000 and often falls below 100 per sq. km. The built-up areas tend to form tentacles along the main lines of communication, the limits usually corresponding to the important termini of the railroads at the limit of the outer suburban area.

The peripheral sprawl of the Paris agglomeration has been so rapid and uncontrolled that it has features in common with the American city.[2] Private builders on the periphery have opened up *lotissements* on 100,000 hectares of which about one-half is so far effectively occupied, housing 1·8 million people with an average density of 35 persons per hectare. More distant centres, 25 to 30 km. distant, have expanded and often coalesced, so as to lose their individuality, and lack adequate services or facilities for a social life. Moreover, building has taken place without regard for terrain or drainage or the need for open spaces for recreation. This sprawl demands a large mileage of roads, the construction of which is beyond the resources of the single commune. Many such areas are undeveloped and incomplete.

[1] This figure is slightly higher than the overall average for the urbanized areas of other great cities.

[2] J. F. Gravier, *Paris et le Désert français*, pp. 228–47.

THE STRUCTURE OF THE CITY

Some kind of central control of this growth has long been needed and in 1932 the Paris Region was created by law, and planning proposals were prepared in the thirties for an area within 35 km. of Notre Dame Cathedral. The Plan was finally approved in 1939, having as its main objectives the reduction of congestion in the central city and the planned development of the outer zones. A new plan, to continue the work of the existing plan, was begun in 1956. The Region now includes the whole of the *départements* of Seine and Seine-et-Oise and Seine-et-Marne and five cantons in Oise to the north. It is divided for planning purposes into four zones: the city of Paris; a so-called central zone that is fully built-up around the city but lies entirely within the *département* of Seine; a peripheral or suburban zone around the latter and extending well beyond the limits of the *département* of the Seine; and, beyond, the essentially urban area, a vast area that is described as the rural zone and extends right to the limits of the Region and covers by far the greater share of its total area.

Current plans as developed in the late fifties seek to check growth by reducing the opportunities for employment and by decentralizing employment. This involves the elimination of uneconomic plants, the transfer of industry to the provinces, and urban renewal. It is estimated that 600 hectares will be made available in this way, primarily for new housing. The programme is under way. Three main ideas lie behind it: first, the reconstruction of the urban centre by constructing buildings in height and providing more open space as land is cleared; second, the decongestion of the city of Paris by shifts outwards along main lines of communication; third, the provision of adequate service centres in the straggling suburbs with shopping centres on the American pattern and cultural institutions. Decentralization will be to the lesser towns in the three departments around Paris. Plants have, indeed, been shifted as far as 250 km. out of the capital. But these areas cannot rely on local labour in the countryside. Houses must be built for new workers from the Paris area. There is scope for the absorption of some 100,000 to 150,000 families adjacent to new plants. And there will be need for the provision of adequate tertiary services to cater for them. There should also be seats of higher learning at Orleans and Rheims with higher institutions also at Amiens, Rouen, Bourges, Le Mans, Troyes, Le Havre, and St. Quentin. The operation is similar to the development of new towns around London, except that here the growth is taking place in existing towns in a dominantly agricultural area.

It is of relevance to note the plans for the future development of the highway system of Paris (Fig. 21). The new plan proposes an inner circular road following approximately the eighteenth-century limits and a network of diverging radial roads connecting this road with the suburban centres over a distance of three to six miles. A perimeter road built round the outside of the present existing circle will complete the system and will receive and distribute traffic coming from the main highways. Adequate parking places will be provided close to the main thoroughfares and the main underground railway stations. There will be also fast regional tube services from existing suburban lines and three deep underground lines crossing the city east–west and north–south between Invalides and Versailles.

4. Examples of Urban Growth: Stockholm

Stockholm has been the subject of thorough geographical analysis in several studies.[1] Like other cities, the urban entity extends beyond the city's administrative limits but there has long been strong opposition by peripheral authorities to absorption in the city. Agreement was finally reached in the fifties for a single regional unit of Greater Stockholm. This includes large rural districts, several small towns, and the coastal archipelago for about 50 miles to the north and south. It reaches far beyond the real limits of Stockholm today. The latter includes inner Stockholm, the densely built-up nucleus; corporate Stockholm; the inner suburban area and the outer suburban area. Greater Stockholm has just over one million inhabitants. Nine-tenths are in the urbanized area proper.

The inner town area covers the site of the medieval town (Staden Mellan Broarna) on an isthmus between two east–west stretches of water and the compact built-up area to the north and the large island of Södermalm to the south. This is a densely and continuously built-up area, with buildings of four to six storeys, and the extensive suburbs around it are divided into eleven sectors by belts of water. Out of a total population of one million, some 390,000 live in this inner area, although the suburbs are increasing rapidly. The distribution of population in this area is shown on Fig. 29.

At the beginning of the century the medieval town on the isthmus was the centre of business and administration and from it radiated the steamboat lines. But today the dense net of trolley lines centres on a flat area on the mainland (Norrmalm), immediately north of the isthmus, which has become the business centre and the terminus

[1] W. William-Olsson, 'Stockholm: Its Structure and Development', *Geographical Review*, Vol. XXX, 1940, pp. 420–38. Also *Stockholm's Inre Differentiering* by H. W. Ahlmann and associates, *Meddelande fran geografiska Institutet vid Stockholms Högskola*, No. 20, 1934, and Sten de Geer, 'Greater Stockholm', *Geographical Review*, Vol. XIII, 1923, pp. 487–500. W. William-Olsson, *Stockholm: Structure and Development*, International Geographical Congress, Stockholm, 1960.

THE STRUCTURE OF THE CITY

of the suburban railway lines, and the focus of the chief traffic and business arteries.

A thorough study has been made of the exact location of functions in 1880, 1930, and 1950. The main conclusions, apart from local detail, are of general significance in the process of urban growth.

The inner town is used alike for residence, work, and recreation.

FIG. 29. The Distribution of Population in Inner Stockholm, 1950 (after William-Olsson *Stockholm: Structure and Development*, International Geographical Congress, Stockholm, 1960).
Each dot represents 25 persons.

Places of work are classified as follows: government offices, public institutions, business offices, retail shops, and industrial establishments. Each group may be subdivided and each subdivision has its special situation requirements in accordance with which significant changes in its position may be traced between 1880 and 1950. A composite map showing the location of the functional areas in the centre of the city is reproduced in Fig. 30.

Government offices have long been concentrated in the northern part of Staden Mellan Broarna, the cluster forming a national administrative centre around the Royal Palace. Many other

THE STRUCTURE OF THE CITY

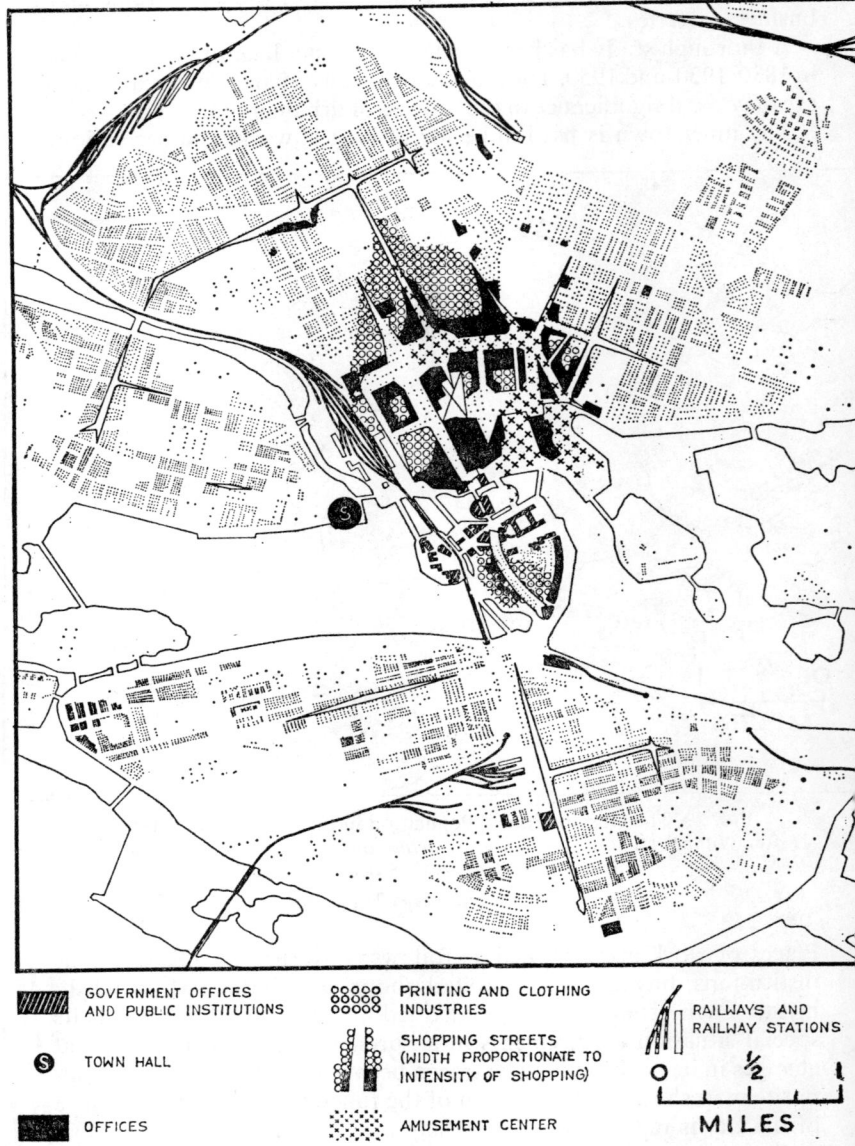

Fig. 30. The Differentiation of Inner Stockholm, 1960 (after William-Olsson).

government offices are located peripherally where they have freedom of choice of location. Those buildings that serve only part of a town—churches, elementary schools, police and fire stations—are normally conveniently located in the part they serve, while those that serve the whole town or State strive for a central position. University buildings, museums, and hospitals do not require a central location (though that is how they usually developed), but they do profit (as they expand) from concentration in one area. The older buildings are situated in the inner area, but the new University is to be built on a vast open area to the north, and there is a group of large museums on the eastern outskirts. These are both common trends in current urban growth.

Business offices direct production and distribution. These include banks, business, and wholesaling. In 1880 the main cluster was south of the administrative quarter, occupying the broad street along the quays and avoiding the narrow alleys of the centre of the island. By 1930 the number of offices had increased many times and they had all shifted to broad streets and open sites in Norrmalm. The trend continued to 1950. In 1880 the banks and stockbrokers' offices—most sensitive of all business activities to situation—were not concentrated; by 1930 they were clustered in the south-east of Norrmalm and formed the true 'core' of the city. Offices require accessibility from one to another, and they are situated by preference in high-class buildings on broad streets and level ground. The great growth of business demanded space such as the congested and historically and culturally valuable medieval town of the Stadsholmen could not provide; moreover, the administration was already there as a competitor for sites. Thus, the business area shifted to the southern part of Norrmalm, where communications were best. Building is spreading northwards into the area of steep narrow streets on the ridge of southern Norrmalm, through which the Kungsgatan (a main street) was cut in 1911. A second road cut is in process of being made.

Retail shops are the last link in the chain of activities by which goods are transferred to the consumer. Distribution, according to this interpretation, includes not only dealings in wholesale and retail trades, but also provision of meals, amusements, lodgings, and hotels. Shops, to be successful, require good contact with the public and are highly sensitive to location. Neighbourhood shops sell goods for daily household consumption and are evenly spread over the city in accordance with the distribution of population. City stores have a specialized character for periodical purchases, with a margin of choice as to qualities and prices. They, therefore, require a central situation for a widely dispersed clientele. The importance of the shop as a distributive organ is most clearly measurable not in the shop-window frontage but in the *rent*. By adding the shop rents of a street-frontage and dividing the total by the length of the frontage there is obtained the shop rent per unit of frontage; and this can be taken as a measure of the shopping intensity of the street. Maps prepared on this basis for 1880, 1930, and 1950 reveal the following facts. The nucleus of the shopping area—the Stadsholmen and the Drottinggatan running north-west to south-east in the centre of Norrmalm —lies in the centre of the town. It remained in 1950, as in 1880, the main shopping area, although extensions had taken place to the north-east towards the wealthier residential districts. The highest shop rents are located on centrally situated street intersections. Since shops prefer level streets of moderate width, the chief shopping streets coincide with the busiest pedestrian thoroughfares, for heavy vehicular traffic is detrimental to shopping streets. Shops at the southern end of Norrmalm have been partly ousted by the banks, and indeed as a rule offices and shops have avoided each other, since their demands on location are different, the first demanding good communication, the second demanding good local contacts with the visiting public, so that competition between the two is rarely keen. Shop rents are normally much higher than office rents, and there is a segregation of different kinds of shops in different streets. In 1880, theatres, places of amusement, hotels, and restaurants were mainly in the south-east of Norrmalm. In 1950 they were found in all parts of the town, hotels being especially localized near the railway stations. Cinemas are located on the main shopping streets of the centre and in the outlying shopping centres.

Industrial establishments.[1] Both factories and small workshops mainly produce metals, paper and printing, foods and tobacco, textiles and clothing. Establishments are mapped in this study according to exact location and by a circle proportional to the number of employees. In 1880 and in 1930 industries are found both in the central fully built-up area and the outer, more open, area, situated especially near the quays and railway sidings. But in 1930 the peripheral sites, which included the largest units, were more widely distributed and further on the outskirts, while the ring of industries of 1880 to the west, south, and east had been replaced by new residential districts expanding from the central town. Industries highly localized in the centre of the town are printing, garment, and needlework

---

[1] Industries occupied 108,000 in 1956. The chief group is engineering (61,000— machinery and electrical apparatus), the plants now being located almost entirely on the outskirts of the city. The other industries are those typical of all great capital cities—printing and publishing (17,500), clothing (6,000), and food (12,000).

trades. The last, depending on the changing fashions and nearness to the shopping streets, made up, in 1950, 80 per cent. of the industries, and were housed in obsolescent buildings in back streets. They had lost their former significance in the industrial scene of the city. Food products and small metal-working industries are widely distributed over the greater part of the town. The large establishments —engineering works, shipyards, etc. seek peripheral locations. A few large concerns remain in the centre as relics of the past, but sooner or later they must shift elsewhere.

Inner Stockholm is surrounded by a ring of industrial suburbs (with a gap to the north-east) that, in 1951, were almost half an hour's journey by tram or bus from the city centre. This pattern was the same on all points in 1850 and 1895. The gap to the north-east has three causes—no good harbour, no railway till 1885 (and this is narrow-gauge), and exclusion of industry by the location of the garden suburbs in this sector. Planning in recent decades has sought to place every home near to at least one area of work and this means the peripheral expansion of both industry and other enterprises.

Residential areas. The distribution of population in inner Stockholm in 1950 is shown by dots in places of residence on Fig. 29. A series of such maps from 1880 to 1950 shows that 'the growth of the town was practically concentric' and 'distribution changed from the high density in the centre and low density in the periphery to the reverse with the formation of a central city district'. The differentiation in these areas by districts rests on a variety of social and economic characteristics. Earlier criteria, chosen thirty years ago for this purpose, were the excess of women to the total population, the ratio of domestic servants, and the number of children per family. These indicators are no longer valid for this purpose, since with the general increase in well-being and the reduction of the birth rate, these are no longer reliable indicators of social status. Well-to-do families often have the larger families and domestic servants have virtually disappeared. Thus, William-Olsson selects new criteria in his recent study (1960). He uses, as general indicators of social and economic status, first, the distribution of the vote between the two major parties, Conservative and Social Democrat; second, the income level per tenant; and third, the classification of the four 'social status' groups used by the Census of Housing in 1951, and based on assessment of education, income, and social status.

The distribution and associations so revealed demonstrate the rule that 'people settle in districts which are homogeneous from economic and social points of view. It is evidently more important to live among one's own kind of people than to live in a central

THE STRUCTURE OF THE CITY

or beautiful place.' This trend, however, does not appear in the new suburbs.

'Although there is little reason to doubt the rule demonstrated, two new facts must be considered (in these areas). First, because of rent control and the long waiting list for housing (100,000 and more), people have not been able to pick and choose where they shall live since the war. Secondly, there is a deliberate policy to eliminate social differences with regard to incomes as well as housing. The standard of living has evened out and earlier contrasts between local districts have become insignificant. Balance of social groups and economic levels is being sought in the newly planned suburban areas.'

Southern Norrmalm was the wealthiest residential district in 1880, and the poorer people lived on the periphery. But since business has invaded the former, the good residential quarter has moved to Ostermalm (immediately east of Norrmalm) by displacing the poorer residences there. Today, Ostermalm is the most exclusive residential district. Vasastaden and Kungholmen (adjacent to the west side of Norrmalm) are the middle-class districts. The outskirts of Södermalm (the large island to the south of the old town), in particular, are the working-class districts.

The changes in the inner town from 1880 to 1950 included no change of relative positions or internal structure, but reflect a development which 'may be likened to a process of growth in which one organ, in expanding, crowds out another, and this in its turn takes up unoccupied space'. The changes are summed up as follows:

'The administrative centre retains its situation but has been enlarged somewhat to the north; office and shopping centres have been developed greatly; and so have the centrally located industries; and all these—which together constitute the working core of the town, its "city"—have spread northward. The best residential district of 1880 has been forced to move farther to the north-east, and lately also to the west, and the better-class dwellings have displaced the poorer residences. These in their turn have pushed the 1880 circle of suburban industries farther out into the country. Finally, owing to the improved communications, large residential suburbs have grown up far from the centre of the town, encroaching on agricultural regions.'[1]

Big changes have taken place in the city and on its periphery, although the general outline of the main districts was the same in 1960 as in 1930. The structure of the city is shown on Fig. 31. The

[1] W. William-Olsson, *op. cit.*

THE STRUCTURE OF THE CITY

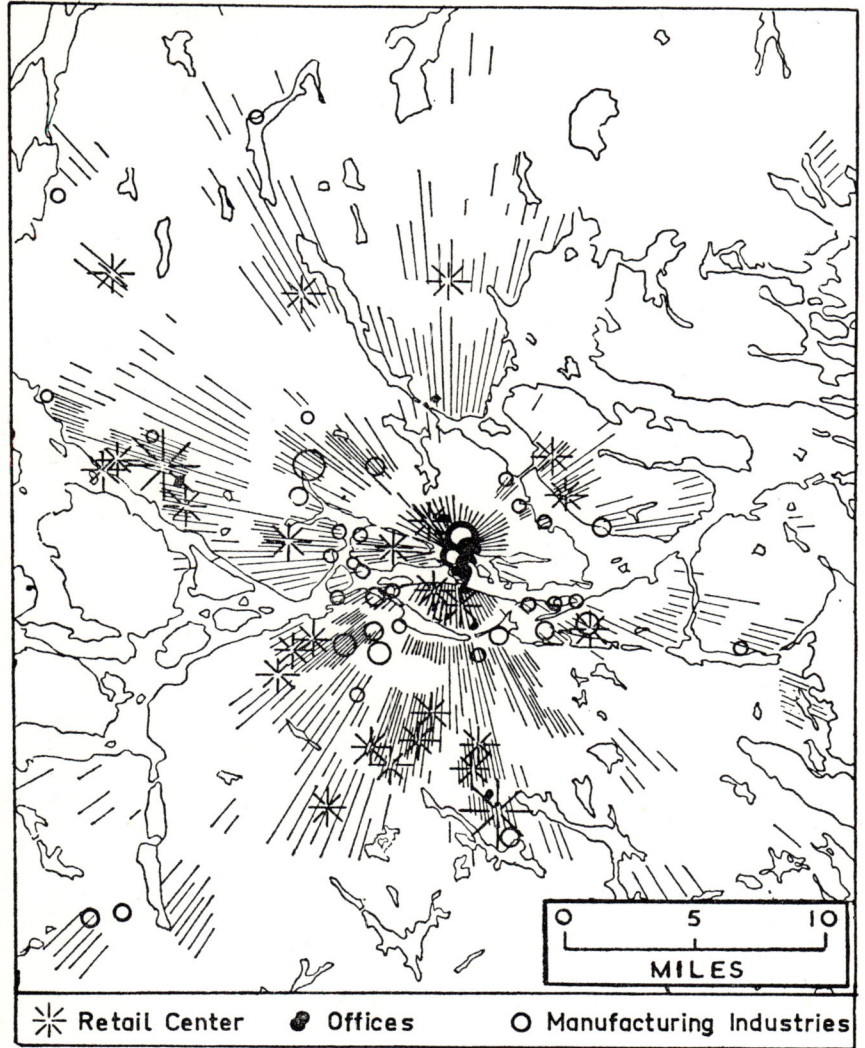

FIG. 31. The Structure of Greater Stockholm (after William-Olsson).

The main features of the structure of Greater Stockholm. The lines converging towards Inner Stockholm show the extension of the suburbs and the density of their population as well as the sphere of influence of the central shopping district. Secondary retail centres are characteristic of the suburbs and the densely populated parts of Inner Stockholm.

THE STRUCTURE OF THE CITY

current developments that are taking place may be summed up as follows in their broad features. They are typical of the problems of growth and planning of all big cities.

Traffic problems are aggravated by the many areas of water that penetrate right to the original island nucleus of the city. This involves great problems of inter-connecting canals and especially bridge construction to accommodate rail and road to and from the city and around it. The crux of the whole traffic system is the bridge over the water in the city centre and the excellent new central railroad station. In 1950 the first part of a new underground rail system was opened (*Tunnelbana*), followed in the fifties by extensions to the suburbs. This system makes it possible to plan Greater Stockholm on the principle that the suburbs will be within forty-five minutes' travel time from the centre. All collective transport will handle 75 per cent. of the rush-hour traffic.

The city centre is being rejuvenated in the area of the steep grades of Norrmalm. The soft rocks of this glacial esker have made it relatively easy to excavate this area. Building is in active progress and there will eventually be five office buildings of eighteen storeys each to dominate the centre, together with a pedestrian precinct, and underground traffic lanes and parking areas at three levels, as well as new roads and flyovers above ground.

The limits of Stockholm, defined so as to include all those inhabitants who 'take part in the life of the town', are revealed by the population trends in the surrounding municipalities. Agricultural areas, untouched by the growth of the city, usually have decreasing numbers. Others with moderate increases have been slightly affected by urban influence. But nearer the city, large increases reflect expansions due to the opening of new communications and the development of new suburbs.

The new suburbs have had to be planned since 1940 in view of the unexpected rapid increase of the total population in the city (see p. 152). Suburbs are growing rapidly both within and without corporate Stockholm. Several principles are being observed in the physical planning. First, new homes are being placed within easy access of at least one major area of work. The decentralization of industry aims at two further objectives: the relief of pressure on space in the city centre; and the increase of traffic outwards to outlying areas in the opposite direction to the inflowing traffic to the centre, so as to utilize idle traffic capacity at rush hours. So far one large suburb is complete at Vällingby. It is a spectacular social and architectural achievement that stands as one of the world's finest examples of city planning.

Stockholm illustrates the tendency for the city to spill over to the

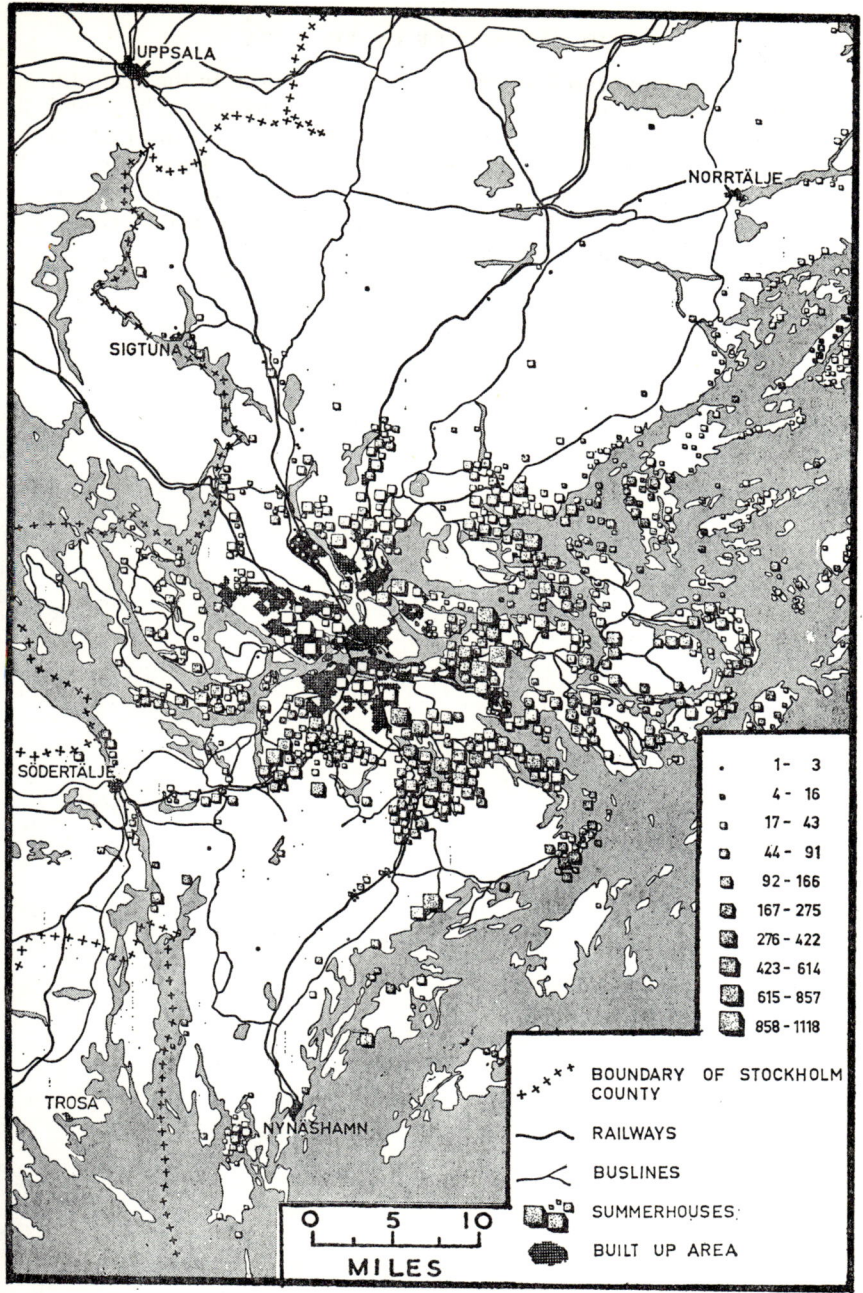

FIG. 32. Summer Cottages around Stockholm, 1953–54
(after William-Olsson).

The cubes denote the number of cottages in accordance with the above key.
No data are available outside Stockholm County.

surrounding countryside in order to seek recreation. In the beautiful landscape of sea, rock, forest, and meadow, there are to be found innumerable timber-built summer cottages. These are located on Fig. 32. The same feature is illustrated in the case of Lyon (Fig. 39, p. 264), where this range of contact similarly reaches far beyond the urban land to remote country sites. This is also a remarkable development around American cities.

Chapter 6

THE CITY AS A WHOLE

In the previous chapter we have discussed the structure of three major cities with respect to their growth as a whole and their distinctive parts. We shall now turn to a general portrayal of the former aspect—that is, the physical structure of the city as a whole.

1. THE GENERAL BUILD OF THE CITY

A large number of cities, in both America and Europe, have been mapped on the same scale by the writer to show the broad categories of land use, the ground plan and density of the built-up land. A general zoning of the urban areas may be recognized and described as follows. Though this broad division is simple, it nevertheless serves as a meaningful framework for understanding the distribution of phenomena in the city and the processes of growth and shifts within it. It should be emphasized that we have reference essentially to the area within the boundaries of the central city.

The Central Zone is the hub of the city and includes the older town and the pre-modern extensions. In it there is the maximum 'friction of space', for it lies at the nexus of communications. All services requiring central locations compete for accommodation in the central zone, with consequent vertical and lateral building expansion and great congestion of traffic. It includes the retail, wholesale, administrative, commercial, and business districts; markets, hotels, residential enclaves for both the *élite* and the poor; and large public buildings that cater for the community as a whole; and railways goods and passenger terminals. It is fully built-up with a minimum area (usually well under 20 per cent.) occupied by streets and open spaces. Its vertical expansion reaches the extreme in the down-town skyscraper district of the American city, with its island of skyscrapers in a sea of relatively uniform built-up areas which are being invaded by sporadically distributed functions associated with the city centre. The same trend is becoming increasingly conspicuous in western Europe, where the skyscraper is now an established feature of the largest cities.

The Middle Zone was built mainly during the second half of the nineteenth century and early twentieth century. During this period most building was effected by private enterprise and there were few restrictions on the density or type of building. Town-planning measures were normally devoted, at best, to street lay-out and street widths. The building blocks are fully built-up and, like the centre, there is little private or public open space. In England, we find the terrace and back-to-back house; on the Continent, as in Paris and Berlin, the tenement; in the United States, the tenement and the frame house. This Middle Zone is mainly 'residential' but contains numerous scattered small factories (the planner's 'mixed uses'). It also contains the sites of early industrial development concentrated on the flat, low-lying land near the river or canal, beside the railway tracks, and around the goods and railway stations. These non-residential areas divide the zone into well-defined residential sectors. Much of this zone, as we shall see later, is usually in a state of deterioration. It is an area of high-residential densities. It contains the main areas of urban blight and houses most of the immigrant and low-income groups. These are what are called the 'grey areas' by American planners, that are ripe for demolition, and present in their future reconstruction a major planning problem.

The Outer Zone is mainly residential land that forms an *inner* suburban zone. Its settlement began by exclusive residential properties in the latter half of the nineteenth century, first by the use of private carriage, then by horse-drawn bus, electric tram and occasionally by electric train, and latterly by car. The main development took place after World War I and has continued to this day so that the area is now fully occupied. It is an area of low-density residential property with plenty of open space, public parks, etc. The older residences have often been transformed and their large lots subdivided. Agricultural land uses, gardens, golf courses, etc. make up a large share, and new industrial plants have been added on the highways. These open spaces serve to divide the residential areas into more or less clearly defined sectors. Urban areas may have grown at strategic points of communications or around a pre-existing nucleus, such as a village, old town market centre, or an old industrial centre. Residences may be widely scattered in a scenic countryside with naturally (or unplanned) winding streets or along a lake shore. Many handsome mansions were built here by the wealthy and are now in process of being converted and their grounds built on as residential expansion proceeds outwards. Many of these mansions are also used by business firms, clubs, etc. in both the European and American cities. Thus the lay-out and growth of this zone varies very widely according to physical build and the mode of expansion. These areas were generally developed in the last seventy-five years as good-class residential districts.

The Urban Fringe is the *outer* suburban zone or, as it is sometimes called, the 'rural–urban fringe'. It generally lies beyond the city administrative limits and is simply a continuation of the same features of development and aspect of what we described above as the outer zone. It is a wide rural area into which residential development is intruding and new industrial sites and other urban uses are in process of development along its main lines of communication, often clustered around existing villages and small towns.

The distinction between the inner suburban zone and the outer rural–urban fringe lies in the fact that the former, when all urban uses are included (both building and open spaces), is almost continuously occupied, whereas the outer rural–urban fringe still contains much farm and woodland with sporadically distributed compact built-up areas and a considerable scattering of urban residences and other uses in rural surroundings. This is the really critical divide between the two, not the administrative boundary, which is simply used here as a matter of convenience, although, as a divide between local government areas, it has a real significance in accounting for contrast between the two zones. The outer limits of the fringes are indeterminate and their definition will be considered on subsequent pages.

These zones taken together form a single social and economic unit in respect of built-up areas, density of population, work, play, interests, and organization. This entity is described below as the urban tract.

2. The Urban Plan

Centrifugal and centripetal forces, the differentiation of functions within the urban area, and the invasion and succession of uses outwards from the centre, and shifts of population are evident at all stages of the development of the city in America and Europe. While centripetal forces were dominant in the past, especially when the wall separated the town from the countryside, and the marketplace served as its focus, centrifugal forces drove certain activities outside the town walls or to the edge of the built-up area, whether inside or outside the walls. The town wall and the land next to it acquired distinct features of build and use that are clearly traceable in the plans of the modern city, as may be seen, for instance, in the case of Paris. The shift outwards from the outworn houses of the centre did not commence on a significant scale until the slum clearances of the nineteenth century on the Continent, but the beginning of the factory era in the last decades of the nineteenth century was marked by the appearance of factories on the outskirts and the growth of houses next to them. The wealthier people settled in their new town houses in the seventeenth and eighteenth centuries (often moving in from the countryside) in the quieter quarters of the town, usually on its outskirts inside the walls or on pleasant sites—high land or a high river bank. In London the wealthy began to shift outwards to Chelsea and Islington so as to avoid the noise and smells of the city. The so-called 'ribbon development' is a natural form of extension consisting of buildings strung out along a main road. It has been a primary characteristic of town growth in all ages, and in the Middle Ages was a mode of suburban expansion along the roads from the gates in the town walls. The earliest maps extant show ample evidence of this. But the dominant trend throughout all the ages until the present was centripetal, for by choice or necessity people and institutions sought a place as near to the centre of the city as possible, and certainly within the city walls.

During the nineteenth century the forces of urban growth were still dominantly centripetal, since through the lack of ubiquitous, cheap, and rapid transport, the concentration of buildings on the smallest and most compact possible area was essential. The situation has changed with the successive advent of the horse-drawn carriage, the electric tram, the inter-urban lines (as they operated in the States down to the twenties and still do to a large extent on the Continent), the occasional suburban line (limited to a single line with a limited number of stations and serving a restricted area), the electric underground in a few large cities, and, since the twenties, the revolutionary and ubiquitous impact of the bus and the private automobile. Each of these means of transport has had its repercussion on both the range and the pattern of residential development. In the last fifty years centrifugal forces have been of increasing importance, involving the spread of urban land uses outwards from the compact urban centre as well as the location of new enterprises on the fringes. The railway permitted the growth of separate urban centres outside the city, both as residential and industrial centres, often arranged like small beads on a chain, focussed on each railroad station. Since the advent of the automobile and the lorry, there has been linear expansion from the compact urban area along the roads. Long tentacles or ribbons extend into the countryside, and the interstitial land is filled up usually at a slower rate especially where unfavourable topographic conditions prevail. The whole process takes place outwards from the fringe of the compact urban area. The railway, offering the quickest means of transport, attracted separate settlements. The waterway, if navigable, has long been selected for industrial sites, but the importance of a valley floor as a zone of urban extension depends entirely on physical and historical conditions. Trends vary from one city to another, depending on the historical development, and the site of the individual city, and on the urban settlements in its near environs. But we may note some broad contrasts between the American, British, and continental city.

The American city invariably has a grid plan—sometimes conforming to one grid, as in Chicago, sometimes made up of a mosaic of grids badly fitted together through the piecemeal development of separate real-estate operations, as in San Francisco and Los Angeles. But over this grid plan one can often trace a radial arrangement of main highways which can sometimes be traced back to the convergence of highways upon a centre which preceded the grid plan, while even the original nucleus of settlement is often traceable from its irregular and crooked streets and irregularly shaped building blocks, dating from origins in the nineteenth and eighteenth centuries (New York, Boston, Philadelphia, Cleveland). The railway pattern above all has a radial arrangement cutting right across the grid of streets and built-up blocks. Expansion has proceeded often by frontal expansion of whole districts as well as along the highways, where, owing to lack of public control, all kinds of enterprises have been localized on approaches to the city.

In the British city a star-like formation is more clearly developed for several reasons. First, the central section, the early nineteenth-century town nucleus, had no walls or other fortifications, to impede expansion. Secondly, the town was almost invariably of 'natural', or unplanned, growth, based on the framework of old highways, some older than the town itself—such as the Roman roads—which were used as the skeleton of the town, about which the new rectangular or herring-bone lay-out of houses was built in the nineteenth century. The result is that there is no clearly defined break in the stages of expansion of the urban areas of a city. Since 1900, its tentacles have extended along the routes from the centre, which has an irregular congested nucleus that is invariably grouped around a marketing place.

In the continental city, we find, on the other hand, great contrasts. In the first place, the nucleus of the town, its modern core, sometimes has an irregular plan with narrow, winding streets and irregular blocks; but it often has, in part at any rate, a rectangular or circular plan and a more open lay-out, dating either from its medieval foundation or from extension and rebuilding of fortifications effected during the seventeenth and eighteenth centuries. Second, the continental town was almost always enclosed by walls right through the Middle Ages down to the nineteenth century. In the growing cities these were eventually replaced by boulevards, in the manner set by the *grands boulevards* of Louis XIV in Paris. New and more extensive fortifications were built farther out, beyond which lay a wide zone in which permanent building was forbidden. These fortifications set clear limits to urban expansion, and beyond them growth continued along the highways. In Germany such ribbon extension is far less marked than in Britain, owing to the greater degree of public control over building rights. The net result is that the continental city shows frequently a double feature, first, one or two circular roads in the built-up area forming wide traffic thoroughfares, and secondly, a radial arrangement of main roads, giving to the whole plan a radial-concentric pattern.

The broad topographic features of the city also depend on the character of its surrounding settlements. In a dominant rural area where the central city far outweighs any competitors, surrounding villages and a few small towns are absorbed by it, and new urban centres bud off from it, though these usually have old nuclei. Such has been the case with the big capital cities such as London, Paris, and Berlin. In other cases, in industrial areas with a long history and a close distribution of industrial centres, depending perhaps upon the use of water power before the Steam Age, several adjacent towns have expanded and merged. One usually dominated the rest, as Birmingham in the Black Country, and Manchester in south-east Lancashire. Separate towns, serving as local market centres as well as seats of industry—and also as local centres for cottage industries in their environs—may expand and then merge through ribbon expansion along roads and valleys. This has been the case typically in south-east Lancashire. The same sort of trend is to be found, for instance, around Chemnitz in Saxony and at Saint Etienne and Lille in France.

Since its appearance in the middle of the nineteenth century, the railway has become a vital factor in the life of the city as well as in the nature and problems of its topographic expansion.[1] Three primary facts appear almost invariably in the development of the railway net of every big city. The first railways sought terminals as near as possible to the city centre, so that today they lie in the heart of the city and are hindrances to the rational planning of its lay-out and traffic-net. The second feature is that the railways naturally radiate

[1] See S. H. Beaver, 'The Railways of Great Cities', *Geography*, Vol. XXII, 1937, pp. 116-20.

outwards from these terminals. The third is that practically every large city during the past fifty years has acquired some kind of a circular or belt line either as a freight or passenger line or as an underground or overground system for urban traffic. The railway is concerned with the transport of both passengers and freight. As regards the first, it must provide (*a*) transport for the suburban worker to and from the city, with marked concentrations of traffic at two specific 'rush-hour' periods; and (*b*) main-line services to other cities, the main stations being either at 'dead-ends' or located on routes which pass through the city. From this point of view, the railway plan should consist of a series of routes, radiating from the city, with branches on its outskirts serving the suburbs. Ideally there should also be transport facilities between the great terminals in great cities—either as a surface or, preferably, as an underground railway—though this, in fact, is seldom the case.

As regards freight traffic, the main problem is to provide efficiently for the import of supplies of food and raw materials for the daily requirements of population and industry. There will also be a great traffic of goods through the city, either for direct transmission or for storage and redistribution. Thus, the belt or girdle line on the outskirts of the city becomes an almost inevitable feature of the railway pattern. Marshalling yards will be built on the outskirts of the city near to the belt lines, while goods stations lie in the vicinity of the terminals in closer touch with the urban areas of the city to and from which goods are distributed and collected.

Thus, the normal historical development of the railway net of a city, varying with its size and location, results in routes through the centre of the city—that is, routes built on what was open land bordering the town—to which the major industrial and built-up areas have largely gravitated; terminals built at the former outskirts of the city and radiating from it; and the final emergence of an interconnecting belt line. 'The ideal railway plan for a large city thus somewhat resembles a wheel; the city is the hub, the main lines are the spokes, and the circumference is the belt line' (Beaver). The symmetry of the railway plan varies, however, according to the conditions of its development and to the topography of the city, its historical development and its present size.

The railroad made its impact on the mode of expansion of the urban area through the development of suburban residential areas, and these were, therefore, of very limited extent. They were located along the railroads at points accessible to the stations on foot. The suburban railroad service was inaugurated in America at Chicago in 1856 and shortly after in New York. The new residential communities emerged like beads on a chain about five miles apart. They gradually coalesced as solid bands so as to form long fingerlike appendages, with large vacant areas in between.

Internal means of communication also affected the urban plan in this period. At first, in the first half of the nineteenth century, when people had to travel on foot and only the wealthy could afford horse-drawn vehicles, building was congested—tenements in New York, row houses in Philadelphia and Baltimore, and houses on both the front and the rear of lots in Chicago. Plank roads in Chicago as early as the 1850's began to spread settlement out on to the prairie. The horse-drawn car appeared in Chicago in 1859, operating on fixed tracks and with a speed of four to six miles an hour. Horse-drawn street cars helped spread the settlement onwards. In the 1880's the cable car speeded up transport to 12 miles an hour. In 1878 in New York and in 1890 in Chicago elevated lines came in, operated first by steam and then by electricity. These stimulated apartment construction along their routes. Then, in 1890 electric surface street cars appeared in American cities and rapidly became the chief form of transport in every city, reaching their peak in 1910.

About 1900 the more rapid form of underground transport was introduced in New York and Boston. This permitted apartment construction along their routes. But only New York, Boston, Philadelphia and, more recently, Chicago and Toronto, have subways. In Europe they have been confined to London, Paris, Berlin, and Moscow, though Stockholm (p. 160) and other major cities are now building their systems. These forms of transport were limited to a few routes along which settlement extended linear tentacles. They resulted in high densities in the centre, and vacant areas in between in which rural land commenced only a few miles from the centre, and urban land extended only a short distance from the transport routes accessible to their terminals. It was on this basis that the central business district rapidly emerged as a focus of great congestion and peak land values. This situation reached its culmination about 1920. In 1910 the value of land in the half square mile of the Loop in Chicago reached a maximum of 40 per cent. of the total value of all land in the city area.

The above circumstances have changed since the advent of the motor-driven vehicle on improved highways in this century. The street-car has been displaced by the bus, and in recent years there has been a great reduction of mass-transit on both the bus and on the railroad in many American cities through the competition of the private automobile. The bus and the car now make every street and road accessible to traffic and the range of commuting to work is thus increased to a distance of some 10 miles for a journey-time of thirty minutes and up to a distance of about 20 miles for a journey-time of one hour. The scale of expansion of the urban area has thus been vastly increased by ever more rapid means of transport. The general trend in the last thirty years has been for both radial expansion and the filling up of the interstices, which become ever wider with increasing distance from the centre. The construction of concrete highways in America from the cities and across the nation rapidly eliminated the horse and buggy and its limited horizons. All places throughout the countryside have become readily accessible to their neighbours and the outside world. After 1935, however, it was suddenly realized that the new concrete highways, the use of septic tanks, power-driven pumps for water, the extension of electric light, water, and gas mains, enabled home developers to utilize farm lands that extended far beyond the main settled areas of cities. Facilitated by Federal Housing Authority financing, whole new communities sprang up within the orbit of the metropolitan centres but at points distant from fixed rails. The lure of cheaper land, more open space, entirely new home communities, and easy financing terms, beckons families to the metropolitan fringe. The unincorporated urban territory is growing much faster than the incorporated central areas which are actually losing population at their centres. Moreover, a large proportion of the wealthier members of the community are going to the 'suburbs', leaving in the central cities families with lower income to support the ever increasing tax burdens of the urban cores.[1]

3. THE RURAL–URBAN FRINGE

On the outer borders of the city, between the areas of rural and urban land use, there is an intermediate zone which shares the characteristics of each. This fringe is invaded by urban uses—by the extension of housing estates, of buildings along the main arterial roads, and by the location of new factories, as well as many other urban features which are excluded for one reason or another from the compact urban area—golf courses, water-works, cemeteries, destructories, parks, allotment gardens, and the like.[2]

Motor transport, far more than the railway, has caused the American city to expand, and to embrace outlying farms, new

[1] Homer Hoyt, 'The Influence of Highways and Transportation on the Structure and Growth of Cities and Urban Land Values', in Labatut and Lane, *Highways in our National Life*.

[2] G. S. Wehrwein, 'The Rural–Urban Fringe', *Economic Geography*, Vol. XVIII, 1942, pp. 217–28. For the meaning of 'central cities' in this context, see p. 198. See in particular G. A. Wissink, *American Cities in Perspective with special reference to the development of their fringe areas*, Geog. Inst., Univ., Utrecht, 1962. Also R. B. Andrews, 'Elements in the Urban-Fringe Pattern', *J. of Land Economics*, Vol. XVIII, 1942.

daughter settlements, and new land uses within its orbit. This 'wild expansion' or 'explosion' of the American city produces premature subdivisions for urban development, in the shape of vacant derelict land, reserved as residential sites and provided with paved streets, water, sewers, gas, and electricity at private or public expense. The result is tax delinquency. The land lies idle and becomes what has been called 'an institutional desert'. New residential areas must rely on rural forms of government to supply their services, though usually they are incorporated as a village or a city, raise their own taxes, and look after their own services. In this way suburban dormitories and factory centres arise upon the fringe of the city, just beyond the limits of its jurisdiction. These find no place in Christaller's theoretical pattern of the distribution of centralized service centres (see Chapter 3). The land use of the fringe is also affected by the recreational needs of the city folk—parks, playgrounds, and golf courses—and also by institutional and legal factors, since obnoxious industries, excluded by zoning ordinances from the city itself, must perforce be dumped on its outskirts. Such uses are slaughter houses, oil storage depots, noxious industries, junk yards—while some city utilities are also given a peripheral location—waterworks, sewage plants, airports, and cemeteries. Thus, the rural–urban fringe is really 'an extension of the city itself, present and potential', and 'since the city or cities of a metropolitan area and the suburban or fringe areas are a unit economically and sociologically, the entire area should be thought of and planned as a unit'.[1]

Residential areas are spreading widely over the countryside. In America, this takes place along and between arterial highways, and whole areas are prepared for building with fleets of bulldozers. Services such as shopping centres, schools, and gas stations, are also widely scattered at strategic points for access to the residential areas by road, as well as along the main radial arterial highways, on which custom is drawn mainly from the car-traveller. Here the urban area really has exploded, since its various functions are widely dispersed, often separated from each other by still open country, but interconnected by a close network of good roads. All such facilities are accessible from home within ten to thirty minutes by private automobile. This new kind of outer zone has recently been described as 'interurbia'. Others are talking of 'the dispersed city'. It extends widely around the city, and between cities, and, when supplemented by the dispersion of recreational week-end and longer activities, these essentially urban activities cover extensive areas, especially in the eastern half of the States. There are also the areas in which a well-to-do élite, that is not required in the office at regular and early

[1] *Ibid.*

hours, seeks to find seclusion in attractive surroundings well removed from association with suburbia. Hence arises around the very big cities, as in New York and Los Angeles and Chicago, the kind of residential community that has been described as 'exurbia'.

The character and problems of the rural–urban fringe are revealed in a study around the city of Flint in Michigan. The author, Walter Firey, a sociologist, reaches the following significant conclusions.

'The fringe area presents the following problems:

(a) It removes land from agricultural productivity.

(b) Platting (i.e. the division of land into building plots) becomes unguided, unco-ordinated, and generally in excess of effective demand, thus creating vast tracts of idle land, irregular settlement patterns and tax delinquent holdings.

(c) Taxes must increase in order to maintain the services necessary in such densely populated settlements; but such taxes commonly exceed the tax-paying capacity of both farmers and shop workers.

(d) Unregulated platting frequently permits tracts to be subdivided with no deed restrictions, thereby ruining adjacent subdivisions that may have started under high deed restrictions.

(e) Fringe dwellers are frequently ill-prepared and ill-informed about buying land, getting implements and cultivating gardens.

(f) The fringe areas boost land values to the point at which it no longer pays to continue agricultural operations.'

The area from which these generalizations are drawn around Flint City, Michigan, is characterized by 'small part-time acreages, platted suburbs, blighted "shack towns", gracious country estates, trailer camps, and other typical fringe manifestations'. It has an abnormally rapid rate of growth. Its occupants have diverse social characteristics and there is a tendency for people of like economic status and like social backgrounds to congregate in homogeneous neighbourhoods. These give rise to 'shack towns' in some portions of the fringe and attractive suburban communities in other portions. In spite of this, however, the fringe has certain common characteristics. These are its high rate of population turnover; high rate of home ownership; high proportion of young adults and many children; heavy dependence on work in the city; inadequate social life and organizational facilities for the people; and part-time farming or gardening on the part of most families.[1]

[1] See W. Firey, 'Social Aspects to Land Use Planning in the Country–City Fringe: The Case of Flint, Michigan'. *Agricultural Experimental Station, Michigan State College, Special Bulletin 449*, June 1946.

THE STRUCTURE OF THE CITY

The European city exhibits the same tendency to extend and explode, but not nearly to the same degree. England and Wales, for example, is the most urbanized country in the world, with well over 80 per cent. of the population classed as urban. But there is a large, essentially urban population living outside the limits of the 'urban' (administrative) districts which is not classed as 'urban' for census purposes, so that the total population which works in urban areas is well over nine-tenths. The large number of cities and the recent spread of the suburban fringe over surrounding areas also means that a large and dangerously high proportion of land is built over.

Expressed briefly, the uses to which the 58,340 square miles of land in England and Wales were being put in 1937 were as follows: some 82·1 per cent. of the total area was in agricultural production (including rough grazings); 1·1 per cent. was open land of various kinds not being used for agriculture but of potential agricultural value; 5·5 per cent. was woodland; and the remaining 11·3 per cent. was covered by buildings, roads and various other forms of constructional development, or was otherwise unaccounted for in agricultural returns.[1] The 41 million people in England and Wales occupied about 4·16 million acres with the various structures associated with their homes and work, so that there were 10 people per acre of land under urban uses.

The impact of urban land uses on the countryside of Britain before 1939 thus assumed alarming proportions, and especially in the thirties. Without any overhead planning control, a colossal redistribution of homes and factories to the borders of the great cities took place—due to the shift of factories outwards from the centre of the cities, as well as to the establishment of new factories to accommodate entirely new industries. During the 1919–39 period four million houses were built and most of them on agricultural land.[2] Another four million houses have been built in the post-war years. The great majority of these lie on the suburban fringes of the great cities, beyond their administrative limits. This is demonstrated very clearly by the map showing the changes in population in the period 1931–38 reproduced in the report of the Scott Committee. This map shows how the central areas of the cities in many cases actually declined in population or managed to maintain a very small increase well below the average for the country as a whole; whereas the outer suburban areas, frequently in non-urban districts and planted in the midst of agricultural land, increased very rapidly. With a few exceptions, the main

---

[1] Report of the (Scott) Committee on Land Utilization in Rural areas, Cmd. 6378, 1942, p. 2. These figures are broadly confirmed by R. H. Best in 'The Urban Area of Great Britain', *Town Planning Review*, Vol. XXVIII, October 1957.

[2] Scott Report, p. 23.

areas of increase in the past forty years are in a belt from south Lancashire to the south-east coast—notably Greater London and the Home Counties and Greater Birmingham.

With reference to the 1931–38 period, it is reported that:

'In every one of the great industrial cities of the central belt there is a *decrease* of population in the centre where commercial buildings replace dwelling-houses, and a huge *increase* in the surrounding fringes, where country is replaced by suburb or town. The continuance of this process we believe to have been temporarily arrested by the war, and we would call attention to the extreme urgency of legislative action to give effect to our recommendations. We are convinced that otherwise the old unregulated sprawl of towns into country with its attendant evils will recommence immediately men and materials are released for the work of physical reconstruction.'[1]

This development in Britain takes many forms—council-housing estates, private building estates on new land or clustered around an existing village or small town, occasional good-class villas scattered irregularly along country roads, usually with an attractive view, or rows of semidetached houses and bungalows strung along the arterial roads. This is frequently accompanied by new factories, which all enjoy the cheapest layout of utility services, gas, sewage disposal, water and electricity and accessibility of transport. Such building disfigures the countryside, and impedes the development of communal living and community consciousness. Factories, lines of houses, wayside cafés, road houses, garages, filling-stations, bill-boards and the like stretch for miles along the arterial roads leading from the cities, and sheltered, pretty nooks along the coast harbour masses of jerry-built shacks and bungalows.[2] Between the roads there are wide stretches of farm land, but much good land has been sold for houses and factories, and much farm land lies derelict, since many farmers and landowners have held their land for sale to builders, and pending such sale have allowed it to lie idle. Under such circumstances land is farmed badly, since the tenant farmer is under constant threat of eviction. This explains the frequent spectacle of derelict land on the borders of our cities with hoardings facing the roadside announcing sites for factories, or desirable residences—which strike one's eye many miles before one reaches the built-up area of the city. 'The threat of the builder overshadowed and sterilized it.'[3] This is a

[1] *Ibid.*, p. 6.
[2] J. A. Steers, 'Coastal Preservation and Planning', *Geographical Journal*, Vol. CIV, 1944, pp. 7–27.
[3] Scott Report, pp. 28–9.

repetition of the 'institutional desert' around the American city and arises from the same causes.

The 1947 planning act in Britain has sought to put a brake on this expansion and to direct the growth of new housing to more desirable channels. This is evident, for example, in the so-called 'green belt' concept. This, when finally defined by each of the planning authorities (country and county boroughs) and approved by the government, will surround each of the major cities with a belt of 'green land' in which building will be controlled. The county boroughs, however, are presented with difficulties by the inadequacy of the land within their boundaries to cope with their housing needs in the foreseeable future. This has already led to various measures for coping with their 'overspills', that is, the population that they cannot house and which must be housed outside their limits by some other authority. Financial arrangements between local authorities permit this kind of development. This situation has also resulted in much land speculation and a remarkable rise in the price of land in the few vacant areas within the borough boundaries that lie between the limits of the existing built-up area and the foreseeable *inner* boundary of the green belt.

This situation has also resulted in a revolutionary change in British building. The multi-storeyed flat, about which there has been unending debate *vis-à-vis* the single family house, has arrived. Ten-storey flats now stand in many cities, as a means of absorbing as many people as possible within the city boundaries as the slums are demolished. There are even plans for blocks with over twenty storeys. The great majority of the $4\frac{1}{4}$ million new houses built since 1945 are in 'suburban' areas—on the city fringes. Unless many more new towns are built, and unless numerous small country towns are revitalized by the growth of industry and the settlement of new residents, the enormous number of new dwellings to be built in the future will have to be built in one of two places, either in multi-storeyed blocks inside the city limits and mostly inside the areas of slum clearance (this has been going on actively during the fifties), or new houses will have to be built beyond the green belt and people commute across it to their daily work in the central city. The last would be a travesty. More effective means of decentralization and even of satellite development in small villages and small towns within and beyond the green belts is an obvious and desirable alternative.

4. The Location of Industry

The growth of factories on the city outskirts is a main feature and cause of the expansion of the modern city. Industries are affected differently by centrifugal and centripetal forces according to their character. *The Regional Survey of New York and Its Environs* in the twenties distinguished light manufacturing and heavy industries, and, though this distinction is open to varied interpretation, the Survey based it on the following considerations. Heavy industries are large in size; the time factor—that is, the factor of immediate accessibility to the market—is unimportant; they demand a large ground area; they frequently have nuisance features such as noise, odours, pollution, fire hazards; they have a serious problem of waste disposal; they require a large plant lay-out; they require large quantities of fuel and water; their products as well as their raw materials are bulky so that they require extensive and contiguous railway or water-transport facilities. All these conditions make the siting of such plants unsuitable for the central districts, and more suited to the fringes, of the urban area, whether they be shifted outwards from the central areas or established in the first place as new plants. Such industries are meat-packing, petroleum storage, smelting, automobile manufacture and assembly, lumber and flour mills, power plants, and gas works. The shift outwards lags behind the need for the move, and plants established originally on the town outskirts are slow in being shifted. They continue, through the inertia of fixed capital as going concerns, to function on their original sites, though unsuited in every way to the well-being of the urban community as well as to the organization of the industry. Many instances of this kind are apparent in Chicago, the outstanding example being the stockyards, which, though originally well sited on the southern outskirts of the town, are now in the heart of it in the midst of an appalling slum.

Light manufacturing industries have the following characteristics. They do not always require buildings of special construction. The time or service factor is of great importance (immediate contact with related industries, transport facilities). They often require highly skilled work. They require little ground space per worker. Obsolete buildings are often suitable since they are carried on in relatively small business units. They are often seasonal in character and have a fluctuating labour demand and they are often conditioned by the vagaries of style, especially in clothing. Finally, their products usually require materials small in bulk often going through several processes, demanding much labour, but little loss of material or bulk in process. Such industries are garment-making, printing, cigar- and cigarette-making, instrument-making and the manufacture of cosmetics. They usually seek a few rooms or an obsolete building or warehouse on the borders of, or as near as possible to, the central business area and draw much of their labour from the poor working-class districts in and around the central business area. Their manufactured goods find their markets in the warehouses and retail stores in the neighbouring wholesale and central business districts.

This broad contrast between the two major sets of industries is sound in considering the growth of the city, but while the heavy industries have definitely this character, many of the so-called light industries may be pursued on such a large scale as to demand, like the heavy industries, an outside location. This process is well illustrated in the case of the industrial districts of north-western London. All modern cities have had large industrial plants established on their outskirts—either as entirely new industries or as old-established ones shifted (often in stages) from the congested city sites. Such plants are situated, according to their needs, on road, rail and canal, and become in themselves the centres of crystallization of housing developments and the foci of daily streams of traffic carrying their workers to and from their homes.

This classification of industry, as devised some forty years ago, seems to be somewhat unrealistic in the light of trends since that date. The demands of heavy industry are the same as ever they were. A petroleum refinery, for example, must be placed as far as possible from a great urban complex, not only because of its unpleasant characteristics, but above all else because of its specific space requirements—a large area of land for equipment and tank storage, water and rail facilities, and adequate surrounding space for protection from the risk of conflagration. On the other hand, the most characteristic feature of new industrial plants in the last generation has been the development of one-storey structures covering large areas, plus space for parking (which in America often exceeds the acreage of the plant itself), recreation grounds, landscaping, and the like. Such plants must obviously be placed on the urban outskirts. This is where they are to be found, especially in America, often employing tens of thousands of workers, who travel long distances from residential areas that are rarely within sight of the plant.

For example, in Chicago there are four major types of industrial plant with distinct locations. First, there are light manufacturing plants which are located mainly in multi-storey buildings on the fringes of the central business district. Examples are the clothing and printing industries. Mixture with older homes near the centre results in a 'hybrid' or mixed agglomeration of land uses. Second, there are manufacturing plants in organized and integrated districts, which are located on either the belt railroads or roads for direct loading facilities. Third, there are the large primary processing refineries, which demand large acreage, and handle large tonnages of raw materials. Many of these were first located on the Chicago River, but many have shifted south to the Calumet River. Fourth, there are the large new war-time plants, built since 1940. These are located on the belt lines and on the major road arteries on extensive sites.

5. The Distribution of Population

The interplay of the centrifugal and centripetal forces in the modern city is most clearly reflected in the distribution and movements of population.

The average overall density of big cities is surprisingly consistent. It is 5,400 per square mile for the metropolitan urbanized areas of the United States, and the average in Great Britain is almost exactly 6,400 per square mile or ten persons per acre. The figure in Germany was 5,000 per square mile in 1951. There are, however, great variations around these averages, and the more densely peopled areas of the big agglomeration—such as New York City, Paris, London, Tokyo—have overall densities of 25,000 to 30,000 persons per square mile. Maxima for small districts seem to be in the order of 100,000 persons per square mile.

In the very large city, densities closely fit with the broad concentric zones outlined above. The cases of Chicago, Paris, and Stockholm have already been noted. The examples of Liverpool and Birmingham are given in the table below.[1] First, the city centre has a relatively low density. It is the heart of the urban organism, throbbing

Density of Population (persons per acre by concentric zones)

	Liverpool (1931)		Birmingham (1938)	
	Acres	Persons per acre	Acres	Persons per acre
Central Zone	1,600	59	3,000	62
Middle Zone (Inner)	3,300	96	9,000	32
Middle Zone (Outer)	2,800	52		
Outer Zone	17,000	17	39,000	15
Total	24,700	34·5	51,100	20
Total Population	855,700		1,050,000	

[1] See the detailed study of Merseyside, and particularly of Liverpool, by Wilfred Smith in *The Distribution of Population and the Location of Industry in Merseyside*, 1942, and the studies of Birmingham in *When we Build Again*, Bournville Village Trust, 1941 and *Conurbation*, Architectural Press, London, 1948.

with activity in the daytime, deserted at night, except for its caretakers, slum pockets, and hotel and apartment blocks (for both rich and poor). For this reason, in cities with under about 750,000 inhabitants, the population of a central census district (such as a ward) includes both the business centre and adjoining slum districts in the transition belt, so that its density of population may be exceedingly high. The general trend, however, is for the slums to be slowly cleared or abandoned and for their inhabitants to shift or be shifted elsewhere. Secondly, around the core is the most closely built-up residential area, which normally has the highest overall densities of population. Farther out, land built up at the end of the nineteenth century until 1914 has more open space and lower densities. Finally, in the suburban outskirts the density—both overall and per acre of built-up land—is lowest.

The Ordnance Survey population map of Greater London shows these features clearly. The central districts—the city of London and the city of Westminster—have about 20 and 50 residents per acre respectively; then comes a surrounding zone, including such boroughs as Stepney, Lambeth, Finsbury, and Paddington, with between 100 and 200 persons per acre (maxima are between 200 and 250). Farther out, a wide encircling belt has 50 to 100 persons per scre, and the outlying suburban districts have under 50 persons per acre.

This decrease of population, while it started in the heart of the city through the expansion of business space, has spread in more recent decades to the zones around it—the zone of transition and even into the middle residential zone of nineteenth-century growth. This shift is due to the bad living conditions in these areas as compared with those in the extensive housing areas that have been built in the suburban outskirts. Sub-standard housing, that is, housing below the minimum standards acceptable in the country, reaches high proportions in many American cities as well as in European cities. In Britain, we find that one-fifth of the dwellings in Birmingham and Manchester are condemned as unfit to live in. The figure in Hull is nearly one-third, and the same figure is undoubtedly reached in other big industrial cities. The replacement of these dwellings by new ones in the coming years will make tremendous demands on the *lebensraum* of every big city.

It should be noted here that this flight from the central city to the suburbs is offset by other population movements in the former. It is a selective process, in the sense that many people choose to stay put or do not have the financial means to move. Such, in particular, in the American city, are the 'problem types' and the members of distinctive ethnic groups. Added to this since 1945 has been the unprecedented immigration of southern Negroes to the inner districts which has often caused their total population to remain stable or to increase in the last ten years.

The examples of Paris and Chicago illustrate these trends (Fig. 26, p. 146, and Fig. 22, p. 138).

The centrifugal drift is illustrated most clearly by comparative figures for American cities. A recent statistical study[1] reveals that the population growth of the metropolitan areas between 1900 and 1950 declined. This was accompanied by a shift of growth from central cities to their outer rings. When growth rates are plotted by five-mile distance zones from the centre to a distance of 35 miles, it is found that growth rates decline with distance from the central city. The range of metropolitan influence as measured by the ratios of growth to total United States rates and by the ratios of zonal rates to central city rates, has progressively extended in the decades since 1900–10. Approximately 25 to 30 miles were added to the radius of metropolitan influence on this criterion. The redistribution of population moved toward concentration from 1900 to 1920 and toward dispersion from 1920 to 1950. Thus, the metropolitan growth in the first half of the century involved, in the first place, a rapid growth of the central cities at the expense of satellite areas: and, after 1920, a centrifugal movement to satellite areas to the detriment of growth in the central cities.

The main features of these trends were summed up for American cities, as follows, nearly thirty years ago.[2]

'1. There has been an exodus of population from the central portions of the city. This exodus is caused in small measure by an increase in the size of central areas utilized for business purposes, but much more largely by the progressive deterioration of structures in large portions of the central areas. The effect of this deterioration is a creeping paralysis, commonly referred to in the United States as "blight".

2. The exodus from the central area, together with the settlement of new populations in suburban areas, has caused a drift of the masses of the population outward radially. Much of this drift is due to the promotional and sales efforts which have been made in connection with the development of new estates.

3. With the outward radial drift of population has come a re-centralization of outlying district business centres, so that they sometimes reach the proportion of satellite business communities.

4. The provision of rapid transport facilities has tended to aggravate further the decline of the central area by providing non-stop highways for automobile traffic.'

[1] Amos Hawley, *The Changing Shape of Metropolitan America*, Glencoe, 1956, p. 161.
[2] McKenzie, *op. cit.*, p. 233.

The study of distribution of land values and of the changes that have taken place in relation to these trends reveals three phenomena:

'the increase in values in the strategically located restricted central areas; the increase in values in the outlying district subcentres; and the decline of values in other portions of the inner area. On the decline of values in inner areas of the city not included in the intensively developed portion, data are not available. It is common observation, however, that this decline has been great and is probably proceeding at an accelerated rate. So rapid has the decline been that in many cities the revenues from taxation of real estate have been shrinking to an alarming extent.'[1]

These trends have continued unabated over the last thirty years. Changes in the fifties will be discussed in a later chapter. The United States is not only a predominantly urban society. It has many characteristics and problems that arise from the predominance of its 'sub-urban' way of life. The essential thing is the contrast between rurality and urbanity. The degree of urbanity diminishes outwards with distance from the central cities and the degree of rurality is highest in areas that are most removed from these centres. In the rural–urban fringe there is an intermixture of both.

Large areas of north-west Europe are even more highly urbanized than the States, and yet there are extensive areas with a high degree of rurality. We require measures of the degree of urbanization so that the limits of the urbanized areas and the semi or demi-semi urbanized areas associated with them may be more exactly defined. We shall return again to this question.

6. Areas of Social Disorganization and Blight

Human ecologists have sought to determine if there is any consistent tendency for social phenomena to segregate within the urban area according to recognizable principles. It is they who have attempted precisely to determine the patterns of distribution (and in recent years often on the basis of complex statistical correlation techniques). In general, two modes of segregation have been recognized, first, in accordance with concentric zones, and second, in particular natural areas. It seems appropriate to summarize here some of these findings with respect to abnormal conditions, both social and physical.

Social disorganization seems to be particularly associated with the outworn, obsolescent areas which are found in areas of high land

[1] McKenzie, *op. cit.*, pp. 232–3.

values and old properties. These are termed by sociologists disorganized areas. Many studies have been made of the exact distribution by place of residence of the victims of such aberrations as delinquency (both adult and juvenile), vice, suicide, mental disorders, alcoholism, divorce, desertion, poverty, mortality and disease, and these traits correlated with community structure as determined by ethnic types, densities of population, and income levels.[1]

Similar trends are found in British and continental cities, although they are less obvious owing to a more homogeneous ethnic composition. There is, of course, in the first place, the general centrifugal drift of people from the older, less healthy, inner housing areas, to the new outer housing areas. This is the most fundamental and widespread feature of the demography of the modern city, and it is probably most characteristic of the British city. It is both a contributory cause and an effect of urban blight in the inner areas. In the early thirties, the Merseyside survey showed that in the inner districts of Liverpool where the slums are, there is a coincidence of high birth-rates, overcrowding, poverty, physical and mental defects, alcoholism, chronic destitution, immorality and criminality, whereas the outer districts show much lower rates. The former phenomena coincided markedly in Black Patch Areas, defined by the Survey as 'streets in which at least one family in every five contains individuals of the chronically unemployed and destitute kind. Such families will not unfrequently be resident in one-room tenements or slums. They will be often in receipt of public assistance and not getting unemployment benefit or transitional payment'. The Survey concludes: 'convinced environmentalists will probably claim that the congestion is the cause of the trouble. The protagonists of heredity will assert in reply that congestion, so far from being the cause, is rather the effect.... No doubt on both sides there is some truth, but the question how much, remains unsettled.'[2] 'Heredity, illness, and "culture shock" are all important elements in the problem. But in spite of that, poverty does appear as the environment in which these disease germs grow most readily.'[3]

This diagnosis and the general validity of the hypothesis of concentric distribution in the city of Liverpool find support in a more recent study.[4] Liverpool falls into three concentric zones— Dockland and the Inner and Outer Residential Zones. Dockland has

[1] D. Caradog Jones (ed.), *The Social Survey of Merseyside*, Liverpool University Press, 1934, Vol. III, Ch. XIX, p. 485.
[2] *Op. cit.*, p. 489.
[3] D. V. Glass, *The Town and a Changing Civilization*, London, 1935, p. 88.
[4] I. M. Castle and E. Gittus, 'The Distribution of Social Defects in Liverpool', *Sociological Review*, Vol. V, July 1957, pp. 43–64. Reproduced in Theodorson, *Studies in Human Ecology*, 1961.

a declining population, owing in part to slum clearance and war damage, with a lot of derelict housing dating back to the 1870's, mainly in the form of terrace housing. The Inner Zone falls into three parts, a southern and a northern part, and an encircling outer ring. The southern part is comparable to the 'zone of transition', though it formerly housed the wealthy merchants and professional classes. The northern part has old bye-law terrace houses, and is now occupied by the Irish and coloured people. From 1931 to 1951 the number of families in this zone increased, but the population sightly declined. The third zone, the outer zone, contains the majority of the new housing estates built since 1930. It has an increasing population and has housed many people from the Dockland area. The distribution of the social defects is shown by wards. The zone of transition seems to have the greatest accumulation of social defects. A high rate is also found in the dockland areas, where there are poor overcrowded conditions. In short, there is a high incidence of social defects in 'the commercial and business wards, in the inner residential areas and more particularly in the part of the city which has been described as the "zone of transition" '. This corroborates the Merseyside Survey of the thirties. The authors thus find the same situation as in New York and Chicago and confirm the Chicago hypothesis that 'if the main trend of city development is from the centre to the periphery, areas in the city centre, where the population is declining, show the highest incidence of physical deterioration and conditions precipitating family breakdown'.

Traits of social disorganization have been exhaustively studied in Chicago. Investigations of the distribution of delinquency rates (school truants, juvenile delinquents, adult offenders, etc.) resulted in important findings. Crime and delinquency tend to be concentrated in specific areas of the city, not evenly distributed according to the density of population. Their incidence was highest near the central business district, and decreased outwards, with higher rates also contiguous to industrial districts such as the stockyards and steel works. The incidence of delinquency was a reliable measure of social disorganization and the breakdown of community life and standards.[1] The gang and gangster thrive also in such areas. They are found in Chicago in a semi-circle around the Loop in the zone of deterioration (as named by Burgess), an area of slight social control where there is lack of law and order.[2] The distribution of

[1] Clifford R. Shaw, *Delinquency Areas*, University of Chicago Press, 1930. Many aspects of this subject in American cities are summarized in the textbooks by Gist and Halbert, *Urban Society*, 1941, and by J. E. Quinn, *Human Ecology*, 1950.

[2] F. M. Thrasher, *The Gang*, University of Chicago Press, 1927.

vice and of homeless men show similar traits since these owe their location to similar causes and are associated with the same unsettled social pattern. Suicide was found to be particularly prevalent in the central business district and the cheap hotel districts near it, in the rooming-house districts of the lower North Side, and in an area between the Loop and the 'black belt'.[1] Cases of insanity psychoses were found to be clustered around the central business district, with a sharp decline of incidence outwards, and in the former there were found interesting associations of particular psychoses with different districts.[2]

It is of interest to report that in a recent study of Negro communities in Chicago[3] there is revealed a concentric arrangement from the centre of a great variety of social and economic data relevant to the Negro population and its movements. The same author later made a study of the Negro community of Harlem in New York. Here the Negroes are highly concentrated in one area. From this nucleus they have spread out radially. The author examines the spread of the Negroes and the incidence of the condition of their buildings (by type, age, and condition), their age and sex distribution, marital status, ratio of children, births and deaths, crime, delinquency, and institutions. He brings out conclusively how these conditions change in the concentric zones outwards from the centre of Harlem. He concludes that while the general hypothesis of concentric growth is borne out in Chicago and elsewhere—'it appears that where a racial or cultural group is stringently segregated and carries a more or less independent community life, such local communities may develop the same pattern of zones as the larger urban community.' In other words, separate ethnic nuclei may serve as independent nuclei of diffusion as is postulated by the multiple-nuclei hypothesis.

One of the most characteristic and serious features of the modern city is the zone of deterioration, to which attention has already been drawn (p. 42), that surrounds normally the city centre, and is also related to areas of industrial slum. The various traits characteristic of this zone are referred to as constituting urban blight, which, beginning on the edge of the central business district, spreads outwards like a creeping paralysis to cover a very large part of the whole urban area—that part mainly with pre-1900 houses. Probably the commonest and best indicator of this phenomenon is the fact of

[1] Ruth S. Cavan, *Suicide*, University of Chicago Press, 1928.

[2] R. F. L. Faris and H. W. Dunham, *Mental Disorders in Urban Areas*, University of Chicago Press, 1939. See map reproduced from this work in Gist and Halbert, *Urban Society*, showing the distribution of schizophrenia cases from 1922 to 1931, p. 221.

[3] E. F. Frazier, 'Negro Harlem: An Ecological Study', in Theodorson, *op. cit.*, pp. 165–74.

both a high density of population (overcrowding) and a decreasing population (removals). A blighted area is thus one in which:

'.... as a result of social, economic, or other conditions, there is a marked discrepancy between the value placed on the property by the owner and its value for any uses to which it can be put, appropriate to the public welfare, under existing circumstances. Old buildings are neglected and new ones are not erected, and the whole section becomes stale and unprofitable. In other words, blight is a condition where it is not profitable to make or maintain improvements.'[1]

Such an area is an economic liability to the community. A slum connotes an extreme condition of blight 'in which the housing is so unfit as to constitute a menace to the health and morals of the community'. It is thus essentially of social significance, the blighted area being primarily of economic significance.

Blight has as its common characteristics:

'high but falling land values; congested but decreasing population; obsolete and unfit housing; a large proportion of abandoned buildings and of rental vacancies; heavily mortgaged property; excessive tax delinquency; low average rentals; generally low economic status of inhabitants; excessive crime, mortality and disease rates; high per capita and per acre governmental costs'.[2]

The pattern of urban blight in America has been summarized by Walker on the basis of Burgess' concentric zones of urban expansion and invasion outwards from the centre. The cases of blight, as defined above, are various and often complicated, but it 'is probably the result chiefly of loss of population, particularly as the more prosperous groups move away', and whether a decreasing population is a cause or effect of blight, it is certainly (if examined in sufficient detail, block by block) the best general criterion of the existence of such a condition.[3]

7. The Journey to Work

The separation of workplace and dwelling-place, rendered possible by the development of cheap and rapid transport, is one of the most fundamental problems of the modern city. This subject has been examined by Dr. K. Liepmann in a volume in this series, and to it

[1] E. F. Frazier, p. 489.
[2] Mabel L. Walker, *Urban Blight and Slums*, Harvard City Planning Studies, Vol. XII, Harvard University Press, 1938, p. 36.
[3] H. Hoyt, *One Hundred Years of Land Values in Chicago*, University of Chicago Press, 1933.

the reader is referred. The following summary comments are drawn from it.[1]

The daily flow of passenger traffic in all its aspects follows a maze of routes and cross-currents. The most marked trend is the movement from residential suburbs or dormitories to business and industrial districts. These streams, and their reverse in the evenings have been described as 'tides of daily ebb and flow'. Workplaces are usually in the centre of the urban complex and residential districts on the fringe so that the tide is centripetal in the morning and centrifugal in the evening. But there are numerous other outstanding flows that cut across these. Thus, with the growth of factories on the fringes, residential districts have grown next to them. But in many cities, especially on the Continent, workers still live in the city and travel daily to the factory on the outskirts. These are *counter-currents* that are the exact reverse of the centripetal movements. There are also *cross-currents*, especially where there are several urban centres within daily travelling distance of each other; these are especially characteristic of the big conurbations. These movements, when considered from the standpoint of the dwelling-place and workplace respectively, may be regarded as movements of *dispersion* from the former—the inhabitants of a neighbourhood leaving each morning in various journeys of very different lengths—and as movements of conflux to the latter.

'Since the needs of industry and commerce have so far been best met by a concentration of the day population, while for residence and domestic purposes converse conditions are preferable, industrial areas are generally associated with a larger number of dormitory areas, and such intersection as takes place is characterized by a daily pulsation between the common industrial centre and a larger number of surrounding residential areas.'[2]

The effect of this mobility on the structure of the city is to permit the separation of residential from industrial and business districts. The daily journey to work also permits the mobility of labour. For good or ill, the house of the employee can be up to a journey of one hour or more, and a distance of 10 to 15 miles, from the workplace. Factories can theoretically be spaced between closely clustered towns and draw upon their reservoir of labour. Large new industrial plants must either draw their workers from a wide surrounding urban area or effect the construction of entirely new settlements. The main

---

[1] Kate Liepmann, *The Journey to Work*, The International Library of Sociology and Social Reconstruction, Kegan Paul, London, 1944, pp. 3–6.
[2] Census of England and Wales, 1921, *General Report*, p. 193, quoted by Liepmann, p. 5.

result of this mobility of labour and the separation of workplace and dwelling-place is to create a 'polarity' in the urban structure, and, among its social and economic consequences, a split of the community interests and financial obligations between the working district and the dwelling district. This is one of the most serious problems of municipal finance.

The following is an important statement on the character of intra-urban movements in the American city which is reproduced here verbatim.[1]

'The commercial–industrial complex of the city is substantially localized with respect to residential areas. Commercial and industrial activities are concentrated in areas of high accessibility—virtually monopolizing the core of the urban area and sharing with intensive residential use the sites adjacent to radial transportation lines. Less intensive residential uses predominate in the areas of lesser accessibility. As a consequence, there is a significant daily movement of population between residential areas and the areas in which industrial and commercial activities are carried on.

'During the day, people are brought together from their relatively dispersed residences to certain focal points in the city where activities essential for its functioning are carried on. Hence, the daytime distribution of population over the urban area differs markedly from the night-time or residential distribution; in fact, the distribution of population over the urban area is constantly changing through a twenty-four-hour period.

'The vast majority of an urban population is involved in daily movement. The most important single component of this movement is that between workplace and residence—accounting for roughly two-fifths of all such movement. The physical separation of residence and workplace varies directly with the socio-economic status of the worker; but, by having access to more rapid and flexible transport means, high-status workers apparently expend no greater time in travelling to work than do low-status workers. The residences of central area workers are more dispersed with respect to the urban core than are the residences of other workers with respect to their areas. And socio-economic status and workplace centralization operate jointly as well as independently to produce high work–residence separation.

'It is true, of course, that large numbers of workers travel long distances on the journey to work; and there is also evidence that, on the average, distance travelled on the journey to work has been

[1] Beverly Duncan, 'Intra-urban Population Movement', in Hatt and Reiss, *Cities and Society*, Glencoe, 1957, pp. 308–9.

increasing. But it is also true that perhaps one-third to one-half of the working force, exclusive of central area workers, reside within two miles of their workplace.[1]

'The literature on intra-urban population movements has been increasing; and a number of recent studies have considered the patterns of movement in relation to ecological, socio-economic, or demographic variables.[2] At present, the static aspects of the ecological organization of the city have been more fully examined than have the dynamic aspects. But improving data-collection methods and analytical techniques should facilitate more adequate study of the patterns of recurring movement within urban areas.'

This closes the quotation. It deals conceptually with the general patterns of daily movements of people in the urban area with respect to places of inflow and areas of outflow. It formulates a field of enquiry that cries out for investigation, to which the individual workers, as well as the team, can make meaningful contributions.

Studies in the United States support the following conclusions.[3] Roughly two out of every five trips fall into the category of the journey to work. This is concentrated at rush hours. The second type of trip is 'socio-recreational' and accounts for about one-fourth of all trips. This is concentrated at night-time. The third category are the shopping and business trips. These are mainly concentrated in the early afternoon (in) and the late afternoon (out).

As regards the journey to work in the United States, the larger the city the longer the journey to work. In smaller cities under 100,000 it takes less than one half-hour. Two out of three workers in Manhattan (the core of New York) spend at least forty minutes in travel each way. The central district is generally the greatest area of 'conflux', the further one lives from the centre the longer is the average journey to work. Trips to work to the central district are longer than trips to work in off-centre industrial districts. Lower income workers tend to live nearer to their work and are less likely to use automobiles. Workers seem to minimize the daily journey, but maximize both employment benefits and residential amenities.

[1] Beverly Duncan, 'Factors in Work–Residence Separation: Wage and Salary Workers, Chicago, 1951', *American Sociological Review*, February 1956.
[2] As examples, see the following: J. Douglas Carroll, Jr., 'The Relation of Home to Work Place in the Spatial Pattern of Cities', *Social Forces*, 30, 1952; Donald L. Foley, 'Urban Daytime Population: A Field for Demographic-Ecological Analysis', *Social Forces*, 32 (May 1954), pp. 323–30; Leo F. Schnore, 'The Separation of Home and Work: A Problem for Human Ecology', *Social Forces*, 32 (May 1954).
[3] Foley, *op. cit.*

THE STRUCTURE OF THE CITY

When trips are classified on the basis of the functional areas to which they are directed, there is an exodus from residential areas to the industrial and commercial areas. A study in five American cities revealed the following. By early afternoon only about three out of every four residents remain in the residential areas. At that time, a peak of 16 per cent. of the residents are in commercial areas. There is a vast rhythmical stream of residents moving to the down-town district in the early morning, and back in the late afternoon. All figures show the tendency for daytime population to concentrate in the metropolitan area and especially in the central business districts.

The increased range of the potential journey to work is causing changes in the patterns of movements and in the configuration of 'labour market areas'. Fifty years ago work-areas were local, tied down in the majority of cases to the distance a worker could walk to work each day. There was some extension of travel by tram, but movement by rail was strictly limited to higher-paid workers in the 'white collar' category. The typical mill settlement in northern England or in New England contained a series of workers' homes within walking distance of the mill or of several mills clustered together in a town. Movement to town centres was limited to the range of rail or tram and clearly did not come within the means of the low-paid factory worker. The range of travel has been greatly increased by the extended use of the bus in western Europe as an addition to the rail (that is still very important in Germany, Belgium, and Holland) and, especially in the States, by the use of the private automobile. Mass transport by rail and bus has become increasingly important and increasingly congested to and from the cities. In the United States the problem is bedevilled by the universality of the automobile that is used today in most cities instead of public transport systems. The latter are slower, more costly, less convenient, and less comfortable than travel by car. Most public transport systems in America are in the red and are faced with real difficulties in trying to adapt their outworn systems to the exacting needs of its potential but discriminating public. The nature of these metropolitan traffic trends in the fifties in the United States is shown in figs. 33 and 34.[1]

Figs. 33 and 34 show metropolitan traffic trends in the United States in the mid-fifties. Fig. 33 shows the extraordinarily low proportion of down-town travel (except New York, Philadelphia and Chicago) and the high proportion of travel by private automobile, especially in the Middle and Far Western cities (e.g., Los Angeles, San Francisco, and Seattle, two-thirds). Fig. 34 shows the changes

[1] W. Owen, *The Metropolitan Transport Problem*, Brookings Institution, Washington, 1956.

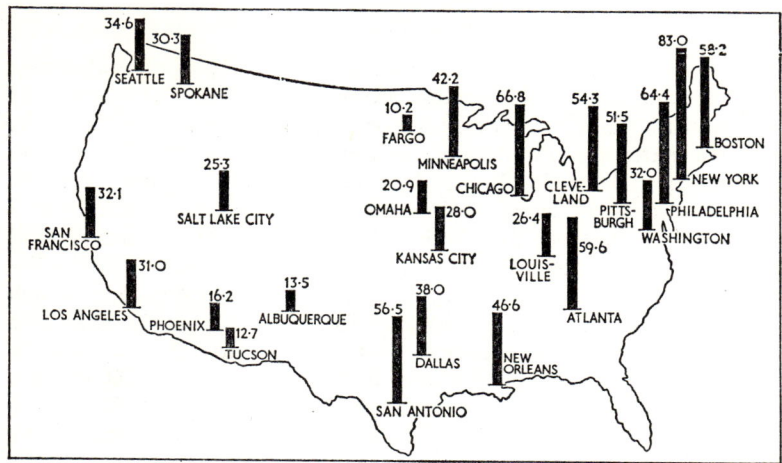

Fig. 33. Cities of the United States: Percentage of Downtown Travel by Public Transport, in early 1950's (after W. Owen).

in modes of travel to the big cities since 1930. Note the great increase of mass transport during the war years, followed in the fifties by an enormous decrease of mass transport (street car, bus and rail) and a continuing increase of travel by private automobile.

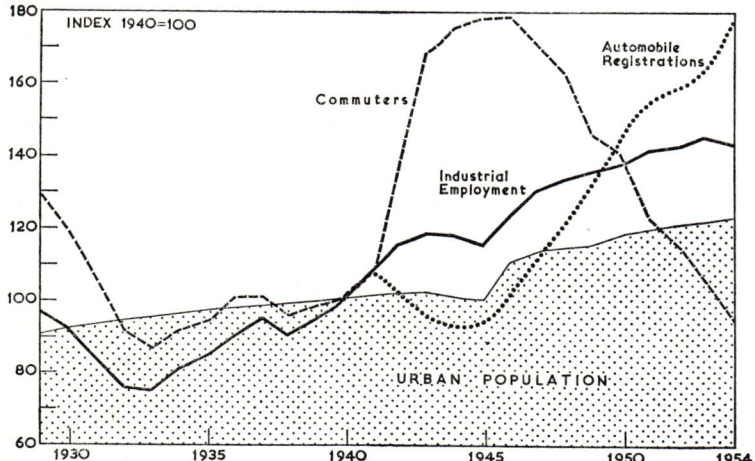

Fig. 34. Cities of the United States: Mass Transport and Economic Growth in the United States (after W. Owen).

8. Traffic Flows

The increasing density of vehicular traffic on roads is one of the most obvious and one of the greatest problems of cities. The business of coping with traffic is one of the major tasks of all planning authorities. Yet we (particularly in Britain) are abysmally ignorant of the nature of traffic and traffic flows—their composition, volume, density, rhythms, kinds of trips, origin, and destination; and of the impact of 'access', 'contact', and 'linkage' on the location of urban land uses, residential and non-residential. One of the primary reasons for this ignorance is the difficulty of acquiring the necessary data, which requires large numbers of workers for recording in the field and processing the data so obtained. Further, there are the great costs of such an operation, as is evidenced by the sum of over £400,000 that has been recently expended merely on collecting such data in a traffic survey of London. This kind of investigation has gone much further in the cities of the United States, although, even there, there is constant outcry about the lack of adequate knowledge and guidance available to the highway engineer or city planner.

Let us be clear that this task demands a conceptual framework on the basis of which traffic data may be recorded, classified, and interpreted. It is not merely a question of mapping traffic flows from data recorded at strategically distributed control points. This is the simplest of the tasks. It is a question of classifying movements in terms of the traffic participating in them, and their daily rhythms and directions. It is also a question of finding measures for determining the relation between land uses and the kind of traffic linkage they require for their efficient operation.

The traffic problems of today are problems of road traffic by car or truck. The railroads are losing out, with the exception of certain bulk commodities and for certain commuting traffic (though even the latter has greatly diminished in American cities). Road and now air transport have stolen both goods and passenger traffic. In Britain, short- and medium-distance passenger traffic goes increasingly by road. Little more than 3 per cent. of the trains around Bristol carry 60 per cent. of the passengers. In long-distance journeys, as many people travel by air between London and Glasgow as go by train. With regard to general merchandize, the situation is grimmer. In 1961 the railways carried 5,500 million ton-miles of goods of general merchandize, while the roads carried nearly five times as much. General merchandise haulage accounts for one-quarter of the vehicle mileage. If all the general merchandise traffic were transferred from rail to road the total vehicle mileage on the roads would increase by less than 5 per cent. And at present, total traffic is increasing

THE CITY AS A WHOLE

at more than twice this rate. The problem of the city lies in road traffic.[1]

The same is even more true in the United States. American planners and other investigators have necessarily paid a great deal of attention to this whole field of traffic analysis, and a broad conceptual framework has recently been formulated in an important work from which the following paragraphs are primarily derived.[2] This kind of investigation goes much further than the collection of Origin and Destination Surveys. It requires thorough analyses of establishments, using this term in the widest sense of a building, its occupants, and its activities (both residential and non-residential). These are examined in relation to the nature of the outside contacts, whether these involve persons, goods, ideas, or organization, that are needed for efficient performance.

The mass movements of persons and goods take three forms. They may involve assembly at points in particular establishments—a factory, a warehouse, or a terminal. They may involve movements of dispersal, as in the case of workers moving from a factory or people dispersing from a football stadium. They may also involve random movements along widely dispersed locations. Assembly may well be focused on a central business district, or an industrial area, or a port area, and the nature of the traffic differs essentially in each case.

Systems of movements of goods are classed as '(1) movement within the marketing process, including production, distribution, and consumption; (2) movement incident to construction maintenance and repair; (3) movement incident to wastage disposal and salvage; (4) movement incident to change of location or groups occupying or constituting establishments; and (5) other movements of special kinds.'[3] The most significant and largest group is the first.

How do such movements affect land use patterns? One of the most important kinds of movement is interlinkage and this has an important role to play in the location of uses. 'The way in which the movement of persons and goods influences an establishment's choice of location is related to its function and activities.'[4] The locational requirements of a department store are very different from those of an automobile assembly plant. This leads us back to Haigh's idea

---

[1] See *The Observer*, London, 18 February 1962. For the latest data and proposals regarding railways, see *The Reshaping of British Railways* (with maps), British Railways Board, H.M.S.O., London, 1963.
[2] R. B. Mitchell and C. Rapkin, *Urban Traffic, A Function of Land Use*, Columbia University Press, New York, 1954.
[3] *Ibid.*, p. 103.
[4] *Ibid.*, p. 106.

of the friction of space, for we are faced with considerations of linkage and proximity.

Establishments are linked if they participate in transactions involving the movements of persons and goods; or when one establishment serves the members of another establishment (e.g. a restaurant serving a factory), or if they serve common consumers (as in the segregation of retail stores or financial houses).

The processes by which land uses sort themselves out in the urban pattern are in large measure a function of the movement requirements of establishments. Specialization of urban activities makes it necessary for establishments to communicate with each other, and consequently there is a tendency for establishments to make accessibility a major locational consideration. For some establishments this means access to the largest number of persons, firms, or households —a central location; for others it means convenience in regard to an inexpensive channel of goods-movement; and in still other cases it means actual proximity. The tendency for certain kinds of establishments to seek proximity is examined in terms of the concept of linkage which aids in understanding the clustering of like and unlike establishments that characterize land use patterns.[1]

In the development of these concepts, both statistical and cartographic techniques have been employed. These include traffic counts, traffic diaries, origin and destination surveys, the site-efficiency ratio of an establishment, the goods–person ratio, the traffic characteristic ratio, the traffic burden index, the paired linkage factor, and the group linkage factor, all of which are used for working out quantitative measures for individual establishments. Such investigations aim at recognizing consistencies in the site of land uses and should be able to assist in remedying undesirable situations.

The enormous development of road traffic in the last fifty years has had to adjust itself in cities to the road net inherited from the past, and the problem for every city is to try to provide a new network to cope with the situation, not only as it is, but as it is expected to develop over a foreseeable period. The two, three, and four level motorways, round, through, over, and under the city, that are found in many American cities, profoundly change this situation, but it is scarcely a realistic prospect in Europe. The essential problem is one of providing main radial routes to and from the heart of the city; circular routes to avoid the centre; adequate provision for access to outlying traffic nodes, such as industrial areas and shopping centres; and parking areas in juxtaposition with places of trip-destinations.

[1] R. B. Mitchell and C. Rapkin, *op. cit.*, pp. 132–3.

THE CITY AS A WHOLE

9. SEQUENT OCCUPANCE: THE CASE OF NEW YORK

The arguments for and against the process of concentric growth and areal differentiation are well brought out in a substantive study of New York in the fifties.[1]

The New York Metropolitan Region is defined by the Regional Plan Association as twenty-two counties in three States that are centred on New York City. It has an area of 6,914 square miles and a population of 15·3 million people with 6·7 million jobs. The Region can be divided into three main zones that differ in the intensity of land use, density of population, and the kind of jobs.

The *Core* embraces the five central counties of New York City. It is grouped around Manhattan, which, in many respects, especially with regard to its southern half, is the central business district. This core has 53·6 per cent. of the population and 64·2 per cent. of the jobs.

The *Inner Ring* embraces the adjacent circle of seven counties and houses 30 per cent. of the people and 23·5 per cent. of the jobs.

The *Outer Ring*, extensive and most of it in non-urban uses and deeply affected in its socio-economic structure by proximity to the city, has 16·7 per cent. of the population and 12·3 per cent. of the jobs.

The great concentration of activities in Manhattan is reflected in the fact that though it has 37 per cent. of the total employment of the Region, it accounts for only 27·4 per cent. of the manufacturing employment as against 58·3 per cent. of the wholesale trade, 66·7 per cent. of the financial employment, and 59·3 per cent. of other office workers and office buildings. Its share of the consumer trades and services, building trades and other forms of employment is a little less than its share of the total employment. Outside the Core with 8·2 million people there are six other cities with over 100,000 that rise as lesser peaks of economic concentration around the Everest of Manhattan.

There are about 1·9 million jobs in manufacturing industries. Manhattan and the six city centres have been growing relatively slowly as seats of manufactures for forty years or more. Manufacturing has recorded a relative decline in the Core and a relative increase in the Inner and Outer Rings since 1889. This trend has accelerated since 1945. Among the basic reasons for this shift to the outer areas is the search for space—for new kinds of structure with space demands different from the rigid framework provided by the building block. Old factories in the Core suffer from the restrictions of space, zoning

[1] E. M. Hoover and R. Vernon, *The Anatomy of a Metropolis*, 1959, being one of nine volumes of the new survey of the New York Region carried out by the Harvard Graduate School of Public Administration.

regulations, and the big costs of additional land. Many lesser firms with small demands on space have also been shifting outwards, though by far the largest amount of rental space is still in Manhattan.

Data on jobs and their locational trends revealed the following. Local manufactures ship over half of their products (by weight) *within* the Region, while national manufactures ship over half *outside* the Region. It appears that about one-quarter of all the manufactures find their market in the Region. One-half of the local industries are located in New York City (nearly two-thirds of those that are consumer-oriented), but only a third of the national manufactures. Garment makers, printers and publishers remain strongly segregated in Manhattan. Wholesale trades, finance and other office employment ('white collar corps') account for 25 out of 100 workers in the Region, as compared with 28 in manufacturing industries, and over 40 in the consumer-oriented (retail) trades. Locational trends are variously represented in these groups. 'Transcending everything else is the fact that the initial lead of the old cities is rapidly being overcome.'

The growth of population by concentric zones reveals that 'at different stages in the Region's development a ring of maximum population growth rate has existed; and as the decades have gone by (since 1900) this ring has moved further out from the centre of the Region'.[1] This, however, is an oversimplification of the process of urban growth. Especially high growth is found in two different and widely separate 'rings'—one with single-family houses in the outer suburbs, and the other with 'second growth' development in apartments much closer to the centre.

The whole process of development of the population distribution in the New York Region and for that matter in any other major American agglomeration has often been described as an outward spread from a core in a series of concentric rings and a process of outward invasion and succession of land uses and occupants from the fringe of the central business district. This view, that undoubtedly is 'not unrelated to reality' must however be modified to fit the facts of growth in the New York Region. In the first place, there is not only one central business district, though Manhattan is by far the largest. There are at least six others and each of these is an independent focus of expansion with its own set of widening ripples. Further, neat concentric zones do not occur because of modifications due to transport, relief, zoning, etc. Again, people do not move house from block to block or even within the same district. They often move to an entirely different and distant district.

There are in other words, several recognizable stages in the sequence of occupance in any one district. These stages are as follows:

[1] E. M. Hoover and R. Vernon, *op. cit.*, p. 186.

First, the earliest phase is residential development in single-family houses. This has been passed long ago in the Core and is in full swing in the outer parts of the Inner Ring.

Second, there comes a transition phase in which there is large increase of population and construction with an increasing proportion of housing in apartments. Some of these replace older single-family housing. Areas of this kind, in which in 1950 over half of the dwelling units are in multi-family structures, are located close to New York City or in large old sub-centres and their suburbs. Nearly all were developed before the period of mass commuting by automobile. In other areas where this process is in swing there are at least 10 per cent. of dwellings in multi-family structures in the fifties—especially in some of the Inner Ring cities and centres, e.g. the well-served communities of Long Island. Most of these areas lie in the inner part of the Inner Ring and the outer fringes of New York City.

In the third phase the older construction (single and multi-family) is being adapted to greater density uses through conversion and crowding rather than reconstruction. It is most clearly revealed by 'slum invasion' in the Core and in and around the other main cities. This is in general a 'down-grading' process, although certain areas may retain their character through high esteem, e.g. Fifth Avenue facing Central Park. The down grading is often associated with the invasion of segregated ethnic groups.

The fourth phase is described as 'the thinning out stage'. The density of people and dwellings is reduced mainly through a decline in household size, helped by vacancy, abandonment, and demolition. No building and a declining population are its hallmarks. These characteristics arise from the excessive overcrowding of new immigrants with growing families in the previous phase. Once these people have settled down and raised their families, the size of the household shrinks. This stage has already been reached in some of the oldest slums that today are far less crowded than they were a generation ago. For example, the lower east side of Manhattan grew from 339,000 to 532,000 between 1890 and 1920 (stage three), but decreased from 250,000 in 1930. The location of similar areas is shown by districts of declining population in the fifties. Thus, out of numerous small Health Districts in Manhattan in 1950, 13 had densities over 192,000 persons per square mile, and all but one decreased substantially in the fifties.

Stage five is marked by demolition and replacement by multi-family housing—though there may not be any substantial change of density. This stage is most important in Manhattan and will extend in the future to other parts of New York. It takes the form of subsidized low income housing (rather than middle income housing) and luxury apartments. Other areas, like Greenwich Village, are 'reconditioned' and 'refurbished'. Most of the redevelopment depends on the public initiative and funds provided by the city government and the federal government. The progress of replacement of dwellings in these blighted areas is very slow—a fraction of one per cent. per year.

Freedom of movement for people with low-income jobs by automobile is the basis of these developments, coupled with the general reduction of daily working hours that increases the time available for travel. In 1907 low-income workers were still rigorously tied down to their work places. There is much reverse commuting today from Manhattan and an actual move out towards houses in the suburbs and this also relieves the situation for those who stay put in the slums. Peaks of high density prior to the thinning out process are not as high as they were. The most crowded slums of 1970 will be roomier (more rooms per person, no matter how inadequate the facilities) than those of today. Areas of blight will become more extensive.

Chapter 7

REGIONS WITHIN THE CITY: THE NATURAL AREA

1. THE NATURAL AREA

In every urban complex there are well-defined geographical areas, called 'natural areas' by the ecologists or 'functional areas' by certain geographers, which are akin to the 'natural formations' of the plant ecologist. Such distinctive areas are formed by the segregation of similar kinds of land uses and population groups. The residential areas normally cover about one-half of the built-up area of a city. They have distinct variations based on, first, the kind of building structure (differing in type, age, and degree of obsolescence); second, the density of the population and its social and economic characteristics; and third, the degree of 'polarization' of the activities and associations of the people around cultural and commercial institutions.

The general procedure in the detailed diagnosis of the spatial structure of a city is well established by many American and continental studies, though it is beyond the scope of this work to deal with the detailed problems involved in such a survey. We may instance the general procedure adopted in a survey of New Haven in Connecticut.[1] First, land use was plotted in the field for every building lot, the classification including single-family, two-family, and multi-family dwellings, commercial buildings, light industry, heavy industry, railroad property, parks and playgrounds, public property, and open spaces. Second, these detailed base maps were generalized on the basis of the percentage of street-frontage devoted to the major categories or urban land use—residential, commercial, industrial, transport, recreational, and institutional. Third, areas which had the same predominant use or continuation of uses were shown on a third map. These are the land use areas of the city. Fourth, the analysis of the socio-economic structure began with the mapping, by

[1] Maurice R. Davie, 'The Pattern of Urban Growth', an essay in *Studies in the Science of Society*, edited by G. P. Murdock, New Haven, 1937, pp. 133–61.

exact place of residence, of such facts as the density of population, nationality, income, delinquency, dependency, and names included on the social registers (indicating social and professional status). These facts were first plotted separately on a series of maps, and then the maps superimposed and it was found that 'to a remarkable extent the various area boundaries coincided'. In this way socio-economic areas were defined and their boundaries were marked on the map of the land use areas. Lastly, by combining the two sets of areas, twenty-five composite 'natural areas', or, as it seems better to call them, functional areas, were discovered (excluding the central business district and the industrial areas). In nearly all cases it was found that physical barriers, such as railways, water, highland, or industrial belts, divided the areas one from another, radial streets usually acting as arteries rather than as boundaries of the regions.[1]

This example of New Haven is a study of a small town. Much more significant is the division of the city of Chicago into 'community areas' as prepared originally by the Social Science Research Committee of the University of Chicago (Fig. 24, p. 142). These areas are groupings of the small census tracts of which there are some 500. They are social units that are best fitted to be used for statistical purposes and for understanding the life of the city. The areas were determined from considerations of non-residential land uses such as railway tracks, streets, major industrial areas, and parks, all of which often serve as barriers between neighbouring communities. The distribution of population by density and ethnic origins, on the lines we have indicated above, as well as case studies of social groups, served as criteria for determining these areas. Detailed analysis was finally made possible by the use of the census tract (first adopted by the Census in 1920). These areas were adopted by the Census in 1930 and by the Chicago Land Use Survey of the Chicago Plan Commission. Such unit areas are badly needed for our British cities as substitutes for the quite arbitrary and heterogeneous and large 'wards' or even the smaller enumeration districts of the British Census.

It needs to be emphasized that the above criteria are based on characteristics by place of residence as revealed by the census of housing and people. There are, however, other socio-economic relationships, which are just as significant, but much more elusive on any kind of census assessment. We refer to the movements and associations of people—the groups to which they belong, the schools the children attend, the institutions they patronize (club, church, chapel,

---

[1] Of many other studies of this type, particular mention may be made of Howard W. Green's work on 'Cultural Areas in the City of Cleveland', *American Journal of Sociology*, Vol. XXXVIII, 1932, pp. 356–67.

REGIONS WITHIN THE CITY: THE NATURAL AREA

synagogue), the shops in which they buy their goods, and the places in the city-complex in which they work. To what extent are such activities, on a house to house basis, polarized around particular centres or places? Are there any clearly defined areas in a city of this kind in which such relations coincide in such a way as to have well-defined limits? And if so, what relation do they bear to the homogeneous areas in terms of type of home and socio-economic status? These questions are clearly concerned with the notion of the 'neighbourhood' as a geographic entity. Do such neighbourhood associations, at different levels, exist in fact in the inherent structure of the city?

2. ECOLOGICAL STUDIES OF NATURAL AREAS

Human ecologists in the post-war years have been greatly concerned with further understanding of the natural areas in the city.[1] They have also made many investigations of particular cities and comparisons of groups of cities. In America, they are fortified by a wealth of data for census tracts and even of individual component blocks. In this way they are able to use statistical techniques to evaluate the correlation between a great diversity of data for each census tract and block, and thus to test, apply, and modify their hypotheses about natural areas. Indeed, such study does not simply amount to the definition of the range and boundary of allegedly homogeneous units. It rests on the determination of the degree of homogeneity between a variety of criteria relevant to the social and economic character of communities, and the incidence of behaviour traits in relation to such socio-economic indices. This becomes a question of determining the quality of 'natural area', i.e. the degree of association of phenomena by small districts, rather than the definition of discrete so-called natural areas. Such refined analysis is just not possible as a rule in cities in western Europe for small areas of the same order, although the Swedish geographers were able to do so in Stockholm. Data for enumeration districts, used by the Census, can be obtained (at a charge) for British cities, although the information has been very little explored.

Special attention is drawn to the research of Gaston Bardet and his associates since the war.[2] This is based upon the minute study of

---

[1] A number of articles are assembled in *Studies in Human Ecology*, edited by G. A. Theodorson, New York, 1960.

[2] Gaston Bardet, *Le Nouvel Urbanisme*, Vincent Freal, Paris, 1948; *Problèmes d'Urbanisme*, Paris, 1948; *Pierre sur Pierre*, 1946; *Mission de l'Urbanisme*, 1946. For a summary of his method see article in *Town Planning Review*, 1951, reproduced in *Studies in Human Ecology*, ed. Theodorson, pp. 370–83.

social characteristics based on house to house enquiries and mapping on a scale of 1 : 2,000. Bardet claims a sixfold hierarchy of social units, three being components of countryside and town, and the other three referring to urban areas. The patriarchal unit or degree is the smallest group above the family and is tied together by acts of mutual aid. It embraces five to fifteen families and is *une constante sociale proprement biologique*. It is located in a row of houses, a small hamlet, a group of farms, or even in a large tenement. In a city it is represented by the people in the neighbouring houses with whom you associate, visit, and help. The next higher unit is called the domestic or economic degree. This is a unit that contains some 50 to 150 families which may be grouped in a village or in a part of a town as a group of streets. This is not a social association of persons like the lesser unit, but of houses and consumers with its focus in a group of shops for daily purchases. These include the *petits multiples*—the general store with a radius of attraction not exceeding some 300 metres. It is a 'geo-economic group'. The next higher unit is the parish degree and this corresponds with the French *quartier* or *faubourg*. It finds its focus in its institutions and monuments, most commonly the church and/or the market place. It is not only a local economic community. It is above all a social group, in the sense that its participants share common institutions. This is why the term 'parish degree' is used by Bardet to define it, since the local church organization in the past has been its predominant unifying force. Its size ranges from 500 to 1,500 families. It has been called by Bardet a 'residential unit', a term which has been used by other scholars as an alternative to that of 'neighbourhood'.

3. The Neighbourhood Unit: A British Study

There are very few British studies of the socio-geographic structure of urban areas. A notable exception is Ruth Glass' work on Middlesbrough.[1] Its findings were as follows.

The neighbourhood has two distinct sets of characteristics and there is, at the outset, no guarantee that they are one and the same. One, as we noted above, is the idea of a territorial unit with common features of physical build and social characteristics of its inhabitants. The other is the idea of a territorial group whose members meet within their area for primary social activities and for both organized and spontaneous contacts.

The physical units in the first sense were defined from eight major indices and maps prepared of each. These were rateable values, age

[1] Ruth Glass, *The Social Background of a Plan: A Study of Middlesbrough*, London, 1953.

of buildings, type of housing, habitable rooms per dwelling, net population density, distribution of the Roman Catholic population (which is a very significant element in this town), births and infant deaths, and head infestations of school children. Four supplementary indices were added to these as checks. These when mapped were all found closely to correspond and 26 composite homogeneous areas were defined. Their boundaries were subsequently slightly modified in order to fit with the 133 small census enumeration districts for which data are available.

The territorial group in the second sense, that is, as a social unit in which the people are associated with each other in terms of social contacts and common institutions, is more difficult to examine and discover. For, in fact, such groups rarely exist. Indices are needed of primary social activities and social contacts within the area of a distinct territorial group as defined above. A series of relevant institutions were selected and located and their catchment areas defined as accurately as possible—elementary and secondary schools, youth and adult clubs, post offices, and shops. From these maps, answers can be found to the three questions: Do the catchment areas coincide? Do they correspond to the physical territorial units already defined? Are social activities concentrated within the areas of the territorial groups? The answers to all three questions were largely negative. The catchment areas of these institutions interlock so much that a generalized boundary could not be drawn, even for one set of institutions (e.g. youth clubs). The catchment areas were found to be widely divergent and the majority 'are completely blurred behind the screen of criss-cross catchment area lines'. Institutions located within a physical neighbourhood were located and their catchment areas mapped so that one could see inflows to the area and outflows from it. It was concluded that on the whole, social activities are dispersed, they are not carried out within the boundaries of distinct territorial groups.[1]

4. The Natural Area as a Planned Unit

The neighbourhood as a planned unit was first clearly expressed in the work of Clarence Perry, written in 1929 for the *Regional Plan of New York*. He wrote as follows.

'The formula for a city neighbourhood, then, must be such that when embodied in an actual development all its residents will be taken care of as respects the following points: they will all be within convenient access to an elementary school, adequate common play

[1] *Ibid.*, p. 25.

spaces, and retail shopping districts. Furthermore, their district will enjoy a distinctive character, because of qualities pertaining viably to its terrain and structure, not the least of which will be a reduced risk from vehicular accidents. . . .'[1]

The neighbourhood was defined by the Stephensons in their study of community centres as follows:

'Among the important things which make up a neighbourhood are, first of all, the houses in which people live and secondly, the various community buildings which they use. These latter consist of shops, cinemas, schools, churches, public houses, etc., which are to be found in a large or small degree at strategic points in any residential area. Such public and commercial buildings tend to group themselves together into some form of shopping or civic centre and to be patronized by the surrounding population. The radius from which people will come to them is decided by the density at which they are housed.'[2]

Further British definitions read as follows:

'It is in turn the social cell of the body of society, and as such the essential group from which emerge the developing folkways, modes and social institutions, the forms and rights of property and of government, the activities of work, of recreation and of learning, of religious ceremonies and beliefs, and of ministrations to the welfare of the community. The locality or neighbourhood group is likewise primary, along with the family, as a basic unit of social control. It is the first grouping next the family through which the individual is inducted into social life.'[3]

'Modern city life has spelled the breakdown of such personal relations. Neighbours, signifying intimate association, have been replaced by nigh-dwellers, this designating adjacent residence coupled with anonymity. While this is true of great cities it has also been shown to be true of smaller towns nearer to them.'[4]

'Although an entire system of government is based on the assumption of the locality group as the unit of representation and

[1] *The Neighbourhood Unit: A scheme of arrangement for the Family-Life Community*, The Regional Plan of New York and Environs, Vol. VII, Neighbourhood and Community Planning, New York, 1929.

[2] F. and G. Stephenson, *Community Centres*, Housing Centre, London, 1942, p. 42.

[3] W. Russell Tylor, 'The Neighbourhood Unit', in *Town Planning Review*, Vol. XVIII, 1939.

[4] *Ibid.*, and E. R. Roper-Power, 'The Social Structure of an English County Town', *Sociological Review*, Vol. XXIX, 1937, pp. 391–403.

REGIONS WITHIN THE CITY: THE NATURAL AREA

administration and that the people living in the same locality have enough interests in common that they may be relied upon to act together for their common welfare, the assumption turns out to be invalid for large cities. . . . We expect concerted action from people who are strangers to one another. Mobility, lack of home ownership, and social distance, all operate in the disappearance of the neighbourhood as an entity possessing social and political values.'[1]

This idea of the neighbourhood is that of an integrated social grouping. As we have seen with reference to rural areas, it refers to the smallest socio-geographic group of families beyond the individual family itself. It may exist in various forms, with varying degrees of strength or weakness, or may be absent, in the texture of an urban community. The smallest unit, that has been found frequently to exist in rural areas, contains some fifteen to thirty families and arises in response to the spontaneous 'neighbourliness' of people with respect to mutual aid or friendliness and association. Such groups occur very rarely in urban areas, and then usually in the longest occupied and poorest sections of the population. The socio-geographic groups in urban areas occur at higher levels and it is this larger group, with 5,000 to 10,000 people, that is usually but erroneously referred to as a neighbourhood. The term community area is more appropriate.

The nature of such a grouping depends on common social relations on the one hand and common use of particular institutions on the other hand. The share of families in such groupings varies, and areas cannot be defined by lines but simply by frequency of association on a house to house basis. Such associations have been fundamental features of the organization of urban communities from the earliest times. The development and planning of such groups was inherent to the structure of the historic city in Europe. It is reflected, for instance, in the institution of the parish and the parish church in a town, by the establishment in the Middle Ages in continental Europe of self-contained and self-governing towns with a few thousand inhabitants each as twin or triplet settlements separated from each other by a wall and gates each with its own plan, institutions, and ground plan. The historic town in this sense was in social and physical proportion. The growth of the nineteenth century upset this situation. While districts are similar in respect to buildings and general characteristics of the people, their social ties and orientations to shop and institution are usually rather widely dispersed.

While the neighbourhood concept has been generally recognized

[1] W. Russell Tylor, *op. cit.*

in principle, it has been neglected in modern housing. The idea persists, however, in the practice of town planners. As stated by Perry in 1929, the general objective is to provide for areas of the order of the neighbourhood based primarily, as a yardstick, on the population needed to support an elementary school in an area that shall be enclosed by traffic arteries so as to have the minimum interference with local traffic and pedestrian movements. It appeared as a basic principle in the *County of London Plan* which proposed to plan on the basis of the existing 'natural (as opposed to the planned) use zoning and community structure'.

In the inner residential areas of London, community areas can often be traced back to their nuclei at important road junctions, or to the original villages, while their limits have often been determined by physical features such as railways, canals, or by industry. These larger communities, such as Finsbury, Lambeth, and Eltham, include smaller neighbourhood units, some well equipped, others lacking suitably located shopping, school, and other communal facilities. More recent housing developments in particular lack such facilities. The residential communities form three fairly distinct groupings. The West Central Group is situated around the West End or comes within its sphere of influence. It is affected by the invasion of the uses of the central area and has a high proportion of large town houses and new blocks of flats, and much property of several storeys let off as flats to small families. The East Central Group, which includes the main areas for reconstruction, comprises the East End, Camden Town, and Kentish Town and the districts on the low-lying ground in the south bank of the Thames. These contain the main areas of slum, obsolescent property and overcrowding, with a profuse 'peppering' of factories. The Suburban Group includes the communities of recent development in which further development requires careful pre-planning so as to prevent ribbon growth along arterial roads, and to preserve open spaces between the community areas. The proposal in the Plan was

'to emphasize the identity of the existing communities, to increase their degree of segregation, and where necessary, to reorganize them as separate and definite entities. The aim would be to provide each community with its own schools, public buildings, shops, open spaces, etc. At the same time care would be taken . . . (not) to endanger the sense of interdependence on the adjoining communities or on London as a whole.'[1]

After very careful consideration, it was decided that the elementary school should be the determining factor in the size and organization

[1] J. H. Forshaw and P. Abercrombie, *County of London Plan*, 1943, p. 28.

of the subsidiary or neighbourhood units of these communities in which large-scale reconstruction was proposed,[1] so as to ensure a maximum walking distance from home to school.

The principle is again evident in a recent report of the Transportation Survey in Chicago. The term neighbourhood or community is here replaced by the other aspect of the concept—a traffic island. This is envisaged as a 'module' of land use in which the building blocks shall be free of traffic and designed mainly from the viewpoint of land use and pedestrian traffic. It would be bounded by main traffic routes. The size of the area will be determined by the size of the elementary school and the density of housing that supports the school, by the arrangement of the street plan, and by the maintenance of a uniform size. The size based on the demands of the school would be about 5,000 (the size accepted hitherto by planners). At suburban densities of housing this will require an area of one square mile. In the densely built inner areas a school will need 9,000 people and, at 25 families per acre, a size of a quarter mile square. These enclosed traffic islands are the neighbourhood groups and they would be the major determinants of the spacing of traffic highways.

The same investigators went a step further by examining the actual pattern of wider community relations—school districts, travel patterns, and social groupings. These revealed 'community areas' in the order of 30,000 to 100,000 people. These were found to be more clearly developed in the suburban areas than in the centre. 'As the urban area grows, it appears that these communities tend to merge and lose their former sharp identity.' There is also strong evidence that the functions of school, shopping, government, and social groupings rarely are co-terminous in the Chicago area, but have overlapping 'trade areas'. Consequently such areas cannot be considered as factors in the spacing of new expressways, but the latter should be designed so as not to damage these individual trade areas.[2] More study on these lines would be extremely rewarding. Traits of spatial unity in areas that are to be demolished could and probably should be preserved in the wholesale shift and resettlement of people from the same locality to a new housing area elsewhere.

It is well known that the planners of new suburbs and towns seek to group houses and institutions in such a way as to permit their occupants to enjoy the social and economic amenities of group living. Hence the ideas of the neighbourhood with the group of shops and institutions, and of the residential court around a central green for

[1] *Ibid.*, p. 28.
[2] *Chicago Area Transportation Survey*, Vol. III, Transportation Plan, April 1962, Chicago.

the small 'face-to-face group'. Some remarkable features are revealed in William H. Whyte's study of the new Park Forest community some 30 miles south of Chicago.[1] Some areas are laid out on 60 × 125 feet plots in curved super-blocks and surrounding a green court. Park Foresters like to call this a social laboratory. Whyte prefers to call it a natural environment.

'Perhaps not since the medieval town have there been neighbourhood units so well adapted to the predilection and social needs of its people. In many ways, indeed, the courts are physically remarkably similar to the workers' housing of the fifteenth century. Like the Fugger house still standing in Augsburg, the courts are essentially groups of houses two rooms deep, bound together by lines of interior communication, and the parking bay unifies the whole very much as did the water fountain of the Fugger houses.'[2]

There are certain cause and effect relationships between the kind of physical lay-out (of which there are many variants in the 105 courts) and the social characteristics and habits of their occupants. Inhabitants of one court tend to take on a particular character. Church leaders tended to be segregated on one court or another rather than being generally dispersed. The same held good for members of certain churches, voting records, group parties (especially where the lay-out encouraged neighbourliness). The character of a neighbourhood develops within months, whereas that of a town, in generations. It is closely associated with the people who first settle in it, when co-operation in many simple but vital ways help people to get to know and help each other. The court becomes a 'hothouse of participation' and the newcomers are absorbed—or else they dislike it and move out. Common hobbies and parties and interests, and even distinct words and phrases, develop.

These comments apply to the court neighbourhood as a whole. There are differences within them, and such differences are closely related to the physical lay-out of the homes and their gardens and their back and front doors. This was checked by an exhaustive survey of the friendship patterns, interests, and backgrounds of all forty-four couples on one court. These were mapped and repetitive patterns and associations were discovered to be intimately related to the physical lay-out of the houses to each other. 'Wherever areas have common design characteristics—such as a cul-de-sac road— the friendship groupings also tend to be similar.' Such groupings were based partly upon participation in parties, which in American

[1] W. H. Whyte, *The Organization Man*, Doubleday Anchor Book, 1956.
[2] *Ibid.*, p. 367.

life are held frequently for children and adults. These spatial relationships were so consistent as 'almost to seem like laws' and were as important in governing behaviour as the desires of the individuals in them. Much of this grows from the habits of the children. A main thoroughfare is a social barrier, a children's play area (where children are exercised by their parents) is a social bond. The location of a house (and its relation to the others in a series) determines your closest contacts—'it also virtually determines how popular you will be'. Social contacts and social traffic develop normally via the front door and not the back that opens out on to the individual yard. Social barriers are drawn as imaginary lines in courts to limit the circle of contacts.

Happiness for the American suburbanite can apparently be virtually guaranteed by physical lay-out! The individual couple, be they introverts or extraverts, can be advised to choose a house in the court which will cater for their type and desires. The people living in these courts are fully aware of what is going on. They like it and thrive on it. If not, they move out. But there is little private life. This is a most interesting investigation of the relations between physical lay-out and social life. Planning on the group principle is admirably adapted to those who thrive on 'togetherness'. It is appalling for those who do not and prefer some privacy of living and routine.

5. INSTITUTIONS AND SERVICE AREAS

Community groupings in the city are effected through service institutions. The distribution and grouping of service institutions in urban areas are determined by the same basic factors as for service centres over the countryside. They depend upon the same principles of centrality. In the urban area these services may be classed broadly, from the standpoint of their clientele, as regional, city-wide, district, and local or neighbourhood services. The chapel, the club, the public-house, the small retail shop catering for immediate everyday requirements, and, above all, the elementary school, tend to be scattered about the residential areas without segregation, although local clusters may occur at street junctions, or, as in the case of shops, along main roads. 'Neighbourhood shops repel, city shops attract, one another.'[1] The elementary school, in particular, should be located, though it very often is not, so as to be within about ten minutes from the homes of its pupils without their having to cross any dangerous main thoroughfares. Above these local services there are those of a higher order, which the consumer requires occasionally

[1] W. William-Olsson, 'Stockholm: Its Structure and Development', *Geographical Review*, Vol. XXX, 1940, pp. 420–38.

THE STRUCTURE OF THE CITY

and with a wider choice, and for which the maintenance of the institution, in view of its more specialized character, demands access to a larger clientele. Such services tend to segregate, normally at fairly regular intervals in the residential districts of the middle zone, though they are fewer and inadequate in the newer suburban areas. In the former, they are found at strategic road crossings and there are often old town or village centres with a parish church near by. In the American city, the 'bright light areas', as they are called, are situated at regular intervals of about a mile at road crossings in the rectangular network of the street pattern. Here are banks and offices, multiple shops, cafes, cinemas, and so on. Above these again are the biggest and most exclusive concerns in all these categories; these are located in the central business zone. The big department stores, newspaper offices, banks and offices, including city and regional head offices, concert halls and theatres, civic buildings and wholesale concerns all compete for space. There is a marked tendency for the central shopping area to shift in the direction of the better-class residential districts, as in the case of South Kensington in London; and for more popular shops not merely to be segregated in separate streets, but to cluster near the centre on the side of the working-class districts. Many instances are found in American cities where the expansion and shift of the central city or down-town district can be clearly traced within the last generation.

In a separate category must be placed special services that are essential to the civic life but are not in everyday demand. Such are the civic buildings, the university and technical schools, hospitals, and museums. Accessibility, plenty of space, and seclusion are the requirements of such buildings. In Britain, as is well known, most of them were built in the latter half of the nineteenth century, and they are in consequence situated in what is now the dilapidated middle zone. In continental cities, on the other hand, such buildings are clustered together in a district near to the city centre but secluded from it. Such an arrangement of precincts has also been achieved in the building of American cities during the last twenty years. In Britain, the regrouping and rebuilding of public buildings is a matter for future planning.

The location and size of all these service institutions depend upon the density of population, the social character, and the standard of living of the areas they serve. Private bodies, which control, for example, cinema and theatre circuits, multiple shops, restaurants and offices, and public bodies, which must allocate space for commercial premises and public buildings, should have thorough information on the relation of these institutions, in size, staff and capacity, to the density of population and its social structure. In

REGIONS WITHIN THE CITY: THE NATURAL AREA

the United States large sums of money have been spent in the detailed mapping of cities, showing such data as the density of population, income levels, and social make-up, upon which basis commercial centres and individual concerns may be rationally sited. Surveys and estimates of the purpose and capacity of the individual concern—whether it be the capacity of a super-market, an elementary school, a clinic, cinema, or a bank—should form the basis of rational planning in our cities. Numerous services in the old middle zone are redundant and should be more rationally distributed. On what principles must this be done and what shall be the relation between the distribution of such services and the future distribution of population? Detailed maps of an urban area can indicate which areas are inadequately served, the nature and volume of the demand for a service, and the best site on which to establish the buildings to perform the service. In the building of new residential areas and community centres, such matters must be considered jointly as part of the problem of build and lay-out of the planner and architect.

The lack of accord between the distribution of services and the distribution of population brought about by the rapid outward expansion of the urban area is well known. One of the main problems of planning is to remedy this. The great concentration of public-houses in the centre and the older districts around it and their virtual absence in the outer, newly built-up areas, has been shown convincingly in a map prepared by the Hull Regional Survey group. This applies to most other service institutions. The church may be taken as an example. As has been pointed out,[1] the church in the centre of a growing city can do one of three things—and this applies equally to any kind of service institution: it can follow its congregation to a different part of the city; remain in the same locality and draw on its old visitors who are scattered in various parts of the city; or endeavour to maintain and build up a congregation from its parish, though its population may indeed be quite inadequate to support it. This is the problem before many British churches in areas of slum clearance. A church, however, in this country, is usually a historic edifice which cannot be moved. It may be changed to meet the needs of a new community, or the building may be put to other uses, such as a warehouse or a community centre. Many a church in English towns stands isolated in the midst of a slum clearance area; its houses razed to the ground and their people transferred elsewhere. New churches of all denominations and of little architectural merit are built in the new residential areas, but naturally they are late in appearing and meanwhile there is absent

[1] H. P. Douglass, *The St. Louis Church Survey*, 1924, p. 76, quoted by Gist and Halbert, *op. cit.*, p. 166.

one of the chief integrating forces of community life. In the United States, where there is less sentimental attachment to historic buildings, the churches move outwards, quickly adjusting their location to population movements. In St. Louis, Douglass found that churches moved consistently westward with the expansion of the city from the old town centre. One Protestant church was rebuilt three times, moving four blocks in 1850, twelve blocks in 1890, and two and a half miles in 1912. Many Jewish churches have moved out to the west side in Chicago, and in Minneapolis there has been a 'retreat before the expanding business buildings and a pursuit of the retreating residential districts'.[1]

6. COMMERCIAL CENTRES IN THE URBAN AREA

This section is concerned with the nature and distribution of commercial, that is, primarily, retail trade, activities.

In a recent study of commercial centres in Zurich, Switzerland,[2] Hans Carol equates the commercial centres of an urban area with the hierarchy of urban centres in general. Zurich has a little less than 500,000 inhabitants on an area of 38 square miles in which there are 26 municipalities. Carol recognizes four types of commercial centre—the local business district, the neighbourhood business district, the regional business district, and the central business district. These he equates with the village in Switzerland (hamlet in the United States); the market centre in Switzerland and Germany and the 'village' as described by Brush in Wisconsin; the town in Switzerland (Christaller's *Bezirksort*, the 'town' in the United States); and the metropolis (Zurich, equated with Chicago). The neighbourhood centre was found to supply and service the goods in regular demand—jewellery (cheaper variety), photography, electrical equipment, hardware, bicycle stores, flowers, drugs, pharmacy, tobacconists, shoes, post office, and doctor. It serves a population of 5,000 to 10,000 people and there are 20 such centres in the city area. The regional business district supplies services of 'middle order' for its own neighbourhood as well as the surrounding neighbourhoods and serves a population of about 60,000 plus a varied wider umland with 30,000 giving a grand total of about 100,000. It has a greater variety and number of services than the neighbourhood centre. There are 15 such districts in the city. The central business district serves the whole city and its umland for middle and higher

[1] Calvin F. Schmid, *Social Saga of Two Cities*, Minneapolis Council of Social Agencies, 1937, p. 51.
[2] H. Carol, 'The Hierarchy of Central Functions Within the City', *Annals of the Ass. of Am. Geog.*, Vol. 50, No. 4, 1960, pp. 419–38.

REGIONS WITHIN THE CITY: THE NATURAL AREA

order services, and its metropolitan services cover the whole of Switzerland.

The same characteristic was recognized by Malcolm Proudfoot in a study of the retail centres of Philadelphia (1937). He wrote as follows:

'The retail structure of many principal cities shows a progressive change in type as follows:

1. The *central business district* has a marked concentration of shopping-goods stores, which serve a substantial proportion of the commodity wants of every city family and which are located within that focal area of intra-city transportation collectively most accessible to the entire city population.

2. The *outlying business centre*, in miniature form is well-nigh identical to the central business district in concentration and in kind of outlet and in transportation accessibility and is distinguished by having a more restricted customer tributary area and by the presence of a greater mixture of convenience-goods stores.

3. The *principal business thoroughfare* is characterized by heavy mass and vehicular traffic between the central business district and outlying residential areas and by shopping and convenience-goods stores catering to and principally dependent on customers derived from its heavy traffic.

4. The *neighbourhood business street* is characterized by dispersed rows of convenience-goods stores within densely settled residential areas, and by having a customer tributary area restricted, for the most part, to within easy walking distance.

5. The *isolated store cluster* is characterized by non-competitive convenience-goods stores grouped to serve the immediate wants of families within an area restricted to easy walking distance.'[1]

This study is based upon a detailed survey of the city of Philadelphia, and is dated from the middle thirties. The scheme is clearly based on a hierarchical concept of the functions of the centres in relation to the extent of their tributary areas.

Since the thirties in the United States there has been a tremendous growth of population outside the reaches of mass transport, depending on the private automobile. Houses in the country depend on septic tanks, private water, and sewerage disposal systems, since they lie beyond the reach of the city utility systems. To serve these areas as well as the greatly expanded rural-urban fringe an entirely new type of shopping centre has come into being. This provides extensive parking facilities for thousands of cars, grouped around a 'mall' so as to eliminate the long walks that would be involved by a 'linear' arrangement.

[1] M. Proudfoot, in Mayer and Kohn, *op. cit.*, p. 397.

THE STRUCTURE OF THE CITY

These new centres are classed by Homer Hoyt[1] into the following categories, that will be particularly interesting to British readers:

'1. Large regional shopping centres with a major department store with over 100,000 square feet of store area covering a total area of 35 to 100 acres. There were 60 such centres in May 1957. The largest of these (over 250,000 square feet) need over 200,000 people to support them.

2. Large neighbourhood centres with a junior department store covering 25,000 to 40,000 square feet and a site of 15 to 40 acres. There was a total of 120 such centres in 1957.

3. Large neighbourhood centres with a variety store or family clothing store of 10,000 to 20,000 square feet and covering 10 to 20 acres. There are probably over a thousand such centres.

4. Small neighbourhood centres, with a supermarket, of 10,000 to 20,000 square feet plus a drug store, hardware store, and "convenience-goods" site of 5 to 20 acres. The number of such centres is not specified, but they are very numerous and for the country as a whole probably run into several thousands.'

The redistribution of population around the cities is going on so fast that there is no doubt that these centres will increase greatly in number and service. Since practically all of the increase of population in the sixties will be concentrated in the fringe areas, it may be expected that new retail centres will emerge and the function of the central business district will change. Moreover, the new centres will be placed at strategic points among the far-flung residential population rather than simply on the edges of the old cities. The growth of outlying shopping centres had repercussions on the central business districts in the fifties. Prior to 1920 over 90 per cent. of the business of all department stores was done in the central business districts. By 1948 this was 70 per cent. in 44 of the largest cities. By 1954 this had fallen to 60 per cent. Today there is no doubt that over a half of the department stores' sales is in the outlying shopping centres rather than in the central business districts.

The growth of shopping centres far out in the urban–rural fringe and beyond will continue in the sixties. Looking to the future of shopping centres Hoyt writes as follows:

'After the present wave of shopping-centre building has passed its crest, there may be a slight lull, but the resumption of the suburban boom in the decade of the 1960's, when the children born

[1] Homer Hoyt, 'Classification and Significant Characteristics of Shopping Centres', in *Appraisal Journal*, April 1958, reproduced in Mayer and Kohn, *op. cit.*, pp. 454–61.

REGIONS WITHIN THE CITY: THE NATURAL AREA

before, during, and after World War II must reach marriageable age, will start a new surge of shopping-centre building.

'The new federal highway pattern, with limited-access roads between major cities and belt highways around cities, will be the primary factor in locating the regional centres of the 1960's. Instead of building centres on the edge of the old cities as the first shopping-centre promoters did ten years ago, the new centres will be located at a central point between a number of large and small cities like Allied Stores North Shore Centre at Peabody, Massachusetts, 20 miles north of Boston, which can tap a population of 1,500,000 living in numerous towns, cities, and villages by means of the Belt Highway, and connecting roads, aptly termed "women's roads" because they are free from the congestion of through traffic.'

Several points of importance may be noted in the development of these centres. In general, they are still primarily shopping centres. There are not yet, in general, many business offices. The largest have branches of the finest department stores as well as large new movies and first-class restaurants. They are depriving the central business districts of much of their business and as one head of a big department store in downtown Los Angeles has said: 'If you can't beat 'em, join 'em.' So they move out to the periphery. This undoubtedly is relieving both pedestrian and traffic congestion in the centres. There are many people in the suburbs of cities with only 250,000 who rarely go 'downtown' except for a concert or a public function. The same trend is evident on the Continent, especially in the cities of Germany, that have been so extensively reconstructed. It is also apparent in the growth of post-war Stockholm. On the other hand, in Britain, conditions outside London are in general as they were before the war. There are few first-class shopping centres outside the cities with good stores, cinemas, spacious lay-out, and freedom from vehicular traffic. These amenities on a small scale will be found in the New Towns. But the New Town is a centre for a population less than the equivalent of the first-class centres noted above. Such a centre, as at Welwyn Garden City, for example, serves a population of some 25,000 people only. The provincial industrial cities in Britain are not only disastrously short of hygienic modern housing. They are so short of regional shopping centres (as opposed to groups of a few private neighbourhood stores) that, although the people 'have never had it so good', they swarm into the central business districts, especially on Saturday for the weekly 'blow out', as a change from the drabness of their home surroundings. They come to 'look' not merely to buy. The cities are crowded with pedestrians in the streets and in the stores to a degree that, together with the congestion of automobile traffic, is making movement and service in the central city during rush hours wellnigh impossible. The fact of the matter is that the shopping patterns of British cities emerged in the late Victorian and Edwardian era and have changed very little since World War I. In the provincial cities there is hardly a hierarchy of centres as Carol and Proudfoot have indicated. There is a large gap between the central business district and the many small clusters of a few private stores serving a local clientele, and the miserable shoestrings of tiny stores that line the main streets through the late nineteenth-century housing areas.

There are signs, however, that the regional shopping centre is arriving in England. The first planned regional shopping centre was being discussed in November of 1961 for Watford, 15 miles outside London. It will aim at transforming 'the shopping geography of the whole area', on lines that are avowedly following the American experience with parking facilities for a thousand cars. It is of interest that the leading figure in this plan is chairman of a big department store that will establish a branch as a nucleus of this development. It is to be called 'Shoppers World'. This trend, it is pointed out, is not entirely new—but, we would add, it is rare indeed, especially in the provinces. The centre planned for Watford will be the first unit built entirely anew exclusively for the purpose of shopping.[1] It will probably serve an aggregate of 50,000 to 100,000 people. There is another case of a department store in central Manchester that shifted to the outer suburbs of the city (Wilmslow) with a parking area for 800 cars. Several other shopping centres are under consideration or being built around London. The existing shopping facilities of the New Towns for 15,000 to 50,000 indicate the kind of centres in considerable numbers that are needed in the outer zones of our provincial cities to relieve traffic congestion and to make life more worth living.

The supermarket has made its debut in England and appears to be gathering momentum. It remains to be seen whether these concerns will choose sites on the suburban outskirts rather than in the middle zone. It must be admitted that the question of access is vital, since shoppers come to shop by bus and a minority by car. It is clear that, with the turnover needs of such a store in mind, careful appraisals should be made of the density and purchasing power and buying habits of the population and the access of the store to an adequate catchment area. A number of geographers in the United States have applied their skills to this task. A whole number of the periodical *Economic Geography*[2] was recently devoted to this kind

[1] *Observer*, 19 November 1961.
[2] *Economic Geography*, Worcester, Mass., Vol. 37, No. 1, January 1961.

of market analysis. This is a problem for applied geography. The recent (1963) decision of a Canadian firm to establish up to 5,000 super-markets in Britain indicates the scope of this need.

The service centres of Greater London have recently been the subject of a thorough analysis as an aid to the royal commission in the redefinition of the local government areas of the London area (p. 486).[1] The status of the service centres was determined from three sets of evidence—a preliminary selection of centres (on which a first basic list of 200 centres was drawn up) from banking, shopping facilities (chain stores, etc.), and entertainment; a second evaluation based on the rateable value of the main chain stores; and a third evaluation based on the frequency of bus services at each centre, as a measure of the degree to which the facilities of the centre are actually used. Carruthers then graded the centres by assessment of these three sets of criteria on similar lines to the studies of the hierarchy of centres for England and Wales, with, it would appear, broadly similar results in the hierarchy of centres. The highest—first and second order—functions (of the metropolis and the provincial capital) are both assumed to be located in central London. The major suburban centres fall into what is called a third order and these again are arranged into three subdivisions of decreasing importance, *a*, *b*, and *c*. They total about 60. Another 40 at the next lower level—fourth-order category—are included. In all, these total about 100 out of the basic list of 200. The remaining 100 are excluded since they are not of direct concern to the problem of defining new administrative units with a minimum population of some 200,000. These third-order centres seem to be broadly comparable with provincial cities of the same order, such as Bedford, Ipswich, or Boston (Fig. 84, p. 323). They are rather regularly distributed and, if their service areas are arbitrarily defined as the area more accessible to one centre than to surrounding centres of the same order, then the population of all 54 third-order centres ranges from 100,000 to 200,000. The 30 chief third-order centres form two rings. One is an inner ring of older centres that have lost some importance owing to the decrease of population in their service areas. The other is an outer ring in the suburban areas, serving extensive outlying sectors. In inner London there is a large number of smaller centres (not graded here) strung along the main highways. The 40 smaller 4*a* centres are particularly active in the outer suburban areas, serving districts that are too far from the main service centres

---

[1] W. I. Carruthers, 'Service Centres in Greater London', *Town Planning Review*, Vol. XXXIII, No. 1, 1962, pp. 5–31. See also A. E. Smailes and G. Hartley, 'Shopping Centres in the Greater London Area', *Inst. of Brit. Geog.*, Publication No. 29, 1961, pp. 201–13.

to be effectively reached by them. It is suggested by Carruthers that the outlying principal suburban service centres could be further developed both as service centres (though they will require more provision of parking precincts) and as sites for office buildings that could be removed from central London.

7. Commercial Centres in the San Francisco Area.[1]

Down to World War I there were three central business districts in the Bay Area, San Francisco, Oakland, and San Jose. Each served a distinct area and was the focus of a close network of street car routes. A number of local shopping centres came into being as residential development spread into the Berkeley Hills. Berkeley developed as a centre for the sale of perishable foods, dry goods, and stock clothing. This pattern was reproduced in a number of other places in the Bay Area at the junction of local street car routes and at more important stations on the railroad routes south of San Francisco in the Peninsula. There were many such units but they were usually small, though the range of goods was small and they depended on 'restricted local support'. The present super-market combines the goods of at least six stores of 1900. Isolated store clusters and individual stores were widespread, primarily for the selling of goods, owing to the absence of mechanical refrigeration. This is still essentially the situation in British towns.

Changes since World War I have been revolutionary in the vast expansion of new residential areas where new factors of location were able to operate. These new factors are associated above all else with the advent of the automobile that has completely replaced the street car and outstripped the bus. The new factors are as follows: first, population has decreased in the central city; second, new housing has located in extensive residential districts without any pre-existing commercial centres; third, increased distance of the new residential districts from the central business districts; fourth, new residential districts were not strategically located with regard to the lines of mass transport and consequently they depended almost entirely on the private automobile; fifth, the new districts were normally provided with 'neighbourhood' stores similar to the staple goods stores in the pre-war towns. What was needed was a projection of the mass selling facilities of the department stores of the central

---

[1] This material is drawn from an article by Mr. James Vance of the Department of Geography, University of California, Berkeley. It is published in the *Proceedings of the I.G.U. Symposium in Urban Geography, Lund, 1960*, ed. by Knut Norborg, Lund, 1962, pp. 485–518.

business districts to districts that were too far removed from the core to use its regular facilities. From 1945 to 1950 there was thus a 'disequilibrium' in the provision of shopping services in these outer districts and it was not until after 1950 that the big downtown department stores and other retail sales outlets began to establish themselves in new regional shopping centres. This shift is reflected in the data of retail sales for 1948 to 1954. In this period the Bay Area increased its population by 53·3 per cent., but the value of retail sales of San Francisco remained unchanged, and its share decreased from 18 to 14 per cent. of the total sales of the metropolitan district. Oakland recorded a loss also, and only San Jose (at the southern end of the Bay Area) showed an increase since it was serving as the centre for the rapidly growing Santa Clara valley to the south of it. The post-war commercial growth of sales has obviously been almost entirely peripheral, and this is especially true of the department stores.

Before the end of World War II there were no integrated regional shopping centres in the Bay Area. Mass selling of goods in the fifties has concentrated in new regional shopping centres and larger community centres. There are 11 definite regional shopping centres, plus 10 lesser community shopping centres, and other business districts. Their spheres of influence were determined from a sample of registration number plates of cars in the parking areas associated with these centres. It was found that in these 21 centres there were 18 department stores' branches with aggregate sales of $130 million, a total equivalent to the sales of department stores in the central business district of San Francisco and Oakland combined. Sharply contrasted with this vast increase of sales is the narrowing of their service basis. In all the regional centres about two-thirds of the customers come from within a tributary area of 4·5 to 5·5 miles and a narrower radius is found in the older non-integrated business centres in outlying areas. This 'equilibrium of location' is reflected in the distribution of these centres that have a median spacing of 9 miles apart. The fact that about half of the customers on the average come from within 3 miles of the centre indicates the closely knit character of the sales areas and the need for a firm to ensure in its mass selling the full patronage of its closely adjacent population—otherwise the store would not pay. 'The core draws widely but selectively, whereas the shopping centre draws narrowly, but necessarily as completely as possible.'

A survey of all the integrated shopping centres (as opposed to the central business districts) in the Bay reveals a total of 145 of which 11 are regional centres, 15 community centres, and 124 neighbourhood centres. There were 9 central business districts in which only 40 per cent. of the total floor space is in retail and service uses as compared with over 95 per cent. in the 145 outlying centres. In the latter, food stores are more important, but household goods space is less than in the central business districts. In the 11 regional centres department stores account for 45 per cent. of all the space, and variety and drug stores for 13 per cent., i.e. mass selling lines. High-style clothing and non-durable household goods are found exclusively in the central business districts. Food stores are far less important (11 per cent.) in the regional centres than in the outlying centres.

Thus, the growth of regional shopping centres, effecting the dispersion of mass-selling of goods, is having its repercussions on the functions and structure of the core. This has already shed much of its retail function and is becoming more a centre for speciality goods and office space. In turn, the regional integrated centre has become the mass-seller to the individual suburb alone, with no other important function.

8. The Structure of the Central Business District[1]

The central business district, or the C.B.D. as it is called in the United States, is the core of the city in which those activities are segregated that seek a central '100 per cent. location' in order effectively to serve and to be accessible to the whole of the city and its region. It has grown in effect over the past hundred years and particularly over the last fifty years, though the tempo of growth varies from one city to another. It is marked by the clustering of stores, offices, governmental buildings, hotels, theatres and restaurants, rail and bus terminals, etc. It has a relatively rapid rate of growth and change in its buildings which have great heterogeneity as to style, function, frontage, and height, ranging from the late medieval to the ultra-modern. It is a hive of people and vehicles in the day and, in its business sectors, is normally deserted at night. It is the focus of daily tidal rhythms of passenger and goods traffic. The skyscraper and the slum are its extremes. It reflects the demands and the rate of growth of the city it serves. It is undergoing significant changes in its function and buildings as the nature of the contemporary city changes. It is growing upwards and outwards. It certainly contains functions that are emphatically central in nature. But it

[1] R. E. Murphy and J. E. Vance, 'Delimiting the C.B.D.', *Economic Geography*, Vol. XXX, 1954, pp. 189–222, reproduced in Mayer and Kohn, *op. cit.*, pp. 418–446. See also W. Firey, *Land Use in Central Boston*, Harvard Sociological Studies, No. 4, Harvard University Press, 1947; John Rannells, *The Core of the City*, Institute of Urban Land Use and Housing Studies, Columbia University Press, 1956.

REGIONS WITHIN THE CITY: THE NATURAL AREA

harbours many activities that are ancillary services or even vestigial remnants from the past, and many of its activities, such as office establishments, could as well be located elsewhere. This area needs to be understood as to its location, growth and extent, and the changing processes that shape it.

Generalizing from their analysis of nine smaller cities in the United States, Murphy and Vance draw certain conclusions regarding the structure and dynamics of the central business district. The tallest buildings and the greatest pedestrian traffic occur somewhere near the centre of it, and less intensely used land grades away from this centre. Moreover, there is a universal tendency for similar kinds of uses to segregate within the district—retail stores, theatres, banks and insurance, and other business houses. The central business district is also in constant process of change. Its main growth took place in Britain in the late Victorian and the Edwardian days down to the outbreak of World War I. Subsequently, there came a period of general stagnation and very few new buildings appeared, so that the buildings of the 'downtown' district of any city in Britain are essentially a reflection of this Victorian era of growth, though there are, of course, some clearances of old buildings and replacement by new office buildings or stores. In America similarly there was a great era of rapid growth of business and building in the last decades of the nineteenth century. The skyscraper became *à la mode* in the thirties not only in the major cities but in every city throughout the Union. A period of stagnation occurred in the days of the depression and then during World War II. In the last ten years, however, there has been a remarkable transformation of the C.B.D. and the next decade will carry this process much further.

A further feature is that the process of functional and physical growth has resulted in both the upward and the lateral growth of the buildings in the C.B.D. Uses have shifted. They have invaded certain areas through extension or overspilling beyond the limits of the C.B.D.; while they have moved away from other areas, which tend to form zones of deterioration with a distinct assembly of low-grade uses.

Underlying this whole process of internal differentiation are several controlling factors. The most important is land values. These were found by Murphy to range down to 5 per cent. of the peak value in the heart of the central business district. This 5 per cent. line closely corresponded with the limit of the central business district as defined by use. In every case it was found that the peak value intersection lay within a few hundred feet of the centre of the central business district. It is also the point with the maximum pedestrian and vehicular traffic.

THE STRUCTURE OF THE CITY

The zone of advance of the central business district is described by Murphy as the 'zone of assimilation' and the zone of retreat as the 'zone of discard'. The central business district tends to extend towards the best residential districts. This may be due either to the positive attraction of the latter, or alternatively to the repulsion from undesirable railroad and wholesaling sectors. In the zone of expansion or assimilation residential areas are invaded by shops, automobile showrooms, drive-in-banks, offices, and newer hotels. At the opposite end of the central business district, directly opposite as a rule to the zone of expansion, is the zone of discard. Here one finds 'pawn shops, family clothing stores, bars, low-grade restaurants, bus stations, cheap movies, credit jewellery, clothing and furniture stores'.

There are several important features about the structure of the central business district that are almost completely ignored by American studies of this subject. The extent and structure of the central business district must be based upon a strict definition of what its distinctive functions are. These functions are those that serve the whole of the city area as well as the tributary region, and indeed the state and the nation. It is for this reason that they are located centrally together. Pawn shops and the like found in the 'zone of discard', however, do not normally draw their clientele from the whole of a city and its environs. They cater to the localized community in which they are situated. In other words, these residential areas (if they may be so called) are more or less dependent or parasitic upon the central business district and are inevitably closely associated with it in many ways. Such are Hobohemia, rooming house areas, and Chinatown. Areas of segregation of undesirable uses and activities may well be located in either the zone of advance or the zone of retreat, both of which are zones of deterioration.

A second point is even more important to the changing structure of the central business district. Many centralized services, that seek a central position accessible to the whole urban area, need not be in the central business district and, in fact, find their best sites outside it. Thus, in America one finds new hotels built on the outskirts or right outside the main central business district, situated on favourable sites—such as the Lake Shore front in Chicago or the site of the Fairmount and Mark Hopkins hotels on Nob Hill in San Francisco. There are many such cases in American cities of hotels built in recent decades. Further, many public buildings, though they need to be in the city, do not need to be located in the hurry, bustle, and congestion of the centre. Museums and civic buildings come into this category and many such are now built well outside the main limits of the central business district.

Finally, the centralized commercial properties are often located right outside the recognized central business district, usually on a wide thoroughfare that offers both space and accessibility from outside. One of the trends in European cities in the past has been the shift of the central business district and public buildings to the wide boulevards erected on the site of the earlier fortifications. Fine examples of this are the *Ring* in Vienna and Cologne, and there are many others. More recently, with the need for access and parking space, this trend is now found on new thoroughfares with the increasing use of vehicular traffic. In San Francisco, for example, the main central business district has extended northwards from Market Street. In recent decades hotels have clustered around Nob Hill. The new civic centre is to the west of the central business district, situated at the junction of Market Street (north-west–south-east from the (old) Ferry Building) and Van Ness Street, which runs from south to north to a dead-end against the area of the Presidio (reserved for the use of the army). Van Ness Street has developed rapidly as a main business thoroughfare and as a segregation of luxury motels and new hotels. Although the city planners of San Francisco seek to have the central business district expanded eastwards to the wholesale and light industrial area between it and the Embarcadero, the most natural trend, that is at present going on, would be for the centralized uses to invade the area to the west, in the wedge between Van Ness and the central business district at the apex of which the civic centre is located. The centralized activities that have clustered to form the central business district are actually expanding over a much wider area than the conventional definition of the central business district. This is likely to be a continuous new trend in city development in America and Europe during the coming decades.

This brings us to a final comment on the definition of the central business district by Murphy and Vance. It is much too narrow. The centralized services—that is, the services that cater to the whole of a city and its region and hence require ease of accessibility with a minimum of friction—are much more varied than the narrowly defined 'business activities'. Even the latter need precise definition in terms of their degree of centrality. Many shops, gas stations, and restaurants, located in sections of the central business district and on its margins, serve the clientele of the environs, be they in a Hobohemia or a Chinatown or a North Beach. Many services such as barber shops and the like in the central business district presumably cater to the regular business personnel. More important, there is little justification for the limitation of the uses of the central business district to retail and office buildings in which there is a 'profit motive'.

This excludes wholesaling (that, it is claimed, depends on transport media rather than the pull of centrality), and certain factories and residential units, since 'though represented in the central business district (they) are not characteristic elements'. The absence of the profit motive leads these authors also to exclude municipal and other governmental buildings, parks, churches, schools, and fraternal orders, since these do not contribute to the 'essential character' of the central business district. It is admitted by Murphy that some wholesaling activities do benefit from a central location. In the larger city, all these activities form an integral element of the historical growth and present character of the inner city. Similarly among industries newspaper publication is highly exacting in its demands for a central situation. Geographically, the fact of the matter is that all these activities, that are excluded by Murphy and Vance, are consistently associated with retail trades and business in the centre of every city, and the process is more pronounced the larger the city. They are not as exacting in their demands and in their competition for the choicest central sites, but they serve the whole urban community and require to be placed in sites accessible to it.

Finally, understanding of the structure of the central business district can only be reached by the historical interpretation of precisely how its functions have segregated and shifted their locations, and how its buildings have been located in terms of site needs and land values. The Swedish studies of Stockholm illustrate the value of this approach. The clustering of the so-called central functions and hence the development of the central business district extend over no more than about one hundred years and the most spectacular changes have taken place since the beginning of this century.[1]

While centralized functions are accumulating in the C.B.D.s of west European cities, thereby adding enormously to their problems of traffic congestion, a reverse trend is already apparent in some American cities. The latter are losing functions to peripheral centres on a large scale. Indeed, there is considerable discussion as to what should be the role of the C.B.D. in the city of the future.

[1] See E. Kant, 'Zur Frage der Inneren Gliederung der Stadt, insbesondere der Abgrenzung des Stadtkems mit Hilfe der bevölkerungskartographischen Methoden', *The I.G.U. Symposium in Urban Geography Lund 1960*, 1962, pp. 321–75.

PART III
The City-Region

Chapter 8

THE REGIONAL RELATIONS OF THE CITY

1. The Concept of the City-Region

The City cannot be fully understood by reference only to its arbitrarily defined administrative area. It has to be interpreted as 'an organic part of a social group'.[1] In approaching the analysis of the four main urban functions—dwelling, work, recreation, and transport—it must be remembered that every city forms part of an economic, social, cultural, and political unit, upon which its development depends.[2] The problem of defining and analysing the functions and limits of the city and the unifying relationships with the surrounding area, is one of disentangling the regional component and examining the multitude of tributary areas served by, and serving, the city. Each group of functions has its particular zone of influence. Consequently, many functional areas have no relationship with each other in their geographical extent—which is often difficult to define. However, they all have a common denominator in their dependence on the city. We may refer to this area of functional association with the city as the city-region.

This concept of the city-region, like all concepts, is a mental construct. It is not, as some planners and scholars seem to think, an area which can be presented on a platter to suit their general needs. The extent of the area they need will depend on the specific purpose for which it is required. The concept of the city-region can only be made specific and definable, as a geographic entity, by reference to the precise areal extent of particular associations with the city. Major determinants of many such associations are transport facilities, and the density and movements of the population. Meaningful definition of city-regions could well be based on such criteria. But when the extent of minor associations is examined together, one can recognize those whose limits coincide and one can pick out zones of similar

---

[1] M. Aurousseau, 'Recent Contributions to Urban Geography', *Geographical Review*, Vol. XIX, 1934, pp. 444–55.
[2] J. L. Sert, *Can Our Cities Survive?*, Harvard University Press, 1943, p. 10.

associations with the city. Probably, and especially if the gradients of areal change are sharp, one can, on the basis of these associations, define the limits of the area which can be regarded as the city-region. It is also possible that selected criteria of city associations may be measured for all places within a given area. Their degree of correlation at each place would then indicate the degree of association with the central city. On this point it is interesting to recall the statement of Amos Hawley, an American sociologist:

'The application of indexes thus far brought into use, however, reveals that the boundaries of the modern community, instead of being precise lines, are blurred, if not indeterminate. Each index yields a different description of a community's margins. . . . In view of this peculiarity, and since each of the available indexes represent a more or less specialized relationship, nothing less than a combination of indexes is adequate for the fullest approximation to an appropriate boundary. But the use of a number of criteria produces a confusion of intertwined lines of demarcation.'[1]

The regional associations of a city, complex and multitudinous as they are, fall into four categories. The first are trade relations that are summed up under the heading of the trade area—again, the concept of a composite that actually contains as many areas as there are individual trading activities. The second are the social relations comprising cultural and educational associations, patronage of theatres, concerts, museums, general social ties and common attitudes and ideas that find their leadership and expression through the voice of the city. Such relations may be expressed in part quantitatively, but can only be fully understood in the light of the historical growth and function of the centre. This may be referred to as the social area. The third is the area of movement of population to and from the central city. This is primarily expressed in the daily journey to work, to shopping, and to entertainment, but it also appears in the wider distribution of seasonal residences and in the ownership of farm land by urbanites, etc. This may be called the settlement area. Finally there is the impact of the central city on land uses—both urban and agricultural—in the area around it. It needs to be emphasized that the role of the city as a regional service centre in terms of 'central place theory', though important, is only one aspect of the relations between the city and its surroundings, and the evaluation of the city as a geographic structure demands that all aspects of their interconnections be given balanced consideration.

This interpretation of the functions of the city as a centre of

[1] A. Hawley, *Human Ecology*, New York, 1950, pp. 248–9.

associations involves a twofold approach: first, an assessment of the character of the surrounding area—its resources and production and its effect on the character of the activities of the city; and, secondly, the effects of the city, as a seat of activity and organization, on the character of its surrounding area. Some attention has been paid to the question of defining the limits of the city as a regional centre. We must now seek to evaluate both the city and its region, however vaguely defined, in terms of their mutual relations and in the light of their historical development.

Settlement, route, and area are the three facets of the geographical interpretation of urban economy. The economic output of an area—farming, forestry, mining, industry, or combinations of these—calls into being centres differing widely in their interest, their commerce and industries. The quantity of output that passes through commercial channels is the total of economic, political, and cultural intercourse.[1] It is, in effect, a measure of the nodality of the urban centres. If all such intercourse were concentrated in one city, then all the commerce for the area would pass through it. The sum total of this commerce would be that total of the city's exports and imports. However, this theoretical state of affairs never exists. The degree of concentration of circulation through one city depends on the suitability of the surrounding area for commerce, relative to the location of the city and its neighbours, on the conditions of historical development, and on the orientation of its routes. The potency and extent of the field of association of a city are to be measured by the degree to which the city controls the circulations of all places in the area around it.

The city produces goods, and processes and stores imported goods not only for a nation-wide market, but also for its surrounding market where it is in competition with its neighbours. In addition to the growth of population in the city by its own natural increase (by excess of births over deaths), the city draws folk from the surrounding area to enjoy its special amenities—to find employment and to enjoy its shops, institutions, markets, art galleries, and theatres. With the growth of employment in town and city in the nineteenth and twentieth centuries, more folk moved to them from the surrounding countryside. Studies of the places of origin of the population of particular cities clearly reveal this trend. The city is a melting-pot and fount of opinion. It disseminates its views, through the medium of the Press, on matters relevant to the life and affairs of its citizens and the people of the surrounding towns. It is a seat of learning, culture, and political life. The city must be fed, with food for its

[1] H. Bobek, 'Grundfragen der Stadtgeographie', *Geographische Anzeiger*, Vol. XXVIII, 1927, pp. 213–24. This is called *Verkehrspannung* by Bobek.

people and materials for its industry. Before the development of rapid transport, every city was almost entirely dependent upon its surrounding area for both. Distant supplies of food, materials, or immigrants were brought by the only means of transport—water. It is therefore no accident that in the past, before the railway era, the chief cities in Europe and America were either ports or cities at the heads of river navigation. In the last hundred years, however, in spite of world-wide movements of foodstuffs and raw materials, there has grown an ever closer relationship between town and country. For all perishable goods must be delivered quickly and daily to the city consumers. Farmers market their products in accessible urban markets. With the increasing complexity of the social and economic structure of society, the city has acquired many new functions in its role as a centre for the distribution of both goods and services. The impact of the city on the surrounding towns and countryside has been greatly extended by the advent of the automobile and by the expansion of urban land uses—for residence, industry, and recreation. The way of life of the city also affects the character of the social and economic life of the people in its hinterland.[1]

2. The Town–Country Symbiosis

The relations between city and countryside vary from city to city in accordance with circumstances of historical development. A French writer[2] has recently emphasized three contrasting kinds of predominant relationships that are so contrasted as to give rise to different kinds of city-regions. He shows how the shift of capital from the country into the town or from the town into the country results in a distinct kind of city–region relationship. Formerly, the Industrial Revolution caused a shift in the flow of capital from the small towns and surrounding countryside to industrial developments in the big cities, especially in the north of France. More recently, however, the direction of flow has been reversed. Capital earned from industry and trade in the cities may now be invested in the purchase and development of agricultural land in surrounding areas. This is true, for example, of investments in the development of viticulture in Bas Languedoc. There the cultivation of wheat and olives met with increasing competition from outside markets and the capital investment needed for a new commercialized agriculture was

[1] For an important discussion of the varied relations between town and country, see G. Friedmann (ed.), *Villes et Campagnes: Civilisation urbaine et civilisation rurale en France*, 473 pp. Centre d'Études Sociologiques, Bib. Gén. de l'École Pratique des Hautes Études, VIe Section, Paris, no date (1952?).

[2] E. Juillard, 'L'Urbanisation des campagnes en Europe occidentale', *Études rurales: École Pratique des Hautes Études*, I. April–June 1961.

beyond the reach of the small peasant's resources. City entrepreneurs were encouraged to make this investment as their own industries (e.g. textiles) began to decline in face of factory competition from northern France. Today, a quarter of the vineyards are owned by 3,000 urban dwellers, mainly in Montpellier, Nîmes, and Béziers. This kind of symbiosis between town and country, dependent on investment of urban capital in the agriculture of the surrounding countryside, seems to be especially marked around the south-western and southern cities of France. The same trend is evident in Italy, where the cities in the north have played a major role in developing agriculture in the Lombardy plain since medieval times. In the south of Italy where ownership of land has always been associated with social prestige, there are numerous townsmen who invest their capital, however small, in the purchase of agricultural land. This forms a valuable addition to their unearned income when rented on insecure terms to poverty-stricken peasants. It is this type of urban-dwelling owner, rather than the large absentee landowner, who constitutes a major problem in the reorganization of peasant agriculture in this area, as in other parts of the world. The problem arises from the old tradition of 'rent capitalism' by which the ownership of tiny patches of land is a major source of income for the owners who live in the towns.

On the other hand, there are cities that are separated from, and indeed alien to, the countryside in which they are located. The traditional symbiosis often broke down during the nineteenth century with the advent of the railroad and urban growth. People left the land, capital was invested in towns, and the countryside was neglected. Supplies of food were shifted from the *umland* to more distant sources. These trends are emphasized where new industries developed and urban centres grew around them. This happened at the end of the nineteenth century, for example, in northern Lorraine with the mining of iron ores and the production of iron and steel. Men and families moved from the village to the work centres or travelled daily to their work, and many simply gave up agriculture altogether. Their parcels of land are retained but lie in fallow, the same as the 'social fallow' (*Sozialbrache*) in Germany. The land carries more people, but they are progressively divorced from the soil. Foreign industrial workers often cluster in the towns and this sharpens the gap between town and countryside.

The same breakdown of the traditional symbiosis occurs in the *Côte d'Azur* in the hills between the high limestone Alps of the interior and the urbanized coast between Cannes and Nice.

'Already in 1860 the economic ties between country and town were enfeebled; on the hills devoted to the traditional Mediterranean agriculture—wheat, vine, and olive—there was little investment of urban capital; indeed little exchange at all, and an appalling net of roads, or absence thereof, contributed to the isolation of its perched villages, which had a very fragile economic equilibrium. And yet there was no lack of towns; Nice, Antibes, Cannes, Grasse. . . . But they were small, and Grasse apart, turned to maritime trade, interested more in foreign markets than in exchange with their rural hinterland.'[1]

The growth of tourism in this area in the last hundred years has accentuated this breakdown and isolation, for beyond the narrow belt of flourishing floriculture around the villages, the interior is sterile. Native folk move out, new residents move in, agriculture declines for lack of capital, and instead of the water being developed for irrigation it is led off to supply the towns and villas. Land lies in fallow and villages are depopulated, and scattered farms are derelict, while new seasonal residences abound so that it becomes *une reserve suburbaine*. The coastal towns are centres of tourism and there is little demand for the daily employment of workers from the country. The interior is becoming a great *banlieue*, with market gardening and floriculture and country residences. The process is described as a 'peri-urban metamorphism'.

Thirdly, there are areas in which the towns serve as a focus of urbanization of the countryside. This may almost be regarded as a phase of development in which the city may completely deluge a countryside, causing the agricultural life virtually to disappear, resulting, as in Belgium, the Netherlands, and Switzerland, in an 'agro-industrial society' through the formation of an extensive *grande banlieue*. Many areas before reaching this phase have not necessarily passed through the phase of decadence of the countryside noted above. There are many *gemeinden* in western Europe where agriculture has been maintained by adaptation to the demands of a nearby market and by additional opportunities for non-agricultural work. The three-field system, for instance, may be transformed to one of consolidated holdings with a commercial agriculture, such as pasture and milch cattle, orchards and market gardening. Local towns may service the country folk, and communes become urbanized. Small factories may grow in the countryside, and such areas become functionally urbanized. 'Not that they have forcibly adopted, in their exterior forms, the urban livery, but because they are functionally and psychologically integrated in the general life of which the centre of impulsion is the city.'[2] This situation is found in the Low Countries, Denmark, Switzerland, and in wide areas of Germany,

[1] E. Juillard, *op. cit.* [2] *Ibid.*

France, and England—though the precise extent of such areas is dependent upon more precise definition. The traditional peasantry has gone, but it has changed with neither a fatal death of agriculture nor with total submergence into characterless suburbia. Many villagers work in the cities, land remains in production or it is developed and preserved. The city is not merely a focus of attraction. There is a rebound of urban settlers and interests in the countryside in settlement, tourism, and recreation. This is a new and, over vast areas, an absolutely inevitable new symbiosis. It is the duty of future planning to provide a sound lead by breaking down (through regional planning) the separation of town from country that is so evident in the division of units of local government. Industrial decentralization, the dispersion of industry in small centres, the preservation of the countryside, and so on, are the needs of this system, in which rural and urban cease to have meaning. The way to effect such a change is through the full development of the hierarchy of urban centres so that all places are within reach of the offerings of modern civilization.

It is appropriate to mention at this stage the idea of the spread of innovations in its relevance to the role of the urban centre. Ideas and techniques spread through the intermediary of the route and the central place. This has been true through history. It is true in our own day in the sense that innovations spread through a country first to its urban centres and thence radiate through the countryside to lesser towns, villages, and homesteads. Work on these lines has been done by Hagerstrand and his associates at the University of Lund in Sweden.[1] Hagerstrand points out that the automobile, radio, and television in Sweden have tended first to concentrate in the towns and spread outwards from them, in such a way that in time and intensity their frequency diminishes outwards from the centre, although the innovation eventually reaches the population throughout the whole area.

3. THE STRUCTURE OF THE CITY-REGION

The limit of the city, when considered as a centre of regional services of collection and distribution in a spatial system of urban centres, may be approached by referring to Figs. 1a and 1b (p. 53). This theoretical distribution of towns is based on the assumption that

---

[1] T. Hagerstrand, 'The Propagation of Innovation Waves', *Lund Studies in Geography*, Series B (Human Geography), IV, 1952. See also S. Godlund, 'Bus Services, Hinterlands'. Special attention is drawn to the very important contributions of the Lund school of geographers to this whole field of study, most of which are published in the above series in English.

places may be graded according to their functional complexity. Consequently, a city of the fifth grade in Christaller's scheme, for instance, will contain all the functions of the four lower grades, in addition to others that set it above them in the hierarchy. The corresponding limits to each set of functions will form a series of concentric circles passing through the towns of the next lower grade. This system is nearly approached in extensive, predominantly rural areas with a uniform distribution of population and occasional, evenly spaced large, dominant cities, as in the Middle West, eastern England, France, or, indeed, in south Germany.

This theoretical concentric structure of the city-region, however, is modified by a variety of other factors, apart from irregularities brought about by surface relief and historical conditions. These cause relatively small deviations in an evenly settled area.

First, growth of population in modern times has been centred mainly in urban centres. This has resulted in the growth of pre-existing towns, and consequently perpetuates the basic pattern of distribution of the historical service centres.

Secondly, the growth of industrial towns, clustered at sites of raw materials or places of assembly, has given rise to new population clusters, which in turn generate new centres of service.

Thirdly, the spread of population from the big city results in the extension of the urban area radially and frontally, merging with, often absorbing, pre-existing centres in its closer environs. These outlying centres, though absorbed in the urbanized area, often retain their functions as commercial sub-centres.

Fourthly, the extension of the big city results in the development of new satellite settlements. These may be independent centres, both legally (if beyond the city boundary) and economically, without any relation to the laws governing the historical distribution of centralized services.

Finally, much evidence has been adduced that major cities tend to usurp the functions of lesser centres around them. Isard and Whitney [1] concluded that 'core cities tend to appropriate trade in general merchandise and apparel at the expense of cities within a 20 miles radius', but that sales of immediate consumer goods (such as foods and drugs) are usurped least.

The zonal associations of cities revealed in numerous studies would seem to suggest an arrangement according to three main groups of functions, and, consequently, three orders of centres from the provincial capital (higher order) downwards. This would explain the fact that there are two or three sharp gradients associated

[1] W. Isard and V. H. Whitney, 'Metropolitan Site Selection', *Social Forces*, Vol. 27, 1949, pp. 263-9.

with a major city and thus two or three broad zones of common association with it. The first is the limit of the city as an urban complex. This seems to reach as far as a sharp break at the outer limits of the compact rural–urban fringe. A second break occurs at a distance of about 15 to 20 miles from the centre, since this limit, as noted above, corresponds with a variety of boundaries of daily transport facilities. It is consequently an area within which the city is accessible in one day for the return trip for work, business, shopping, or entertainment. A third limit is the outer range of the sphere of influence. This is more sharply defined when the neighbouring capitals of the same order are more closely spaced and forms a wide indeterminate when the competitive cities are far apart.

The same idea of zonal arrangement is expressed by L. P. Green in a study of Johannesburg. He distinguishes between the city hub or central business district and the rest of what he calls the metropolitan zone, which embraces the population in daily contact with the hub and whose limits determine the second of the main boundaries (beyond the urban complex). A more distant area, although not in daily contact with the city, is economically dependent on it for many specialized services. 'Its boundary, in itself an indeterminate and shifting zone, marks the confines of the metropolitan region and the limit of the hub's regional attraction.'[1]

The outer area associated with the metropolis and dominated by it was referred to as its hinterland by Gras, its *umland* (the land around) by German scholars, and its region by McKenzie. Bogue[2] prefers to speak of the metropolitan community as comprising the metropolis itself and the surrounding area over which it has a dominating influence. This area, he writes, owes its unity to a system of interdependent spatial relationships. These are in certain respects derived from the metropolis and pervade all its parts. Many, however, are affected indirectly, reaching the dispersed population of consumers through the medium of lesser urban centres distributed throughout the area. By biological analogy, Bogue refers to the metropolitan centre as the dominant, the hinterland city as a sub-dominant, the rural non-farm populations (the village and the small country towns) as influents, and the rural-farm population as sub-influents. The decreasing values along this scale refer to two kinds of change in this spatial dominance; first, the decreasing range or

---

[1] Article by L. P. Green on Johannesburg in W. A. Robson, *Great Cities of the World*, London, 1957. The same author definitely refers the measurement of basic and non-basic occupations to the framework of the region, not to the city centre.

[2] Donald J. Bogue, *The Structure of the Metropolitan Community*, University of Michigan Press, Ann Arbor, 1949.

THE CITY-REGION

area of dominance (the farm operating unit being the smallest areal functional unit, the metropolitan hinterland the largest); and, second, the decreasing number of functions by which the dominance is exercised. The influents and sub-influents are considered outside the range of Bogue's investigation. With respect to the metropolis and its hinterland cities, he considers that to the extent that all hinterland cities are patterned with respect to the metropolis, even while dominating smaller areas, we may call such cities 'sub-dominants'. It would be arbitrary to set the lower limit of sub-dominance at a population figure of 2,500, writes Bogue, but places less than this size have few specialized service institutions and they serve an area of only a few square miles, and, even more important than the absence of specialized retail services is the absence of wholesale services and manufacturing. Bogue defines the metropolitan regions of the United States on this basis, and the map is reproduced and discussed on p. 314.

Further data on the range of urban associations around cities is given in Bogue's studies of 67 American cities. The first 25 miles he refers to as the 'zone of direct participation'.

'The level of land occupancy is high; dormitory towns are numerous; the cities located there are more deficient in retail trade, wholesale trade, and services than are the cities lying in other parts of the hinterland. Because they provide space and yet are able to participate directly in the advantage of the metropolis, the principal hinterland cities in this zone attain a high degree of manufacturing specialization.'

Beyond 65 miles radius there begins the general rise in services in cities, indicating the sub-dominance of these cities in their own hinterlands. Standard commodities are provided by small cities but they depend on the metropolis and the larger hinterland cities for their specialized needs. This is called a 'zone of exchange'. Its centres are seats of collection and distribution and there is little manufacturing.

Between 25 and 65 miles is a mixed zone. It may therefore be called a 'zone of interchange', since 'it mediates between the metropolis and its direct participants and the outlying zone of exchange. From the outlying centres in this zone secondary highways radiate to the more remote portions of the hinterland, and for this reason the cities in this zone may be called "hinterland-access cities".' [1]

The city-region, as suggested above, is arranged into three main zones, which can be described as the central *urban tract*, the *city settlement area*, and the *city trade area*.

[1] D. Bogue, *The Structure of the Metropolitan Community*, 1949, p. 54.

THE REGIONAL RELATIONS OF THE CITY

The term *urban tract* is used to define the compact and continuous built-up area, in preference to the term 'conurbation'. The latter term was coined by Patrick Geddes fifty years ago. He had in mind the continuous urban area that stretched across the boundaries of several contiguous administrative districts. But he had more than this in mind, for he also thought of cities that were physically separate, but close enough to present the possibility of coalescing in time. South Wales (or Waleston), for example, was such an extensively urbanized area. C. B. Fawcett gave to the concept a much narrower definition by including within a conurbation the areas occupied by a continuous series of dwellings, factories, and other buildings, harbour and docks, urban parks and playing fields, etc., which are not separated from each other by rural land; though frequently such an urban area includes enclaves of rural land which is still agricultural.[1] This assumes that the conurbation ends with the limit of the compact built-up area. In fact, there is invariably a fringe of rural–urban uses, a fringe that is wide and irregular so that it is extremely difficult to run a line around the outer limits. Moreover, an urban area, however large, provided it lay inside one administrative boundary, presumably would not qualify as a conurbation under this definition. In many cities the administrative boundaries have been extended with the growth of the urban area, or the urban area itself has grown by the coalescence of separate units. These may be independent towns, villages, or satellites around a central city, that have been absorbed in its expansion. Moreover, the peripheral rural–urban fringe is so diffuse that there arises the problem of deciding whether to include places that are cut off from the main area but sufficiently near to it to be a part of its economic and social organization. In other words, on the margins, the emphasis in definition must shift from compactness of urban uses to functional association and accessibility. As time goes on, the definition of an urbanized area in terms of continuous urban land uses becomes increasingly elusive.

The *City Settlement Area* is the zone between the urban tract and the rural–urban fringe, as we have described it in a previous chapter. A journey-time of one hour is usually considered to be the main limit of daily travel for the city worker, and dormitory settlements lie, within a radius of about 20 miles, on the main railway routes and highways outside the greatest cities. This outer area, however, is not merely one of residential and industrial settlement. It supplies the city with milk and vegetables and receives many goods from the city's wholesale warehouses and retail shops. It is sufficiently accessible to permit regular visits to the city. It forms a part of the labour

[1] C. B. Fawcett, 'Distribution of the Urban Population in Britain in 1931', *Geographical Journal*, Vol. LXXIX, 1932, pp. 100–16.

market of the city complex and has intimate social and economic associations with the activities of the city. The area has been appropriately called by Chabot the *zone du voisinage*.[1] It is called the *umland* by P. Schöller (Ch. 4) in an attempt to give this term a specific connotation as opposed to the hinterland. The primary determinant of these associations is ease of access—for daily travel or weekly trips to the city, and for the daily delivery of goods and the daily operation of services. Its characteristics are summed up by the relatively high densities of population, intermediate between the urban tract and the country, but more significantly, by its high rate of increase of population.[2]

The *City Trade Area* is the wider and more extensive area with more occasional circulations to and from the city. The great bulk of local circulations, within it, are directed to the local towns. The city is the head of affairs, the seat of opportunity, offering in all fields things the local town does not possess. Clearly the connections with the big city are occasional and diffuse. Except for through routes these connections are not reflected in terms of traffic until the threads collect on the main roads near to the urban fringe. The city settlement area is, of course, served by a net of railroad routes and highways. The outer limit of this circulation is fixed principally by the accessibility of the city relative to surrounding cities offering the same service. In fact, the limits will coincide in the peripheral towns, where such goods and services are received for distribution to their local service areas. It is normal for towns of medium size with considerable functional independence to be placed on the border of the sphere of influence of two cities, with close relations with both.

4. The Urban Tract

Many criteria have been used to define urban areas on the basis of average densities of occupants per square mile. It is of interest that the data of all countries, including Japan, give an average density of population in cities of about 5,000 to 6,000 per square mile. Many years ago, the geographer Mark Jefferson suggested a minimum of 10,000 persons per square mile for areas that were fully built-up. There is also the question, here our main concern, of the selection of the minimum density that may be taken as the outermost limit of an

[1] G. Chabot, 'La Determination des Courbes Isochrones en Géographie Urbaine', illustrated by reference to Dijon in *Comptes Rendus du Congrès International de Géographie*, Tome II, *Géog. Humaine*, Amsterdam, 1938, pp. 110–13.
[2] A particularly interesting study in the *banlieue* of northern Paris will be found in R. Clozier, *La Gare du Nord*, Paris, 1940.

urban area against the rural areas around it. The United States Census in defining 'metropolitan districts' took the very low figure of 150 persons per square mile for *minor civil divisions*. In 1950 a *cluster of dwellings*, with, in effect, a density of 2,000 persons per square mile, was considered to define the periphery of an 'urbanized area', since this is the minimum density associated with a closely spaced street pattern. The British Registrar General accepted the idea of the conurbation for the major urban aggregates in 1951, but adhered strictly to the existing local administrative boundaries in defining their limits. The urban aggregates in France were defined for the 1954 census as those contiguous communes which were associated primarily in terms of family associations (*cadre de l'existence familiale*). This means the geographic framework of the family—the schools for the children and shopping places for the wife, but *not* the working places of the breadwinners.[1]

The Ordnance Survey, in the gradation of densities on a population map of Great Britain (10 miles to one inch), defines 'urban' densities as exceeding 6,400 persons per square mile (i.e. 10 persons per acre) whilst the minimum density for 'suburban and industrialized rural' areas is taken as 400 persons per square mile. Crozier takes 250 persons per square mile for the extreme limit of the Paris urban area, and 1,250 per square mile as the limit of the compact and continuous urban tract of Greater Paris. O. Boustedt in his study of urban agglomerations in Germany takes the same limits, with densities of 1,250 per square mile for each *gemeinde* as the criterion for inclusion in an urban core area. We found in mapping the urban areas of the countries in north-western Europe that the density of 500 per square mile (200 per square kilometre) was the best criterion for the definition of urbanized areas, and this is the basis of the map on Fig. 56.

Let us now illustrate the question of definition of the urban tract by special reference to the cases of Germany and the United States.

There is no official definition by the census authorities of Germany of an urbanized area, but various attempts have been made to define it. This field of study demands a functional typology of *all* settlements. Detailed information for this purpose is not available

---

[1] 'Dès que les pôles d'attraction, pour les questions comme les magasins, les spectacles, les sociétés sportives, etc., sont nettement différenciés, de sorte que les ménagères pour les achats à rythme relativement fréquent, et les membres de la famille pour occuper leurs loisirs, ne passent pas habituellement d'une commune sur l'autre, nous considérons que les deux communes ne font pas partie de la même agglomération.' *Villes et Agglomérations Urbaines*, Inst. National de la Statistique et des Études Économiques, Paris, 1955, p. 11. See also E. Benard, 'L'Étude des Agglomérations françaises', *Population*, January–March 1952.

for parishes in Britain nor for the enumeration districts of the Census within its urban areas. Nor is it available in the United States for the rural townships. But a variety of data are available for the local communities in continental countries. In Germany, for example, data of occupational structure, commuting, etc. are available for the 24,000 *gemeinden*, so that extremely detailed spatial analysis is possible. Studies of this kind have been undertaken by German geographers for many years, beginning with suggestions by Alfred Hettner in 1902,[1] and continuing with various statistical typological studies for the tiny *gemeinden*. One of the latest of these studies is that of an agrarian economist, P. Hesse,[2] who, in 1950, published a work on south-west Germany. In this he recognized the following types of *gemeinden* on the basis of accurate statistical analysis: (i) industrial communities (*gemeinden*); (ii) workers and residential communities; (iii) workers and peasant farmers communities; (iv) small farmers communities; and (v) farming communities. As criteria he uses (1) the proportion of landless families; (2) the percentage of all employed in agriculture and forestry; and the following ratios:—(3) out-commuters to total resident workers; and (4) in-commuters to total workers; (5) percentage of small holdings to total holdings; and (6) percentage of large holdings to total holdings. On this basis, Hesse recognizes fifteen types of *gemeinden*. Such a classification, when mapped, gives as clear an indication as is possible of the range of urbanization and the degree of rurality.

More specifically with reference to the definition of the city-region, O. Boustedt has used the following criteria: (1) the percentage of resident workers in each *gemeinde* who depend on agriculture (the degree of rurality); (2) the percentage of all out-commuters who work in the central city; and (3) the density of population, the critical figure for the boundary of the central urban areas being 1,250 persons per square mile.[3]

The *Stadtregion*—the city-region—is divided into sections (Fig. 68, p. 374). The core contains one or more contiguous administrative urban units and adjoining *gemeinden* that have the same urban characteristics as the central cities. The urbanized zone (*verstädterte zone*) contains *gemeinden* adjacent to the core that are structurally akin to and economically intimately associated with the core. The fringe zone is a zone of transition between the urbanized area and

---

[1] K. Haubner, 'Methoden zur Raumgliederung ins besondere im Bereich von Stadt und Umland', in *Stadtregionen in der Bundesrepublik Deutschlands*, Forsch. v. Sitzungsber. d. Akad. f. Raumf. u. Landesp., 1960, Band XIV.

[2] P. Hesse, *Grundprobleme der Agrarverfassung*, Stuttgart, 1949.

[3] O. Boustedt, 'Die Stadt und ihr Umland', *Raumforschung und Raumordnung*, 11 Jhg., 1953, pp. 20–9.

THE REGIONAL RELATIONS OF THE CITY

the surrounding rural areas. The outer zone includes the whole area of the urbanized and fringe zones between the core and the country. The occasional isolated dormitory settlement (*trabantenstadt*) is separately designated. Beyond lies the wide area of the *umland*, within which, on the basis of specified criteria, the influence of the central city area is predominant.

We may now turn to the *standard metropolitan area* as defined by the United States Bureau of the Census. The definition has been modified slightly at each census since 1910. The 1910 and 1920 censuses defined the metropolitan district as a city of over 200,000 population, together with every contiguous civil division in which the density of population exceeded 150 to the square mile, the whole or the major part of whose area or population lay within ten miles of the boundary of the central city. In the cases of cities with 100,000 to 200,000 inhabitants, the whole of the area within this radius was included.

The Bureau undertook further investigation of this idea for the 1930 census and it deserves to be quoted.[1] A committee appointed by the Industrial Bureaus of the Chambers of Commerce reported in 1927 as follows:

'The real city today, because of the automobile, the telephone, and other distance diminishing agencies, extends not only beyond existing city boundaries, but beyond the boundaries of any area which might be annexed. Because of this there are students of the subject who incline to oppose further annexation except in the cases of obviously misfit or irregular boundaries and to favour the creation of a new unit, the metropolitan region, which shall have charge of certain common public services—such as main highways, water supply and sewage disposal, parks systems, police and fire protection, etc., leaving the municipalities within the region autonomy as to their individual concerns. A clear definition of such metropolitan regions, capable of application to all situations, is still to be worked out. There are, however, certain considerations that should be borne in mind when drawing the boundaries of a metropolitan region, i.e. it is an area within which the conditions of manufacturing, trade, transportation, labour, and living, in brief the daily economic and social life, are predominantly influenced by the central city.'

Pursuing this idea, the United States Chamber of Commerce, with the approval of the Bureau of Census, sent a circular letter to the Chambers of Commerce of towns of over 50,000 population,

[1] *15th Census of the United States: 1930, Metropolitan Districts, Population and Area*, 1932, pp. 5–6.

inviting them to supply maps and data defining a metropolitan district (or region) as determined by certain control factors.

'These factors included telephone services, electric power service, retail store delivery, commuting service, water service, gas service, mail delivery, sewer service, residential membership in social and athletic clubs, operation of local real estate companies, and soliciting and collecting routes. A subsequent study of the extent of these factors, their relations one to the other, and the general interpretation made of these by local organizations, made it evident that there was more or less inconsistency, and that if the metropolitan districts were made to be uniform and comparable with one another, some factor should be used which would be applied uniformly and consistently to every city.'

It was found that in preparing their maps the local organizations were thinking of an industrial or trade area, rather than of the continuously urbanized area around the large central city. The problem for census purposes was to establish the latter so as to show 'the principal population centres taken as a whole by including in a single total both the population of the central city itself and that of the suburbs and urbanized areas surrounding it—or, in some cases, the population of two or more cities which are located in close proximity and that of their suburbs'. The districts were finally defined in the 1930 census as including 'in addition to the central city or cities, all adjacent, contiguous civil divisions having a density of not less than 150 inhabitants per square mile, and also, as a rule, those civil divisions of less density that are *directly* contiguous to the central cities, or are entirely or nearly surrounded by minor civil divisions that have the required density'. The minimum aggregate population was taken as 100,000.

The definition of these areas was changed once again in the 1950 census, in such a way as to provide 'the closest approximation to the theoretical ideal concept of an economic base, that it is practically possible to attain'. The general concept was that an area should be an integrated economic and social entity, with a large volume of daily travel and communication between the central city and the outlying parts of the area. The new unit was called a standard metropolitan area (S.M.A.). Unlike previous definitions, that were based on minor civil divisions, the 1950 definition is normally based on larger county units (except in New England), so that the area involves a central county in which the major city is situated, plus other contiguous counties that are essentially metropolitan in character, and are socially and economically integrated with the central city.

The criteria of metropolitan character relate primarily to the character of the county as a place of work and as a home for concentrations of non-agricultural workers and their dependents. Specifically, the criteria may be listed as follows, according to the 1950 census.

'The areas to be included in an S.M.A. are as follows: First, there should be a central city with at least 50,000 people and the whole area must have more than 100,000 people. Second, two cities will ordinarily be included in the same area. Third, adjacent counties with two cities with over 50,000 people each and within 20 miles of each other will form one area, provided that they form an integrated economic and social unit. Each county included in an S.M.A. must have either 10,000 non-agricultural workers or 10 per cent. of the non-agricultural workers in the area, or over one-half of the county's population must be included in the metropolitan district as defined in 1940 (i.e. in terms of the minor civil divisions used at that date) and non-agricultural workers must constitute at least two-thirds of the total labour force of the county. Fourth, each peripheral county in the S.M.A. must be economically and socially integrated with the central counties of the area. The criteria of integration are (*a*) 15 per cent. of the workers in the county work in the central county of the S.M.A., or (*b*) 25 per cent. of those working in the county live in the central county of the S.M.A., or (*c*) telephone calls from the county to the central county average four or more toll calls per subscriber per month. Other criteria, such as retail trade or banking, were abandoned as impracticable for purposes of definition.'

It should be noticed that these criteria are based on daily associations with the central city. This is undoubtedly the best basis on which to define a single urban economic and social entity. It was the criterion used by the International Research Unit at Berkeley in *The World's Metropolitan Areas*,[1] and gives a reasonable basis for the comparison of the world's urban areas.

The *urbanized area* included in the 1950 census is a new definition. It includes the central city with over 50,000 people plus its so-called *urban fringe* which lies outside the administrative limits of the central city. The criteria for inclusion in the urban fringe are as follows:

'(1) Incorporated places with over 2,500 inhabitants or more. (2) Incorporated places with less than 2,500 inhabitants in which there is a concentration of 100 dwelling units with 500 units or more per square mile, this being about 2,000 persons per square mile and normally is the minimum found associated with a closely spaced street pattern. (3) Unincorporated land with at least 500 dwelling

[1] See Chapter 12.

units per square mile. (4) Territory devoted to commerce, industry, transport, and recreation, and other purposes functionally related to the central city.

'Outlying non-contiguous areas with the required dwelling unit density are included if they are located within one and a half miles of the main contiguous urbanized area measured along the shortest connecting highway; and other outlying areas, within one half mile of such non-contiguous areas, which meet the minimum residential rule. Second and third cities near a 50,000 city may qualify as central cities provided they have a population at least one-third of that of the largest city, and minimum of 25,000 inhabitants.'

Many outlying 'suburban areas' around the big cities, which were previously termed 'rural', are now included in the 'urbanized area'.

Various slight changes were made in the 1960 census in the definitions of both the standard metropolitan areas and the urbanized areas. These are placed in an appendix to Chapter 10.

5. Zurich: An Example

The procedure of definition of a city-region has been well demonstrated by Hans Carol in a study of Zurich. This map is shown on Fig. 35. He first defines the urbanized area as one of continuous urban land uses. The edges of this area are defined by excluding built-up sectors that were more than 350 metres apart from the next built-up area. The suburban area (*Vorortsbereich*) contains communities which look to the urbanized area for their work and entertainment. There is here a close personal and daily relationship. The proportion of out-commuters to resident workers is taken as the primary indicator of these associations, which fall into three zones— the extended area of 42 *gemeinden* from which 5 to 10 per cent. of the resident workers commute to the city; an intermediate zone of 44 *gemeinden* with 10 to 25 per cent.; and an inner zone of 28 *gemeinden* sending over 25 per cent. of their workers. The last zone actually makes up one-half of all the commuters moving daily into the city. The whole of this area with 476,000 people has a star-like shape with extensions radial from the city centre.

The outer field of city associations is determined by the range of central services. Carol recognizes theoretically three orders of centres —lower, middle, and upper. These correspond broadly with *Marktort, Stadt,* and *Großstadt* (*Landesmetropole*) of Christaller. The tributary area of a centre is the sum of its service areas. Since these do not correspond, Carol distinguishes between a small, medium, and larger

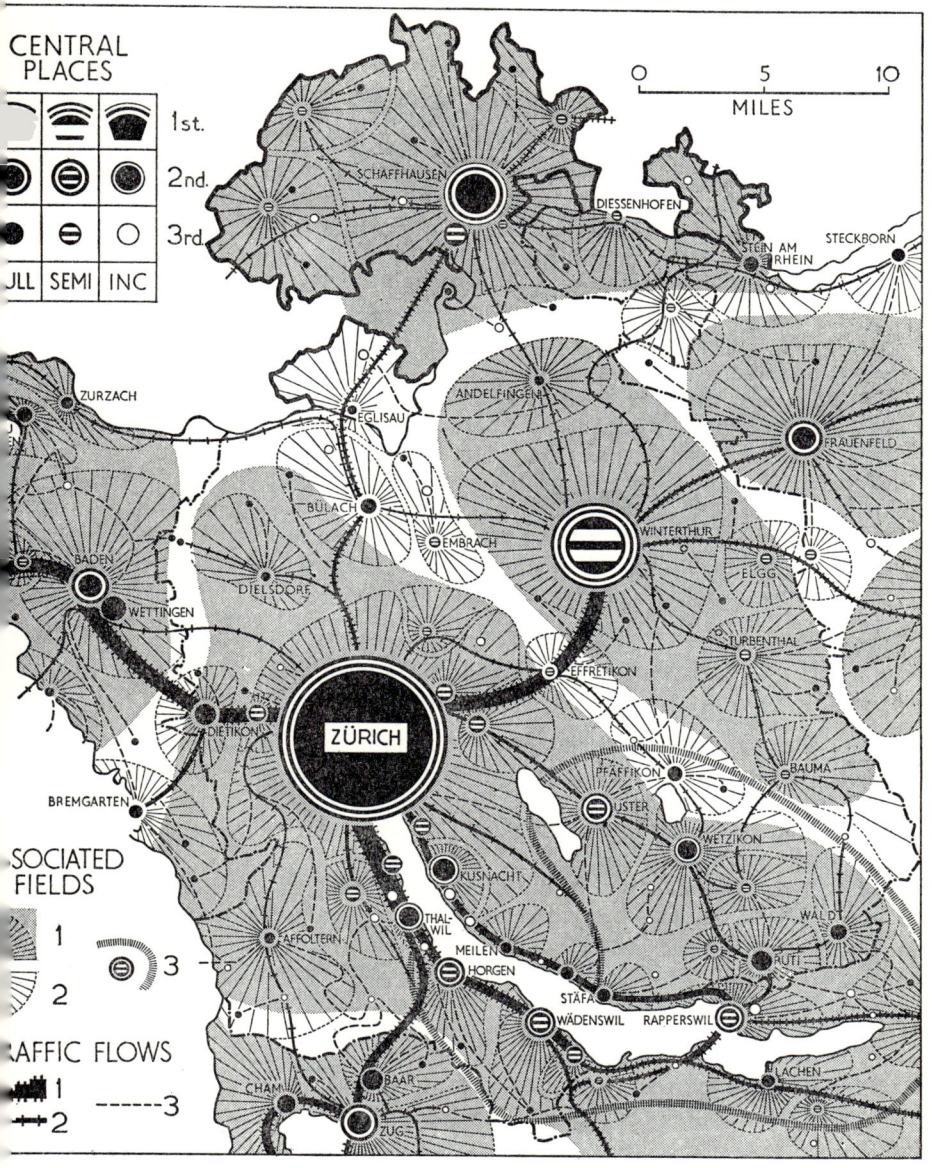

FIG. 35. The City-Region of Zurich (after Carol).

Central Places of the 1st, 2nd, and 3rd orders (upper, middle, lower), graded according to full, semi-complete, or incomplete range of services. Associated fields: 1. 1st and 2nd-order centres, full service. 2. 3rd-order centre, full and semi-complete service. 3. 2nd-order centre, semi-complete service. Traffic Flows: Width of band proportional to number of units per day—1. Express trains. 2. Slow trains. 3. Post-buses.

tributary area appropriate to a centre of the lower, middle, and upper orders respectively.

The composite tributary area of each order falls into an *internal area*, by which is evidently meant the built-up area itself, and an *external area*. He divides the latter into a *relative tributary area*, in which the connections with a centre of a certain order exceed the connections with all other centres of the same order; and a *core area* in which the connections with the centre dominate over relations with all other centres.

In the case of Zurich, the three orders of places are graded as follows. Low-order centres have 12 selected traits and are described as full-central, semi-central, or sub-central, from the number of these services they perform (10 to 12, 6 to 9, or 3 to 5). Middle-order centres have a high school, plus the above services. Upper-order centres have a University. Each of these orders is divided into the three above categories with respect to their services. The composite picture of the graded central places and their service areas is shown on the map. This is the arrangement of central places in the city-region of Zurich. A planned decentralization of activities, Carol argues, should build upon this framework.[1]

6. The Regional Impact of the City on Rural Economy

The city exerts powerful influences on the social and economic structure of the territory around it. These influences are expressed in the types of rural land use and farm economy, in the nature of urban land uses, and in the social and economic structure of the villages and towns affected.

As soon as a city arises it exerts an influence on the agricultural uses of the land around it according to a principle that was clearly expounded by Johann Heinrich von Thünen in his *Isolierte Staat*—the Isolated State—first published in 1826.[2] The principle was worked out in respect of rural land use by imagining one large city in the centre of the State in a plain with uniform soil and climate. Types of land use would then be conditioned by the economic factor of distance by road from the city to the market centre, the cost of production of the product, and the price offered for it in the central city

---

[1] Hans Carol, 'Sozialräumliche Gliederung und planerische Gestaltung des Großstadtbereiches', *Raumforschung und Raumordnung*, 14 Jhg., Heft 2/3, 1956, pp. 80–92.

[2] J. H. von Thünen, *Der Isolierte Staat in Beziehung auf Landwirtschaft und Nationalökonomie*, 1826, reprinted, with introduction by Heinrich Waentig, Gustav Fischer, Jena, 1910.

market. The State, served by the one city, is assumed to be surrounded by a wilderness completely cutting it off from the rest of the world. The type of crops grown and their location will be determined by their price in the city and the cost of transport to it. Six concentric zones surround von Thünen's city, namely—a small zone just outside the city producing perishable commodities that cannot stand long-distance transport, e.g. milk and vegetables; a narrow zone of forest, wood being used in this pre-industrial era for fuel and building, placed near to the city owing to its bulk and high cost of transport; third, a zone of rotation grain cultivation; fourth, a zone of less intensive rotation cultivation with pasture and fallow; fifth, a wide area of three-field farming, the dominant system in western Europe until the end of the eighteenth century; and finally, a zone of cattle-raising and hunting. According to von Thünen's calculations, cereal cultivation would cease at 31·5 miles from the city. It is the competition of land uses that explains these concentric belts of land use in a theoretically isolated state. The use which can pay the highest rent at a particular place occupies the land.[1] In pioneer areas, where crops were carried to railhead (rather than to a city) by wagon on rough roads, the limit of profitable transport was 15 to 25 miles, though the bulk of the goods came from a five-mile radius of each railhead. In Rhodesia thirty years ago the limit was 15 miles by wagon. 'Roughly the zones are "farm land" within 25 miles of the railway, "ranch land" 25 to 50 miles, and land beyond 50 miles is of little practical value to the settlers.'[2] Indeed, even today there are still large areas of the world, in which the villager 20 miles from a railroad is inaccessible to the resources of civilization since 'the cost of transporting any substantial quantity of his produce to the market in exchange for them is almost prohibitive'.[3] Medieval conditions still prevail. But much wider areas are today within reach of the world of exchange for, where roads exist, the truck greatly extends the range of profitable transport.[4]

This effect of the modern city on the rural land uses and the crops grown in its environs is related to two basic trends: first, the orientation of commercialized farm output towards the city market; secondly, the effect of the spread of the urban area on the values of open land around it. Such land is likely to be used in the future for urban uses and, in anticipation, will therefore rise in value with the

[1] R. T. Ely and G. S. Wehrwein, *Land Economics*, New York, 1940, p. 135.
[2] *Ibid.*, p. 136, and I. Bowman, *The Pioneer Fringe*, American Geographical Society, 1931, pp. 216–19.
[3] Colin Clark, 'Transport—Maker and Breaker of Cities', *Town Planning Review*, Vol. XXVIII, pp. 237–50.
[4] Many interesting examples on this theme will be found in M. Chisholm, *Rural Settlement and Land Use*, Hutchinson University Library, London, 1962.

result that farming will be intensive in order to get the maximum returns. Alternatively, if there is immediate likelihood of its being sold for building, it will lie unused in the hands of the speculative builder, awaiting a purchaser. The location of commercialized horticulture near to cities is due to the high price of land as well as to the proximity of an immediate market. For the same reason the demand of the city market for fresh milk has a marked influence on the spread of dairy farming around cities, irrespective of climate and soil. In the United States it has been shown that there is a tendency for the formation of concentric zones around the city market, the sequence being milk production, feeding grains, bread grains, and ranching, each fading into the next by a zone of transition from one type of land use to another.[1] The influence of the city market upon the kind of land utilization is thus based on the factor of distance from the market. This theoretical pattern of land use trends around the great European cities has been summarized by Olof Jonasson.[2]

The same principle of concentric zones may be applied to the delivery of goods outwards from a centre. If, instead of von Thünen's single city market, there are several competitive market centres, and providing these centres serve as equivalent sources of supply and distribution, the price to the consumer becomes the cost price plus the transport charge. Around each centre lines (*isotims*) may be drawn to show the limits to which any commodity can be delivered for the same price, and where the lines of neighbouring centres meet is a transition zone in which it is immaterial whence the product comes, or *vice versa*, in which centres it is marketed. Given the same cost of production, the centre enjoying the more convenient, more efficient, or cheaper, form of transportation will penetrate the market area of the other. This principle is of special importance in respect to retail and wholesale distribution.

[1] Ely and Wehrwein, *op. cit.*, pp. 133–8.
[2] *Horticulture.*
    Zone 1. City, plus greenhouses and floriculture.
    Zone 2. Truck products, fruits, potatoes, and tobacco.
Intensive Agriculture with Intensive Dairying.
    Zone 3. Dairy products, beef cattle, sheep for mutton, veal, forage crops, oats, flax.
    Zone 4. General farming—grain, hay, livestock.
Extensive Agriculture.
    Zone 5. Bread cereals and flax for oil.
Extensive Pasture.
    Zone 6. Cattle (beef and range), horses (range), sheep (range), salt, smoked, refrigerated and canned meats, bones, tallow, and hides.
Forest Culture.
    Zone 7. Outermost peripheral areas. Forests.
Olof Jonasson, 'The Agricultural Regions of Europe', *Economic Geography*, Vol. I, 1925, pp. 284–7.

7. The Regional Impact of the City on Industrial Location

The urban centre is a focus of economic forces, that, other things being equal, diminish with increasing distance from it. This was the basic contribution of von Thünen over a hundred years ago, and latterly (1933) of W. Christaller, with particular, though by no means exclusive, reference to services.

New industrial plants are located at peripheral sites either as new concerns entering the area, or as old concerns already located in the urban area, that move outwards to a new site. Industrial plants, according to their nature, are predominantly oriented to raw materials, markets or labour. New industrial concerns may be located as vast industrial plants independent of a pre-existing town (e.g. oil refinery) in which case houses must be built nearby or workers come in from a wide surrounding area; or smaller plants may be located in small towns and villages and the labour be drawn locally; or the plants may be located on the periphery of a big city in order to 'cash in' on the facilities already available in the city. The last category is our primary concern. The facts of growth around big cities have been assessed. Notable, for example, in the United States, are Bogue's studies.[1] More recently a German geographer, E. Otremba[2], has sought to generalize regarding the spatial factors involved in such industrial locations.

Two fundamental processes seem to affect the spatial arrangement of industrial enterprises with respect to the urban focus. First, the stronger the interlinkage of a concern, the stronger does it seek for a place in an urban system; whereas concerns with few needs for such regular contacts—in the exchange of products or sharing of processes or in management and sales, etc.—can well be sited on the periphery or even right outside the urban system. Second, industries that are concerned with the production of consumer goods tend to locate in accordance with the distribution of population. In the production of goods of general and regular consumption, Christaller's market principle operates. The more expensive goods of occasional consumption by those with higher income levels will tend to find their optimum site conditions in the major cities.

Thus, the spatial distribution of industries with respect to the attractive power of the urban market, permits four generalizations.

[1] D. J. Bogue and E. M. Kitagawa, 'Suburbanization of Manufacturing Activity within Metropolitan Areas', Scripps Foundation, Oxford, Ohio, 1955, and 'Suburbanization of Service Industries within Standard Metropolitan Areas', ditto, 1955.
[2] D. E. Otremba, 'Raümliche Ordnung und zeitliche Folge im industriellgestalteten Raum', *Geographische Zeitschrift*, 1963, Heft I, pp. 30–53.

THE CITY-REGION

1. In the core of the urban area, industry has no further space owing to the competition of such uses as offices and retail stores that must have the most central sites. The result is high land prices that industrial concerns with large space demands cannot carry. Even residential occupance is being forced out of these central areas. Certain manufacturing industries are found in city centres, but they are there because of the demands of centrality (e.g. printing industries) and interlinkage (e.g. garment making).

2. On the periphery of the urban area the dominant factor is access to the residential areas of the labour market and access to transport routes. Here there develop distinct interdigitated sectors of residence and industry. It is the outer limit of commuting that sets the outer geographical limit to this industrial-residential zone. This is the limit of the settlement area. Wage rates are uniformly high throughout this urban area, but land costs and taxes are substantially lower than in the central city itself.

3. With increasing distance from the periphery, with a smaller and more scattered autochthonous population, there occurs a fall in wage levels. The type and size of plant is determined by the labour potential and its skills and the industries are normally labour (i.e. wage) oriented rather than dependent on high capital investments. There are numerous examples of such dispersion of industry from the city to the villages and towns around it. Such are the shift of the textile and engineering industries from Berlin[1] and Lyon,[2] and the printing industries from London. It is clearly evident in the changing distribution of industry around many other continental and American cities. Local markets are inadequate to support the production of specialized consumer goods, and these must be imported from the urban focus. The availability of cheap labour for simple jobs is a decisive attraction for certain industries rather than the costs and congestion of the city centre. Examples are the light fabricating industries, more or less foot-loose, that have developed in the villages and towns of Württemberg (machine tools, electrical apparatus, etc.) and in the southern Netherlands (e.g. electrical apparatus at Eindhoven and adjacent towns).

4. At still greater distances removed from the urban core, and especially with a decreasing density of predominantly rural and often unskilled population, this principle is reversed, for the lack of labour results in a rise in wage rates (often for imported labour). This demands high capital investments in order to cancel these disadvantages. Thus, the highest levels of technical perfection are reached in the heart of the urban area and places furthest removed

[1] R. E. Dickinson, *West European City*, 1962, p. 240.
[2] See Chapter 9.

from it. Such industries will be those for which there is a compelling reason for their localization in sites far from the major urban foci in which are the primary sources of labour, capital, and interlinked producer goods. They are normally based on the production of raw materials.

The whole of this system, in a growing economy, where it is most clearly recognizable, is evident in the form of a series of impulses emanating from the urban centre and manifesting themselves in the type and spatial arrangement of industrial enterprises. The system is most clearly developed when the urban centre is growing rapidly in an agricultural area with few competitors of equal status at distances of hundreds of miles apart. It is not normally strongly developed in Britain since cities are so close together. It is well developed in the United States. The system develops most clearly in the under-developed areas where one great centre dominates a backward agricultural and self-subsisting hinterland.

The role of distance from the metropolis in the arrangement of economic activities has been demonstrated by D. Bogue from 67 metropolitan communities in the United States. He writes:

'On the average, as the distance from the metropolis increases, the number of persons per square mile of land decreases. With increasing distance, each square mile of land area supports steadily decreasing average amounts of retail trade, services, wholesale trade, and manufacturing activities.'[1]

These regularities with distance hold for each size class of metropolitan region, though with different rates of change.[2]

8. THE REGIONAL IMPACT OF THE CITY ON SOCIAL AND ECONOMIC CONDITIONS

The impact of urban influences on the country and smaller towns has many and deep-seated effects on their social and economic structure, such influences normally being most intense near the city and decreasing outwards from it. An obvious method, at any rate in theory, for examining the nature of the relations between town and country is to examine various conditions statistically on the basis of small administrative units in the environs of the town. No such studies appear to have been undertaken in Europe, but an attempt has been made in the American researches of Brunner and Kolb in their *Rural Social Trends* monograph.[3] Eighteen cities were selected with

---

[1] D. J. Bogue, *The Structure of the Metropolitan Community*, Ann Arbor, 1949.
[2] See also W. Isard, *Location and Space Economy*, London, 1956, Ch. 3.
[3] E. de S. Brunner and J. H. Kolb, *Rural Social Trends*, Chapter V on Rural–Urban Relationships, 1933, pp. 141–2 and 151–2.

populations ranging from 20,000 to over half a million. A statistical analysis of concentric zones round each city was made, taking as limits for the area the limits of the wholesale trade area for the city. The county in which the city is situated was taken as a unit, and the counties contiguous to it were called Tier One, counties contiguous to Tier One were called Tier Two, and so on up to Tier Four. The outer boundaries of each tier from the boundary of the city county are approximately 6, 12, 18, and 24 miles respectively.[1] There averaged nineteen counties to each city, covering 10 per cent. of the population of the country. Liberally hundreds of indices were taken in these studies, and the characteristics of the tiers or zones in 1930, and the changes in these characteristics since 1910, were determined. The indices include fertility rates, sex ratios, ratio of children, proportion of land in farms, average acreage of improved land per farm, value per acre of farm property, and of farm crops, and value of dairy products. Several significant 'gradient relationships' were discovered in the successive concentric zones. The ratio of children under ten years of age to women of reproductive age increased with distance in the first three tiers but declined in the fourth tier. The birth-rate tended to increase with distance from the city. Distance from the city was found to have an important effect on farming. The percentage of farms devoted to dairying tended to increase with distance in the first three tiers and declined rather sharply in the fourth tier. The percentage of truck farming (market gardening) declined in the first three tiers, but showed a slight increase in the fourth. The percentage of poultry farms declined through all four tiers, while the proportion of stock farms increased with distance in all four tiers. The farms tended to increase in size with increased distance from the city. The value per acre of farm land decreased consistently with distance and the value per acre of all farm products also decreased with distance. The value of dairy products per acre tended to be lower in the first three tiers and higher in the fourth tier. These data were then examined for the 1910 to 1930 period and the following conclusions were drawn.

The City County and, to an increasing extent since 1920, Tier One, are likely to be given over to smaller farms for market gardening, fruit growing, and intensive dairying. This means more compact communities and relatively high densities of population. It means more frequent contacts with the city centre. Demographic trends are akin to those of the city. Tier One, and especially Tier Two, show an increasing specialization on dairying. Tier Three has many markedly

[1] Wholesale trade areas were taken from the *Market Data Handbook of the United States*, by P. W. Stewart, published by the U.S. Department of Commerce, Domestic Commerce Series, No. 30, 1929.

transitional features. Tier Four and beyond, until the influence of another urban centre is reached, form what is described as an outer zone. It has larger farms but fewer cultivated acres per farm. Population densities are lower, communities larger, and there are fewer contacts with the city. City influence in retail sales declines beyond Tier Two, although there is some dependence on the city stores and mail-order houses for clothing, furniture, and household effects. But most remarkable are the demographic trends in Tier Four that stand in fundamental contrast to the inner Tiers. There are more children under ten to women twenty to forty-five years of age and there are higher birth-rates. There is a higher proportion of males to each 100 females, and this in turn is reflected in the marriage ratios. Children are more numerous among the farm populations removed from urban influence, and they have been becoming more so, even though the general differences between rural and urban populations in this regard are tending to decrease.[1]

Changes in farming conditions with increased distance from the city were revealed some years ago in a study of Louisville. Within 8 miles of the city market place market garden products and potatoes provided 68 per cent. of the farm income, whereas at a 15 miles radius only 20 per cent. were drawn from this source, even though the soil that is especially suitable for market gardening extends more than 20 miles along the river. At 15 miles or more dairying and general farming took the place of the intensive crops. The greater intensity of land use near the city was shown by the smaller farms, greater operating expenses, and higher expenditure on fertilizers. Gross earnings were five times higher per acre at 9 miles from the city than at 16 miles, and this was reflected in rents paid and land values.[2]

A similar investigation was made by the Urbanism Committee of the National Resources Committee.[3] A grouping of the counties was based upon the major cities. The county which has a city containing over 100,000 inhabitants is allocated one tier of contiguous counties. A second tier was added to the eight cities with 500,000 to one million inhabitants thus showing their greater range and potency of influence. A third tier was added to those cities with over a million inhabitants. On this basis, regions were established around the counties containing the 93 cities which contain over 100,000 inhabitants. Data considered were the growth and density of population,

---

[1] Brunner and Kolb, *op. cit.*, Chapter 5, especially pp. 141–2.
[2] Ely and Wehrwein, *op. cit.*, p. 137, quoting J. H. Arnold and F. Montgomery, *Influence of a City in Farming*, U.S. Dept. of Agriculture, Bulletin 678, 1918.
[3] *Population Statistics, 3. Urban Data*, National Resources Committee, October 1937, pp. 43–5.

industry, income, occupations (grouped as agriculture, industrial non-service occupations, and industrial services),[1] and the percentage of total population gainfully employed. This investigation showed that an increasing proportion of the total population of the country is concentrating in these regions, and that settlement is, as it were, segregating in wider areas around the central urban districts. The character of these city-regions varies from one part of the country to another. In the Atlantic Seaboard, the Great Lakes, and California, population is highly urbanized and concentrated and is becoming increasingly so and increasingly industrialized. In the rest of the States, the cities have a more limited range of influence and lead 'a more isolated and independent existence'. They are primarily commercial centres for their agricultural hinterland. It was, moreover, clearly revealed that the city was predominantly engaged in the service trades and professions, as compared with less than a half so engaged in the outlying counties, and 25 to 60 per cent. (an average of 40 per cent.) in all the outlying areas. The city is thus clearly revealed as 'the centre of managerial, commercial, clerical, and professional functions'.[2]

These relations have been extended and intensified since World War II. The rural fringes in the United States suffer from lack of public services—sewerage, water, police and fire protection, garbage disposal, health services, and recreational facilities. These offset the attractive force of a new home with a large 'yard' and fresh air, and the short-sighted attraction of lower taxes than in the city. The husband pays the price of a greatly extended daily journey to work with a big addition to his expenditure. The lack of service proportionate to the expected needs is due to the lag of capital improvements behind the relatively rapid growth of housing and population, and to the miscellany of local government authorities and their interlocking areas. In no sense is there in such areas a 'harmonious association' of characteristics that can be designated as 'urban'. They are usually good residential areas (though by no means necessarily so) in which many of the urban amenities are absent, at any rate for the time being.

The ecological changes in the urban–rural fringe in America include the continued deconcentration of industry in the forties and fifties (Bogue calls it the suburbanization of manufacturing). Building permits issued in 1955 show that two-thirds of the new industrial buildings in the standard metropolitan districts took place

[1] These included all those engaged in transport, trade, public service, professional service, domestic and private service, and industry not specified.
[2] *Population Statistics, 3. Urban Data*, National Resources Committee, 1937, p. 45.

in their outer rings. Similarly, the same survey revealed that two-thirds of the new stores and commercial buildings were located in the outer rings.

Rural land values were on the increase. Studies in the Middle West show that the value of agricultural land per acre is highest in the townships nearest to the cities. Similar quantitative changes in tiers of townships are found in the level of income, age, and sex composition and fertility.[1]

Indeed, this impact is proportional to the degree of dependence on urban, as opposed to farm or village, employment. In effect, these are measures of contrast between the degree of rurality and vice versa the degree of urbanity. The latter is strongest in the cities but decreases with increasing distance from the big cities, while conversely the degree of rurality is highest in the areas furthest removed from the radii of urban influence and urban innovations.

Other investigators in the United States have commented as follows on the same trend.[2]

'It is possible to delineate on maps with remarkable precision the gradients which urban cultural patterns take on in the rural areas contiguous to a city. Data on birth-rates, on delinquency, on subscription to daily newspapers, on living levels, and on many other significant items show more or less typical concentric tiers surrounding a central city, each tier revealing successively less urban acculturation as one goes outward from the city.'

This is illustrated by the work of the Planning and Traffic Division of the Michigan State Highway Department. It shows that the flow of traffic to and from centres is highly correlated with their socio-economic characteristics (such as population, bank resources, newspaper circulation, etc.). On this basis, 1,306 centres in Michigan were classified in 1950 as follows—neighbourhood centres or small retail outlets which offer some of the requirements of the immediate surrounding area; minor market centres or those which offer services usually sufficient to meet the general requirements of the centre and its trade area; complete market service centres, or those offering services usually sufficient to meet the general requirements (including some recreational and cultural advantages) of the centre and its trade area; regional centres, or places which offer complete market

---

[1] J. Martin, 'Ecological Change in Satellite Areas', *American Sociological Review*, Vol. XXII, April 1957, pp. 173–83; and B. G. Zimmer and A. H. Hawley, 'Approaches to the Solution of Fringe Problems: Preferences of Residents in the Flint Metropolitan Area', *Public Ad. Review*, Vol. XVI, 1955, pp. 258–68, and articles reproduced in Theodorson, *op. cit.*

[2] W. Firey, C. P. Loomis and J. A. Beegle, 'The Fusion of Urban and Rural', in Labatut and Lane, *Highways in our National Life*, Princeton, 1950, p. 161. A short but very important study of this topic.

services sufficient not only to meet the needs of one community and its trade area but also to serve as a principal wholesaling centre; and metropolitan centres which not only offer complete market services sufficient to meet the needs of the trade area, but also serve as major trade centres in the national economic structure.

In these ways, 'rural centres are becoming culturally urbanized'.[1] Through the medium of the highway, rural and urban activities are fusing, and there is emerging a universally accepted value system.

[1] D. G. Marshall, 'Hamlets and Villages in the United States; Their Place in the American Way of Life', *American Sociological Review*, April 1946, pp. 159–65. Firey, Loomis, and Beegle, *op. cit*. Quotes are from the latter article.

Chapter 9

THE REGIONAL RELATIONS OF THE CITY: CASE STUDIES

There are numerous studies of individual cities in which the regional relations receive varied treatment. There are few, however, that handle the matter with any thoroughness and the modes of approach vary considerably. Several case studies are selected here to illustrate these varied aspects of the city-region from the standpoint of the geographer. We have endeavoured to select one case from each major country with which we are concerned. These are Lyon, Cologne, Leeds–Bradford, and Salt Lake City.

1. Lyon[1]

The lands between the Alps and the Upper Loire, in the middle valley of the Rhône, are characterized by great diversity of relief and economy, but they are welded together by the development of the radiating influence and integrating activities of one city—Lyon. Lyon has some 650,000 inhabitants. Together with St. Etienne on the coal-field 25 miles to the south-west, and with the small towns between them, there is a total urban population exceeding one million inhabitants. The whole area tributary to this urbanized area can justifiably be described as *La Région Lyonnaise*.

The heyday of Lyon as the capital of Roman Gaul was followed by a thousand years of decadence. The revival of trade with the Mediterranean lands in the early Middle Ages caused the city to revive as a trade centre. In the thirteenth century it was already a city of repute, though it never became the capital of a province as

---

[1] This section is based on two works by Jean Labasse, his definitive study entitled *Les Capitaux et la Région: Étude géographique, essai sur le commerce et la circulation des capitaux dans la région Lyonnaise*, Cahiers de la Fondation Nationale des Sciences Politiques, No. 69, Paris, 1955, pp. 532; and *La Région Lyonnaise*, Paris, 1960, a general geographical work, with an excellent closing chapter on the role of Lyon as a regional capital. This section is largely taken direct from the latter source with selections from the major work.

was usual among other cities of France. In the sixteenth century it was a great seat of collection and distribution for the woollen goods produced in the surrounding area and for luxury goods imported from Italy, although the printing trades and banking, the hall-marks of the really great city, were ill-developed. During the eighteenth century it began to extend its range of influence. The Canal du Centre was opened in 1791, between the Loire and the Rhône and it permitted the transport of coal to Lyon, and facilitated further contacts with the Forez and Auvergne. The coal of St. Etienne replaced the timber of the Jura. The annexation of Piedmont by Napoleon brought French-controlled territory right across the Alps and permitted the development of Alpine routes. It was the trade in silk, however, that increased the ties of Lyon with its environs during the early nineteenth century. Spinners and silk-throwers in Vivarais and in the Rhône valley delivered raw silk and finished products to merchants of Lyon. Weavers of silk, troubled by social crisis in the city, spread to the surrounding towns and countryside. Thus, thousands of craftsmen moved to the countryside of Beaujolais, Forez, and Dauphiné, where they found running water to serve as motive power. This is clearly reflected in the distribution of silk workers today as shown on Fig. 36. This map gives one of the clearest indications of the extent and uniqueness of the region of Lyon.

In the second half of the nineteenth century all forms of industry between the Loire and the Alps found financial support in Lyon for their further development. Capital from Lyon supported the principal mining concerns of the St. Etienne area, assisted on a more modest scale in the growth of hydro-electricity at Grenoble, and played a dominant role in the spread of power throughout the south-east. The gas industry throughout this area was controlled from Lyon and the enterprises in the engineering and charcoal industries (1875–1914) found their support from the city. All these contributions added to the power of Lyon in the economic development of the whole of south-east France.

This growth was associated with the development of banking. Banking was begun in the sixteenth century by the Florentines, but did not develop until the nineteenth century, when credit establishments with multiple branches were founded. These were the *Crédit Lyonnais* and the *Société Lyonnaise des Depôts*, which covered a large area with a network of branches in the 1860's and after. By 1900 Lyon was the financial centre for the south-east and had an international reputation. Great sums were invested in the area after 1880—for the distribution of coal, ferrous and non-ferrous metals, dry goods, provisions, and the commercial production of milk, leather, and other products. 'Based upon the factory and the bank, Lyon, spreading its craftsmen and capital over a radius of 150 km., built a dependent region that permits the retention and employment of men on land that, on the basis of its natural resources, is absolutely incapable of supporting them.' Thus, 'Ce n'est pas la région qui c'est donné une capital, c'est la ville qui a forgé sa région.'

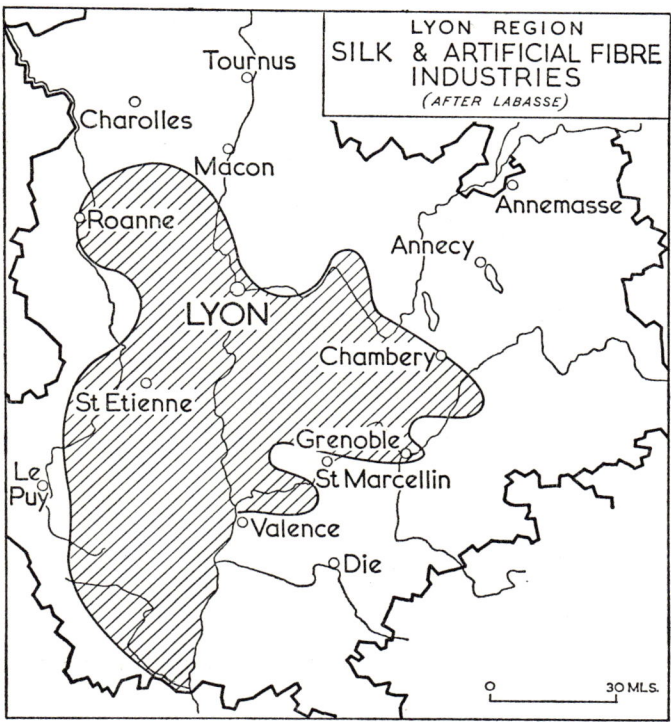

Fig. 36. Lyon Region: Distribution of the Silk and Artificial Fibre Industries (after Labasse).

The framework of these relations is afforded by the route net. The railroad complex centred on Lyon is second only to that of Paris. There are nine stations in the city receiving more than 3 million tons of goods per year, and despatching over 1 million tons outwards. There are two great marshalling yards. Eighteen express trains leave daily for St. Etienne in each direction, 11 to Grenoble, 10 to Roanne. Lyon is not so much a link between Paris and Marseille as it is a nexus of regional routes. Great streams of traffic ply on the roads to the Mediterranean coast via Vienne and Valence, west to St. Etienne, and east to Geneva and Grenoble (over 5,000 vehicles per day in each direction.) The airport is the fourth in France (after Paris, Marseille, and Nice) and over a third of its traffic is with its region, notably with St. Etienne and Grenoble.

The invisible circulation represented by telephone and banking

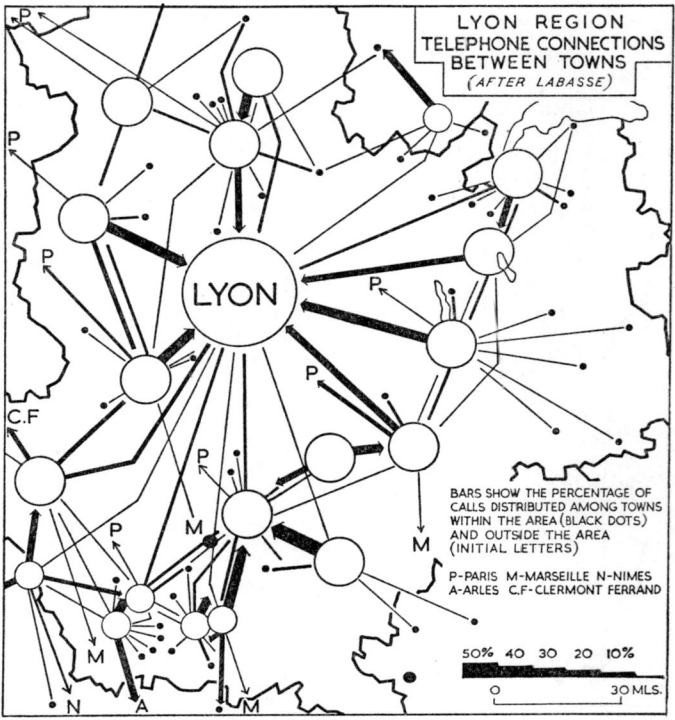

FIG. 37. Lyon Region: Telephone Connections between towns (after Labasse).

is less tangible but more expressive of the regional relations of the contemporary city. The distribution of telephone calls between Lyon and its neighbouring cities is shown on Fig. 37. It reveals the outstanding status of Lyon as a centre of business. The cities of its region have their own orbits, but are closely connected with Lyon. Such are St. Etienne and Grenoble in particular and secondary centres such as Macon, Valence, Annecy, and Chambery. More than one-half of the financial transactions of the region are effected in

Lyon—the centres next in order being St. Etienne with 15 per cent., Grenoble with over 10 per cent., Chambery and Roanne with about 3 per cent. each. This illustrates the role of Lyon as both a distributor and a user of regional products. Vegetables and fish are purchased from the Dombes, fruits from the orchards of Savoie. Industrial products are brought from the iron and steel workshops of St. Etienne and electrical apparatus from Haute Savoie, and textiles from the whole area. Trade is derived from the provision of products and services to its region on a far greater scale than its purchases. The region has in consequence great diversity that does not disrupt its unity.

There are, however, weaknesses in the organization of the industrial infra-structure. These include the costly production of coal, the small and inferior coal reserves, and the lack of mineral resources. Such inadequacies in raw materials are also found in other ways. The decline in silkworm breeding in the nineteenth century deprived the industry of its local resources. The chemical industry began using local pyrites, mineral salts and residues (superphosphates, bone glue, wood waste, coal tar, extract of chestnut). Industries are typically small concerns with skilled craftsmen who display a sturdy individualism and are averse to large-scale organization. The skilled mechanics of the local crafts participated early in the development of the automobile, but most of them succumbed to competition from elsewhere. But one name at least has attained renown, Marius Berliet, who established a large automobile concern in Lyon that now employs 12,000 workers. The industries of the area are remarkably adaptable and have gone through many changes. An example is the replacement of natural by artificial silk. The Gillet group, for example, since 1900 has established plants throughout the region.

Industries are generally in small and widely scattered plants. The spread of the textile industry was encouraged by the scattering of the Lyon weavers and by the availability of a cheap and skilled labour supply, especially the peasant-weaver who is ready to leave his loom when business is slack and turn to his fields. The progress of decentralization is still going on. Silk and other textile workshops have spread around St. Etienne and new plants are steadily being established in the valley of the Rhône. Many of these do not develop from local enterprises but from the enterprise of concerns from Lyon. Lyon is an entrepôt centre. It has been a great centre for the organization of the distribution of coal and coke and in this respect the range of its business extends to northern Italy, northern France, and England. The Lyon coal merchants have been involved in the development of water transport. After World War I, they participated in opening the Rhine–Rhône canal from Strasbourg. Commerce in metals has also developed in Lyon and most of these products sold in the region are negotiated by its firms. Building materials are normally provided through local channels but the city again occupies a pre-eminent position for tiles and bricks, concrete blocks and tubes, and pre-fabricated woodwork. A large measure of commercial control is exercised over trade in foodstuffs. Refrigerator equipment is supplied over a wide area. Chain stores have their head offices in Lyon, notably three firms with a total of 1,500 branches, although they have to meet competition from similar organizations in St. Etienne and Chambery.

The city has lost something of its autonomy as a business centre for it is not a centre for the initiation of finance. The market is too limited. Evidence of this is found in the meagre transactions of the local *Bourse*. The control of banking from Paris has increased greatly in this century, but in the 1900's Lyon was approached directly by American financiers to assist the financing of the St. Louis and San Francisco Railway and by official Russian authorities to finance the Russian treasury. Initiation and direction today lie much more in Paris. Indeed 'les 4/5 environ du potentiel économique lyonnais sont mus sous l'impulsion de Paris'. This stands in marked contrast to the status of metropolitan cities in Germany and Italy, such as Munich and Milan. It does, however, remind one of the situation in Britain, in which business affairs are similarly concentrated in London, with the possible exceptions of Manchester and Glasgow. In such cities new office buildings are erected to create an ever-changing central business district, whereas Lyon lacks a central business nucleus worthy of its economic importance. She lacks the presence of leaders of business and finance and the buildings in which to accommodate them and their staffs.

Substantial changes, however, are taking place in the realm of industry, organized, in large measure, within the framework of the National Plan. Big industry has made its appearance in recent years on the periphery of the city, and in the towns of its orbit. An Institute of Applied Science is now in being, in conjunction with the University, which is a new development in technical education in France. Meanwhile, the railroad depots, aerodrome, facilities for the International Fair, and the wharf facilities on the river (above the projected dam below the confluence of the Rhône and Saône), the building of the road-tunnel under the Croix Rousse, and new urban highways, are either achieved or planned. The physical equipment of the city is being modernized to meet its growing part in the total economy of France and in its relationship with its region.

From the standpoint of administration, Lyon is outstanding among the French provincial capitals. It is the headquarters of some

REGIONAL RELATIONS OF CITY: CASE STUDIES

twenty-four of the major administrative divisions of the country and ten *départements* of the south-east are customarily grouped around it (Rhône, Ain, Isère, Loire, Haute Loire, Ardèche, Drôme, Savoie, Haute Savoie, and Saône et Loire). For certain purposes St. Etienne and Grenoble serve their own districts, independent of

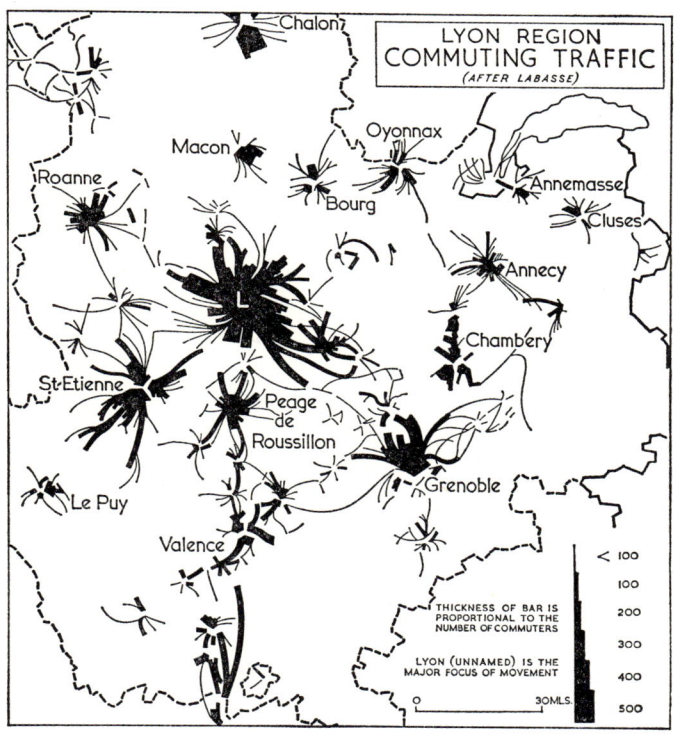

Fig. 38. Lyon Region: Commuting Traffic (after Labasse).
Thickness of bar is proportional to the number of commuters. Lyon (unnamed) is the major focus of movement.

Lyon. In 1956 an important society for the regional development of the south-east was formed, reaching to the ten *départements*. The great majority of the large enterprises which act within the framework of the current National Plan are called upon to organize their commercial services by regions and many use Lyon as their centre and the ten *départements* as their area.

Finally, social services are rendered to the region. Many kinds of mutual aid and sports activities are held in the city. Civil hospitals have charge of fourteen establishments with facilities for 9,000 patients. The cultural services are represented by the University which is a little more than fifty years old. It is now the second largest in France with a reputation in medicine and chemistry. The city has an active theatrical life with splendid open-air theatres, a museum of fine arts, and a renowned museum of textiles. It is the headquarters

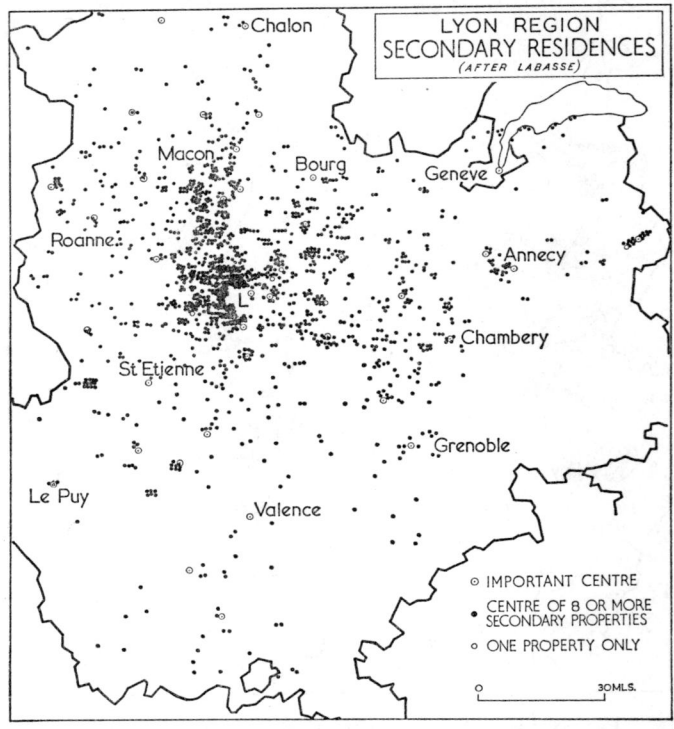

FIG. 39. Lyon Region: Secondary residences in the Region (after Labasse).

of French missionary work in Africa and an important theological centre.

The cohesion of the region is strengthened by the impact of the city upon the rural economy. The food demands of its population provide a market for the peasant cultivators who, in general, have small holdings of 6 to 12 hectares. The city folk need milk, meat, fowl, vegetables, and fruit. It is owing to the commercialization of its agriculture that the Dombes area has ceased to be ridden by poverty. The 'milk shed' of Lyon reaches from the Lyonnais to the

REGIONAL RELATIONS OF CITY: CASE STUDIES

Jura and even into the Prealps. The meat market is the second largest in France. Fat stock are drawn from as far afield as the Central Massif and the Alps, and at the big fairs the merchants of Lyon compete with those from Paris.

The close ties of each city with its surroundings are revealed by the range and density of commuting as shown on Fig. 38.

A further tie with the environs is found in the ownership of property by Lyon people. This goes back to the sixteenth century when landowning city dwellers drew food supplies from their country properties. A rural bourgeoisie is also attracted to Lyon by the call of industry and commerce. Fig. 39 shows secondary residences of the *bourgeoisie* of Lyon. To this, one has to add the tiny plots of land held by humble peasants who have moved into the city. The Lyon ownership of land has many repercussions on the mode of agriculture in the Dombes, and along the western border of the southern Jura, where vineyards in the latter area are frequently the property of Lyon people.

2. COLOGNE

The city of Cologne is one of the most historic cities of Germany, and one of its greatest centres of industry, commerce, and culture. It is closely associated with its environs and, though never a political capital, it is an old-established regional metropolis. The city was devastated during World War II, but it rapidly recuperated and expanded in the fifties and has now been entirely rebuilt, and has resumed and increased its pre-war regional relations. This city is an excellent example of the structure and organization of the city-region.[1] The population was 756,000 in 1933 and 791,000 in 1960—the third city in West Germany, after Berlin and Hamburg.

The Romans chose the site of Cologne for their camp, the *Colonia Claudia Agrippensis*, at the last point at which firm rising ground reaches the bank of the river Rhine before the flood plain widens northwards and makes approaches to the river difficult. It lies at the centre of a fertile lowland embayment that juts south into the Rhine Plateau. The river was far too wide for bridging until the nineteenth century (1859) and, in fact, the river has always played the role of a frontier in the political divisions of the lowland. Cologne was originally an outpost against the non-Roman lands to the east. The main north–south Roman road, that continued in use in the Middle Ages and remains to this day as a great trade artery, formed the axis of the old town.

[1] Based upon Bruno Kuske, *Die Großstadt Köln als Wirtschaftlicher und Sozialer Körper als Beitrag zur allgemeinen Großstadtforschung*, Cologne, 1928. This is one of the few studies of the regional aspects of a great city's development.

THE CITY-REGION

Thus established as a Roman centre, Cologne early became the seat of a bishopric, and grew to be one of the greatest commercial centres in Europe in the Middle Ages. It lay at the junction of the north–south route from the towns of north Italy and south Germany along the Rhine valley to Flanders and the North Sea ports. Like many other cities of less importance in the Rhinelands, the political disintegration of the lands around it after the sixteenth century hampered the free flow of goods, and this restricted relations with its environs. Cologne was an Imperial Free City, but immediately beyond its boundaries lay the territory of the archbishop of Cologne, stretching as a long belt on the west side of the Rhine from near Bonn to Krefeld, while to the west and east, the extensive territories of the dukes of Julich and Berg respectively stretched to the edges of the Rhine plateau.

At the beginning of the nineteenth century the city fell to the Prussians and was then developed as a frontier fortress against France and passed through a period of relative decline. The chief administrative centres of the newly established Rhineland Province were located at Koblenz and Düsseldorf. The old University at Cologne, that dated from the fourteenth century, was closed down. A new University was founded at Bonn and a Technical High School to serve western Germany was placed at Aachen. The present University in Cologne dates from the twentieth century and did not reach this rank until after 1918. Cologne's administrative status has been confined to that of a centre of a *Regierungbezirk*. It is thus pre-eminently an economic metropolis. It is a seat of old-established skilled industries, which produce high-quality finished goods. Heavy engineering, chemicals, and other industries have developed in the last two generations. It is also a pre-eminent seat of commerce, serving the daily needs of its inhabitants and industries, as well as controlling a large share of the trade and organization of the Rhineland province and neighbouring areas in north-western Germany.

The general layout of Cologne and its environs is shown on Fig. 40. The old city is sited on flat land on the left bank of the Rhine. It has a marked spider-web plan, in which, with the concentric semi-circular belt formed by its ancient town walls and the series of nineteenth-century fortifications, four zones may be recognized: the inner old town (*Altstadt*, *Ring*, and *Neustadt*); the inner suburbs (*Vorstädte*); the outer suburbs (*Vororte*); and the outer industrial–agricultural areas, that are allied, socially and economically, with the city.

The Prussian fortifications were built against the medieval wall of the *Altstadt* in the 1820's. The whole of these fortifications were destroyed in the 1880's and replaced by the *Ring*, and a wide semi-circular belt of the *Neustadt* developed between the Ring and the new

REGIONAL RELATIONS OF CITY: CASE STUDIES

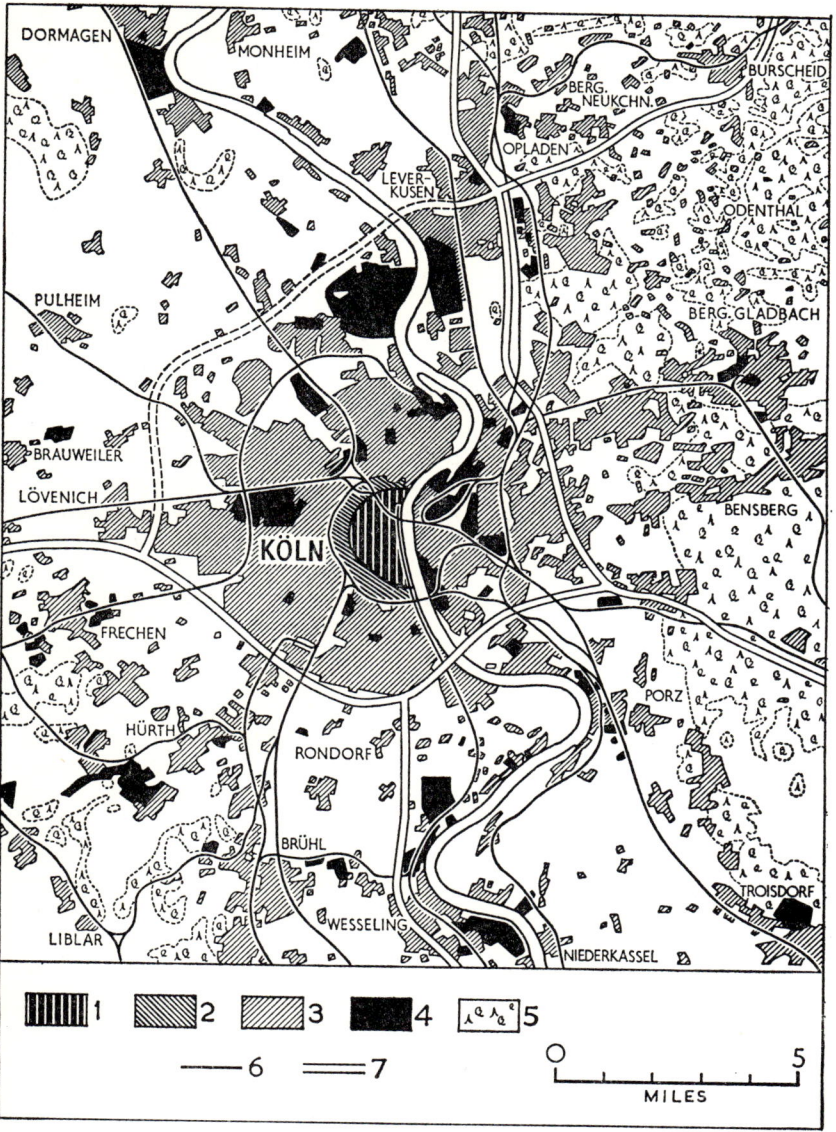

Fig. 40. Cologne Region: Land Use.
1. Medieval Town. 2. Neustadt (late nineteenth century). 3. Modern residential extensions. 4. Industrial areas. 5. Woodland. 6. Main railways. 7. Motorways.

fortifications. Along the outer side of the new wall (1880's) encircling railway tracks were built, and on their outer side a belt, or *glacis*, 600 yards wide, was forbidden for permanent building, as in Paris and other big continental cities. This system of fortifications became obsolete almost as soon as complete, and was completely demilitarized between 1906 and 1914, and a circle of detached forts beyond the *Vororte* then formed an outer fortified zone. The administrative limits of the city ended at the inner fortifications. Beyond, for centuries, it was ringed in by the independent state of Kurköln, so that the suburbs were independent of the city. The suburbs (*Vorstädte*) outside the fortified zone grew as independent administrative units—both towns and villages—two or three kilometres from the centre of the city—in the first half of the nineteenth century. They rapidly assumed full urban character, as sites for villa residential quarters, but, above all, for new industries. Each was a separate built-up area, with its axis on a main radial route from the city, and occupied a sector of a great semi-circle round the city of Cologne. The right bank was at last drawn into the orbit of urban development. The only settlement here hitherto was the small fortified bridge-head settlement of Deutz, designed to protect the approach to Cologne across the Rhine, that was without fixed bridges until the middle of the nineteenth century. Though not a national or political boundary, the Rhine was a frontier between German states and communes on its banks for centuries, and the right bank had no important towns until the late nineteenth century.

The railways on the east bank were laid out as independent rail terminals opposite Cologne before the first iron bridge across the Rhine was built in 1859. Here, in contrast to the skilled industries handled by small concerns in Cologne, heavy industries such as engineering and chemicals, with extensive plant lay-outs, together with working-class quarters, grew up on the open land near the railways and the river at Mulheim and Kalk. The conditions of the peace settlement at the end of the 1914–18 war resulted in the complete demilitarization of the outer circle of forts on the boundary of the *Neustadt*. This facilitated the expansion of the great city complex, notably the establishment of industrial sites on the Rhine, improved diagonal and circular roads, and the expansion of the housing area.

This urban expansion, that had commenced during the nineteenth century, was reflected in the expansion of the administrative limits of the city (Fig. 41). The first expansion in 1888 added the inner suburbs, and the city area was thus increased from 2,500 acres to 27,500 acres. More right-bank annexations were made in 1910 and 1914 bringing the city to its present eastern limits. The city now had a symmetrical shape on both banks, its frontiers to north and south lying opposite to each other on the Rhine. The Rhine frontage measured nine miles on each bank and the city stretched about 13 miles at its widest from east to west. But expansion had not ceased. With a view to acquiring land for industrial sites and a harbour on the Rhine front, extensive open areas were acquired by the city to the north along the Rhine in 1922, in a part of the old fortified zone. This forms an isolated prong jutting northwards from the compact administrative area. Since the last war Worringen has been added to it. Opposite this northern prong are the great chemical works of Leverkusen and Wiesdorf. The total administrative area amounts to about 100 square miles. After Berlin it is second in area of the German cities.

The city was wellnigh obliterated during the second world war and both the centre and the nearer suburbs have been largely rebuilt. There has also been large extension of the built-up area. In spite of its large administrative area, the built-up land has now reached its roughly circular administrative limits in most sectors on both banks of the river. Only the northern part in Worringen provides space for further expansion and here a new satellite town is being built. Today the built-up land reaches out without interruption to the surrounding *gemeinden* of Porz, Bensberg, Bergisch, Gladbach, and Leverkusen.

Cologne has spread its net of urban expansion and influence still further, from the brown-coal industrial areas of the Ville to the west and to the wooded Berg Uplands to the east. This wide area was, until the end of the nineteenth century, predominantly agricultural. Today, though it has much productive farm land, its economy is predominantly industrial and its settlements urban. Moreover, while the latter are oriented to their local plants, a large part of their workers travel daily to work in Cologne. The railroad net and the Rhine bridge of 1859 offered the framework for this development. Cologne plants at an early date began to be moved out beyond the *glacis* of the 600 yard zone of the Prussian fortifications. The exploitation of brown coal in the Ville, and zinc, lead and iron ore mining in the Berg land to the east of Bensberg, offered a material base for new heavy industry.

The city-region or *Großstadtraum* is shown on Fig. 41. This area has a diameter of some 25 miles and embraces 1·3 million people of whom nearly 800,000 are in Cologne itself on an area of 100 square miles. The whole area embraces the urban core of Cologne, including the areas incorporated in 1883; the area of the city of Cologne, in 1960; the fully built-up areas both in and outside Cologne (the urbanized area); and the urbanized border *gemeinden*.[1]

[1] See E. Meynen, 'Die Randstädte Kölns', in *Köln und das Rheinland, Festschrift zum XXIII. Deutschen Geographentag*, 1961.

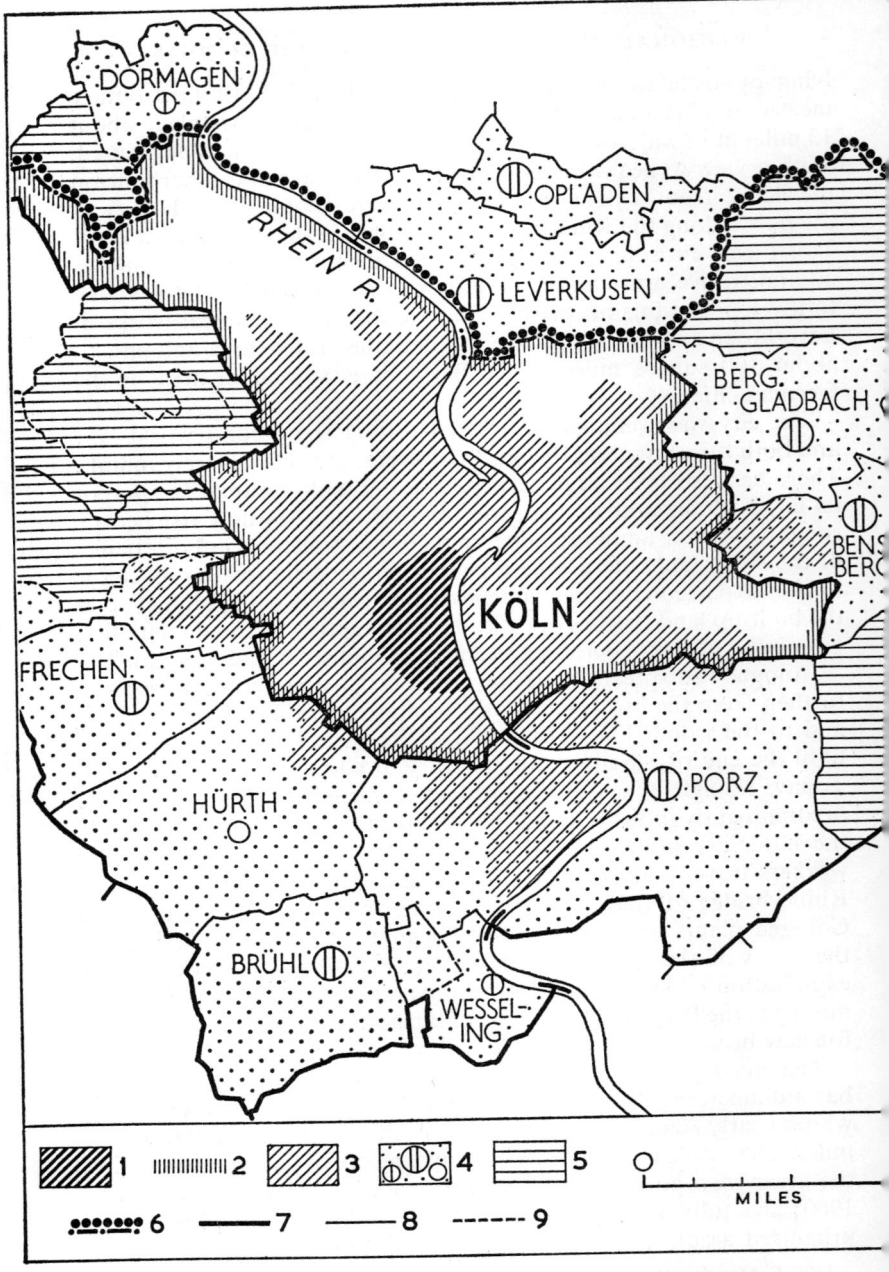

Fig. 41. Cologne Region: Growth Trends (after Meynen).

1. Cologne administrative area in 1883. 2. Annexations down to 1960. 3. The core urbanized area. 4. Urbanized rural *gemeinden* and towns. 5. Partly urbanized *gemeinden* of the environs. 6. Administrative boundaries of *Regierungsbezirk*. 7. *Landkreise*. 8. *Ämter*, and other towns. 9. *Gemeinden*. *Note:* This map is on the same scale as Fig. 40.

REGIONAL RELATIONS OF CITY: CASE STUDIES

There is a sharp functional division between left- and right-bank sectors. On the right bank there is an alternation of small agricultural and industrial settlements. On the left bank lies the extensive brown coalfield in the Ville district that runs as a strip from north-west to south-east. This area produced 30 per cent. of (pre-war) Germany's enormous production of brown coal. It is today the *Bund's* main source of supply and is closely integrated with the Ruhr and the whole of north-west Germany. It has great electricity plants, which supply power to Cologne, the Ruhr, and throughout north-western Germany, as well as briquette, brick, and other works. Here there is a north–south series of small industrial centres six to nine miles apart, all of which are old agricultural villages that have been industrialized.

The majority of the plants of Cologne are situated in the suburbs outside the compact central city on both banks of the river. The two greatest industrial complexes lie alongside the river to the north and to the south of the city. Niehl, to the north, was selected as a new industrial area and port in the twenties and here were erected the Ford plant (since 1930) and the *Glanzstoffwerke* (1926) and, further north, an area of four square kilometres of industrial land developed in the 1950's, as the site of the Esso refinery and other chemical plants. Across the river is the giant chemical plant of Leverkusen (population 100,000). This is the greatest single industrial complex between the Ruhr and Mannheim. To the south, at Wesseling (population 16,000), there was little development in the thirties, though it was an outlet for the shipment of brown-coal products from the Ville. It is now a big heavy industrial complex with chemical plants, a Shell refinery, depending on a pipe line for oil from Wilhelmshafen, and port facilities for shipments by the river. Other industrial developments are dwarfed by these two giants.

The whole of this outer zone is a transition belt from the urban area to the open country, in which industries are based in large measure on local resources—sugar, brown coal, and stones and earths. Established within it are those industries which sell their products in the Cologne market, and take advantage of local labour and cheap land.

The range of influence of the city may be clearly indicated from two criteria that are mapped on Fig. 76 on p. 384 and Fig. 67 on p. 372. The first shows the *gemeinden* from which more out-commuters worked in Cologne than in any other city. The second shows the *gemeinden* in which the majority of the workers are dependent on non-agricultural occupations.

The outstanding nodality of Cologne is reflected today in its radial routes, several of which follow the lines of Roman highways (Fig. 40). There are two autobahns, one parallel to the east side of the Rhine (from Frankfurt) and the other running along the border of the Rhine Plateau from Aachen to the Ruhr. With the construction of the route through Leverkusen, the city-settlement area will be encircled by motorways. Railroads were actively constructed from Cologne, backed by its own capitalists, and it is today one of the greatest railroad centres in western Europe. The environs are served by a dozen electric railways and many omnibus lines, with terminals averaging 20 to 25 miles from the city centre, though some reach distances of over 40 miles. Several of these lines on the right bank have branch routes 6 to 12 miles long that reach as far as the edge of the hills towards Solingen. The main railways parallel to the river keep well away from its banks so that villages on the Rhine are somewhat isolated and unaffected by urban trends. Until the advent of the electric railway these were connected with Cologne by steam-boat.

The city enjoys high status as a centre of business. It has the headquarters of fifty insurance companies and nearly thirty banks. The system of production of a great city such as Cologne has various bases. Old handicrafts contribute, through historical development, to the growth of modern finished industries of high-quality wares. A large number of people have to be provided with their manifold requirements, by both handicrafts and industry. Modern industrial and commercial development has been favoured by the geographical situation of the city in relation to the densely peopled industrial areas of western Europe—the Low Countries, and the lower and middle Rhinelands. Hence, its historic importance as a seat of transit and exchange. In this respect it is basically different from the other big cities of the lower Rhinelands that depend principally on one set of primary industries and the secondary industries dependent on them. Cologne's varied industry is based on its commercial position, and, from medieval times, goods have been imported for processing in the city, not only for consumption in the city, but for despatch to outside markets wherever they could be found. In 1959, the railroads received 1·3 million and despatched 1·0 million tons, while the harbours received 2·3 million and despatched 2·9 million tons.

In view of its historic role as a commercial centre, Cologne early became the seat of supply for the area around it. The old city supplies the surrounding specialized industrial districts with material and equipment such as machinery, installations, chemicals, and furnishings. It is able to supply from its plants many goods to the Ruhr and the Sauerland, while these latter supply the city with their special consumer goods, and coal, iron, and steel for use in its own industries. Thus, in addition to the vast variety of highly skilled industries, producing goods of high quality and demanding complicated processing, there are the more recent heavy industries, producing goods made from raw materials and semi-manufactured goods imported from the Ruhr. There is thus a most intimate interchange of goods between Cologne and other Rhine cities and the industrial districts of the lower Rhinelands, especially the Ruhr.

Many concerns in the surroundings have headquarters in Cologne and Cologne men have long occupied leading posts in concerns over a wide area. Business, trade, and professional organizations of all kinds for Rhineland and Westphalia have their headquarters in Cologne. Several great insurance firms have branches throughout western Germany, Holland, and Switzerland. Here are two of the biggest wholesale houses in Germany. It is an important banking centre, and the headquarters of many industrial firms whose plants are in the Ruhr, Aachen, Wuppertal, and the Siegenland. Cologne capital created the heavy iron and steel industries in the city, and helped finance the coal mining of the Ruhr and the brown-coal mining in the Ville.

The hinterland of Cologne in all these respects may be divided, as Kuske suggested forty years ago, into three areas. The 'local' market area covers the city and its closely associated environs—the city settlement area—which together have a population of over one million inhabitants. The 'provincial' market area covers the province of Rhineland and western Westphalia, for which it is the undisputed commercial metropolis. The 'state' market (*Landmarkt*) is a wider and less clearly defined area for which, in respect of specialized commercial functions, Cologne is a service centre. This is the area which is often referred to as the Lower Rhinelands. 'This area,' wrote Bruno Kuske, 'is one of the main regions into which Germany may be divided in regard to the organization of modern civilization. It has its independent commercial headquarters in the city, which has become one of the first centres of such economic radiation in the structure of the national market.' Cologne is a modern metropolis of the highest order.

3. LEEDS AND BRADFORD

We now pass to a brief treatment of the regional relations of two industrial cities in Britain—Leeds–Bradford—that jointly serve as an outstanding regional focus.[1]

Owing to the complex physical configuration of the site of the west Yorkshire conurbation, its lack of direct contact with the sea, and the rapid growth of Bradford in the nineteenth century, displacing Leeds as the merchanting centre of the woollen and worsted industries,

[1] R. E. Dickinson, 'The Regional Functions and Zones of Influence of Leeds and Bradford', *Geography*, Vol. XV, 1930, pp. 548–57.

THE CITY-REGION

there is in the industrial area of the Aire and Calder valleys not one principal nucleus as in other British conurbations, but two—Leeds and Bradford, and there exists a subdivision of regional functions between them. The West Yorkshire conurbation has a population of about 1·7 millions, and Leeds and Bradford, its largest centres, have about 500,000 and 300,000 respectively. The total population has remained constant for at least fifty years.

Bradford is the hub of the commercial organization of the woollen textile industries. The area tributary to it in this capacity is suggested by the distribution of members of the Bradford Exchange and the Chamber of Commerce. It is co-extensive in the main with the distribution of woollen textile workers, as given in the Census, in the Aire and Calder valleys west of Leeds. In this connection the close association of Keighley, Halifax, and the Spen valley with Bradford should be specially noted. The character of the commercial activities of Bradford is dominated by the woollen industry and its broader regional activities are of little importance. Leeds, however, with numerous industries, a large population, and a central location, has acquired functions of a more general and varied character. It is the headquarters of many industrial associations, and societies established in the interests of the industries pursued in the conurbation; the variety of pursuits undertaken in the city itself fostering this development. It is pre-eminent in Yorkshire as a centre of branch offices and depots established by firms with their works outside the conurbation. Such offices are generally located at Leeds, Sheffield, and Newcastle. The area in which business is transacted from the Leeds centre, though varying widely according to the nature of the business and the number of competitive branches, exhibits some consistency in that it regularly excludes Cleveland and south Yorkshire, the former being controlled from Newcastle and the latter from Sheffield. Hull and the East Riding are less frequently detached from the Leeds office.

Leeds is also prominent as a banking and insurance centre, though, in contrast to what has happened at Manchester, no banking house has resisted amalgamation and there is not one insurance company with its head office in Leeds or Bradford. In the development of banking in Yorkshire, each of the west Yorkshire towns played a prominent part and no one centre was dominant. The largest private banks had their headquarters in Leeds (2), Bradford (1), Halifax (1), and York (1). Today, though all these banks have been absorbed by the Big Five, there is still some measure of administrative control centred in Bradford and Leeds. The Stock Exchanges at both cities are negligible and are of no higher status than similar exchanges at Halifax and Huddersfield. The lack of a

REGIONAL RELATIONS OF CITY: CASE STUDIES

dominant focus is one of the most notable features of the financial organization of the West Riding, in striking contrast to the extreme concentration of the financial activities of south-east Lancashire and Manchester. Insurance development, however, lends itself admirably to regional treatment. In Leeds there are the district offices of almost a hundred insurance companies.

A regional capital functions as a general distributing centre through the agency of the wholesale markets, wholesale provision merchants, distributing depots of confectionery and kindred firms, and the retail shopping trade. The areas served in these capacities, based upon data of the areas served by individual concerns, were mapped for the distribution of fruits, vegetables and wholesale provisions, and retail trade areas.

The sphere of influence of Leeds and Bradford as cultural centres is more difficult to define. It may be estimated from the circulation of their principal newspapers, and those of competitive regional centres, the extent of the 'Yorkshire Region' adopted by educational and political societies with branches or headquarters in either city, and the areas served by the higher educational institutions (notably the University, Training College and College of Commerce in Leeds, and the Technical College in Bradford). From the evidence culled from these various sources we conclude that Cleveland and north Yorkshire have intimate relations with north-eastern England and its capital at Newcastle; south Yorkshire and north Lincolnshire with Sheffield. Doncaster divides its allegiance, having close relations with both West Yorkshire and Sheffield. Hull and the East Riding are more often than not associated with Leeds, but Hull today has its own University and certainly functions as an independent centre for the East Riding.

As an administrative centre, Leeds is of outstanding importance and ranks with the British provincial capital cities. This contrasts with the relations of Bradford, whose commercial and administrative functions are mainly concerned with the woollen textile industry. There are located in Leeds the divisional offices of government departments, railway and post office areas, and trade and professional societies.

From a consideration of the areas served by Leeds and Bradford in their various regional relations (a total of several hundred maps, plus a circulated questionnaire to a majority of clerks of parish councils throughout the county), and of the factors which condition their extent, we indicated the limits of their sphere of influence (Fig. 42). The area thus defined we have named the 'Yorkshire Region'. It is served from Leeds by the district branches of many business firms and insurance companies; it is the area adopted by the 'Yorkshire' trade, professional, and voluntary associations; it is served by the Leeds and Bradford newspapers and higher educational institutions, by the large retail shopping firms (mainly furnishers and high-class drapers), and the regional secondary industries. Leeds is its principal administrative and business centre, and Bradford the hub of its chief manufacturing industry.

The Middlesbrough industrial area has intimate relationships with

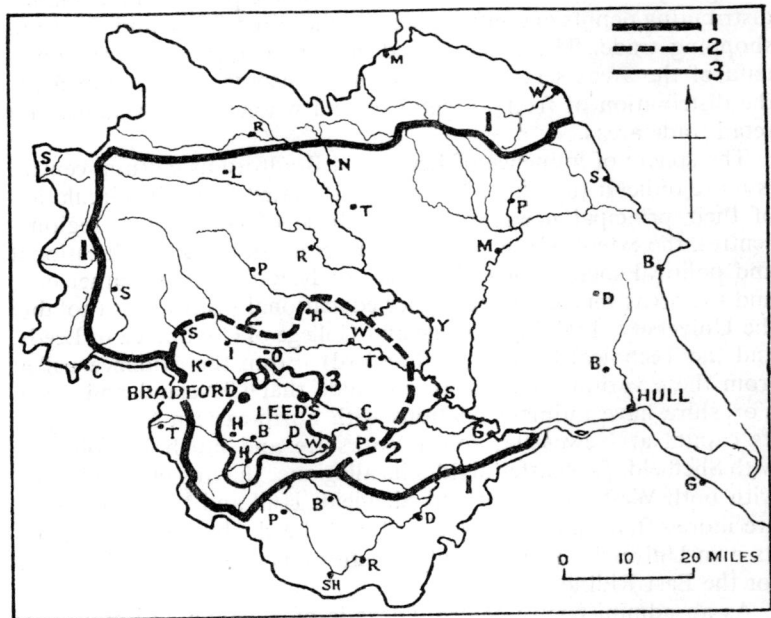

FIG. 42. The Zones of Influence of Leeds and Bradford.
1. The Yorkshire Region. 2. The Conurbation and Outer Suburban or Commuting Area. 3. Boundary of the West Yorkshire Conurbation.

north-eastern England and is too remote to be effectively controlled from West Yorkshire; indeed, it lies definitely within the Tyneside sphere of economic, administrative, and social influence. The West Riding falls into two clearly defined industrial areas focused upon the west Yorkshire and south Yorkshire conurbations and separated by the Calder–Dearne watershed. Thus the woollen textile industry of the Aire and Calder valleys has its southern limits in the urban districts of the Upper Colne Valley centred on Huddersfield; to the south the iron and steel industry is dominant. The Yorkshire coal-field is similarly divided into two sections, the west Yorkshire field centred on Wakefield, and embracing Huddersfield, Halifax and Bradford to the west, and Pontefract to the east; and the south Yorkshire field with its two chief centres at Barnsley and Doncaster. The orientation of these two fields towards Leeds-Bradford and Sheffield respectively is indicated, for example, by the distribution of members of the Leeds and Sheffield Coal Exchanges and the West and South Yorkshire Coal Owners' Associations. Thus, south Yorkshire, with a distinctive group of related industries, reflected in a community of economic organization and interests, is to be regarded as a portion of a separate region with its capital at Sheffield. The limit of the west Yorkshire sphere of economic influence is similarly set on the south-western borders in the Pennine valleys of the West Riding by the appearance of the cotton industry in places which are definitely oriented in every respect to Manchester. Hull and the East Riding are to be included in the west Yorkshire sphere of influence, for this area is regularly included in the Yorkshire districts of Leeds branch offices, insurance companies, and 'Yorkshire' administrative areas. In all these respects Hull possesses no fundamental regional functions. It is primarily a great port, but is acquiring increasing importance as a centre of regional integration. Moreover, its very existence as a great port is dependent upon its trade relations with the West Riding industrial areas. Yet it is such a large city that a separate organization of various purposes is essential, and in the interests of economy and in view of the relative inaccessibility of most of the East Riding from West Yorkshire, the East Riding often forms a separate district with Hull as its centre. As a large city, it is also a good shopping centre for the thinly populated area which surrounds it. It now has its own University.

Within this region there is a zone which has more intimate relations with Leeds and Bradford. This embraces two main areas. The first is the conurbation and its associated industrial towns. This may be divided into two sections, each with its predominant industries; the first, to the west of Leeds, concentrates upon the textile and engineering industries, and has its specialized commercial focus at Bradford. The second section, to the south and south-east of Leeds, is the principal coal-mining area and has intimate commercial relations with Leeds. Secondly, there are the residential areas lying to the north and north-east of the conurbation, including middle Wharfedale and Harrogate, the residential spa.

Most of this zone is accessible to either Leeds or Bradford by rail in under one hour, and there are daily reduced fares on most lines. All parts are served by through bus routes to one or both of the cities. That portion of the zone west of a line from Otley to Dewsbury, extending south to include Halifax and Brighouse (but not

Huddersfield and its tributary area in the Colne Valley), is more accessible to Bradford by bus and rail than to Leeds. It is these travelling facilities that mainly account for the coincidence of the zone with the shopping and insurance areas of the two cities and their daily inward and outward movement of workers. The whole zone is served by the four chief towns of the conurbation, but Bradford and Leeds are the principal distributing centres, and Leeds in particular distributes occasionally throughout its whole extent.

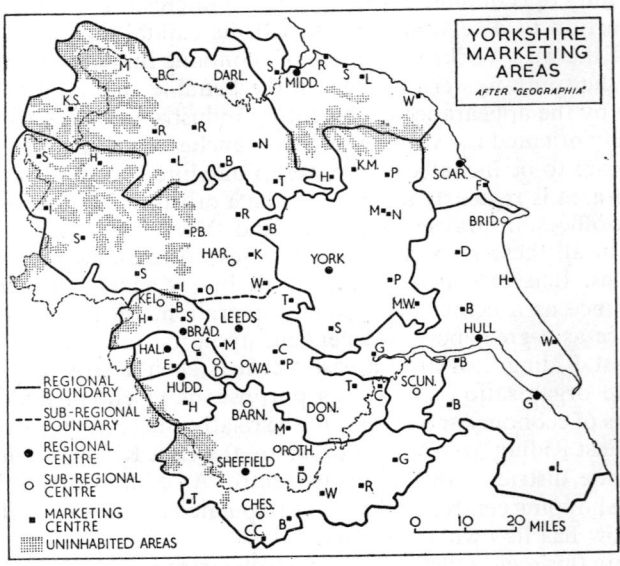

Fig. 43. Yorkshire Marketing Areas (after *Geographia*).

In the light of the investigations of F. H. W. Green into the bus service areas of centres, we have some modifications to add to our investigation. The map of Yorkshire on Fig. 43 shows, according to Green's method, the regional centres of Yorkshire grouped into one major province, the outer limits of which are defined on the basis of television patronage. The important point is that the Leeds regional service area—fed by its evening papers and drawn on primarily for purposes of special shopping facilities—is not circular, as shown on our map, but elongated from north-west to south-east, so as to include the Wakefield and Doncaster market areas and the Yorkshire Dales with Harrogate.

This area impinges on the market area of York to the east and of Sheffield (with Barnsley) to the south. The immediate market area around Leeds is thus smaller than shown on our map. The paper circulation and special shopping facilities of Bradford include a larger, but a still quite restricted, area. This map is, in fact, not a substantial modification of our earlier effort. It is a more precise definition of what we defined in more general terms.

4. SALT LAKE CITY[1]

Salt Lake City is the capital of the state of Utah, the seat of a religious denomination, the Mormons. It has played a dominant role in the regional development of America, and serves as an important basis of regional integration, a nucleus of commercial and financial enterprises, and a focus of transportation, a leading centre in educational activities. It is the largest city in a vast section of the United States. In many ways this city of only 200,000 inhabitants both serves and dominates an extensive tributary area that may be called its region. This region has an area of about 200,000 square miles and a population of about one million inhabitants (cf. England, 51,000 square miles and 40,000,000 inhabitants). It includes Utah, southern Idaho, eastern Nevada, and south-western Wyoming (see Fig. 44).

Salt Lake City has a well-balanced occupational structure. Its 54,000 gainfully employed persons in 1930 were occupied as follows: manufacturing and mechanical industries 25 per cent., trade (wholesale, retail, and other) 20 per cent., clerical occupations 15 per cent., transport and communications 11 per cent., domestic and personal service 12 per cent., professional services 11 per cent., public service 3·4 per cent. It was estimated that a fifth of the total gainfully employed were in occupations over and above the needs of Salt Lake City and its immediate environs—that is, that a fifth of the employed were concerned directly with meeting *regional* as opposed to *local* needs. These 'represent merely the elemental occupational base upon which are pyramided many other occupations serving chiefly the inhabitants of the city itself'. On this basis Salt Lake City had 62 per cent. of the clerical occupations; 71 per cent. of the wholesale trade; 46 per cent. of the retail trade (which is more evenly distributed with the population in accordance with local needs); 56 per cent. of other trades (bankers, brokers, and money-lenders 61 per cent.; insurance agents, managers and officials 60 per cent; commercial travellers,

---

[1] *Salt Lake City, A Regional Capital*, by C. D. Harris, published by the University of Chicago Press, 1940, Private Edition. We summarize the findings of this work since it illustrates excellently the viewpoint and technique of our approach and the study in itself has a very limited circulation and will therefore not be generally accessible. Map reproduced with the kind permission of the author.

65 per cent); 59 per cent. of public service (mainly military service, since the city is a garrison centre); 42 per cent. of professional service;[1] 37 per cent. of transport and communication. Wholesaling is a main regional function, the 40 establishments handle two-thirds of the wholesaling of both producers' and consumers' goods of Utah. Manufacturing is not a dominant activity in the occupational structure of Salt Lake City. It produces about a quarter of the value of manufactured products in the state of Utah. But manufactures are none the less important, and figure large in the life and structure of the City.

The region serving Salt Lake City has a populous core, and scattered oasis and mining settlements in the midst of grazing and desert lands. The boundary of the region is therefore a wide no-man's land in which there is really no effective competition, with other regional capitals. Boundaries are, therefore, more clearly defined in the populous sectors along the main lines of communication. The region was determined by studying the areas served by a number of important regional functions, as shown on Fig. 44. Each of these service areas covers a distinct area that is limited by different factors. Twelve areas were defined and superimposed. The service areas for retail trade, wholesale grocery trade, wholesale drug trade, radio broadcasting, and generalized trade were all taken from published sources. All of them are the result of careful statistical studies by competent authorities. Newspaper circulation and the extent of the Mormon religion are also based on statistical study. The former is a good indicator of potency and extent of metropolitan influence. The latter is a feature peculiar to the state of Utah, which gives to Salt Lake City special claims to leadership over a wide area. Established as the capital of the Mormons in 1847, the settlement of much of the surrounding lands was effected by the religious leadership of the Mormon community, which directed the exploration of irrigable lands, the lay-out of new villages, and the settlement of European immigrants. Mormons are still today in a majority throughout Utah and in sectors of southern Idaho (except the Twin Falls district), and throughout a wide surrounding area they make up to 10 to 20 per cent. of the total population. Interviews provided the data for the extent of telephone, bakery, and petroleum distribution areas. From these twelve areas a generalized boundary was drawn (Fig. 44).

The retail trade area (which was prepared for department stores, clothing, furniture, and jewellery stores rather than for grocery and drug stores) differs from the rest in having a very small service area.

[1] Publishing 66 per cent., banking 60 per cent., clothing 58 per cent., petroleum refining 100 per cent., managers and officials 55 per cent., building (the second largest group) 38 per cent., all other (the largest group) 31 per cent.

REGIONAL RELATIONS OF CITY: CASE STUDIES

Higher priced goods have larger areas—both from the point of view of the consumer travelling to the centre, and of the goods being

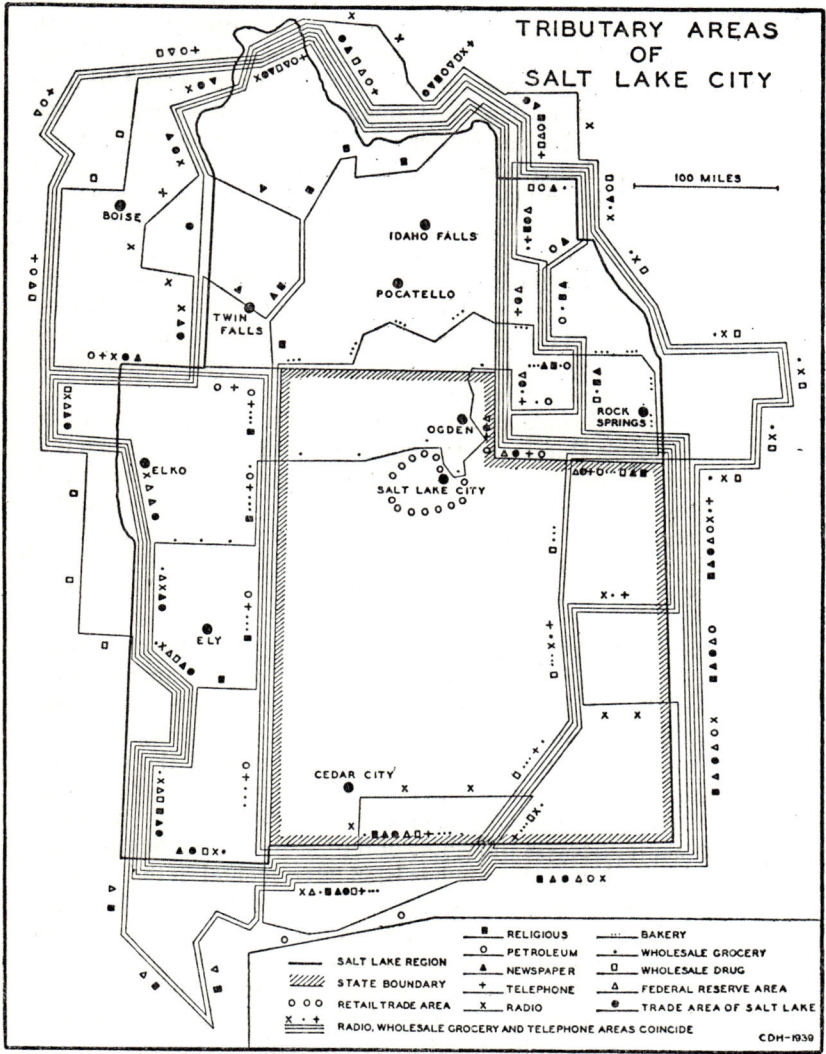

FIG. 44. Salt Lake City: Tributary Areas.

delivered to him. Occasional deliveries (or visits) may cover a long distance, but the retail area considered is that of regular service.

THE CITY-REGION

There are other areas of similar restricted extent, such as milk supply and professional service.

Beyond this smaller area comes the wholesale trade area, which again is fixed by the distance factor and its effect on transport costs. Groceries being relatively bulky will not stand the cost of long-distance deliveries from one centre, and smaller towns tend to have their own distributing depots—though the advent of cheap road transport has extended the sphere of delivery from Salt Lake City. Bakery products, being both bulky and perishable, have a range of distribution that is limited by time, as well as by transport costs.

Beyond these areas again are the religious, newspaper, and generalized trade areas. The first is estimated from the area in which the Mormons form over 20 per cent. of the population, though a smaller proportion occurs over a much wider territory. The limits of newspaper circulation tend to follow a 'time divide' between competing metropolitan centres. These two areas are of the highest significance as cultural and economic agencies.

The generalized trade area is the result of a careful synthesis by the United States Bureau of Foreign and Domestic Commerce and closely corresponds with the extent of the region as finally defined. Five areas extended still further to the north-west—radio broadcasting, finance, telephone, wholesale drugs, and petroleum service—since these are concerned with services in which the item of transport cost is small and the widest area of distribution is an economy in service.

The Wasatch Oasis, with its combination of agriculture, mining, and transport facilities, is the chief supporter of the capital, and is the section of the region most tied up with it. The irrigation and settlement of this whole area were planned and financed by Salt Lake City and its Mormon community. The very size of the city as a consuming market encourages the specialization and commercialization of farming in the Oasis. The influence of the city in all its regional relations covers the whole of the Oasis, and the business and financial leadership of the city has been instrumental in the development of its transport facilities. The impact of the city on the types of commercialized farming on the irrigated land is reflected in the importance of dairying, for the Oasis produces half of the milk of the state, and 80 per cent. of the fluid milk consumed in the Oasis is produced in it. There is also a marked specialization on the production of fruit, vegetables, and other perishable products.

Salt Lake City, together with Ogden, forms an important nucleus of railways, while the Oasis, in addition to being a focus, has a closely knit net of electric inter-urban lines. In contradiction to this complicated pattern with its two foci in Ogden and Salt Lake City, the highways are centred on the latter, eight of them radiating in all directions. The business activities of the city and its region are reflected in the trade flows as canalized on rail and road. Railways dominate this goods traffic. This falls into three categories: through traffic (from California to East or Middle West) making one-half of the total carload traffic of the region; inter-regional traffic which either originates in, or terminates in, the Salt Lake City Region, one-fifth; and intra-regional traffic, which both originates and terminates in the region, one-quarter.

The role of Salt Lake City in these traffic movements may be viewed from the standpoint of either the service areas or the mapped streams of traffic flow in which the services are canalized. Ogden is a transfer point between major railway systems, a despatch centre for certain raw materials such as live stock, and an industrial satellite of Salt Lake City, with railway workshops, meat-packing plants, and flour mills. Salt Lake City handles the trade in diversified wholesale goods, and while Ogden is a through route centre for rail traffic, Salt Lake City is by far the more important terminal for goods and passenger traffic. Inbound shipment of goods far exceeds outbound shipments at Salt Lake City in contrast to Ogden, for it imports valuable and diversified products for distribution (often including processing in the city) by rail and lorry throughout the region. The carloads of goods (in and out) handled by Salt Lake City (1932) amounted to a sixth of the total for Utah, and some of these products were handled dominantly by the City for distribution in the region—petroleum at the refinery; miscellaneous products through the hands of the distributors; ores and concentrates terminating at refineries in neighbouring satellite towns; imported products such as automobiles, furniture, and machinery; and paper and paper products.

The city plays a much smaller part in exports from the region, for products from seats of specialized production proceed direct to their regional or national markets. Goods sent to Salt Lake City are mainly consumed in the city itself—milk, building materials, manufactured goods (sugar and canned goods), coal, and coke. Three bulky commodities made up two-thirds of the freight handled in the city: coal, ores, and petroleum. Like a great national inland port the city also handles a complex variety of goods for distribution to its hinterland. The total tonnage figures of the Salt Lake City yards, like those of the great ports, are dominated by a few bulky commodities. It owes this function, not to its location at a physical break of bulk point in the transport system, but to a break in this transport system devised and developed to serve a particular region around it.

Chapter 10

THE CITY-REGION IN THE UNITED STATES: I

1. DEVELOPMENT OF THE METROPOLITAN REGION

Three of the most remarkable trends in the development of the United States in the first half of the twentieth century have been the continuous increase in the proportion of the population living in cities, so that today it is essentially an urban society; second, the increasing concentration of affairs in mammoth cities—the 'megalopolitan civilization' that is the target of Lewis Mumford's gloomy invectives; and third, the suburban sprawl of low-density housing and other urban land uses around and between the mammoth cities, so as to produce vast urbanized regions which are making alarming inroads on the land and amenities of the country. Innumerable collections of statistics, books, and commentaries have been written on these themes and there is certainly nothing new that can be added here. We shall, however, try to put these trends into a perspective that is relevant to understanding the relations between the city and its dependent region. This calls for a brief review of the growth and spread of urban population and urbanized areas, for an appraisal of the functions of the metropolitan cities, and for a definition of the areas dependent upon these cities in respect to the distinctive production and demands of their regional economies.

With a population of over 180 million people living on three million square miles, the United States is the world's greatest producer of agricultural products, yet it is essentially an urban society. In 1900, 60 per cent. of its population was classed as rural and 40 per cent. as urban. In 1960 seven-tenths, indeed, close on three-quarters, could be classed as urban. In fact, less than 10 per cent. of the population is actually dependent on farming and about a third of these are part-time farmers. The full-time farmers make up a tiny fraction of the total working population of the country.

The main phases in the economic development of the United States are clearly reflected in the growth of its great cities. In the pre-railway era, until the middle of the nineteenth century, settlement was confined for the most part to the Atlantic coastal belt east of the Alleghany Mountains, with sporadic pioneer settlement beyond these mountains along the river courses. Settlement was mainly rural. Towns were small service centres and the largest were situated on the Atlantic coast. The second period of settlement corresponds with the expansion of the railway network between about 1850 and 1900. Settlement spread westwards across the continent. During this period, the United States was primarily an exporter of foodstuffs which amounted to two-thirds of its exports in 1900. Cities grew both as centres for the collection of agricultural products and for the distribution to the farmer of supplies brought in from the manufacturing centres on the Atlantic Seaboard. The principal cities were located at the crossways of railway and water transport. They all developed as railway centres. Local transport was by covered-wagon or horse and buggy on badly-maintained and often dangerous earthen tracks.

Towards the close of the nineteenth century great changes marked the emergence of the modern United States—the development of the manufacturing industries, the great influx of European immigrants, the advent of the internal combustion engine and the automobile, and the development of electricity. Industries grew both at the seats of natural resources and also in the great cities. The cities supplied their market areas with the manufactured goods which, in the earlier phase, they had imported from the east. The advent of the automobile has brought about a much greater mobility and diffusion of both persons and goods than was possible by the railway. Whereas under the influence of railway transportation there was an ever-increasing concentration of population in cities, the automobile has permitted the outward expansion of the city and has enabled it to establish much more intimate relations with the surrounding towns, villages, and farms. Consequently, the city or metropolitan community, extending far beyond the limits of the city as an administrative unit, is now an established and important fact in the framework of American society.

The last stage of this growth has been the emergence of financial centres, independent of New York. The great commercial centres of the nineteenth century have become 'million' cities, seats of commerce, industry, finance, and culture. Within the span of fifty years each of these great cities has attained metropolitan proportions, first as collectors and distributors of products drawn from their hinterlands, then as producers of those very goods which hitherto they had imported from distant producing areas; and finally, as independent centres of finance and culture. There is no mistaking about a dozen of these cities. There are, however, marked variations in their

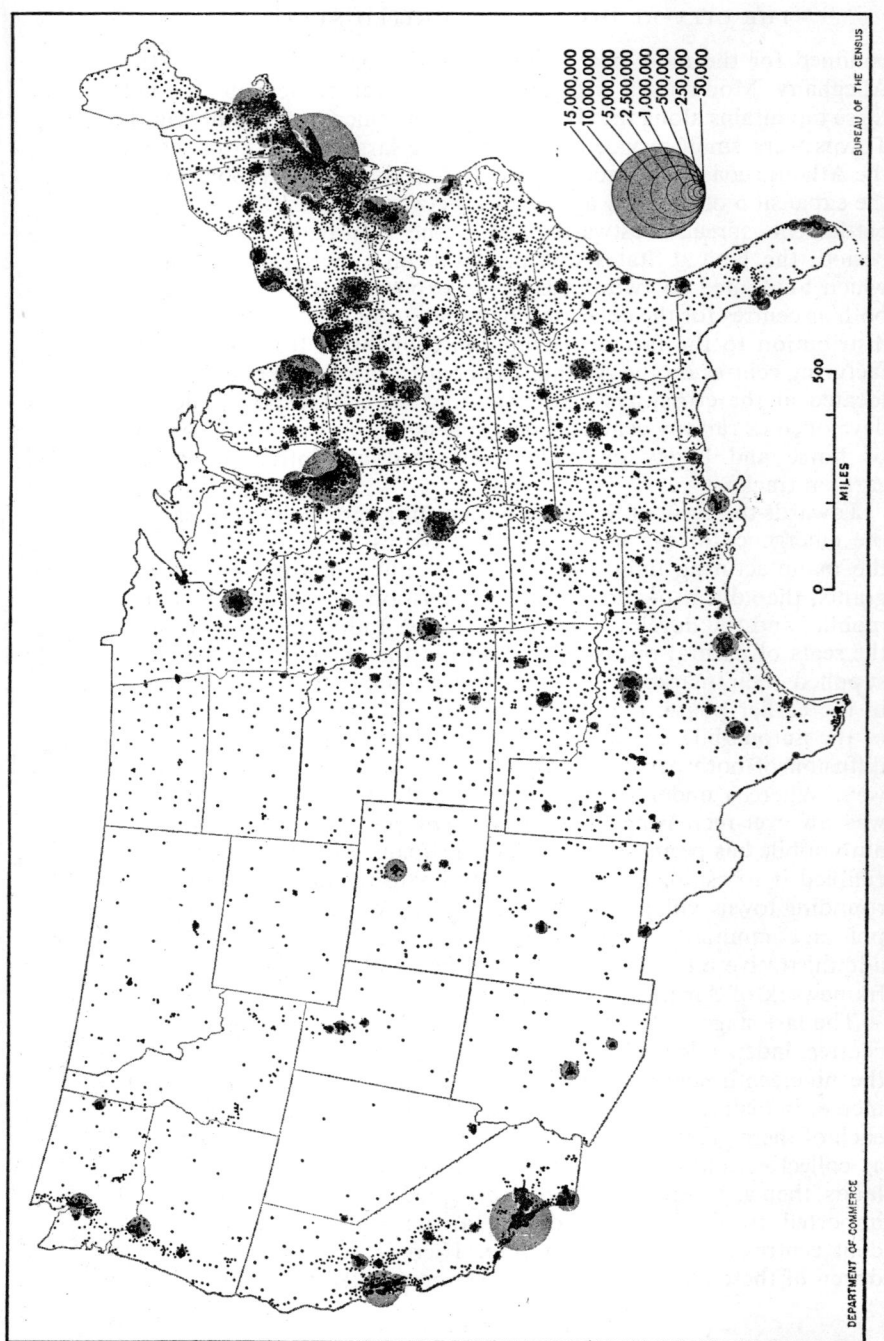

FIG. 45. United States: Population Distribution, 1960 (from U.S. Census of Population, U.S. Summary, PC(1), IA).

functions, depending upon the character of their hinterlands, whether concerned with agricultural production, industry, or the production of raw materials, such as oil. But all have the same essential characteristics. They are capitals for wide tributary areas, which they serve as leaders in economy and culture, interests, and aspirations.

The idea of the economic metropolis has come from the United States. Owing to the great size of that country, the absence of tariff barriers and rapid settlement in the last hundred years, the stages in the development of the metropolis—the commercial or wholesaling phase, the industrial phase, the transportation phase, and the financial phase—can be traced over a few generations. In this development there has been acute rivalry between cities—New York, New Orleans, and Montreal in the early nineteenth century; Chicago and St. Louis as rivals for the leadership of the Middle West; the Twin Cities (Minneapolis and St. Paul) and Kansas City, with the opening of the grain and cattle-raising lands of the western states during and after the nineties; and San Francisco, Los Angeles, and Seattle in the Pacific West. But the fiercest competition has been between the cities on the Atlantic Seaboard, especially New York, Boston, Philadelphia, and Baltimore. Backed by closely settled hinterlands, this cluster of old cities in the north-east is an important outlet for the entire Middle West.

'By every peaceful means possible, each of these cities had endeavoured to outdo its rivals, by constructing highways, canals, and railroads, ... by establishing transatlantic lines for freight and passengers, and by setting as low land and water rates from and to its ports as could be secured. They have been rivals for grain, cattle, coal and general merchandise, and the passenger trade.'[1]

In examining the extent of their tributary regions one sees 'a see-saw of unending struggle, not marked by political elections, or military engagements, but by advertising, the circulation of newspapers, the activities of commercial travellers, the struggles of boards of trade, rate wars, and the migration of workers and business men'.[2] Gras, on the basis of his definition of a fully-fledged metropolis, considered that there were (in the twenties) eleven metropolitan cities in the United States—New York, Chicago, St. Louis, the Twin Cities (Minneapolis and St. Paul), Kansas City, San Francisco, Baltimore, Boston, Cleveland, and Cincinnati. The above-mentioned stages in the development of these cities during the last hundred years are

[1] N. S. B. Gras, *Introduction to Economic History*, pp. 286–7.
[2] *Ibid.*, p. 298.

especially evident among the cities of the Middle West and the Far West. Each began as a commercial centre, then added manufacturing to its activities, and finally emerged, in varying degree, as a dominant seat of finance and business.

2. Growth of Urban Population

The population of the United States increased by 19 millions in the decade 1940–50. This increase soared to about 28 million in the fifties and by 1960 the population had reached a total of 178·5 millions, an increase of 18·4 per cent. since 1950. This figure is more than 30 per cent. greater than in the decade 1940–50. This remarkable trend is due to a continued high birthrate since the war of a little less than 25 births per 1,000 people. This trend completely explodes the views of demographic experts in the thirties that the higher the level of living the lower the birth rate. This revolutionary change, whereby America is not only an urban society but also a family society, is basic to an understanding of American society and its problems of building and social provision.

'Urban population' was redefined in 1950 to include all places with over 2,500 inhabitants and the densely settled fringe around the cities with 50,000 people (meaning places with at least 500 dwelling units per square mile or contiguous non-residential areas).[1] The rest of the population was classed as rural, in the categories of rural-farm and rural-non-farm. In 1950, 64 per cent. of the population of the States was urban in this sense and one-third rural, but only 15 per cent. lived on farms. Full data of the 1960 census are not yet available but 70 per cent. is classed as urban and 30 per cent. as rural. During the period 1950 to 1958 the farm population declined by 17 per cent. The urban population increased by 9·4 per cent. and comprised over half of the total growth. It is the rural non-farm population, located primarily at the margins of the cities, which experienced the most rapid growth—roughly one-half, a great acceleration over the 1940–50 rate. This was due to the unprecedented extension of suburban areas. The increase in these areas (outside the central cities) was 16·8 millions as compared with 9 millions in the urban areas, though the latter contained 63·1 per cent. of the total, as compared with 23·8 per cent. in the rural non-farm areas.

A comparative study of the growth of the Standard Metropolitan Areas from 1900 to 1950 may now be made. There were 168 according to the 1950 census definition. This area, except for New England,

[1] This is a generalized statement. See a discussion in D. J. Bogue, *The Population of the United States*, Free Press, Glencoe, 1959.

THE CITY-REGION IN THE UNITED STATES: I

is a county or a group of contiguous counties with at least one city with 50,000 inhabitants or more, provided that such counties are 'essentially metropolitan in character and socially and economically integrated with the central city'. The list of criteria defining such integration is discussed in Chapter 8. Modifications of this definition enabled Bogue to compare the population growth of the S.M.A.s from 1900 to 1950. In 1950, 56·8 per cent. of the population of the United States lived in the S.M.A.s that covered 7·1 per cent. of the land area. Moreover, the number of S.M.A.s has steadily increased from fifty-two in 1900, in which year they contained 32 per cent. of the total population. The rate of growth has been much greater than in the non-metropolitan areas. In the 1940–50 decade the S.M.A.s accounted for 80 per cent. of the total increase of population. In the 1950–60 decade it amounted to 85 per cent. There was no slackening of the trend in the fifties, for S.M.A.s, by the 1960 definition increased by 25 per cent. They accounted for 85 per cent. of the increase and contained 63 per cent. of the total population of the nation in 1960.

The United States today is an urbanized society and the overwhelming majority of its people live in cities on a fraction of its area. The table shows that the most highly urbanized States in the Union are in the north-east, Illinois and California. Rhode Island is 87 per cent. metropolitan, New York 86 per cent., Massachusetts 85 per cent., and New Jersey, Connecticut, Pennsylvania, Maryland, and Illinois are all over 75 per cent metropolitan. The really high

UNITED STATES: PER CENT. OF POPULATION
IN URBAN AREAS—1940–60

	Per cent. Urban		Per cent. Change	
	1950	1960	1940–50	1950–60
U.S.A.	64·0	69·9	19·5	29·3
New England	76·2	76·4	7·8	13·1
Middle Atlantic	80·5	81·4	7·1	8·1
East North Central	69·7	73·0	14·6	24·8
West North Central	52·0	58·8	17·1	23·8
South Atlantic	49·1	57·2	30·0	42·9
East South Central	39·1	48·4	28·9	30·0
West South Central	55·6	67·7	48·0	42·1
Mountain	54·9	67·1	39·8	65·1
Pacific	75·0	81·1	43·3	52·9

SOURCE: *U.S. Census of Population, 1960, U.S. Summary, Number of Inhabitants*, PC(1), Table 20.

rates of increase were located in the predominantly desert states of the south-west (Phoenix, Tucson, Las Vegas, Albuquerque, Denver, and Pueblo). Certain features of this growth in the deserts of the south-west are summarized on p. 304. The metropolitan population of Florida almost doubled.

3. Urban Regions

The phenomenal expansion of urban land uses around and between the central cities has not merely resulted in the growth of conurbations, but also in the coalescence of such areas to form predominantly urban regions in which cities compete with each other in the extension of their functional orbits.

The great cities are expanding on their peripheries at a phenomenally rapid rate. Comparable rates of growth are found nowhere in western Europe. The urbanized areas are spreading to the boundaries of the S.M.A.s and even beyond them. Not only are many S.M.A.s contiguous, but their urbanized areas are now expanding and merging into one another. This process of 'regional urbanization' is producing continuous clusters of large cities interconnected by sprawling and heterogeneous urban land uses. How are we to determine the extent of these areas? There are obviously degrees of urbanization, that depend not only on the extent of the urbanized areas and their immediate peripheries, but also on the facility with which homes in the country are accessible to work and service in city centres.

Fig. 46 shows the distribution of the standard metropolitan areas. There were according to the 1960 census 208 such areas but 107 of these can be grouped in 25 contiguous clusters of two or more S.M.A.s. These may be described as urban regions. They are listed at the end of Chapter 11 on the basis of the 1960 figures. There are also 38 single S.M.A.s, each with over 250,000, four of them with over one million inhabitants—St. Louis, Buffalo, Kansas City, and Atlanta.

The most obvious feature of the distribution of these metropolitan areas is the great stretch of almost continuously urbanized land which extends a distance of over 600 miles from Portland in Maine to Norfolk-Newport News in Virginia. It contains 33 S.M.A.s, including Boston, New York–New Jersey, Philadelphia, Baltimore, and Washington. Here in 1950 there was a population of 27·3 millions and in 1960 31·6 millions. This is an increase of about 18·1 per cent. in the decade, comparable to the national increase of 18·4 per cent. If you travel from Boston to Washington by air on a clear night, the lights clearly indicate the continuity of urban occupance. There

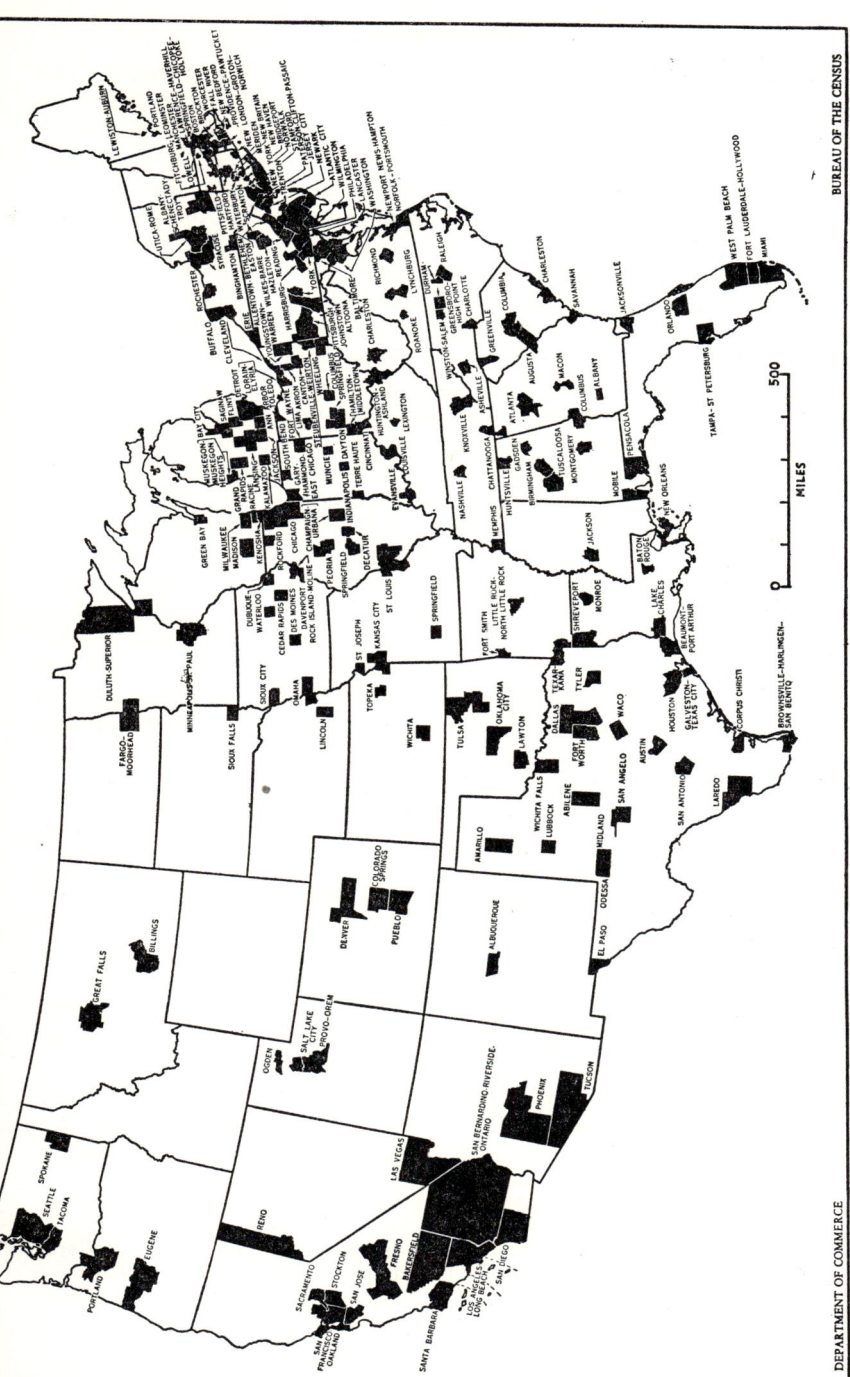

Fig. 46. United States: Standard Metropolitan Statistical Areas, 1960. (Source as for Fig. 45.)

are open spaces, of course, but they are rapidly being filled up, and all parts are drawn closely into the functional orbits of the major places of work. The farmsteads in the rural islands are lived in today by professional people, factory workers, and others who travel daily to their plants and offices. For here and elsewhere, growth takes place most rapidly along the highways. Miles of ribbon development—bill-boards, cafés, hot-dog stands, drive-in theatres, amusement parks, petrol stations, and even specialized stores—herald the approaches to every city. Bulldozers clear the way for housing developments that are completed within a few months, swallowing up farms and woodlots. Regional shopping centres emerge between outlying suburban subdivisions and are often physically removed from the actual residential areas. Industrial plants, covering hundreds of acres each, are located in the open countryside and workers' cars are accommodated on parking lots that far exceed the ground area of the plants themselves. Big city department stores open up large branches in the suburban outskirts. The Eastern Atlantic Seaboard has become the continuous urbanized area that Geddes and Wells envisaged fifty years ago and has recently been named Megalopolis by Jean Gottmann.[1]

Outside the Atlantic Seaboard, there are five other such clusters that dwarf the rest. Chicago–Milwaukee had 8·2 millions, but on the basis of access this area reaches further afield, extending north along the western shores of lake Michigan, and eastwards through Michigan City to link up through the cities of southern Michigan with the Detroit region. The latter has some 5·0 millions and is closely linked with its neighbours. Cleveland and Pittsburgh with their intermediate cities form a vast urban agglomeration with 6·3 million people. Together with Cincinnati (2·1 millions) this whole cluster in Ohio–Pennsylvania has an aggregate population of about 14 millions. The next two giants are located in California, the most rapidly growing state in the Union. San Francisco and the Bay area has over 4 million people. Los Angeles, with 9 millions in 1960, is the second largest aggregate in the nation and the fastest in growth. Eight other such city clusters have around one to two million inhabitants each, quite a drop in size from the major clusters.[2] We should include with these, five 'single' metropolitan areas of about one million inhabitants each—Kansas City, St. Louis, Buffalo, Atlanta, and Denver. Below the figure of about one million down to

---

[1] J. Gottmann, *Megalopolis: The Urbanised Northeastern Seaboard of the United States*, Twentieth Century Fund, New York, 1961, 810 pp.

[2] Minneapolis–St. Paul (1·5 m.), Seattle–Tacoma (1·4 m.), Dallas–Fort Worth (1·6 m.), Houston–Galveston (1·4 m.), Syracuse–Utica–Rome (0·9 m.), Phoenix–Tucson (0·9 m.), Miami (1·5 m.).

THE CITY-REGION IN THE UNITED STATES: I

250,000 there are 47 agglomerations. Especially noticeable are the two north-east–south-west series in the south-eastern States, one from Birmingham through Chattanooga to Knoxville, and the other from Montgomery to Atlanta and thence through the cotton manufacturing towns of the Carolinas to Greensboro and Winston Salem. The eastern coast of Florida is rapidly becoming a narrow urbanized coastal strip. The Puget Sound cities of Seattle, Tacoma, and Portland are closely interrelated but they are still physically separate. Of particular interest is the east–west series of cities in the Middle West that is bounded by Chicago and St. Louis. This series runs through central Illinois and Indiana from Indianapolis through Peoria to the Mississippi Valley and thence into central Iowa.

The rates of increase of these metropolitan areas are shown in the table (end of Ch. 11) for 1940–50 and 1950–60. The Eastern Seaboard belt increased by 18·1 per cent. in the last decade and its number of S.M.A.s increased from 24 to 33. This increase compares with 18·4 per cent. for the nation as a whole. While some S.M.A.s within the belt continued to grow rapidly (that is, above the national average), others show sub-normal increases. The areas of most rapid growth in the nation were Los Angeles and San Francisco (1940–50, roughly 60 per cent., and the same in 1950–60 decade)—fantastic rates for metropolitan areas of such a vast size. At the end of 1962 the 17 million Californians surpassed the population of New York State, thus reflecting one of the most phenomenal migrations in history. Remarkable among the larger cities with over one million inhabitants are Dallas–Fort Worth and Houston–Galveston in Texas. Also highly significant are the tourist and retirement agglomerations of the south-west. Phoenix–Tucson almost doubled in both decades. Florida also had great increases. Miami and West Palm Beach (1950–60, 161 per cent., 1940–50, 80 per cent.) are 70 miles apart but are rapidly expanding towards each other. Tampa nearly doubled, and Jacksonville increased by one-half. Lesser areas also recorded large percentage increases, such as Albuquerque.

The flood of urban expansion is in full spate and there is no apparent limit to it. It is likely that, if present trends remain unchecked, by A.D. 2000 the Atlantic Seaboard belt will spread westwards through central New York State and Pennsylvania, through the Middle West past Chicago, and possibly to Kansas City. It will expand southwards beyond the southern fringe of the so-called Manufacturing Belt into Kentucky and Tennessee. New manufacturing centres are already growing in these latter States. The president of one of the greatest trucking companies in the States has said that in ten years one may have to travel 150 miles to get really clear of the big city of Chicago and he envisages a 'super-metropolis' in

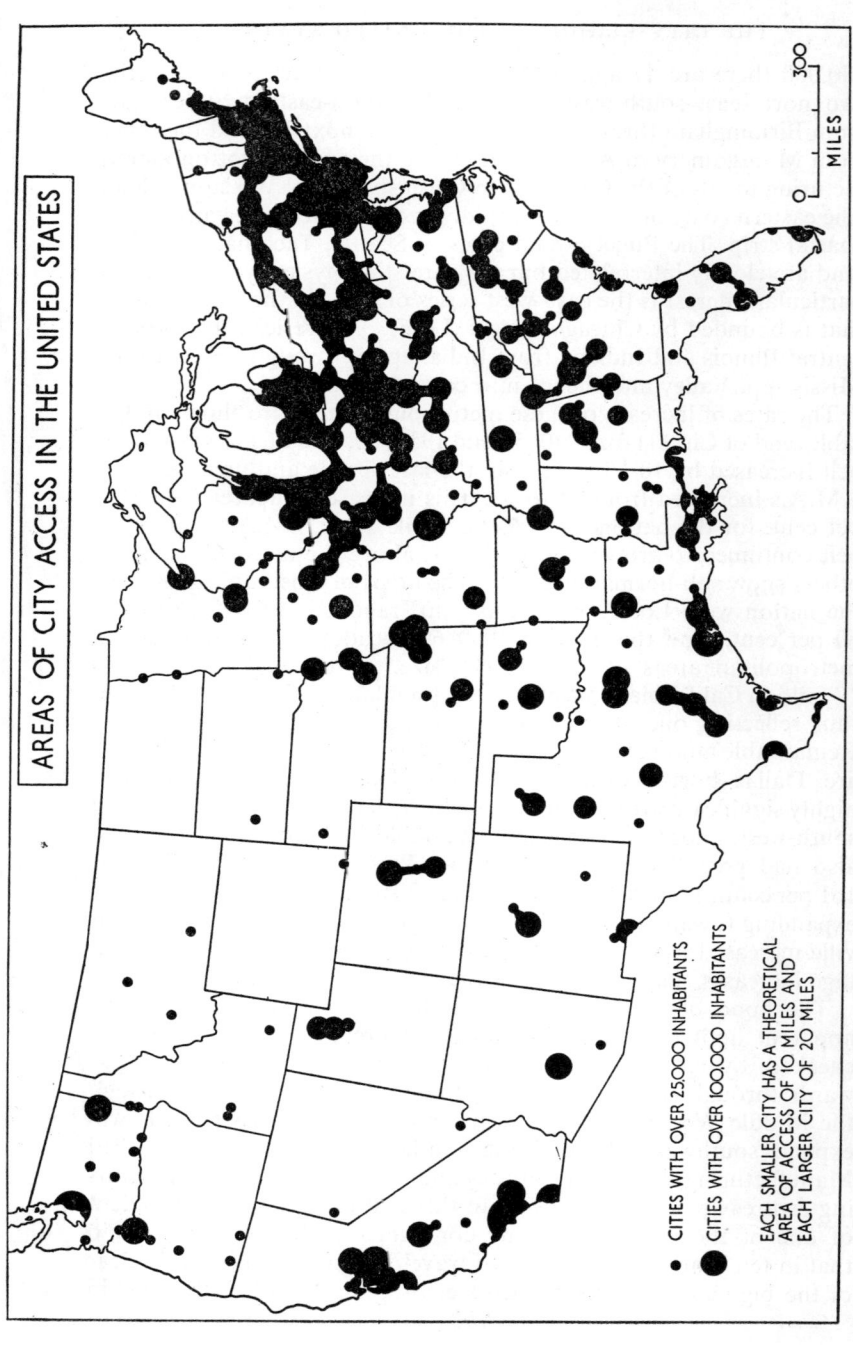

Fig. 47. United States: Areas of City Access. All places in black that lie within 20 miles radius of a 100,000 city, or 10 miles radius of a city with 25,000 to 100,000 people. For further detail see text. The map is on the same scale

THE CITY-REGION IN THE UNITED STATES: I

the Middle West running from Milwaukee through Chicago to Michigan City. He states that 'the new interstate highways, the vast urban airports, and the huge industrial and residential growth along the expressways will run the big urban areas together into a blending of population and commercial enterprise'. Blending is hardly the correct word for such a scrambling of uses, but it gives a general picture of what is taking place.

This expansion of urban uses is dependent on rapid transport mainly on highways between cities. Accessibility is a primary determinant on the range of urban expansion. The United States Census has not yet undertaken a thorough census of workplaces and consequently there is no basis for nation-wide assessment. We have adopted a simple, but effective, device to show the areas that are closely associated with central cities. Fig. 47 is an attempt to mark out the areas in which all places are within easy reach of service and work in a large and well-equipped city. The standard metropolitan areas have each been given a radius of 20 miles, measured from the outer limits of their urbanized areas. All other towns outside these radii with over 25,000 and, in effect, less than about 100,000 inhabitants, have been given a radius of 10 miles. All places within these circles are definitely within the reach of work and services of a well-equipped city centre. These urban fields have been linked together when the circumferences of two major cities lay within 20 miles, or of two minor cities within 10 miles, and of a major and a minor city within 15 miles. The resultant areas are marked out in black. This is a conservative estimate of the extent of the urban and interurban areas.

Notice the extension of the Atlantic Seaboard area through Upstate New York and central Pennsylvania to the Middle Western States as far as the Mississippi, including the whole of southern Michigan. In this vast area there are three inliers, one in the Catskills, a second in the northern Appalachian plateau, and the third in the Middle West, south of the Chicago belt. The groups of cities in the south-eastern states do not quite qualify, on this basis, to be called a continuous belt, but the closeness of these lesser clusters indicates that here is one of the major urban regions of the nation. The Los Angeles and San Francisco regions are rapidly spreading into central California at an alarming rate. Houston–Galveston (plus Beaumont and Lake Charles) and New Orleans are extending tentacles towards each other and will soon merge. Seattle–Tacoma and Portland are substantial in size, and though functionally interrelated, they are still widely separated. It seems safe to say that these areas indicate the outer framework within which the urban growth of the next few decades will take place.

4. THE CHANGING STRUCTURE OF THE CENTRAL CITY

Fundamental changes in the distribution of population are also going on within the standard metropolitan areas. These are divided by the Census into the Central City and the Outer Ring or Satellite Area. From 1920 to 1950 the central cities grew less rapidly than the nation as a whole and half as rapidly as the outer rings. This trend has been greatly accentuated since 1950, and will become more marked in the future decades. It is having profound effects on the demography of the nation. The far-flung suburban fringe of the big urban areas is the new frontier zone in America. The Bureau of Census estimates that in the period 1955 to 1975, the great population increase of the country will be distributed geographically as follows—38·3 millions in the outer rings as against only 8·2 millions in the central cities, whereas throughout the rest of the nation there will be an increase of only 16·8 millions. In other words, over 60 per cent. of the nation's estimated increase of population will be located in the existing suburban areas of the cities.

The standard metropolitan areas increased from 89 millions in 1950 to 113 millions in 1960, that is, by 26·4 per cent. (1940–50, 22·6 per cent.), as compared with 18·4 per cent. increase for the nation. The central cities increased by only 10·7 per cent. (1940–50, 14·7), and the rings outside the cities increased by 48·6 per cent. (1940–50, 35·9). The central cities accounted for only 20 per cent. of the total national increase of population, the suburban areas for 60 per cent. The suburban increase was from 37 to 55 millions, that is, 18 millions out of a total increase in the S.M.A.s of 23·6 millions. The focus of suburbanization is even more highly localized than appears, since the 'urban fringes' of the 'urbanized areas' (that is that part of the urbanized areas outside the boundaries of the central cities) increased by 81·4 per cent., from 21 to 38 millions. In other words, this is practically the entire increase of the standard metropolitan areas and 60 per cent. of the total increase of population in the nation.

It should be emphasized, however, that while the central cities record sub-normal increases of population, they are undergoing profound changes in the composition and distribution of population. The population of the central city in the last twenty years has been increasing at a rate well below the average for the country as a whole. There is a substantial net emigration of families from the central city to the suburban ring. Many districts are declining in numbers. This flight to the suburbs has become a surging tide in recent years. It has been counterbalanced, however, in the largest cities by a great influx of Negroes from the Deep South. New York, in addition, has received large numbers of Puerto Ricans. These people have settled in the central cities, on a much bigger scale than after World War I. The ethnic difference between the central city and the suburban ring has become accentuated in many cities. New York City is receiving 30,000 Puerto Ricans and 10,000 Negroes and loses 50,000 whites annually. At this rate by 1970 it will be 28 per cent. Puerto Rican and Negro, and Manhattan will have over one million, representing 50 per cent. of its total population. Chicago receives 35,000 Negroes per year and by 1970 at this rate it will have one million, or one-quarter of its total population Negro. About 15,000 Whites move out of Chicago annually. Cleveland has received 6,500 Negroes a year for fifteen years and the city today is 26 per cent. Negro which by 1970 will increase to 40 per cent. In St. Louis the Negro population has increased from 12 per cent. in 1940 to 30 per cent. today, but if the population stays at only 875,000, by 1970 at this rate the city will be 50 per cent. Negro.

Still another essential feature is that there is a strong contrast between the families with a predominantly 'average' or above average income in the suburban ring and the numerous families with below average incomes who occupy large areas of the blighted and older sections of the central city. These phenomena are reflected in a remarkably consistent political contrast between the central areas that are frequently Democratic in their voting, as opposed to the outer suburban rings that vote Republican.

The character of the central business district is also undergoing change. It is losing much business to the shopping centres of the suburban periphery. Recent statistics demonstrate this trend. The value of retail sales from 1948 to 1954 in 24 standard metropolitan areas increased by 32 per cent. The trade of their central business districts, however, increased by only 2 per cent., while that of the central city increased by 20 per cent. and the outer suburban ring increased by 50 per cent. During the fifties, the big city department stores opened spacious extensions in these suburban areas. Even in medium-sized cities, such as Syracuse with some 250,000 inhabitants, the central business district is sharing to only a very small degree in the great upsurge of retail buying. It is becoming more of a business centre—a nucleation of multi-storeyed office buildings, hotels, theatres, and other public buildings, with open spaces and structures for the parking of cars.

One of the first regional shopping centres to be built after the war was on the periphery of Stamford, Conn. It cost 6·7 million dollars and has 30 stores and parking space for 1,000 cars. Much larger centres than this are now to be found around most cities. Los

Angeles has two shopping centres that cost 10 million and 40 million dollars respectively, and each has branches of 2 or 3 down-town department stores and 50 to 150 branches of other stores. The downtown store executives follow the dictum 'Join 'em if you can't lick 'em'. Minneapolis has a mammoth centre seven miles out of town. It cost 20 million dollars to build and has 72 stores with parking for over 5,000 cars. All stores are under one roof with a centre court so that in winter shoppers may circulate in comfort with warm indoor temperatures.

The obsolescence of physical plant is one of the main characteristics and problems of the central cities. And this applies not only to buildings, but to street layout, sewage systems, and water supply. Tearing down and rebuilding is a necessity for urban growth. In general, the process is one of replacement and refurbishing—better sanitation and water supplies are brought into obsolescent homes, electricity replaces gas, bath and toilet are installed, and rooms put to new uses. More affluent people can move to new houses with the new equipment. As Henry James wrote in 1881:

'... At the end of three or four years we'll move. That's the way to live in New York—to move every three or four years. Then you always get to the last thing. ... So you see we'll always have a new house; you get all the latest improvements.' [1]

This has been described (incidentally with reference to the same movements in The Hague in Holland) as 'urban nomadism'. The 'underprivileged', however, are unable to make such moves. They must stay put. But the American is inclined to retort that anyone has the chance to make money and better himself. It is only the 'problem types' who stay put and they would be unlikely to benefit anyway by moving into a better subsidized home. This undoubtedly helps explain the reluctance of Congress to vote large funds in support of public housing. It is argued that good housing to suit the middle-income groups who are stepping up the economic ladder is the solution to the housing problem.

The tendency to move from one home to another produces a typical growth pattern in the central cities that proceeds outwards in concentric rings. In all cases the central city shows a tendency to decline relatively to the whole metropolitan area. Eventually it begins to show an absolute decline in numbers, beginning from the central district and spreading outwards. After the middle-income groups move out, their houses are occupied by another group lower

[1] Quoted by R. Vernon, *The Changing Economic Function of the Central City*, Committee on Economic Development, New York, 1959, p. 41.

down the income ladder, and these begin to overcrowd the structures into which they move, maintenance deteriorates, and the area becomes a slum. Then these slums go through another cycle. This overcrowding is followed by another tapering off of the population. 'The ring of slum population growth crawls outward from the centre of the city in a belated imitation of the middle-income group that preceded.'[1] Demolition has usually not kept pace with this population decline, and so we get the reduced use of old slums and the development of new slums in another section of the city to replace them.

The central cities have passed their peak as industrial centres, and they have long been declining in relation to their suburban hinterlands. In recent years—from 1947 to 1954—the cities of Boston, Chicago, Detroit, Pittsburgh, St. Louis, and San Francisco, recorded not only a relative decline, but also an absolute decline in the number of industrial jobs. One of the most important factors in causing these changes has been the obsolescence of existing plant and the lack of space for adequate reconstruction.[2]

Commercial activities that are located in offices tend to continue in the central cities, but even here there are hopeful suggestions of a contrary trend. The immigration of new groups, largely Negroes, will displace the white labour force to the suburbs, particularly young women, on whose work the office largely depends. Further, most office work does not actually need a central location. It may be that the office will begin to move out from the central business district to other less congested locations, closer to the homes of their workers.[3]

Thus, in the housing areas of the central cities, especially in their inner districts, there is likely to be in the future a long-run decline in the intensive use of space as sites for jobs and homes. This presents a problem of the proper use of these areas following housing demolition. Vernon suggests two possibilities in the States. Middle-income families could return to the city in large numbers, or, with the aid of government finance, low-income housing with open spaces may be expanded over considerable areas. The first is unlikely and undesirable as a major trend. The second is the major challenge and will demand great financial expenditure. It is the major problem in urban renewal in Britain. America hardly seems to have faced it as yet.

[1] *Ibid.*, p. 42.
[2] *Ibid.*, p. 49.
[3] Large new multi-storeyed office buildings have been observed (1963) on the outskirts of such contrasted cities as Minneapolis–St. Paul and Lincoln, Nebraska. This is a rapidly increasing new development.

5. The Urban Impact on the Countryside: The Highway

Urban expansion extends over wide areas beyond the limits of suburbia. The highway is the axis of this expansion and ribbon growth, so much deplored in Great Britain in the thirties, stretches for miles across the countryside well beyond the city and often linking it with lesser neighbours. Here are the scenes known by every motorist in the United States—uncontrolled uses, that stretch for miles on the approaches to every city, all drawing on the great volume of passing automobile traffic. Throughout large areas around and between the big cities houses are widely dispersed but urban services are easily reached within a matter of minutes. Distances must be judged in these terms. Christopher Tunnard writes as follows, with reference to a part of Connecticut that has seventy-nine urban cores each surrounded by an urban–rural fringe:

'This is the kind of district where a housewife's remark that she is just going to step out to take the children over to the neighbour's house means that she is going to drive them five miles down a country road. Or if she says she's just running down to the store, she may drive fifteen miles to a shopping centre or a supermarket or an upholsterers.'[1]

These areas he describes as 'interurbia'. Shops, offices, schools, and factory are available in a variety of places over a range of rapid travel. In all Connecticut only 3 per cent. of the population live on farms. This kind of density and arrangement is characteristic of all the areas that lie in between the closely packed urban regions of the north-eastern States, as well as on the Florida coast, the south-eastern States, Gulf Coast, Puget Sound, and California. Fig. 47 is, in effect, an attempt to portray the extent of 'interurbia'.

The wider countryside is affected by the urban impact. Industrial plants are being located along the main highways as well as in small cities outside the urban areas, and their workers travel by automobile over distances up to 20 miles. It has, moreover, become fashionable for people to buy some land with an old house or disused farm (or to build a new house on the land) and to live there at the weekends during the summer, or even continuously. Most of the open land in Vermont, much of it formerly in agricultural uses, is used in this way. Similarly, attractive scenic areas are sought out for seasonal residences by city dwellers. The shores of numerous lakes, 50 miles away or more from large cities of 100,000 upwards, are lined with cottages, camp sites, parks, and bathing beaches. The highlands of the Adirondacks and the Catskills, the wooded lands

[1] C. Tunnard, 'America's Super-Cities', *Harpers*, August, 1958, pp. 59–65.

of northern Maine, and the hill country of New Hampshire, are essentially vast recreation grounds for the city dwellers of New York State. New England is thickly studded with tourist homes and tourist facilities. Along the coast of southern New England it is difficult for the individual to find access to the sea-shore, for most of the beaches are in private ownership. The government is turning to surveys of its coasts and of the Great Lakes so as to preserve some of the natural amenities from the vandalism of the private speculator and even from the exclusiveness of private ownership. The business of recreation or tourism is one of the fantastic developments in the United States that belittles similar remarkable developments in western Europe in recent years.

The Federal Highway Act of 1956 provides for 41,000 miles of interstate super-highways in ten years at a cost of 40 billion dollars—the costs thereof to be derived principally from federal tax on gasoline. The total cost of construction for all types of highway in this period will be a hundred billion dollars. The aim of this programme is to outpace the demand for space by vehicles. Its purpose is 'to disperse our factories, our stores, our people, in short, to create a revolution in living habits'.[1] America's top highway experts declare that the modern controlled access highways are and will continue to be the greatest stimulant to economic development in America in the last half of the twentieth century. They will be as important as the railways were in the preceding century.

Interstate super-highways will revolutionize the impact of the city upon the land and introduce a widely extended urban impact.

'There is little doubt that the gigantic highway engineering programme now under way will have far reaching effects, influencing hundreds of communities either directly or indirectly. The system will promote geographic mobility; populations will shift; services and industry will decentralize. Politically, new alignments will arise; additional annexations will occur; pressure groups will develop and formalize; municipal, state, and federal governments will be harassed concerning locations, relocations, zoning, planning, and development. Ecologically, land uses will change; property transfers will increase; the process of concentration, decentralization, and invasion will be simultaneously fostered and fought. In point of fact, in many places these developments have already occurred or are now in process. Yet the full extent of these changes may not be realized until after the interstate system has been completed.'[2]

[1] *The Exploding Metropolis*, by The Editors of *Fortune*, New York, 1957.
[2] H. K. Dansereau, 'Some Implications of Modern Highways for Community Ecology', in Theodorson, *Studies in Human Ecology*, pp. 175–87.

THE CITY-REGION

The impact of the highway is already widely apparent, and will become increasingly widespread on land values, land uses—commercial, industrial, institutional, and residential.

'From the standpoint of supply and demand, highways permit population dispersion which in turn creates a demand, first for minor highway-oriented business sites and then for residential properties. Open land immediately beyond the existent suburbs or at super-highway interchanges provide the supply. Following or concurrent to the residential development, retail and service development can be expected, creating even further demand.'[1]

In this process of spatial impact of the highway there is a remarkable interdependence of a diversity of variables—surface relief, traffic volume, accessibility of highway, number of real estate transfers, zoning and planning laws of local government authorities, availability of public utilities, etc. These all interact along the line of impact of the highway. The spread of urban land uses causes a great reduction of the farm land since the farmers fall for the profits to be derived from land that greatly increases in value in the immediate proximity of the road. By-passes frequently cause much opposition from the business people in the community to be by-passed. But many studies indicate that once the by-pass is complete, there is in general a substantial *increase* in business in the by-passed community. This has been proved by a number of studies particularly in California and elsewhere. Interchanges become great potential transport junctions. At the intersection of two super-highways north-west of Philadelphia (Pennsylvania Turnpike and Schuylkill Expressway) the demand for open farm land was so great that values rose from 500 to 700 dollars to 9,000 to 12,000 dollars per acre. Community planners have an opportunity (and a duty) here to plan orderly land development.

What controls exist in order to check and guide the new uses of land along the existing and future super-highways? While there is evidence all over the States of lack of control, there is also plenty of evidence of first-class controls and of beautiful landscaping through magnificent country. The general verdict to date is one of failure, and fear for the future. There is now widespread awareness of the need for control of land uses along arterial highways. Before the advent of motor transport, a highway was a means of reaching the farm and village in the country from the urban centres. The enormous increase of vehicular traffic has caused this 'local' traffic to be mixed with a great increase of the 'through traffic', that

[1] H. K. Dansereau, *op. cit.*, p. 176.

demands a minimum of obstructions and maximum speeds. Mixture of the two kinds of traffic causes accidents, congestion, and high cost of operation. In order to cope with this problem the new highways are being provided in most States with controlled access facilities. Frontage roads are provided off and parallel to the highway for local shopping and services. There are today numerous examples of this system from the superb net of freeways of New York to those of Los Angeles in California. Public authorities are empowered in some States to acquire lands marginal to the highway; then roadside development can be controlled in the public interest. The highway can be insulated from growth on either side of it, even though it may be for only a few hundred yards. This is a 'green strip'. It involves the power of purchase or condemnation by the State, with fair compensation, of individual property rights. Land-use control may also be effected by zoning and subdivision control, bill board and set-back regulations. Though this is customary in urbanized areas throughout the States, it has not yet developed far in respect of land marginal to highways. Such regulations, however, prevent ribbon development and all its accompanying ills. Another possibility is control through the acquisition of highway development rights. This could be effective along all new highways and is the kind of power that is needed by the federal authority in building the new super-highways. It would mean appropriation by the State or its subdivision of the right of private property owners to improve road margins. Owners would not have the right of development along the strip within 100 to 200 feet of the highway. Such rights of way, however, are difficult to get since the law differs from State to State.

The impact of the super-highway on the face of America is evident all over the country especially within the wide orbits of the cities. Hundreds of miles of super-highways *preceded* the present programme. Examples are the overhead highways that encircle the urban area of San Francisco, and the magnificent 500-mile-long New York Throughway from New York to Buffalo, now complete to Cleveland, and thence to Chicago. Fleets of bulldozers, operating high above the existing highway, have pierced a new interstate route on Highway 40 right through the Sierras from Sacramento. These new highways are attracting industries and settlement which centre around the interchanges where traffic joins or leaves the expressways on the far outskirts of existing urbanized areas. There are many staggering examples of rapid growth of this kind—the Eastshore Freeway (built before 1956) on the east side of the Bay of San Francisco; the Garden City Parkway in New Jersey, the axis for a settlement with 200,000 houses built by a private New York syndicate; and the New York Throughway.

THE CITY-REGION

The New York Throughway has had a speedy and spectacular impact on industrial, commercial, and residential development since its opening in 1954. Syracuse has acquired a vast new industrial area on its northern outskirts just south of the access to the highway, involving to date 78 million dollars. The General Electricity Company contributed 28 million dollars to this development in its so-called Electronics Park, and its other plants are located with access to the throughway at Schenactady (west of Albany), Utica, Auburn, Clyde, Brockport, and Buffalo. Cheekowaga, N.Y. had 45,000 people in 1949 when work on the throughway began, and its livelihood depended on crab-apple trees. Today it has over 75,000 people and land formerly valued at 400 dollars per acre soared to 10,000 dollars per acre in 1959. Some hundred million dollars of capital are involved, invested by sixty industrial firms. This nation-wide programme has only just begun. As the work and momentum increases, the impact will be revolutionary on land use and economy.

One of the most interesting and challenging aspects of the spread of homes in the open country is the fact that the old terms of rural and urban cease to have any real significance over large areas. For these reasons the Census introduced a category described as 'rural-non-farm' population. No matter how 'urban' a person's occupation may be, he is not classed as urban unless he lives in a place with over 2,500 inhabitants. Thus, the lesser central places in the countryside are described as rural. The rural-non-farm population are those households in rural areas that are *not* located on farms as opposed to the rural farm population.

The non-farm population includes local service workers, but abnormal numbers are due to the 'adventitious element'. These are the urban dwellers who live in these areas, be they productive workers or retired 'senior citizens'. The distribution of the non-farm population is shown on Fig. 48 on the basis of counties. The most striking features are the high percentage of rural-non-farm population to total population in rural areas in the whole of the south-western States as well as in the western districts of Washington, Oregon, and western Montana; the high proportions in Florida; and the high proportions in and around the urban areas of the north-east, especially in New England, eastern New York, and Pennsylvania. Various factors are involved here, but three can be emphasized. First, there is the suburbanization of the rural territories on the outskirts of the cities in the north-eastern States. Second, there is the growth of the retired and resident elements in the rural districts of Florida. Third, there is the fantastic growth of homes for the retired in the deserts of the south-west. The spread of scattered homes and of new small settlements (as well as new cities,

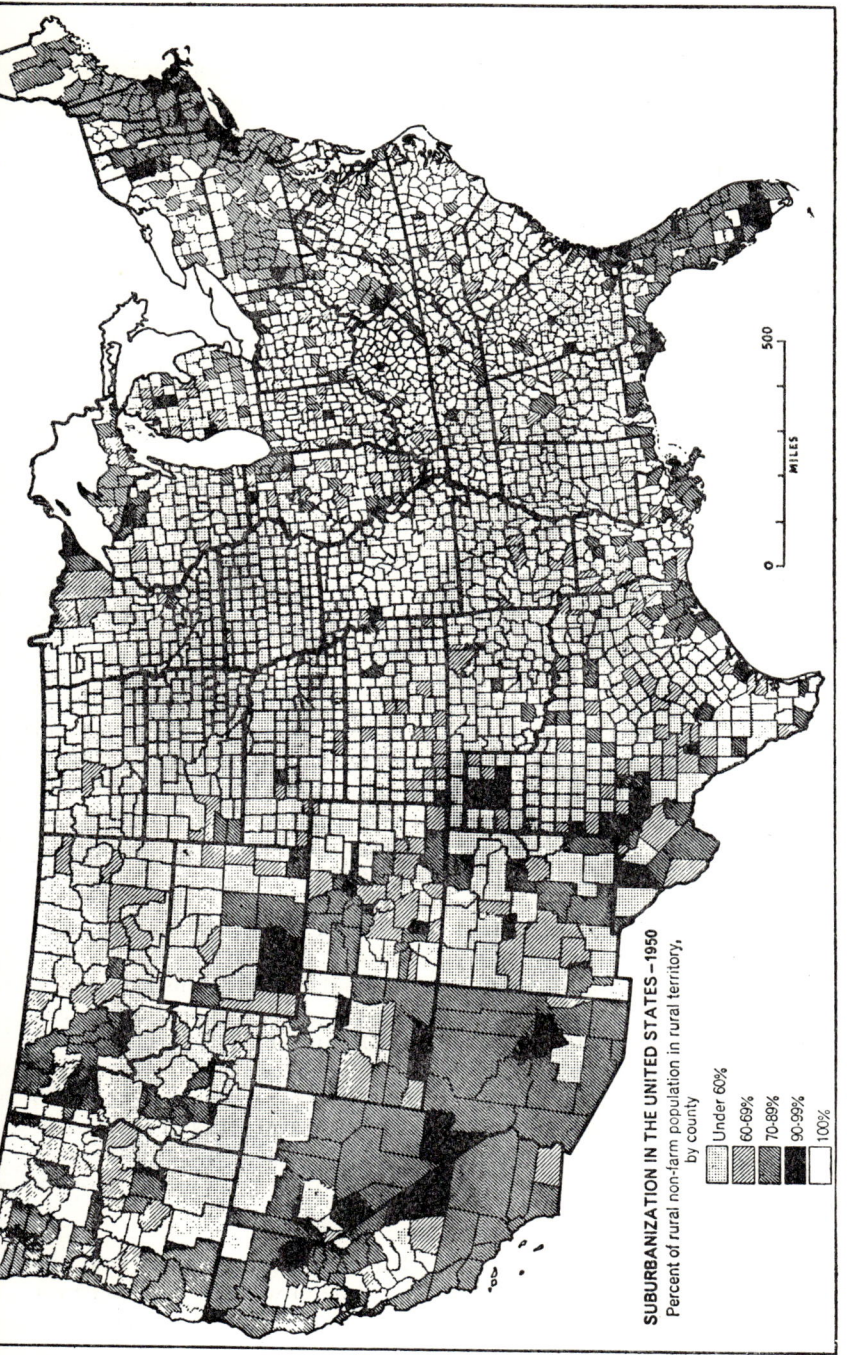

Fig. 48. Suburbanization in the United States: Percentage of rural non-farm to total population in rural territory by counties (from U.S. Census, and after Gottmann).

many of them still on paper) in the desert of the south-west is one of the most remarkable developments in the changing distribution of population in the United States.

APPENDIX TO CHAPTER 10

Definition of the Standard Metropolitan Statistical Area and Urbanized Area according to the United States Census of Population, 1960

[From *U.S. Census of Population, 1960. New York, Number of Inhabitants*, PC(1), 34A, pp. vi–viii.]

Standard Metropolitan Statistical Areas.

Except in New England, a Standard Metropolitan Statistical Area (S.M.S.A.) is a county or group of contiguous counties which contains at least one city of 50,000 inhabitants or more or 'twin cities' with a combined population of at least 50,000. In addition to the county, or counties, containing such a city or cities, contiguous counties are included in an S.M.S.A. if, according to certain criteria, they are essentially metropolitan in character and are socially and economically integrated with the central city. The criteria followed in the delineation of S.M.S.A.s relate to a city, or cities, of sufficient population size to constitute the central city and to the economic and social relationships with contiguous counties that are metropolitan in character.

1. Each S.M.S.A. must include at least:
(*a*) One city with 50,000 inhabitants or more, or
(*b*) Two cities having contiguous boundaries and constituting, for general economic and social purposes, a single community with a combined population of at least 50,000, the smaller of which must have a population of at least 15,000.

2. If two or more adjacent counties each have a city of 50,000 inhabitants or more and the cities are within 20 miles of each other (city limits to city limits), they will be included in the same area unless there is definite evidence that the two cities are not economically and socially integrated.

The criteria of metropolitan character relate primarily to the attributes of the outlying county as a place of work or as a home for a concentration of nonagricultural workers. Specifically, these criteria are:

3. At least 75 per cent. of the labour force of the county must be in the nonagricultural labour force.

4. In addition to criterion 3, the county must meet at least one of the following conditions:

(*a*) It must have 50 per cent. or more of its population living in contiguous minor civil divisions with a density of at least 150 persons per square mile, in an unbroken chain of minor civil divisions with such density radiating from a central city in the area.

(*b*) The number of nonagricultural workers employed in the county must equal at least 10 per cent. of the number of nonagricultural workers employed in the county containing the largest city in the area, or the outlying county must be the place of employment of at least 10,000 nonagricultural workers.

(*c*) The nonagricultural labour force living in the county must equal at least 10 per cent. of the nonagricultural labour force living in the county containing the largest city in the area, or the outlying county must be the place of residence of a nonagricultural labour force of at least 10,000.

5. In New England, the city and town are administratively more important than the county, and data are compiled locally for such minor civil divisions. Here, towns and cities are the units used in defining S.M.S.A.s. In New England, because smaller units are used and more restricted areas result, a population density of at least 100 persons per square mile is used as the measure of metropolitan character.

The criteria of integration relate primarily to the extent of economic and social communication between the outlying counties and the central county.

6. A county is regarded as integrated with the county or counties containing the central cities of the area if either of the following criteria are met:

(*a*) If 15 per cent. of the workers living in the given outlying county work in the county or counties containing the central city or cities of the area, or

(*b*) If 25 per cent. of those working in the given outlying county live in the county or counties containing the central city or cities of the area.

Only where data for criteria 6(*a*) and 6(*b*) are not conclusive are other related types of information used. This information includes such items as average telephone calls per subscriber per month from the county to the county containing central cities of the area; percentage of the population in the county located in the central city telephone exchange area; newspaper circulation reports prepared by the Audit Bureau of Circulation; analysis of charge accounts in retail stores of central cities to determine the extent of their use by residents of the contiguous county; delivery service practices of retail stores in central cities; official traffic counts; the extent of public transportation facilities in operation between central cities and communities in the contiguous county; and the extent to which local planning groups and other civic organizations operate jointly.

7. Although there may be several cities of 50,000 or more in an S.M.S.A., not all are necessarily central cities. The following criteria are used for determining central cities:

(a) The largest city in an S.M.S.A. is always the central city.

(b) In addition, one or two additional cities may be secondary central cities on the basis and in the order of the following criteria:

(1) The additional city or cities have at least 250,000 inhabitants.

(2) The additional city or cities have a population of one-third or more of that of the largest city and a minimum population of 25,000, except that both cities are central cities in those instances where cities qualify under criterion 1(b). (A city which qualified as a secondary central city in 1950 but which does not qualify in 1960 has been temporarily retained as a central city.)

8. The titles of the S.M.S.A.s consist of the names of the central cities followed by the names of the States in which the areas are located.

Urbanized Areas.

The major objective of the Bureau of the Census in delineating urbanized areas was to provide a better separation of urban and rural population in the vicinity of the larger cities, but individual urbanized areas have proved to be useful statistical areas. They correspond to what are called 'conurbations' in some other countries. An urbanized area contains at least one city of 50,000 inhabitants or more in 1960,[1] as well as the surrounding closely settled incorporated places and unincorporated areas that meet the criteria listed below. All persons residing in an urbanized area are included in the urban population.

It appeared desirable to delineate the urbanized areas in terms of

[1] There are a few urbanized areas where there are 'twin central cities' that have a combined population of at least 50,000. See the section on 'Standard Metropolitan Statistical Areas' for further discussion of twin central cities, neither of which has a population of 50,000 or more.

the 1960 Census results rather than prior to the census as was done in 1950. For this purpose a peripheral zone around each 1950 urbanized area and around cities that were presumably approaching a population of 50,000 was recognized. Within the unincorporated parts of this zone small enumeration districts were planned,[1] usually including no more than one square mile of land area and no more than 75 housing units.

Arrangements were made to include within the urbanized area those enumeration districts meeting specified criteria of population density as well as adjacent incorporated places. Since the urbanized area outside of incorporated places was defined in terms of enumeration districts, the boundaries for the most part follow such features as roads, streets, railroads, streams, and other clearly defined lines which may be easily identified by census enumerators in the field and often do not conform to the boundaries of political units.

In addition to its central city or cities, an urbanized area also contains the following types of contiguous areas, which together constitute its urban fringe:

1. Incorporated places with 2,500 inhabitants or more.
2. Incorporated places with less than 2,500 inhabitants, provided each has a closely settled area of 100 dwelling units or more.
3. Towns in the New England States, townships in New Jersey and Pennsylvania, and counties elsewhere which are classified as urban.
4. Enumeration districts in unincorporated territory with a population density of 1,000 inhabitants or more per square mile. (The area of large nonresidential tracts devoted to such urban land uses as railroad yards, factories, and cemeteries, was excluded in computing the population density of an enumeration district.)
5. Other enumeration districts in unincorporated territory with lower population density provided that they served one of the following purposes:

(*a*) To eliminate enclaves.

(*b*) To close indentations in the urbanized area of one mile or less across the open end.

(*c*) To link outlying enumeration districts of qualifying density that were no more than $1\frac{1}{2}$ miles from the main body of the urbanized area.

Contiguous urbanized areas with central cities in the same standard metropolitan statistical area are combined. Urbanized areas with

---

[1] An enumeration district (E.D.) is a small area assigned to an enumerator which must be canvassed and reported separately. In most cases an E.D. contains approximately 250 housing units.

central cities in different standard metropolitan statistical areas are not combined, except that a single urbanized area was established in the New York–Northeastern New Jersey Standard Consolidated Area, and in the Chicago–Northwestern Indiana Standard Consolidated Area.

The boundaries of the urbanized areas for 1960 will not conform to those for 1950, partly because of actual changes in land use and density of settlement, and partly because of relatively minor changes in the rules used to define the boundaries. The changes in the rules include the following:

1. The use of enumeration districts to construct the urbanized areas in 1960 resulted in a less precise definition than in 1950 when the limits were selected in the field using individual blocks as the unit of area added. On the other hand, the 1960 procedures produced an urbanized area based on the census results rather than an area defined about a year before the census, as in 1950.

2. Unincorporated territory was included in the 1950 urbanized area if it contained at least 500 dwelling units per square mile, which is a somewhat different criterion than the 1,000 persons or more per square mile of the included 1960 unincorporated areas.

3. The 1960 areas include those entire towns in New England, townships in New Jersey and Pennsylvania, and counties that are classified as urban in accordance with the criteria listed in the section on urban–rural residence. The 1950 criteria permitted the exclusion of portions of these particular minor civil divisions.

In general, however, the urbanized areas of 1950 and 1960 are based on essentially the same concept, and the figures for a given urbanized area may be used to measure the population of that area.

Chapter 11

THE CITY-REGION IN THE UNITED STATES: II

1. THE FUNCTIONAL CLASSIFICATION OF CITIES

The functional classification of cities, in terms of their occupational structure, has been worked on by various investigators in recent years. In spite of their more or less sophisticated statistical techniques, they do not bring us nearer to a meaningful assessment of the role of the city as a regional focus. Chauncy D. Harris[1] presented a quantitative, but subjective, classification of American cities. This classification is based on an analysis of the 605 functional, rather than political, units, with over 10,000 inhabitants, 140 were metropolitan districts with one city of over 50,000 inhabitants. The study arrived at nine principal types of towns as follows—manufacturing cities; retail centres; diversified centres; wholesale centres; transport centres; mining towns; University towns; and resort and retirement towns. There is a marked concentration of the manufacturing towns (44 per cent. of the metropolitan districts and 43 per cent. of the smaller cities) in the Manufacturing Belt north of the Ohio and lower Missouri and east of the Mississippi. There is also a secondary concentration in the south-eastern States from Virginia to northern Alabama, with a sprinkling of such cities on the Pacific littoral. The retail centres have over one-half of their workers in retailing out of the total in manufacturing, wholesaling, and retailing. They are mostly smaller cities outside the main manufacturing belt (under 10 per cent. of the metropolitan districts and 20 per cent. of the smaller cities). About one-half of these cities lie in a north–south belt between the ninety-fifth and hundredth meridians near the eastern margin of the High Plains and near the western limit of arable agriculture. This is a continuously settled area of highly commercialized agriculture in which there is certainly little manufacturing, and servicing is a primary function of its urban centres. The diversified cities with a good representation of trade and manufacturing (25 per cent. of the metropolitan districts and 20 per cent. of the smaller cities) include four of the five

[1] C. D. Harris, 'A Functional Classification of Cities in the United States' *Geographical Review*, Vol. XXX, January 1943, pp. 86–99.

largest cities in the country. They are especially numerous in the transitional area between the manufacturing belt and the band of retail centres noted above. They include major cities in the manufacturing belt (New York, Chicago, Boston) and five state capitals. A number of these cities also lie in the transitional zone towards the belt of retail centres (St. Louis, Nashville, Birmingham, Minneapolis, St. Paul, Des Moines, Kansas City, Little Rock, Montgomery, and Tampa). Still others are the oil-refining and flour-milling centres in the belt of retail centres. Wholesale cities include cities engaged in the assembly of agricultural products and large cities engaged in general distribution. Transport cities include eighteen railroad centres and fourteen ports. There are only fourteen mining towns (e.g. Butte for copper mining), most of which are smaller centres. Although mining may be important in larger cities it is obscured by other activities. There are seventeen University towns, all small centres, and twenty-two resort and retirement towns.

Harris recognizes regional centres in general, but not as types based on particular criteria. He concludes that 'such a centre is a large, centrally placed city dominating and serving a wide tributary region'. In general, these centres are important wholesale, financial, and office centres. A high percentage of their gainful workers is engaged in professional and clerical occupations. One good criterion of such a centre, he writes, is newspaper circulation. Of the forty-one regional centres defined by metropolitan newspaper circulation all except four had important wholesaling functions. These regional centres comprise nine wholesale cities, nineteen diversified cities (all with a strong emphasis on wholesaling), eight manufacturing cities, and five other types. With reference to location, Harris writes, 'The central location theory, in which centrality within a productive hinterland is stressed, is illustrated best by the distribution of wholesaling centres, which are usually large cities centrally placed within a smaller area'.[1] There is no doubt that out of this listing, the two principal indicators of the role of the city as a regional focus are the wholesale and retail trades.

These are interesting indicators, but it is surprising that neither this study nor its successors (Nelson, Frazer Hart, Alexandersson, etc.) have sought a consistent quantitative measure of the regional status of towns. The nearest approach is that of Philbrick discussed in Chapter 3. This evasion may well be because the regional role embraces part of all the specialized functions and defies meaningful quantitative measurement from census data. The reality can only be adequately appraised from the investigation of groups of towns in relation to the areas they serve.

[1] C. D. Harris, *op. cit.* See also Gunnar Alexandersson, *The Industrial Structure of American Cities*, London and Stockholm, 1956.

2. The Definition of Metropolis and Region

Various attempts have been made to divide up the United States entirely into areas tributary to a selected list of cities. Our own attempt, published in 1932, was one of the first of these and is shown on Fig. 49. We should note other more recent interpretations. A system of metropolitan regions was drawn up by Donald J. Bogue in 1949. The map is shown on Fig. 50. It is far less 'real' than our own map. The method was arbitrary, in that it took no account of actual service

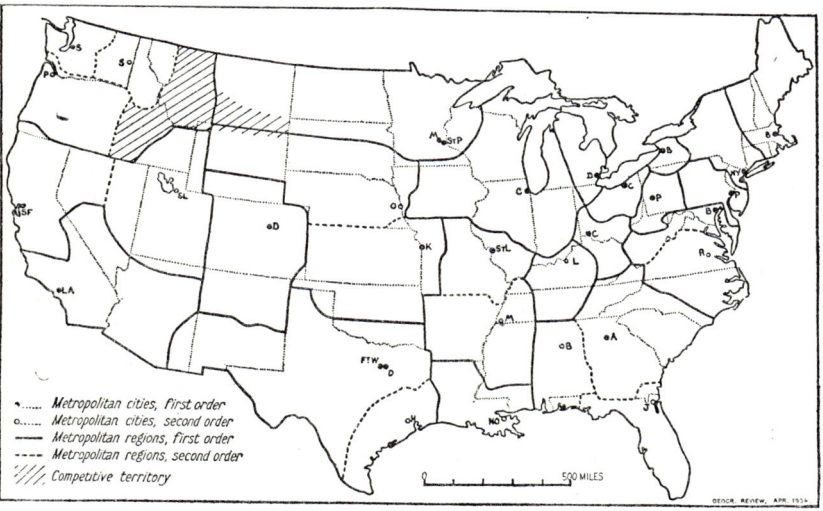

Fig. 49. United States: Metropolitan Regions (by the author, 1932).

areas or relations, but simply assumed that accessibility between one centre and another was a basic determinant of city-regional relations. The sixty-seven centres were selected which had over 100,000 inhabitants and a 'sizeable' hinterland. The boundaries were drawn in such a way as to be equidistant from each centre, but the lines were drawn so as to coincide with the county boundaries. The assumption was that 'a metropolis can dominate all of the area which lies closer to it than to any other similar city, even if the other metropolis is larger'.[1] A study based on the actual data of city-regional relations was prepared by two authors in 1953[2] and the results shown on Fig. 51. These are reproduced for comparison with our own effort.

[1] D. Bogue, *The Structure of the Metropolitan Community*, Ann Arbor, 1949, p. 17.
[2] L. F. Thomas and R. M. Crisler, *A Manual of the Economic Geography of the United States based on Trade Areas and Geographic Regions*, St. Louis, 1953.

Fig. 50. United States: Metropolitan Regions (after Bogue, 1949, from Duncan *et al.*).

The map as devised in our study is based on a great variety of evidence. The metropolitan cities with over 50,000 inhabitants were selected on the basis of the following criteria—sales *per capita* of retail and wholesale goods; the value added by manufacturers for all cities with over 50,000 inhabitants; the volume of merchandizing

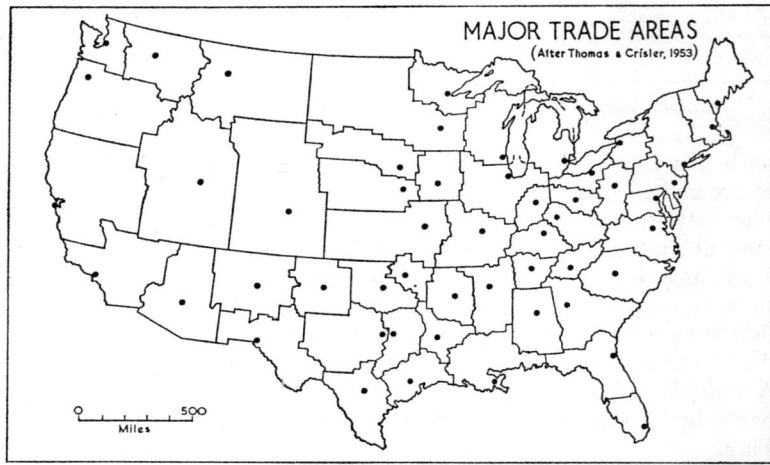

Fig. 51. United States: Major Trade Areas (after Thomas and Crisler, from Duncan *et al.*). Cf. Rand McNally, *Commerical Atlas*, 93rd ed., 1962, Trading Area Map. This shows 494 'basic trading areas' and 50 'major trading areas', each grouped on a major trading centre.

warehouse space; the location of branch offices of twenty outstanding national concerns; and the location of Federal Reserve banks and branches. From these data we concluded that there were two orders of metropolitan cities. The first included Atlanta, Baltimore, Boston, Buffalo, Chicago, Cincinnati, Cleveland, Dallas–Fort Worth, Denver, Detroit, Kansas City, Los Angeles, Minneapolis–St. Paul, New York, Philadelphia, Pittsburgh, St. Louis, and Seattle. The metropolitan cities of the second order included Birmingham, Jacksonville, Omaha,

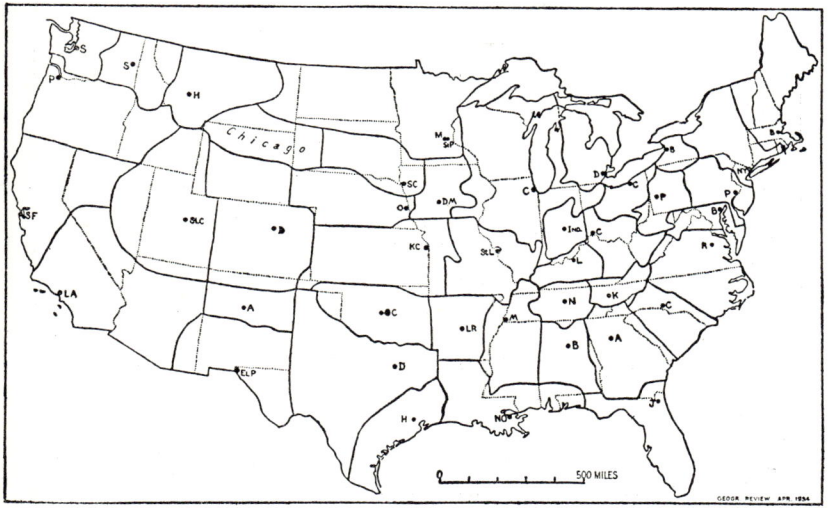

Fig. 52. United States: Newspaper Circulation Areas.

Richmond, Houston, Memphis, Portland, Salt Lake City, Louisville, Milwaukee, New Orleans, and Spokane.

The regions dependent on these metropolitan centres were then derived from a variety of maps of specific areas of collection and distribution of goods and services. These areas included wholesale trade areas, newspaper circulation areas (Fig. 52), the marketing of agricultural products that figures largely in the industries and wholesaling of cities, the car-load shipments by counties of livestock products and grain, and finally the federal reserve districts (Fig. 53). The resultant composite trade areas are in considerable measure arbitrary, especially in areas far removed from the central cities, with a very scattered distribution of population. Indeed, unless one criterion be rigidly followed, the exact placing of a boundary is largely a matter of personal judgment. In any case, the extent of the area depends not only on the degree to which boundaries of specific areas coincide, but also on the number of cities that are selected as centres. While not existing as exact regions with discrete linear boundaries, these city-regions are realities and the additional data given in Duncan's recent study help considerably to refine their definition.

Vance and Smith, in their important work on the southern States,[1] while concluding that our own study of the metropolitan cities 'has been the most sophisticated attempt to differentiate the true metropolises from the other large cities', rightfully regret that it was then 'twenty years old'. However, they had used more up-to-date figures

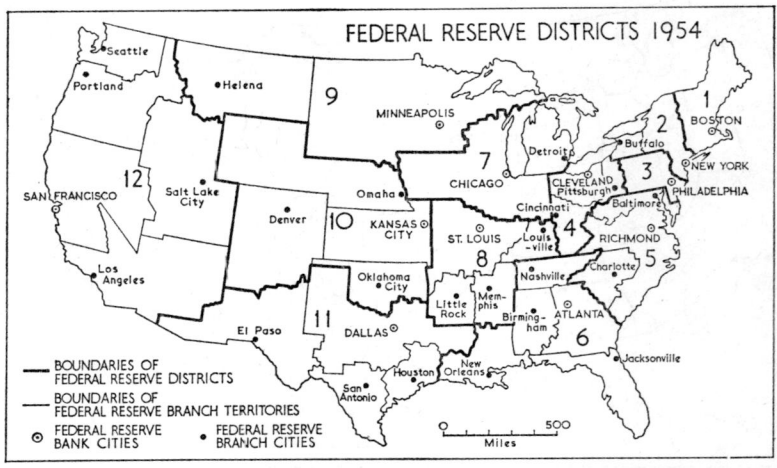

FIG. 53. Federal Reserve Districts and Branch Territories, 1954 (after Duncan et al.).

(including some of ours) in order to arrive at a classification of cities by metropolitan (regional) status in the south. They used the following data: wholesale sales (1948), business services receipts (1948), number of branch offices (using our data as an 'excellent index'), as the most decisive indicators, and weighted two to one. The remaining three are retail sales, bank clearings, and value added by manufacturing. The cities with over 100,000 people in the south were ranked on this basis and divided into second-order metropolises (directly below New York and Chicago)–Atlanta and Dallas; third order (five); sub-dominants with some metropolitan characteristics (twelve); and sub-dominants (ten).

The relations between the city and its region have been thoroughly

[1] Rupert B. Vance and Sara Smith, *The Urban South*, University of North Carolina Press, 1954.

treated by Otis Dudley Duncan and his associates[1] and we shall draw on this as a check against our own earlier work. Duncan makes an analysis of the functions of the fifty-six metropolitan cities with over 300,000 inhabitants and seeks to evaluate the extent of their dependent trade areas and the relations that exist between the two, metropolis and region. The activities of the cities are interpreted in terms of their inputs and outputs, that is, the source of the raw materials used in the industry (input), and the distribution of their products (output). These sources are estimated on the basis of a threefold geographical division of their market areas. The 'local' metropolitan region is defined 'operationally' as the standard metropolitan area itself. The wider 'trade area' corresponds with what we have called the city or metropolitan region. A third division is not in any sense a continuous geographical area. It is a 'residual category' that embraces all origins and destinations of goods and services outside the trade area, be they in the national market as a whole or in any foreign territory.

Let us now turn to the elaborate analysis of cities undertaken by O. D. Duncan and his associates.[2] The forty-one principal groups of the industrial classification of the census were arranged as follows—extractive industries (agriculture, forestry, fisheries, and mining); processing industries (mainly first-stage resource users); fabricating industries (mainly working materials that have been through an initial processing stage); and service industries.[3] The last include local services that have an appreciable or preponderate proportion of non-local consumers.

The difference between the two categories of services (as indeed between the two groups of industries) is a fine one and must be based on a subjective grouping of the industrial classification of the census. The local services include retail trades, retail services, private household services, utilities, and personal service, such as laundering, cleaning and dyeing, and professional services, such as welfare, religious and legal and other professional services. The non-local services are those that remain and that have a large proportion of consumers

[1] Otis Dudley Duncan *et al.*, *Metropolis and Region*, Johns Hopkins Press, Baltimore, 1960, 587 pp.
[2] *Ibid.*
[3] The industrial classifications devised for purposes of this study are as follows: Primary resource extractors with production for non-final market; first-stage resource users with production for non-final market; first-stage resource users with production for final market; second-stage resource users with production for non-final market; second-stage resource users with production for final market; resources of indirect significance with production for non-final market—service industries local, service industries non-local, service industries may be local or non-local, construction, and industry not reported. *Ibid.*, p. 205; a full listing is given on pp. 206-8.

outside the city community. These include transportation services of all kinds, wholesale trades, banking and credit agencies, brokerage and investment companies, advertising, hotels, radio and T.V., federal and state public administration. Some services are 'border line' cases, and are classed as either local or non-local. These include insurance, hospitals, educational services. Out of all the urban places in the States with over 50,000 inhabitants in their various size categories about one-third of their total employed were in non-local services and just under 30 per cent. in local services. In smaller places with more than 2,500 people, the percentage is 28 per cent. in non-local services and increased slightly to 32 per cent. in local services. The proportion in all urban centres, irrespective of size, is about 60 per cent. in all services and 25 to 30 per cent. in manufacturing.

A selection of thirty-eight metropolitan centres is based upon the following criteria—(1) a population of over 300,000—this being taken as presumptive evidence of functions described as metropolitan; (2) value added by manufacture (1947), wholesale sales (1948), business service and receipts (1948), non-local commercial loans (1950), and demand deposits (1950). All data are expressed on a *per capita* basis in dollars.

These thirty-eight metropolitan centres, though varying greatly, all have levels of wholesaling and manufacturing above 'a bare minimum'. They fall into the following categories.

The national metropolises with over 3 million people are New York, Chicago, Detroit, Los Angeles, and Philadelphia.

Diversified manufacturing centres with metropolitan functions include Boston, Pittsburgh, St. Louis, Cleveland, Buffalo, and Cincinnati. There is a similar group with few metropolitan functions. These include Baltimore, Milwaukee, Albany–Schenectady–Troy, Toledo, Hartford, and Syracuse.

The type described as a regional metropolis includes San Francisco, Minneapolis–St. Paul, Kansas City, Seattle, Portland, Atlanta, Dallas, and Denver.

The regional capitals of sub-metropolitan character as distinct from the metropolis is a group that turns largely on size. These include Houston, New Orleans, Louisville, Birmingham, Indianapolis, Columbus, Memphis, Omaha, Fort Worth, Richmond, Oklahoma, Nashville, and Jacksonville. The division is largely based on a subjective judgment of the distinction on the basis of the criteria used. Thus, New Orleans and Atlanta have the same population, but Atlanta leads in all indicators used and is a federal reserve city, whereas New Orleans is only a branch city. Houston, though a little larger than Dallas, is second to Dallas as a financial and trade centre.

Special cases include Washington, San Diego, San Antonio, Miami,

Wilkes Barre, Norfolk, Portsmouth, Tampa–St. Petersburg, Knoxville, and Phoenix. Each owes its size to the predominance of one highly specialized group of functions, such as Washington with government, Miami with the tourist trade, San Diego with naval installations, and Wilkes Barre with coal mining.

This classification is summarized here in deference to the most recent study of the matter. It should be pointed out, however, that thirty years ago we adopted the same procedure, and, though without the exact banking returns, federal reserve status was taken into account, together with the same criteria used by Duncan. If the special cases be omitted, the listing of the metropolitan centres is essentially the same, though the data on which they are based are nearly thirty years apart.

3. THE REGIONS AND THEIR CAPITALS: THE MANUFACTURING BELT

We may now briefly review the characteristics of the cities and their regions.

The main manufacturing belt, in the north-eastern States,[1] is the area of most advanced metropolitan development, in which the metropolitan centres are the commercial and cultural centres for tributary industrial towns. This manufacturing belt contains about 70 per cent. of U.S. manufacturing industries and 40 per cent. of the U.S. population. A westerly extension of it includes the State of Iowa and the sections of the adjoining States, together with the southern portions of Wisconsin and Michigan. These additional areas have 5 per cent. of the manufactures and 7 per cent. of the population. This is the area of greatest intensity of traffic flows in the nation. It reaches south to include St. Louis and west to reach Kansas City and Omaha. It includes the continuous urban belt of the Atlantic Seaboard from eastern Massachusetts through to Washington D.C.; the series of Up-State New York cities; the Cleveland–Pittsburgh complex; the middle Ohio urban complex (Cincinnati); the south Michigan complex (Detroit); the Chicago–Milwaukee complex; and the east–west series of lesser cities in the centre (Ohio,

---

[1] Sten de Geer, 'The American Manufacturing Belt', *Geografiska Annaler*, Vol. IX, 1927, pp. 233–359. Compare the grouping here suggested with Jefferson's regional grouping of population, 'Some Considerations of the Geographical Provinces of the United States', *Annals of Association of Geographers*, Vol. VII, 1917, pp. 3–15. Also the map on Fig. 106 by Helen Strong reproduced from 'Regions of Manufacturing Intensity in the United States', *Annals*, etc., Vol. XXVII, 1937 pp. 23–43. This is one of several such maps prepared in the late thirties. See also H. H. McCarty, *Geographic Bases of American Economic Life*, New York, 1940.

Indiana, Illinois, Iowa). All places are within 20 miles of a big city (Fig. 47). Here too are some of the most productive agricultural areas of the country—the Corn Belt, the Hay-Pasture-Dairying Belt, and the Truck Farming Belt on the Atlantic Seaboard. The remainder of the country receives the bulk of its manufactured products from the manufacturing belt. On the Atlantic Seaboard, Boston, New York, and Philadelphia have central wholesale markets, which distribute food products and raw materials. Each city has its distinctive industries, and each has the characteristics of a full-fledged metropolitan centre. Yet the similarity of urban pattern and functions, freight-rate structure, and the dominance of New York give to this Atlantic group a certain measure of unity.

The main urban region of the nation lies along the Atlantic Seaboard. Its general extent has already been noted on p. 290 and its component metropolitan areas are listed on p. 335. The area is a continuous sequence of metropolitan districts plus a contiguous tier of counties. In terms of population it contains the fully built urbanized areas with over 1,000 persons per square mile, then outer partly urbanized areas with 500 to 1,000 persons per square mile, and surprisingly large areas, both inland and on the coastal belt, with under 150 persons per square mile. The total area is given by Gottmann as 53,575 square miles or 1·8 per cent. of the land area of the nation, and its population reached 32 million in 1950 as against 37 million in 1960, about 20 per cent. of the national total. The overall density of population is 700 persons per square mile so that it is one of the largest and most densely peopled areas in the world. The area has recently (1961) been subjected to a searching and brilliant geographic analysis by the French geographer, Jean Gottmann for the Twentieth Century Fund.[1] He names the area Megalopolis and describes it as the 'main street', the 'cross roads', and the 'hinge' of the continent. It stretches over a distance of over 600 miles along the axis of Highway U.S.I. and has a width of 30 to 100 miles. It interconnects six of the nation's major metropolitan areas—Boston (2·6 m.), New York (10·7 m.), Philadelphia (4·3 m.), Baltimore (1·7 m.) and Washington (2·0 m.)—and includes also at least a dozen other major cities with populations ranging from 200,000 to close to one million. New York, with its 11 million people, has been examined in Chapter 6, p. 195. We would stress here its regional associations in terms of the areas which it dominates and the areas in which it competes with its giant, but lesser, neighbours. From Gottmann's work, we venture one quotation that is relevant to the regional impact of these major cities.

[1] Jean Gottmann, *Megalopolis: The Urbanized Northeastern Seaboard of the United States*, Twentieth Century Fund, New York, 1961.

THE CITY-REGION IN THE UNITED STATES: II

'New York City's economic role makes New York the most important State in the nation. Whether that city prospers or declines is a concern not only for its residents and of the state government in Albany. It is also very important for the neighbouring states of Connecticut and New Jersey, because so many of their activities are tied to the dynamism of New York city and could shift to other areas if what is now concentrated in Manhattan could be easily decentralized. Similar relationships exist for Boston and Philadelphia, for Baltimore and Wilmington. The weakening of one of the hubs, the chain of which constitutes the framework of Megalopolis, would necessarily affect the others and all the areas between them and around them.'[1]

Boston (2·6 m.) has a variety of specialized industries, and also serves as the focal point for commerce and finance in New England, although the south and south-west are more closely related to New York than to Boston. Boston is also the principal port for New England, except the southern half of Connecticut. The Boston wool market is the largest in the States and second only to that of London.

The location of the boundary between the hinterlands of New York (10·7 m.) and Boston, though indicated roughly in several nation-wide studies of metropolitan hinterlands—including one by the present author that is shown on Fig. 49—has been recently studied.[2] Fig. 54 shows the median limits of seven criteria. The following criteria were used for which quantitative measures of areal relationships were available—transport, newspaper circulation, telephone calls, markets for agricultural products, recreational areas, manufacturing, and finance. Rail freight today is of little importance. Passenger commuting traffic was mapped from point to point ticket-sales on the railroads. As regards shipping of goods by rail, New York handles almost all the traffic from the whole area of New England, only 10 per cent. going through Boston. Truck traffic is important, but it is difficult to get reliable data. There are indications that Boston dominates the traffic within a radius of about 35 miles, but the rest of New England is served by New York. The Audit Bureau of Circulation issues figures of newspaper circulation and these are mapped. Telephone calls are an equally valuable measure of metropolitan influence and the 50–50 limit is very similar to that of newspaper circulation. There is no sharp line of demarcation in the movement of agricultural products of the two cities, for the intermediate cities consume most of the surpluses of their environs.

[1] *Ibid*, p. 750.
[2] Howard L. Green, 'Hinterland Boundaries of New York City and Boston in Southern New England', *Economic Geography*, Vol. XXXI, 1955, pp. 283–300. See also Mayer and Kohn, *op. cit.*

New York and Boston have extensive and ill-defined 'milksheds', since the intervening cities consume most of their local production. New York draws its supplies from the west and Boston from New York and New England. Vacationing areas are located in the hinterlands and the data reveal a two-pronged movement of New York–New Jersey residents during vacation seasons: one advance is made

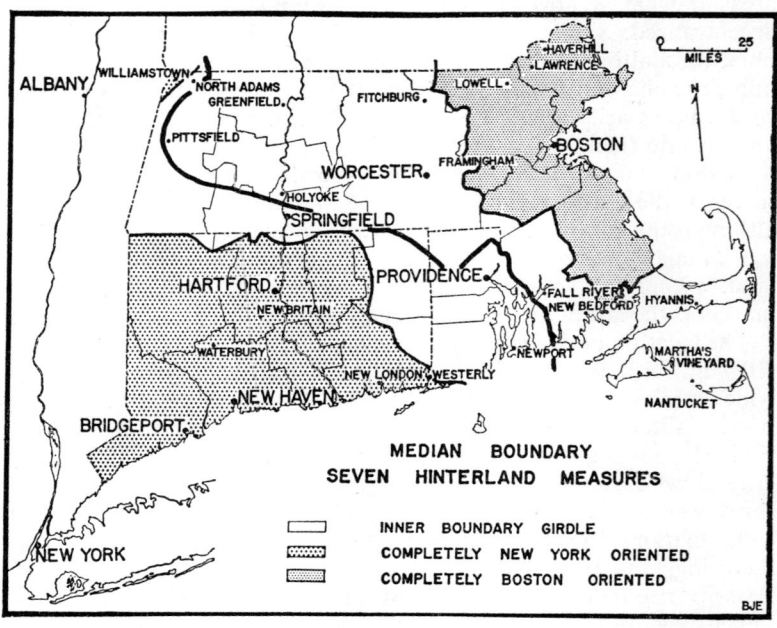

FIG. 54. The Competitive Hinterlands of New York and Boston
(after H. L. Green).

northwards into the interior hill country of Connecticut and Massachusetts; the other (probably embracing more people) along the Atlantic shore line toward Cape Cod. Massachusetts residents go south to Cape Cod and north to Maine and New Hampshire coastlines, with a second extension into the hill- and lake-country of New Hampshire. The financial connections of the New England area are estimated from Federal Reserve Bank data. Two indicators are used—votes by banks for choice of Federal Reserve City and New York and Boston banks that are listed as correspondents of hinterland banks. Seven functional indicators are thus mapped. A median or middle boundary is interpolated from these and the result shown on Fig. 54.

Providence (816,000), in spite of its large size as a textile manufacturing city, is completely overshadowed by Boston with regard to financial, commercial, and wholesale activities. Similarly Hartford (525,000) is an important seat of aircraft production and insurance business, and a centre for the Connecticut valley, with its tobacco production, but it lies within the orbit of Boston and, to a lesser degree, of New York.

The central section of the manufacturing belt consists of a large number of industrial towns, which fall into four groups, each with its distinctive industries and focused upon a metropolitan city— Detroit, Cleveland, Pittsburgh, and Buffalo. In each of these cities metals and minerals form the chief item of the wholesale trade. The group of four regions is like the Atlantic Seaboard group, in the hay-and-pasture belt, and each metropolis has a considerable livestock market serving a local hinterland.

Buffalo (1·3 m.), because of its lakeside location, is a big centre for the processing and transmission of wheat, received from the Middle West, and of iron and steel production. Its trade area covers the ten counties of western New York State. Detroit (3·7 m.) is the centre of a close group of industrial towns in southern Michigan that are associated with automobile and wood-working industries. Pittsburgh (2·4 m.) is a large producer of coal and iron and steel and these occupations dominate its industrial profile. Its trade area includes 'the coal areas of Pennsylvania and West Virginia as well as a considerable section of south-east Ohio'.[1] Many corporations with headquarters in Pittsburgh dominate the manufacturing localities of western Pennsylvania, the panhandle of West Virginia and east central Ohio. Wheeling and Youngstown are a continuation of the Pittsburgh complex.

Cleveland (1·8 m.) is a manufacturing city, dominated by blast furnaces, steel works, and rolling mills. It receives ores via the lakes and fuel from Pennsylvania. A variety of industries diversify its profile, including synthetic fibres, paints, and varnishes. It is the head of a federal reserve district, though second to Pittsburgh, and serves as a commercial centre to north-central Ohio and the lake shore centres within a radius of 50 to 75 miles.

Indianapolis and Columbus are both meat-packing centres and dealers in agricultural products. Both are also State capitals.

The western section of the manufacturing belt is served mainly by the metropolitan region of Chicago, which also embraces the greater part of the corn-and-hog belt. This city, the economic epitome of the Middle West, combines the functions of both primary and

[1] McCarty, quoted by Duncan, *op. cit.*, p. 300.

central wholesale markets. It is still a vast livestock and grain market, though some of the packing plants have moved out west to the cattle raising area (e.g. Omaha City, Kansas). It is also a great food processing centre. It has varied industries that are typically concerned with the needs of its hinterland. The chief are slaughtering and meat packing and the manufacture of iron and steel and machine products—the last being the largest employer of labour. But in addition there is a multitude of miscellaneous industries, of which the most important are clothing, electrical supplies, chemicals, and printing and publishing. Grouped around Chicago there are a number of specialized local markets and industrial centres. The former in particular are largely dependent on truck haulage and draw supplies from a 75 to 100-mile radius. Such towns are Peoria, Indianapolis, and Milwaukee. The major relations of Chicago with its trade area in the mid-thirties were examined on a statistical basis. Statistics were available, for example, of the movement of livestock market centres, and of grain to grain elevators. About 70 per cent. of the cattle handled in the Chicago market, 85 per cent. of the pigs, and 35 per cent. of the sheep were drawn from the States of Illinois, Iowa, Indiana, southern Minnesota, and Wisconsin. The boundaries of each area from which over 50 per cent. of each class of livestock were transported by rail (from each county) to Chicago closely corresponded. Consequently, one can speak of a composite livestock market area of Chicago. As a grain market, Chicago is the main centre for the western corn belt, including the States of Illinois, Iowa, northern Indiana, southern Minnesota, with two main areas of outward consignments, northern Illinois and the north-centre of Iowa. The limits of the Federal Reserve Banking District give a broad indication of the sphere of economic influence of Chicago. This includes southern Wisconsin, Iowa, Illinois, Indiana (except their southern parts), and western Michigan (except the eastern part of the State which falls to Detroit). Two other criteria of orientation are the railway commuting zone, which was defined on the basis of numbers of season tickets issued from stations; and the circulation of Chicago newspapers. These are delicate and reliable indicators of the influence of the city upon its environs. All these areas have been mapped and there is a remarkable coincidence between their boundaries. These are fixed partly by consideration of access to Chicago in terms of both mileage and cost in relation to other metropolitan cities such as St. Louis, Minneapolis–St. Paul, and Detroit. One can, without hesitation, define the major hinterland of Chicago on the basis of these criteria. Chicago is also the largest inland port of North America, and its traffic is increasing now that the enlarged Seaway is open.

4. Centres of the Middle South

To the south of this group of metropolitan regions there is a second east–west tier, the centres of which are in part related to the manufacturing belt but also have relations with, and primarily serve, the Middle South. These are the regions of St. Louis, Louisville, Cincinnati, and Baltimore, which form a belt closely corresponding with the corn-and-winter-wheat belt, with tobacco as its chief money-crop. St. Louis, indeed, is at the junction of the hog, cattle, cotton, and wheat belts—a favourable location, reflected in its marketing activities and its varied industries. Its historic relationships have been principally with the south-west, where it previously shared with Kansas City an undisputed monopoly of the distributive trades. Indeed, this in some measure still holds good, for it handled in the thirties almost 40 per cent. of the hardware distribution in the south-western states. Owing to the development of the Gulf South-west, however, the principal sphere of influence of St. Louis now lies in the middle Mississippi basin. St. Louis is one of the largest diversified manufacturing centres in the country. It is located on the western edge of the manufacturing belt as well as being in close touch with the agricultural areas to the west and south. It has important stockyards and meat-producing industries, drawing supplies of livestock from the latter areas. Its wholesale grocery areas cover eastern Missouri and the south-west of Illinois, but a large part of the south-west has long been served also. The scope of St. Louis trade has been restricted by the competition of Chicago, but it remains an outstanding business and banking centre.

The Louisville and Cincinnati regions serve the Ohio basin, which includes one of the major areas of tobacco production. Cincinnati has a trade territory that covers much of the Blue Grass region of Kentucky and the lower Miami valley and south-west Indiana. Approximately one-fifth of the wholesale trade of Louisville is in farm products, mainly tobacco derived from Kentucky and Tennessee (grain mill products, distilled liquor, tobacco, hardwood furniture). To the east, Richmond and Baltimore have similar characteristics. The manufacture of tobacco products is the chief industry of Richmond, situated in the middle of a second major area of tobacco production. Tobacco products account for 20 per cent. of its wholesale trade and 30 per cent. of its occupied workers. Baltimore is the focus of the small Atlantic winter-wheat area. It is the only seaboard city of the Middle Atlantic Group with a grain consignment trade, and it leads in grain-elevator capacity. It has large industries, owing to its seaboard location, and a large distributing trade in Maryland and the Virginias. It serves, with Norfolk and Newport News, the West

Virginian coal-field. Thus, like St. Louis and Cincinnati, it is closely linked with the manufacturing belt, while metropolitan functions for a large region to the south are shared with Richmond. Richmond (408,000), a regional capital, is an outstanding centre of tobacco manufacturing in the States and also of textile-mill products, especially synthetic fibres. In all of these there are strong ties with raw materials in its hinterland—tobacco, cotton, and woodpulp. It is the main city in the Virginia Piedmont, has a small port and is a leading tobacco market. But as a commercial centre its status is subordinate to the giants on the Atlantic Seaboard. Nashville (400,000) is a regional capital with varied industries, as well as being the capital of Tennessee and the seat of a federal reserve branch. It is a seat of synthetic-fibre production (rayon), cotton spruce woods being the raw materials derived from the hinterland. Meat products also stand high in its activities. Its primary trade base is the central section of Tennessee.

5. The Cotton Belt (The South)

The southern tier of metropolitan regions closely corresponds with the cotton belt. Freight-rate structure has had an effect on urban development here very different from that of the northern states. In the latter, with the westward progress of the railway, the existing cities that had large distributing trades were able to attract the railways and become 'basing points', with special through rates, but from bases, within a definite area, cumulative freight rates were operative. This rate structure had the effect of assisting the concentration of wholesaling in those cities that were basing points. In the South, however, a number of small towns became local basing points, with special through rates to the north. This permitted the growth of small wholesaling centres, and, in addition to the special economic character of the South, tended to prevent the dominance of any one centre.

In the South two rapidly growing centres of metropolitan integration are Atlanta and Dallas–Fort Worth. This is indicated by their large population increase—40 per cent. for Atlanta and 46 per cent. for Dallas in the 1950–60 decade. 'Regional headquarters for national distributors, central banking institutions, and large merchandizing concerns have given Atlanta a metropolitan character and a direct dependence upon the prosperity and progress of every mining, lumbering, manufacturing, and agricultural enterprise in the area.'[1]

[1] J. M. Hager, *Commercial Survey of the Southeast*, U.S. Bureau of Foreign and Domestic Commerce, Domestic Commerce Ser. No. 19, 1927, p. 142.

Dallas also claimed thirty years ago to have the south-western headquarters of more than 2,000 concerns of sectional or national importance, and 100 of its 750 manufacturing plants are branch plants.[1] Farm supplies (livestock and grain) form over two-thirds of the wholesale trade of Fort Worth and 45 per cent. of Dallas's (cotton). These two cities, however, share the metropolitan functions of the south-west with Houston–Galveston. Similarly, Birmingham and Jacksonville are subsidiary to Atlanta in the south-east. Birmingham has industries based on local supplies of iron and coal and is the trade centre for northern Alabama. Jacksonville is the centre for northern Florida and southern Georgia; it has important tobacco industries as well as being a port and a resort centre and an outstanding transport centre in the south-east.

Between these two regions is that of Memphis, again primarily a cotton market (one-half of wholesale sales), but with well-diversified activities. It is to be considered, however, as subordinate to St. Louis, for the livestock marketing of the whole area is focused on the latter and much of the distributive trade and other economic relations is directed therefrom. Several of the industries of Memphis have strong regional ties—cotton, hardwoods, tobacco. As a wholesaler it serves the western third of Tennessee and surroundings.

Finally, New Orleans is essentially a through-commodity port and not a centre of metropolitan integration. It has an extensive hinterland, serving the whole of the Mississippi basin. When the Federal Reserve Bank centres were being selected, New Orleans claimed as its hinterland the whole of the South, but the banks that expressed a desire to be associated with New Orleans were, however, located almost entirely in Louisiana and Mississippi. Dallas and Atlanta were therefore selected as more suitable centres.

Houston (1·4 m.) has gas extraction and petroleum refining prominent in its industrial profile, and both are based on the materials of its hinterland. It is also a port with important trade in cotton and oil. The port enjoys freight rate advantages in all Texas and the eastern half of New Mexico, south-west Kansas, and Oklahoma, west of the city. The great agricultural and oil-producing areas contribute most of the export tonnage of the port. New Orleans (868,000) has canning and preserving industries that are dependent on the Gulf fisheries (shrimps and oysters). There are also sugar-refining and vegetable-oil industries. The 'local' hinterland of the port reaches Memphis and to the east competes with Mobile, to the west with Houston. It is a big wholesaling centre for southern Louisiana.

[1] C. V. Wallis, *The Southwest Market and Dallas as its Geographic and Economic Center*, Dallas, Texas, 1930, pp. 43–5.

6. THE WEST-CENTRE[1]

The Twin Cities region closely corresponds with the spring-wheat belt. In the marketing of grain the Twin Cities are partnered by Duluth. The large stock-market of St. Paul is a reflection of the size of its supply area and not of intensity of production. Four-fifths of its supplies come from Minnesota and nine-tenths arrive by truck. Large quantities are shipped elsewhere for feeding. The area extends west to the 'economic divide', though in southern and western Montana livestock shipments are principally directed to Chicago. The distinctiveness of the Twin Cities is further reflected in the great importance of their flour milling (though decreasing), wholesale trades, and varied light manufactures and assembly plants.

One of the first studies of the sphere of influence of a metropolitan city was Mildred Hartsough's examination of the Twin Cities (1·5 m.).[2] Areas were plotted which were tributary to the cities in respect of grain trade, livestock trade, wholesale (jobbing) trade, and the Federal Reserve banking area. The smaller commercial and industrial centres tributary to Minneapolis and St. Paul were also indicated. These areas were shown only generally, and they have since been studied more exactly from statistical data—notably for newspaper circulation and for livestock and grain trade, the two primary functions of the Twin Cities. While these areas do not exactly coincide, the composite map shows that the Twin Cities dominate Minnesota, northwestern Wisconsin, the Dakotas, and part of Montana. This area, be it noted, has its nucleus in the great spring-wheat growing area, with the addition of the semi-arid stock-raising areas on its western border towards the foot of the Rockies, and the wooded dairying area of northwestern Wisconsin.

Today the Twin Cities is the commercial, industrial, and financial centre for Minnesota, North and South Dakota, eastern Montana, and western Wisconsin.[3] St. Paul serves northern and western Wis-

[1] Special attention is drawn to the work of the Upper Midwest Research and Development Council, the University of Minnesota, and the Twin Cities Metropolitan Planning Commission. We have reference particularly to the monograph on *Trade Centers and Trade Areas of the Upper Midwest* by John R. Rorchert and Russell B. Adams, an Upper Midwest Economic Study, Urban Report No. 3, Sept. 1963. This study applies the concepts discussed in this book to the problems of metropolitan growth in this area. The hierarchy of trade centres in six grades and their service areas are thoroughly worked out, and changes evaluated in the post-war period.

[2] M. Hartsough, *The Twin Cities as a Metropolitan Market*, Studies in Social Sciences, Research Publications of the University of Minnesota, No. 18, 1925.

[3] See R. Hartshorne, 'The Twin City District, A Unique Form of Urban Landscape', *Geographical Review*, Vol. XXII, 1932, pp. 431–42. Also J. R. Borchert, 'The Twin Cities Urbanized Area: Past, Present and Future', *Geographical Review*, Vol. LI, 1961, pp. 47–70.

consin and southeastern Minnesota, whereas Minneapolis serves western Minnesota, North and South Dakota, and Montana.[1]

The Twin Cities is one of the top cities in respect to wholesale sales *per capita*, with grain and livestock as the outstanding sales, together with a great variety of manufactured products, such as groceries and automotive equipment. Areas of service differ for different products.

Taking the wholesale hardware trade area as a basis of definition of the general wholesale trade area, Minnesota and eastern North Dakota are responsible for 70 per cent. of the trade, and the remainder is transacted with the rest of the Dakotas and Montana to the west, while the trade area falls off sharply to the east and south of Minnesota.

'Since one of the major wholesale functions performed by the S.M.A. involves the distribution of manufactured products from the industrial belt, it is clear why the hinterland extends much further in a westward direction than an eastward direction.'[2]

To the south there is the Omaha–Kansas City region, closely corresponding with the western—and principal—section of the corn belt, serving the beef-cattle area farther west. These two cities, with Sioux City and St. Joseph, are all located at the western extremity of the corn-and-hog belt. This is reflected in the overwhelming importance, in their wholesale trade, of farm products (livestock and grain) and, in their manufactures, of slaughtering and meat-packing. Some two-thirds of the wholesale sales of Omaha (458,000) are farm products. Nine-tenths of its livestock are drawn from Iowa and Nebraska and considerable numbers from Wyoming. Its primary wholesale territory is in Nebraska but it reaches out to the adjacent states.

Kansas City (1·0 m.), with 45 per cent. of its trade in this group, is a larger centre, with a greater diversity of commercial and industrial activities, particularly the processing of agricultural products, with a big warehouse storage capacity. It is definitely metropolitan on all criteria; hence it is selected as the principal centre. Its trade area covers Kansas and western Missouri, though it has contracted substantially in the last fifty years.

Oklahoma City (512,000), a regional capital, is a seat of crude petroleum and gas extraction and of meat-product industries, all depending on resources derived from its region. The Mid-continental Oilfield is connected with the city by a close network of pipelines. Located at the contact of the winter-wheat belt and the cotton belt,

---

[1] Duncan, *op. cit.*, p. 348.
[2] *Ibid.*, p. 350.

it is a headquarters for grain, livestock, and cotton interests. Non-local services make up nearly a quarter of all its workers. Its trade area covers Oklahoma State and the Texas Panhandle, though Tulsa and Dallas are strong competitors.

7. The West

The western states, including the intermontane belt and the Pacific Seaboard, are largely dependent on the East for manufactures. San Francisco is still the chief centre of distribution—a fact reflected in its many sales-territory organizations and in the extent of the western Federal Reserve district, for which it is the headquarters. The Panama Canal has brought the intermontane belt considerably nearer to the Pacific ports, which now compete more effectively with distributors and manufacturers from the Middle West. The historic trade monopoly of San Francisco has, however, been broken in this century by the rapid metropolitan development of Los Angeles and the ports of the Pacific North-west.

San Francisco (4·2 m.) is the hub of the Central Pacific Coast Area and its influence dominates from San Luis Obispo and the Tehachapi Pass north to the Oregon border.

'Rail lines, highways, and waterways, branch out to connect the port with Sacramento, San Joaquin, Salinas, Santa Clara, Pajara, Sonoma and Napa valleys—rich irrigated soil basins that produce the major part of Californian agriculture. This is the local market or jobbing area in which, in competition with the large Pacific Coast ports, Bay Area shippers and distributors have a freight rate advantage. It has been estimated that 90 per cent. of the imports entering San Francisco Bay are for use in the area, and that an equal percentage of exports originated there.'[1]

San Francisco is a seat of trade, service, and finance for its hinterland, though the growth of Los Angeles in the south has inevitably curtailed its impact. It is one of the few cities in the States in which a single bank, the Giannini concern, formerly the Bank of Italy and now the Bank of America, developed by establishing many branch banks throughout a hinterland. Branches were established throughout and beyond the State in order to cater for the varied needs and seasonal demands of the highly contrasted and localized types of agriculture in this area. The development of this concern is a unique example in the States of the regional growth of a city as a seat of banking in the service of the agricultural enterprises of its hinterland.

[1] Duncan, *op. cit.*, p. 340.

Los Angeles (8·9 m.) did not arise in response to a demand for metropolitan integration: this came subsequently. The city has, however, rapidly acquired metropolitan characteristics and for that reason may be regarded as serving a separate region, though it is closely related to San Francisco. It is the third largest city in the United States, and has grown with phenomenal rapidity since the 1880's, especially with the advent of motion pictures and aircraft assembly. This sprawling urban area, sometimes described as 'forty suburbs in search of a centre', can in some respects be regarded as one with San Diego to the south, which also has over a million inhabitants giving a total of about 9 millions. This complex dominates the southern counties of California, south of San Luis Obispo and the Tehachapi Pass.

San Diego (1·0 m.) is an important seat of canning and preserving of regional products—fruit, vegetables, and sea food (notably tuna fish). It is also outstanding as a tourist centre, based upon its magnificent natural harbour and its attractive climate. In spite of its size (that nearly doubled in the fifties) many of its services are derived from Los Angeles.

Spokane, Salt Lake City–Ogden, and Denver are the metropolitan centres for the intermontane belt. They are the chief centres of collection and distribution of commodities, which are purchased from Pacific or mid-western manufacturers. Manufactures are low but have increased in recent years through both the growth of local concerns and the establishment of branch plants. Each is the centre of a distinct region, and though small cities (Spokane, 278,000, and Salt Lake City, 490,000), they certainly have metropolitan characteristics of the second order. Spokane is the undisputed focus of a region of agriculture and lumbering, the so-called 'Inland Empire'; one-third of its wholesale trade is in lumbering materials. Denver and Salt Lake City have mining interests and are also large store-stock markets and general distributing centres. Spokane is tributary to Seattle, and Salt Lake City to San Francisco. Denver (929,000) is a meat-packing and sugar-refining centre and it has the largest lamb market in the country. It is an important commercial and financial and wholesaling centre for a large area of the western States. These functions are in large measure due to its location at the contact of the range lands of the Great Plains and the irrigated areas to the north of the city, especially in the Platte valley. As a wholesaler, Denver dominates Colorado and southwest Wyoming, and is considerably larger than the other two and higher in metropolitan status. It has acquired in the post-war years many federal research and military establishments. The 'zone of transference' in Montana and Idaho has several small mining towns and draws supplies from, and sends products to, both East and West. Denver increased rapidly, by one-half, in the fifties, an

THE CITY-REGION

indication of its great importance as a regional focus and its steady climb towards the status of a first-order metropolis.

The Pacific Northwest[1] forms a distinctive geographical unit, focused on the Puget Sound area, with Seattle as the metropolitan centre but sharing its functions with Portland. Some two-thirds of the total wheat production of the whole region (Washington, Oregon, Idaho, northwestern Montana) moves through these two ports.[2] An increasing proportion of its stock is also being diverted to these centres from the primary markets in the Middle West. Regional distribution is effected by importing goods from San Francisco by water, or by local manufactures, which are increasing rapidly. To the east the region includes the Spokane area and western Montana, from which the movement of grain and stock is directed mainly to the Pacific Northwest, while general distribution from Seattle and Portland in competition with the Middle West is rendered possible on an equal freight-rate basis.

Seattle (1·4 m.) has saw mills and wood-working industries based on the surrounding forested areas, the main area of commercial timber in the nation. Aircraft production and assembly is of first importance here, with its raw materials drawn from widely scattered points beyond the hinterland, though the electric power is drawn from the Northwest. It is a commercial city dependent on its port facilities, and non-local services occupy one-fifth of all its workers. As for its wholesale sales, McCarty writes that it 'includes not only the forest and farm lands of the Puget Sound Valley but also the vast productive area in eastern Washington and adjacent Idaho and Montana. To these lands Seattle acts as a gatherer and distributor.'[3] It gathers wheat, fruit, and flour, animal and mineral products. It distributes manufactured goods and other consumer goods. It is an outstanding financier of its shipping interest, lumbermen, and fish merchants in the north-west of Alaska.

Portland (822,000) is not far behind its rival in size. It serves central Oregon and parts of Washington and Idaho. It too is an important river port with a 35-foot channel on the Columbia river. Situated in the Willamette valley, it assembles a great variety of agricultural products.

---

[1] Edwin Bates, *Commercial Survey of the Pacific Northwest*, U.S. Bureau of Foreign and Domestic Commerce, Domestic Commerce Ser. No. 51, 1932. Also O. W. Freeman and H. H. Martin, *The Pacific Northwest*, New York, 1954.

[2] *Ibid.*, p. 6, and other ports in the *Port Series* of the U.S. War Department Corps of Engineers.

[3] H. H. McCarty, *The Geographic Basis of American Economic Life*, New York, 1940, pp. 116–17.

APPENDIX TO CHAPTER 11

Single Standard Metropolitan Areas (S.M.A.) with over 250,000 Inhabitants (in thousands), 1960

S.M.A.	Population			Percentage Increase	
	1960	1950	1940	1950–60	1940–50
1. St. Louis (Mo.)	2,060	1,719	1,464	19·8	17·4
2. Buffalo (N.Y.)	1,307	1,089	958	20·0	13·6
3. Kansas City (Mo.–Kans.)	1,039	814	687	27·6	18·6
4. Atlanta (Ga.)	1,017	727	559	39·9	30·1
5. Denver (Col.)	929	612	445	51·8	37·5
6. New Orleans (La.)	868	685	552	26·7	24·1
7. Portland (Oreg.)	822	705	501	16·6	40·6
8. Louisville (Ky.)	725	577	451	25·7	27·8
9. Tampa–St. Petersburg (Fla.)	722	409	272	88·8	50·4
10. Indianapolis (Ind.)	698	552	461	26·4	19·7
11. San Antonio (Texas)	687	500	338	37·3	48·0
12. Columbus (Ohio)	683	503	389	35·7	29·5
13. Memphis (Tenn.)	627	482	358	30·0	34·7
14. Rochester (N.Y.)	586	488	438	20·3	11·3
15. Oklahoma City (Okla.)	512	392	299	30·4	31·2
16. Omaha (Nebr.)	458	366	325	25·0	12·7
17. Toledo (Ohio)	457	396	344	15·5	14·9
18. Jacksonville (Fla.)	455	304	210	49·8	44·7
19. Tulsa (Okla.)	419	328	290	27·8	12·9
20. Richmond (Va.)	408	328	266	24·5	23·2
21. Nashville (Tenn.)	400	322	257	24·2	25·1
22. Knoxville (Tenn.)	368	337	246	9·2	37·0
23. Fresno (Cal.)	366	277	179	32·3	54·9
24. Wichita (Kans.)	343	222	143	54·4	55·1
25. Orlando (Fla.)	318	142	92	124·6	53·5
26. Mobile (Ala.)	314	231	142	36·0	62·8
27. Peoria (Ill.)	289	251	212	15·3	18·3
28. El Paso (Texas)	314	195	131	61·1	48·8
29. Chattanooga (Tenn.–Ga.)	283	246	211	14·9	16·5
30. Spokane (Wash.)	278	222	165	25·6	34·6
31. Duluth–Superior (Min.–Wis.)	277	253	254	9·4	−0·5
32. Charlotte (N.C.)	272	197	152	38·1	29·8
33. Davenport–Rock Island–Moline (Iowa–Ill.)	270	234	198	15·3	18·3
34. Des Moines (Iowa)	266	226	196	17·8	15·4
35. Albuquerque (N. Mex.)	262	146	69	80·0	109·9
36. Huntington–Ashton (W. Va.–Ky.–Ohio)	255	246	226	3·7	8·9
37. Charleston (W. Va.)	253	239	196	5·5	22·5
38. Erie (Pa.)	251	219	181	14·3	21·3
United States	178,464	150,697	131,669	18·4	14·5

GROUPS OF CONTIGUOUS STANDARD METROPOLITAN AREAS
(S.M.A.) WITH OVER 250,000 INHABITANTS (IN THOUSANDS), 1960

S.M.A.	Population			Percentage Increase	
	1960	1950	1940	1950–60	1940–50
1. Eastern Seaboard (33 S.M.A.s)	31,625	27,323	23,979	18·1	14·4
2. Los Angeles–San Diego–Bakersfield & San Bernardino	8,878	5,605	3,607	61·8	70·1
3. Chicago–Gary–Hammond, Milwaukee	8,232	6,728	5,879	25·7	18·1
4. Cleveland, Youngstown, Pittsburg, Steubenville–Weirton, Wheeling, Johnstown, Altoona	6,359	5,740	5,210	14·4	9·9
5. Detroit–Flint–Saginaw–Lansing	5,037	4,016	3,175	25·8	27·3
6. San Francisco–Oakland	4,178	3,010	1,941	62·8	57·9
7. Cincinnati–Springfield	2,097	1,682	1,387	26·3	22·2
8. Dallas–Fort Worth	1,657	1,137	783	45·8	47·2
9. Miami–West Palm Beach	1,497	694	388	161·9	79·7
10. Minneapolis–St. Paul	1,482	1,151	967	28·8	19·0
11. Seattle–Tacoma	1,429	1,121	776	23·8	46·8
12. Houston–Galveston	1,383	910	610	39·1	45·9
13. Phoenix–Tucson	930	473	259	94·0	86·0
14. Syracuse–Utica–Rome	895	749	669	18·8	6·3
15. Norfolk–Newport News	804	601	352	37·3	69·1
16. Birmingham–Tuscaloosa	744	653	526	14·7	22·6
17. Albany–Schenectady–Troy	732	656	592	11·2	10·0
18. Wilkes-Barre–Scranton	582	649	743	−11·2	−12·7
19. Grand Rapids–Muskegon	513	411	341	24·7	22·8
20. Salt Lake City–Provo	490	357	269	34·9	36·3
21. Columbia–Augusta	477	349	273	36·6	27·8
22. Beaumont–Port Arthur	451	296	220	46·6	51·7
23. Greensboro–Winston–Salem	436	337	280	29·3	19·8
24. Texarkana–Shreveport	373	312	265	13·4	16·7
25. Raleigh–Durham	281	238	190	34·1	51·3
26. Springfield–Decatur	265	230	203	15·5	14·1
27. Colorado Springs–Pueblo	263	165	123	62·2	34·4

THE CITY-REGION IN THE UNITED STATES: II

GROUPS OF CONTIGUOUS STANDARD METROPOLITAN AREAS (S.M.A.) WITH OVER 250,000 INHABITANTS (IN THOUSANDS) IN THE EASTERN SEABOARD AREA (1960)

S.M.A.	Population			Percentage Increase	
	1960	1950	1940	1950–60	1940–50
	31,625	*27,323*	*23,979*	*18.1*	*14.1*
1. Lowell	158	136	133	16·2	2·5
2. Lawrence–Haverhill	188	182	178	2·8	2·3
3. Boston	2,589	2,411	2,210	7·4	9·1
4. Worcester	323	303	276	6·7	9·6
5. Brockton	149	120	110	24·8	8·4
6. Fall River	138	137	135	0·6	1·6
7. New Bedford	143	142	138	0·8	2·8
8. Springfield–Chicopee–Holyoke	479	413	372	15·7	11·8
9. Hartford	525	407	337	29·2	20·6
10. Waterbury	182	155	139	17·4	11·4
11. Providence–Pawtucket	816	760	695	7·4	9·3
12. New Britain	129	104	90	24·1	15·2
13. New London–Groton–Norwich	157	123	106	27·4	15·9
14. Meriden	52	44	39	17·6	11·6
15. New Haven	312	270	244	15·6	10·4
16. Bridgeport	335	274	225	22·2	21·5
17. Norwalk	97	66	51	47·3	29·0
18. Stamford	178	135	99	32·3	36·4
19. New York	10,695	9,556	8,707	11·9	9·8
20. Patterson–Clifton–Passaic	1,187	876	719	35·5	21·9
21. Newark	1,689	1,468	1,291	15·0	13·7
22. Allentown–Bethlehem–Easton	492	438	397	12·4	10·4
23. Reading	275	256	242	7·7	5·7
24. Lancaster	278	235	213	18·6	10·5
25. Harrisburg	345	292	252	18·1	15·9
26. York	238	203	178	17·6	13·9
27. Baltimore	1,727	1,405	1,140	22·9	23·3
28. Washington	2,002	1,464	968	36·7	51·3
29. Philadelphia	4,343	3,671	3,200	18·3	14·7
30. Wilmington	366	268	222	36·4	21·0
31. Atlantic City	161	132	124	21·5	6·7
32. Trenton	266	230	197	15·9	16·5
33. Jersey City	611	647	652	−5·7	−0·7

Chapter 12

THE CITY-REGION IN WESTERN EUROPE

We have discussed in the previous chapter the characteristics of the metropolitan city and the expanding impact of urbanism in the United States, with its 180 million people in an area of 3 million square miles. It would now seem appropriate to attempt a similar portrayal of western Europe. Europe without the Soviet Union has about 400 million people living on 2 million square miles. The more restricted area of Britain, Scandinavia, Germany, the Low Countries, Switzerland, Austria, France, and Italy has an area of about one million square miles and 210 million inhabitants. The structure of the city-region and the practices of city, regional, and national planning vary considerably from one country to another. However, we shall briefly bring out some general aspects of special interest to our theme, with a view to comparison with the United States. We shall discuss, first, a selection of the metropolitan cities; second, the limits of the urbanized regions; third, the range of the daily journey to work and fourth, the city-regions. Britain will be dealt with in more detail in the next chapter, and the special aspects of regionalism and the problems of city planning in the last chapters of the book.

1. URBAN AGGLOMERATIONS

The continuous urban aggregates in western Europe have been defined, officially and unofficially, in various ways in different countries. Since we want a common standard of measure we shall take the data provided by the International Urban Research Group in its book on *The World's Metropolitan Areas*.[1] Their definition of an urban aggregate, described as a metropolitan area, is as close as possible to that of the standard metropolitan area according to the United States Census. These areas have over 100,000 inhabitants, with at least one city over 50,000,

[1] International Urban Research Group, *The World's Metropolitan Areas*, University of California Press, Berkeley, 1959. These are the areas used in this chapter, with populations converted for 1960 or 1961.

plus the contiguous administrative divisions which have over two-thirds of the population engaged in non-agricultural occupations, or, alternatively, a density of population at least one-half of the density of the central urban core, or at least twice the density of the next ring of divisions at a greater distance from the urban core. On this basis, Europe, excluding the Soviet Union, had fifty agglomerations each with over one million inhabitants. The list of agglomerations exceeding 250,000 is given at the end of the chapter.

Britain has seven major agglomerations. Three others approach the million mark through the coalescence of neighbouring cities—Sheffield, Nottingham–Derby and South Wales. Outside these, there are 20 with 250,000 to 750,000, and 30 with 100,000 to 250,000 inhabitants. Ireland has three 100,000 cities—Belfast, Dublin, and Cork.

Germany (East and West) has 51 urban aggregates with over 100,000 people each, including West and East Berlin as one. Berlin has 4·2 millions and the Ruhr 5·7 millions. Six others have between 2 and 1 millions (Cologne, Frankfurt, Hamburg, Mannheim–Ludwigshafen–Heidelberg, Munich, and Stuttgart. Düsseldorf, Hanover, Wuppertal, Nuremberg, and probably Leipzig, are very close to this mark, below which there is a big drop to the next largest city.

France has 30 agglomerations with over 100,000 people. These are dwarfed by Paris with over 7 million. Near the million mark, and greatly exceeding all other cities, are Lille–Roubaix–Tourcoing, Lyon and Marseille.

Belgium has five agglomerations. These are headed by Brussels with 1·5 millions, followed by Antwerp (870,000), Liège (600,000), Ghent and Charleroi (each with just under 500,000).

The Netherlands, although much less urbanized than Belgium, has roughly the same total population. It has a total of 14 agglomerations exceeding 100,000. These cities, together with Haarlem and Utrecht, form a hollow *Ring* with a diameter of 40 km.. There is here a total of 3·5 million people, one-third of the population of the Netherlands. Amsterdam and Rotterdam are each just in the million mark.

Switzerland has five 100,000 cities of which the largest is Zurich with about 600,000. Austria has five large cities, with nearly 2 millions in Vienna. In Scandinavia, Copenhagen (1·3 m.) has a fifth of the total population of Denmark, Stockholm has one million inhabitants, and Oslo reaches half a million. There are no other cities in Scandinavia with over 100,000 inhabitants.

We have calculated the percentage growth of population in these metropolitan areas over the period 1950 to 1960. The results are shown on Fig. 55 and the data listed at the end of the chapter.

THE CITY-REGION

The symbols are proportional to the population, the largest corresponding approximately with the limits of the metropolitan area. Each is shaded according to percentage annual increase in relation

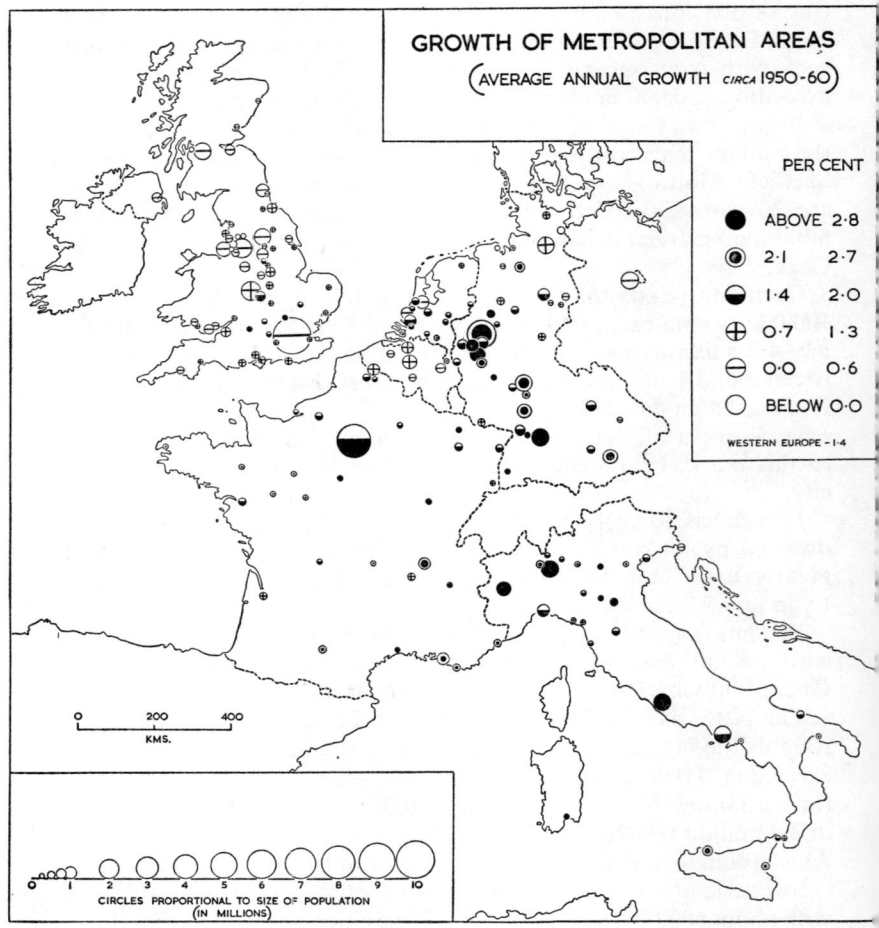

FIG. 55. Western Europe: Growth of Metropolitan Areas, 1950–60.

to the growth of metropolitan areas as a whole. The growth rates for each country are as follows for 1951–61 (adjusted): Britain 3·5 per cent., France 9·0 per cent., Belgium 5·6 per cent., Netherlands 13·3 per cent., West Germany 9·6 per cent., and Italy 6·2 per cent.

The metropolitan increase accounts for virtually all of the growth in the countries of western Europe. The agglomerations on the continent had a remarkably rapid growth in contrast with the situation in Britain, where the provincial conurbations (except Birmingham) all show increases well below the small national increase. It is in these areas that economic growth is concentrated. Here are new industrial complexes on the urban peripheries. Here are the new and rapidly growing central business districts. Road and rail routes bring in tens of thousands of daily commuters to each big city over journey distances of up to two hours, so that actually their orbits extend not only to residential peripheries but beyond these into rural areas in which, though with an agricultural base, the bulk of the workers commute to distant places of work in the big agglomerations or small neighbouring towns.

The three greatest metropolitan agglomerations (by the same definition in 1961) are in London with 10·7 millions, Paris with 7·7 millions and the vast aggregate of the Ruhr with 5·7 millions. London increased in the period 1951–61 by 4·5 per cent., Paris by 7·5 per cent. from 1946 to 1954 and 15 per cent. from 1954 to 1962, the Ruhr by 24 per cent. from 1950 to 1961. Many other cities have increases over the decade in excess of 20 per cent. Relatively few show increases below the averages, and few have actual decreases. The last are conspicuously located in Britain. The rapidly growing cities, together with their dependent orbits, form a belt from the southern Netherlands right through the western portion of West Germany to northern Italy, with a few rapidly growing centres in southern Italy, wherein there are prospects of rapid growth in the next decade. The small cities of France record significant increases, but particularly significant is the high increase of Lyon and (a much smaller city) Grenoble, together with Marseille. This whole region of the south-east is a major pole of attraction in the post-war development of France.

2. Urbanized Regions

It has already been emphasized that urbanization extends today beyond the limits of the metropolitan areas in such a way as to interconnect separate urban agglomerations. The conurbations as defined by Geddes have merged with each other or are rapidly doing so. The next step then is to define those areas that are so closely interconnected in their land use and functions as to be regarded as continuously urban. From a consideration of the outer limits of a number of various cities in north-western Europe we have found the density of 500 persons per square mile per commune to be the

THE CITY-REGION

best indicator of the outer limits of the urbanized areas as against contiguous rural areas. This figure corresponds with Gottmann's estimate of 469 per square mile in the areas of eastern Atlantic Seaboard of America that lie outside the main cities. The result,

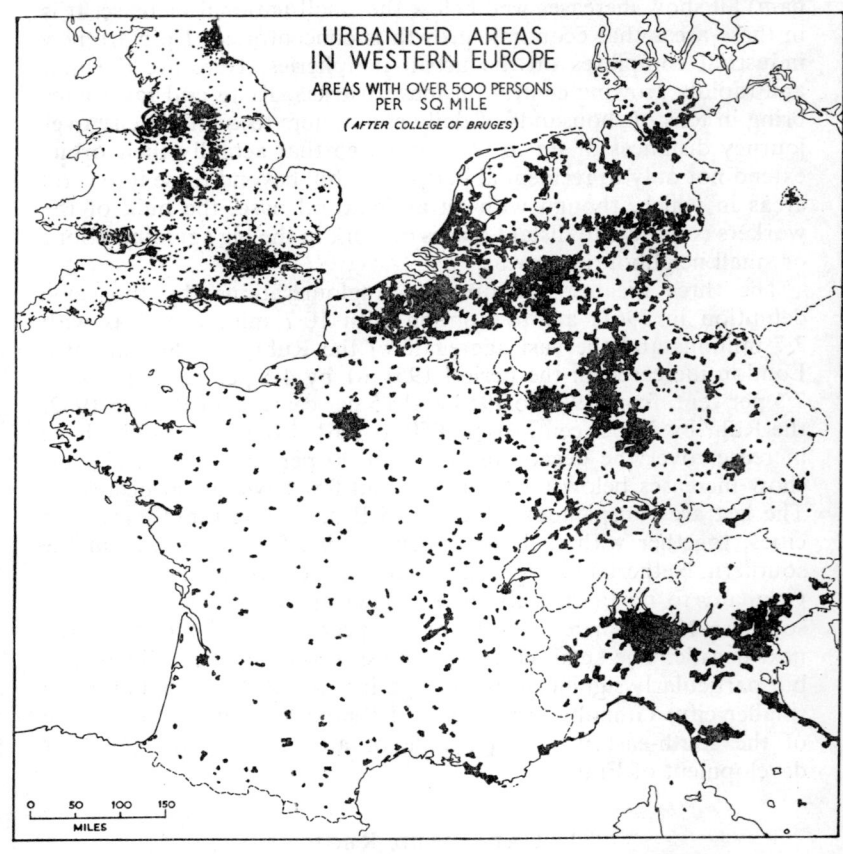

FIG. 56. Urbanized Areas in Western Europe, circa 1950.

Areas with over 200 persons per sq. km. (500 per sq. ml.) (after map of the College of Bruges, scale 1 : 2,000,000). This map is *double* the scale of the maps of the United States on Figs. 45, 46, and 47 in Ch. 10.

taken from the map of Dr. Koomoss of the College of Bruges (scale, 1 : 2,000,000), is shown on Fig. 56. This is based on small units with densities for around 1950.

On the Continent, we note the continuity of the belt through northern France and Belgium and the Netherlands to the central axis of Germany with its southerly extension through the Rhineland and its outliers to the west in the Saar and Lorraine and to the east in the Neckar basin. We note in France the dominance of Paris and the frequency of the small and separate town outside the major agglomerations of the Nord, Lorraine, Lyon, and Marseille. Jean Labasse referring to the growth of the south-east of France, speaks of the Lyon–St. Etienne–Grenoble triangle. The so-called A.B.C. triangle of Amsterdam, Brussels and Cologne is extended by a recent British writer to refer to the 'golden triangle' of London, Paris, Cologne, the area of greatest urban concentration in western Europe. We hear again of the Genoa–Milan–Turin triangle. One has recently suggested Lonbirm as the name for the urban region in southern and central England. These names indicate the groups of conurbations that form extended urbanized regions of economic activity and population. These are in all essentials, comparable with Gottmann's Megalopolis on the Atlantic seaboard of America.

Urban development is almost entirely responsible for the more substantial growth of total populations in western Europe and it is therefore appropriate and illuminating to look at the trends of population growth during the fifties. Fig. 57 shows the growth of total population by districts of approximately the same order of size in each of the countries of the Common Market, together with Britain, Northern Ireland, and Eire. Rates of growth are given in each country in relation to the increase of the group as a whole.

Areas with increases above their national averages include the following: the Midlands and south-east England; the western *Regierungsbezirke* of West Germany together with the southern section of the Netherlands and north-central Belgium; the departments of south-eastern France; and the departments grouped around Greater Paris. Smaller isolated areas are Lorraine, the Nord and lower Loire (Nantes) in France; north Yorkshire (due to the increase in Teesside), and several individual departments in the Pyrenees.

The areas with the greatest increase, with over double the rate of increase of the countries in which they are situated, are the London region, the Paris region, Marseille and the Riviera (the example *par excellence* of the pull of tourism), Westphalia, and south-west Germany (Baden and north Württemberg). It should be noted that the Netherlands has in fact the largest of all the national increases of total population—13·9 per cent.—due in large measure to its high birth-rate. In consequence, its areas of high increase as shown on the map have bigger rates of growth than districts in other countries. The southern Netherlands is, in fact, one of the areas of greatest percentage increase of population. Its adjacent areas in Belgium include Antwerp, Brussels, and the Campine. In Belgium, where, as in England, over 80 per cent. of the population is urban, the rate of growth is small, and the areas of smallest increase are in the old coalfield and industrial areas of the Sambre–Meuse and in the rural

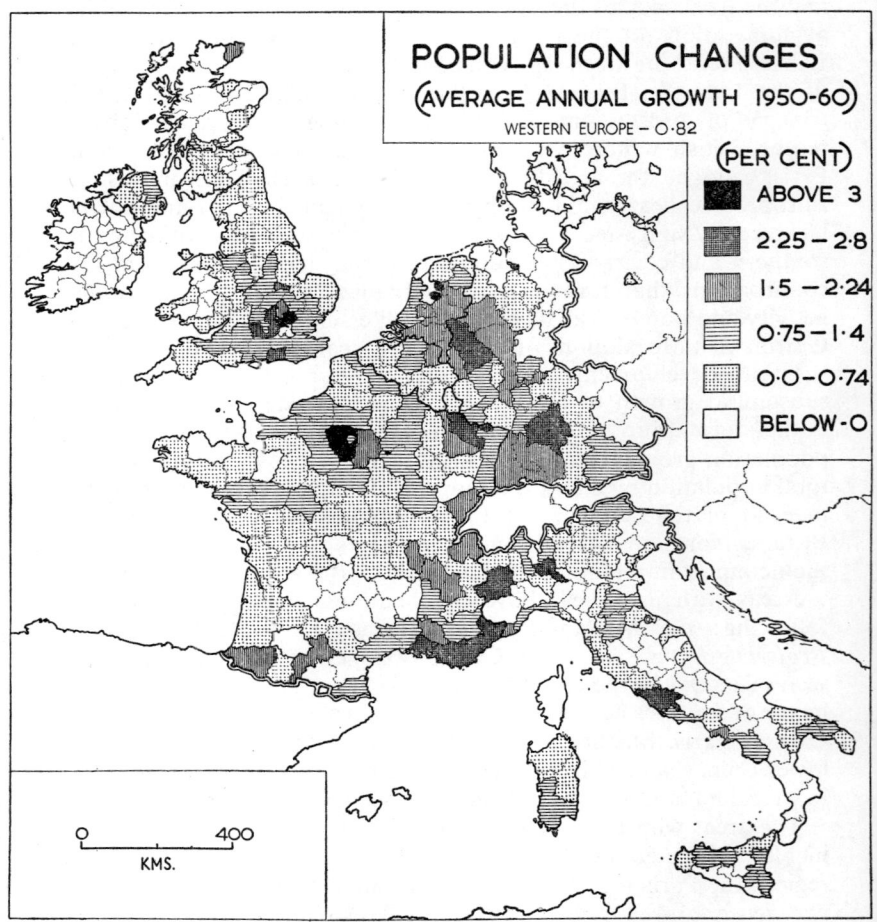

FIG. 57. Western Europe: Population Changes, 1950–60.

and textile areas of Flanders. In fact, these areas of Belgium, together with the Ardennes and the agricultural provinces of northern Netherlands, are the sub-normal provinces of these two countries. In Italy the increase of population from 1951 to 1961 was 6·2 per cent. Above this average were the three regions covering the Milan, Turin, Genoa triangle. This is the great pole of attraction in the

Italian economy. The Region of Lazio, centred around Rome, also records a big increase. Campania owes its high increase predominantly to urban growth in the wide orbit of Naples. (Sardinia owes a high rate to its high birth-rate and small emigration.) These areas in western Europe are the poles of economic growth into which population has been flocking continuously through the fifties.

Next we note the areas with either small increases below the national averages or with actual decreases in absolute numbers of population. The areas of absolute decrease include the districts of west Germany that lie along the border against the Iron Curtain, and suffered from an excessive increase by the emigration of refugees after the war, feel the pinch of geographic aloofness from the main poles of economic growth in the Bund, and have lost many of their surplus of refugees since 1950 by migration westwards into the areas of employment demand in the western provinces. The growing Braunschweig–Salzgitter–Wolfsburg complex has withstood these trends and the decrease in the fifties is mainly associated with Schleswig-Holstein and eastern Bavaria.

In France, while the whole of the south and west has generally experienced small increases (except the Clermont Ferrand area), the main areas of continued decrease are in Brittany, the southern departments of the Central Massif and several departments of the south-west. Great areas of positive decrease are located in Britain—in Wales, the south-west, northern England, the Scottish Highlands, and most of Ireland. Here are recorded the biggest losses of population in the whole of western Europe. These are the underdeveloped rural areas of Britain. Areas of decrease in Italy were in the agricultural areas of eastern Lombardy and in central Italy (notably Marche and Abruzzi). The southern Regions have a relatively high natural increase and this more than offset their large emigration to the North. They managed to maintain a small increase, though Calabria, a great reservoir of emigration, recorded no change, which is indicative of its traditional status as a reservoir of emigration. The emigration from southern Italy to the north became a torrent in the fifties and over a million people moved there in this period. In fact, the South lost an aggregate of 2 million people between 1950 and 1960.

We may now briefly comment on certain significant features in the growth of these countries since 1945.

Germany, in all its three parts—west, east, and the Polish areas—has experienced profound changes in the composition of its population in the last twenty years. As far as Potsdam Germany is concerned, two features are outstanding. Firstly, there has been the large immigration of 13 million 'refugees' into the Soviet Zone and especially into West Germany. Secondly, there was the stagnation and decrease of all the cities due to war-time devastation and population shifts, in the period 1939–46. During the fifties, however, with the economic revival of the country, the overcrowded eastern provinces of West Germany have lost large numbers of people through emigration into the western provinces where, with the industrial revival, job opportunities were available. Innumerable industrial plants have been established both within the major cities and in the wider lands around them, as well as in the small towns throughout the countryside. An unprecedented growth of the big cities and their environs has thus taken place.

From 1946 to 1954 while the eastern provinces of West Germany (as well as almost all East Germany) showed a decrease in numbers, the districts in the Rhinelands showed a remarkably rapid increase of population. This was true for most of Rhineland-Westphalia, Hesse, Rhineland-Palatinate, and Baden-Württemberg. In the eastern section, the major cities also showed large increases—notably in Munich, Nuremberg, Braunschweig, Hanover, Bremen, and Hamburg. While the total increase for the Bund was 14 per cent., extensive areas had increases of 15 to 25 per cent., while there were also large areas with increases of 25 to 35 per cent. during the eight years. This is unprecedented in any area at any time in western Europe. All of these are urban areas. They include the Lower Rhinelands—the whole of the Ruhr with its corners in Aachen, Bonn, Dortmund, and Münster; the Upper Rhinelands—Mainz–Frankfurt and Ludwigshafen–Mannheim; and the great area of the Neckar lowlands on the axis of Heilbronn–Stuttgart south to the shores of Lake Constance, together with the southern Black Forest area.

There is rapidly emerging an ever closer integration of groups of cities and of lesser industrial satellites around them to form what the Germans call *Ballungen*—urbanized regions.

The extent of these regions has been worked out by G. Isenberg,[1] and data are given of their size and rates of growth. A core area is defined so as to have at least 500,000 people on 500 sq. km. Administrative limits are taken as the basis, and may consist of one city or two or more contiguous cities. The surrounding contiguous *Landkreise* (administrative districts) are described as the border area (*Randgebiet*), with over 100 persons per sq. km. (250 per square mile). Such districts may be included even if not contiguous, provided that their main centres are not more than 30 km. from the boundaries of the core, and provided they have an overall density of over 300 per sq. km. (750 per square mile). Any other separate

[1] G. Isenberg, 'Die Ballungsgebiete in der Bundesrepublik', *Inst. f. Raumforschung*, Bad Godesberg, March, 1957.

towns are included if they lie within the 30 km. radius. If a separate city has more than 300,000 it is included as a second core city. There are nine of these major areas (see Fig. 58).

Lesser aggregates are nine in number. These are Bonn, Kiel, Lübeck, Braunschweig, Bielefeld, Aachen, Kassel, Karlsruhe, and Augsburg. They range from about 250,000 to 600,000. The 14 smaller agglomerations are also clearly marked off from the medium-sized ones. These, together with their adjacent *Gemeinden* (*not Kreise*), rarely have more than 150,000 and the average size is about 100,000. The densely settled industrial zones are singled out for special indication since they do not have a dominant central city. They include the Hof area in northern Bavaria, the Neckar lowland and the Swiss border in Württemberg; the eastern half of the Rhine Massif; and the textile and engineering areas of Westphalia.

In aggregate these urban areas cover much of the north-west (Rhineland and western Westphalia) and stretch over much of the south-west from the Rhine–Main complex to Karlsruhe and the Neckar basin above Stuttgart. Note also the close proximity of the Hanover complex to that of Braunschweig. Otherwise, the major cities are well spaced and serve distinct hinterlands, containing many separate cities, which are either rapidly merging with each other or lie so near together as to be functionally closely associated around one or two major central cities.

These major urbanized regions are listed below, with their populations and their rates of growth in the early fifties. They contained in 1955 42·4 per cent. of the total population of the Bund as compared with 39·2 per cent. in 1950 and 44·0 per cent. in 1939. Their numbers

GROWTH OF URBANIZED AREAS 1950–1955 (after Isenberg).

	Population (000)		Percentage Growth 1950–55
	Whole Area	Core	
Rhine–Ruhr	10,010	6,730	16
Hamburg	2,240	1,780	7
Rhine–Main	2,170	1,110	16
Stuttgart	1,640	600	17
Rhine–Neckar	2,380	970	11
Munich	1,270	970	15
Hanover	930	530	9
Nuremberg	930	520	9
Bremen	720	510	8
Total Urbanized Areas	21,460	13,190	13·7
Bundesgebiet:			5·5

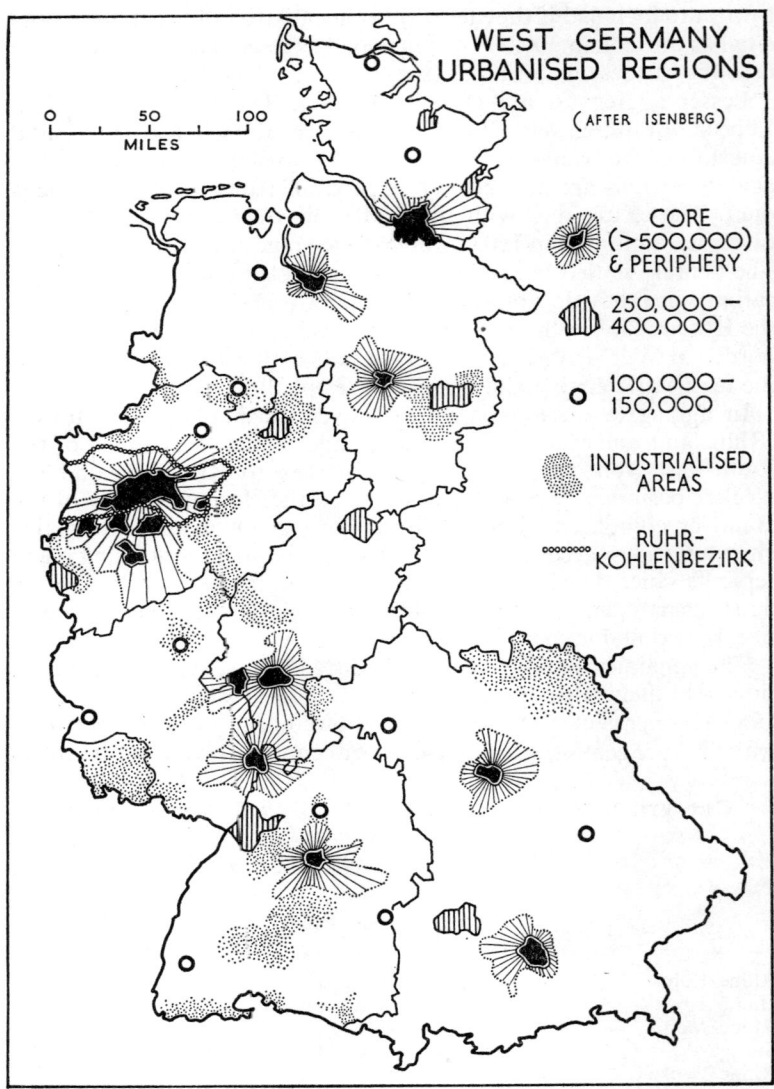

FIG. 58. Urbanized Regions of West Germany (after Isenberg).
1. Urban core (over 500,000) with suburban periphery. 2. Medium-sized agglomeration (over 250,000). 3. Small agglomeration (over 100,000). 4. Industrialized Zone without large agglomerations. 5. Boundaries of Germany (31.12.37). 6. Boundaries of *Länder*. 7. Area of the Ruhr-Kohlenbezirk. For further detail see text.

increased from 17·3 millions in 1939 to 18·8 millions in 1950 to 21·4 millions at the end of 1955. They increased nearly three times as fast as the Bund as a whole. These growth trends continued with great rapidity in the late fifties.

In Holland attention has been drawn in recent years to the so-called *Randstad* Holland. This, shown on Fig. 59, is the grouping of the Amsterdam and Utrecht conurbations to the north and The Hague and Rotterdam conurbations to the south. These are in effect almost joined up both along the coast and between Utrecht and Rotterdam to form an 'annular' or ring-shaped belt of urbanization with a relatively thinly peopled centre. By 1980 this may extend to include Arnhem at its eastern wing and Eindhoven, Tilburg, and Breda at its southern wing. An increase of population to 1·3 millions by 1980 is expected in the Rotterdam area, since this port far exceeds its pre-war traffic and is developing rapidly with the construction of the vast *Europoort* on the south side of the waterway between Rotterdam and the Hook.

In the late fifties this urbanized region had 4 million inhabitants, or 37 per cent. of the population of the Netherlands, concentrated on a fraction of its total area. It is estimated that this will rise to 5·5 millions in 1980, and that, at a more liberal estimate, including the centres indicated, it could reach a total of 7 to 7·5 millions in 1980. The diameter of the ring is about 40 km. This fact is the major reality of the Netherlands that must underlie all its development plans for city, region, and nation.

In Belgium, the three main urban agglomerations of Brussels–Antwerp, Liège and Charleroi form a triangle with an agricultural core south of Brussels. The development of the coalfields in the Campine is taking place north of the Antwerp–Liège side of the triangle which is adjacent to the growing industrial area in south Holland just across the border. Beyond Liège, this area continues into north-west Germany where there is the great nexus of the Ruhr with a number of large cities, including Aachen and the coal-field of southern (Dutch) Limburg that connects with Liège. In all three countries, in fact, there is one great urbanized complex in which there is taking place active economic growth with an increasing concentration of people and increasing location of heavy industry and residential development.

In France, it will be noted that, with the exception of Paris, the single giant agglomeration (7·7 m.), the other major urbanized areas are located along the northern and north-eastern border of the State. The northern coalfield forms a more or less uninterrupted series of coal-mining and industrial towns with a population of some 750,000 people. To the north of the latter and in many ways part of it is the

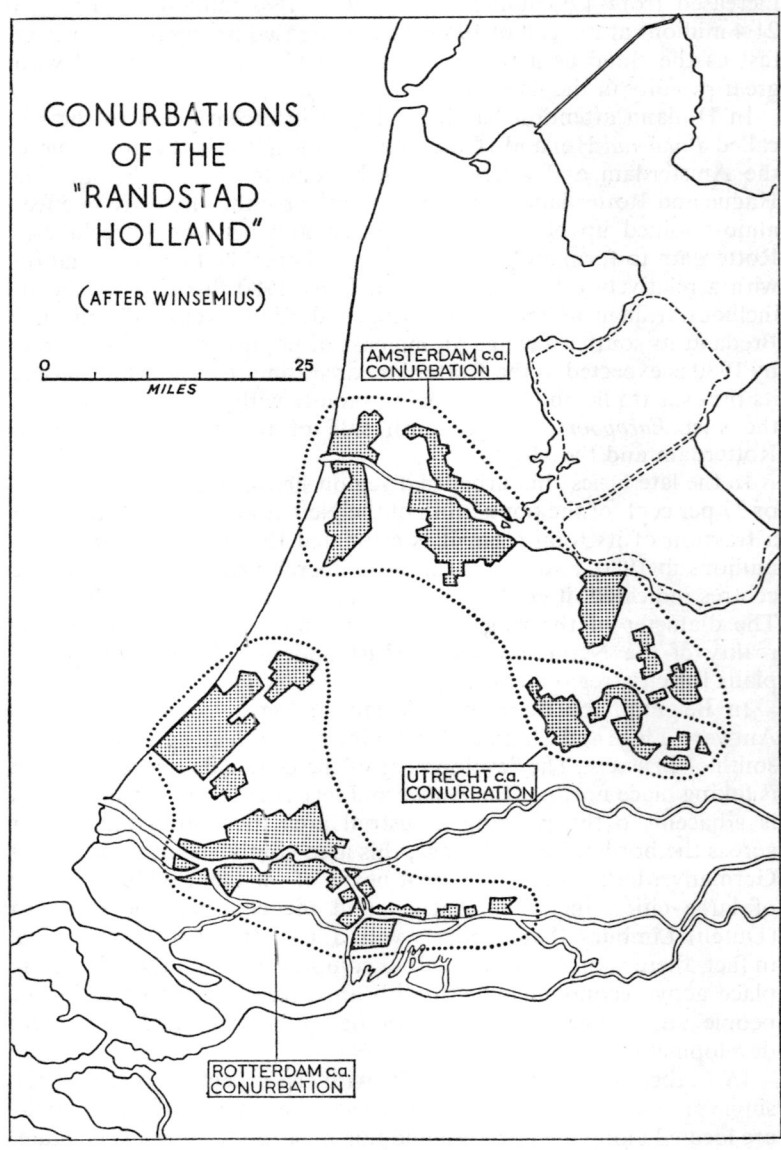

FIG. 59. Conurbations of the 'Randstad Holland' (after Winsemius).

agglomeration of Lille and Roubaix–Tourcoing (with 1 million people). In contrast, there exists a peculiar situation in Lorraine. There is no really large city, but there are smaller closely spaced mining and iron-working communities north and north-west of Metz and Thionville with 400,000 people. Nancy and its adjacent communes has about 500,000. This north–south axis of industrial Lorraine has thus about one million people. The major city and its historic capital is Nancy. Lyon and Marseille are the other two aggregates. Lyon with St. Etienne, and their intermediaries, has nearly 1·5 million people. Marseille has a population of 1 million. These are double the size of the next largest cities of Bordeaux and Nancy, and represent the great urban agglomerations of France.

Several special features brought out by Fig. 56 may be noted with regard to France. A continuous zone of high density connects Marseille and Toulon and a very narrow continuous strip on the Riviera links Nice with Genoa. Note similarly the continuous strip of St. Etienne–Lyon; and the 'discontinuous strip'—centres that all are in fact closely functionally interrelated—in the north of Lorraine, stretching from Longwy on the Luxemburg border south through Metz to Nancy. A similar discontinuous strip is apparent in the plain of Alsace (to which high agricultural densities contribute) from Strasbourg south to Mulhouse.

France has experienced profound changes in demography and policy which are reflected in the growth of its urban population. The demographic erosion of the thirties has been followed by a 'renaissance' in the fifties. The higher birth-rate has been due to the liberal allowances and privileges afforded by the government as well as to conditions of full employment. The rate in the mid-fifties was 18·9 births per thousand, which, unlike the thirties, is considerably higher than in most west European countries. The economic revival began with the first programme of Jean Monnet in 1946. This continued with the development of regional planning in the fifties and a policy of decentralization of industry from the Paris region. This programme began with the establishment of the *Fonds National d'Aménagement du Territoire* in 1950–51. Industrial shifts included, for example, part of the Renault operations from Paris to Le Mans and of Citroen to Rennes.

The 1954 census revealed an increase of 2·2 millions in eight years, as compared with 1·2 millions over the twenty years' period since 1936, an increase over the twenty years of 3 per cent., with an accelerated increase since the war. In 1954 there were 10·3 million people living in urban places with over 100,000 according to the census definitions, that is about 24 per cent. of the total population. While this total population increased by 5·6 per cent. in the 1946–54 period, the big cities increased by 7·7 per cent. and the total urban population by 9·6 per cent. For the first time since 1890 the gain of the Paris region was less than that of the provinces—487,000 as against 720,000. The rate of increase of Paris was 7·6 per cent., but it was not accompanied by an aggregate decrease in the rest of the country.

The areas with a decrease in numbers of over 10 per cent. from 1936 to 1954 include central Brittany, the Argonne and Ardennes, the central Alps, practically all the Central Massif, and the viticultural areas of Languedoc. The areas with the greatest increases are rather widely dispersed. They include—the Paris region and the lower Seine, the northern coalfield (with a high birth-rate), industrial Lorraine, the valleys around Grenoble, maritime Provence (except Marseille and Toulon), the Toulouse area, the lower Rhône and Durance, the Basque coast in the far south-west, the periphery of Bordeaux, the *pays de la Loire* around its medium-sized urban centres, and the area of Caen.

Growth is around, rather than in, the cities. This is the same trend that one finds in the United States and elsewhere in western Europe. For the period 1936–54 the growth in these areas was as follows—Paris, 2·7 per cent., suburban fringe, 23·7; Marseille, city, stationary, periphery, 40 per cent.; Lyon, city, 2·5 per cent., periphery, 24·5 per cent.; Bordeaux, city, 6 per cent., periphery, 27 per cent.; Toulouse, city, 26 per cent., periphery, 49 per cent.; Clermont, city, 12 per cent., periphery, 19 per cent.[1] These peripheral increases in the countryside are attributed by Gravier to *motorisation et confort*. Especially important in the fifties was the advent of the *cyclomoteur* or moped. Its prodigious increase in the fifties, with a consumption of only 1·5 to 2·0 litres for 100 km., permits a journey to work of 12 to 20 km. in half an hour. According to Gravier this is changing the structure of urban and rural areas. He quotes the case of the area of Cholet (E.S.E. of Nantes) where small industries are able to draw on workers from a wide radius.

A further feature, generally characteristic of other countries, is the relatively rapid growth of many small and medium-sized towns with 5,000 to 50,000 inhabitants. These benefit from the growth of the tertiary sector and also from the increasing use of the automobile. Small towns that have been side-tracked by the railroad have been revived by the use of the car. An outstanding instance is Aix en Provence (30,000 in 1911 and 54,000 in 1954 and 62,000 in 1962). Such small centres owe their growth to the factor of regional service.

In other cases, this has been due to industrial growth. Examples are the watch-making centres of the Jura, and the industrial villages of the district of Cholet, 30 miles south of Angers (see below).

[1] J. F. Gravier, *Paris et le Désert Français*, 1947, p. 109.

Such changes are tied up, since 1954, with the policy of industrial decentralization, and especially with shifts from the Paris region. In three years, 1955 to 1957, there were 300 transfers or extensions

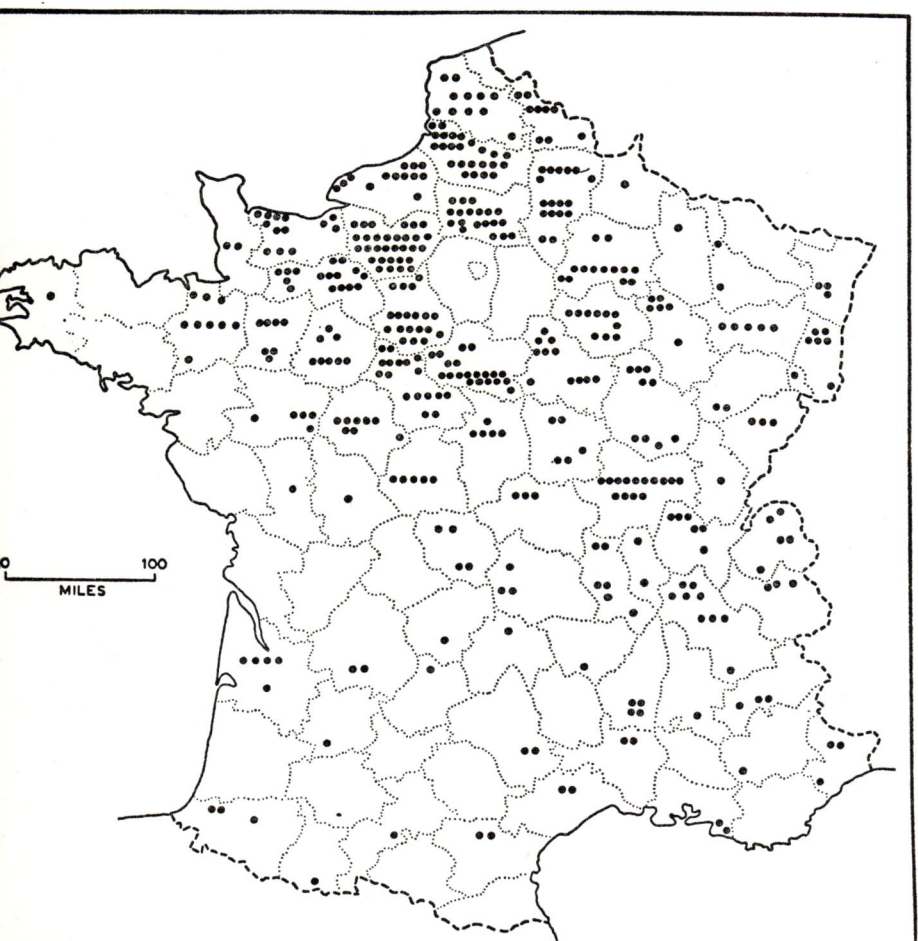

FIG. 60. France: Location of Decentralized Industries, 1950–58 (after Faucheux). See *Raumforschung und Raumordnung*, 1962, p. 109.

of Paris industries in the provinces, involving a total of some 70,000 to 80,000 workers. It is claimed that this movement is comparative to the development of the new towns in Britain.[1] These are mainly

[1] *Ibid.*, p. 115.

light foot-loose industries. Determining factors in their localization are the availability of labour, the attractions offered by municipalities, and the availability of factory space. (See Fig. 60, p. 351).

Apart from the compact industrial zone within an urban area, there are three other kinds of industrial spatial structure in France. The first takes the form of a constellation with the development of several small centres around a central town, each drawing on the labour of the surrounding countryside. This type is found on a large scale in the Lyon region, but there are other examples, such as Strasbourg. Secondly, there is the industrial axis formed by a series of plants on a chain, either along a valley, a railroad, or a route. This pattern is found in the valleys of the Vosges, along the Meuse in the Ardennes from Mouzon to Givet, a distance of 100 km., and in the upper valley of the Marne from Chaumont to St. Dizier, a distance of 75 km. Another such industrial zone has been in the process of growth since 1955 in the middle valley of the Loire between Cosne and Angers as a result of decentralization from Paris. Thirdly, there is the *nébuleuse industrielle* marked by the scattering of small plants in the communes of a considerable area, usually around a town. In a small way, this is a common feature of the small industrial plants of France. The district of Cholet in 1956 had 130 plants on 2,000 sq. km. each with over fifty workers, producing boots and shoes, electronics, and textiles. About a third to one-half of the workers in each commune are engaged in agriculture and a quarter to one-third in industry. No farm is more than 8 km. from a plant and almost all the workers have a bit of land. This kind of socio-economic space-structure is also characteristic of large areas in Germany and the Low Countries, but is relatively little developed in the English countryside. It ensures a social equilibrium that permits crises to be circumvented. Any workers can choose between a number of different places of employment which these days are easily accessible by motor-cycle.

3. The Areas of City-Access

An attempt has already been made, in the case of the United States, to indicate the extent of the areas that are sufficiently accessible to a large city to participate in its daily life. We shall now attempt to determine the same areas in western Europe on the same basis and scale so that the two areas may be compared at a glance.

We have indicated graphically on Fig. 61 the areas that may be regarded as accessible to each city for purposes of work, shopping, and entertainment. Around each city with over 100,000 inhabitants there is shown a circle of 20 miles radius. This is assumed to be the maximum extent of the area within a journey-time of about one hour from a large city. This is probably on the liberal side, in terms of distance, although it is effective for the large cities with several

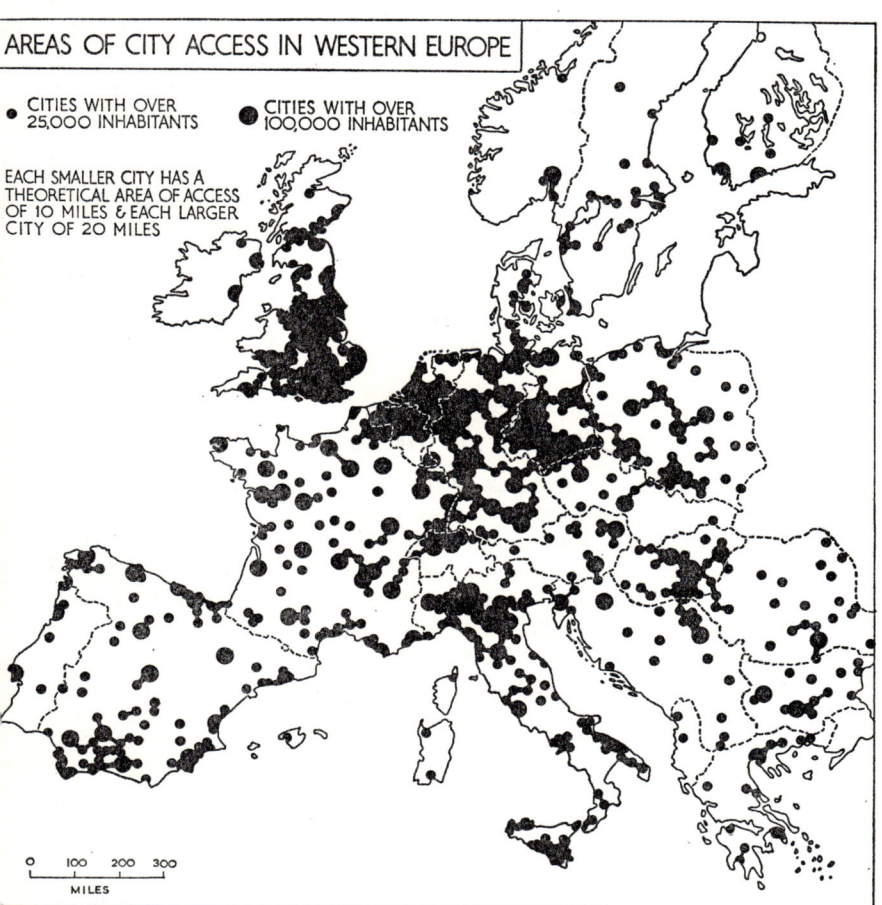

Fig. 61. Areas of City Access in Western Europe. This map is on the same scale as the similar map of the U.S.A. (Fig. 47, p. 294).

million inhabitants. In smaller cities the pull will be much less and the range not so effective. But, at any rate, this is the potential limit of daily impact of the central city, and every place within this area should be accessible to the city in at least one hour and at the most two hours. The lesser cities, with 25,000 to 100,000 inhabitants, are able to offer the amenities of modern living and also employment, although on a smaller scale. We have given to these cities a potential radius of 10 miles. Where the circles lie closer together than the diameter of the circle, they have been joined up. All areas shown in black are areas within which all places are within one hour's journey-time of either a large city or a small city.

Western Europe has a main area of greatest accessibility to cities comparable to that of the north-east and centre of the United States. This area covers most of England, Belgium, and the Netherlands and the greater part of West Germany, with the contiguous areas of eastern and northern France and Switzerland. There are relatively remote areas in Germany, though in general these are thinly populated. France is characterized by its relatively small cities with large areas actually well over 20 miles, often over 50 miles, from the nearest major city. This is the largest area of western Europe in which many people in the countryside are far removed from daily urban associations.

4. The Functions of Cities

Comparative study of towns on the basis of occupations in western Europe has to overcome the obstacles of differences in the census classifications of each country. There are studies of individual countries, but the economic map of Europe by W. William-Olsson of Stockholm is the nearest there is to an overall classification. This has a simple but consistent basis of classification. All agglomerations are shown that have over 10,000 inhabitants. Places with over one-half of their people engaged in 'areal activities' (that is agriculture, forestry, and mining) are called 'villages'. This type occurs in the Mediterranean countries and in Hungary. Agglomerations with 25 to 50 per cent. of their population supported by these occupations are described as 'village-towns'. Examples are the places that cultivate flowers and vegetables in the Netherlands and England and the fishing settlements of northern Scandinavia. They are few in number, rather specialized, and sporadic in distribution. When an agglomeration has 75 per cent. of its population engaged in 'local activities', that is, non-agricultural occupations in which the place of work is a centre rather than an area, it is called a town. Such local production is divided into industry and handicrafts on the one hand, and service on the other hand. The latter includes communications, trade, administration, medical and social services, artistic activities, hotel and restaurant trades, and domestic service. If half or more of the urban population is supported by these service occupations, the centre is described as a 'service-town'. If half or more is dependent on industry and crafts, then the settlement is described as an 'industrial town'. William-Olsson then goes on to group the industrial towns according to their predominant industry. He recognizes one-industry towns in which over one-half of all the workers in industry are in one

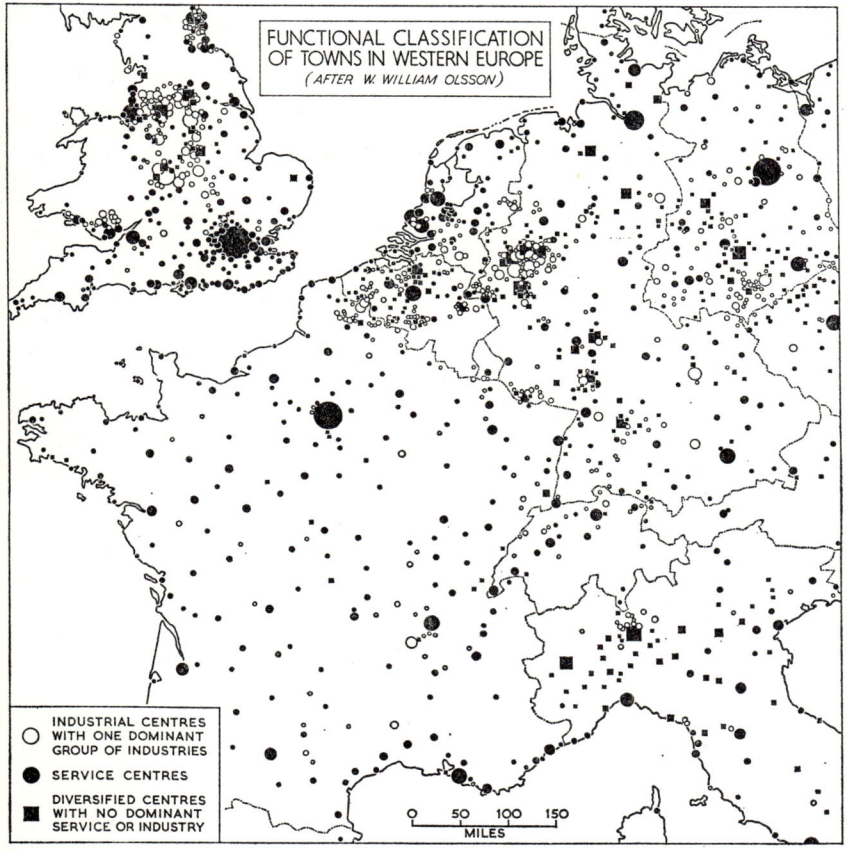

FIG. 62. Functional Classification of Towns in Western Europe (after W. William-Olsson, *Economic Map of Europe*).

industrial group. A diversified industrial town has no single branch dominant and two-thirds of the industrial population is supported by two branches of industry.

The broad features of distribution of the service-towns, the specialized industrial towns, and the diversified industrial towns, are shown on Fig. 62. The service centres embrace major commercial centres, including ports, but also a large number of lesser regional service centres, which, particularly in France, are more or less evenly spaced. Since these symbols are based on occupations by place of residence (not of work), two areas in particular reveal interesting clusters of 'dormitory' communities, even on this small scale. Such are the places on the periphery of London, and those grouped to the south-east of Amsterdam between it and Utrecht. Presumably the other major cities are so extensive that few dormitory communities lie outside their boundaries.

The industrial centres are, in general, rather few in number and sporadically distributed, but they are highly localized in a few areas. These are central England, the north-east coast, and south Wales; the industrial belt of central Europe (northern France, Belgium, north-west Germany, middle Elbe basin), the Saar and Württemberg in south-west Germany. A number of large cities stand out as predominantly industrial. Apart from the obvious towns of England (e.g. Birmingham) and the Ruhr, one notes cities such as St. Etienne, Nuremberg, Braunschweig, and Chemnitz. Note also the clusters of small industrial towns around Milan, Stuttgart, and Lyon.

The diversified towns, in which no group of manufacturing industry is predominant, are conspicuously rare in Britain but, as one would expect, include the so-called 'regional capitals' of the industrial conurbations (e.g. Leeds, Manchester, Birmingham, and Nottingham). They are also conspicuous by their absence in France. But they are frequent and indeed typical of the mid-European industrial belt, and occur throughout Germany, where diversified industries frequently obscure the important regional services. The diversified industrial town is also very characteristic of the highly urbanized area of north Italy.

5. COMMUTING PATTERNS

The journey to work from home to workplace is a primary determinant of the spatial extent and internal structure of the urban community. It is, in effect, one of the most meaningful criteria for defining the range of influence of an urban centre and the extent to which urban associations reach out into the countryside.

The daily movement of populations is of such tremendous importance that most countries in western Europe now have a detailed census of these movements for the smallest local government units—*commune* in France, Italy, and Belgium, *Gemeente* in the Netherlands, and *Gemeinde* in Germany, and corresponding units in the countries of Scandinavia. In Britain, the first census of this kind was taken in 1921 and repeated in 1951. The 'rural districts' (including a considerable number of parishes) are the statistical units in the country areas, not the individual 'parish', which would be the equivalent of the continental unit. The daily movements of workers in Britain, in other words, cannot be subjected to nearly such a refined analysis outside the urban areas as is the case on the Continent. Recall, for example, that there are 24,000 *Gemeinden* in West Germany, for each of which commuting data are available. The nature of the recorded data varies from one state to another, but they normally include the numbers of workers who work outside the communes in which they live and the numbers of workers who move in to a place of work. In addition such information as the mode of travel, time of travel, sex, nature of the occupation, whether a holder of land or not, are variously available in different countries. We have here then the means to determine the range and intensity of the influence of urban associations throughout these States for the smallest statistical units.

The journey to work as between one community and another really started with the advent of the railroad net in the last decades of the nineteenth century. It was greatly facilitated for workers by the provision of reduced railroad fares at the end of the century, in which Belgium seems to have taken the lead. Great extension of the daily journey was also facilitated by the steam and electric railroad tracks in the cities and on their outskirts and interconnecting them. The so-called interurban lines played an extremely important part in urban expansion in the United States and in western Europe. Though they have virtually disappeared in the former, they are still operative with comfort and speed in considerable areas on the Continent—in Belgium, Holland, and Germany, in particular. The bicycle enabled much more frequent travel by many workers over relatively short distances. A big further increase took place between the wars with the development of the bus, which in west European countries in general still remains a primary means of public transport. The growth of the private automobile has played a part on both sides of the Atlantic, but while it has become wellnigh universal in the States, virtually replacing both the bus and the commuting train, it is still of relatively small, though rapidly growing importance in the European countries. It is also important to note the effects of social changes. The advent of the eight-hour day in the thirties and the five-day week, especially since the war, though not universal, have had a big influence in reducing the fatigue in travel and making it possible to do more out-of-door work at home. Finally, since the war, the moped has greatly added to the facility and the range of travel, doubling the normal journey by bicycle up to distances of 20 miles, while taking no more time than the slower means of travel before the war.

A final point of paramount importance should be noted in this connection. The journey to work to urban centres is usually undertaken by people who have moved to work in the city and live on its outskirts. This is the normal mode of suburban growth. There are also, however, those workers who were born and bred in the country and frequently own a piece of land, small though it may be. They have the opportunity of working in a factory in a neighbouring town or city, but choose to stay in their native village, remain among their friends and relations, and retain their piece of land, which is a source of pleasure, livelihood and insurance. This type of worker is frequently found on the Continent. The practice is to be distinguished from the alternative solutions for obtaining a livelihood—of either moving into the impersonal and costly life of the nearest city itself or of migrating elsewhere. A journey to work of up to two hours each way per day has become a normal pattern in areas like Württemberg and the Palatinate (where they move mainly to the vast chemical works in Ludwigshafen).

Two examples of the journey to work are shown on Figs. 78 and 79 (p. 386–7). Both of these are large concerns employing over 30,000 persons and drawing many of their employees from the surrounding countryside. One of these is the Volkswagen plant at Wolfsburg. This is one vast plant adjacent to which a small new town was established by the Nazis. This grew so rapidly after the war that in 1955 nearly 20,000 workers, a large part of them refugees, were drawn by bus from the villages over a radius of some 30 miles, as against 12,000 who lived in the town of Wolfsburg.[1] The second example is the vast chemical plant of the B.A.S.F. at Ludwigshafen, a unifunctional town with a population of about 150,000. Some 10,000 workers, one-third of the workers in the plant, are drawn from the villages of the rich agricultural land of the Palatinate. This area has long been a seat of emigration overseas. But many of its people stay put in their villages and work in Ludwigshafen and other smaller towns. This is an old-established practice in this area, as in other parts of south-western Germany, and is accepted by the people and the managements as a healthy social and economic condition.

The situation may be briefly summarized in West Germany, Belgium, and the Netherlands.

In *West Germany*[2] in 1950 commuters made up 14·5 per cent. of

---

[1] See R. E. Dickinson, 'The Braunschweig Industrial Area', *Economic Geography*, Vol. XXXIV, 1958, pp. 249–63.

[2] R. E. Dickinson, 'The Geography of Commuting in Western Germany', *Annals of Association of American Geographers*, Vol. 49, December 1959, pp. 443–56.

the total number of workers. Fig. 63 is a general map on which the movements for each *Gemeinde* are aggregated within each *Kreis*, each of which contains some 40 to 50 *Gemeinden*. There are 556 districts (urban and rural *Kreise*). It will be evident that there are large areas in which over 25 per cent. of the workers are out-commuters, and near the big cities this proportion reaches 40 to 50 per cent. This means that these *Gemeinden*, most of which are basically agricultural communities situated in the open countryside are, in fact, mainly dependent on factory or office work in urban centres. The main areas are located in the south-west of Germany and along the populous west–east belt around the Ruhr, in the Bielefeld–Osnabrück area, and around Braunschweig. The area of the Ruhr, it will be noted, is one of relatively short daily movements which are mainly movements from one urban area to the next. Commuting stops rather abruptly on the edges of the industrial area, especially to the north. The reason is that most of the miners in these areas live within relatively short distances of the coal-mines—they do not usually travel beyond the limits of their *Gemeinden*.

Among the places with large numbers of in-commuters it should be emphasized that the numbers are not proportional to the size of the city. The largest influx of workers is recorded at Frankfurt (70,000) and Stuttgart (62,000). Actually in July of 1958 the latter had 110,000 in-commuters, a number which is still rapidly increasing and presents a host of problems.

Württemberg and the Palatinate are classic areas of commuting, that dates back a hundred years. The vast chemical plant at Ludwigshafen from its inception in the 1850's has drawn on labour from the densely peopled villages of the Palatinate plain and still draws many thousands by rail and bus from a wide area (p. 387).

Württemberg also has long fostered the growth of industry in small country towns and labour is drawn from the countryside. The reservoir of labour is associated with the tiny holdings of the cultivators, inherited by the sub-division of parental property (*Realteilung*). Such holdings are too small and the plots too scattered to provide adequate work or income to the cultivators to maintain them at a respectable standard of living. For long, cultivator and craftsman have stayed put in their villages but sought work in the towns, and this practice has grown rapidly in the post-war years. Stuttgart has drawn numerous workers, and many places in the area, that fifty years ago were agricultural communities, are today manufacturing towns, producing a variety of textiles and metal-wares. A substantial part of the workers live in the countryside. They may allow their land to lie idle, or they may rent it, or plant it with conifers (with state aid), but they rarely dispose of it.

THE CITY-REGION

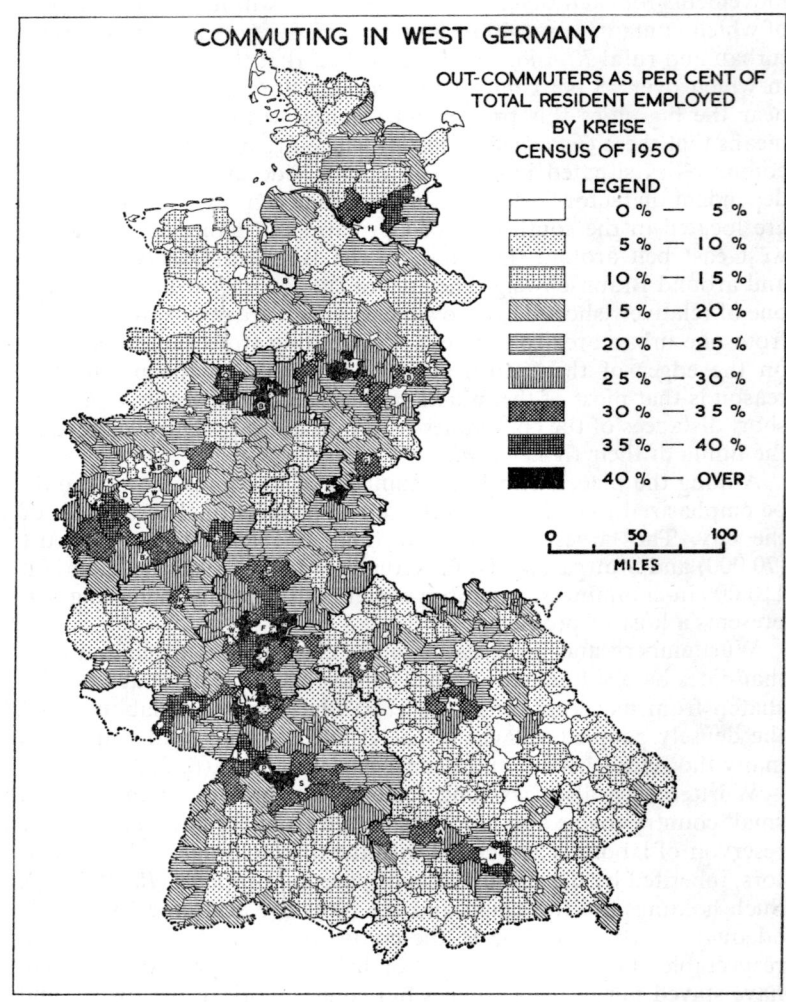

Fig. 63. Commuting in West Germany (by *Kreise*).

Out-commuting in the *Kreise* of West Germany. Out-commuters as percentage of total residents employed by *Kreise* (i.e. as an aggregate of data for all *Gemeinden* in the *Kreis*) (1950). Letters indicate the cities with over 10,000 in-commuters.

THE CITY-REGION IN WESTERN EUROPE

Belgium and the Netherlands (Fig. 64).[1] About one-third of the total population of over 11·5 millions in the Netherlands is concentrated in the province of Holland in the *Randstad*. About 15 per cent. of the workers are classed as commuters. One-half of these travelled by bicycle, 16 per cent. by train, 14 per cent. by bus, and 7 per cent. by tram. Most of the commuting areas are concentrated

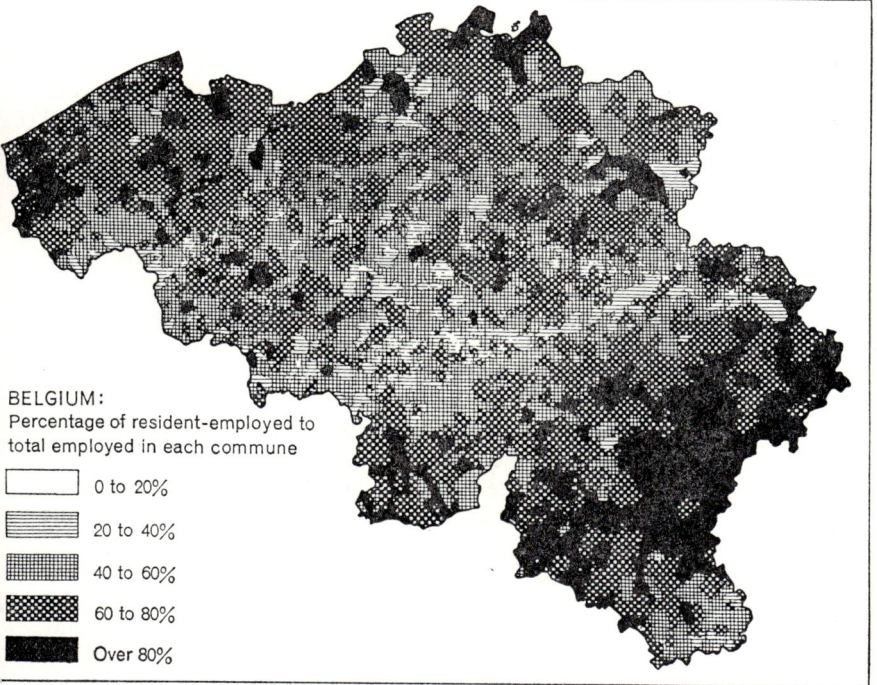

Fig. 64. Commuting in Belgium: Percentage of resident-employed to total employed in each commune (after O. Tulippe: *La Population active en Belgique*).

in the province of Holland and also among the predominantly coal-mining communities of Limburg. It is significant to note the range of travel. Most people travel by bicycle or tram and there is a break in the frequency of journeys beyond a distance of 15 km. Beyond this distance numbers drop rapidly and bicycle and trams are replaced by bus and train, to a distance of 30 km., representing a journey time of about one hour.

[1] R. E. Dickinson, 'The Geography of Commuting: The Netherlands and Belgium', *Geographical Review*, Vol. XLVII (1957), pp. 521–38.

Belgium has 9 million people and it is highly and widely industrialized. It has developed the most elaborate system of commuting in the western world. In 1910 the railroad was still the main means of travel. It was pointed out at that date that workers were able to travel to all parts of the country. 'There is developing in this way a mixture of populations, a better understanding of each other, a blend of aptitudes and needs, that serves more effectively to unite the whole nation. This is social integration.'[1] There has been a tremendous increase in the numbers of commuters and the range of their daily journey to work in the last fifty years. In 1947, 40 per cent. of the workers worked in places outside the commune in which they lived. Brussels serves as a main focus of these movements. It had 137,000 in-commuters in 1947, a figure that today almost certainly exceeds 150,000. Some 54 per cent. were drawn from a radius of 25 km. and 33 per cent. from 25 to 50 km. Two-thirds of the commuters came in by train and one-quarter on the interurban lines.

In 1896 the workers were mainly drawn from the environs of the city and, to a lesser degree, from the industrial areas of the Sambre Valley, Antwerp, and Ghent. In the 1900's there was a large influx of workers from the agricultural countryside, the result of growing numbers and a surplus of workers and, above all, the advent of the bicycle. From 1910 to 1930 the increasing inflow was due to the decreasing demand for labour in agriculture and to the introduction in 1921 of the eight-hour day, which gave time to work a small piece of land in the country in the evenings. The large increase from 1930 to 1947 was due to the steady mechanization of agriculture, the higher wages offered by the industrial centres, and the greater security of industrial jobs. There was a tendency for workers to have no land or to give up their piece of land, and the question now arises whether the advantages of living as well as working in the city may not in the future more than offset the advantages of living in the village or small town. If this is so, there will be a much greater demand for dwellings nearer to the place of work.

Certain significant developments may be noted in Belgium in the post-war years and they are repeated in the Netherlands, Germany, and France. The post-war period in Belgium has seen two significant trends. First, industry's demand for labour has greatly and rapidly expanded, so that employment in specific centres has far exceeded construction of housing. Second, the invention of a small motor that can be attached to a bicycle has reduced the time and more than doubled the range of commuting. The result is that since the 1947 census, there has been a large increase in labour mobility and in the number of journeys to work.

[1] R. E. Dickinson, *op. cit.*

It is clear that in certain areas many autochthonous commuters still prefer to live in the country for personal reasons. Moreover, many new plants employ female labour, and girls who live with their families have no objection to a long daily journey to work for a few years before marriage. Again, if industry is scattered in smaller centres, a dwelling in the country offers a wider choice of jobs, journeys in any case are short, and there is no 'big city' attraction. But it is also clear from enquiries of workers in many large plants that the majority would prefer to live nearer to their work and preferably in the same town. It is largely a question of the lack of housing and high costs in the big city, as compared with the country village. Moreover, plants that draw on local labour and often subsidize travel costs, such as the Philips concern in Eindhoven, have reached a stage at which it is uneconomical to bring in labour over long distances. Philips must now establish branches in neighbouring towns that can draw on an area of some 6 to 10 km., from which the workers can reach work by bicycle or bus within about half an hour. This labour orientation is now being adopted as a definite policy in the Netherlands for the location of new industry, and for the relief of underemployment and low living levels in rural areas.

6. Capitals and Their Regions: France[1]

We may now turn to the question of the selection of the metropolitan cities in their various orders and the extent of the areas dependent upon them. We repeat that in western Europe the status of a city is not only a question of size. Nor is it only a question of economic dominance. The role of a city is closely associated with the conditions of its historical development. The cases of Lyon and Cologne demonstrate this point. We shall now examine briefly the metropolitan regions of France and Germany.

The idea of the regional capital in France was developed long ago by Vidal de la Blache and R. Blanchard. It involves the following characteristics for the recognition of a capital. Each is an historic centre, first as a Roman settlement, then as the capital of a fief, a *gouvernement* or *généralité*, and a seat of the *Parlement*. They are outstanding centres of population. They carry important regional administrative functions. Each is a cultural focus, with a University and other institutions of higher learning, and literary and artistic groups. Each is a centre for the liberal professions—lawyers, doctors, architects, etc. Each is the seat of economic direction for a large

[1] The latest discussion is in J. Coppolani, *Le Reseau urbain de la France*, Paris, 1959.

surrounding province, usually a group of several *départements*. Such are the regional grouping of Chambers of Commerce, banks, professional organizations, and wholesalers. Each is a centre of rail and bus communications, which interlink the surrounding towns of a lower order, and each has interconnections by air with other sister cities and capitals. Each is an outstanding industrial centre, although the 'tertiary workers' normally exceed the industrial workers.

Brief comments may be made on these capital cities. Marseille and Lyon, incontestably modern metropolitan centres, do not have the historic importance as regional centres of other capitals of France. Marseille shares some of its regional functions with Aix and the two may be regarded as one conurbation with about a million people. The ten cities in the next grade of size are not all capitals. Thus, Roubaix–Tourcoing is essentially an industrial complex (two-thirds industrial and one-third tertiary, as compared with 50–50 in Lille), and the two together with Lille form a conurbation comparable in size and status with Marseille and Lyon. Nice owes its remarkable growth from 36,000 in 1861 to 355,000 in 1962 to the development of tourism. It is the centre of a coastal strip 100 km. long with 500,000 people. Nice lacks the administrative and intellectual attributes of the regional capital and its sphere of influence is confined to the coastal strip, backed by the thinly peopled southern Alps and connected by communications across the water to Corsica. Nantes, on the other hand, should rank with the major capitals, although many of the regional functions for the province of Brittany are in Rennes, which is the capital of the military region and of the courts of appeal and of the University. Thus, the outstanding regional capitals of France are eight in number—Lyon, Marseille, Lille, Strasbourg, Toulouse, Bordeaux, Nantes, and Rouen. These cities are very widely spaced from each other and most of them are long distances from Paris. Intervening areas are served by lesser regional capitals. These are the cities with 80,000 to 200,000 inhabitants.

The biggest distances between the main capitals are between Paris and Toulouse, a direct distance of 470 km. across the difficult country of the Massif Central. Two cities serve this area, which is too remote to be effectively influenced by either Paris or Toulouse. These are Limoges and Clermont Ferrand. Though active regional centres, they are not used as capitals in the major administrative network of the country, and Limoges does not have a University and that of Clermont Ferrand is not fully-fledged in the sense of enjoying representation of all faculties. But they completely dominate the life of a widespread tributary area.

Nancy, with 316,000 people, occupies a similar position between Paris and Strasbourg (450 km.). This city was the ancient capital of the dukedom of Lorraine and enjoyed eminence as a ducal capital in the seventeenth and eighteenth centuries. It is also an outstanding intellectual centre, with a University, but regional administrative functions are shared with Metz. Nancy has developed as a large industrial and commercial headquarters for the new industrial nexus of Lorraine and is the capital for most of old Lorraine.

Dijon (170,000) lies between Nancy and Lyon. This is a small and historic city and is an outstanding administrative regional centre with a University. Its area of influence reaches north to Langres, west to the Côte d'Or and Morvan, and reaches the orbit of Lyon between Macon and Châlon-sur-Saône, while to the east it extends almost uninterruptedly to the Swiss frontier. Besançon (73,000), though a Roman settlement and the medieval capital of the Franche Comté from the ninth century until 1789, is a small city with specialized industry of clock- and watch-making; its University is one of the smallest of the French institutions. Large areas are more closely allied with Dijon than with Besançon and the whole province is to be included in the Dijon sphere of influence.

Rennes (190,000) in Brittany, in spite of its nearness to Nantes, has retained its role as a capital. It was the capital of a historic dukedom until 1789 and is today selected as a centre for over thirty administrative purposes—slightly more than in Nantes. It has a University and one of the strongest provincial newspapers. It is the capital of Brittany, whereas the orbit of Nantes extends eastwards outside Brittany. It has hitherto had little industrial growth but this is planned for the immediate future in order to absorb some of the surplus of rural labour in Brittany.

Montpellier (125,000) lies midway between Toulouse and Marseille. This city is the ancient capital of Languedoc. It has a University and is the headquarters of about thirty regional administrative functions. Yet, like Besançon, it has certain weaknesses. It suffers from the competition of two large neighbours, Nîmes and Béziers, each distant only about 50 to 70 km. respectively. It has little industry and the wine-making is centred on Béziers. Montpellier is thus primarily an economic focus.

Grenoble (240,000) is the Alpine capital *par excellence*. Industry is growing steadily and is closely associated with the University. But the city is losing significance as a regional capital. This is due to the ease of access of Lyon (104 km. distant) to the whole of Grenoble's hinterland. The spheres of influence of the two meet in Voiron and Rives. Vienne and Bourgoin are directly dependent on Lyon, and Valence and Romans are more attracted to Lyon than to Grenoble; and, to the south, Gap looks definitely to Marseille. Grenoble is the seat of only some fifteen administrative regions and its future lies in industry rather than in serving as the 'capital of the French Alps'.

Each of the above fourteen or fifteen cities serves a region with a population of about one million or 4 to 5 millions for the larger cities. A number of them might well be named after the historic provinces with which they broadly coincide; Brittany for Rennes, Normandy for Rouen, Alsace for Strasbourg, Lorraine for Nancy, Burgundy for Dijon, Limousin for Limoges, Auvergne for Clermont Ferrand, Provence for Marseille, Dauphiné for Grenoble, Languedoc for Toulouse, Guyenne for Montpellier, and Gascogne for Bordeaux and Toulouse. Only Lille, Nantes, and Lyon are not associated with historic provinces.

Paris is the focus of a large area between the orbits of Lille to the north, Nancy to the east, Dijon to the south, and Rouen to the west. But along the border of the vast tributary area of the capital there is a series of lesser capitals of a lower order in size and service than those already considered. These include Rheims (147,000), Amiens (96,000), Poitiers (52,000), and along the Loire, Orléans (148,000), Tours (170,000), Angers (150,000), Bourges (56,000), and Le Mans (164,000). To the east, Rheims, Chalons, and Troyes lie in the historic province of Champagne, but in general the districts they serve are very small, comparing with the extent of a *département*. Rheims was the capital of the Roman province of Belgian Gaul and later became the seat of an archbishopric, but as an administrative centre it was later supplanted by Chalons. It is, however, an important industrial centre and an important route focus and has acquired a variety of administrative functions, as opposed to Chalons. But they are both within the economic region for which Nancy is the capital and both are so near Paris (160 km.) as to be restricted in their growth. Amiens is the centre of an economic region to the north of Paris; but the pull of Paris and Lille is so strong throughout this area that one doubts the existence of an independently functioning sphere of relations.

A 'Région de l'Ouest' is generally recognized and Poitiers is its capital. This is an ancient city, and is today both an intellectual centre, with a distinguished University, and an administrative centre on the national scale. Yet Poitiers is a small city (52,000) and its influence restricted by the orbits of Nantes, Limoges, La Rochelle, and Bordeaux, so that its orbit is very small, covering two *départements* only.

The lands of the middle and lower Loire occur in a variety of administrative groupings of *départements* without any one centre emerging as a consistent choice as capital. There are five small cities, each serving at the maximum two *départements*. Orléans has declined since the loss of navigation on the Loire and is stifled by its proximity to Paris. Bourges, located in the heart of France, lies in 'un angle mort' between two north–south axes to Paris. To the west, a group of some three to seven *départements* appears frequently as a single administrative unit, and its administrative functions divided between three small cities—Angers, Tours, and Le Mans. Angers and Tours have both institutes of higher education, that give them a University status. Orléans and Bourges formerly had Universities, but they were suppressed in 1783. None of these cities can be described as genuine regional capitals. They are a cluster of sub-capitals, situated in the heart of France and subjected to stagnation by their inadequate resources and location for industrial growth, and throttled by their proximity to Paris.

These smaller cities are described by Coppolani as *villes-relais* and *capitales secondaires*. In their institutional status and economic importance these secondary or sub-capitals are between the grades of regional capital and *ville maîtresse*. They are defined by Coppolani as follows. 'Une ville grande ou moyenne, qui possède une partie des attributs, soit historiques, soit économiques, soit institutionnels, d'une capitale régionale, mais qui dépend d'une ou de plusieurs capitales véritables dans d'autres domaines et n'a pas l'ampleur de rayonnement qui caractérise ces dernières.' An example of this kind of city is St. Etienne, a sub-capital of the Lyon region. Grenoble falls into the same category; also Pau and Perpignan at the extremities of the Pyrenees; and Nice on the Riviera. Other examples are the towns noted above in the Paris Lowland—Poitiers, Angers, Orléans, Tours, Bourges, Le Mans, and Amiens. Most of these cities find themselves under the influence of two major cities, and, though locally active, they have not been subordinate to a more effective and larger city, such being the case of Caen (with a University) *vis-à-vis* Rouen, or Besançon *vis-à-vis* Dijon, and Metz *vis-à-vis* Nancy.

There are, therefore, some thirty cities in all that are in one of the categories of sub-capital or regional capital. These are the first and second order capitals in France.

The *ville-maîtresse* we may repeat (from Ch. 4) is the typical *département* capital with 30,000 to 50,000 people with an urban field of some 45 km., e.g. Agen, Annecy, Chartres. There are about 120 cities in this category that lie between the *Bezirkstadt* and *Gaustadt* of Christaller.

The spheres of influence of the cities of France have recently been studied by Professor George Chabot. His map has been used as the basis of Fig. 65. The zones of influence of cities with over 50,000 inhabitants are mapped from a variety of criteria and many studies of individual cities. The criteria of association listed and mapped are the daily journey to work, place of birth of the inhabitants of the city, immigrants to the city, frequentation of the city markets, telephone connections, provision of milk ('milk-sheds'), range of multiple chain stores from the central headquarters, range of business of city concerns, banking connections, operating territory of salesmen, medical clientele, range of week-end journeys (often with places

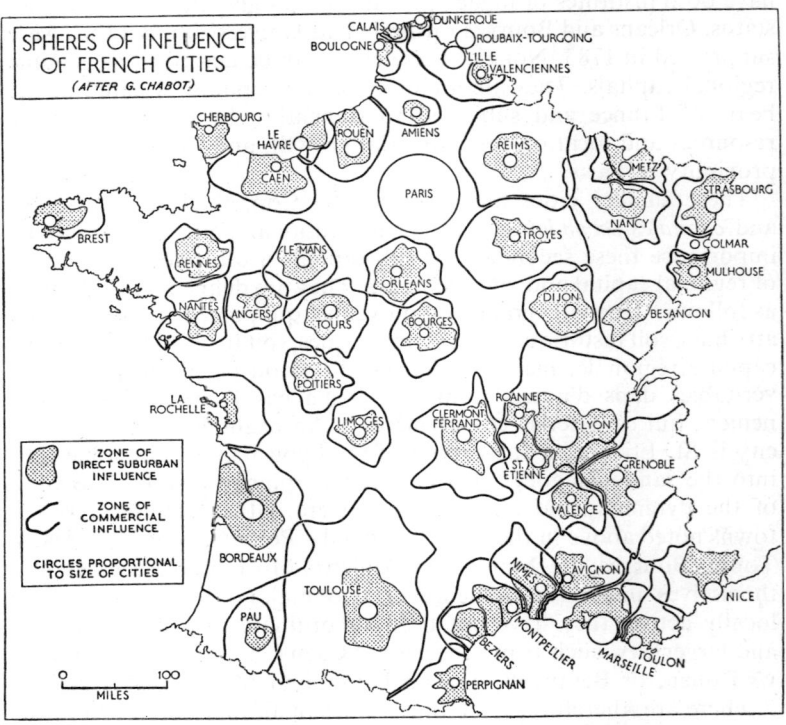

FIG. 65. Spheres of Influence of French Cities (after G. Chabot).

of temporary residence or ownership of farm properties or other land), distribution of newspapers, recruitment of students in the higher institutions of learning. Many of these data were mapped, and their geographic limits result in a number of overlapping lines grouped around each city. Thus Chabot used what he calls synthetic curves, that is, he drew one generalized line where there was a close coincidence of a number of lines which indicated a sharp gradient from one set of relationships to another. In this way he defined three curves or limits which defined three zones. The innermost zone nearest the city is an area of undisputed influence, in which no other city is able to compete with the central city. This is what he called some years ago the *zone du voisinage*. It corresponds with Schöller's notion of the *umland* and Bogue's zone of direct participation. It is intimately associated in all respects with the central city. It corresponds with the main commuting area, it is the undisputed shopping and business area, of the city. Secondly, further out there is 'an economic curve', which is determined by commercial and banking relations. Here he defines not a median line but the outer limit of the most far-reaching relation that embraces all the others. For this reason, the outer ranges of neighbouring cities often overlap. Thirdly, he defines 'a cultural curve' that is fixed by the range of the sphere of influence of the University and of the outstanding newspapers. This also embraces the range of hospital patients, and the area in which there is a sense of 'belonging' to the central city. This outer area is not shown on Fig. 65.

The hierarchy of centres has been even more recently enumerated by Gravier.[1] The status of a centre, he writes, is based essentially on the importance of its tertiary sector, including commerce, insurance, banking, entertainment, and public and private services. As an example, in the *Nord* a true town is represented by Arras with 65 per cent. of its active population in the tertiary sector and 18 per cent. in industry. Boulogne and Bethune are in the same category. Examples of unifunctional industrial centres in the same area, with little genuine town character, are Lens, 31 in the tertiary sector and 62 in industry, and Lievin 19 in the tertiary sector and 77 in industry.

The service centres are placed into a hierarchy by Gravier as follows. The regional capital has a minimum population of 70,000 serving an area with a radius of 100 to 150 km. with about one million inhabitants. It ranges from Besançon and Caen to 'twin' cities in one region such as Nancy and Metz. Secondary capitals have 50,000 to 100,000 inhabitants with a sphere of influence of 60 to 80 km., a total population of 300,000. Examples are Boulogne and Poitiers. The smaller cities, industrial or commercial, have 15,000 to 50,000 inhabitants, with 30 per cent. or less in the tertiary sector. They play a major role in the daily activities and contacts of the people over much of the country. They are of the order of Aurillac and Le Puy in the Central Massif (in fact the only two of that order, as compared with five in the *département* of the Nord). The smallest centres have 5,000 to 15,000 inhabitants, and their primary function is to provide the urban facilities of the lowest order for the surrounding population—*urbanisation en profondeur*. This grouping broadly corresponds with that outlined earlier in this chapter.

The dominance of the regional capitals over their respective regions

[1] J. F. Gravier, *Paris et le Désert Français*, 1947.

is well shown by the flows of vehicular traffic on the main highways. This is shown on Fig. 66. The major centres are clearly defined by their patterns of radial flows. Apart from Paris, examples are

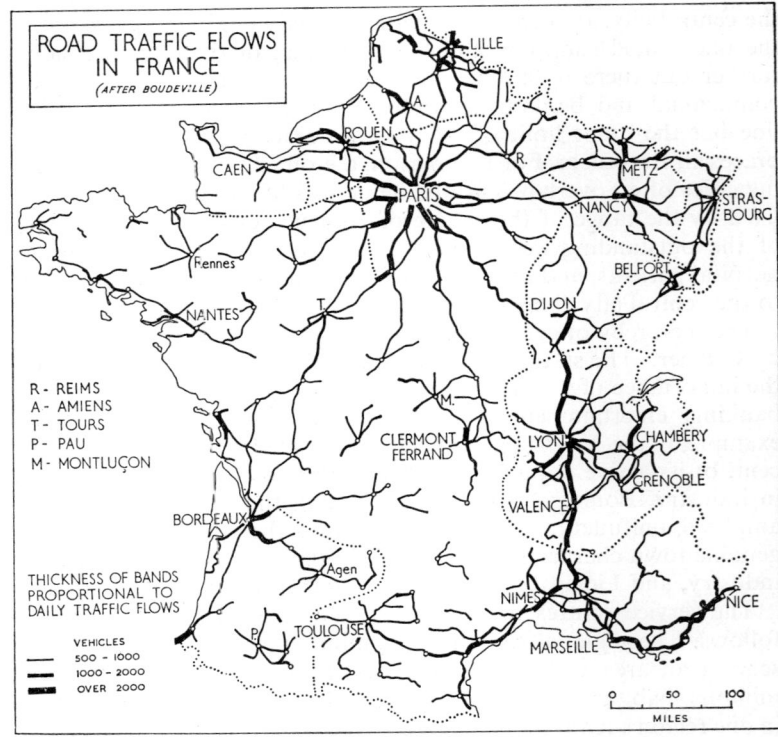

FIG. 66. Road Traffic Flows in France (after Boudeville).

Bordeaux, Toulouse, and Lyon. Further, the local spheres of influence of a great many lesser cities are shown by the convergence from a distance of some 50 km. of several traffic routes. Good examples are Rennes and Montluçon.[1]

7. Capitals and Their Regions: Germany

The role of the cities in polarizing the activities of the lands around them has been given much attention over many years in Germany, as in France, in view of the need for the reorganization of its political

[1] Jacques-R. Boudeville, *Les Espaces Economiques*, *Que Sais-Je* Series, Paris, 1961, for the map and an excellent discussion of the regional problem in general.

territories. The present author made an analysis of the various distributions and movements involved in Germany in the thirties and produced a map, which, although now thirty years old, is still substantially correct and fits in closely with the post-war trends and commentaries. No apology is offered, therefore, for referring to it again in this context. But reference will first be made to new evidence and criteria.

Three kinds of accurate distribution have been used in Germany to define the degree and direction of urban associations. The first is the definition and exact mapping of those areas that may be described as urban. The second is the functional classification of the 24,000 *Gemeinden* in West Germany on the basis of which the associations and orientation of local communities (*Gemeinden*) may be measured. The third is the volume and direction of the daily journey to work by *Gemeinden*. There still remains the need, of course, for the more exact definition of the trade areas of the individual cities as has recently been done by Chabot (see below). Traffic flows offer the best general indicator.

In the first place, Fig. 67 shows the types of economic structure in West Germany on the basis of the individual 24,000 *Gemeinden*, which are normally comparable in average extent to an English parish and a mere fraction of the size of an American township. The classification is based on the percentage of employed workers engaged in agriculture, industry, and services. The detailed map is prepared by the *Bundesamt für Landeskunde* on a scale of 1 : 1,000,000. It is here generalized to show three categories of *Gemeinden* arranged in three areas. The boundaries are the limits of the *Gemeinden*. The unshaded areas have one-third to over two-thirds of the workers engaged in agriculture, with less than a third engaged in either industry or services. This is the normal occupational structure for areas with a dominant agricultural base. The second areas, shown in black, are mainly engaged in manufacturing industries, to the extent of one-third to over two-thirds of all workers. These *Gemeinden* with up to two-thirds of their workers in service are unquestionably cities. Those cities that lie within the main industrial areas are also shaded in black. The stippled areas show *Gemeinden* that have an agricultural base (one-third to two-thirds of their workers), but they have over one-third in either service or industry. Towns embedded in agricultural areas are shown by circles according to whether they are mainly industrial or mainly service centres. This is an effective method, then, of showing 'urbanized areas' on the basis of the data of occupations. It should be emphasized, however, that these areas show occupation by *place of residence* not by *place of work*. The widespread distribution of industrial occupations is in

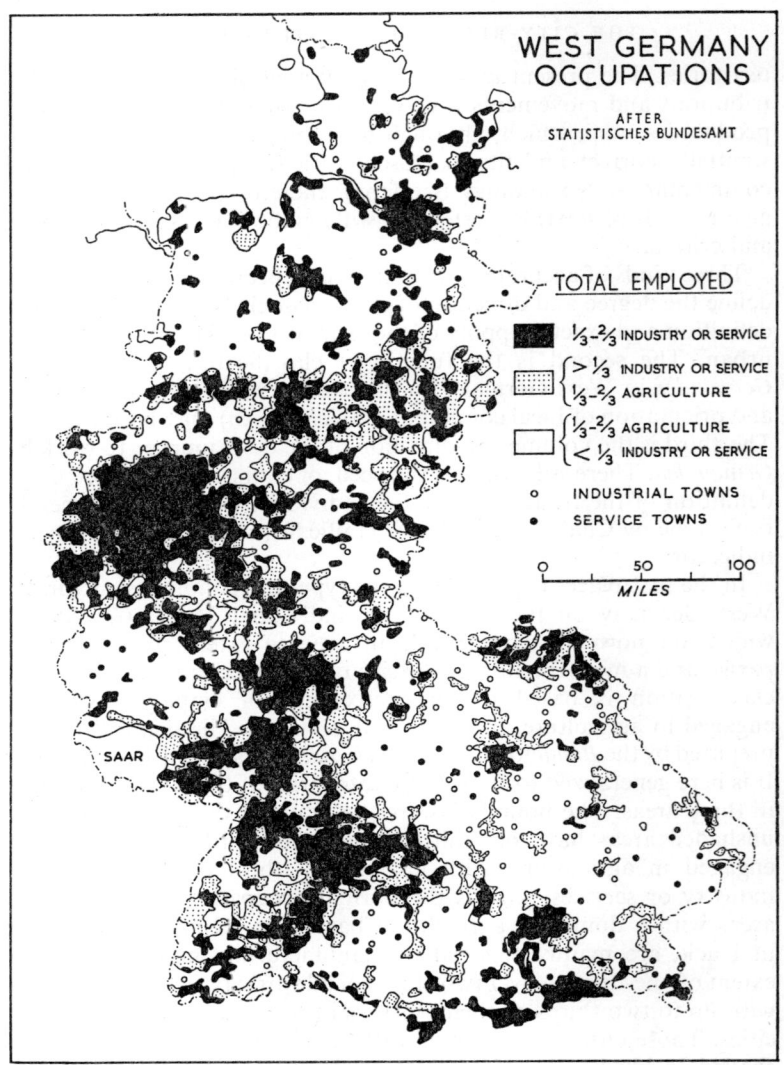

FIG. 67. Occupational Structures in West Germany (after *Die Erwerbspersonen nach Vorherrschenden Wirtschaftsbereichen*, 1950).

1. Mainly industrial or service, including groups as follows: (*a*) One-third to over two-thirds engaged in services or industry; but less than a third in other occupations. (*b*) One-third to two-thirds in either industry or services, but with over a third either in agriculture or in services, or in industry. 2. Mainly agricultural (one-third to two-thirds), but over one-third in either services or industry. 3. Mainly agricultural (one-third to over two-thirds) with less than one-third in either services or industry. Category 1 includes the main service centres. Places outside the main industrial areas are shown by symbols. 4. Mainly industrial (less than one-third in services). 5. Mainly services (less than one-third in industry).

large measure to be interpreted in terms of an extended journey to work.

A second important indication of the range of urban influence is the journey to work. This has been discussed earlier in this chapter and attention is drawn to the map on p. 360.

A third problem is to define the limits of the urbanized area. The method of the Californian group and of Isenberg noted above define rather extensive areas. A more limited and exact definition is that provided by Boustedt as shown on Fig. 68.[1] The *Gemeinde* is again the basis of this study. The core city consists of contiguous *Gemeinden* that have either more than 2,000 in-commuters, or more than 40,000 inhabitants. The associated areas contiguous with the central city have (1) less than 10 per cent. of their workers engaged in agriculture, and (2) a density of population exceeding 500 persons per sq. km. (say 1,250 per square mile). These two areas together form the urban core (*Kerngebiet*). The outer areas are grouped together as the *Umland*. These include *Gemeinden* that have densities of more than 200 persons per sq. km. (say 500 persons per square mile). These fall into two groups: (1) the urbanized zone, with less than 30 per cent. of the workers engaged in agriculture, over 30 per cent. of all workers and 60 per cent. of all out-commuters working in the central core; and (2) the fringe areas (divided into two divisions), in which 30 to 65 per cent. of the workers are engaged in agriculture, but having densities over 200 per sq. km. with over 20 per cent. of all workers and over 60 per cent. of out-commuters working in the central core. Only those agglomerations so defined were described as *Stadtregionen* if they had more than 80,000 inhabitants (with a few exceptions).

It should be noted that the density criterion of 200 persons per sq. km. (500 per square mile) is the same as the criterion used in our definition of the urbanized areas on Fig. 56 on p. 340.

A total of 54 city-regions in this sense were defined as on Fig. 68. They contained in 1956 a total population of 24·5 millions or 50 per cent. of the total population of West Germany, with an increase of 13·5 per cent. from 1950 to 1956. The Ruhr (4·8 m.), Hamburg (2·0 m.), Stuttgart (1·3 m.), Frankfurt–Offenbach (1·2 m.), Munich (1·2 m.), and Cologne (1·2 m.) were the largest and contained 21·5 per cent. of the total population. Next in order are Wuppertal, Düsseldorf, Hanover, Mannheim–Ludwigshafen, Nuremberg and Bremen, the last with 600,000 inhabitants.

A fourth criterion of great importance, as we have emphasized in previous chapters, is the amount and direction of traffic. The data

[1] O. Boustedt, *Stadtregionen in der Bundesrepublik Deutschland*, Forschungs und Sitzungsberichte der Akad. f. Raumforschung und Landesplanung, Band XIV, Raum und Bevölkerung, I, Bremen, 1960, pp. 5–29.

of traffic flows by the trade districts of the Bundesbahn give indications of the orbits of the big cities (some of which are treated

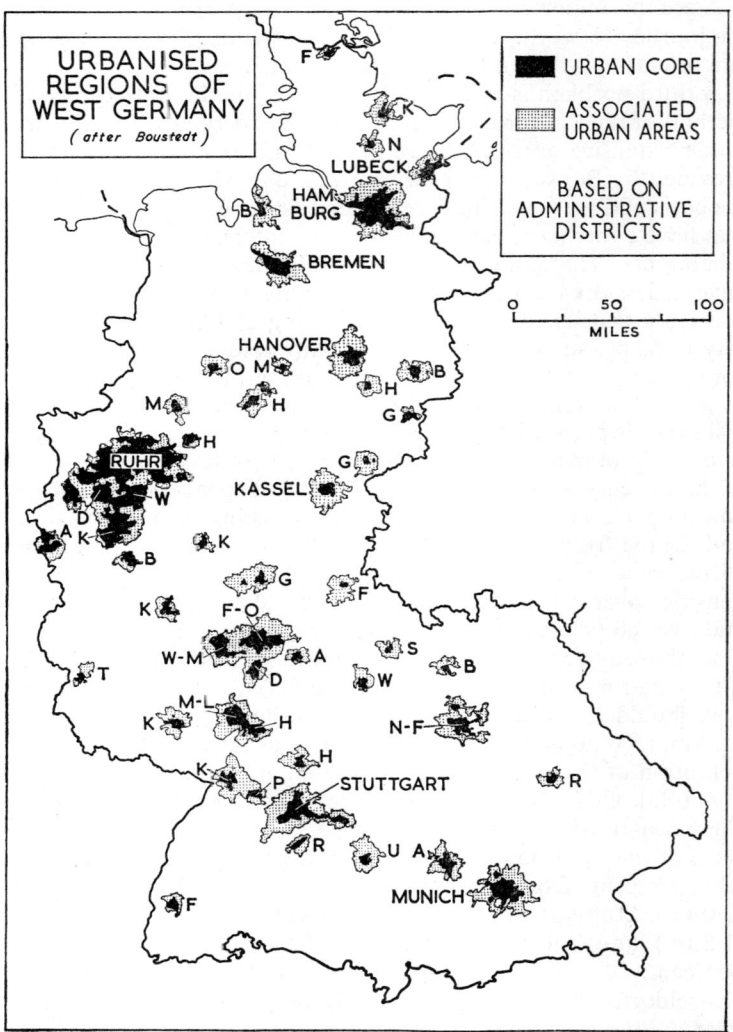

FIG. 68. Urbanized Regions of West Germany (after Boustedt).

separately as trade districts). Traffic flows, especially by road, are further important indicators. These are shown on Fig. 69 for a part of West Germany. An elaborate map of this kind (including both

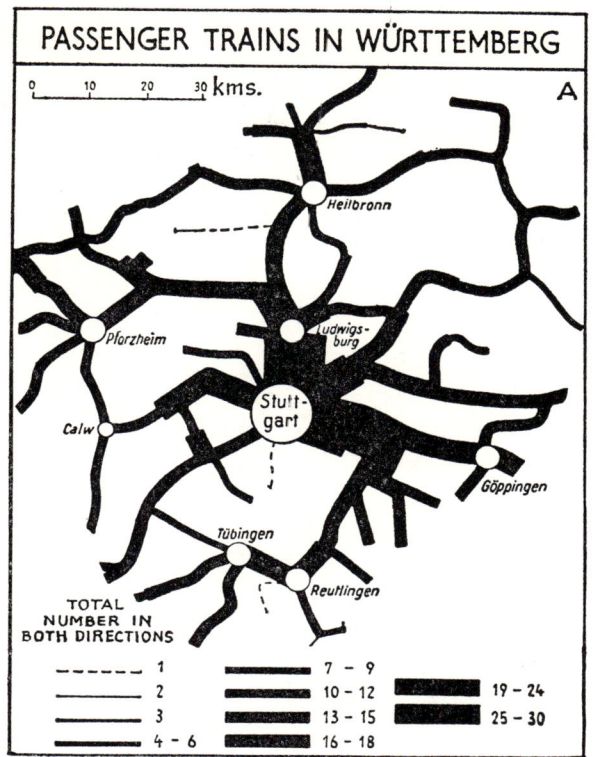
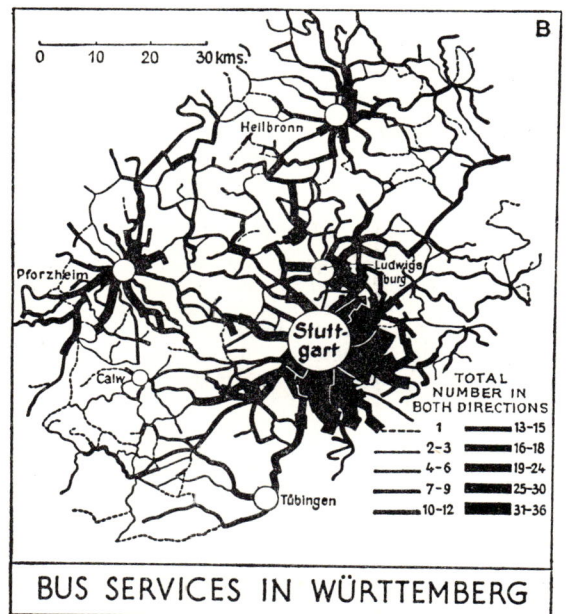

Fig. 69. Traffic Flows in Württemberg (after R. Hoffmann).

(a) Passenger Trains, bands proportional in width to total number of trains in both directions. (b) Buses, bands proportional to number of buses in both directions.

railroad and road routes) is included in the *Gutachten* of the Luther Commission, but this is much too complicated to be reproduced here. Traffic divides, however, can often be taken to indicate the limits of influence of particular cities, as is shown on Fig. 69B.

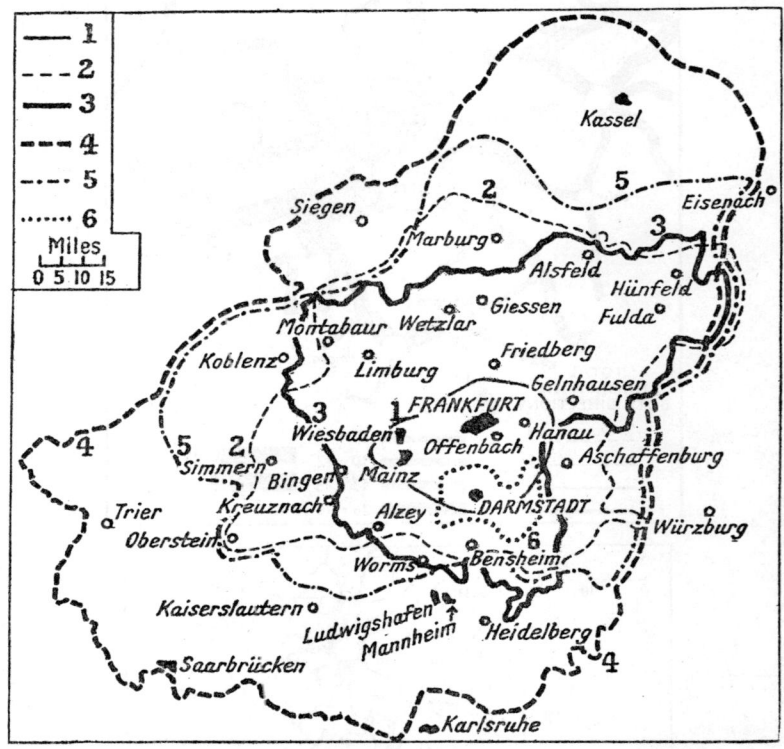

FIG. 70. Zones of Influence of Frankfurt-am-Main (after Schrepfer).

1. The Nuclear Region. 2. The Economic Region (after Schrepfer). 3. Boundary of the *Rhein-Mainischen Industrie- und Handelstages* (seat at Frankfurt). 4. Limit of the Outer Rhine-Main Region and 5. of the Inner Rhine-Main Region, after Otto Maull. 6. Sphere of Influence of Darmstadt, after M. Schilling. The towns shown have independent local spheres of influence. After Schrepfer, *Über Wirtschaftsgebiete, Geographische Wochenschrift*, Hefte 21–2, 1935.

The details of traffic flows according to trade districts are available and have been used in this study. In general, it can be said that of the four or five districts that may make up one area, one-third to one-half of all their trade is with each other, the rest being spread over the other districts of the country. Having selected the capital cities, their respective tributary areas may be defined by marking all the points of equidistance by rail and road or by marking breaks in traffic flows between the cities.

A fifth criterion is the definition of the 'zones of participation' of each city. For this purpose, as for western Europe as a whole, we may simply assume a radius of about 15 to 20 miles, since close studies of all cities on the same basis are not available. An example of

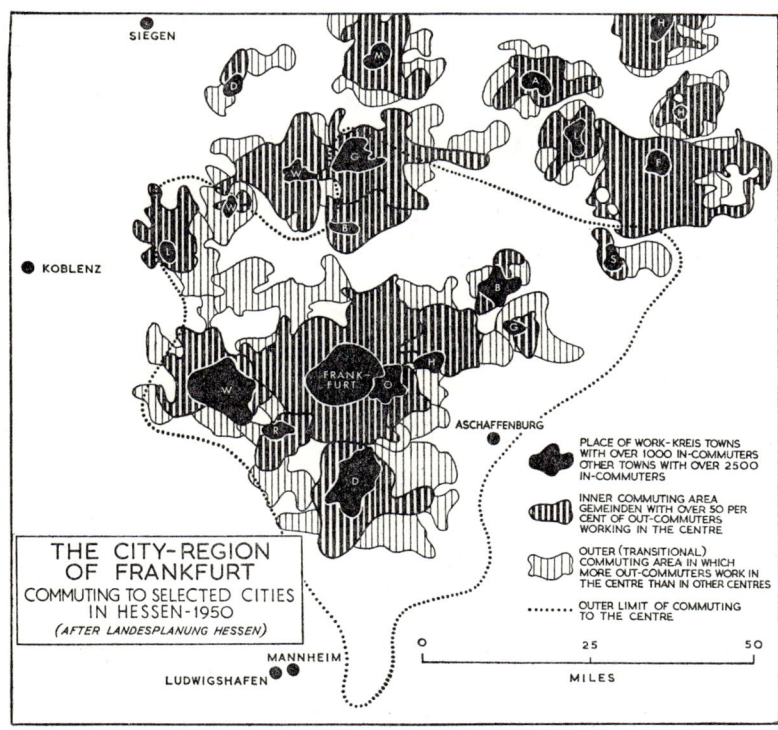

FIG. 71. The City-Region of Frankfurt: Commuting to Selected Cities in Hessen, 1950 (after Hessen, Einzugsbereiche, 1950, Hessischen *Ministerpräsidenten Landesplanung*).

a trade area is given for the case of Frankfurt on Fig. 70. The commuting patterns and newspaper circulation in the same area for the post-war years are shown on Figs. 71 and 72.

A final criterion to be considered here is historical. Historical provinces and ethnographic and cultural associations assist in defining the associations between one area and another. An old-established boundary, that may be a thousand years old, and in most cases dates from the Middle Ages, has often grown to have much meaning in the traditions and attitudes of the people living on either side of it. This is shown on Fig. 73, reproduced from the *Gutachten*.

All these data have been considered in defining the regions and their capitals in West Germany on Fig. 74.

There remains of course the question of selecting the cities that

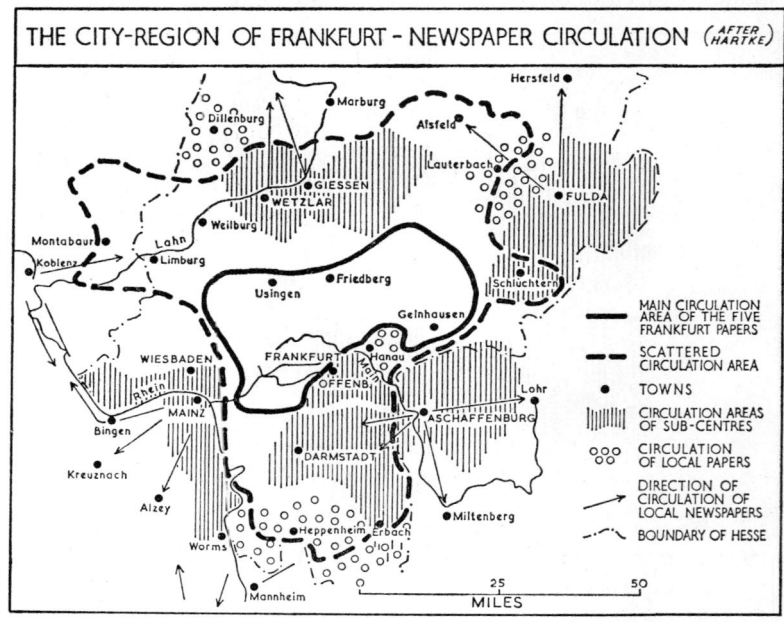

FIG. 72. The City-Region of Frankfurt: Newspaper Circulations of the Central Places (after Hartke, *Die Zeitung als Funktiom sozial-geographischer Verhältnisse im Rhein-Main Gebiet*. Rhein-Mainische Forschungen, Heft 32, 1952.

1. Main circulation area of the big Frankfurt 'local papers' (containing local news and adverts of all kinds). Frankfurt has 5 papers of this kind appearing daily; Offenbach has one. 2. Scattered circulation area. 3. Towns. 4. Main circulation areas of sub-centres. 5. Strong circulation of local papers. 6. Important directions of circulation of newspaper centres. 7. Boundary of the *Land* of Hesse.

may rank as metropolitan cities. West Germany, with approximately the same population as Britain and France, may be considered to have about the same number of outstanding metropolitan cities. But there is a steady gradation of cities downwards and the question is one of assessment. In the thirties various quantitative measures of central status were made, and we have always found that of Otto Schlier to be the most practical. He listed from the German Census all those occupations that could be considered as essentially 'central'

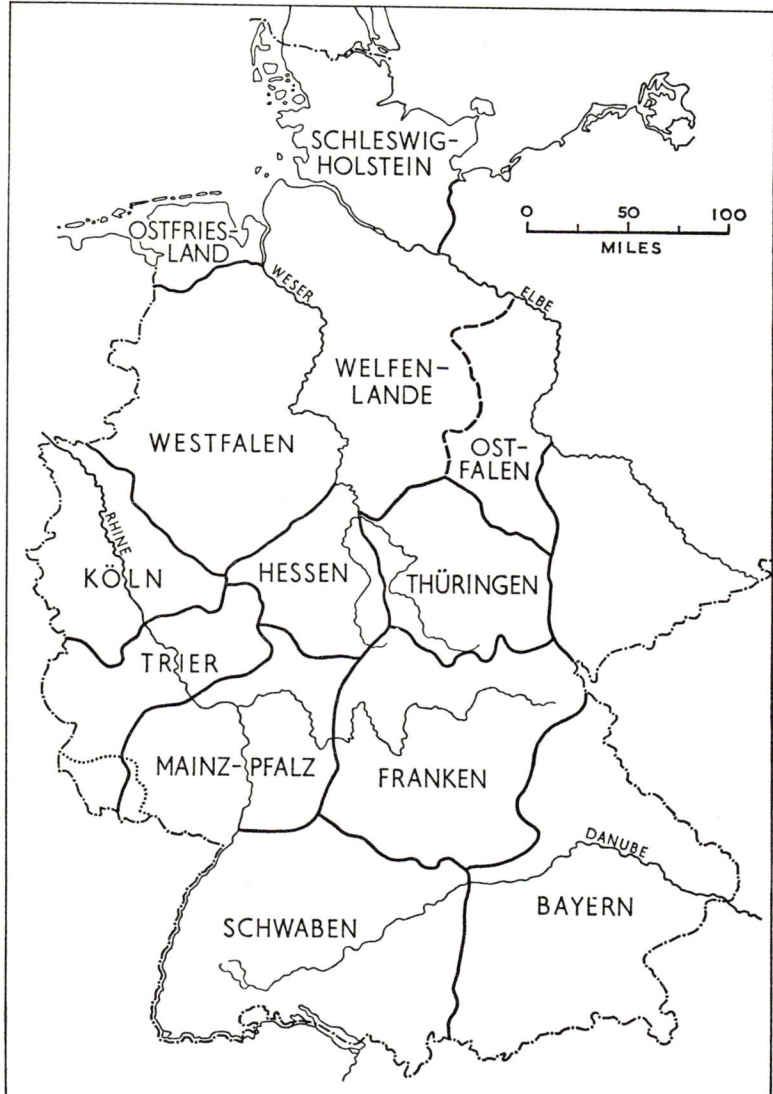

Fig. 73. Historical Provinces of West Germany (after *Die Neugliederung des Bundesgebietes*, Gutachten des von der Bundesregierung eingesetzten Sachverständigenausschusses, 1955).

in character and listed the cities in order of their total number employed in the 'central services'. These are the figures used on Fig. 74 in order to show the capitals. The boundaries were based on the criteria discussed above in order to define their orbits of association.

Fig. 74 reveals a number of cities which are quite outstanding as metropolitan centres. These are Cologne, Düsseldorf, Essen, Frankfurt, Stuttgart, Nuremberg, Munich, Hanover, Bremen, and Hamburg. To these should be added Berlin, Leipzig, and Dresden in East Germany. Below them, there is a considerable number of cities of the second order. These are Kiel, Mannheim, Dortmund, Duisburg, Kassel, to which should be added in East Germany, Magdeburg, Halle, and Chemnitz—a short list of cities that would be placed much below the order of the top list even on the basis of a general 'impression'. The other centres of a much lower order are more numerous and fairly evenly spaced over the land, and would seem to correspond, functionally, with Coppolani's sub-capitals in France.

The regional boundaries are based on many overlapping areas, so that they are extremely generalized on this small scale. But the regions and their centres are real and could, on a larger scale, be divided in their allegiance, both in terms of their orientation to cities, and, indeed, in terms of their association through history with contiguous political divisions and cultural groups. Three of these were shown on this map in 1938 and the same three areas are still being discussed as to their future political fate. These include a central belt of the Rhine Plateau grouped on Trier and Koblenz. This may indeed be extended still further east through the Westerwald to the second area we have shown around Kassel. A third area that is traditionally divided in its associations is in the Weser Upland between Rhineland and Westphalia to the west and the old kingdom, and later Prussian province, of Hanover, known today as the *Land* of Niedersachsen, to the east. In this area there is a nest of small and for long independent political territories, whose people still have a strong sentiment of 'togetherness'. It lacks a single dominant city, though it has several small old capitals (e.g. Detmold) and several important industrial cities, like Bielefeld. The boundaries of the regions, in general, are thus often indeterminate, since the change from one polarized region to the next is gradual. But the core of each region provides a definite nucleus.[1]

North-west Germany is a good example of a major regional complex made up of a variety of component political and populous entities.

[1] This is a general discussion of the problem. A summary description of the regions will be found in our book on *Germany: A General and Regional Geography*, 1961, pp. 280–5.

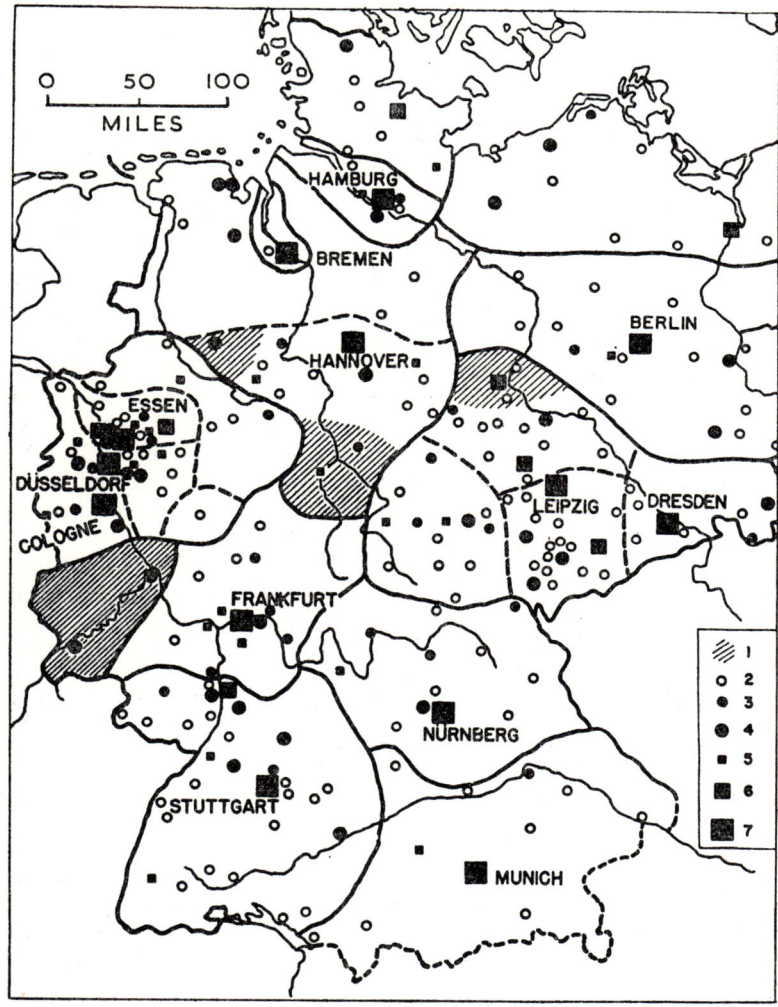

Fig. 74. Metropolitan Cities and their Regions in West Germany (according to the author).

1. Transitional areas; Persons in centralized services: 2. Under 5,000. 3. 3,000–8,000. 4. 8,000–15,000. 5. 15,000–30,000. 6. 30,000–50,000. 7. Over 50,000.

THE CITY-REGION

This area consists politically of the two provinces of Rheinland and Westfalen, with the boundary between them located about five miles east of, and parallel to, the Rhine. Its nucleus is formed by the coalfield and the industrial concentration of the Ruhr conurbation. Around it, however, are grouped other separate but interdependent industrial clusters and cities: Wuppertal and Solingen–Remscheid; the textile area to the west of the Rhine centred on Krefeld and Mönchen–Gladbach; the Aachen district; the Siegerland (Fig. 10, p. 97;) and the large cities of Düsseldorf and Cologne. These clusters are set in the midst of agricultural areas, into which, however, industrialism and commuting make deep inroads.

The two provinces emerged with their present boundaries as provinces of Prussia in 1815. It should be noted that historically and economically they embrace two belts of country that have their allegiances directed in large measure outwards. The first is the Moselle valley and the Westerwald that have long had close associations with the Hesse nucleus to the south. The second is the Weser Upland, with its splintered political territories and its predominantly light textile and engineering industries, centred on Osnabruck and Bielefeld. This area is closely associated with the politico-cultural realm of Lower Saxony with its capital in Hanover.

The whole of the densely populated areas in and around the Ruhr, however, are intimately tied up by rail and road networks and their traffic flows, as well as by orientation to ports on the Rhine river. The commuting patterns, for example, are shown on Figs. 75 and 76. These show that though the journey to work is extremely important over short distances in the Ruhr industrial area the more extended movements stop abruptly at the edge of the populous area. This is associated on the northern border with the fact that workers in the coal-mines and associated industrial plants live near to their work and long-distance commuting from the countryside is relatively unimportant. It will be noted, however, that Düsseldorf and particularly Cologne, draw their workers from an extended area by train and bus and that the agricultural areas west of the Rhine send large numbers of workers, living in their villages, to daily employment in the cities and in the industrial area of the Ville. Note also that eastern Westphalia has a number of closely spaced small towns as centres of the textile and other industries which draw up to one-half of their workers from the surrounding countryside. This is an industrial complex quite distinct from the Ruhr and physically separated from it.

The service areas of the Ruhr are shown on Fig. 77. This map shows the areas that trade predominantly with the Ruhr and the more restricted trade areas within the Ruhr. The latter are exemplified

THE CITY-REGION IN WESTERN EUROPE

by the grocery-trade areas of Essen, Duisburg, and Dortmund. On the other hand, extensive and fairly well defined trade areas occur around Münster (at the heart of an agricultural area to the north),

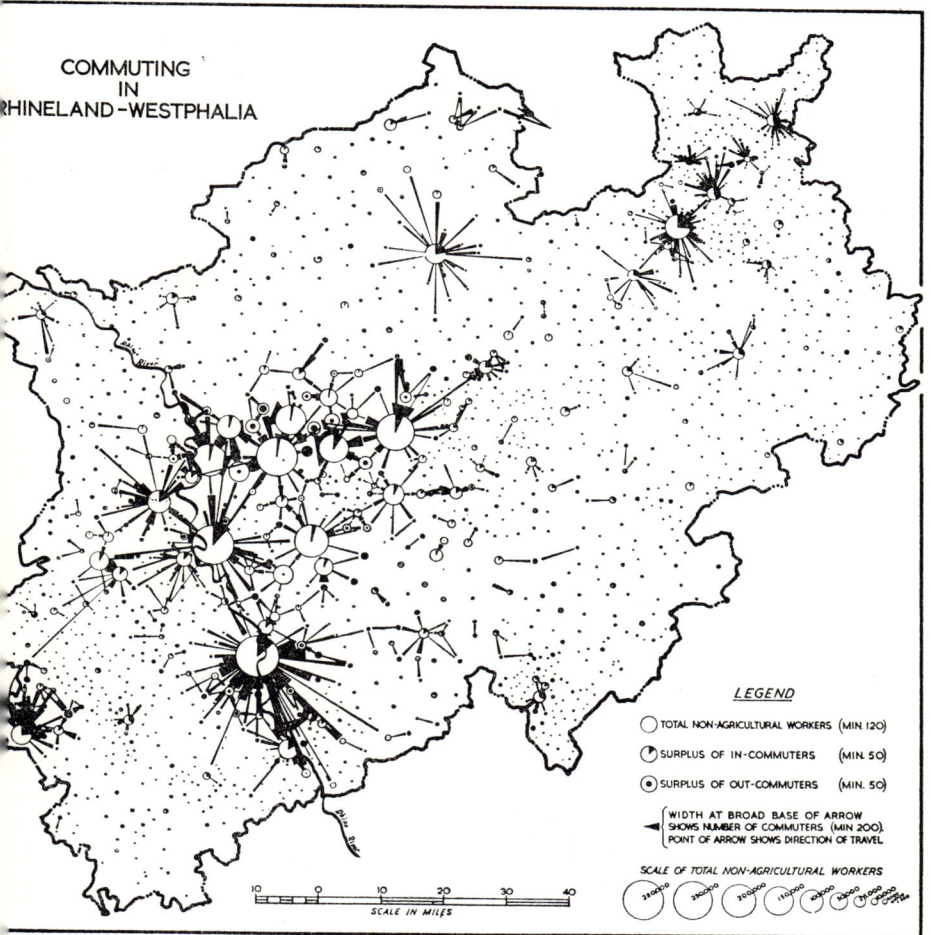

Fig. 75. Commuting in Rhineland-Westphalia (Cities may be located from Fig. 76) (after *Landesplanungsstelle*, Düsseldorf, map on scale of 1 : 300,000).

and Cologne to the south. The main direction (indicated by arrows) of movement of milk supplies to the Ruhr is shown, and the same orientation holds good for the movement of livestock for meat consumption into the cities.

THE CITY-REGION

Administrative organization shows only a partial adjustment to these spatial relationships. The most remarkable feature, of course, is that the boundary between the two major provinces cuts right through

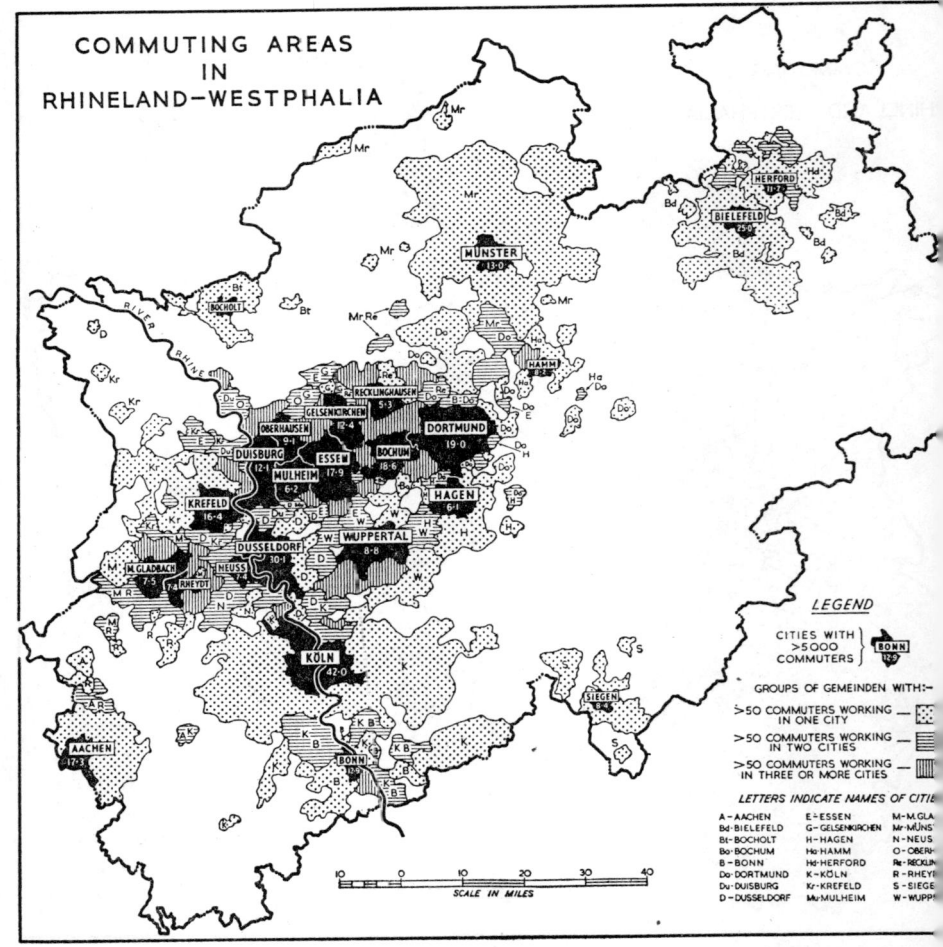

FIG. 76. Commuting areas in Rhineland-Westphalia (drawn direct from data in the Census of Rhineland-Westphalia).

the Ruhr complex from north-west to south-east and the Rhine river itself has always interposed a physical barrier to local movements and organization which was not effectively overcome until the construction of bridges in the later nineteenth century. The great planning

THE CITY-REGION IN WESTERN EUROPE

district of the *Siedlungsverband Ruhrkohlenbezirk* roughly covers the iron and steel and coal and coke producing areas, that is, the industrial Ruhr together with its westward continuation into the lower Rhine lowland to the Belgo-Dutch frontier. The limit is approximately on the line of the Lippe river to the north and just to the

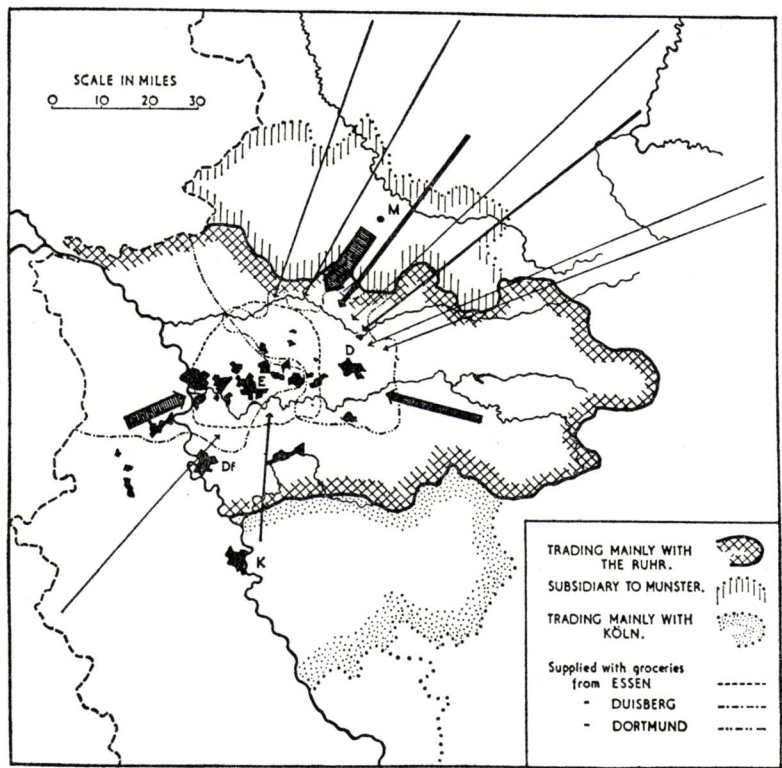

FIG. 77. The Service and Supply Areas of the Ruhr east of the Rhine (after Pounds).

south of the Ruhr river to the south, with the inclusion of Hagen. Within this area the Ruhr Authority has powers to plan the zoning of land uses, transport, open spaces, water-supply, and amenities. Düsseldorf serves as a high-class centre for shopping, entertainment, and business for the Ruhr. Cologne, in these respects, is rather too distant to serve as a regular focus, but, as indicated in a separate chapter, it has served in many ways historically as the dominant

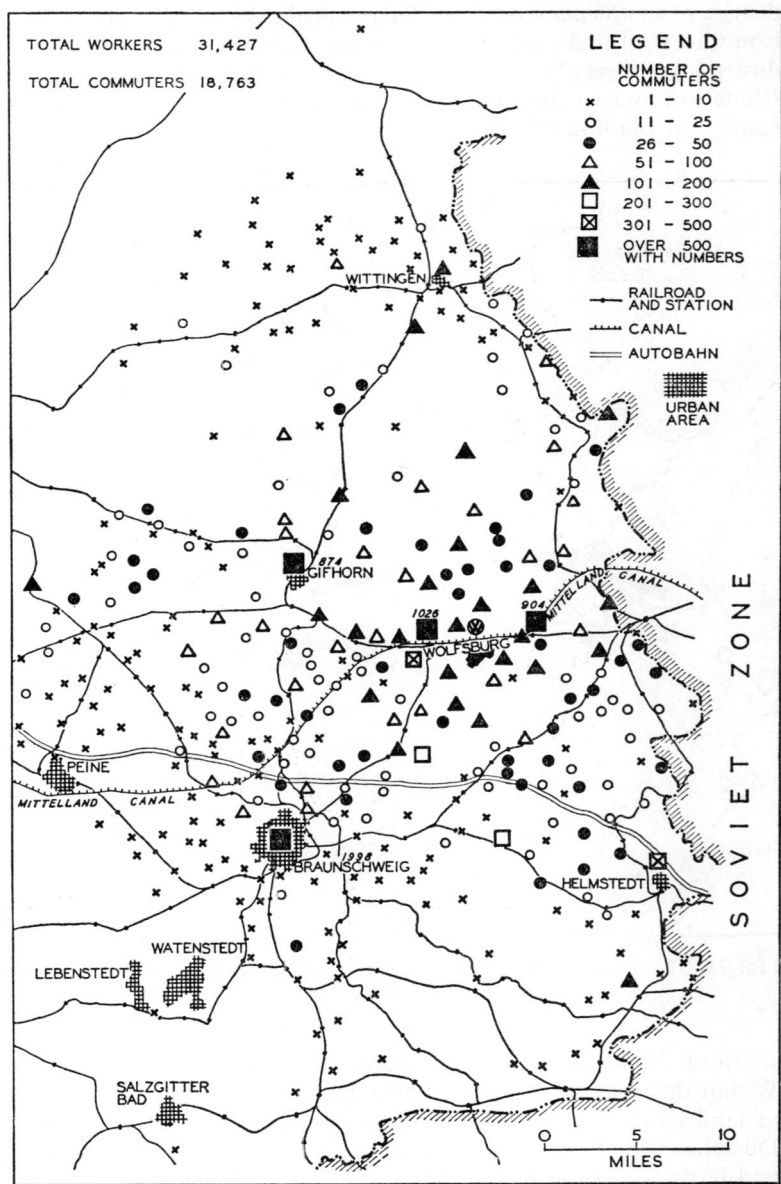

FIG. 78. Commuters to Volkswagen Plant, Wolfsburg, June 1955 (data from the Wolfsburg plant).

metropolis of the whole north-western complex. The planning areas are shown on Fig. 123, p. 546.

Further spatial relationships of the area may be examined on the

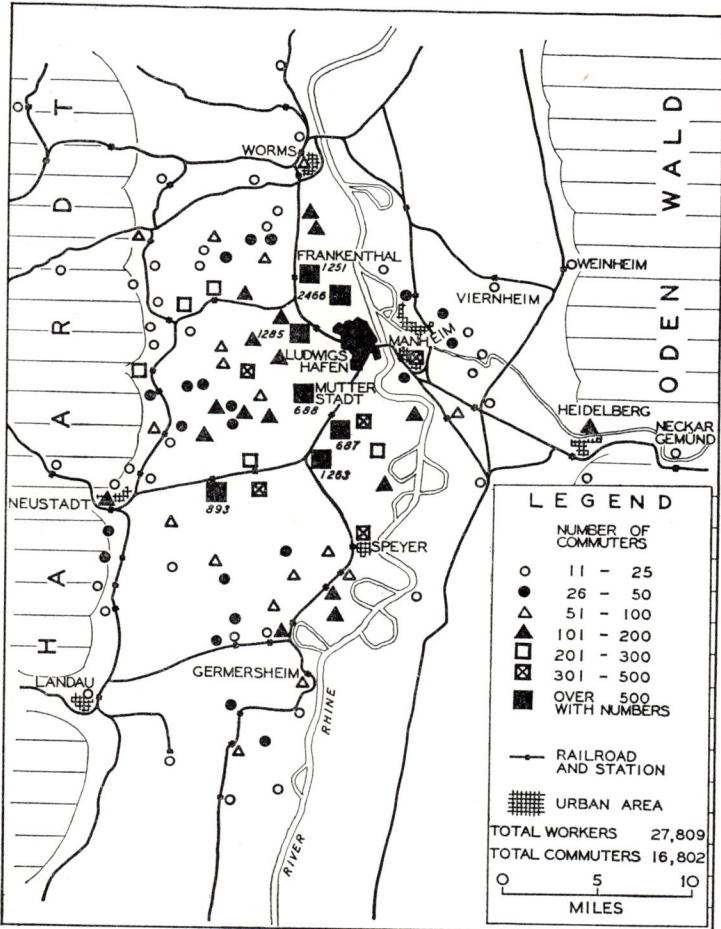

FIG. 79. Commuters to B.A.S.F. (Badische Analin- und Sodafabrik, Ludwigshafen, June 1955 (data from the B.A.S.F.).

maps of West Germany in Chapter 18. They all serve to demonstrate the clear but complex unity of much of this great area, the cohesion of its sectors, and the divided allegiances of its distinct eastern and southern border areas.

8. A Theoretical Hierarchy of Cities

An interesting attempt has been made by Walter Christaller to establish a hierarchy of major central places in western Europe on the purely theoretical basis of his principles of centrality, discussed in Chapter 3.

Following these principles Christaller works out a scheme of distribution of orders of major cities and their tributary areas in western Europe. This is shown in Fig. 80. The system is based first on the

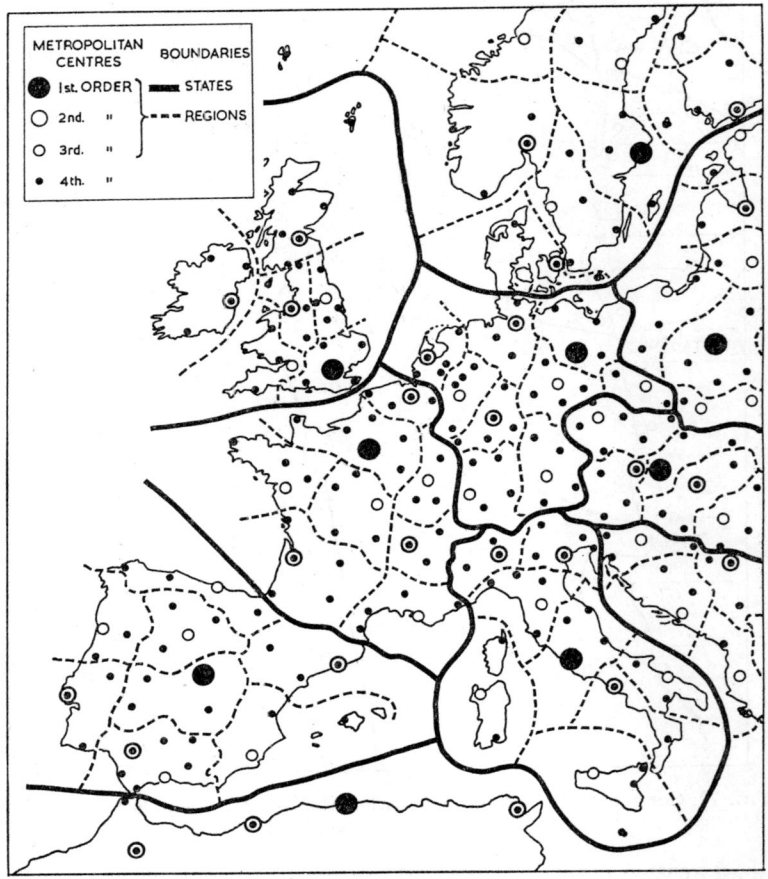

Fig. 80. The Hierarchy of Capitals and their Regions in Western Europe (after Christaller).

Central Places are arranged in four orders described by Christaller as: 1. Reichsmetropole. 2. Nebenmetropole. 3. Regionszentrale. 4. Landeszentrale.

selection of the metropolitan capital, of which there are nine (a figure that reappears in the major divisions of several west European countries). It is pointed out that these capitals form the corners of hexagons based on a series of east to west, south-east to north-west and south-west to north-east lines. Where capitals are missing at the corners of a hexagon, major cities can usually be located nearby that are described as sub-metropolises (*Nebenmetropole*). Liverpool and Hamburg are examples. Several sub-metropolises are located in accordance with the regional principle in the centre of a triangle formed by three capitals (Milan, Lisbon, and Frankfurt). More frequently, they are located in accordance with the traffic principle, that is, along the main interconnecting lines between two capitals. Two lower orders are recognized with their associated tributary areas. These are the regional centres and the metropolitan centres. *Land* centres are also shown but not their tributary areas. Christaller, though showing tributary regions, nowhere indicates how he has defined their boundaries, but it is of interest to note than in general in each region there is the capital with three or four lesser *Land* centres. There are in the whole of western Europe (west of Russia proper) *nine* major divisions, based on the major historico-political units, namely, Scandinavia, Baltic Lands—Poland, Balkans, Danube Lands, German Lands, Italy, France, Iberia, British Isles. Within these there are 33 major State divisions, 76 Regions, and 338 Lands. There are thus 7 to 9 major regional divisions in each of the large countries.[1]

This map may be criticized as a mere *Spielerei*, but, whether acceptable or not, it presents an interesting attempt to treat the cities of Europe as a whole in respect of their role as regional centres. The real meaning of a city, however, can only be grasped in terms of the country in which it is situated. The statistical generalization takes us far from the real state of affairs.

[1] W. Christaller, 'Das Grundgerüst der Räumlichen Ordnung in Europa, *Frankfurter Geog. Hefte*, 1950.

THE CITY-REGION

METROPOLITAN AREAS WITH OVER 250,000 INHABITANTS

As defined by International Urban Research, Institute of International Studies, University of California (Berkeley) 1959

ENGLAND AND WALES 1951–61		1951	1961	% increase
London	M.A.	10,282,928	10,743,533	4·5
	City	3,347,956	3,195,114	−4·6
Birmingham	M.A.	2,520,880	2,694,596	6·9
	City	1,112,685	1,105,651	−0·06
Manchester	M.A.	2,509,870	2,525,349	0·62
	City	703,082	661,041	−6·0
Leeds–Bradford	M.A.	1,909,004	1,927,142	1·0
	City	505,880	510,597	0·9
Liverpool	M.A.	1,600,853	1,620,836	1·2
	City	790,838	747,490	−5·5
Newcastle-upon-Tyne	M.A.	1,128,080	1,158,270	2·7
	City	291,724	269,389	−7·7
Sheffield	M.A.	744,974	751,485	0·87
	City	512,850	493,954	−3·7
Nottingham	M.A.	602,761	645,199	7·0
	City	306,055	311,645	1·8
Bristol	M.A.	599,017	642,406	7·2
	City	442,994	436,440	−1·5
Cardiff-Rhondda	M.A.	590,603	608,024	2·9
	City	243,632	256,270	5·2
Coventry	M.A.	515,929	597,465	15·8
	City	258,245	305,060	18·1
Middlesbrough–Stockton– W. Hartlepool	M.A.	483,367	537,915	11·3
	City	147,272	157,308	6·8
Stoke on Trent	M.A.	489,128	505,933	3·4
	City	275,115	265,506	−3·52
Leicester	M.A.	427,644	466,262	9·0
	City	285,181	273,298	−4·2
Newport-Pontypool	M.A.	414,653	426,642	2·9
	City	106,420	108,107	1·6
Portsmouth	M.A.	366,828	410,475	11·9
	City	233,545	215,198	−7·9
Southampton	M.A.	356,525	401,452	12·6
	City	189,821	204,707	7·8
Brighton	M.A.	362,728	399,153	10·0
	City	156,486	162,757	4·0
Hull, Kingston upon	M.A.	334,759	345,656	3·3
	City	299,105	303,268	1·4
Swansea–Neath	M.A.	305,057	306,643	0·52
	City	160,988	166,740	3·6
Wigan–Leigh	M.A.	299,560	297,056	−0·84
	City	84,560	78,702	−6·9
Preston	M.A.	272,667	282,569	3·6
	City	121,367	113,208	−6·7

		1951	1961	% increase
Bournemouth–Poole	M.A.	252,850	272,707	7·9
	City	144,845	153,965	6·3
Plymouth	M.A.	253,262	254,773	0·60
	City	208,012	204,279	−1·8
Blackpool	M.A.	230,414	251,880	9·3
	City	147,184	152,133	3·4

SCOTLAND 1951–61

Edinburgh	M.A.	591,300	*	
	City	466,761	468,378	0·35
Glasgow	M.A.	1,878,911	1,905,034	1·4
	City	1,089,767	1,054,913	−0·32

FRANCE 1954–62

		1954	1962	% increase
Paris	M.A.	6,736,836	7,739,614	14·9
	City	2,850,189	2,751,014	−3·5
Lyon	M.A.	817,832	972,473	19·0
	City	471,270	524,569	11·3
Lille–Roubaix–Tourcoing	M.A.	898,524	965,051	7·4
	City	194,616	195,798	0·6
Marseille	M.A.	797,873	941,780	18·0
	City	661,492	773,006	16·9
Bordeaux	M.A.	460,079	492,227	7·0
	City	257,946	249,019	−3·5
St. Etienne	M.A.	367,878	399,099	8·5
	City	181,730	199,497	9·8
Rouen	M.A.	334,837	382,805	14·3
	City	116,540	121,227	4·0
Lens–Henin–Lietard	M.A.	363,617	420,992	15·8
	City	40,753	41,743	2·4
Toulouse	M.A.	300,289	365,912	21·9
	City	268,863	324,258	20·6
Strasbourg	M.A.	316,783	358,183	13·1
	City	200,921	229,417	14·2
Nice	M.A.	299,621	355,097	18·5
	City	244,360	290,712	19·0
Nancy	M.A.	278,634	316,138	13·5
	City	124,797	130,893	4·9
Nantes	M.A.	274,951	311,863	13·4
	City	222,790	240,938	8·1
Toulon	M.A.	247,015	297,662	20·5
	City	141,117	168,777	19·6

WEST GERMANY 1950–61

		1950	1961	% increase
Essen–Portmund–Duisburg	M.A.	4,597,223	5,696,707	23·9
(Inner Ruhr)	City	605,411	726,550	20·0

THE CITY-REGION

		1950	1961	% increase
West Berlin	M.A.	2,146,952	2,197,607	2·4
	City	2,146,952	2,197,607	2·4
Hamburg	M.A.	1,951,988	2,190,485	12·2
	City	1,605,606	1,832,374	14·1
Frankfurt	M.A.	1,308,531	1,671,540	27·7
	City	532,037	683,081	28·4
Stuttgart	M.A.	1,129,111	1,518,490	34·5
	City	497,677	637,539	28·1
Munich	M.A.	1,109,846	1,422,684	28·2
	City	831,937	1,084,474	30·4
Cologne	M.A.	1,059,609	1,412,816	33·3
	City	594,941	809,247	36·0
Mannheim-Ludwigshafen–Heidelberg	M.A.	1,145,547	*	
	City	245,634	313,890	27·8
Dusseldorf	M.A.	707,635	973,423	37·6
	City	500,516	702,596	40·4
Hannover	M.A.	786,615	941,009	19·6
	City	444,296	573,124	30·0
Wuppertal-Solingen–Remscheid	M.A.	763,297	901,169	18·1
	City	363,224	420,711	15·8
Nuremberg	M.A.	632,293	744,397	17·7
	City	362,459	454,520	25·4
Bremen	M.A.	616,865	*	
	City	444,549	564,517	27·0
Krefeld-Mönchen-Gladbach–Rheydt	M.A.	597,812	707,262	18·3
	City	171,875	213,104	24·0
Bonn	M.A.	460,131	573,763	24·7
	City	115,394	143,850	24·7
Karlsruhe	M.A.	444,826	527,398	18·6
	City	198,840	241,929	21·7
Braunschweig	M.A.	444,670	452,841	1·9
	City	223,760	246,200	10·0
Wiesbaden-Mainz	M.A.	365,333	445,926	22·1
	City	220,741	253,280	14·7
Aachen	M.A.	351,768	428,736	21·9
	City	129,811	169,769	30·8
Saarbrucken	M.A.	355,920	390,717	9·8
	City	244,224	260,012	6·4
Kassel	M.A.	333,460	373,174	11·9
	City	162,132	207,507	28·0
Darmstadt	M.A.	268,356	331,106	23·4
	City	94,788	136,412	43·9
Lubeck	M.A.	345,428	323,678	−6·3
	City	238,276	234,643	−1·5
Augsburg	M.A.	266,826	312,066	17·0
	City	185,183	208,659	12·7
Bielefeld	M.A.	254,897	304,106	19·3
	City	153,613	174,642	13·7
Kiel	M.A.	254,449	273,227	7·4
	City	254,449	273,227	7·4

		1950	1961	% increase
Osnabrück	M.A.	227,072	259,677	14·4
	City	109,538	138,777	26·7

NETHERLANDS 1947-61

		1947	1961	% increase
Amsterdam	M.A.	936,896	1,052,496	12·3
	City	803,847	866,342	7·8
Rotterdam	M.A.	836,199	998,569	19·4
	City	646,248	729,744	12·9
The Hague	M.A.	687,742	767,641	11·6
	City	532,998	605,876	13·7
Utrecht	M.A.	333,484	*	
	City	185,246	256,332	38·4
Haarlem-Velsen	M.A.	280,868	336,013	19·6
	City	156,856	169,497	8·1

BELGIUM 1950-61

		1950	1961	% increase
Brussels	M.A.	1,323,394	1,439,536	8·8
	City	185,141	170,489	−7·9
Antwerp	M.A.	798,278	872,739	9·3
	City	261,412	253,295	−3·1
Liège	M.A.	572,270	604,177	5·6
	City	156,193	153,240	−1·9
Charleroi	M.A.	440,123	461,340	4·8
	City	25,662	26,175	2·0
Ghent	M.A.	444,790	459,191	3·2
	City	166,171	157,811	−5·0

* The definition includes administrative units which are not listed in the respective censuses (c. 1960), so that an accurate figure cannot be given for the last census date for these Metropolitan Areas.

Postscript
For more recent data on the growth of cities, see H. Fehre, 'Zur Bevölkerungsentwicklung der deutschen Stadtregionen von 1939 bis 1960', *Raumforschung und Raumordnung*, 21, Jg., 1963, Heft 3, pp. 129–48; and Ph. Pinchemel, *Le Fait Urbain en France*, 1963.

Chapter 13

THE CITY-REGION IN BRITAIN

Great Britain is the most fully urbanized land in the world. Eighty per cent. of the population is classed as urban. Over a half of the total population and two-thirds of the urban population live in urban local authority areas with 50,000 or more population. One-third of Scotland's people live in Clydeside and one-fifth in the six smaller conurbations. In fact, nearly two-fifths of the total population of Britain live in the seven major conurbations.

The extent of the 'urbanized areas' in the wider sense is shown on Fig. 56 (p. 340) and the criterion for this definition was taken as 500 persons per square mile. The Ordnance Survey map of Britain places the break in density at 400 persons per square mile and this is the limit on Fig. 81 opposite. It shows clearly the extended urbanized areas around each of the major conurbations. These are, in effect, interconnected urban tracts. Note particularly the great U-shaped area in the Midlands, with its base in the Black Country and reaching north into Lancashire and Yorkshire on either flank of the Pennines. Note also the long stretches of urbanized land—mainly formed through resort or port development—along the south coast. Many of these are dormitories or resorts for the Greater London area. The great area from Merseyside and west Yorkshire through the Midlands to Greater London and the south-eastern counties is the equivalent of Gottmann's Megalopolis on the Atlantic Seaboard of the United States. One should emphasize, however, the break of this belt in the waist-line of the Midlands, although industrial growth is going on rapidly here also. Much more evident than this axial belt is the great concentration around London and a second (actually numerically much greater than that of Greater London) in the Midlands, together with Lancashire and Yorkshire. In Scotland, Clydeside and Edinburgh with their intervening urban areas form in effect one great urbanized complex in the central lowland stretching from the lower Clyde to the Forth.

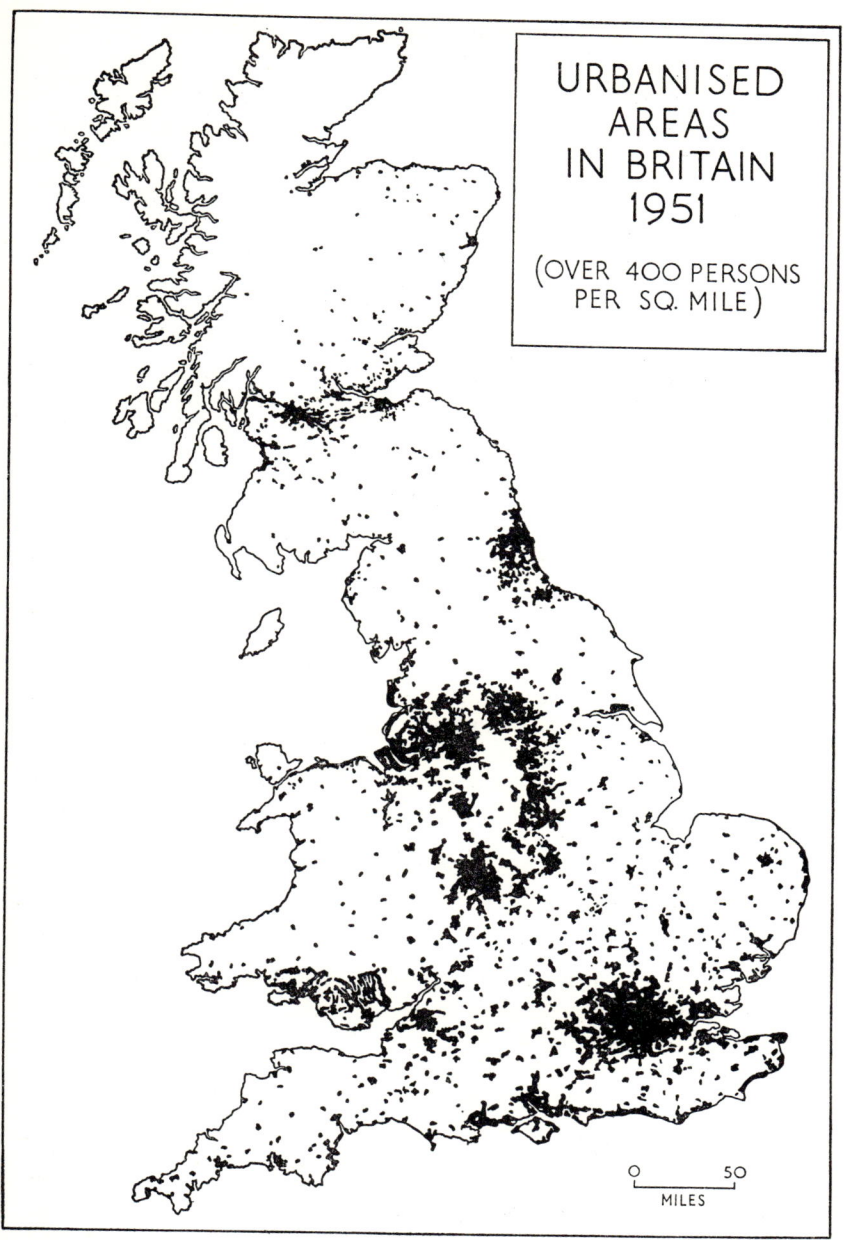

FIG. 81. Urbanized Areas in Britain, 1951 (after Ministry of Housing and Local Government, 1951 census).

THE CITY-REGION

1. Definition of the Conurbations

The major conurbations were defined by the Census in 1951 as 'aggregates of local authority areas'. These, it is claimed, are similar to the 'standard metropolitan areas' used in the U.S. Census as 'all-purpose statistical units'. Three factors were considered in defining them.

'First, that the conurbations generally should be a continuously built-up area, but on the one hand this should not include ribbon development, and on the other it should not necessarily exclude a built-up area separated by a narrow strip of rural land from the main built-up areas to which it was strongly attached for employment or other reasons; second, that a local area should be considered for inclusion in the conurbation to whose focal centre it was strongly attached as a centre for work, shopping, higher education, sports, or entertainment; third, that some consideration should be given to population density.'

The weight given to these factors will obviously vary, but in general 'the criterion for inclusion or exclusion was community of interest, considered from many aspects, but taking into account mainly the degree of centripetal attraction exerted by the central areas, especially as regards employment, on those surrounding areas which, prima facie, would seem to form part of the continuous urbanized area'. If there were any doubt in definition as between a narrower and a wider area, the latter was adopted.

Six conurbations were so recognized in England and Wales—Greater London, west Midlands, south-east Lancashire, west Yorkshire, Merseyside and Tyneside. To these should be added Clydeside in Scotland. Each of these was in turn divided into 'divisions and sub-divisions' suitable for economic and social research, using, where necessary, the boundaries of areas (in boroughs) or parishes (in Rural Districts).

The minor conurbations may be defined as towns with over 50,000 inhabitants. They have been listed by Freeman and are shown on Fig. 82.[1] The population figures are for 1951. They fall into two groups, those with 250,000 to 700,000 inhabitants, and those with 50,000 to 250,000 inhabitants. They are groups of administrative units that lie within one continuous urbanized area.

The larger group, fourteen in number, contains 5·5 million inhabitants. The chief are the South Wales Coalfield (666,000) and Sheffield with Rotherham (614,000). Both of these were defined by Geddes as conurbations with the names of Waleston and South Riding respectively. The half million mark is nearly reached by Nottingham and

[1] T. W. Freeman, *The Conurbations of Great Britain*, Manchester, 1959.

Bristol, and the Lancashire Coalfield group (St. Helens and Wigan). The next in order are the Potteries, Portsmouth, Coventry, Hull, Teesmouth, Brighton, Barnsley, Leicester, and Cardiff. Some of these

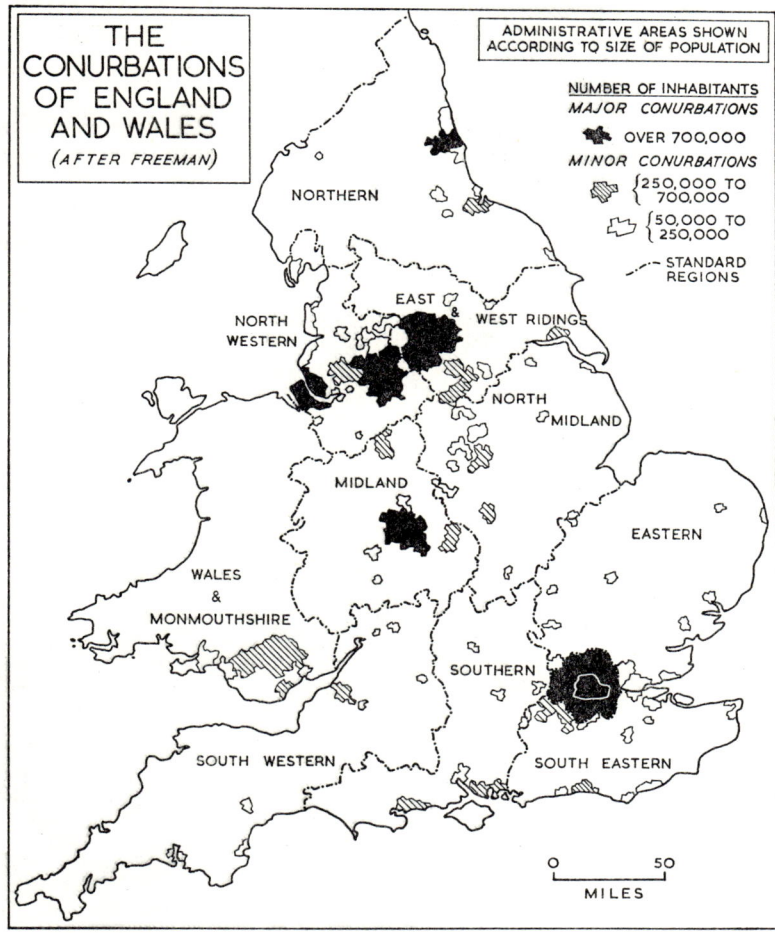

Fig. 82. The Conurbations of England and Wales (after Freeman). Regions modified since 1957: see *Ministry of Labour Gazette*.

are rapidly expanding and merging. The South Wales Coalfield area is almost linked with the centres on the coast (Cardiff and Swansea) and the whole of this area has over one million people. Similarly Nottingham and Derby have almost joined up and this aggregate is not far short of the million mark (850,000). The Sheffield–Rotherham

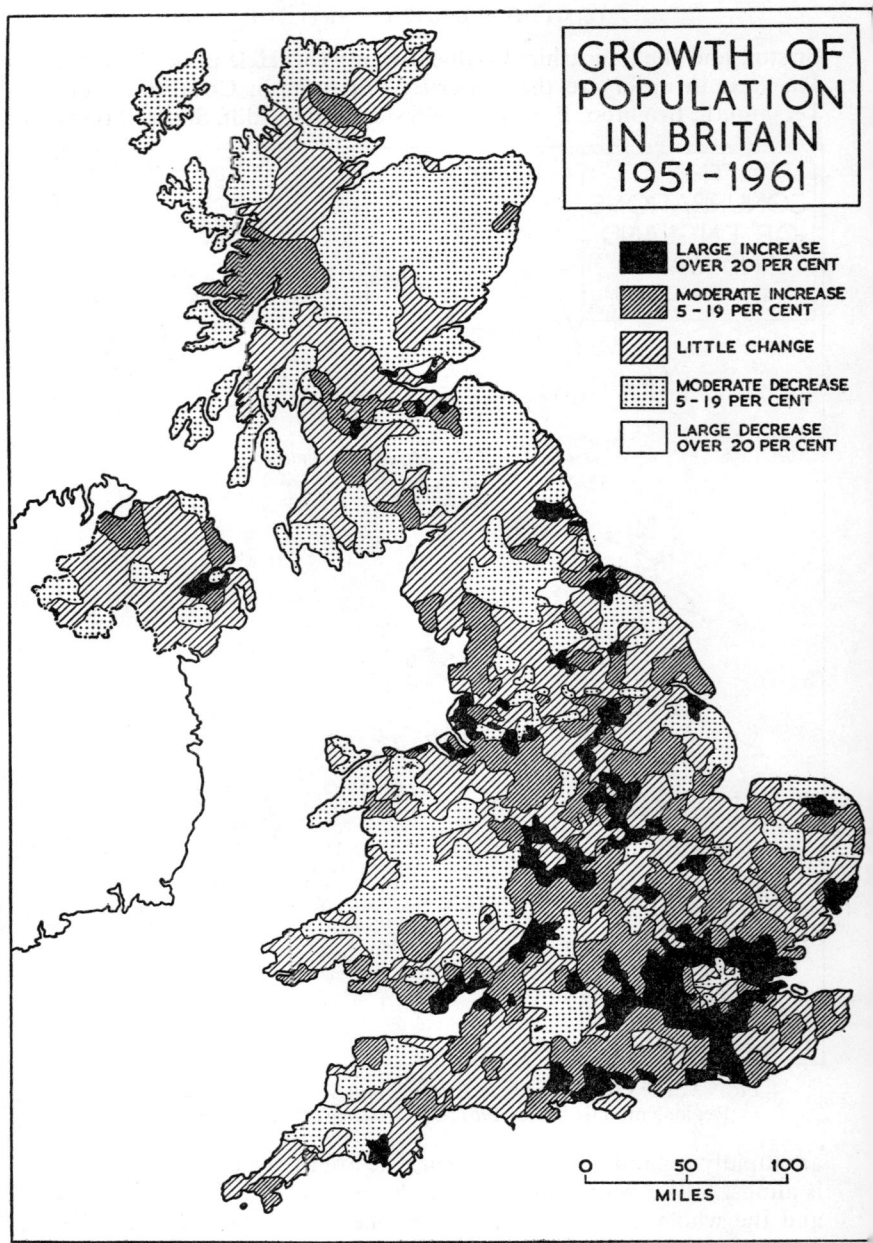

FIG. 83. The Growth of Population in Britain, 1951–61.

unit stretches north through the Dearne valley to Barnsley, and is also near the million mark (854,000).

The smaller conurbations, with 50,000 to 250,000 inhabitants, are 75 in number and total 7·6 million people with one-fifth of the total population. Freeman puts them into seven types—industrialized old towns; ports and naval centres; railway towns (e.g. Crewe); older industrial areas, mainly coal, cotton, and wool textile towns in Lancashire and Yorkshire (growing rapidly in the late nineteenth century, and stable or declining in numbers for at least fifty years); newer and expanding industrial areas, mainly the rapidly growing towns of recent decades on the peripheries of London and Birmingham; residential and holiday towns, which have grown rapidly over the last fifty years or more on the coasts of England and Wales, as well as at certain inland resorts (e.g. Harrogate); and London 'overspill' towns, which are attached or very near to the periphery of Greater London and record rapid increases in the past three decades.

Since these urban areas embrace most of the population of the country, it is appropriate to look at the rates of growth of the total population. The areas with the largest increases of population between 1931 and 1951 (at least 25 per cent.) were mainly located in the south-eastern section centred on the Home Counties around London, and reaching north-west *en bloc* as far as the lower Severn. A second less extensive, though rapidly growing area, was found in the Midland counties, centred on the Black Country and its environs, and the Derby, Nottingham, and Leicester area. A third area of increase was in west Lancashire behind the coast at Liverpool, Preston, and Blackpool. Areas showing a decrease in numbers corresponded to the major uplands. Elsewhere, in city and countryside alike, the rate of increase was below the national average. The really important feature here is the concentration of economic growth—new factories and new homes—in the belt from Lancashire through the Midlands to the outliers of London on the south-east coast.

These trends were continued in the fifties in spite of government efforts to check them. The geographical distribution of rates of growth in the 1951–61 decade is shown on Fig. 83. The total increase of the United Kingdom was 3·5 per cent. The main regional trends as revealed by this map are as follows. First, the areas with the largest increase, over 20 per cent., are located in south-eastern England outside Greater London. Second, similar large increases occurred in the Midlands—in the Black Country (around Greater Birmingham) and in the East Midlands (around Derby and Nottingham). There were also substantial increases at several sea-board locations, notably South Wales, Southampton, Teesside, and Merseyside. Third, an outstanding feature is the marked localization of areas of moderate increase of 5 to 20 per cent. (that is, well above the national increase), together with the previous areas of rapid growth, to form a continuous belt from Lancashire through the Midlands to the south-east. This is the main axis of growth in Britain and continues the pattern of the 1931–51 period. Fourth, extensive rural areas record little change or absolute decreases of population (5 to 20 per cent.)—much of northern England, Wales, most of the south-west, and the highlands of Scotland. Fifth, the map shows, though not so clearly in all cases, the slow growth or little change in the major conurbations, to which further reference will be made below. The six English conurbations actually decreased by 0·2 per cent. Urban areas with over 100,000 people increased by only 2·6 per cent., while those with 50,000 to 100,000 people increased by 14·8 per cent. The new towns recorded abnormally rapid increases, their aggregate population growing from 135,000 in 1951 to 426,000 in 1961.

Scotland has a total population of about 5 millions. Over one-third live in Clydeside, and Edinburgh has well over 500,000. There are five other lesser conurbations with over 50,000 and only two of these, Aberdeen and Dundee, are outside the main centres of population in the central lowland. From the lower Clyde to the Forth, with centres in Glasgow and Edinburgh, and including three lesser conurbations, there is indeed one great urbanized complex. The two main centres, however, remained virtually stationary during the fifties.

We turn now to the growth of the conurbations.

In 1851 the Census reported that there were 580 towns in England and Wales, and 225 in Scotland. These fell into three groups—market towns, where men could meet weekly, do business and get back home on the same day; country towns, centres of administration in which the country gentry and others could meet for business and for social occasions; and large towns around London. It was reported that there were 21 villages (centres where 'men, women, and children can assemble weekly') to one town, each in the middle of a square of 110 square miles or a circle with a six-mile radius, at an average distance apart of 10·8 miles. All were growing rapidly but particular note should be made of three other groups—watering-places, ports, and mining and/or manufacturing towns. The railway stimulated the growth of such centres which were recognized as 'of an inferior order' in their 'local relations' although in industry, commerce and wealth they had 'almost acquired a metropolitan character'.[1]

The conurbations were already apparent in skeleton outline in the mid-nineteenth century, although at that time they consisted of con-

[1] T. W. Freeman, *op. cit.*, pp. 205–6.

gested and compact cores, plus, however, some sprawl along the interconnecting turnpike roads and around the mills that were located either on the streams or near the coal-pits. The horse omnibus and private carriage permitted expansion up to some five miles from the town centre for the wealthier people, though workers' homes down to the end of the century were usually tied within walking distance of their places of work. Better-class 'suburbs', grouped around a pre-industrial village, were already in being at mid-century. Suburban growth occurred frequently (though not necessarily) along railways up to distances of ten miles from the city centre. The suburb often became the seat of a vigorous social community. The tram, that replaced the horse-bus in the last decades, permitted many more people to travel to work, but a half-hour journey reached no more than about six miles and the dense net of tram-car lines served industrial built-up areas rather than opening up new ones. The big acceleration to urban expansion came with the advent of the bus after World War I, for by this means seven to ten miles could be covered in the same time. Tram, bus, and railroad (especially when electrified) have permitted the outward spread of urban areas in the last fifty years. The bus has now taken the place of the tram almost everywhere. The last impetus comes from the private automobile, though its impact on the dispersion of housing has been far less significant in Britain than in the United States.

People refused to move out from the centres of the towns a hundred years ago. The first signs of an outward shift in the provincial towns appeared at mid-century. Properties were needed for railroads and factories. Slum clearance, however, as a deliberate policy, did not begin, and then only on a small scale, until the end of the century. The decline in numbers began in the centre and spread outwards to the middle sections. Vast areas of dreariness, blight, and dereliction of the paleotechnic era, give the essential keynote to the major urban areas of Britain, apart from the inner islands of more attractive, though now often obsolescent, Georgian and Victorian housing. The residential areas were built on the edges of the old centres. The 'suburb' was, however, the recipient of new 'immigrants' to the city, coupled as well by those who, by choice or necessity, left the old houses of the centre for the new houses on the periphery. This process has been going on steadily for some time. What needs to be emphasized are the tens of thousands of old blighted houses in every city whose occupants sooner or later must be rehoused either on the spot or in other centres, or in new centres in the countryside. In 1955, 68,000 dwellings in Manchester out of a total of 208,000 were unfit for habitation. Virtually the whole of the land within its administrative boundaries is built-up. Moreover, its population is declining, but the number of dwellings is increasing, and households are becoming smaller (earlier marriage age and smaller families), so that this is a still further demand over and above the needs of slum clearance. All British cities reveal these features and they are causing ever-increasing encroachment on the countryside.

It is particularly enlightening to look at the growth of the conurbations over the past fifty years or more. The data are shown on the table below. From 1901 to 1911 the growth of West Yorkshire was already well below the national average and the others oscillated around the national figure of 10·9 per cent. Since 1911 West Yorkshire, south-east Lancashire and Greater London have been below the normal, with the exception of Greater London's big increase in the 1921–31 decade. The two textile areas owed their slow increase to their exceptionally low birth-rates, that undoubtedly have been associated with the employment of women in the textile industries. On the other hand, Tyneside and Merseyside (and we may add Clydeside—not shown here) kept up a slightly higher increase because of their higher birth-rates among their high Roman Catholic population and their very low proportion of female employment. In the

PERCENTAGE RATE OF GROWTH OF THE SIX PRINCIPAL ENGLISH CONURBATIONS AND CHIEF CITIES

Conurbations and Chief Cities	1891–1901	1901–1911	1911–1921	1921–1931	1931–1951	1951–1961	Population in 1961 in 000's
West Yorkshire	8·1	4·3	1·5	2·6	2·3	0·6	1,703
Leeds	16·7	4·1	0·9	4·2	4·6	0·9	510
Bradford	5·3	3·1	−0·9	2·5	−2·1	1·2	295
South-east Lancashire	11·8	10·0	1·4	2·8	−0·2	0·2	2,427
Manchester	7·6	10·8	2·2	4·2	−8·3	−6·0	661
West Midlands	11·8	10·2	8·5	9·0	15·7	4·8	2,344
Birmingham	9·2	10·7	9·4	8·7	11·0	−0·6	1,105
Tyneside	23·5	13·7	6·4	1·4	1·0	2·0	852
Newcastle	15·6	7·9	3·2	3·3	1·9	−7·7	269
Merseyside	13·4	12·3	9·2	6·6	2·7	0·0	1,386
Liverpool	8·8	5·9	6·6	6·3	−7·9	−5·5	747
Greater London	16·8	10·2	3·2	9·7	1·6	−2·1	8,172
London County	7·3	−0·3	−0·8	−2·0	−23·9	−4·6	3,195
Outer Ring				27·1	30·9	−0·5	4,976
England and Wales	12·2	10·9	5·0	5·5	9·5	5·3	46,072

SOURCE: *Census 1951: England and Wales, Report on Greater London and Five Other Conurbations*, 1956, and *Census 1961: England and Wales* Preliminary Report, 1961.

period 1931–51 there is a slow growth in the filled-up area of Greater London but a big increase in the counties around it where industry and people concentrated in the thirties. On the other hand, Birmingham alone also grew rapidly in this period, since it attracted many of the new industries, such as artificial fibres, electrical appliances and above all automobiles. The other conurbations were identified with the old-established basic export industries—coal, textiles, shipbuilding—and were largely dependent on them. They were hit hard by unemployment in the dark days of the depression. These areas, as well as South Wales, lost heavily by emigration to the south-east. It is this drift to the South that has continued in the fifties, in spite of the efforts of the government to divert new industries to the depressed areas, and to encourage existing industries to shift their plants from London.

2. The Build of the Major Conurbations

The major conurbations in Great Britain can be briefly portrayed as follows.

Greater London. London is continuously expanding in area and the criteria used in defining it are quickly outdated. In 1931 Greater London of the Census was regarded as the extent of the Metropolitan Police District although there were many contiguous and outlying urban areas that would bring the total population at that time up to 10 millions—a quarter of the population of England. From 1931 to 1951 the population increased by 1·6 per cent. There was, however, a decrease of one million in the inner area of the County of London, a loss of 23·9 per cent., as against a vast increase of 30·9 per cent. in the Outer Ring, between the County and the limits of the Census area. The last decade (1951–61) revealed a continuing loss in the County and a remarkable halt in the growth of the Outer Ring (−0·5 per cent.). Expansion is going on rapidly beyond the Census area of the conurbation. Hence the growth of 14·2 per cent. in the 'remainder' of the South-eastern Standard Region outside the conurbation. These outer areas should now be included in the Census definition. The whole of the London area has about 12 million inhabitants.

Greater London is divided into six sections. The metropolitan commercial and administrative centre reaches from Paddington in the west to the City of London in the east. Around this are the high-density and old residential, industrial, and dockside areas, that reach eastwards as a belt as far as West Ham and west to Kensington. Dense residential areas, mainly pre-1914 in date, cover a large area mainly to the north and west of the preceding divisions, with very limited extension to the south. Three kinds of outer residential area are named in the Census. The 'Hampstead type' is, in fact, limited to the 'Garden Suburb' of that name, laid out in north-west London. The newer residential and industrial suburban districts cover vast areas in a circle up to 15 miles radius of the city. Outer-residential areas form a single tier of administrative divisions impinging on Romford to the east, Hatfield to the north, Leatherhead and Reigate to the south.

South-east Lancashire. The name as given by the Census to this conurbation is an unfortunate one, since large residential areas to the south, in the county of Cheshire, are a part of it. The whole area owes its identity to the dominance of the central city of Manchester and the prevalence of cotton textile and related industries. It developed during the nineteenth century as an assembly of closely spaced, but physically separated towns. These have merged by ribbon growth to form a continuous urban area with a radius of some eight to ten miles from Manchester Town Hall. It has a total population of about 2·5 millions. The whole area occupies the upper basins of the rivers Mersey and Irwell, which are encircled by hills to the north and east. The various towns and industrial villages have merged both through ribbon development and by the extension of residential areas around them. The lesser conurbation of the Central Lancashire Coalfield, including St. Helens and Wigan, now virtually links the Manchester with the Merseyside conurbation. The forecast of their coalescence by Geddes has today become a reality. Residential development has been particularly extensive on the south of the conurbation in the countryside of Cheshire. The older industrial towns in the northern part of the conurbation have remained stable or have actually declined in numbers.

The conurbation falls into five divisions (Fig. 88e, p. 43). The centre is the commercial and industrial core plus the high-density buildings, and (closely related to the previous division on the north and south sides of Manchester–Salford) the older residential areas (pre-1914). Extensive residential areas built since 1914 lie mainly in the southern third of the conurbation south of the core. Mixed areas with post-1914 residential development lie for the most part in a belt some 4 miles wide encircling the north and east of the central core. The crescent of individual industrial towns, another four miles in width, form a second semi-circle to the north and east, penetrating in valley-strips into the surrounding Pennine hills.

The West Midlands is the conurbation centred on Birmingham. It has its core in what is traditionally defined as the Black Country. Its early industrial history was associated with the working of coal and iron and a great range of fabricating iron and steel industries. The widespread sprawl and dereliction which dates back to this development accounts for its name and the fact that one-tenth of the area is waste land. New industries have grown rapidly in the twentieth century in this area, especially on its outskirts. It has attracted immigrant labour and has experienced continual growth. In 1921 the population reached 1·75 millions, in 1931 2 millions, in 1951 2·25 millions, and in 1961 2·3 millions on an area of 209 square miles. The population growth from 1931 to 1951 was 16 per cent., double the rate of the country as a whole. In the fifties it experienced a slower rate of growth. At least one-third of the houses are unfit to live in. Many factories are old and congested. Much of the derelict land is being now used for housing and industry. Over one-half of the population lives in Birmingham and the other million lives in the twenty-one other towns of the conurbation. It lies on the southern edge of the south Staffordshire coalfield and is on relatively high ground (400–450 feet), though the coalfield today has a negligible production. It is drained in all directions by rivers which are linked by canals that pass through Birmingham.

The west Midlands is divided by the Census into three kinds of area. The industrial and commercial centres with the old residential districts reach continuously along an axis from the centre of Birmingham north-west to Wolverhampton. Residential areas of varying age and type surround the first in a zone two to four miles wide and are most extensive in Birmingham itself. The new residential fringe areas (post-1914) cover the northern tier of units in the conurbation.

West Yorkshire lies in the valleys of the Aire and Calder rivers and spreads across the higher land which separates them at the northern extremity of the Yorkshire coalfield. The tract measures about 30 miles from north-west to south-east, and 20 miles from north-east to south-west. Its two chief cities lie in the Aire valley, Bradford situated in a southern cul-de-sac surrounded by high land, reaching 1,000 feet, and Leeds at the place where the Aire valley opens out to the plain of York. In the Calder and its tributary valleys are Huddersfield, Halifax, and Dewsbury. The intervening high land is not closely built-up but there are many smaller centres—village nuclei with factories, some bearing town character—along the main roads. The total population is about 1·7 millions.

The area contains thirty-three boroughs over an area of 481 square miles. No city dominates the whole and indeed there is a popular aversion to regarding the area as a unit, so strong are the feelings of separateness of the major centres. It is particularly identified with the wool and worsted textile industries, but the eastern border includes coal-mining communities. Engineering industries are widespread. Ready-made clothing manufactures are especially characteristic of Leeds. The Census area had 1,703,000 people in 1961. Its growth has been sub-normal for sixty years, and most of its towns have actually been stagnant or decreasing in numbers in this period. It is divided by the Census into the compact industrial communities and old residential cores of the main towns; the area of mixed development of smaller towns around the central cores; the suburban fringe areas of the larger towns; and the predominantly rural countryside with scattered residential and industrial centres.

Merseyside lies on both sides of the Mersey estuary. Liverpool, on the north side, contains over two-thirds of its population. The Wirral Peninsula, on the south side, has its main nucleus in Birkenhead but residential areas extend along the estuary and into the centre of the peninsula. The total population is nearly 1·4 millions—almost double the population of Liverpool, its central city.

The conurbation owes its existence to the port of Liverpool, which accounts for one-third of the foreign trade of England and Wales. The conurbation has grown outwards in all directions from a nucleus on both banks of the Mersey. Around its dockside and commercial cores are arranged the static inner residential area, built before 1914. Beyond this are the expanding residential and industrial areas (a great arc on the inner side of Liverpool and Bootle), and the greater part of the peninsula of Wallasey south of the Mersey. Down to 1921 the area maintained a relatively high increase of population, due to a high immigration rate, but particularly to a high birth-rate among its Irish Roman Catholic population. However, its normal increase in the 1921–31 period was followed by a low 2·7 per cent. increase (England and Wales 9·5) for the 1931–51 period, while the city of Liverpool actually decreased by 7·9 per cent. In the fifties there was no change in numbers.

Tyneside, though the smallest of the conurbations, is very distinctive in every way. It lies along the lower river Tyne, below Newcastle and Gateshead, reaching down to the mouth of the river. The traffic of the river is its lifeblood. Sunderland is slightly outlying and might be considered a part of it functionally, though it is excluded from the Census definition. The population is under one million, but its capital Newcastle combines the feature of a historic town and a small though very distinct regional metropolis. Shipbuilding, mining, and engineering are the economic mainstay of this area. The 852,000 people occupy only 90 square miles divided between thirteen administrative units. Immediately behind the Tyneside tract are many coal-mining communities and these, together with new industrial sites, constitute an urban periphery around the heart of the conurbation. Like Merseyside, it increased rather steadily until 1931 and then was terribly hit by the depression in the thirties. Its growth since 1931 has been almost stationary (through emigration). The area is divided into the commercial and administrative centre of Newcastle; the main industrial and pre-1914 residential area back from the river; and the newer residential areas, plus holiday centres on the coast; and the inland rural mining villages.

The Clydeside Conurbation in Scotland is situated on the lower Clyde, with Glasgow as its dominant focus. It covers 320 square miles and has 1,758,000 inhabitants, one-third of the population of Scotland. Glasgow has 1,090,000 people on 60 square miles. It grew up at the lowest bridging point on the Clyde. It is a historic city and a great modern metropolis—the shipbuilding, industrial, commercial, and cultural centre of south-west Scotland and the west Highlands. It is also an appalling example of bad nineteenth-century housing. Its population increased rapidly in the Victorian era, but since 1911 the growth dropped dramatically from 11 per cent. (1901–11) to 3–5 per cent. (1911–21) and only 4·5 per cent. for the period 1931–51.

The conurbation clusters around seven town centres, the chief of which is Glasgow itself with one million inhabitants. This city grew up on the north bank of the Clyde, but extensions since 1800 now straddle the river to a distance of about five miles. The industrial and dock areas and congested and obsolescent housing extend along the Clyde for nearly ten miles, both above and below the city, as far as Motherwell and Clydebank respectively. The major residential areas stretch over large areas to the north and south of the pre-1914 core.

It is appropriate to draw attention here to the three other urban clusters that are entitled to be regarded as conurbations with close on one million inhabitants.

South Wales is marked by the concentration of coal-mines and their associated settlements in the narrow valleys which dissect the moorland plateau; and by the series of urban centres off the coalfield on the coast. In these parts are located the iron and non-ferrous metal smelting industries, based on coal from the valleys and imported ores. The chief centres are Swansea and Cardiff. The latter has many of the traits of a provincial capital.

The Sheffield area is focused on this central city at the convergence of valleys deeply sunken in the Pennine moorlands. This is an ancient seat of iron and steel fabricating industries. Its urbanized area stretches to the coalfield areas of Barnsley to the north and down to the Don Valley to include Rotherham. The population increased by 5 per cent. in the 1931–51 period and by under 1 per cent. from 1951 to 1961.

Mid-Trent has its centre in Nottingham, a definite and growing provincial capital. The city has now almost coalesced westwards with Derby and it extends without interruption northwards to include

Mansfield and Chesterfield, with coal-mining, steel workers, and engineering industries. Nottingham itself has hosiery manufactures and lace-making, in addition to mining and engineering industries. The Nottingham cluster alone has about 500,000 people and increased by 20 per cent. between 1931 and 1951. This is one of the growing urban areas in the country. The capital itself increased by only 1·8 per cent. in the 1951–61 decade, but the whole area increased by 7 per cent.

3. Recent Growth Trends: Greater London

A paramount feature of the changing distribution of population in Britain is the decline of the provincial conurbations and the drift of population to the South.

Extension is going on far beyond the limits of the conurbation of Greater London. Increases of population and of the range of commuting to London together warrant the recognition of an area with a radius of 40 to 50 miles from central London in which there live 12 million people. South-east England is undergoing a tremendous shift in the dwelling-places of its workers from the centre to outlying places. It is serving as a magnet for employment. The south coast also attracts people in retirement.

The growth of the fifties has added to the national significance of London as a port and seat of industry and commerce.[1] Many new office buildings reflect these advances in business. Extension of industry, notably television and electronics, has continued. It appears that, in spite of controls exercised through the Board of Trade, further industrial employment is inevitable. So that 'the continued economic expansion of south-east England as a whole is a basic economic fact which must underlie all realistic planning for the future'.

The trends have been investigated for the period 1951 to 1958 by Powell. The daily movement of workers gives the keynote to this expansion of Greater London. The decrease of population in the built-up areas of Greater London continued in the fifties, with a total migration of over 400,000. There is a great belt of continuous population increase *beyond* the boundaries of the conurbation, where increases were of the order of 10 per cent. and more, compared with an average of 3 per cent. for the country. This belt had in 1958 18 per cent. more people than in 1951—the census reveals around 25 per cent. for the decade. The area extends way beyond the Green Belt, encircles the New Towns, and stretches along all the major highways.

A remarkable redistribution of people is evidently taking place.

[1] A. G. Powell, 'The Recent Development of Greater London', *Advancement of Science*, Vol. 17, No. 5, May 1960.

Between 1951 and 1958 120,000 were moved to the new towns, 45,000 to London County Council estates on the edge of the conurbation, and 10,000 to more recently expanded towns. The same total moved voluntarily to places in and beyond the Green Belt. These have been short-distance moves by the new immigrants from somewhere in the London area. A main factor is the completion of electrification and diesel development on the railways. Car owners in the London area nearly doubled from 1952 to 1958. New workers and their families are moving into the Region 40–50 miles radius and retired people in particular are moving out.

Unfortunately these shifts of people to the outside are not being accompanied by commensurate shifts of places of employment. In the fifties one-half of the increase of insured workers occurred in south-east England, and most of that increase was concentrated within 40 miles of the centre of London. While this wider London Region received over 40 per cent. of the new employment, the Greater London Conurbation received 21 per cent., and 12 per cent. of the total was in the city centre. Changes in employment from 1952 to 1958 reveal five trends—the great attraction of central London where the numbers of employed steadily increased; the steady growth of industry in the north and western outskirts of the London Region; the growth of new centres on the whole periphery of the conurbation ('industry moves and expands—population follows'); the continued growth of a heavy large-scale industry on Thames-side itself from Reading to Southend (e.g. the Ford plant, power plants); fifth, the rapid growth of the New Towns. Small-scale industrialization is found throughout the areas north of the Thames—in towns, village, and countryside alike. 'It is this general spread of small-scale industrialization which . . . promotes the matrix which wields together the larger, independent urban blocks into the solid conglomerate of the conurbation.' This expansion is shared by larger and independent towns that lie well beyond the main area of the London Region—Reading, Chelmsford, Southend, Luton. Little growth takes place, however, to the south of the Thames; these areas are semi-residential or rural.

'The extended conurbation consists basically of a number of industrial centres, expanding independently and with industrial workers travelling not much more than ten miles from their home to work. These separate industrial entities are knit together into a composite and recognizable greater whole—firstly, by the inter-movement of workers between them, and secondly, by the superimposition upon them of the great and increasing daily flow of commuters to central London which forms a web uniting all parts of the whole and which is further reinforced by the daily flows to the shopping and entertainment areas of the centre.'[1]

This new post-war expansion of the Greater London conurbation raises problems of social and physical planning that far out-date the Barlow Report and the Greater London Plan. These growth trends will continue and demand a reorientation of planning concepts and practices.

4. The Growth of the Central Business Districts

One of the big factors of urban growth in the post-war years is the development of the tertiary activities of business, organization and administration. The county of London has over a million daily in-commuters, most of whom are white-collar workers. Central London has acquired an extra 15,000 office jobs annually over the past ten years. Offices represent three-quarters of the rateable value of the City of London and 40 and 30 per cent. in Westminster and Marylebone. Among the provincial towns only Manchester exceeds 10, with Liverpool at 8·2 and Newcastle 6·9 per cent. In Birmingham, where growth is now proceeding rapidly, it stands at 5·5 per cent. The main attractions in London are the access to other fields of business in the same spot and access to the general consumer market. There is also the trend towards larger units with the growth of offices in London. Other factors are the proximity to the London airports and to the port of London. All the other metropolitan districts have their central business districts and there are indications here of the increase of both office space and retail shopping space, but they are in the aggregate out-shadowed by London, though it would be a mistake to let the growth of London obscure what is going on in the provinces even though such changes have come tardily. It is important to note that none of these cities complain of an excessive commuter problem to the city centre, for the majority of workers travel no further than half an hour each way to their work. Only in Birmingham, one of the most extensive and rapidly growing, is the journey time somewhat larger, at about three-quarters of an hour.

This growth is expressed in demolition and reconstruction. It means emergence of tower buildings in London that punctuate its skyline, rather than growing in clusters as is characteristic of the down-town districts of the United States. It means the increased tempo of destruction and building in the last ten years in the provincial cities with the advent again of the skyscraper. It means empty areas of demolished slum in derelict areas that surround the central

[1] Powell, *op. cit.*

business district of every big city—for these areas are awaiting redevelopment. The Victorian face of England's city centres is changing at last in all the provincial cities. In other words, as urban areas expand, business is being more highly centralized in the city centres. It should be added, however, that slum demolition did not begin until the mid-fifties and it is only in recent years that the construction of commercial buildings has got under way in the provinces.

The most spectacular programme of central area development is probably in Birmingham, with the aid of Dr. Gropius and Mr. Cotton. Plans include a multi-million shop and office scheme, as well as other blocks of shops, offices, hotels, a theatre and technical college buildings, and an inner ring road, 3·5 miles long, begun in 1957, to encircle the business centre and seal it off from through traffic. Manchester, with bold plans in 1945, has made slow progress, though it now has one of the tallest buildings in Britain. Liverpool and Newcastle have their plans but have as yet made little headway. Leeds has several large shops and office blocks under construction (1963), and is shortly to begin an inner ring road, and to clear a large area of slum to make way for the expansion of the University and the hospital buildings. The Victorian railroad stations in Britain are in general a disgrace to the nation, and their reconstruction goes on slowly or has often reached no further than the planning stage. But the centres are expanding and this will be facilitated as the slums around them, in the zone of deterioration, are cleared. What is now to be feared is unchecked growth, with increasing congestion through the lack of co-ordinated development of inner ring roads and radial highways, and without the far-seeing development of regional shopping centres, instead of the frequently spaced and tiny clusters of neighbourhood shops that do little to relieve congestion in the centres.

In a White Paper published in February of 1963 the government claims to be firmly resolved in checking the drift to the South. The Abercrombie Report planned for a static London. This is no longer realistic. The net loss of population to the conurbation in the fifties was half a million, but the population fell by less than 200,000 owing to the natural increase. About 40,000 new jobs a year have been added to the conurbation since the mid-fifties, most of which were service employment, only 20 per cent. in industry. There has been an increase of one-third of the floor space in offices over pre-war and half as much again is to be constructed. About 15,000 new jobs a year are being added to the central area alone, so that in a decade 150,000 people have been added to the daily peak-hour travel. It is presumed that this general trend in the structure of our urban society will and must increase. The rate of office growth in the centre, however, must be stopped, and more evenly distributed through the conurbation. The government propose to get as much of its work as possible done outside London and to encourage the establishment of offices in other cities than London and in the towns of the outer London region.

5. THE MAJOR CITIES AND THEIR REGIONS: FOOD SUPPLIES

Each of the conurbations has a dominant central city, which is the main focus of its activities. They differ from each other in certain important respects. London, Glasgow, and Newcastle have sites with marked nodality. As a bridge-town at the head of navigation of a river, where natural land routes converged, each of these historic cities has emerged as the nucleus of a conurbation with a large tributary area around it. Merseyside has a similar unity, since it is grouped around the harbour on both its banks. Birmingham is similarly a dominant unchallenged focus. Manchester–Salford, though a great industrial centre, is also a metropolitan centre of the highest order, serving the many smaller industrial towns around it. The west Yorkshire conurbation is unique. It has no natural dominant focus, and lacks a tradition of unity. Bradford is the specialized commercial focus of the wool and worsted textile industries, and Leeds is its general business and administrative centre.

Let us first examine the regional functions of the cities as commercial and cultural centres. In the first place, they are the principal nodal points for the distribution of produce. This trade is effected through three main channels, the wholesale markets, wholesale merchants, and branch depots.

The distribution of meat is handled by about twenty wholesale deadmeat markets in England and Wales, located in those towns which contain, or serve areas which contain, a population exceeding about 500,000[1]. Those with the largest annual turnover are naturally situated in the chief cities.

The trade in imported meat, both fresh and refrigerated, is dominated by London to the extent of about 40 per cent. of the total for the United Kingdom. However, the meat imports of Liverpool and other ports have increased in recent decades at the expense of London, in that an importer requiring meat at a provincial market arranges for direct consignment, in order to save the extra rail and handling charges entailed by redistribution from London. Furthermore, apart

[1] Ministry of Agriculture and Fisheries, Economic Series, No. 14. *Reports on Markets and Fairs in England and Wales*. Part II, *Midland Markets*, 1927, p. 16. F. J. Prewett, *The Marketing of Farm Produce*. Part I, *Livestock* (1926), Part II, *Milk* (1927), Oxford.

from London, imported meat is not stored at the ports but is delivered direct to the consuming centres, where cold storage accommodation is provided at convenient centres for distribution. Smithfield Market handles about one-half of our meat imports, and it has been estimated that between the wars almost all of its supplies were consumed in the Metropolitan and Home Counties Area.[1] Though London and Liverpool are the giants of the imported meat trade, the smaller importers tend to serve distinctive hinterlands, although there is much overlapping of service.

Newcastle serves the coal and steel areas of the North Riding of Yorkshire, Northumberland and Durham, and Cumberland. Hull is well placed for the West Riding and the north-east Midlands. Manchester and Liverpool serve Lancashire, Cheshire, West Riding, Midlands, and North Wales. The Bristol Channel ports serve South Wales and the Lower Severn Basin, and Southampton and the southern counties; London serves the south-eastern counties and the south Midlands.[2] Similar factors control the distribution of imported dairy produce. London imports 50 and 70 per cent. of butter and cheese imports respectively.

From the wholesale meat markets home-produced, and, to a smaller extent, imported meat are regularly distributed to the principal towns within a radius of 20 to 30 miles, where, by means of rapid motor transport, fresh supplies can be delivered and offered for sale by retailers on the same morning as they are purchased.

Fifty years ago the provincial wholesale markets dealing in fruit and vegetables[3] were concerned with trade in local produce. They obtained all other English, continental, and imported produce from Covent Garden, and to a lesser extent from the port auctions. Now they receive home-grown and continental supplies direct from the centres of production, and are rapidly increasing in importance as distributors, independent of Covent Garden. The re-consignment trade of the latter is now mainly restricted to imported fruits and expensive luxury out-of-season produce.

The wholesale trade of Covent Garden, the principal market in southern England, may be divided into four categories. For the distribution of expensive luxury produce there is a national market. Produce is distributed to the large provincial markets, although this trade has been decreasing with decentralization and provincial

[1] Report on the Linlithgow Committee on the Distribution and Prices of Meat, Poultry and Eggs, Cmd. 1927 (1923), p. 84.

[2] Ministry of Agriculture and Fisheries, Economic Series, No. 6. *Report on the Trade in Refrigerated Beef, Mutton and Lamb*, 1925, p. 35.

[3] Ministry of Agriculture and Fisheries, Economic Services, No. 15. *Report on Fruit Marketing in England and Wales*, 1927. Report of the Linlithgow Committee on the Marketing of Fruit and Vegetables (1924).

competition. Supplies also reach retailers and small wholesale merchants who visit the markets in person. With rapid motor transport, the area served by this means has a radius of about 50 miles. In southern England agricultural districts with a small population are able to supply most of their own requirements locally. They only require imported and continental fruits, and these can be obtained cheaper, with better choice, and often better transport facilities, from Covent Garden than from local wholesale markets. Gloucestershire, Wiltshire, Dorset, and the south-west find their distributing centres in Bristol and Plymouth, although large quantities of imported and luxury produce are preferably obtained by local merchants and retailers from London.

The chief markets, with their areas of distribution, in northern England are as follows: Manchester–Liverpool serves Lancashire, Derbyshire, north Staffordshire, Cheshire, North Wales, and the Isle of Man. Newcastle serves Northumberland, Durham, and Cumberland. Leeds serves a radius of about 40 miles and Sheffield serves a radius of 20 miles, including Barnsley, Doncaster, and Chesterfield. Hull serves the East Riding and north Lincolnshire. In the Midlands, Birmingham is the market for the four surrounding counties and central Wales. Nottingham, Derby, and Leicester serve areas with a radius of about 20 miles. In South Wales the main distributing centres are Swansea and Cardiff. The former supplies the thinly populated western portion of South Wales; the latter serves the densely populated valleys from Newport to Swansea.

In the pre-railway era the movement of fluid milk was limited to a few miles. More distant areas made butter and cheese. With the coming of rail, plus the development of wholesaling, this distinction disappeared. Producer-retailers, however, long survived around the cities. In the twenties such producers still supplied one-quarter of Great Britain's retail milk, and one-half that of the provincial towns. By 1936 this was reduced to one-sixth and in 1945 only 15 per cent.—mainly in country villages. The urban markets are now supplied almost entirely by purchasing dairymen who receive their milk direct from farms.

London's fluid milk market dominates the situation in England. In 1861 most of the milk (70 per cent.) was provided by stall-fed cattle in the metropolitan area; only 4·4 per cent. came in by rail. By 1891 this urban contribution had fallen to 15 per cent., and 85 per cent. came in by rail. In 1954 about one-half came in by rail and one-half by road (with, incidentally, a sixfold increase of total consumption in sixty years). This meant that the milk-shed of London has steadily been encroaching on other milk-sheds throughout the country. In the twenties 'London's supply area was essentially

Lowland Britain south of the Wash–Mersey line, except for a west Midland salient sterilized by the local demand of the Birmingham area'.[1] In the mid-twenties the flows of milk were directed to six main consuming areas, while that of London dominated the south-east. Of the other areas, the north-east drew heavily on south-west Scotland. Other milksheds were the north-east, north-west, West Riding, west Midlands, South Wales. Cities like Hull, Bristol, and Nottingham were supplied by their immediate environs.

There were only minor changes in this pattern before the war. A commission reporting in 1935 thought that only London needed to seek milk more than 50 miles distant, and certainly no more than 100 miles. The main increases in production during the war were in the west and south-west. These surpluses had to reach increased consumer areas in the conurbations; and particularly in the London area (where supplies from the Midlands have decreased with increased consumption in that area). One must note the 'progressive decline in importance over the past century of proximity to markets among the factors influencing the location of milk production for fluid consumption'. Milk can now be carried without depreciation from almost any producing area to any market in the country.

The Milk Marketing Board was 'born out of chaos' in 1933. It rationalized collection and prices and minimized transport costs within the framework of its eleven regions. This has greatly reduced the importance of distance from urban markets in fixing the location of dairy farming.[2] Sales of fluid milk have doubled in twenty years.

The distribution of provisions is effected by independent wholesale merchants, branch depots, and the headquarters and branch warehouses of multiple-shop companies. The existence of port facilities has a profound effect on the nature of the business of the first group of distributors and the extent of the areas served by them. In the port of Manchester, for example, large wholesale importing houses specialize in one line of business, and distribute to the smaller wholesalers of surrounding towns for local redistribution. On the other hand, Leeds, Sheffield, and Birmingham receive supplies for redistribution from the ports. Many large provision and confectionery firms have adopted a system whereby distributing depots are located at large towns throughout the country to supply the chief consuming areas. Such depots are, therefore, nearly always situated in the big cities. Motor transport is the chief means of distribution used by these firms. Their areas of regular distribution are

[1] F. A. Barnes, 'The Evolution of the Salient Patterns of Milk Production and Distribution in England and Wales', *Trans. Institute of British Geographers*, 1958.
[2] E. S. Simpson, 'Milk Production in England and Wales: A Study in the Influence of Collective Marketing', *Geographical Review*, January 1959, pp. 95–111.

conditioned by the fact that, first, the maximum limit of distribution will be that distance which can be conveniently covered by road in one day, an approximate radial distance of 60 miles; and second, delivery over such distances is not regularly practised because the demand in rural areas and scattered small towns is not sufficient to require full and frequent loads. Consequently, provision distributors generally serve an area within a radius of 20 miles by road, comprising the conurbations and their contiguous suburban and rural areas. The same factors condition the distribution of fruit and vegetables and meat from the wholesale markets, and the extent of the areas drawn upon by road by the conurbations for their milk supplies.

A great variety of firms, in addition to those engaged in the provision trades, have also established provincial offices and depots. In all cases, the areas served vary widely according to the nature and amount of the business of each company. Such offices are usually situated in London, Birmingham, Manchester and/or Liverpool, Leeds and/or Bradford, Newcastle, Cardiff, and Bristol. They are also occasionally found in Sheffield, serving south Yorkshire and part of Derbyshire, Nottinghamshire, and north Lincolnshire, Plymouth serving Devon and Cornwall, Southampton for Hampshire, and Nottingham for the east Midland counties.

6. Business and Finance

The chief city in each conurbation is the centre of the economic activities of the surrounding industrial towns, and in it there are, therefore, located the Exchanges, the scenes of the daily activities of the business men. Examples are the Manchester Royal Exchange, the principal transaction centre for the cotton industries of south-east Lancashire, the Iron and Steel Exchange at Birmingham, the Bradford Exchange serving the wool and worsted industries of the west Yorkshire conurbation, the Newcastle Commercial Exchange, formerly a coal and coke market, now handling varied engineering and shipping interests, and the Sheffield Exchange, the centre for the iron, steel, and coal trades of south Yorkshire, Nottinghamshire, and north Lincolnshire. Also located in the city are the registered offices of firms with their factories in the surrounding industrial districts; and the headquarters or branch offices of industrial and trade associations established in the interests of the principal regional industries and general welfare of those whom they employ. An excellent example of a trade association which has adopted a regional system is the Federation of British Industries with eleven districts in England, excluding the London City area. The extent of each district of these trade associations is determined by the nature of its business. One district branch is concerned as far as possible with one group of related industries, in a district which is within easy reach of the centre.

The zoning system used during the war parcelled out the whole country into areas, each being served from fixed centres of distribution for certain commodities, so as to eliminate, as far as possible, long and uneconomic hauls. Reference to the zones for particular commodities shows that they broadly corresponded with the normal service areas of the principal cities described in this chapter.

The amalgamation movement in English banking,[1] dating from the third decade of the nineteenth century, bears ample testimony to the function of the great cities as regional financial centres. At first, joint-stock companies and private banks established in the cities extended their influence in all directions by absorbing small banks and by opening up new branches in surrounding towns, mainly to cater for the growing financial requirements of their principal industries. The amalgamation movement, however (while enhancing the financial strength and individuality of the principal cities in the middle of the nineteenth century), proceeded so far in the latter half, that today only four important independent banks remain, the Lancashire group with headquarters in Manchester and Liverpool. The large provincial cities, however, do possess distinctive functions which tend to offset excessive centralization in London. There are ten branches of the Bank of England doing business in the chief commercial centres. The organization of absorbed banks has also in some cases been maintained and their provincial headquarters still retain their original capacity in a modified form; and district boards have been organized in recent years, with their headquarters in large cities.

The insurance companies of England are mainly concentrated in London, though a reliable indication of the status of a city as a financial centre is afforded by the number of branch offices and headquarters of insurance firms which it contains. Insurance business, owing to its need for constant personal contacts and to rapidly increasing business connections throughout the country, lends itself to the organization of districts which are administered from main district branch offices. Every important insurance company exhibits this tendency, as we have seen in the case of Leeds and Bradford (p. 273). The extent of the districts controlled from the branch offices of a firm varies widely according to the nature and amount of its business, but the main factors which are generally considered in their delimitation are: first, the amount of business of a district should not be too great for efficient and prompt attention at one office, and second, all parts of the district must be easily accessible to its branch office to facilitate efficient control and supervision.

[1] J. Sykes, *The Amalgamation Movement in English Banking*, London, 1926.

THE CITY-REGION

The cities of Newcastle, Leeds, Manchester, Liverpool, Birmingham, Bristol, and Cardiff are pre-eminent among provincial cities as centres for the location of district branch offices and the headquarters of provincial companies. All the large insurance companies originally established branches in these cities, although the growth of business has often necessitated a still further step in the process of decentralization, whereby smaller districts with independent branches have been established. Thus, Bristol was originally the centre for the lower Severn and south-west counties, but now the latter have often a separate branch office at Plymouth or Exeter. Leeds was the original centre for all Yorkshire, but it has lost Cleveland to Newcastle, and south Yorkshire to Sheffield. London was, in many cases, the original headquarters for south-east England, but now many firms have district branches in Norwich and Southampton, the London district being restricted to the Home Counties. These regional orbits are not watertight catchment areas. There is much overlapping. But major areas can be defined within which the influence of one city is dominant. For example, as we have already noticed, the west Yorkshire wool textile and south Yorkshire iron and steel areas have their respective centres in Leeds–Bradford and Sheffield. On the western slopes of the Pennines, the compact industrial area of south-east Lancashire has its focus in the city and port of Manchester. This city has attained a much more advanced stage of metropolitan development, so that its influence, along with that of its partner, Liverpool, penetrates into the West Riding. Thus, several banks with their original headquarters in the Yorkshire centres have been absorbed by Manchester firms. The West Riding lies in the hinterland of the Lancashire ports, and several Manchester retail firms have branches in Leeds and neighbouring towns.

It may be noted that north Wales lies definitely within the sphere of influence of Manchester–Liverpool, and central Wales has close relations with Birmingham and the Midlands. The Potteries district is very divided in its allegiances to Manchester and Birmingham. Lacking an effective capital of its own, the north Staffordshire Potteries is oriented towards Manchester and Birmingham.

'The proximity of Manchester to the north and of Birmingham to the south even suggested the superfluity of such a capital, a point which national administration in its delimitation of local government regions seemed to underline, and north-west Staffordshire would seem to be falling more and more into the position of a satellite to the west Midland capital, Birmingham. Local feelings now have been subordinated to a truer regionalism, though Newcastle and Stoke have still to work out its full significance for themselves, and also jointly the relation of this regionalism itself to the larger provincial loyalty.'[1]

In south-eastern England, on the other hand, the regional capitals are not independent foci. Metropolitan England, as its name indicates, is dominated by the influence of London. Here again, however, for many commercial purposes, the south-western counties have their separate headquarters in Bristol, and sometimes in Plymouth, and the eastern counties often have separate headquarters in Norwich and Cambridge.

7. The Major Cities as Cultural Centres

It is extremely difficult to assess the actual role of a city as a cultural centre and more so to define the range of its regional associations. This is, however, one of the most important and lasting functions of a genuine metropolis. One has reference to educational facilities, professional and learned societies, concerts, sports, and the like, and most intangible of all, the ideas and movements that the city has developed and propagated through its history on behalf of the people of the city and its environs. There are two direct ways in which one can measure this association and leadership. One indication is found in the presence of a University, Technical College, or other institutions of higher education, and the residence of their students. Another guide is in the circulation of the principal newspapers, both the main morning papers (e.g. *The Guardian*), and the evening papers which come out in several editions and are distributed locally to the whole population and reflect their interests in what may be called regional news and activities (e.g. *Manchester Evening News*). These are substitutes for the less tangible manifestations of such ties which are reflected in the stuff of local history.

The Universities known as Redbrick, for the edification of the American reader, are those institutions that started in the big provincial cities some fifty to seventy-five years ago. London and Durham in England started over a hundred years ago, and the Scottish Universities are almost medieval in origin and cannot, accordingly, be defined in these terms. The two older Universities are referred together, popularly, as Oxbridge. Both are situated in rural counties in the waistline of the industrial axis of Britain. It is true that today all Universities draw a large number of students from other parts of the country (many more than before the war), but the Redbrick Universities are essentially regional in function and serve most of the

---

[1] A. H. Morgan, 'Regional Consciousness in the North Staffordshire Potteries', *Geography*, Vol. XXVII, 1942, pp. 95–102.

local schools and are responsible for the guidance of education in many ways in school and college of their environs. The technologies are also closely linked with the industries of their regions.

A further important feature is that full University status has been granted to colleges that formerly took the external degrees of the University of London (Nottingham, Leicester, Hull, Southampton, and Exeter). The first new University at Keele in North Staffordshire was established shortly after the war. Current plans will establish new Universities, seven in all, at York, Lancaster, Coventry, Canterbury, Norwich, Colchester, and Brighton. The last opened its doors in October of 1961. Note that these are not all in 'regional capitals' of a high order. Other factors have entered in the choice, for it is intended that these Universities should remain relatively small (c. 3,000 by 1970) and be primarily residential. They will serve areas that obviously lie well outside the commuting radius of the existing Universities.

It should also be noted that Scotland has four Universities of old standing between which the country is 'neatly regionalized'. Each draws the majority of its students from its local area and there is remarkably little interchange between the areas. The principal daily papers are also published in the following cities—Glasgow 4, Edinburgh 2, Dundee, and Aberdeen 1 each.[1]

Circulation provides a second general indicator of regional associations. This embraces the circulation of newspapers, and, in these days, the range of radio and television broadcasting from provincial stations. The mapping of these areas has been a major contribution of F. H. W. Green and will be referred to directly.

The assessment of the role of the city as a leader in the thought and aspirations of its dependent areas is a matter that needs to be evaluated historically. The outstanding feature in Britain is the role of Manchester in the free-trade movement in the nineteenth century, as opposed to the protectionism of Birmingham. Both these policies were associated with personalities, but they are also deeply rooted in the contrasted needs of the dominant industries in the two areas. The cotton textile industries needed free access to foreign markets. The miscellaneous metal fabricating industries of the Black Country, dependent on human skills and a shortage of local raw materials, favoured a protected market. Similar evidences of the protagonism of ideas and leadership in thought and policy are to be found in Glasgow and to a lesser degree in other cities.

The outstanding cultural characteristics of the big provincial cities

[1] See R. Miller and Joy Tivy (eds.), 'Glasgow's Spheres of Influence', in *The Glasgow Region: A General Survey*, Glasgow, 1958 (British Association volume). New Universities are now chartered at Dundee and Glasgow.

are also reflected in their institutions and public buildings. In them are to be found art galleries, museums, and the chief concert and assembly halls, and exchanges, most of which are heavy and outmoded Victorian structures. The Free Trade Hall of Manchester is an example. Here too are literary, musical, and artistic societies. The provincial symphony orchestra has become an institution: the famous Hallé orchestra of Manchester is an example. Liverpool and Birmingham also have their orchestras and repertory companies, but other cities apparently have difficulty in supporting them. Concerts, festivals, etc., though held elsewhere also, are important features of the big provincial city. The theatre, too, is outstanding. Almost all of them, both 'legitimate' and 'music hall' (vaudeville to Americans), were built in the Edwardian era and still carry top-line shows, though a number of them have closed down in the post-war years. In general, the cultural facilities of this kind seem to be well below the levels of continental cities, and, indeed, in the post-war days, of American cities.

8. The Urban Hierarchy and Urban Fields

The variety of services of the major cities discussed above is reflected in their total significance as regional centres. Such functions are the *raison d'être* of all urban centres and their measurement forms the basis of the concept of a hierarchy as has already been discussed in a previous chapter. Services segregate in a steady gradation so that the break between one order of centre and the next is difficult to determine. The differences are nonetheless real, so that several distinct orders can be recognized. Smailes, on the basis of an assessment of key services, recognized the orders of sub-towns, towns, major towns (or minor cities), and major cities (p. 78).

Further assessment on these lines has been undertaken by F. H. W. Green,[1] and still more recently by W. I. Carruthers. Green recognizes five grades of towns as service centres on the same lines as Smailes. Omitting his city of the first order, the only one of which is London, and the small market villages (the fifth or lowest order), there remain three orders (Fig. 84). These are the second order or provincial centres (e.g. Birmingham); the third order or regional centres (e.g. Ipswich and Exeter); and the fourth order or district centres, or small towns with a minimum number of urban functions. Each town performs its own distinctive functions, plus those of the lower orders. Green has been especially concerned with the centres of the fourth order, and obviously all the other centres of higher order with respect to their fourth-order functions. Places were selected as

[1] F. H. W. Green, 'Urban Hinterlands of England and Wales: An Analysis of Bus Services', *Geog. J.*, Vol. CXVI, 1950, pp. 64–88.

such centres if they had a bus service which served no place larger than themselves. When each centre was selected its hinterland was drawn by joining up the ends of the routes serving it, as opposed to routes serving neighbouring centres. There are about 700 of these in England and Wales (900 in Great Britain) a figure that is identical with that of Smailes who classed the small towns on the basis of their having a minimum number of specified services. The average size of the service area is 87 square miles (median 61). The average population of the hinterland is 16,500 (median 8,500). It was found that in agricultural areas served by country market towns, the ratio between the population of the town and its hinterland was 3 to 5. These local hinterlands, within which a central town is more accessible than any other, serves as a framework for the use of common central services and for the development of a community of interest. They have been shown to correspond with the areas of a variety of voluntary organizations, retail trade areas, and the range of the regular journey to work. They are the areas of regular daily or weekly participation in the facilities of the centre. This approach and its findings find remarkable parallels in studies carried out in Sweden, Germany, and the United States, as discussed in Chapter 4.

The third order of centres defined by Green, are called regional centres (Fig. 84). These are roughly the same as Smailes' minor cities and major towns of which there are sixty-five in Britain. They have been selected on the basis of their having an *evening* paper, and they are centres for more occasional visits for the purchase of furniture, clothing, and household durables. Their accessibility areas are defined in the same way on the basis of bus services or sometimes of rail services. Green notes that the use of the private automobile results in a catchment area that is essentially the same as that by rail and the two broadly correspond with the area of bus accessibility. Their areas are defined as a group of district areas of fourth-order centres and sub-regional ('regional service areas').

The second-order centres are the major provincial centres. Their service areas are shown on Fig. 84. While evening papers were taken as the criterion in defining the regional centres, the primary criterion of a provincial centre is the possession of a daily morning paper. The areas contain a group of regions and the boundary is generally fixed by the limits of the service areas of the commercial television stations. With varying emphasis given to these and other factors, the following appear as indubitable provincial capitals—London, Bristol, Birmingham, Manchester, Liverpool, Leeds, and Newcastle. Others with varying degrees of certainty are Nottingham, Plymouth, Norwich, Cardiff, Sheffield, and Bradford; Darlington, Ipswich, and Leamington; and in Scotland, Glasgow, Edinburgh, Aberdeen, and Dundee.

We would emphasize that the provision of special programmes and the broadcasting of 'regional news' by commercial television within

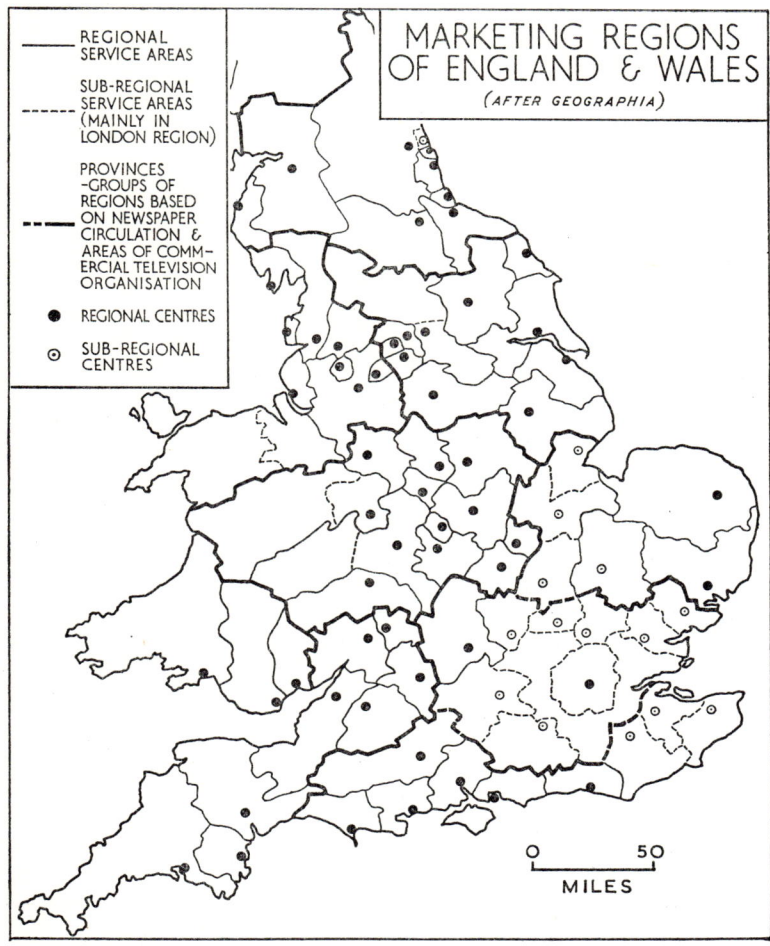

Fig. 84. England and Wales: Marketing Regions
(after 'Marketing and Media Survey' by *Geographia*).

specified areas both reflect and create interests, attitudes, and shopping habits. These areas, shown in heavy black on Fig. 84, have a special significance as indicators of regional cohesion beyond the tributary areas of the regional centres. A group of regions corresponds broadly with one of the eleven television or provincial areas.

THE CITY-REGION

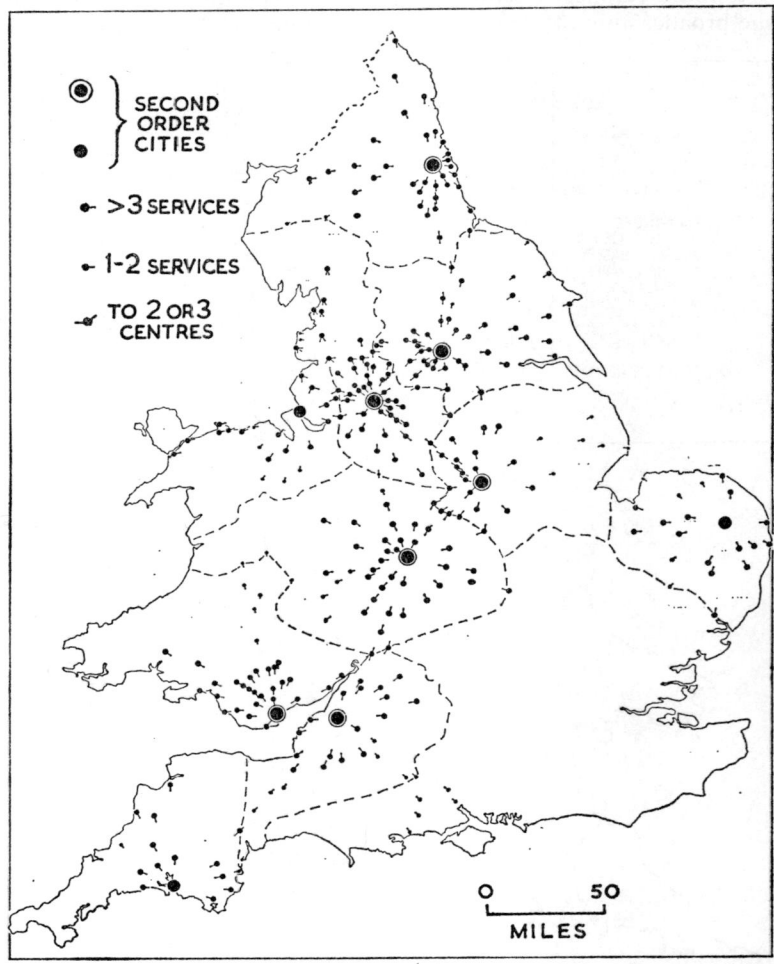

FIG. 85. England and Wales: Second-order Centres and their Hinterlands (after Carruthers).

The status of centres is based on journeys by public road transport. Second-order cities (as distinct from London in the first order) are in two grades, described as 2a and 2b. Journeys to 2a or 2b centres from other centres: 3 or more journeys daily, 1 or 2 journeys daily, or services on certain days only. Centres with services to more than one 2a or 2b centre have additional arrows in appropriate directions. Services from London are excluded. The hinterland boundaries of second-order cities are shown by dashed lines.

In a more recent paper Carruthers[1] examined further the provision of bus services and recognizes centres of four orders. The first of these is represented by London only. The second-order centres are Birmingham, Bristol, Cardiff, Leeds, Manchester, Newcastle, and Nottingham. Liverpool, Norwich, and Plymouth are also outstanding. Based on the frequency of journeys by public bus transport from particular places to these centres, their fields of accessibility were defined as shown on Fig. 85. These cities have extensive hinterlands in which they are more accessible than the other competitive provincial cities. Their hinterlands closely correspond with the major areas of service and organization as discussed on previous pages. Note, for example, the area of Leeds, that here includes Sheffield and north Lincolnshire, an area that occurs in many business and administrative organizations. Note also the large undisputed catchment area of London.

9. Commuting Areas

Data of the daily journey to work were made available in the Census of Workplaces for 1951, in which data are given for Urban Districts of all categories and for the Rural Districts. The same data were recorded in the 1921 census for the first time. Though the latter have been used for many years in town-planning studies, they have never been mapped systematically for the whole country. (The author prepared such a map many years ago and it is reported on, though not reproduced, in the first edition of this book.)[2] The data for 1951 have, however, been recently mapped and published, as is the case for several continental countries noted in the previous chapter. In a study of the Greater London area, Westergaard,[3] by using a formula described as the 'job ratio' (similar to many continental studies of this kind), is able to distinguish administrative areas on the basis of the ratio of total workers to total resident workers.

It has long been evident that the great majority of commuters indulge in an average of 30 to 45 minutes of travel time by rail or bus or car. This isochrone (i.e. line of equal time-distance to or from city centre) is normally about 10 miles from the centre. The total time from home to office or bench will cover about one hour. But many workers come from greater distances, and residential centres at much

---

[1] Ian Carruthers, 'A classification of service centres in England and Wales', *Geographical Journal*, Vol. CXXIII, September 1957, pp. 371–85.

[2] This work has finally been undertaken by R. Lawton in 'The Journey to Work in England and Wales: Forty Years of Change', 8 maps, *Tijdschrift v. Econ. en Soc. Geografie*, 1963, pp. 61–9.

[3] J. Westergaard, 'Journey to Work in the London Region', *Town Planning Review*, Vol. XXVIII, No. 1, 1957.

greater distances send in more workers to a city centre than to other competitors. But the spatially continuous area of contiguous communities that send out over one per cent. of their resident workers to

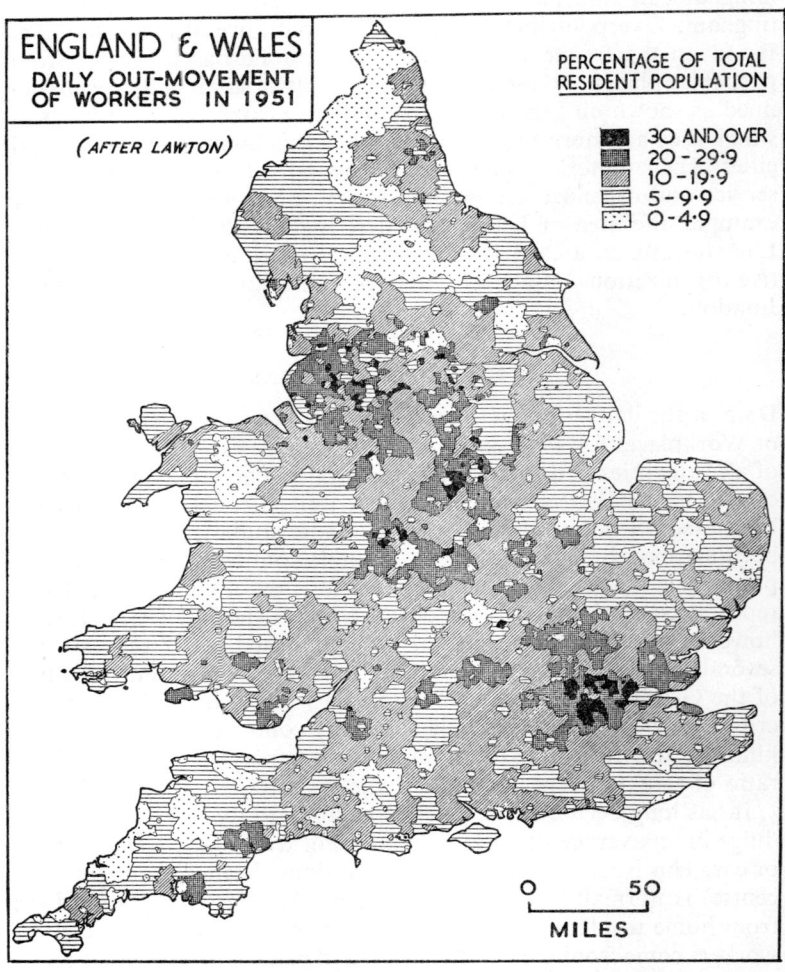

FIG. 86. England and Wales: Daily Out-movement of Workers in 1951 (after Lawton).

a central city gives a reasonable definition of the commuters catchment area. Such an area, in a big city like Manchester, has an outer limit of about 15 to 20 miles and an inner area of some 30 minutes' journey to town and a distance of some 10 miles. The Manchester core draws 75 per cent. of its in-commuters from the inner zone, and 18 per cent. from the outer zone. The remaining 7 per cent. come from

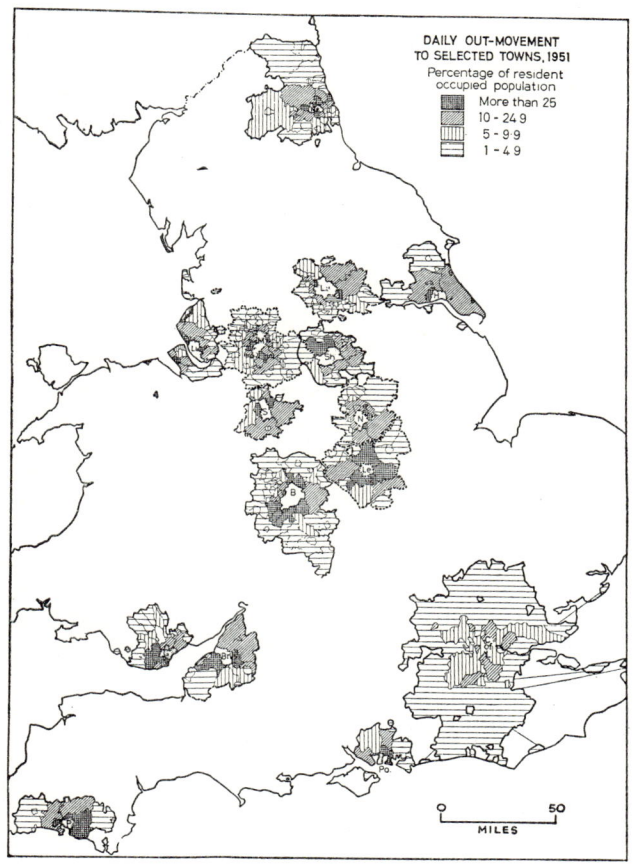

FIG. 87. England and Wales: Daily Out-movement to Selected Towns, 1951 (after Lawton).

widely scattered places. This pattern is general to all the major urban regions.

The general pattern of commuting in England and Wales is shown on Fig. 86.[1] This shows the daily out-movement of workers from administrative areas. Lawton concludes from this that 'any simple

[1] R. Lawton, 'The Daily Journey to Work in England and Wales', *Town Planning Review*, Vol. XXIX, No. 4, January 1959, pp. 241–59.

idea of movement towards a number of centres of attraction, weakening with the size of such centres or with distance from them, cannot be maintained'. The 'axial belt' from Lancashire to Greater London has everywhere a daily movement in excess of 10 per cent. of total resident population. The areas of the most intensive movement (over 30 per cent.) are mainly confined to the suburban districts close to the major centres, although areas with over 20 per cent. are particularly extensive, and obviously give the clue to the main areas of commuting.

Fig. 87, also prepared by Lawton, shows the daily movement of commuters outwards to selected major cities. It demonstrates clearly that the bulk of the commuting takes place to the provincial cities within a radius of about 20 miles. London, on the other hand, draws from a wider radius, reaching out to about 40 miles.

Lawton concludes in the following terms:

'The concentration of modern economic life on the hierarchy of urban centres has been demonstrated from another point of view. Even greater concentration of workplaces than of population in relatively few centres is implicit in the contrast between the few areas of large-scale in-movement and the many areas of large-scale out-movement. This is confirmed by the analysis of job ratios. The present patterns of movement are, however, very complex. They consist not merely of flow towards the industrial and commercial centres within large cities, but of counter-flow and cross-currents from older residential areas to new industrial sites on the periphery, and between adjacent towns. Where such towns are close together daily population movement is creating still closer links and this, together with new industrial development, is helping to foster incipient conurbations or to further extend the present conurbations.' [1]

10. STRUCTURE OF A CITY-REGION: METROPOLITAN LANCASHIRE [2]

The structure of a metropolitan region and the problems involved in its government are illustrated by the case of Manchester and its associated area in south-east Lancashire and north Cheshire. Our purpose here is twofold. The first aim is to seek appropriate criteria on the basis of which the unity and limits of a metropolitan complex can be defined. The second aim is to examine this area as an example of the complexity of the geographical pattern of government

---

[1] R. Lawton, *op. cit.*, p. 255.
[2] L. P. Green, *Provincial Metropolis: The Future of Local Government in Southeast Lancashire*, London, 1959.

which has grown up in the conurbations. It is generally agreed that this area needs a co-ordinated system of government divisions which shall be more realistically related to the problems of spatial organization—particularly of physical planning and government.

Fig. 88 shows the general extent of the built-up areas of south-east Lancashire and north Cheshire, and the boundary of the conurbation. The main divisions of the conurbation are shown in Fig. 88e. The phenomenal growth of the area as a seat of cotton textile industries in the mid-nineteenth century was accompanied by shocking housing conditions and chaotic sanitary arrangements throughout the area. There were no building byelaws and the area was swept by waves of cholera, smallpox, and typhus. There are still 13,500 houses in Manchester dating from before 1850. The second half of the century down to 1914 brought 'prosperity', with increasing specialization in textiles. The conurbation grew from one million in 1851 to 2·3 millions in 1911. Commercial cores began to develop in the middle of the century in the centre of the towns and civic buildings were erected. A spate of legislation sought to improve living conditions, but the great majority of the houses built before 1900 are obsolescent and ripe for demolition. Their occupance is reflected in high infant mortality and ill-health. The fragmentation of administrative boundaries also inherited from this period have long proved to be unsuitable for such services as transport, hospitals, higher education, sewerage, water, electricity, gas, police, and finance. The local areas have long been inadequate to cope with the needs of service and rehabilitation. For while in 1896 43 per cent. of the national tax revenue in the country was derived from local rates, by 1946 this had diminished to 8 per cent. and in 1956 central grants from the government reached £581 million as against only £91 million from local rates. Since 1914 the area has ceased to expand. It was badly hit by the years of depression. Many towns are losing people. New towns were built in outlying areas, especially to the south, based on the new transport facilities afforded by rail, bus, and telephone. In 1945 the city of Manchester still had 68,000 houses unfit to live in although they housed over 200,000 people. In the oldest areas in the centre of Manchester and Salford and their neighbours 60 to 75 per cent. of all houses lack a fixed bath and figures in the northern crescent of towns are not much less (45 to 60 per cent.).

What are the factors of cohesion in this area? The primary criterion is the daily journey to work. Fig. 88b shows the percentage of resident workers employed in the core of the conurbation—its industrial and commercial core (Manchester, Salford, Stockport, Stretford, and Urmston). The wider area may be called Metropolitan Lancashire. An inner area has 16·8 per cent. and over of its resident workers

THE CITY-REGION

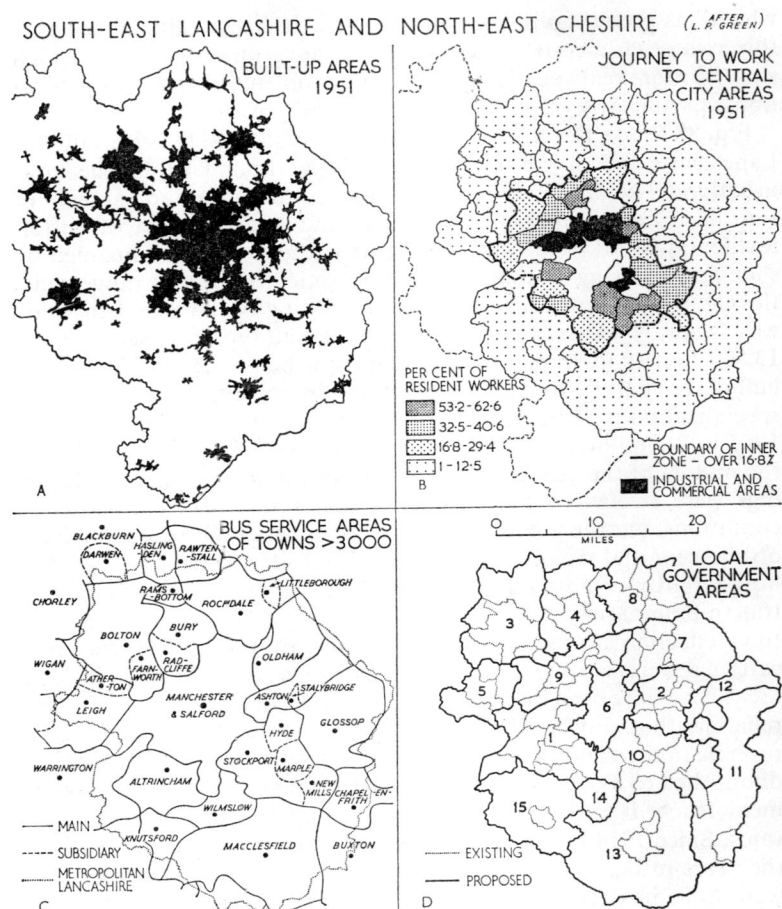

FIG. 88a. South-east Lancashire and North-east Cheshire: Built-up areas in 1951 (after L. P. Green).

FIG. 88b. Journey to Work in Manchester, Salford, Stockport, Stretford, and Urmston, 1951, for Local Authority Areas (after L. P. Green).

FIG. 88c. South-east Lancashire and North-east Cheshire: Bus Service Areas of towns with Populations of 3,000 and over in 1946–47 (after L. P. Green).

This is based on the Ordnance Survey Local Accessibility Map, 1955. 1. Main Service Areas. 2. Subsidiary Service Areas. 3. Metropolitan Lancashire.

FIG. 88d. Metropolitan Lancashire: Proposed Two-tier Reform of Local Government Areas (after L. P. Green).

1. Existing Local Authorities. 2. Proposed Local Authorities.

employed in the core area; and from this area the core drew 71 per cent. of its workers. The outer limits of the continuous catchment area are approached about 15 to 20 miles from the centre of Manchester and 45 minutes by train. This is a wide transition zone of towns and villages from which in general at least 25 workers travel daily to work in the centre. Outlying towns like Wigan and Warrington are separate areas and send few people to Manchester. Bolton,

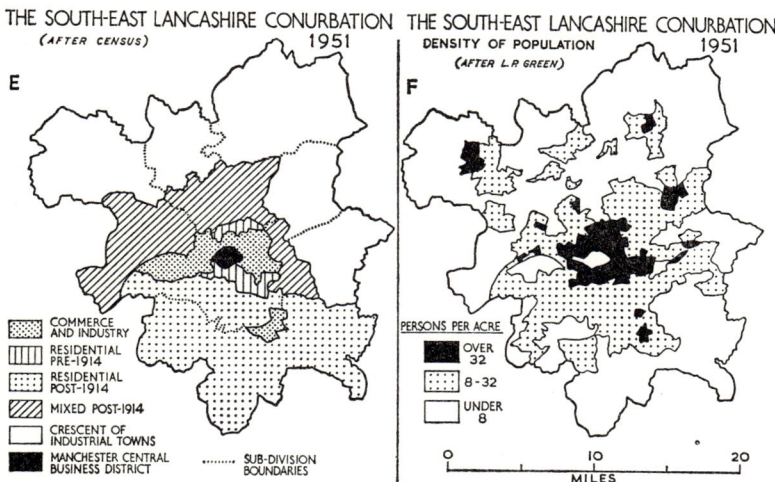

FIG. 88e. The South-east Lancashire Conurbation, 1951 (after the Census).

FIG. 88f. The South-east Lancashire Conurbation: Density of Population, 1951 (after L. P. Green).

on the other hand, has only 2·2 per cent. of its workers employed in the Manchester area, but they make a total of nearly 2,000 per day.

A second criterion of cohesion is the range of the journey to market and entertainment. These areas may be generally defined in terms of the accessibility by bus of the chief service centres. The hinterland on Fig. 88c show the areas more accessible to one centre than to the other neighbouring towns.

The circulation of newspapers has already been emphasized as an important indication of social relations, shopping habits, and entertainment. On the basis of the news advertisements, the newspaper circulation areas were defined. There are eighteen service areas in the inner metropolitan zone. These boundaries support the definition of both the inner and outer zones of metropolitan Lancashire.

It is on the basis of these criteria of local 'community of interest' that Green has submitted a proposal for the reorganization of the local government areas of south-east Lancashire. His suggestion of a two-tier arrangement is shown on Fig. 88*d*. This is one of a number of proposals that have been put forward. A solution of this problem, that is of paramount importance in each of the conurbations, is at present the task of the Local Government Commission whose work will be referred to in a later chapter.

Note: see postscript to Chapter 16.

PART IV

Regionalism and the City-Region

Chapter 14

THE CASE FOR THE REGION

So far we have discussed the role of nucleated settlements—village, town, and city—as regional centres. We now come to consider the major social groupings within the State and the various ways in which these find expression. The metropolitan or city-region is the most potent single force in the formation of these modern groupings, but other conditions—historic, cultural, and economic—also contribute to their characterization. Our concern is not with the constitutional intricacies of the regional movement, but with the characteristics of the major social groupings inherent in society, for it is upon these that any reorganization of new political divisions must be based. After a general discussion of Regionalism we shall pass to a brief review of its particular aspects in France, England and Wales, Germany, and the United States.

1. THE REGION AS AN INTERMEDIATE AREA BETWEEN LOCAL UNIT AND STATE

The prominence accorded by the public to the idea of the Region is the spontaneous expression of an urgent need in the life and organization of modern society. The great mobility and the complex structure of modern society in Europe and America have meant that new areas of organization are needed for all aspects of national life, and that existing local government areas have been outmoded by wider areal organizations, and act as deterrents to the efficient functioning of public services. The idea of the Region has also developed in relation to the movement for the decentralization of authority from the central national government to a limited number of provinces, which would relieve the central government of its too onerous responsibilities, foster the development of local responsibility in the truest democratic tradition, and foster provincial and regional differences of tradition and culture. Regions, in the sense of more or less arbitrary groups of contiguous local government authorities, have been established since 1918 in all the countries with which we are concerned, as a necessary extension of the planning of individual towns. This is probably the widest use of the term Regional Planning. There is also a demand for the delimitation of major homogeneous divisions of the State, to serve as a framework for the long-term development of national resources, and for physical and economic planning. This is the type of region which seems to be the ultimate goal of Regional Planning as the counterpart of National Planning. It figured prominently in Germany and the United States and has become of increasing significance in the west European countries since the war. The problem is to demarcate a few areas throughout a country larger than the existing political divisions. For many purposes, the *County* in Britain, the *Land* in Germany, the *Département* in France and the *State* in the United States are, in each case, either too small or too unrelated to the practical needs of modern life to serve as effective units for large-scale planning on a nation-wide scale.

2. Cultural and Political Regionalism

The problem of Regionalism in its broadest European aspect was admirably summed up by Patrick Geddes and Victor Branford[1] at the close of World War I:

'The industry and the politics of the nineteenth century progressed alike through extension and unification. Larger industries, further reaching and swifter transports, wider markets, became naturally also associated over greater areas, and these into larger unities of administration and government. Railways and telegraphs, steam-routes and cables at once enlarged industrial towns to world markets, and aggrandized their metropolitan cities into imperial capitals. Practical life and political endeavour were thus at one; hence the expansion of England; the centralization of France, the American War of Union, the unification of Germany, and even of Italy, are now seen as kindred processes.

'Exceptions to these processes, even dissents from them, were noticeable. But these were simply explained, in terms of limitation or backwardness, e.g. geographical for Switzerland, linguistic for Hungary, sentimental for Alsace and Lorraine, legendary for Ireland, and so on; and thus as so many survivals, destined to disappear with progress or education, or at worst as petty self-assertions, to be repressed with such firmness as need be. The sun of Progress

[1] Editors' Introduction to C. B. Fawcett's *The Provinces of England: A Study of Some Geographical Aspects of Devolution*, London, 1919.

THE CASE FOR THE REGION

shone essentially from the ever-growing capitals over their extending empires, and illuminated the unification of their nationalities, under due predominance of their metropolitan types.

'Yet, despite Vienna and Austria, Hungary achieved her equality in Empire; and thus diffused a more European influence and example than she knew. The separation of Norway from Sweden was a more peaceful case of this process, albeit a more extreme one: and now after the war, we see not only the conversion of the small nations, but the rise of new ones—witness the complete break up of Austria into its units, the reunion of Poland, the disintegration of "all the Russias", and the growing detachment of German States from Berlin and Prussia. The decentralization of "all the Spains" from Madrid is also under discussion; and, most significant of all, it is from France, though the earliest and most fully centralized of all countries, and most unanimous of all throughout the war, that we have longest been receiving alike the best descriptions of her component regions and the most definite projects of legislation towards their renewal. "Regionalism" was indeed a French word; and this not merely in geography, but also in politics, and long before the war. From Brittany to Provence its studies and policy have long been preparing; and now still more definitely with the return of Alsace and Lorraine. The United Provinces of France are thus in the remaking.

'For most of the older generation, whether industrial and liberal, or of imperialist and financial outlooks, this newer movement has seemed reactionary or perverse, and of course not always without cause. Yet as students of social life and its processes we are learning to recognize that every society is a complex web, with its relatively fixed geographical and historic conditions, its regional warp, as the very basis of its economic and political woof. Economics is thus fundamentally regional, since sources of food, materials, and power, conditions of transport and more, are of Nature's making, which we utilize more than we modify. Hence since politics cannot but follow economic lines, it has to become inter-regional as well; not simply super-regional—i.e. uni-regional, if not positively irregional—as metropolitan bureaucracies are increasingly felt by their external provinces to be. So far as the war settlement and the League of Nations are recognizing these conditions and dual requirements, the regional and the general, their work may thus be effective, and become stable; or conversely.

'Hence this new movement towards regionalism, and all over Europe, despite the impatiences, or even excesses, with which it may be chargeable, is by no means the mere mental disorder or material revolt so alarming to the metropolitan view-point; since its inmost purpose is not the disruption of larger ties, so far as vital ones, but the legitimate development of local life; which has been at best but insufficiently fostered, if not positively repressed, from distant centres substantially unacquainted with it. As the first claims of this regional life are granted, inter-regionalism cannot be advanced anew: hence the most discerning, and therefore the most intensive regionalists of today are also among the most appreciative of truly comprehensive politics such as the League of Nations. Though the embers and sparks which actually kindled the war were largely from among the Balkan people, in their long ill-centralized and still unadjusted regions, it is the well-adjusted cantons of Switzerland, with their different races, languages, and religions, their varied yet mutualized sympathies and interests accordingly, and the United Provinces of Holland, of Belgium, the Scandinavian peoples, and of course the United States, which are leading the Great Powers into that League of which they have each so long been samples and examples, in their various ways.

'So indeed it is for the British Empire, for which the crude separatism of one generation, and the crude centralization attempted by the next, have in ours been reconciled through wise and large measures of devolution; and with increasing moral solidarity accordingly, as the war has so vividly shown. Why not then the like in our own islands? Ireland's predominant demand is not their only difficulty, nor yet Ulster's more exasperated regionalism. Wales, for matters of church, education, etc., Scotland too for her own concerns, and also north England, the Midlands, and more, are all claiming more understanding, and affirming more urgency, for their own affairs, than an overworked central government can give them.

'Hence the need of regional geography; and for this survey, this necessary description and diagnosis before treatment, England offers one of the best fields, the more so since undivided in language or sentiment. . . .'

The regional movement began in France and has assumed prominence more recently in Britain, Germany, and the United States. In France, regionalism had an early and energetic start as a means of offsetting the excessive centralization of affairs in Paris and giving greater scope to the development of regional culture and representative self-government. Numerous schemes have been put forward during the past fifty years for the division of France into regions, and many treatises written on the theory of regionalism and the practical form it should take. Many proposals have been made for the erection of new Regions to displace the *départements* as political units, and although they came to nothing, many *ad hoc* divisions have long been in use. It was not until the late fifties (1955), however, that the first steps towards a nation-wide system of regional planning were initiated. In Britain, interest in the question was active immediately after 1918. The need for national planning during and after World War II stimulated public and government interest in the whole question. Big changes have been made in the fifties, but the urgent problem of reorganizing local government areas is still under discussion. In the United States the problem has been tackled by geographers, sociologists, and economists. Marketing areas, newspaper circulation areas, and zones of influence of metropolitan cities, have been the subject of careful investigations, and the regional treatment of planning and the development of resources in the United States were examined under the auspices of the National Resources Committee, established in 1935.

Since World War II, the phenomenal expansion of cities and the complexity of their government have given special focus to the problem. The reorganization of the political framework of Germany has been a matter of continuing concern since the end of World War I. Exhaustive unofficial and public enquiries have been made of this matter, but it still awaits solution by the central government. Spain, Italy, and Yugoslavia have their problems of regional devolution, and the U.S.S.R. has effected a revolutionary reorganization of its component divisions. In all these cases the problem is to establish new political units which will harmonize with the existing geographical structure and the need of society for efficient government and organization.

3. REGIONAL TOWN PLANNING

In the broadest terms, compulsory town planning on a nation-wide scale did not appear until the beginning of this century. The co-operation of contiguous neighbouring public authorities for the investigation of joint problems began in the years following the 1914–18 war. Such inter-town, or, as they are generally called, 'regional' groupings, normally have no legal status; they exist to study problems of planning and to make proposals; action depends upon the consent of all constituent authorities. From this point of view,

'a region may be imperfectly described as a rural or urban or rural–urban area having common needs and interests, linking up its economic and social life, and forming a unit, with physical conditions and boundaries appropriate for the purpose of planning its future developments'.[1]

[1] Thomas Adams at the International Town Planning Conference, Amsterdam, 1924, *Proceedings*, Part I, p. 51. See also 'The Preliminary Survey of the Region, by P. Abercrombie in the same volume.

'It is not a community structure in the sense of being an administrative unit, such as a county or borough. It is a composite of different municipal units in juxtaposition to each other and having common or overlapping problems relating to their economic life, means of circulation, and land uses.'[1]

The fact that bodies of this kind in the past have only had *advisory* functions, and no legal executive authority, needs the strongest emphasis. Regional planning in the strict sense has now come to mean the organization of an area of operation large enough in extent to permit long-term designs for the distribution of population and the uses of the land and the organization of services and recreation. The authorities in control of such areas must have the legal power not only to prepare plans but also to put them into effect. This would mean the coalescence of contiguous local government units, and the surrender to such new authorities of some, if not all, of their rights and responsibilities. In a sense, the term regional planning has been used in practice in the past as a convenient label, for the simple reason that such groupings do not exist. The great obstacle in establishing them in all countries is to decide on what principles they should be based and their boundaries defined, and to overcome the resistance of the local authorities.

Local government authorities are jealous of their powers, and in spite of the obvious difficulties in the field of planning, they seek to find local solutions through compromise rather than by the annexation of territory by certain large units at their expense. This problem is particularly acute in Great Britain, especially as the very business of changing local government boundaries is a long and complicated procedure. The problem of the conurbations and their outmoded local government divisions is common knowledge. On the Continent, the expansion of the city administrative area has been a quicker process. There are cases where large cities have expanded their administrative limits well beyond their present built-up areas to embrace the whole of their 'potential settlement areas', and such cities are able to enforce throughout their administrative area town-planning measures which regional planning authorities cannot do. Thus, Amsterdam, Rome, Hamburg, and Cologne have their plans. A further variation is the particular case of special planning powers being given to a large region round a city. This was enacted by law for the Paris Region in 1932 to cover an area within a radius of thirty-five kilometres of the city, modified in 1941 to include the whole of the *départements* of Seine-et-Oise, Seine-et-Marne, and five cantons of Oise. In the United States, cities expand rarely by annexation,

[1] Thomas Adams, *Recent Advances in Town Planning*, 1932, p. 114.

and federation of contiguous authorities (achieved with remarkable success in Toronto) is a rarity. There are often *ad hoc* associations of authorities, but there is essentially a welter of tiny and interlocking districts in all the big urban areas.

Regional town planning units, that is, groups of contiguous municipalities, have the merit of being larger units for the purpose of planning than the town, which is too small independently to carry out the very functions with which it has been legally endowed. But a larger area defined in this way is often no more a unit than the single local government unit. This is evident from the extent of such 'town-planning regions' in the United States, Great Britain, and Germany, for they frequently cut across areas that are closely interdependent and are, indeed, in themselves closely tied up with other areas contiguous to them. In other words, a programme for joint town-planning areas automatically involves a further consideration of planning on a nation-wide scale, for which there is need for a framework of definite provinces which should incorporate several regional town-planning units. The case of north-west Germany illustrates this point.

The Ruhr Regional Planning Federation is the outstanding example of a regional planning *authority*. It was established in 1921 with legal powers to control matters of traffic, housing, open spaces, and light-railways traffic. The area covers the whole of the Ruhr east as far as Hamm, and west of the Rhine as far as the Dutch frontier, an area of 4,600 sq. km. with a population of over five and a half millions. The rapid growth of this area as the greatest coalfield in Europe and the seat of four-fifths of Germany's coal and pig-iron production, the concentration in it of through east–west railways, the complex pattern of its local communications, the spread of its great cities, the need for adequate houses and open spaces, and the need for an adequate water supply, all raised problems demanding the supervision and guidance of a central authority. But though a unit in these senses since 1921, it is quite impossible for the Ruhr Authority to handle its problems of economic development, land planning and the rest, without reference to the areas around it. The new brown-coal industrial area south-west of Cologne, the new heavy industries concentrated on the Rhine, the close economic interrelations between Cologne, Düsseldorf, and the Ruhr, bind this whole area into one economic unit that needs to be planned as a whole. The range of these associations reaches further, for not only is north-west Germany closely allied with the rest of West Germany, and especially the Rhinelands, it also has strong and old ties with kindred industrial areas in Holland and Belgium, and here too north-west Germany finds access to foreign markets through the ports of the Low

Countries. The regional net reaches across frontiers to acquire an international significance.

This example illustrates very clearly the need for the planning of land and resources in very densely peopled areas, with a close network of settlements, routes, open spaces, and interspersed farm land. It is also obvious that such areas should be linked in some way with the areas around them with which they are closely related economically, socially, and historically. Planning on such a scale demands national or State supervision of some kind with a framework of provinces covering the whole country, an organization for collaboration, a programme and technique of research, and means of carrying proposals into effect. The mention of provinces on this scale brings us face to face with a wider issue, namely, the case for the reorganization of major administrative units, for the decentralization of administration, and for the development of a more lively and responsible system of local government.

4. Practical or *Ad Hoc* Regions

Britain, France, Germany, and the United States are divided into districts for a great variety of purposes—for the collection of statistical data, for administration by departments of State, for the organization of numerous trades and professions, for the planning of natural resources, and for military purposes. These districts, defined as a rule quite independently of each other, vary greatly according to their purpose. Many are based on the existing political divisions; others adopt quite new boundaries; some are simply determined by the amount of business which a single office staff can conveniently handle; others hinge on the distribution of one or more occupations, on questions of accessibility, or distribution of population. Each country is divided into districts by numerous private concerns which have regional offices, depots, or warehouses, to facilitate nation-wide organization and service. This procedure is adopted by State departments, by trade and professional organizations, and by business concerns dealing in consumers' goods so as to ensure effective and regular contact with all retail dealers, and by nation-wide health services and water and electricity supply. Practically every aspect of business, commerce, and administration is now 'regionalized' in this sense, with the services concentrated in the principal cities. It should also be noted that while these *ad hoc* regions differ widely, often necessarily so, from each other, many show a remarkable similarity in their geographical extent, especially around the great cities. They are built in large measure on existing administrative units which are often anachronisms. Regions have been established for such special purposes as medical services, education, and industrial and social organizations, each with a set of units and authorities suited to its particular problems.

5. Problems of Regional Development

The problems falling within the purview of the national planning of resources were considered by an American writer in 1936, with particular reference to the United States, to embrace such matters as land use, population, resettlement, land improvement, water use—including drainage, irrigation, and navigation—transport, reafforestation, preservation and development of wild life and fisheries, use and conservation of power resources, industrial development (including mining), and social and economic improvement. The American nation, it was argued, is too large to be dealt with as a unit for these purposes. Moreover, there are great differences of sentiment and attitude in different parts of the country.

'One of the major concerns of the planner becomes, therefore, a search for a sphere of jurisdiction—a unit of area which will provide both reasonable physical and economic homogeneity, and approximate unity of public opinion. Regional planning centres should be established in those areas where there is a major clustering of related resources coincident with a marked regional consciousness among the inhabitants.' [1]

Problems of planning would be centralized and co-ordinated from regional headquarters, but 'regions' for specific purposes would vary considerably. The outstanding instance of the planned development of an area is the Tennessee Valley Authority, and it still serves as a model for large-scale planning in the other parts of the world.

In the post-war years, the problems of regionalism, in their varied aspects, have continued to occupy a central position in the affairs of States in all parts of the world. There has been a phenomenal growth of new nation-states in territories that were formerly colonial possessions in Africa and southern Asia. The internal organization of these new States has often involved the delimitation of new internal divisions on a federal basis, whereby differences of ethnic composition, traditions, aspirations, and economies, have found recognition in new systems of regional government. This is true for example of India, Nigeria, and, more recently, of Kenya.

Questions of *internal* territorial organization, of the simplification

[1] G. T. Renner, in *Our Natural Resources and their Conservation*, edited by A. E. Parkins and J. B. Whitaker, New York, 1936.

and co-ordination of areas of government, as well as the establishment of regional self-government, are continuing and mounting problems of the occidental nations. There has, however, been a shift in emphasis in the approach to such problems. This is associated, above all else, with the increasing concern of governments, both within the States of the Industrial Society, and among lesser developed countries, with the assessment and development of natural resources and the general improvement of their social and economic conditions. We have not found among the academics in recent years so much preoccupation with the theoretical definition of new multi-purpose regions as before the war. It is generally realized now, as stated above, that areas must be defined for specific purposes. Thus, the matter of reorganizing the chaotic multiplicity of administrative units in the sprawling metropolitan cities is still unsolved. Much thought and study have been given to this problem; the difficulty is to get action. The phenomenal expansion of urban areas, far beyond their pre-war limits, accentuates the anachronism of small and independent local government units, and here, as in international affairs, ways must be found of retaining what is appropriate in local government, but rising to the organization of larger integrated administrative units.

Further, it has become apparent in recent years that social, economic, and physical conditions are localized in different sections of a country (and they are not always coincident), and that their regional variants call for special treatment. These variations prohibit the use of a blanket legislation in all parts of a country, simply because conditions and problems vary from one part of the country to another. The more the State becomes involved in economic and social welfare, the more must it pay attention to these differences, both in the advanced countries as well as in the underdeveloped countries. Pockets of unemployment, for example, must be located before the jobless can be given jobs accessible to their homes. The advent of the Common Market in western Europe is exposing certain weak industrial areas to foreign competition. Examples are the old-established (and old-fashioned) little industrial areas near tiny coalfields on the periphery of the Central Plateau of France that face the competition of their mightier competitors in northern France and Germany. These areas are being studied in order to detect new possibilities of industrial employment and the places in which new factories may be located. Backward areas, like Brittany or south Italy, need to have more jobs, but the conditions of employment vary generally from place to place in each of these large areas. Large numbers of surplus farm labourers need to be given industrial jobs in local towns to stop their inevitable drift into the big cities (a shift that is going to increase in magnitude in the coming decades). In a word, in both the United States and in western Europe (and especially on the Continent) attention has turned increasingly in the fifties to the study of problems of areal or regional economic development, based upon studies of the distinctive existing conditions of areas. Such studies seek to measure and localize the variants of the standard of living of the people and their physical environment (including the man-made infrastructure) in order to improve conditions—consolidate tiny strips of farm land, enlarge farm-holdings, provide surplus agricultural workers with new jobs, provide homes, public utilities, roads, etc. Such changes are inevitably associated with the growth of urbanization. Since the war, the major cities have grown rapidly and urbanized areas have expanded. One of the aims of areal development, no matter how small its achievements, has been to check this trend and canalize growth to lesser cities that are widely distributed over the countryside, and to try to find principles of lay-out on desirable economic and social principles to replace suburban sprawl, and to work out principles of 'recentralization' of urban activities.

Thus, for these varied reasons, research since 1945 has been directed to the analysis and locale of social and economic conditions, of natural resources, and of human populations—since these must serve as the datum line for plans of economic development and social welfare. Social scientists are devising new techniques and applying their expertise to this end, as is abundantly evident in the United States, in France, in Germany, in the Low Countries. Indeed, the more these countries become involved in the 'welfare' of their people, the more must they call on the expertise of the diagnostic and regional expert. Areal physical planning, in particular, must be concerned with the theory of location of places and their relations with each other—in other words, with the principles of regionalization.

A Commission of the European Economic Community has recently made a report on the question of regional delimitation of their six countries for purposes of economic and social development. They defined a region from this standpoint as

'a certain number of territorial units united by complementary and strongly interrelated economic activities, gravitating around urban centres in which are localized important economic activities, in particular functions of decision. Further, these centres enjoy almost always a very important intellectual and cultural role. These agglomerations have thus an essential importance for the identification of a territorial unity the limits of which, in the first approximation, correspond to those of the areas of influence of its principal agglomerations.'

The concept of such a 'socio-economic region' is clear, the limits are not. 'As regards the placing of boundaries, there is a certain indeterminateness between contiguous regions, so that their limits may be defined with a certain liberty of judgment.' In defining the regions in the Community a start was made with the existing divisions as a basis—the 22 planning regions of France, the administrative *regioni* in Italy, and 23 groups of *Kreise* (24 with Berlin) in Germany. These were grouped again into major regions—'grandes régions socio-économiques'. In Germany the grouping of 8 regions respected the boundaries of the *Länder*. France has 9 major regions, Italy 10. The Netherlands is divided into two major regions (east and west) while Belgium and Luxemburg each are treated as one. These are general divisions of convenience. We need much more empirical and theoretical analysis of the geographic patterns on which they are allegedly based.

Chapter 15

REGIONALISM IN FRANCE

1. THE REGIONAL MOVEMENT

The regional movement was born and cradled in France. During the nineteenth century the country suffered from the excessive concentration of both national and provincial affairs in the national capital, and that was the main cause of the growth of the regional movement. Many schemes were put forward for the creation of new political divisions in place of the *départements*, including those of Auguste Comte, the philosopher, and Frédéric Le Play, the sociologist. In 1898 the *Union Régionaliste Bretonne* was founded, and in 1900 the *Fédération Régionaliste Française* came into being with the objects of affording a link between all advocates of regionalism and of providing for the propaganda and defence of regional ideas and interests. Its organ was *L'Action Régionaliste* and its chief exponent M. Charles-Brun.[1]

This movement aims at the decentralization of administrative, economic, and social activities from the capital, and the revival and free development of regional cultures, activities, interests, and aspirations. The excessive centralization of affairs in Paris failed to recognize that within the State there exist such distinct regions, whose requirements cannot be satisfied by uniform treatment from a national centre, detached, ignorant, and unsympathetic, and too burdened with its manifold duties of State and Empire to devote adequate attention to vital questions of high regional priority and significance. The movement aimed ultimately, as one of its main objectives, at the creation in place of the *départements* of entirely new provinces with a large measure of democratic self-government. The enthusiasm with which the problem was tackled is evident from the many schemes of regions and outlines for the machinery of regional government which appeared in the years immediately preceding the 1914–18 war.

The regional movement was further fostered by the emergency of

[1] J. Charles-Brun, *Le Régionalisme*, Bloud, Paris, 1911.

the 1914–18 war. The idea was discussed in the Chamber, the Institute, the Academy of Moral and Political Sciences, and the Faculty of Law at Paris. However, proposals for the effective establishment of political regionalism by creating entirely new major regions and abolishing the *départements* have all failed. Jean Hennessy put a proposal before the Chamber on 29 April 1915 which would have suppressed the *départements* and established elected regional assemblies with a large measure of administrative and legislative decentralization. Similar abortive proposals were made by Etienne Rognon in 1916 (proposing thirty-four regions), Victor Peytral and Henri Roy in 1917, and M. Bellet in 1923 (proposing twenty-eight regions). Though in the strict sense political regionalism was not realized, many aspects of political life and organization have, in fact, since been regionalized.

The chief of these are the regions of the Chambers of Commerce.[1] On July 22 1915, M. Jean Hennessy, with the aim of 'completing military mobilization by economic mobilization', invited the government 'not to lose sight of the fact that in a country composed geographically as ours, the component regions differ from each other', and proposed that there should be a technical council on economic matters in each existing military region (as organized in 1914). The decree of 25 October created this organization, the economic council[2] in each military region being charged with 'investigation of measures to maintain and develop the agricultural, industrial, and commercial activity of the region, notably by the rational employment of civilian and military man-power and the use of local resources'. There were twenty of these military regions, but they did not serve effectively as economic units. For this reason Hennessy proposed in 1916 that the committee would render more useful service if the economic units centred in the great cities, as suggested by Vidal de la Blache (see below), were adopted as their spheres of activity instead of the military regions. This proposal was not immediately adopted, but in the spring of 1917 M. Clementel, as Minister of Commerce and Industry, undertook an investigation of the economic regions of France under the direction of Fighiera and Hauser. The decree of 5 April 1919 permitted the organization of 136 Chambers of Commerce into seventeen economic regional groups—increased later to twenty. These regions are today of fundamental importance in the organization of the economic life of France, their committees functioning as intermediaries between the central government and the region they represent. The extent of these regions as fixed in 1939

---

[1] See F. Prevet, *Le Régionalisme Économique: Conception et Réalisation*, Paris, 1929.

[2] *Comité Consultatif d'Action Économique.*

is given on Fig. 89. Their activities cover such important matters as the development of port facilities, navigation, industrial development, afforestation, irrigation, and general economic surveys.

By 1939 practical regionalism was an established fact in the life of France. There is a regional system for the administration of justice, for education, for military organization, and for the associations of

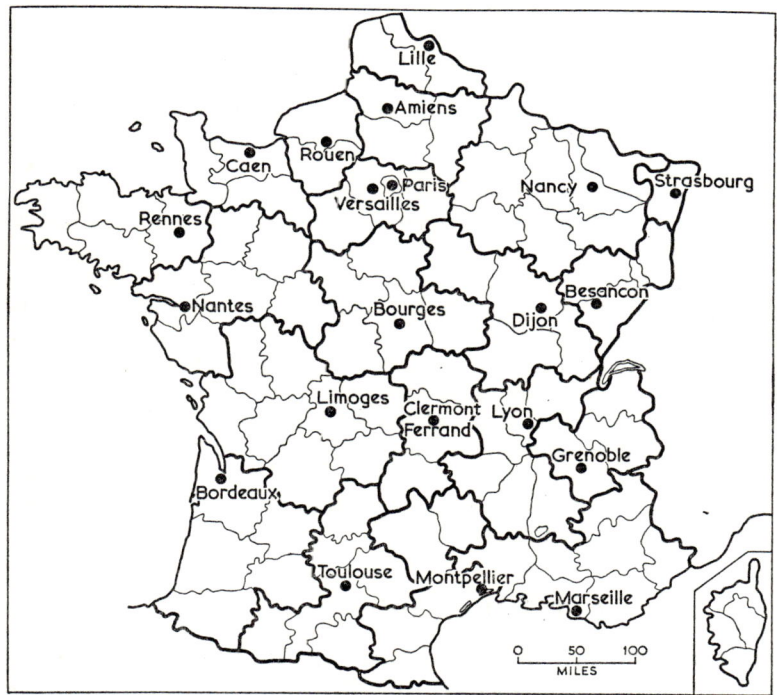

FIG. 89. France: Economic Regions (after Coppolani).
These are the areas of associations of the Chambers of Commerce.

the Chambers of Commerce, to name but the most important purposes. 'Spontaneous regionalism' had developed in the cultural activities of the provinces. It also was apparent in the organization of the activities of the country around the cities which, with their roots in the distant past, have emerged in the last hundred years as outstanding cultural and economic centres of metropolitan character.

Under the Vichy Government emergency regions were established. Pétain encouraged the regionalist idea and sponsored official investigations into the administrative reorganization of France on the basis of new provinces made up of groups of *départements*. Fourteen industrial regions were organized for supervision by the Inspectors-General of Production. In 1941 Pétain decreed the formation of eighteen emergency regions under Prefects who had special administrative, economic, and juridical powers. The *Comités d'Organisation Professionnelles* have different *ad hoc* regional divisions to suit the needs of particular industrial occupations. The *Charte de Travail*, effected in 1941 for the settlement of disputes between employer and employee and of personal problems of the latter, provided for the groupings of occupations into syndicates, each group having its own committee (*Comité Social*), with regional unions of the syndicates serving as the link between the *Comité Social* and the Federations at the centre.

Regionalism was defined by the Académie Française in 1934, as 'une tendance à favoriser tout en maintenant intacte l'unité nationale, le développement particulier autonome des régions et à en conserver les mœurs, les coûtumes, les traditions historiques'. This definition, writes Barathon[1] in a pamphlet dedicated to Marshal Pétain, is inadequate, for regionalism is now a doctrine rather than a tendency. It aims not at favouring the development of regions but at creating or reviving them, and has more than the sentimental idea of merely conserving traditions. It is defined by this writer as 'une doctrine politique dont le but est d'instituer, au sein de la nation, des groupements régionaux autonomes dotés d'une vue propre'. In this sense, regionalism should be clearly distinguished from federalism and from administrative decentralization.

2. The Historical Provinces[2]

Paris has dominated the life of France since the Revolution to such a degree that the State has been referred to as a brain-centre with atrophied limbs, and, more recently, J. F. Gravier has written of 'Paris and the French desert'.[3] It is also true however that France, more than any other country, reveals with the greatest clarity the arrangement of town and countryside in small units of human life and organization with a popular consciousness of that unity. This applies both to the very small human units called *pays* and to the larger pre-1789 units called *provinces*. These are alike in the sense

[1] Claude Barathon, *Le Régionalisme d'hier et de demain*, Les Œuvres Françaises, Paris, 1942.

[2] See Jean Brunhes, *Géographie Humaine de la France*, in G. Hanotaux's *Histoire de la Nation Française*, Tome I, Vol. I, 1920, pp. 337–410.

[3] J. F. Gravier, *Paris et le Désert Français*, Flammarion, Paris, 1947, revised 1958, 314 pp.

that they have been for centuries units of social life and their names are ancient in origin and popular in their usage.

The initial divisions of France were those of the Gallic tribal groups (French *nations*), and the Roman *civitates* (French *cités*) which often broadly corresponded in extent with the areas of the Gallic tribal groups. The ecclesiastical dioceses followed broadly the outline of the *civitates* and in the great majority of cases the bishoprics were established in the Roman *castra*, the capital of the *civitates*. Then the Frankish period witnessed the formation of the medieval territorial pattern. The *civitas* was broken up into two or more smaller parts called *pagi* (French *pays*), though some retained the outline of the *civitas*. The medieval unit of the *comté* broadly corresponded with the smaller *pagus* or *pays* and had its capital in the central town.

Under the *ancien régime* France was divided into ecclesiastical, judicial, financial, military, and administrative divisions. The judicial divisions were the *bailliages*, of which there were about 250. For financial matters there were the *pays d'état* and the *pays d'élections*. In the former there were provincial assemblies for voting taxation, while in the latter, covering three-quarters of the area of the country, the representative of the king ruled as a virtual viceroy. The *gouvernements* were military districts for the levying of troops under the supervision of a Lieutenant-General. The *généralités* were by far the most important divisions of the *ancien régime*. They began in the sixteenth century as representations of the authority of the king for the survey of justice, finance, and general administration. In 1523 there were ten of them, including Normandy, Languedoc, Picardy, Burgundy, Provence, Guyenne, Dauphiné, Brittany. Under Louis XIV, the number was increased to twenty-one and in 1789 there were thirty-four. Some of these divisions in 1789 embraced several provinces, and several were sometimes embraced in one province, as in the case of Normandy, which was divided into the *généralités* of Rouen and Caen. The Intendant, who was the real administrator of the realm, presided over the *Parlement* and controlled the legal and financial administration. It was said in the days of Colbert that 'L'intendant c'est le roi dans la province'. *Parlements* were held in the *pays d'état* at Rennes (Brittany), Rouen (Normandy), Arras, Douai, Metz, Nancy (Lorraine), Dijon (Burgundy), Besançon (Franche Comté), Grenoble (Dauphiné), Aix (Provence), Toulouse (Languedoc), Perpignan (Roussillon), Pau (Bearn), and Bordeaux. Each of these was also the seat of its *gouvernement* and *généralité*. Cities that were the seats of both a *gouvernement* and a *généralité* were as follows: Tours, Orléans, Lille, Amiens, Strasbourg, Lyon, La Rochelle, Moulins, Bourges, Poitiers. Cities that were seats of either one or the other but not of both were as follows: Boulogne, Angers, Troyes, Chalons, Toul, Valenciennes, Nevers, Saintes, Guéret, Riom, Limoges, Trévoux, Soissons, Alençon, Montpellier, Auch, and Montauban.

The names of the *pays* and *provinces* have persisted to this day. They are attached to a particular part of the country with a distinct human individuality. The same name has been given to various political divisions of the country that roughly correspond with the same area. Some of the provinces have their origin in the Roman *civitas*, such as Touraine (*civitas Turonum*, the Gallic tribe of the *Turones*); others in the areas of the Gallic tribal groups such as Poitou (the Gallic tribe of the *Pictones*); while the majority emerged as political groupings in the Middle Ages, such as Champagne, Languedoc, and Aquitaine. Some of the smaller provinces emerged from *pagi*, as Aunis from the *pagus alionensis*, Senonais from the *pagus senonicus*. The names of the provinces were in popular usage on the eve of the French Revolution, and although some of the political divisions carried the name of a province, these divisions varied in extent. Thus it is impossible to define the province exactly, any more than one can precisely define, for example, the limits of the Cotswolds or the Weald. 'Malgré les fluctuations historiques, malgré les vicissitudes des rattachements ou des sectionnements politiques, il est un certain nombre d'ensembles provinciaux majeurs qui ont conservé ce que nous pourrions appeler une certaine continuité de personnalité, et cela jusqu'à notre siècle même.' [1] This unity is often reflected in 'un esprit provincial, un art provincial, une littérature provinciale',[2] and indeed the very mention of the name of a province, writes Brunhes, 'éveille et réveille d'un seul coup des ensembles de souvenir, de pensées, de coûtumes, de passions, et d'images correspondant à des séries seculaires de connexions humaines dont la synthèse est encore un fait social, historique et géographique tout actuel'.[3]

The *pays* is usually smaller than the *province*, but, like the latter, it is essentially a social unit. This unity it owes to the distinctive mode of life, common interests, and traditions of its inhabitants. Though the *pays* sometimes corresponds with a distinctive physical unit, it is far more characteristically, like the *province*, an amalgam of two or more distinct types of country whose people are interdependent by reason of the exchange of goods and ideas through the medium of a central capital town, from which it often takes its name. Examples

---

[1] Brunhes, *op. cit.*, p. 344.

[2] Claude Barathon, *Le Régionalisme d'hier et de demain*, Les Œuvres Françaises, Paris, 1942, p. 13.

[3] Brunhes, *op. cit.*, p. 342.

are Touraine, capital Tours; Anjou, capital Angers; Poitou, capital Poitiers; Lyonnais, capital Lyon; Limousin, capital Limoges; Périgord, capital Périgueux; Angoumois, capital Angoulême; Bordelais, capital Bordeaux; Agennais, capital Agen; Maconnais, capital Macon; Laonnais, capital Laon; Soissonnais, capital Soissons.

There are certain contrasts in the character of the social groups that have developed historically in the north and in the south and west of France.[1] In the north, in the area characterized in the past by the compact village with a three-field system of cultivation worked on a compulsory communal system, space-groupings have been more permanent and are more real than in the west and south, where the isolated farmstead has been dominant. The *pays* of Beauce, Brie, Vexin, and Valois are ancient names antedating that of France itself. Their origins date back to the Gallic tribal divisions and the Roman *civitates*, through the *pagus* to the medieval *comté*. The same stability is characteristic of the *commune*, the successor in 1789 of the parish, which in effect was the village community area. In the south and west, on the other hand, the parish was not so clearly defined, as the dispersed farmsteads and hamlets were not suitable for the erection of parishes centred on one village. With the formation of the *communes* as civil units in 1789, these had to be imposed on the countryside, since there was no existing village community area.

In the north, the *arrondissement*, established in 1795, also became a real unit and shows the same cohesion as the *commune*. 'C'est une véritable société homogène, consciente, bien ordonnée autour de sa petite ville comme autour d'une capitale.' [2] It is often coincident with the ancient *bailliage* and this, in turn, was frequently based on a seigneurial district or a fief. In the west and south, space-groupings are neither so homogeneous nor so clearly defined. *Commune* and *arrondissement* are somewhat arbitrary units, since there were no clearly defined social units in 1789 on which they could be based. Ancient *noms de pays* of Gallo-Roman origin are rare. Feudalism did not have nearly the same hold as north of the Seine. The farming family was the primary social unit situated in the centre of its own lands, and above it was the château of the nobility, which formed a distinct aristocratic class, frequently in opposition to the peasantry.

The historical provinces are shown on Fig. 90. Brunhes divides them into six groups, according to their geographical location and the character of their historical development.[3] A group in the centre of the Seine basin, the middle Loire, and the basin of the Garonne,

---

[1] See Philippe Aries, *Les Traditions sociales dans les pays de France*, Les Editions de la Nouvelle France, Paris, 1941.

[2] Philippe Aries, *op. cit.*, p. 23.

[3] Brunhes, *op. cit.*, p. 342, *et seq.*

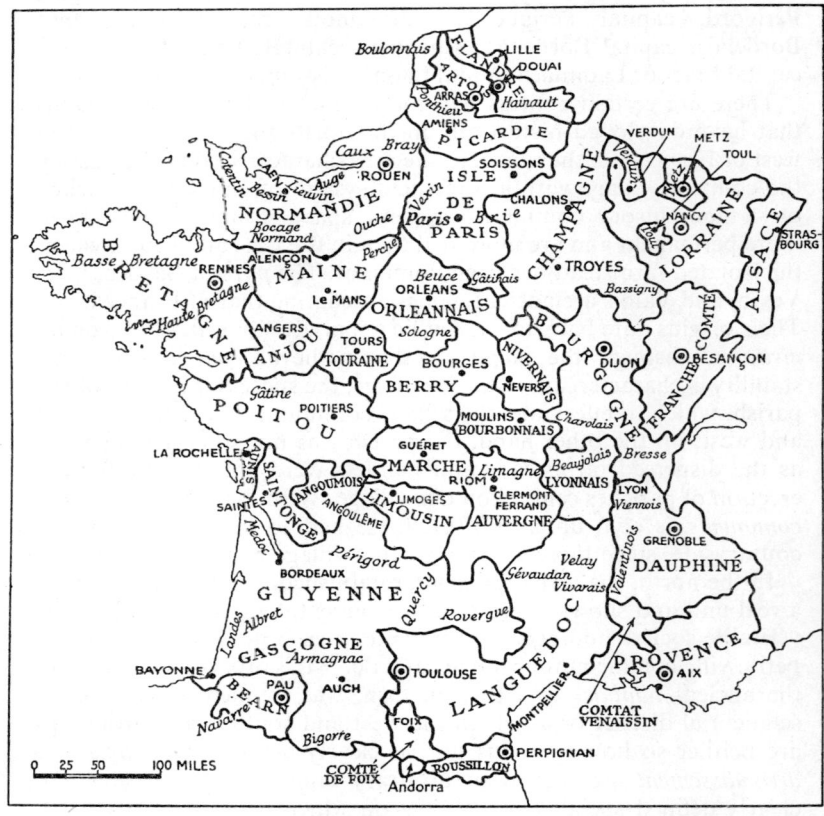

Fig. 90. France: Historical Provinces.

The thirty-three political units of the *gouvernements* and their capitals, as shown in this map, give the clearest indication of the approximate extent of the historical provinces. The *pays* are shown in italics. The Comtat Venaissin (1791) and the Comtés of Nice and Savoie (1860), when absorbed by France, became *Départements*. The cities shown were capitals of the *gouvernements*, and most of these were also capitals of the *généralités*, the most important administrative divisions at that time. Ten cities, however, were the headquarters of *généralités* only. Cities shown with a dot and circle were also the seats of *Parlements*; they were the outstanding provincial capitals. (From F. Schrader, *Atlas de Geographie Moderne*, 1907, Carte 13. See also W. R. Shepherd, *Historical Atlas*, University of London Press, 1922, pp. 146–7) (For *Beuce* read *Beauce*).

served as nuclei of crystallization for distinct provinces. These are the Ile de France; Guyenne and Gascony; Lyonnais, Forez, Beaujolais; Touraine, Maine and Anjou; Alsace. A second group lies on routeways astride the great lowlands—Poitou, Champagne, Picardy and Artois, Burgundy (with Nivernais) and Languedoc—each of which had a wide field of influence, intellectual, commercial, and political. A third group contains what were formerly outstanding centres but are now of secondary importance. All of them are situated in the centre of France, between Chartres in the north and Saint-Flour in the south. They include Auvergne, Berry, Bourbonnais, Orléannais, and Nivernais. These provinces have suffered particularly through the lack of capital cities sufficiently strong to offset the dominating influence of Paris. The fourth group are isolated, thinly peopled provinces in the barren high plateau of central France; nevertheless, these provinces are distinct, and their names and character are strongly entrenched in popular feeling and usage—Limousin and Marche; Périgord and Quercy; Rouergue; Gévaudan; Velay and Vivarais. The fifth group are the frontier provinces which have been absorbed in part or in their entirety into France when it was expanding, in the seventeenth and eighteenth centuries, towards its so-called 'natural frontiers' on the Rhine and the watersheds of the Alps and Pyrenees. These provinces are Roussillon and Cerdagne in the eastern Pyrenees; Foix, Andorra, Quatre-Vallées, and Bigorre in the central Pyrenees; Béarn, Navarre, and the Basque country in the western Pyrenees; the Dauphiné, Briançonnais, and Savoy in the Alps; Flanders, Lorraine, Barrois, and the three bishoprics (Metz, Toul, and Verdun) in Lorraine; and Franche Comté in the east. The sixth group includes the maritime frontier provinces of Provence in the south-east, with Corsica across the water; Brittany and Normandy in the north-west; and Aunis and Boulonnaise, two small provinces on the western and northern coastlands respectively.

The scheme drawn up by the *Comité de Constitution* in 1789 for the new administrative departments was based upon these historical provinces, although the names of the provinces were dropped and the *départements* named after principal topographic features. Several *départements* corresponded usually to one province. They all have roughly the same area and were so designed that the central city could be reached within one whole day by road. 'D'un chef-lieu, la puissance publique doit pouvoir atteindre, entre le lever et le coucher du soleil, toutes les points de la circonscription' (J. Barthelemy).[1] Each *département* was divided into three or four divisions called *arrondissements*, and these again into about ten divisions, called

---

[1] Quoted J. F. Gravier, *Regions et Nations*, 1942, p. 37.

cantons. The same principle of approximately equal size with a centrally placed town as administrative centre was observed throughout.[1]

A main political problem, that has persisted since the French Revolution, is that of offsetting the centralization of affairs in Paris by democratic government in units larger than the *départements*. This has taken many forms—separatism, federalism, administrative decentralization, and regionalism. Though these solutions differ in their political aspects they have a large measure of common ground in that they recognize the need for new units that are neither the *départements* nor an attempted revival of the provinces, but are based on the real socio-economic groupings of today.

Growing partly from the ancient provinces, but in large measure reoriented around the chief regional centres, there have emerged in the last hundred years new provinces or regions. Here have crystallized both the imposed regionalization of nation-wide activities, and the spontaneous development of regional activities, with their founts in the leading cities. The problem of defining new Regions is, in fact, an attempt to define the areas of social and economic association that have emerged in the structure of modern society.[2]

3. The Modern Regions and Their Capitals

A main problem of political regionalism in France is the definition of appropriate new regions. M. Charles-Brun[3] set out the factors which should be considered and, though old, his enunciation of principles is still of interest. He began with general matters of climate, geology, relief, orientation, natural products, race, customs, history, and language. Next, he pointed out that 'homogeneity, which is the fundamental feature of the *pays*, should not, in so far as the region is concerned, be exclusive of a certain amount of variety'. The region should 'combine opposed elements'. Thirdly, he argued that new tendencies, particularly of an economic character, should be

[1] An even distribution of urban settlements permitted the formation of a geometrical pattern of administrative divisions, each with its central capital. '*Chefs-lieux* de départements et arrondissements y sont disposés comme les pièces d'un damier à distances convenables, chacun avec son rayon limité d'action.' Vidal de la Blache, in the symposium *Les Divisions Régionales de la France*, 1913.

[2] The best general work that deals specifically with these problems is a symposium entitled *Les Divisions Régionales de la France*, 1913. It contains articles on the regions of France, the geographical divisions of France in 1789, the development of transport in the nineteenth century, the growth of urban agglomerations, the development of ports, and studies of individual regions—Brittany, Lorraine, and the regions of Nantes and Rouen. All were written by outstanding scholars.

[3] Charles-Brun, *Le Régionalisme*, Paris, 1911.

taken into account, since professional organizations will be based on a regional system. Under this head he includes population and commercial relations. Finally, he considers size. The new regions should be large enough, not only in area, but also in resources and population, to withstand the influence of Paris, and they should all be roughly of the same size. This last requirement, he realized, could

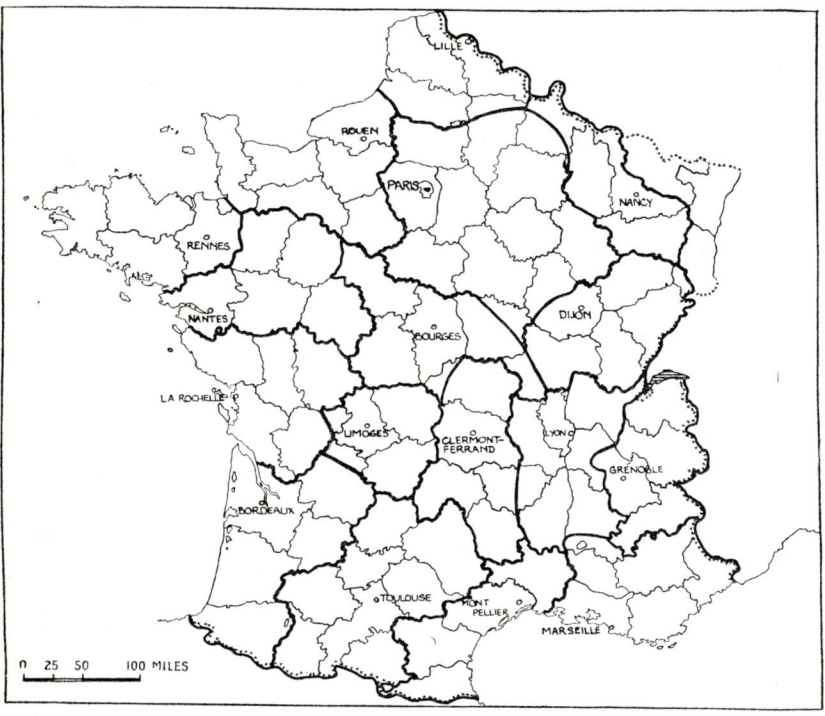

FIG. 91. France: Regions proposed by Charles-Brun (1911).

not be fulfilled with mathematical exactness, since Nature does not permit absolute equality of treatment, but some rough correspondence should be attained so that all regions might be sufficiently strong and vigorous, absorption by the stronger and bigger would be avoided, and equilibrium would be maintained. His scheme of regions is shown on Fig. 91.

This heterogeneous collection of criteria does not greatly help in providing for specific needs. It has often been pointed out by French regionalists that the definition of new regions does, in fact, involve a dual problem. The region must function as an effective unit of government, so that every part is easily accessible to the centre; and it must be a balanced economic unit, that is, it should possess a common basis of activity and interests. Further, the regional capital should be strong enough in virtue of its history and tradition, and of its large population and modern commercial importance, to withstand the influence of Paris, and should in fact be the principal natural (real) centre for the activities and organization of its region. In other words, the regional capital should function for the region as the national capital functions for the State.

French students of the problem have long been agreed that the extent of the sphere of influence of the dominant cities is of paramount importance in defining such homogeneous human units. The regional capitals are 'large cities indispensable to the development of the areas which surround them and throughout which their influence radiates',[1] and around which 'new regions are gradually evolving from the ancient provinces, shattering the restricted framework of the administrative *départements*'.

France is mainly rural and its cities small. Consequently, the influence of the city, if judged by the amount of brick and mortar, is not very extensive—with the exceptions of Paris, Marseille, Lyon, and Lille–Roubaix–Tourcoing. Very large areas are far removed from the dominant influence of any great urban complex so that the small historic city plays a correspondingly important role as the focus of human activities. For this reason (as evident in Ch. 12), it is not possible to define regions clearly on the basis of service areas of a few large cities. Thus, while many schemes for new regions of government and most important of all, that of Vidal de la Blache (Fig. 92),[2] include from twelve to seventeen large regions, there is bound to be an arbitrary factor in the definition of such large units.

New economic regions, as Brunhes argued,[3] cannot be resolved simply by the compass or by railway time-tables and bus services, that is, on the basis of accessibility of the suggested capital city. Moreover, there are many other regional factors to be taken into account, such as types of farming and industry, and regional needs and interests. In order to meet these needs, Brunhes maintained that effective human units must be smaller in size, and, still adhering to the basic idea of the city as the focal point of the region, he suggested about twenty-five to thirty regions, each with a historic and modern

[1] Jean Hennessy, *Régions de France* (1911–16), Paris, 1916.
[2] P. Vidal de la Blache, 'Les Régions Françaises', *Revue de Paris*, December 1910.
[3] Jean Brunhes and Pierre Deffontaines, *Géographie Politique et Géographie de Travail*, in G. Hanotaux's *Histoire de la Nation Française*, Tome II, Vol. II, 1926, pp. 51–78.

'regional metropolis' as its focus. These regions in groups of two or three would form in some cases the major regions. The following is his selection of centres. Rouen and Caen are capitals for eastern and western Normandy respectively. Orleans, Tours, Angers, and Bourges are capitals and serve the middle Loire lands—and to these we would add Poitiers. Rennes and Nantes serve the west, the first for Brittany,

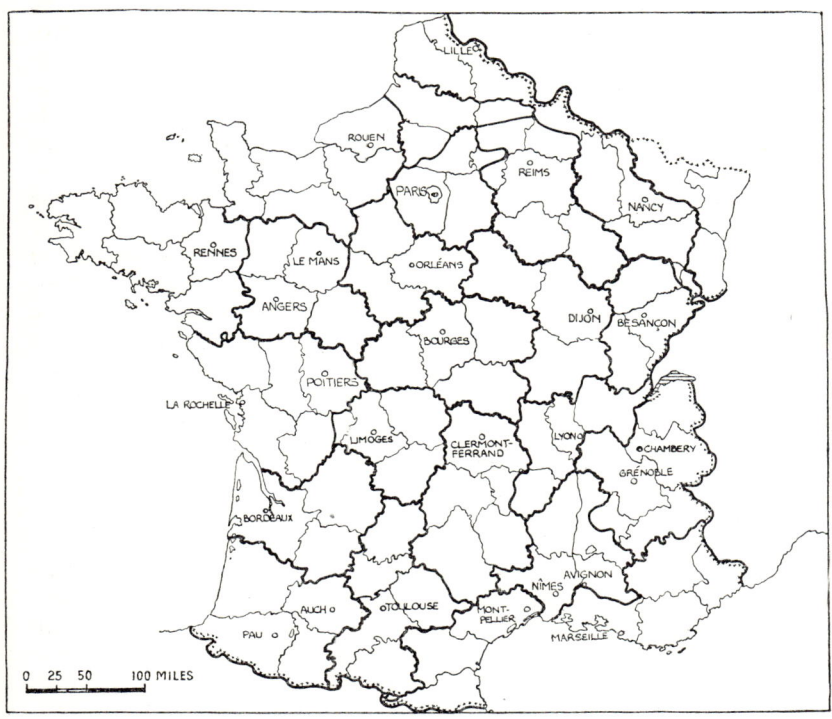

FIG. 92. France: Regions proposed by Vidal de la Blache (1910).

the second for that portion of the province of Brittany and the lower Loire lands which is centred on Nantes and its outport of Saint-Nazaire. Bordeaux is the capital for the south-west, and La Rochelle for the lands between Poitiers and the Garonne, and Limoges and the west coast. Limoges serves the west of the Central Plateau, with its nucleus in Limousin, and Clermont-Ferrand the heart of the Central Plateau, with its nucleus in the lowland of the river Loire and the province of Auvergne. Toulouse and Montpellier are pre-eminent historical and cultural centres in the south, with, to name but one trait, Universities dating back to the thirteenth century.

Lyon, Marseille, and Grenoble are the capitals of the south-east of the Rhône lands and the Alps. Lyon, the capital of the silk textile industries, is an admirable example of an economic metropolis in the fullest sense of the term, with a regional role as great as that of Paris itself (see Ch. 9). Dijon and Besançon are capitals for the ancient provinces of Burgundy and the frontier province of the Franche Comté. Strasbourg, Nancy, and Metz in the east are the capitals of Alsace and Lorraine, the latter of special modern economic importance owing to the development of the iron and steel industry. Reims, Amiens, and Lille are capitals in the north of France, the last in particular being the centre of the great textile industrial area and the coal-field which serves as the hinterland for the port of Dunkirk. This gives a total, excluding Paris, of twenty-five cities, and it includes almost all the leading cities of the country.

Two other cities, however, might be added. Their claims to be independent centres of a high order are evident from their insistence on being treated as separate units in the regional organizations of the chambers of commerce. They are Saint-Etienne (350,000) and Nice (270,000). Saint-Etienne is an ancient and modern industrial centre complementary to, but in large measure independent of, Lyon. It is the centre of a small conurbation on a coal-field with about 350,000 inhabitants, and the focus for the industries—engineering, ribbon wear, and knitted goods—in the homes and small workshops of the *pays* of Velay and Forez. The Saint-Etienne district long lay outside the organization of economic regions and did not accept till lately absorption into the Lyon region. The second, Nice, is a new city, the centre of a horticultural and luxury residential area, which has become the capital for the whole of the Maritime Alps north to the Var river. It may be noted that in the organization of the economic regions, Nice preferred union with Grenoble rather than with Marseille.

In the schemes for fewer larger regions on the lines of Vidal's plan, the following cities appear almost always as the suggested capitals, and may, therefore, be regarded in fact as the outstanding cities with real metropolitan character: Clermont-Ferrand, Limoges, Dijon, Rennes, Grenoble, Lille, Toulouse, Nancy, Lyon, Marseille, Rouen, and Nantes. These are the cities of the first order in France; the remainder, noted above, are of the second order.

The sequence of the historical development of these natural capitals of France is much the same in all cases. Each began as the centre of a Gallic tribe, usually on a hill-top. This was followed by the location of the Roman settlement on the flatter land by the river-side commanding the river crossing, the centre being the headquarters of a *civitas* that in turn was based on the area of the Gallic tribe. The same centres and areas were used in the Middle Ages for the siting of bishops' seats and their dioceses. In the same period they became outstanding commercial and industrial centres for their surroundings. Under the *ancien régime* they were capitals of provinces, several had their own Parlements, and all were seats of the nobility. They also had Universities. Deprived of many of their functions in 1789, they obtained a new lease of life with the coming of the railway and the growth of industry and commerce. Most of them have regained their historical status, in modified character and degree, as regional seats of commerce, industry, culture, and administration.

4. Post-war Planning Regions

Town planning has had a slow development in France and regional planning has made very little headway. There are several reasons for this. The landowner in France has almost unlimited rights over his land, rights that are considered as one of the essentials of individual liberty. Further, land is extremely divided into tiny plots both on the land and in the towns. This presents a basic problem in all matters of private and public enterprise in land-use planning. Problems of town planning in general have presented less urgent situations than elsewhere. About one-half of the population still lives in the country or in small towns and the problems of large urban growth are highly localized in a few major areas, the biggest of them being the capital city itself. A further point that has been advanced by a French authority is that the French have not attached such importance to housing conditions as other peoples, although, in general, the housing conditions in France compare very unfavourably with other countries.

Very little progress was made between the wars. Change came with the Town Planning Act (*Loi d'Urbanisme*) in 1943, which obliges all towns to prepare a planning scheme which, when approved, shall become binding on the community and upon all private parties. The commune remains the basic unit of the planning process as of the system of taxation. The problem of building new towns is hardly encountered in France, but considerable attention is being given to suburban development within communes. Much haphazard growth has taken place around the major cities, notably Paris, and steps have been taken to check this. The present policy of decentralization encourages the expansion of small towns. The reconstruction of war-devastated areas has followed closely on the pre-existing layout and property divisions and new ideas have thus not had much scope for development. Recent legislation now allows expropriation of land by public authorities for development and a special national fund is now available to permit communes to acquire land.

With the exception of Greater Paris, there has been very little progress in the co-ordinated planning of adjacent communes, and the planned development of wider areas is still in its infancy. 'The tradition of administrative centralization and the apparent stability due to a rather stable population did not foster regional initiative or bold plans for great changes. After World War II, the economic rhythms were accelerated, the population grew and many areas were confronted with new problems arising either from rapid growth or from the economic stagnation that threatens decline.'[1] In consequence, laws have been passed to encourage regional initiative in planning. The law of 1955 established the *Commissariat Général du Plan* and the government was given special powers for the planned development of the country, under the *Direction Générale de l'Aménagement du Territoire*. A decree of June 1955 provided for the formulation of regional plans for development, in particular in those areas that suffer from underemployment and a low level of economic development. Such programmes will seek to co-ordinate the action of the various administrations and of regional public and private authorities. The plans will determine the works to be done and the action to be taken. A number of government departments, through their regional divisions and officers, are legally involved in these plans —the ministry of finance and economic affairs, the ministry of the interior, the ministry of industry and commerce, the ministry of agriculture, the ministry of public works, transport and tourism, the ministry of reconstruction and housing, the ministry of labour and social security, and the Secretary of State on economic affairs. A law of November 1956 established the regions that should be used for these comprehensive planning purposes. They are shown on Fig. 93. There are twenty-two such regions and plans have been published for a number of them. Apparently maps are under preparation for each of the regions.

There is at present, however, a discrepancy between two sets of areas, first, the nine areas of the Inspectors who are responsible for the plans, and second, the twenty-two planning regions. The various central ministries also have regional divisions that differ one from the other. Co-ordination is thus extremely difficult. In 1948 there was established the *Inspecteur Général de l'Administration en Mission Extraordinaire*, often called Super-Prefect, who is charged with the maintenance of order in his territory. He was further empowered in 1951 to 'co-ordinate the economic life' and is assisted by an *Inspecteur*

[1] Jean Gottmann, 'Regional Planning in France', *Geographical Review*, Vol. XLVIII, 1958, pp. 257–61.

Général de l'Economie Nationale. He thus has charge of the preparation of the regional plans. But his executive powers are limited. There is need for the co-ordination of territories and of authorities, for the regional officers are responsible to their heads in Paris and not to the regional inspector. The Inspectors General are responsible for the execution of the regional plans, but they operate within nine military

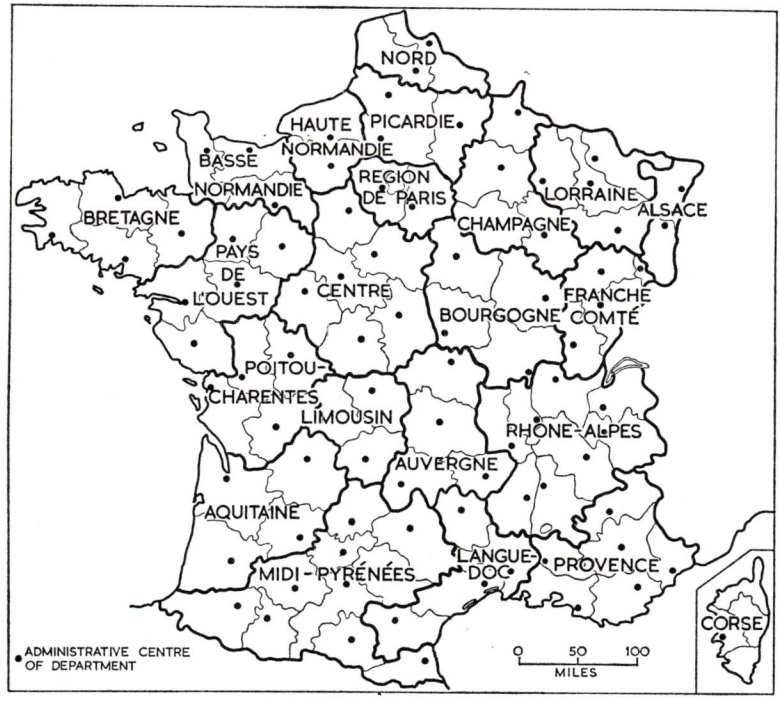

FIG. 93. France: National Planning Regions.

regions, whereas there are twenty-two planning regions as defined in November 1956. The military regions, comparable to the Civil Defence regions in Britain, are much too large for planning purposes.

The twenty-one planning regions (twenty-two with Corsica) are preferable comprehensive planning units, in terms of size, balance of population, accessibility to a central capital, and their community of interests. They often correspond with the historic provinces. It will also be noted that the number of these regions corresponds with the number (not always the boundaries) of divisions of various central ministries (e.g. postal service, statistical institute, education, health).

Particularly important as indicators of regional community of interest are the regions of the Chamber of Commerce, which are active channels of public opinion, since they are free associations of local chambers of commerce throughout the country. They also number twenty-one and are thus of the same order as the planning regions. Thus, it would appear that, in general, the new planning regions could be used as a framework for the co-ordination of administrative areas of government ministries. They could also serve as effective units of regional planning and administration, and even as eventual successors to the *départements*. The military districts are much too large and impersonal for these purposes, but they could be modified by a regrouping of two or three regional planning districts. At any rate, here is an effective framework for the major aims of the French national plan towards regional economic development and the decentralization of economic activities and people from the large urban centres, especially from Paris. This is now the national policy.

It will be clear that many of the proposed and existing divisions of France make a total of eighteen or twenty. These include the 'regional capitals', some of which, however, are small with a limited range of influence, and are dependent upon a larger metropolitan centre. It has been suggested that these regions are too numerous for the effective organization of the country. Jean Labasse, in pursuing this contention, works from the region of Lyon outwards throughout France. He suggests a total of nine major metropolitan regions with their capitals in Lyon, Lille, Nancy, Marseille, Toulouse, Bordeaux, Nantes, Clermont-Ferrand, and Paris (i.e. Paris as the capital of the Paris region). He writes as follows:

'We are far from the confusing conception that guided the public authorities when they established some five years ago [decree of 30 June 1955] twenty-two planning regions. For it is evident that a country like ours, less anciently industrialized and urbanized than its neighbours, cannot be divided among twenty-two major regional centres. Further . . . when a programme of regional action, such as that for Poitou–Charente, recognizes that "le Centre–Ouest cannot find a symbol in the name of a metropolis", this is a confession of an error from the outset in the concept of a region. It is to be hoped, therefore, that these programmes may be used as a provisional framework for the collection of information and for the distribution of credits, so that they may be merged as soon as possible into a more coherent regional structure, capable of serving as a basis of a policy of planning.'[1]

[1] J. Labasse, 'A la recherche d'un cadre régional', *Économie et Humanisme*, Lyon, 1960, pp. 68–74.

Gravier has recently tackled the question of a revised system of territorial units and their corresponding centres. He argues that the *commune, canton, arrondissement,* and *département* were devised before the advent of the railroad, when movement was by foot, wagon, or horseback, and they are in need today of drastic revision in the light of modern needs. The commune depends primarily on face-to-face contacts. Its needs and services demand a minimum population of 500 people. A journey of half an hour by bicycle and quarter of an hour by moped fix its frame with a radius of 8 km. to its remotest hamlets. The size of the units would vary with the density of population.

The *canton* would normally contain two or three communes—as, in fact, is the case in the Midi. Its focus should be a small *bourg* with notary, doctor, and pharmacist and probably a weekly market, with a total population of some 3,000 inhabitants. Its school would cater for the eleven- to thirteen-year-olds with a radius of action of some 15–20 km. The development of school buses would permit centralization in these centres.

The sub-prefecture with college and seats of apprenticeship training would operate over a radius of 30 km. This function is well suited to the *arrondissement* with its centre at the focus of local road communications with a good shopping centre for a radius of 30 km. This centre would play a most important role in the commerce, culture, and administration of the countryside.

The regional capital with ubiquitous road transport would serve an area of some 150 km. radius. A fundamental need for such a centre is a University, for, 'il n'y a pas de vie régionale sans cerveau'. A good press is another essential trait, with a circulation of at least 100,000. The area of service should have at least one million inhabitants. Some cities possess several, but not all, of these functions.

Gravier suggests eighteen regions as shown on Fig. 94. This number he compares with the average number of other divisions. There are sixteen Universities, eighteen divisions of the Institute of Statistics, twenty-two planning regions, etc.

These divisions, continues Gravier, would have real and independent powers of government by means of: (*a*) the transfer to them of certain public services which in other countries are exercised by provincial authorities (instruction, public health, police, etc.); (*b*) the transfer of fiscal powers; (*c*) the administration of the regional budget by a permanent commission; (*d*) the creation of a regional economic council by means of reform of the existing Economic Regions.[1] These changes would be effected by evolution rather than revolution. The region would become above all an economic entity and

---

[1] Gravier, *op. cit.*, p. 145.

organization, bound together by its system of government, by educational institutions, by banking facilities, and planning authorities. At a later phase one could establish the complete and

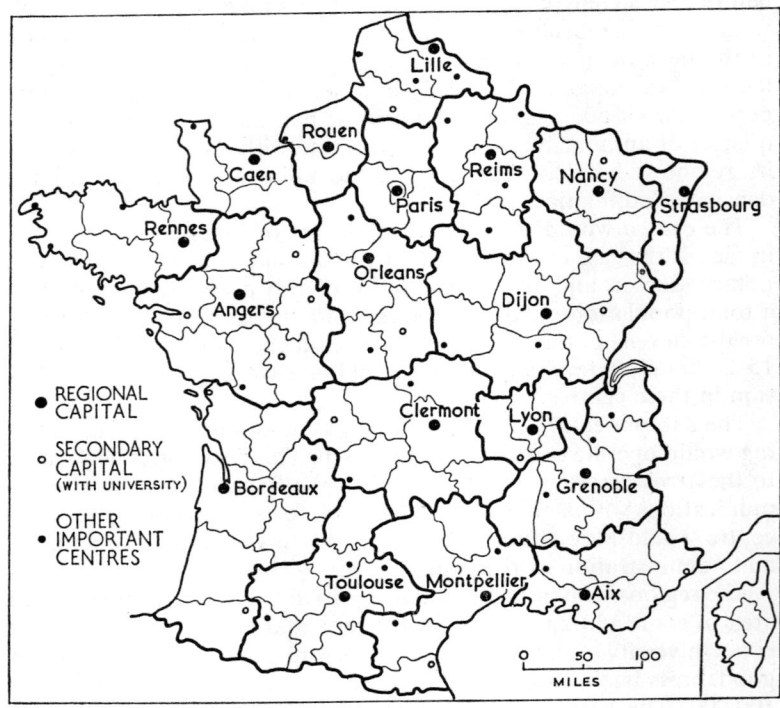

FIG. 94. France: Regions proposed by Gravier.

formal regional structure. The region would then be comparable to the nineteen regions of Italy or the provinces of the Netherlands. It is possible in time that some *départements* would disintegrate by absorption into the orbits of new *arrondissements* around small towns, or that two or more would group together around one major metropolitan city.

Chapter 16

REGIONALISM IN BRITAIN

1. THE DEMAND FOR NEW REGIONS

Regionalism has never been as popular a movement in Britain as in France. It has, in fact, been confined to a few scholars—geographers, economists, and political philosophers—and it is only in the last few years that it has become a subject of wider interest and concern. This interest centres on the administrative aspect, that is, the question of reorganization of local government districts and the devolution of administrative authority from Whitehall. Indeed, regionalism is usually considered in Britain as synonymous with administrative devolution in a framework of new local government units.

The local government of England is carried out in three tiers of areas—the Counties, the Districts, and the Civil Parishes. The Rural and Urban Districts, formed in 1894 from the sanitary districts of 1872, were based upon the Poor Law Union Districts which were created under the Poor Law Amendment Act of 1834. Before this date, the triple system consisted of the County, the Hundred, and the Parish, and it can be traced back to the Norman Conquest.

The geographical counties are 52 in number and include the boroughs that lie within them. The administrative counties, 62 in number, were formed in 1888, and the extra 10 counties were formed by dividing up several of the old geographical counties. They exclude the County Boroughs. The latter, now 83 in number, were also formed in 1888, though a further 24 have been added since that date. These function independently of the administrative counties. The right to become a County Borough has been raised from a population of 50,000 in 1888 to 100,000 in 1945. Within the counties are the Municipal Boroughs, Urban Districts, and Rural Districts, all of which are subject to the authority of the County Council. The Urban and Rural Districts were created in 1894. The former number 572 and have populations ranging from 700 to 210,000! There are 475 Rural Districts with populations ranging from 1,200 to 80,000. The parishes, the oldest units in Britain, number 14,000 in England and Wales. Every parish with over 300 persons has an elected council, and this applies to about one-half of the total.

The County or Shire is the major statutory administrative unit in Britain. It was already in existence before the Norman Conquest. The counties south of the Thames and in eastern England were recognized as 'shires' in the time of King Alfred. Some of them correspond with the initial areas of settlement of the Anglo-Saxon tribes, so that each had a nucleus of open, settled land and a periphery of marsh and forest on the lower land. In the densely wooded and thinly peopled lands of central England, which was then the kingdom of Mercia, the shires came into being during the tenth century. Each was defined as a group of Hundreds conveniently accessible in one day to a fortified administrative centre, which became the county town. These midland counties, each with the suffix 'shire', are all approximately of the same size, and the shire bears the same name as its capital. The counties in the north and south-west of England are the largest; they were not organized as definite county administrative areas until the twelfth century, and were not effectively absorbed into England until after the time of the Tudors. In Wales the political divisions that existed before the English conquest were based on the ancient tribal groupings of pastoral communities who lived on the lower slopes of the hills below the moorlands and above the forested river valleys. The hierarchy of tribal space-groupings culminated in nine major areas each under the rule of an overlord. By the Statute of Rhuddlan in 1284, Edward created the Principality in West and North Wales with five new counties based on the tribal overlordships. The March remained under the disputed control of about 150 marcher lords until 1536, when by the Act of Union five more new counties were created, the boundaries of which were based on those of the lordships and not upon physical divides.

The main fact we would emphasize in connection with these counties is that they came into being before the Norman Conquest and already in the Middle Ages their boundaries had often become areas of close settlement. This has been greatly emphasized in the last hundred years, so that today there is often little relation between the county boundaries and the present distribution and movements of population.

Regionalism as a popular cultural movement (though not bearing this name) has been mainly associated with the linguistic revivals in Scotland, Wales, and Ireland, each of which has expressed itself in more or less degree in a Home Rule Movement. These movements are analogous to the claims to autonomy of groups inside the west European States, such as Provence, Brittany, and Alsace-Lorraine in France, Flanders in Belgium, and Catalonia in Spain, although such movements on the Continent have been regarded as endangering the unity of the State and have been treated with suspicion. In England proper there are no deep-seated cultural differences. There is, of course, a popular consciousness of regional association, as manifested by a regional literature—Hardy's Wessex novels, for example—and by differences of dialect, popularized in some measure by the wireless. There are also 'regional' or 'district' social, cultural, and trade associations. But in its national and cultural life, England is a unit, for reasons of history and because of the small size of the country, and perhaps most of all because of the overwhelming dominance of the urban way of life. The rural way of life—dialect, customs, temperament, and the like—has been swamped by the influence of city ways.

There are big differences between France and Britain in socio-geographical structure. In France the old political divisions and the very names of the provinces were abolished in 1789 and the new and smaller *départements* established. In Britain, the counties are historical provinces and have persisted, unchanged, with real administrative significance, to this day. Nevertheless, there have been periods when larger units were required. The chief of these were the military governorships established under Cromwell. Among the few popular names applicable to such larger areas are East Anglia, the Fens, Wessex, and the Weald. Britain, however, is lacking in geographical names that refer to permanent social groupings like the *pays*. Possible examples are the Craven, Hallamshire, Forest of Dean, and Holderness districts, but these are of little significance today. This whole question, it may be added in passing, deserves much more careful study than it has yet received. Lastly, with few exceptions, urbanism has not seriously affected the traditional social patterns in France. In Britain, especially in northern England, the Midlands, the Home Counties, and central Scotland, these have been profoundly changed. Yet the county has always been the chief social and political unit in Britain and still is a popular unit for business, professional and cultural associations, army regiments, football and cricket clubs, and the like. It is most popular in rural areas, but in the vicinity of the great cities the old-time associations have been all but obliterated, and here the need for a reorganization is most urgent and most needed. Any scheme to introduce new divisions and abolish the old must contend with very real and valuable social forces of tradition and conservatism.

But if the movement for the creation of entirely new divisions to replace the counties has never been widespread in Britain, in practice, as we have already seen,[1] regions exist for a great variety of purposes,

---

[1] See above, Chapter 11.

and in recent years the need for new regions for many aspects of public life has become more obvious and urgent. As far back as 1905 the Fabian Society championed the idea of regionalism with a series of pamphlets called *The New Heptarchy*. The first of the series[1] declared that 'the great towns of Liverpool, Manchester, Birmingham, Newcastle, Nottingham, Leeds, etc., must be considered as centres, and not as self-contained units for all local government purposes, particularly in regard to such services as transport, electricity, and water supply'. This idea of a new Heptarchy attracted some attention and was worked out in greater detail by C. B. Fawcett, G. D. H. Cole, and W. A. Robson.

A number of official reports have presented somewhat similar conclusions, as the Report of the Hadow Committee on the training of Local Government Officers (1934), the Report on Greater London Drainage (1935), the Report of the Royal Commission on Local Government in the Tyneside Area (1937), and more recently, the Report of the Royal Commission on the Geographical Distribution of Industrial Population (1940), the Report of the Scott Committee on Land Utilization in Rural Areas (1942), and the Report of the Uthwatt Committee on Compensation and Betterment (1942).

Meanwhile, the needs of the last war led to the setting up of Civil Defence Regions (Fig. 95). These were administrative regions designed to co-ordinate the functions of the various government departments. Regional divisions of the country were suggested during World War II in reports and Bills for purposes of education, employment, medical services, and the organization of the coal industry. A basic and comprehensive survey of the major regional divisions was put forward at that time in an article in *The Times*, for purposes of industrial reorganization and development.[2] Thus, while scarcely agreeing that 'at last we have established regionalism', as is claimed by a writer on the Civil Defence Regions,[3] it is undoubtedly true that regional treatment is now generally recognized as an urgent need in the solution of domestic problems.

'The obsolete and inefficient character of our local government organizations became increasingly obvious. Every extension of the scope of the functions which local authorities were required or permitted to discharge emphasized the hopeless inadequacy of the existing system of areas. Far larger units of administration were needed not only for relatively new services, such as town and country

[1] W. Stephen Sanders, *The Municipalization by Provinces*, 1905.

[2] 'An Industrial Survey, The Role of Regional Research and Development', *The Times*, 3 April 1945.

[3] *Regional Government*, published by the Fabian Society, Research Series, No. 63, 1942.

planning, housing, electricity supply, road passenger transport, higher and technical education, but also for the older functions such as police, highways, and sewage disposal. The expansion in the area of

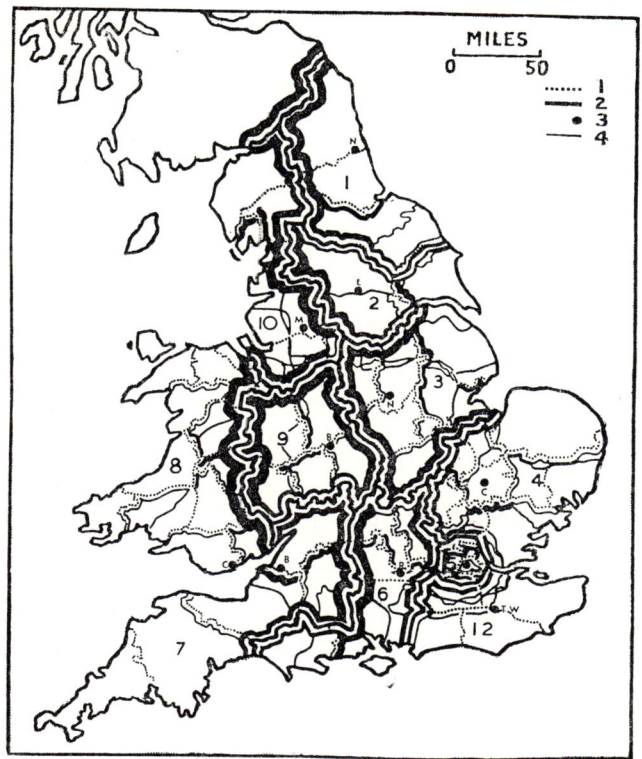

Fig. 95. England and Wales: Civil Defence Regions and twelve other Administrative Divisions.

1. County boundary. 2. Composite boundary varying in width according to the number of Government Departments that use it. 3. Civil Defence headquarters. 4. Civil Defence Region with number. Thin lines are boundaries used by only one Department. Prepared and reproduced by permission of the Association of Planning and Regional Reconstruction.

the daily movement of the people for economic, social, and political purposes, consequent upon improved methods of transport and communications, has for long necessitated a corresponding extension in the units of local government; for no principle of political organization is more firmly established than that the areas of public administration should approximate to the areas of diurnal movement.

Above all the dichtomy between town and country, which is implicit in the rigid separation of county councils and county borough councils, became manifestly absurd when vast numbers of persons who work and earn their living in cities were enabled to live in semi-rural or suburban dormitories, situated at considerable distances outside their boundaries. An enlargement of local government areas on the one hand, and an integration of town and country authorities on the other, thus became insistent needs, which no amount of obtuseness or resistance to reform on the part of local councils or their associations could overcome. The facts were too eloquent to be silenced.'[1]

2. THE TOWN-PLANNING REGION

Town Planning in Britain has proceeded, in the phrase of Sir Patrick Abercrombie, from the particular to the general. During the nineteenth century, as a result of private enterprise, much pioneer work was done in estate and village planning. Well-known villages attached to factories, the co-partnership tenants' estates, and the great achievement of Hampstead Garden Suburb, all aimed at the reform of the domestic environment. The need to extend those principles to the town led to the first Town Planning Act in 1909. In its somewhat grudging treatment of old built-up areas this act showed a strong bias towards suburban if not estate planning, and in due course it was found inadequate. The next Act of 1919 led to the treatment of towns in their relationship to neighbouring towns and to the wider setting of the town in the countryside. Thus, regional planning was almost unconsciously initiated, and there were in the thirties more than a hundred advisory town-planning authorities covering all the most populous areas in a belt from the Solway Firth to the Straits of Dover, as well as elsewhere in the country.[2] The disadvantages of such regions have already been indicated in general terms. Here it may be added that they frequently do not coincide with the natural geographical region (as defined in this book), and this, in turn, does not coincide with existing administrative boundaries.

The problem of the town-planning regions is well illustrated by the case of Manchester,[3] the administrative area of which stretches for

[1] *Regional Government*, Fabian Society, Research Series, No. 63, 1942.

[2] See a useful summary by C. B. Fawcett on Regional Planning in England and Wales, in the Report of the International Geographical Congress, July 1928, and a more recent report by G. L. Pepler in *Städtebau und Wohnungswesen der Welt*, published under the auspices of the *Deutsche Verein für Wohnungsreform*, edited by Bruno Schwan, 1935.

[3] Sir Ernest D. Simon, *The Rebuilding of Manchester*, London, 1935, and, more recently, in *Rebuilding Britain, A Twenty Year Plan*, London, 1945, and L. P. Green, *Provincial Metropolis*, 1961.

twelve miles from north to south but only three and a half miles from east to west. Contiguous to it are closely built-up areas like Salford, Sale, and Stretford, and the small towns of north Cheshire, that are its best residential areas. About two million people live within a radius of ten miles of the Town Hall of Manchester. This city is the capital for a densely populated industrial area with an aggregate population, according to Simon, of 4 millions.[1]

The city of Manchester has grown 'from the centre outwards by continuous additions on the fringe of the existing built-up area, and as new districts which adjoined the city were developed they were incorporated by an extension of boundaries'. In consequence, the city falls into four broadly concentric belts that coincide broadly with the belts discussed in Chapter 13, Section 10, and on Fig. 88*e*. The business centre is an area of one square mile in which much of the property is old and will have to be rebuilt and streets widened. The slum belt is a circular zone about half to two miles wide around the business centre with buildings erected before 1890—a mixture of houses, factories, and warehouses. There are 80,000 houses in this belt, out of a total of 180,000 for the whole of Manchester, on an area of 3,000 acres. The suburban belt falls into two concentric zones, the inner one containing by-law houses built between 1890 and 1914, that are 'dreary, and depressing' but not 'unhealthy or unsanitary'; the outer one containing inter-war housing estates, including the best residential districts to the south of the city and including Wythenshawe south of the Mersey.

The reconstruction of the slum belt is the greatest problem of every British city. The scheme put forward by the City Council in Manchester in the thirties aimed at converting the slum belt into 'a really fine, healthy, and attractive residential area' by a comprehensive replanning scheme that made provision for new roads, parks, schools, playing fields, and the best lay-out of blocks of flats at a density of forty to the acre, with the relegation of industry to the zones in which it is segregated near the railways and canals. This scheme, however, would permit building on only one-third of the whole area of the slum belt of 3,000 acres, housing a total of 40,000 families. This leaves the other half of the houses in the belt, plus an outstanding deficit of 20,000 houses, to be built on the periphery of the built-up area. It is proposed to build these as single-family houses. There is room for 5,000 new houses in the present city and 25,000 in Wythenshawe, so that about 25,000 houses will be needed outside the city area.[2] The

---

[1] See Simon, *Rebuilding Britain*, 1945, pp. 194–212.
[2] The Reconstruction Committee of the City Council recommended the construction of 75,000 new houses, 50,000 of which should be built *outside* the present area of the city, thus allowing for an overspill of 150,000 persons. See Simon, *Rebuilding Britain*, p. 204.

demand for the extension of the city's administrative boundaries is obvious. Manchester, Salford, Stretford, and north Cheshire ought at least to form one administrative unit. At present the people living in the best residential districts in north Cheshire (Bowdon, Knutsford, Alderley, Wilmslow) for the most part work in Manchester and enjoy its amenities, but escape local rating obligations for its upkeep.[1] Moreover, the boundary between Manchester and Salford runs through the built-up area along the river Irwell and is almost contiguous with the city centre of Manchester, so that all plans for the reconstruction of Manchester—its core, its slums, its outer fringe, its ring and radial roads and the rest—must be dependent on some sort of adjustment to the needs and plans of the Salford town council. This state of affairs is repeated in practically every British conurbation.

3. REGIONAL SCHEMES IN THEORY AND PRACTICE

We have seen how nation-wide and town-planning regions have grown up in Britain. The purpose for which the former have been created are so varied that a single set of regions cannot possibly serve them all. But we ought to be clear about the purposes and about the principles which are to be observed in the delimitation of new regions. Mr. G. D. H. Cole has asked these questions: Planning for what purpose? Planning by what machinery? Planning under what auspices? In answer to the first it has already been made clear that widely different considerations arise. Industry, electricity supply, banking organizations, and so on, require different regions. In the second question we must distinguish between decentralization of the national government, and the reorganization and development, in large units, of local government. For the former, large regions like the Civil Defence Regions may best serve, and those who have primarily considered this need think in terms of such regions. For the latter, small units are required for the effective working of local government. Mr. Cole's 'basic conditions' are 'that there shall be *some real consciousness of unity* [italics ours] among ordinary citizens extending over that region as a whole, and marking it off from the other regions in the country'. Such a region should be thought of in terms of 'a biggish town, or sometimes a group of very close

[1] This is one of the most serious problems raised by the explosion of the big city beyond its administrative limits. The shift of the wealthier people from the less desirable residential areas in the city to the pleasanter sites outside it is reflected in the reduction of rateable values in the city by 5 per cent. and a tremendous increase (85 per cent. between 1928 and 1938) in the surrounding districts. There is also a wide disparity in the rates between the two. See Simon, *op. cit.*, p. 209.

together biggish towns, together with the surrounding country, which is served by that single town or by that conurbation'.[1]

These views closely resemble those of Dr. W. A. Robson, who writes:[2]

'If we examine the demands for larger areas put forward by official committees and various disinterested experts, or survey the territories comprised in the most promising developments in electricity, town planning, and numerous other services, we shall find that what is required is not a single set of areas, however large or comprehensive, but a whole series of different areas for separate and distinct purposes. There is no division of the country which will suit all municipal functions.'

While these areas will and must differ from each other, continues Robson, 'the essential principle is that diverse areas should be built up from certain more or less stable units'.[3] Thus both writers accept the principle that two types of region are required. The large region is necessary for decentralization, for national planning in all its aspects, and for statistical purposes: the smaller region is necessary for purposes of local government. The latter units do exist, in fact if not in name, and are mainly centred around the metropolitan cities of the country. Such a region is that centred on Manchester, which we have already discussed with particular reference to town planning. It remains to examine the schemes which have been put forward for new regions, and the *ad hoc* regions which have come into existence.

Lord Passfield (Mr. Sidney Webb) considered the problem[4] but paid no attention to the delimitation of the region and the nature and function of its capital. His main purpose was to discuss the organization of the region in a scheme of administrative devolution based upon the principles of socialism. Professor C. B. Fawcett[5] and Mr. G. D. H. Cole[6] both produced a scheme of regions (Figs. 96, 97). The latter, although claiming not to have based his suggestions 'on any one predominant principle, least of all that of geography' (by which he evidently means hills, valleys, and rivers), none the less adheres throughout to considerations of human geography, as understood by geographers, although not suggesting such radical changes

---

[1] 'Discussions on Geographical Aspects of Regional Planning', *Geographical Journal*, Vol. XCIX, 1942, p. 65. See also leading articles in *The Times*, 5, 6, 7 October 1944, quoted on pp. 2–3.
[2] W. A. Robson, *The Development of Local Government*, London, 1931, p. 130.
[3] *Ibid.*, p. 140.
[4] Sidney and Beatrice Webb, *A Constitution for the Socialist Commonwealth of Great Britain*, 1920.
[5] C. B. Fawcett, *The Provinces of England*, 1919.
[6] G. D. H. Cole, *The Future of Local Government*, 1921.

in the existing country boundaries as does Professor Fawcett. Cole located the regional capitals and then traced very roughly the boundaries of the regions[1] around them which are sparsely populated. The six 'axioms' enunciated by the late Professor Fawcett, who was a

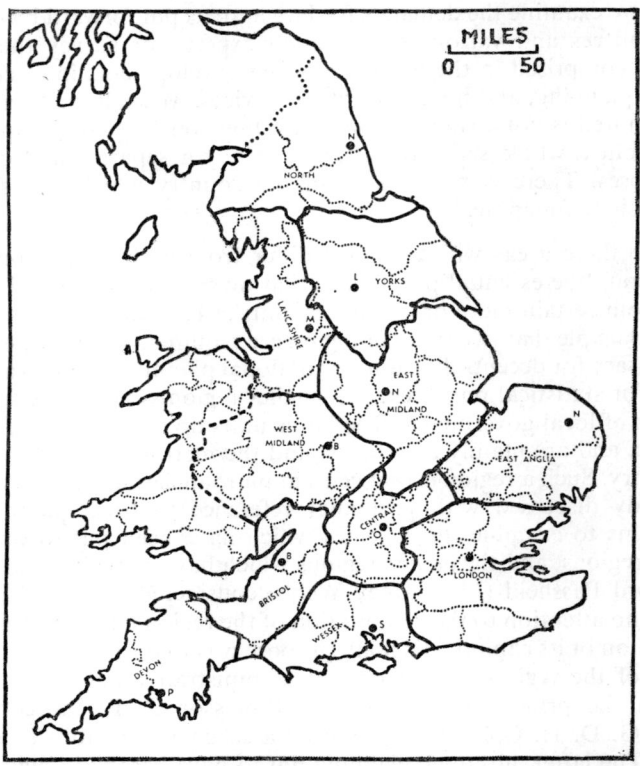

FIG. 96. England and Wales: Divisions proposed by C. B. Fawcett, 1917, revised in 1942.

geographer, in the delimitation of his twelve provinces are as follows:

1. The provincial boundaries should be so chosen as to interfere as little as possible with the ordinary movements and activities of the people.

2. There should be in each province a definite capital, which should be the real focus of regional life. This implies, further, that the

[1] For Cole's general definition of a region, see p. 474.

area and communications of the province should be such that the capital is easily accessible from every part of it.

3. The least of the provinces should contain a population sufficiently large to justify self-government.

4. No one province should be so populous as to be able to dominate the Federation.

Fig. 97. England and Wales: Regions proposed by G. D. H. Cole, 1921.

5. The provincial boundaries should be drawn near the watersheds rather than across the valleys, and very rarely along streams.

6. The groupings of areas must pay regard to local patriotism and to tradition.

The methods and conclusions of both writers are broadly similar, though Cole, as an administrator, devoted more attention to 'the coming of the region' and to the evolution of a system of regional government, than to a detailed study of the character of the regions he suggests. Another scheme was suggested some forty years ago in a series of articles entitled *Towards a National Survey* [1] (1921). This scheme was drawn up for the development of a national housing policy based upon a regional plan, and not with any idea of a provincial system of government. Yet the principles upon which the divisions were made strikingly resemble the axioms of Professor Fawcett. Since this scheme is not so generally known as it deserves, we quote in full the principles adopted.

'The aim has been in the first place to form areas which have a community of economic interest. Such an aim necessarily cuts across many local government boundaries . . . but it is recognized that it is very undesirable to do this more than is absolutely necessary. Generally speaking, therefore, the areas of the boroughs, and urban and rural districts have been adhered to, but it has been found necessary in many instances to ignore the county boundaries.

'For the first broad division of the country, the principal watersheds have been taken as guiding lines. Following these but without adhering to them too closely where other factors seem to counteract their influences the country has been parcelled out into 15 main divisions (see Fig. 62). These main divisions have been subdivided into 59 "regions" which have been in most cases again subdivided into groups. For the purpose of these subdivisions a number of factors have been taken into consideration. In some cases, of course, there is practically an industrial identity between adjoining districts. Far more frequently one area acts as a dormitory for another. Communications by road and rail have a very strong influence on the grouping of areas and it is recognized that a river, where its banks are used for industrial purposes . . . should be looked upon as the centre of a unit.'

Another type of scheme was prepared by a committee of geographers appointed by the Standing Committee on Regional Surveys and Local Studies of the Geographical Association, for submission to the Ministry of Reconstruction during the 1914-18 war.[2] Their conception of a province and the function of its capital differ from the others in two respects.

1. 'The Provinces should not . . . be uniform in character throughout, but should have diversity within unity. . . . In other words, a satisfactory province would be one which contained several *pays* or sub regions each with its distinctive individuality, but yet so related to one another as to form a natural whole.' The average size of a province, based on three regions in Europe which have been distinct

[1] Published by the Ministry of Health in *Housing*, November 1921.

[2] H. J. E. Peake, 'Devolution: A Regional Movement', *Sociological Review*, Vol. XI, No. 2, 1917.

provinces throughout recorded history—Wales, Brittany, and Tuscany—is calculated at 5,000,000 acres.

2. The second difference lies in the conception of the function of the Regional Capital. It is suggested that in each region, instead of all its activities being focused on one capital, 'there should be towns of contrasted types in each province; and region centres representing different kinds of activities, rather than a single metropolis dominating the life of the provinces', since this would 'tend somewhat towards decentralization within the province'. A suggestion put forward is Wessex, with Winchester as the administrative centre; Southampton as the industrial and commercial capital; Oxford as the intellectual and educational capital, and Salisbury as the ecclesiastical capital.

In recent years, and especially since 1940, with the growing attention given to problems of post-war reconstruction, the question of new regional divisions has been increasingly prominent. Two geographers, Professor Eva G. R. Taylor and Professor E. W. Gilbert, have made notable contributions.[1] The Association for Regional Planning and Reconstruction was also actively interested in the problem and has issued broadsheets devoted to it. Professor Taylor suggested a division (Fig. 98) which broke away completely from existing county boundaries while Gilbert reluctantly, but wisely, uses them as far as possible. The latter course is more practical both from the point of view of expediency and because the county, in spite of all that can be said against it, is an established unit and often has popular associations. Gilbert (Fig. 99), unlike most other contributors, made the fullest use of the Civil Defence Regions.

The Civil Defence Regions came in for much criticism; they were too large and too arbitrary to serve as effective political units, and they paid little attention to the facts of regional cohesion. Several of them were no more than groups of counties.

The Civil Defence Regions in England and Wales are shown on Fig. 95, together with the counties and the divisions of eleven Government Departments. The Regions are numbered and their boundaries are shown by black lines. The heavier black lines that run on both sides of the boundaries of the Regions are proportional in

---

[1] Professor Taylor's suggested regions are in the *Geographical Journal*, Vol. XCIX, 1942, p. 62, and those of Professor Gilbert on p. 76 of the same volume. Professor Gilbert's valuable paper, 'Practical Regionalism in England and Wales', *Geographical Journal*, Vol. XCIV, 1939, p. 29, should be consulted for a variety of *ad hoc* regions. Some of these are reproduced on Figs. 61 to 67 with the kind permission of the *Journal* and of Professor Gilbert. A. M. Carr-Saunders and D. Caradog Jones, *A Survey of the Social Structure of England and Wales*, 2nd ed., 1937, pp. 25-32.

Fig. 98. England and Wales: Regions proposed by E. G. R. Taylor, 1941.

width to the number of boundaries of Departmental divisions that were coincident. The Government Departments so considered were as follows:

NUMBER OF DIVISIONS IN GREAT BRITAIN

Civil Defence	12
County and County Divisions	84
Ministry of Labour and National Service	11
Ministry of War Transport	12
Ministry of Food	8
Board of Education Inspectorate	13
Factory Inspectorate	12
Ministry of Works Contractors	15
Ministry of Agriculture Advisory Provinces	16
Ministry of Agriculture Statistical Divisions	15
Board of Trade Census of Production, 1935	17
Registrar General for the Census	16
Post Office Regions	8

Scotland and Wales each formed one Civil Defence Region, with capitals at Edinburgh and Cardiff. England was divided into ten Regions—northern (Newcastle), north-eastern (Leeds), north Midlands (Nottingham), eastern (Cambridge), London (Metropolitan Police Area), southern (Reading), south-western (Bristol), midland (Birmingham), north-western (Manchester), and south-eastern

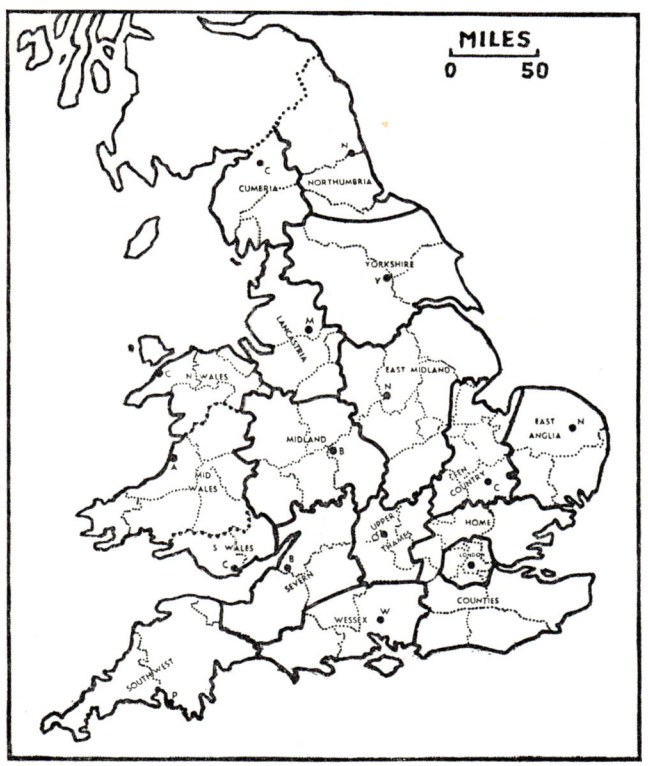

Fig. 99. England and Wales: Regions proposed by E. W. Gilbert, 1941.

(Tunbridge Wells). The Regional Commissioners had three war-time tasks—to represent the central government in each Region; to carry out the government's Civil Defence and A.R.P. measures; and to take the place of the central government in the event of a breakdown of communications. Their duties and powers were thus somewhat nebulous. But it is especially important to note that many government departments appointed Divisional Officers in each Region, so that there was a co-ordination of areas and duties within each

Region. These departments included the Ministries of Food, Information, Health, Labour and National Service, Supply, Aircraft Production, War Transport, Works and Buildings, Mines Department, Petroleum Department, Post Office, Assistance Board, and the Ministry of Home Security.

These Civil Defence Regions were thus administrative regions,

FIG. 100. England and Wales: Standard Regions of the Census, 1946. See p. 397.

organized by the central government as a means of devolution. They were not intended as planning regions and they did not carry out any functions with regard to land planning. They were also not local government regions with elected local representatives. If larger regions are to be formed as units of democratic government with elected legislative bodies, and legislative powers over regional affairs, this larger region would probably be the higher of a twofold order of regions, for smaller districts will be required to replace the county and county authorities. The Civil Defence Regions are a long way from satisfying the demands of regionalism, if the principles discussed above are sound, and substantial adjustments would have to be made to make them into coherent units. For example, there is much to be said for including northern Nottinghamshire with Sheffield. Reference to the city trade areas discussed in the previous chapter gives some further indication of changes. More detailed study of the space

Fig. 101. England and Wales: Regions of Electricity Boards, 1947.

relations of border areas, like the Potteries, which are divided in their allegiance between two centres—in this case between Birmingham and Manchester (see quote on p. 418)—and yet possess a lively regional consciousness of their own, would assist in a refinement of solutions. The essential fact remains that the Civil Defence Regions came into being for the first time as co-ordinated administrative units.

The country is divided into major divisions for a great variety of purposes of administration.[1] Important changes have been made since 1945 in terms of both nation-wide devolution and regional integration. The Civil Defence Regions were eliminated for defence purposes. In 1946 the Treasury adopted a set of eleven 'standard regions' that are, in fact, successors of the Civil Defence Regions, with some minor variations (Fig. 100). These regions are used by

FIG. 102. England and Wales: Regions of Hospital Boards, 1945.

various Ministries and by the Registrar General. Some Public Utility services have also been transferred from the local authorities to the counties or to new *ad hoc* regions. These include electricity, gas, hospitals, the coal industry and the railways. As regards electricity supply the Act of 1947 stated that 'Electricity supply is a service of

[1] A list and discussion is in C. B. Fawcett's *Provinces of England: A Study of Some Geographical Aspects of Devolution*, revised by W. G. East and S. W. Wooldridge, 1960, pp. 35–6.

social and economic significance and the areas for distribution of electricity should as far as possible be natural areas, with strong local outlook and interests'.[1] There are twelve areas for England and Wales (Fig. 101). Gas supply is arranged by eleven areas boards, each with its nucleus in a big urban area. Both the coal industry and the railways were regionalized when they were nationalized,

FIG. 103. England and Wales: Regional Planning Organization of the Ministry of Town and Country Planning in 1946.

but they have quite unique areas, depending on their historical development. Hospital service was regionalized on the basis of fourteen areas in 1946, each grouped around a University city with a school of medicine, so as to eliminate the inadequacies of the existing local government units that are too small to support and maintain

[1] E. W. Gilbert, 'The boundaries of local government areas', *Geographical Journal*, Vol. CXI, Nos. 4–6, September 1948, pp. 172–206, with important discussion and a series of maps.

properly equipped institutions (Fig. 102). In 1947 the Town Planning Act took the administrative counties and the county boroughs as its official planning units (Fig. 103).

4. LOCAL GOVERNMENT AREAS

As regards local government,[1] some functions have been transferred to the county boroughs and county councils—public health, secondary education, town-planning functions. Some other functions have been removed from the local authorities and transferred to the central government. The essential fact, however, is that the local government authorities still persist in their little domains. The unity of the areas focused on the cities has not yet been recognized as a basis for defining new units of metropolitan government. A royal commission was appointed after the war to examine this question and its findings were commented on by E. W. Gilbert in 1948. He rightly criticizes the existing system for its lack of effective units of local representation government, whether at the level of the parish in the country or the neighbourhood in the city (as a substitute for the 'ward' that is merely an electoral division). He points out that the existing boundaries of boroughs and urban districts divorce the town from the country around it, but with which it is intimately associated. New types of districts are needed to eliminate the break between country borough and the predominantly rural districts of the country around it (especially in these days of expanding cities and their demands for expanding their boundaries); and, within the county, to bring the borough and the Urban District into closer touch with their natural market areas. These criticisms are particularly cogent in the conurbations, that are split in such a way that all kinds of administrative areas are intermixed. Various official bodies have already recommended that they all be grouped into a single unit—the problem is one of ways and limits (e.g. the Royal Commission on local government in the Tyneside area recommended a single central authority). Finally, the present system disregards the major geographical groups or regions of the nation. These criticisms are obviously the main contentions of this book and they apply in other countries with the same urgency as in Great Britain.

The question of revising local government areas is still under review. The Local Government Boundary Commission came into being in 1945 and made its first report in 1948. It was directed to make recommendations for 'individually and collectively effective and convenient units of local government'. The criteria it was asked

[1] See in particular, L. P. Green, *Provincial Metropolis, The Future of Local Government in Southeast Lancashire*, London, 1959.

to use are of special relevance to our theme and may be listed here: (*a*) community of interest; (*b*) anticipated development; (*c*) economic characteristics; (*d*) financial resources; (*e*) physical features, including accessibility to centres; (*f*) population (size, distribution, and characteristics); (*g*) record of administration by the local authorities; (*h*) size and shape of the area; (*i*) wishes of the inhabitants. Note that these are listed in alphabetical order, so that the wishes of the people come last. The criterion of 'community of interest', though first on the list, constitutes together with accessibility the two considerations that have long been maintained by geographers (among the others), and have received a good deal of attention in official quarters in recent years. (It seems certain that this idea has penetrated from the work of geographers in the research division of the Ministry of Housing and Local Government.)

The commission found its powers too limited to make effective recommendations to its directive. It recommended 200,000 as the minimum population for an effective major local government unit. It laid down four main principles.

(*a*) There should be three main types of local government unit—counties, county boroughs, and county districts.

(*b*) The whole country should be divided into new counties that would generally correspond to the existing counties, but some would be combined (if less than 200,000) and others divided (if over one million people). Twenty large cities would become new counties.

(*c*) New county boroughs would be the middle-sized towns with between 60,000 and 200,000. They would be part of the administrative county and would depend on it for some public services, such as police and fire, but they would form a new and intermediate level of authority with responsibility for education, health, etc.

(*d*) The County Districts would include all the non-county boroughs, Urban Districts, and Rural Districts, and the distinction in title between the last two would have been abolished.

It is an incredible fact that the reports of this royal commission included no maps, so that it is difficult to understand the implications of their proposals. This was the purpose of Gilbert's investigation, to which reference may be made by the reader. As examples, Lancashire would be divided into five new counties and there would be combinations with areas in adjacent existing counties. Yorkshire would be divided into eight counties. Staffordshire would fall into three parts—Potteries (one-tier), Black Country, and agricultural central area (two-tier). Of the unions suggested, one example is that Rutland, the smallest county with only 18,000 people, should be combined with Leicestershire. Twenty urban clusters are suggested as large enough to become one-tier new counties (e.g. Potteries and Brighton–Hove). Some sixty-three towns were suggested as new County Boroughs. The Commission made proposals for the regrouping of the counties of Wales so as to create larger units.

As regards the conurbations, the commission was not consistent. It recognized some as new single units, but rejected the union of Birmingham with the Black Country around it as a one-tier unit since it would be too large. The conurbations of Liverpool and Manchester would each become new counties, but they made (probably with good justification) no such recommendation for a naturally divided west Yorkshire. Bradford and Leeds would be separate one-tier counties. Nor did it propose the union of Sheffield with Rotherham. Yet in regard to Merseyside, it says 'Where a concentration of 1·4 million persons in an area of this type have so many common interests in life, in business and in local government, they should, through their representations, study and decide their wider problems in the common meeting grounds of one county council.' These principles, if valid here, should apply in all the other conurbations.

Finally, there is no suggestion here of a few major regions to serve between the many new local government areas and the central government in London. Under a new 'Heptarchy' the counties and county boroughs 'could continue but would also be represented in regional parliaments'. Thus recommends a former head of the Civil Service.[1]

The Commission finished its assignment in 1948 but its recommendations were rejected by Parliament. The conurbations present the major problem, that is, whether they should become single units of government or whether they should be a part of a reorganized two-tier system. Investigations continued during the fifties. A White Paper in 1956 suggested either the continuance of the patchwork of local government authorities, though fewer in number; or a new grouping of a few county boroughs (minimum population 100,000) to cover the whole area of each conurbation. The Local Government Act of 1958 provided for a complete review of the five conurbations, now defined as 'special review areas', by a Local Government Commission. London has been investigated by a separate commission, and its report was published in 1961 and an act has been passed by the Commons. It makes provision for the establishment of a Greater London, based on the definition of the census, with a reduction of the boroughs from ninety-four to thirty-two in a two-tier system. This, of course, will mean the elimination of the London County Council, and the whole matter is at present very much under dis-

[1] Sir Warren Fisher, quoted by Gilbert, *op. cit.*

cussion. The work of the Commission on the conurbations is in progress and its proposals for the 'special review areas' are under discussion. They will be briefly examined below, after first considering one conurbation in more detail.

5. METROPOLITAN ORGANIZATION

The problems of organizing the territorial government of a conurbation may be illustrated from south-east Lancashire. Here, there are seventy-two urban and rural local authorities, and four county authorities. 'Geographically and administratively, functionally, and financially, the local government machinery is not equal to our task.'[1] Local government authorities are losing their place in public life; the central government is playing an increasing role in local affairs and is taking over many of the 'universal services' from the citizens. Notable among the new regional services administered by the central government are the Health Service (since 1946), operating through the counties and the county boroughs, with seventeen committees operating in Metropolitan Lancashire. Four public corporations are the Coal Board, Transport Commission, Electricity Authority, and Gas Council. The county boroughs and county councils still enjoy highly important responsibilities of local government, notably public health services, water supply, sewerage, transport, police and fire services, education, libraries, planning, buildings.

Four sets of areas are shown on Fig. 88 (p. 430). These show how the area of Metropolitan Lancashire is subdivided into overlapping districts for several of these activities. With regard to general planning and development, there is no single authority for the area as a whole. As Green wrote in his 1959 study:

'There is no authority charged with the fundamental responsibility of regional planning and control over development. The Lancashire Development Plan is bereft of the important industrial and commercial areas in the county; the Manchester Development Plan cuts through the region's heart and severs it from its tributary hinterland. Instead of co-ordinated reserves, planning and development, we have a series of development plans (prepared by the county boroughs and the counties, the planning authorities) for areas having little community of interest in terms of geography, economics, or human society.'[2]

[1] C. W. Key, Parliamentary Secretary to the Minister of Health, quoted by L. P. Green, *op. cit.*, p. 167.
[2] L. P. Green, *op. cit.*, p. 201.

The same situation holds in all of the conurbations and is one more major reason for the creation of new units of government and a co-ordination of their spheres of responsibility.

The problem of local financial resources versus necessary expenditure has been noted and may again be exemplified from Metropolitan Lancashire. The situation is that the expenditures of the local government authorities cannot be met by their local revenue. Today the great block of their funds is derived from central governmental grants. In 1956–57, 40 per cent. of local authority expenditure on revenue account was devoted to education, 10 per cent. to personal health and welfare services, 15 per cent. to planning and construction, 15 per cent. to environmental health services, and 20 per cent. to other activities. To meet this the authorities derived about a third from rates assessed on immovable properties (their one source of local revenue), near 40 per cent. from Exchequer grants, and 30 per cent. from rents, fees, recoupments, and trading profits. With regard to the expenditure *per capita* of rate-borne income the geographic pattern reveals 'a core of peak expenditure (in the industrial and commercial core) surrounded by successive rings of high, medium, and low expenditure, with a definite weighting in favour of the southern parts of the region, where expenditure per head tended to be higher than in the north'.[1] The distribution of real wealth, as evidenced by rateable values per head in each local authority area, is remarkably consistent with rate-borne expenditure in its geographic pattern. Values *per capita* were in general higher in the southern part of the region, and lower in the north (except for Manchester). The actual rates levied bear out this contrast between the newer residential and the older Lancashire and 'working-class' sectors and the unique position of the inner core; the wealthier and the poorer sectors, the new and growing, and the old and stagnant sectors. But each of these areas was 'integral to a metropolitan region, whose every part was neither socially, economically nor financially self-sufficient'.[2] Thus, concludes L. P. Green—and he is quoted at length, since this problem is here admirably presented on the basis of a concrete study—

'The burden of dealing with the region's most urgent problems of rehabilitation, traffic, housing, health, and welfare falls primarily on the shoulders of the local authorities where they arise. Although these problems are metropolitan in nature, the fragmentation of the region's administrative structure stands as a permanent barrier to their solution by metropolitan means. . . . (The) financial capacities of these local authorities tend to vary in inverse proportion to their needs. . . . (The financial axis of the region is a line drawn from

---

[1] L. P. Green, *op. cit.*, p. 207.   [2] *Ibid.*, p. 211.

Golborne to Glossop.) To its north lies the sector of greatest needs, to its south lies the sector with the greatest taxable resources per head. To the north lies the sector of high average rates, to the south the sector of low average rates. Within each sector there exist a number of zones with varying needs and resources, and within each zone there is often a valuable node ringed by less valuable areas. But the general picture is one of imbalance between needs and resources—and . . . the nodes are frequently the most highly rated in their particular zones.'[1]

Manchester at the heart of the region is its financial giant. It is able to balance its needs and resources owing to the great geographic diversity of its uses over a wide area. But even so, it is not a 'self-sufficient economic or social entity, as it is wedded to a vast hinterland stretching to the farthest corners of Metropolitan Lancashire'.[2]

With variations, these conditions are repeated in all the major conurbations and present the same problems. Housing is a major problem everywhere. Manchester and Salford, for example, require overspills for some 250,000 people. There is also the problem of communications. There is the problem of guided industrial development. There is the problem of co-ordinating the services of government and the reduction of government units from the present areas of seventeen central departments, seventy-six local authorities, and seventy-six committees and boards. Local government boundaries are 'artificial antiquated relics of the past', since 'the social unit is no longer the old local community of town or city delimited by the official municipal boundaries, but is the metropolitan zone of contact and accessibility extending over a number of towns and cities which are linked together by circulation of people, goods, and services between them'. The basis of this whole system lies in the specialization of functions by places with areal forces of cohesion based on the separation and interlinkage of workplace and residence—the journey to work, shopping, and entertainment.

The problem of the reorganization of systems of government in metropolitan areas reveals two kinds of recommendations, either to co-ordinate the activities of existent component government units; or to reorganize radically the whole structure of local government. The first would establish, for example, *ad hoc* bodies, with representatives of all the local government bodies for particular purposes. Bodies of this form are old-established and include, for example, the London Metropolitan Board of Works in 1855. Others are public utility corporations such as the Metropolitan Water Board in London founded in 1902.

[1] *Ibid.*, pp. 213–14.   [2] *Ibid.*, p. 214.

The complexities of this kind of development have led to the second kind of solution. The most obvious is the annexation of adjacent local government units by the central city, but this is not possible for the case of considerable clusters of contiguous units. An association of local authorities over the whole area may be formed with advisory or co-ordinating and planning functions. There are many such cases in the United States but this solution has not been successful since the advisory authority lacks executive power. Finally, some kind of two-tier administrative system may be established. Such a system was first established in London by the Acts of 1888 and 1899, in the London County Council, though it has had a stormy political history. It has no control of the city of London, with its one square mile in the centre, while its authority does extend over the area of the Metropolitan Water Board, established in 1855, and has no control over the vast area that now lies outside it. Many *ad hoc* authorities have been organized and the overhaul of the government system has recently been reported on by a royal commission but no action has yet been taken. In Canada a two-tier system has been introduced in Toronto over an area of 245 square miles and a population of 1·1 million people, and it seems that such an organization could be well adapted to many of the major urbanized areas.

6. Post-war Town and Country Planning in its Regional Aspects[1]

In 1943 a Ministry of Town and Country Planning was created in accordance with the recommendations of the Barlow Commission. The Barlow, Scott, and Uthwatt reports provided an enormous amount of information and sound advice on problems of the geographic distribution of the population, the proper utilization of rural land, and the thorny question of compensation and betterment in the buying and selling of land. There also appeared a number of quite outstanding advisory reports on city plans: Abercrombie's plans for the County of London and Greater London and for Plymouth, the city of Manchester plan, and the reports of Thomas Sharp on Exeter, Durham, and Oxford. Action was taken by the Labour government in the form of the New Towns Act in 1946 and the basic Town and Country Planning Act of 1947. This act, as far as our interest is concerned, removed planning powers from the lesser urban authorities and vested them in the County Councils alongside the County Boroughs (that is, the principal cities). There are now 145 of these planning authorities as compared with 1,441

[1] L. B. Keeble, *Town Planning at the Crossroads*, London, 1961, is a good critical survey of this field.

before the Planning Act of 1947. Each authority is obliged to prepare detailed plans of land uses for future development. The National Parks and Access to Countryside Act was passed in 1949. The Town Development Act of 1952 was passed so as to facilitate the expansion of existing towns rather than the creation of more new ones. This has made slow progress, since it contains no provisions for the implementation of regional proposals, and merely facilitates 'bargaining between importing and exporting authorities' (the method whereby one authority helps to pay another authority for unloading the so-called 'overspill' of population which it cannot accommodate). Without some arrangement whereby overspill housing can be shared between the reception authority, the exporting authority and the central government, any real advance in regional planning is impossible.

In spite of these great changes in planning legislation in Britain in the last twenty years, regional planning, in the sense of groups of contiguous authorities planning and acting as a single unit, has virtually made no headway at all. It is true that many *advisory reports* have been written for such areas, such as the Greater London Plan, the South Wales Plan and the west Midlands Plan, and though they have not acquired any legal force, they have a pronounced influence. The fact is that there is still no legal provision or organization for regional planning. The division between planning authorities has certainly hindered co-ordinated and decisive action. The county authorities indeed often cover large areas, but they have no authority to deal with questions of the redistribution of population and employment, and they have no authority to cope with the problems of county boroughs (cities) that are separate and independent, even though they are often embedded in the midst of the county area. The plans of the two area authorities are made separately and in terms of land use they are simply not properly co-ordinated. It is very well to say that they can live together amicably and reach agreement, or call in the Minister as go-between, but this is not the same as single action within one major area.

Problems of post-war growth that cry out for regional treatment—that is, power to operate over the land independent of the boundaries of local government authorities—include the large increase of office space in the city centres. The Board of Trade has had the power to control the location of industry, but no authority has been concerned with the location of offices and this is one of the main causes of urban congestion. Further population will have to be shifted in great numbers from the obsolescent areas of housing. 'The current policy of leaving Local Authorities to their own devices to make their own agreements for the exporting and importing of overspill population with the Ministry acting as arbitratory or honest broker between them, is futile.'[1]

The case of London is well known. That of Manchester is of equal significance. The city requested overspill accommodation in Cheshire at two places, as it had done before the war by the outright purchase of land at Wythenshawe beyond its boundaries. It claimed the need for 17,000 houses at a place called Lymm. The local people in Cheshire were opposed, public hearings were held, decisions were twice made against Manchester. Manchester claimed at the hearings that it needed 83,000 new houses in all (62,000 being replacement of houses unfit to live in). The Manchester authority planned to build in this area at 90 habitable rooms per acre and refused to increase to 120, as they were requested by the Ministry, since it would not be in the interests of their people whom they were moving. In the public enquiry on this matter, writes Keeble, 'Neither Manchester nor the Ministry seem to be worried about the establishment of a proper physical pattern for the Manchester city-region in relation to accessibility to centre and open country, and the distribution of local shopping, schools, and open space.'[2]

There are finally the changes in town-planning legislation and their adequacy to cope with problems of urban expansion. Only the main relevant facts can be noted here. Since 1947 the official planning authorities are the Counties and the County Boroughs, and every local government authority in the country has prepared a detailed local development plan for every acre of its territory. It should be remembered that the central government, through the Board of Trade, has sought to direct industry to 'development areas, and has sought to preserve the best agricultural land from the incursion of urban land uses'.

The main points to emphasize here concern the inevitable demand for more land for the expansion of the existing urban areas, and especially the conurbations. The problems of urban expansion in Britain are in part concerned with economic growth and the consequent influx of workers and their families. This growth is reflected in abnormal growth curves, and it is to be found for the most part in the Greater London and Midland areas and a number of smaller cities located in this belt. On the other hand, the major problem concerns the shift of the present populations from obsolescent houses into new flats or houses within the cities or on their outskirts. In such areas, the population is stationary, indicating on balance an emigration of workers and their families. This is the case in such areas as the textile areas of west Yorkshire and Lancashire, as well as Tyneside, Clydeside, and South Wales.

[1] L. B. Keeble, *op. cit.*, p. 62.   [2] *Ibid.*, pp. 66–7.

The new towns have been established since 1946 by government action. Two of these, Letchworth and Welwyn Garden City, located 30 and 20 miles respectively due north of London, were established as private organizations before the war on the lines inspired by Ebenezer Howard. They had a precarious financial development in their early days, since this is not the kind of investment that draws private capital. After the war, the government sponsored fourteen new towns on virgin sites, eight of which are in the periphery of Greater London. During the fifties these towns more than doubled their population and accounted for one-quarter of the total increase of urban population. After a long interval and several long disputes regarding the claims for new towns by cities as a means of disposing more quickly of their overspill, the government has approved five more towns,[1] bringing the total to twenty, with the early possibility of a sixth for the much-disputed claims of Manchester. There is talk of the last housing as many as 150,000 people, whereas the others will average around 50,000. It is possible that by 1970 these new towns will house about one million people. Though the British are justifiably proud of the new towns, it should be recalled that the great majority of the $4\frac{1}{4}$ million dwellings built since the war are located in the suburbia of the conurbations. Moreover, the latter are sorely in need of regional shopping centres in their peripheral areas. Each of the major outer sectors of every large city has 25,000 to 50,000 people and could support a regional shopping centre with liberal parking areas of the same order as a new town centre, a provision that is clearly necessary to relieve the congestion of the central business district. No wonder that the super-market chains are preparing plans for thousands of stores in new shopping centres, and meeting with the resistance of the conservative provisions of the planning authorities. New towns, too, are needed, probably one hundred in all, if there is to be effective decentralization. New sites will have to be found well removed from the existing conurbations along the highways and in contact with the depopulated rural areas, that could be assisted by the provision of services and work in the new towns.

The urban areas must expand to rehouse their people. Tens of thousands of derelict houses in every major city must be demolished and their occupants rehoused. Over $4\frac{1}{4}$ millions have been built since 1945, and there is talk at the time of writing of 'an onslaught on the northern slums' and the construction of three million homes in the next ten years. This sounds impressive, but it is still not catching up with the demand for a solution of the problem in our

[1] Dawley and Redditch, near Birmingham, Skelmersdale and Runcorn, near Liverpool, and Livingstone, near Edinburgh. Washington, near Newcastle, was approved in 1964.

time. The rate of 300,000 new units per year reached in the last few years needs to be nearly doubled to equal the current achievements in West Germany—in order to 'solve' the problem in the lifespan of those now in their twenties. This means building new homes at a fast enough rate so as to meet the demands by a specified date—say 1980—of houses long condemned for demolition, the annual addition of further derelict property, and the outstanding and increasing annual demand for new homes by newly married couples. There is at present no sign of catching up with this need that, on a 'conservative' estimate, reaches a total of over 10 million dwellings.

Many people can be put into new dwellings within the city boundaries, and since the war, after decades of discussion, the 'high-rise' apartment blocks have finally taken hold and skyscrapers ten to twenty storeys high are to be found in the large cities. But, even so, the cities will have many more people than they can accommodate with acceptable densities. They must look outside their boundaries. This is described as 'overspill'. Under the present system, these people must be housed in another administrative and planning unit. The arrangement at present is that the central city and the proposed receiving authority reach agreement and the former makes a contribution to the cost of housing people coming to the receiving authority, and the bulk of it from grants from the central government. London, for example, has negotiated the export of 10,000 people to King's Lynn. There is the notorious case of Manchester *v.* Lymm, when public hearings were held for Manchester's case for planting 18,000 of its overspill at a place called Lymm. The case was defeated. The fifteen new towns are now growing rapidly, but in recent years the government, rather than authorize still more new towns, has agreed to finance schemes for the reception of overspill into existing towns, where there is scope for growth. As noted above, the government has approved a further five new towns and more are to come.

The planning authorities have sought to check and direct the expansion of urban land uses, and the shifts and growth of urban populations. Two major matters are of primary importance in this context.

First there are limitations on urban expansion. Several controls are in operation. The Ministry of Agriculture does not exercise any control over land use (except market gardening) inside the limits of urban areas, that are demarcated by the 'Urban Fence'. In the proposed use of land outside the urban fence, the Ministry of Agriculture must be consulted. Outside the fence, there are often areas in which urban expansion could take place with relatively little harm to, or absorption of, good farm land. These are called, in the Ministry, Brown Areas. Most of the land outside the cities in the agricultural areas of the country are described as White Areas, that is, farm land in which no urban land uses are permitted. Here arises the concept of the Green Belt. This, originally formulated by Howard and Unwin, sixty years ago, has been adopted by some authorities and has become since 1955 a matter of government policy. A Green Belt is an area that is not to be used for urban purposes and should be reserved for agriculture, woods, golf courses, playing fields, cemeteries, parks, etc. It is designed to surround a city or lie between cities so as to prevent them from merging into each other. It is an extension of the idea of prohibiting ribbon growth, a law passed in 1935. Each of the planning authorities has been asked to submit an exact plan of the lands reserved for its Green Belt (Fig. 104). This means drawing with precision an inner boundary (around the city) and an outer boundary (in the countryside), between which will be the controlled Green Belt. Since the cities are normally fully built-up right to their limits (or soon will be), they just do not have enough land to provide themselves with an effective Green Belt. They do not even have the land on which to rehouse their people. In other words, Green Belts can only be effectively defined as to location and width over a long period in co-operation with the surrounding authorities. The policy is having an unpleasant impact on land values. Within the city boundaries there are often stretches of open land that lie between the existing edge of the built-up area and the (proposed) inner edge of the Green Belt. Prices of land for residential use are skyrocketing in these areas and are jealously sought after by private speculators and municipal builders. Further, the overspill population of the city will have to be moved outside its boundaries and thus across the Green Belt (however wide it may be) to places beyond. This will mean that either these people will have to be provided with employment in the outlying villages or country towns (i.e. that places of employment will have to be shifted from the city), so that they may become self-contained communities on the lines of the New Towns; or, alternatively, the people will have to travel daily over a long distance across the Green Belt to their work in the city. The problem is at present rendered more acute since Green Belts are normally in the form of proposals, so that there is an element of uncertainty about the whole idea. All these trends are evident in different parts of the country. They point quite clearly to the need for some kind of 'regional planning authority', that shall cover areas large enough to combine the cities and their wide environs, so as to plan effectively for the redistribution of houses, industry and shopping centres, the disposition of their Green Belts, and the further development of villages in the countryside, irrespective of the local boundaries. The latter are too tightly

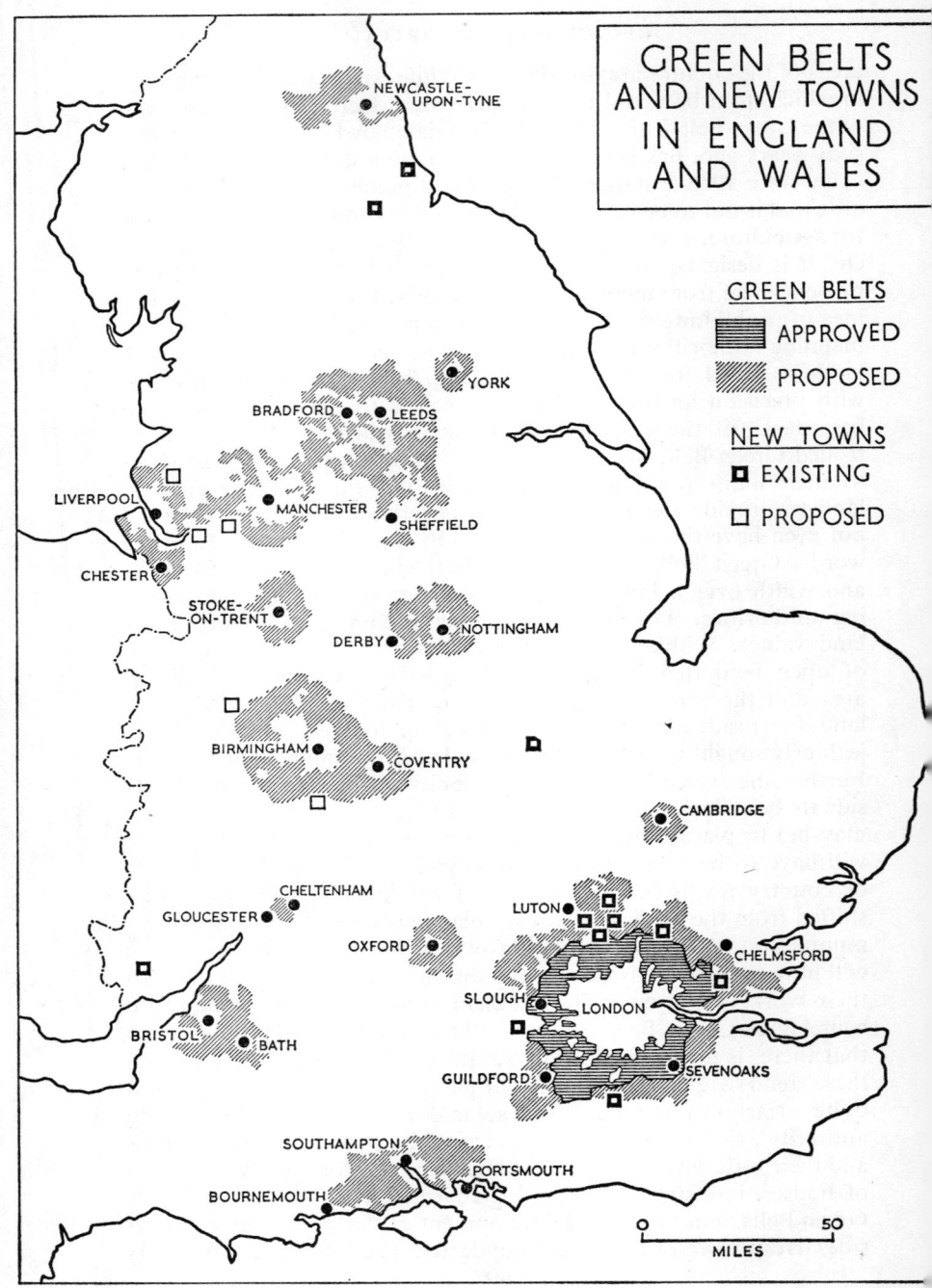

FIG. 104. England and Wales: Green Belts and New Towns (after Ministry of Housing and Local Government, *The Green Belt*, 1962).

drawn around the cities to permit them rationally to plan their own land in relation to the major regional complex of which they form a part.

Finally, there is every indication that in the post-war years the government has not been able to check the major trend in the country —the continual growth of London and the south-east. It was recorded by the Royal Geographical Society to the Barlow Commission in the thirties that between the wars there was a strong tendency for jobs and people to increase in a belt from west Lancashire through the Midlands to London and the south-eastern counties. At this same time, the industrial conurbations of South Wales, the textile areas of Lancashire and Yorkshire, and the coal and industrial areas of the north-east, were terribly hit by unemployment and had a declining population through emigration to the south. In spite of the efforts of the government to direct industry to these 'development areas' since 1945 (Fig. 105)—and there has been some remarkable progress, especially in South Wales—the growth of the so-called 'coffin belt' (so named from its shape) has continued, especially in the south-east. The agricultural area between London and Birmingham, that contains Oxford and Cambridge, has towns of rapid industrial growth, both on the new iron-ore fields and in the medium-sized cities of the area, of which Oxford, with its B.M.C. automobile works, is one, and Luton another. The construction of the first motorway from the outskirts of London to Birmingham provides a great axis in this belt, that will still further canalize this concentration of industry. This is rapidly becoming one great urbanized region comparable to Gottmann's Megalopolis. Everything points to continued concentration of growth within it, in spite of the fact that such growth is contrary apparently to government policy. This is not merely a 'Greater London' problem. It is a problem of nation-wide planning. Far more drastic action is needed at the national level than has been given to it if the trend is to be effectively checked or directed. These are some of the problems of regional planning, indeed, of national planning, in England and Wales, and it is obvious that they need co-ordinated planning both on a national scale and within the framework of effective regional units of self-government and administration.

7. Realism and the New Regions

Under the above title the leading editorial article in the British *Observer* on 9 December 1962 critically appraised the proposals of the bill then before Parliament for the revision of the structure of government in the London area. This proposal arose from an

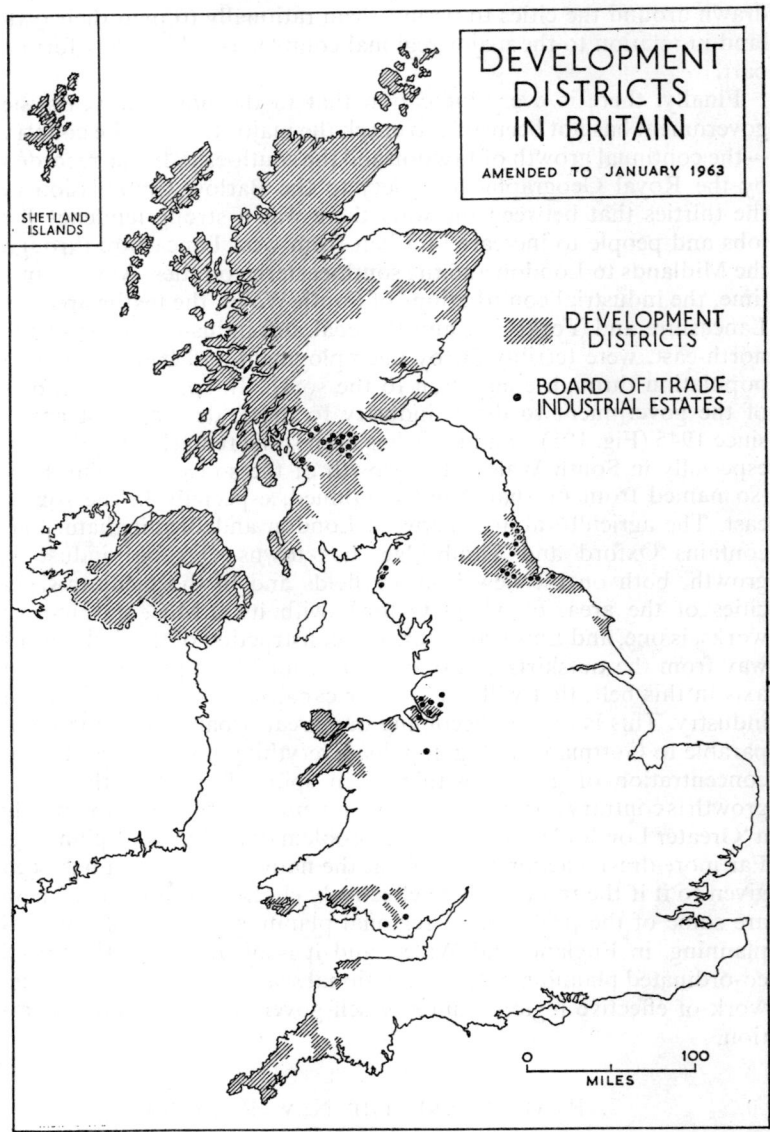

FIG. 105. Great Britain: Development districts in Britain (after Manners).

Towns and areas eligible for government assistance under the 1960 Local Employment Act. Corrected to January 1963. The circles show government industrial estates. Ulster is a development area with its own legislation.

enquiry by the Herbert Commission, separate from that of the royal commission on local government which is concerned with the rest of the country. The proposal for Greater London will bring into being by 1965 a new Greater London area to displace the existing London County Council and the administrative area of its competence. It will also establish thirty-two new component boroughs, with populations ranging from about 170,000 to 340,000. The new Greater London area will extend to the limits of the main built-up areas and their enclosing 'Green Belt'. It will absorb the administrative county of London as well as most of Middlesex and large slices of the counties of Surrey, Kent, and Hertfordshire. As defined by the Herbert Commission in 1959, it is a modification of the Metropolitan Police District (with which its investigation began) by the exclusion of some peripheral districts. This area, continues the editorial, is coincident with Greater London as defined by the Registrar General for the census. It had an area of 826 square miles and a population of 8,740,000 in 1959. The proposed new Greater London area will thus 'bring London as a unit of local government into line with London as a social, industrial, and economic unit'. So far, so good.

One of the main criticisms of the bill, however, is that the government should have defined a much more extensive area, since the relations of Greater London extend far beyond its built-up limits. 'The myth of London as a city has been allowed to predominate over the reality of London as a region.' This view re-echoes the main theme of this book. In other words, the new unit is defined in terms of the built-up area of the conurbation, but excludes the wider, though admittedly much more ill-defined, reality of the more extensive regional hinterland. This hinterland is most clearly indicated by the extending range of commuting to London and in the wide range of the L.C.C. arrangements for the housing of its overspill population, to places as far afield as Thetford, Ashford, Haverhill, Basingstoke, and Swindon. It even extends beyond the large area of Abercrombie's Greater London Plan. This wide area, marked generally by its growth of population, has been discussed in a previous section. Broadly speaking it embraces the area that has been defined by various authorities as south-eastern England or the London Province by Fawcett. This concept, as we have seen, has been developed for nearly fifty years particularly by geographers, beginning with Sir Halford Mackinder's notion of Metropolitan England. It should be noted that some argue that the Greater London of the present proposal is an essential step in the direction of the ultimate nationwide recognition of larger regional units, of which the London Region will be one. The new organization will become effective in 1965.

Similar proposals are being currently put forward by the local government commission and by the various local government authorities in their own recommendations to the commission. For example, Manchester has suggested a new county council to replace the 'patchwork or hotch-potch of local bodies' in south-east Lancashire and north-east Cheshire. There would be only nine county boroughs, including Manchester (in place of the existing fifty-five authorities), each responsible for a wide range of local services but leaving control of regional services to the new county. It is claimed that this area has close similarities to the London area, and that such a reorganization would meet the demands of current growth and development. 'Indeed it has been said that deliberate planning was always distorted by obstinate historical claims and by using the existing framework of local government instead of moulding it so that it is in keeping with contemporary needs and the techniques of new services.'[1] It is important to note that these Manchester proposals are considered to be 'totally unacceptable to most of the authorities in the review area since they would thereby lose their identity'.

A new Merseyside County Council has been proposed to the commission by the city of Liverpool. This would stretch from the Ribble river in the north to the Dee river in the south, and take in a large part of the 'hinterland of south-west Lancashire'. The existing local government units would be retained in a two-tier government with a new regional authority for the whole proposed region.

'In putting forward this proposal, the committee had in mind that there are a number of services vital to the economic life of Merseyside that need to be planned on a broad basis. The committee also has in mind that under overspill arrangements there must be a massive deployment of the Merseyside population if people are to be properly housed. The committee feels that the county council now proposed would be strong enough to tackle all these major problems for the benefit of Merseyside.'[2]

The commission itself in investigating the special review areas had already made proposals for the reorganization of the other conurbations. Two-tier government is proposed in the Birmingham and Tyneside conurbations, with the recognition of a single new unit for the whole conurbation with the status of a new county. West Yorkshire lacks a predominant focus of population and its existing local government authorities have a strong feeling of independence. It has been proposed to form nine new districts by various permutations and combinations of existing divisions and by the creation of a new

[1] Report in the *Guardian*, 20 October 1962.
[2] Report in the *Guardian*, 10 October 1962.

borough in the heavy woollen area of Dewsbury and Batley. Such moves have been made necessary since of the existing thirty-three districts twenty have populations under 20,000 people and are quite incapable of attending adequately, in terms of finance and staff, to the matters of government for which they are responsible. Many lesser cities have presented proposals to the commission for the extension of their boundaries with a plea for an extended *lebensraum*. Equally emphatically, however, as always, the lesser surrounding authorities that are to be absorbed or deprived of land, vigorously protest against such incursions on their independence.

All these cases illustrate the fact that the definition of new regions has to contend with two spatial realities. First, the administrative limits of the town or city must be adjusted to the range of the regular daily participation in its social and economic life—the notion of the urban tract developed in a previous chapter. Second, the region is the much larger entity, whose communities have a wide measure of common relationships and interests. These are tied up in part with the extended range of commuting to the cities and overspill population from the cities as well as with the orientation of common activities and interests to one or more major capital cities. It would appear that regions can only be effectively realized on the basis of a nationwide definition. Their acceptance will be a slow process—the last fifty years has witnessed very little permanent progress—since such regions would, in many ways, ultimately replace the counties as the effective seats of government and administration.

The need for immediate action in the establishment of regional divisions is currently receiving much attention at high levels. There will be in the next decades a drastic cut in the length of railroads and concentration of passenger and freight traffic on fewer lines, if the recommendations of Dr. Beeching's report are acted on. There must also be a big increase in the mileage of motorways. Both these trends will inevitably increase concentration of traffic to, from, and around the conurbations. The government's plans for economic rehabilitation in the north-east and in Clydeside are apparently to be carried out on a wide regional basis. The Buchanan and Crowther reports (1963) on urban traffic—a monumental diagnosis and blueprint for this formidable and desperately urgent problem—give primary emphasis to the need for regional agencies for urban modernization. Traffic surveys are being planned in the conurbations on the lines of the current survey in London. The Crowther report insists that co-ordination within wide regional divisions is essential for the future development of traffic and housing. The government claims, however, that before such drastic action be taken, the recommendations of the royal commission on local government areas should first be given a trial—and this must take many years. Sir Geoffrey Crowther replies to this 'I am willing to lay all Lombard Street to a china orange that it does not work'.[1] In these words, he is reiterating —on the basis of a formidable body of evidence and opinion—what has been obvious to serious observers for over a generation. The spatial needs of modern transport and traffic, housing, recreation, utilities, and government, demand areas of 'living space' that far transgress the horizons of the restricted boundaries of counties and boroughs. These arguments have been milled over by informed observers for nearly sixty years. Drastic and immediate action is needed, especially with the rapid increase of road transport, for the rebuilding of the urban society of Britain within a rational geographic framework.

Postscript

The following government publications have appeared since the above was written: Reports of the Steering and Working Groups, appointed by the Ministry of Transport on *Traffic in Towns; A Study of the Long-term Problems of Traffic in Urban Areas*, 1963; *The Southeast Study*, 1961–1981, prepared by the Ministry of Housing and Local Government (1964), and the White Papers on programmes of regional development and growth for *The Northeast* (Cmnd. 2206) and for *Central Scotland* (Cmnd. 2188).

Special reference should be made to the following new works: *Land Use in an Urban Environment: A General View of Town and Country Planning*, ed. by Dept. of Civic Design, University of Liverpool (essays by nine authors), 1961, and Peter Hall, *London 2000*, London, 1964.

[1] *Manchester Guardian Weekly*, 5 December 1963.

Chapter 17

REGIONALISM IN THE UNITED STATES

1. THE DEMAND FOR NEW REGIONS

The United States is of special interest in connection with the study of all aspects of regionalism. Its vast area is roughly three-quarters that of the whole of Europe, but it forms one political and economic unit. It has had a rapid modern development and transformation from a producer and exporter of primary products to a dominantly manufacturing country, absorbing the great bulk of its own agricultural production. It has experienced a great and rapid growth of its large metropolitan cities and is today primarily an urban society. The recent development of federal enterprise has displaced the 'rugged individualism' of the nineteenth century. There is an awareness of the need for the development of principles of nation-wide planning based on the conception of regional development. Two chief problems in the field of regional planning have received much attention in recent years. First, there is need for the conservation and scientific development of the country's natural resources. Second, changes have been brought about in the social structure by the increasing dominance of city life, made possible, above all else, by the advent of the automobile, which in the United States is not a sign of affluence, but a first claim by every citizen. The boundaries of the constituent States of the Union and their divisions—country and township—are entirely arbitrary and there is need for the creation of new units, large and small, more in conformity with the distribution and movements of population and with conditions of living and organization.[1]

What has been called 'the urban explosion' presents particularly complex and urgent problems in regional organization in the United States. This matter has been given attention for several decades, but

[1] *Our Cities: Their Role in the National Economy*, National Resources Committee 1937, and *Regional Factors in National Planning and Development*, National Resources Committee, Washington, D.C., 1935. M. Jensen (ed.), *Regionalism in America*, Madison, 1951. Twenty essays by various authorities.

has been most cogently expressed in a recent investigation in the following terms:

'The metropolitan areas—that is core cities with 50,000 people plus the urban areas around them—have been the fastest growing sectors of the American economy since the beginning of this century. This has been occasioned by the steady immigration of those seeking economic opportunities coupled with the exodus of people from the central city to the periphery, a movement primarily of younger people with children seeking more elbow room, that results, however, in urban sprawl, crowded and inadequately staffed schools and spiralling taxes. Shopping firms and industrial plants have also sprung up in suburbia. These major shifts of people and industry have strained the social fabric and overloaded time-honoured institutions. Sixteen thousand local jurisdictions in fewer than 200 metropolitan areas have struggled hard to maintain a semblance of orderly growth and to supply the increasing demands for public service of their area residence. But the unit costs of these efforts have been high; a team of mules is not as efficient as a single diesel engine. And although our local governments have kept things going in metropolitan areas they have failed in one crucial area of public responsibility; they cannot plan, budget, and programme ahead for the entire metropolitan region. The heart of the problem is the use of land and of other economic resources, particularly public revenue resources, in our metropolitan areas in the most efficient manner.'[1]

Planning in the United States is based on the existing administrative units and began in the twenties. The city is in many ways inadequate as such a unit, and the metropolitan district or the county has been adopted frequently in its place. The county with a city as its centre is a second type of unit, and is adopted by many planning organizations. It has the great advantage of being a single administrative unit, as against the metropolitan district which is a contiguous cluster of many independent municipalities. Two additional areas, larger than the above, are also used for planning, namely, the State itself, and a large area cutting across State boundaries within an arbitrary limit. In many ways the State is a good unit for planning, primarily because it is an existing political unit. It is a good unit for the study of natural resources and conservation problems. The collection of basic data, the formulation of a plan, and the eventual carrying out of the plan are also facilitated by State arrangements. But many aspects of planning within the State demand that its

[1] *Guiding Metropolitan Growth*, A Statement of National Policy by the Research and Policy Committee of the Committee for Economic Development, August 1960.

regional contrasts should be given full recognition. The Tennessee Valley Authority governs the best-known area of the second type, the boundaries of the region being the watershed of the Tennessee river.

In January 1937 there were over 1,500 city, town, metropolitan, and county planning agencies in the United States. There were just over 500 metropolitan and county agencies as compared with 85 in 1933. Metropolitan plans include those of Boston and New York. Other such regions organized for planning are Philadelphia, Chicago, St. Louis, Washington, and Los Angeles. More than 250 counties had been organized for regional planning, and in these cases the county was usually a predominantly rural area with a few small towns. There are also instances of a country plan which in effect was a metropolitan district and had been organized primarily for the purpose of metropolitan planning. State planning organizations are now in existence in all the States of the continental United States.

2. STATE PLANNING

State planning began in 1933 in the New Deal Period with the appointment of the National Planning Board, later called the National Resources Planning Board and finally the National Resources Planning Board (1939–43). Before this there had been independent State planning arising from such matters as the conservation of forest resources, the improvement of cut-over land, highway planning, heath and park-lands. The Board established State Planning Boards in relation to the federal government's public works programme, as well as for such matters as land use and transport. Within two years there were State Planning Boards in all of the States. These Boards were concerned with such matters as land classification, surveys of water resources, forests, minerals, and fisheries.

State planning was defined by the National Resources Planning Board as 'the systematic, continuous, far-sighted application of the best intelligence available, to programmes and problems of State development and organization, in order to provide higher standards of living and greater security for the people of the State'. There has been a rapid development of State planning in recent years, since the State is the largest existing political unit available for planning of resources. The abandonment of hill farms, and the deterioration of the soil in New York State led to a report in 1920 by the New York State Commission of Housing and Regional Planning, which is generally considered to be the first comprehensive planning report in the United States. The problem of deteriorated and tax-delinquent land led to such investigations as that of the Michigan

Land Economic Survey and the Land Economic Inventory of the State of Wisconsin.

The National Planning Board aided in the organization of planning boards in all the States, and assigned to them regional planning consultants, so that State planning rapidly gained momentum. State planning reports were drafted under the National Resources Board (1934) on the resources of the individual States, and on the basis of these reports the National Resources Board submitted to the President in December 1934 a most thorough inventory of national resources.[1]

Notwithstanding the great importance of the State as both a planning unit and a planning authority, one must recognize the fact that there are regional variations in type of country and types of resources with distinctive problems calling for special attention.

3. Regional Planning

Regional planning[2] has come into being from 'grass-roots', to use an American term (as opposed to the totalitarian system of imposition from above), through educational institutions as seats of research; semi-public commissions, such as the New England Council; Regional Planning Commissions, such as the Pacific Northwest Regional Planning Commission (consisting of the heads of the State planning boards of Washington, Oregon, Idaho, and Montana); commissions derived from 'Interstate Compacts', such as the Colorado River Compact (1922) between seven States for the equitable division and apportionment of the waters of the Colorado river system, and federal regional development agencies, the most famous is the Tennessee Valley Authority (T.V.A.), established in 1933, based on hydro-electric development in that river basin but covering a great number of planning problems associated with it.

Of special significance are the Regional Planning Commissions in and around the great metropolitan cities, that were established in the twenties and thirties as voluntary bodies, with the task of making

[1] The major items dealt with in these planning reports are: land resources, water resources, mineral resources, manufacturing resources, commerce and commercial assets, transport facilities and patterns, urban formations and their problems, population trends, recreational needs, social conditions and institutions, local government, public services, and public works.

[2] See Galloway and associates, *Planning for America*, Chapter 26, 'Regional Planning', by Earle S. Draper. The general trend in these programmes was towards 'comprehensiveness' in planning, without focus on particular problems, and as public works plans diminished in the late thirties the State planning activities diminished and their place was taken by 'development agencies' and other departments.

surveys and advising on future developments. A Committee on 'The Regional Plan of New York and its Environs' was organized in 1922. It published an extensive survey—the Regional Survey of New York and Its Environs (1927-29)—which is the most comprehensive programme ever formulated in the United States. The survey ran into ten volumes. The boundaries of the environs are described by the planners as follows: '(1) the area within which the population can and does travel in reasonable time from home to place of work—commuting area; (2) the large outlying recreational areas within easy reach of the metropolitan centre; and (3) the cities and counties at the periphery of these areas'.[1] The actual plan, however, was limited to the area immediately contiguous with the city, that is, it applied especially to the Metropolitan District of New York City as defined by the Census.

The Chicago Regional Planning Association sponsored many particular scientific surveys on a far more modest scale than the New York survey. Much, however, has also been achieved by it in the realm of practical city and regional planning, including the creation of a system of highways outside the city, the development of an outer belt of parks for public recreation, and the reclamation of land along the Lake Shore front.

In 1934 the St. Louis Regional Planning Association, in connection with the National Planning Board, made a detailed survey of the St. Louis area, covering 3,000 square miles within a radius of thirty-five miles of the city centre. This survey is the basis for a comprehensive regional and city plan. The Regional Planning Federation of the Philadelphia Tri-State District was active in the thirties in the preparation of a regional plan, inspired by that of New York. The Los Angeles County Regional Planning Commission, created in 1922, has a plan covering many cities and open areas outside the metropolis but inside the county. The Massachusetts Division of Metropolitan Planning is mainly concerned with the problem of co-ordinating transport in the Boston area. A plan has been initiated for the Washington-Baltimore-Annapolis area. Mention may also be made of the Milwaukee County Regional Planning Department and the Alleghany County Planning Commission for Pittsburgh, both of which, within the county, include the city and its wider environs. The greatest of all 'regional' planning programmes, endowed with authority to carry out its proposals (as opposed to the above surveys, where ability to carry out proposals is not known), is the Tennessee

[1] *The Regional Plan of New York and Its Environs* (two volumes), New York, Vol. 1, p. 133, 1929. The Survey has recently been repeated in nine volumes by the Graduate School of Public Administration of Harvard University for the Regional Plan Association Inc., under the direction of Dr. Raymond Vernon.

Valley Authority (T.V.A.). This covers a large area in the Tennessee river valley and embraces cities, towns and villages, and a vast rural area.[1] T.V.A. initially had 'the duty of making surveys and plans for the general purpose of fostering an orderly and proper physical, economic, and social development' in the area. In recent years this function of comprehensive regional planning has been eliminated, and in its place there has emerged a pattern of agreements with other government agencies such as State and local planning bodies, so that T.V.A. now functions as 'encourager, adviser, and technical consultant'.[2]

4. GEOGRAPHICAL REGIONS[3]

In a country as large as the United States there are many great contrasts in physical conditions, historical development, and economic and cultural conditions, which cut across the artificial State boundaries. Such regions have already been the subject of much scientific investigation as ends in themselves and as a means to the solution of particular problems. Physiographic regions have been the special contribution of American physical geographers. Geographers and agricultural specialists are concerned with 'agricultural regions' (Fig. 106), determined on the basis of common systems of farming. Sociologists have elaborated the concept of metropolitan or city-regions (Fig. 108), based on the spheres of influence of the principal cities, as a framework for the understanding of many fundamental social and economic problems of the day that are associated with city life. Still broader socio-economic divisions have been put forward as on Fig. 114. The National Resources Committee suggested a regional division for planning problems in connection with natural resources, which corresponds closely with the accepted agricultural regions (Fig. 109).[4] The United States Census Bureau uses a threefold division into North, South, and West, with subdivisions, bringing the total number of divisions to nine, though these statistical divisions rarely correspond with the other geographical units. An interesting and extremely useful type of region is the manufacturing region to

[1] For a full discussion of the programme and achievements of this organization, see David Lilienthal, *T.V.A.: Democracy on the March*, New York, rev. ed., 1953.

[2] See R. C. Martin, *T.V.A.: The First Twenty Years*, University of Alabama Press, 1956, p. 265.

[3] Figs. 106 to 114 are reproduced from *Regional Factors in National Planning and Development*, 1935, by permission of the U.S. Government Printing Office, Washington, D.C.

[4] *Regional Factors in National Planning and Development*, National Resources Committee, 1935, p. 166.

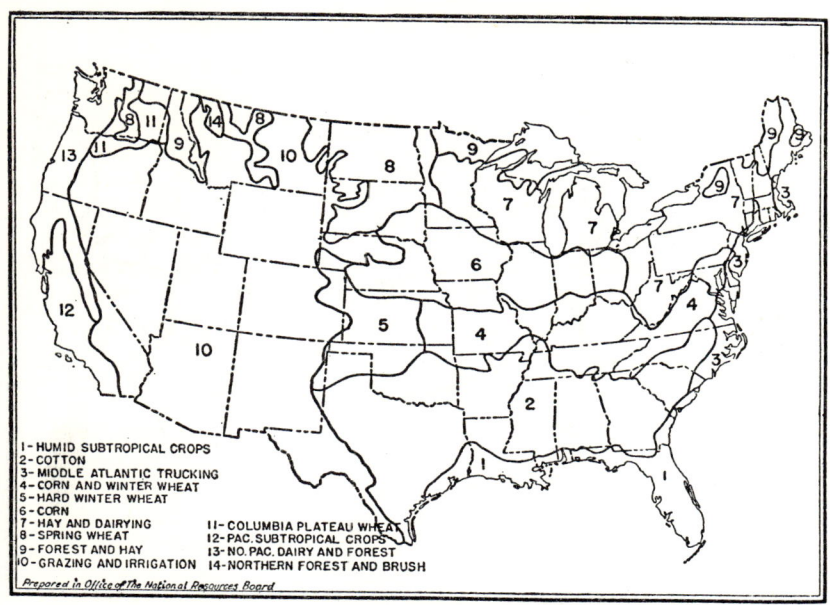

FIG. 106. United States: Agricultural Regions (after Baker).

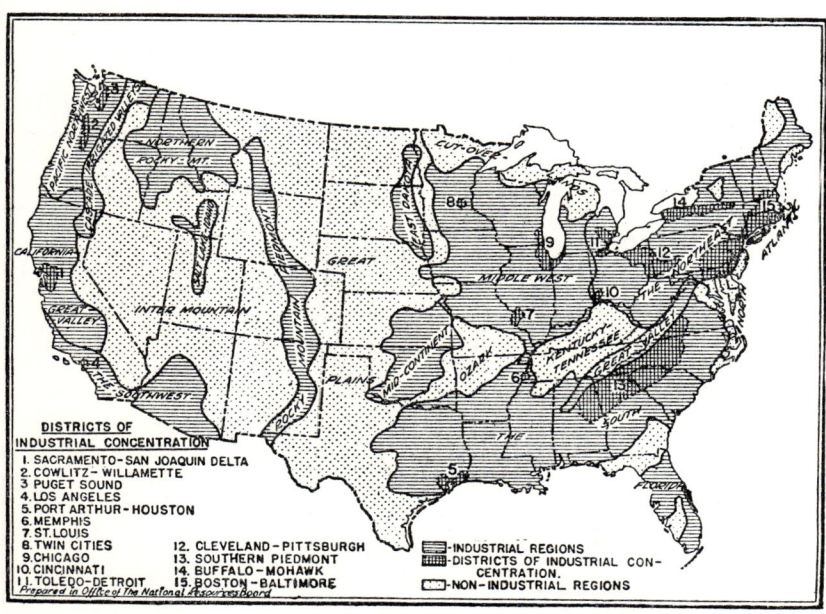

FIG. 107. United States: Regions of Manufacturing Intensity (after Strong).

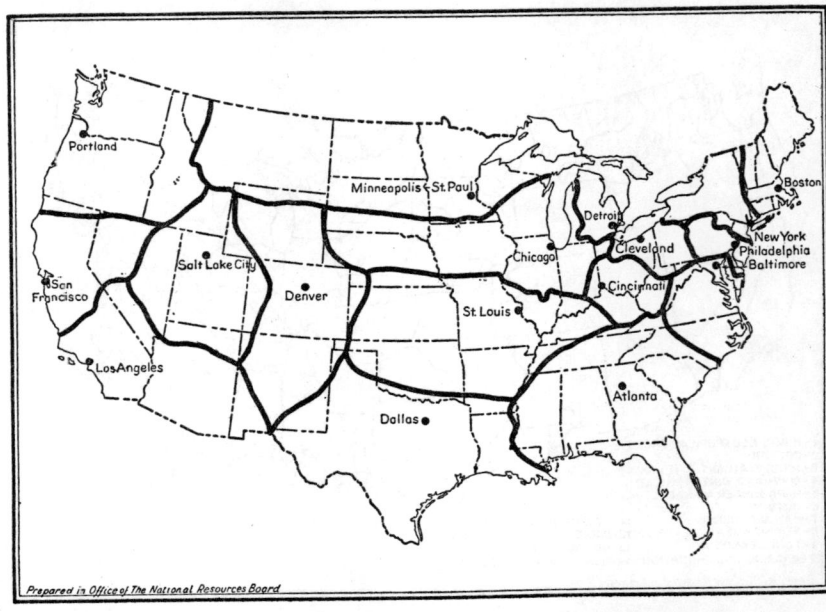

FIG. 108. United States: Possible Planning Regions based upon major Metropolitan Influence (after National Resources Board).

FIG. 109. United States: Possible Planning Regions based upon composite Planning Problems.

which geographers have given attention in America (Fig. 107).[1] Each of these types of homogeneous region is distinguished by a particular range of characteristics and therefore forms a useful basis for the investigation of particular problems.

An important system of economic areas has been worked out by Donald Bogue (1954), for the analysis of Census statistics pertaining to demographic, social, economic, and other data (Fig. 110). The threefold regions and the nine geographic divisions as used by the

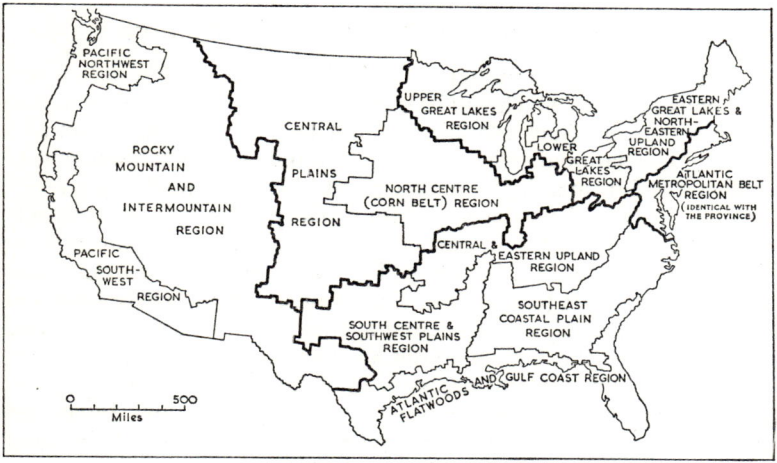

FIG. 110. United States: Economic Provinces and Economic Regions (after Bogue).

Census are unsatisfactory for statistical analysis since they are not in any way homogeneous. With the object of defining units that shall be homogeneous with regard to selected criteria, Bogue subdivides the country into five economic provinces, 13 economic regions (subdivisions of the provinces) (Fig. 110), and further subdivides into 119 economic sub-regions, and 501 State economic areas (subdivisions of sub-regions, which also recognize State boundaries, and are subdivisions of States). Within this system, each standard metropolitan area having over 100,000 inhabitants is recognized as a separate State economic area. In defining these regions a search has been made for

[1] A. J. Wright, 'Manufacturing Districts of the United States', *Economic Geography*, Vol. XIV, 1938, pp. 195–200; C. F. Jones, 'Areal Distribution of Manufacturing in the United States', *Economic Geography*, Vol. XIV, 1938, pp. 217–22; Helen M. Strong, 'Regions of Manufacturing Intensity in the United States', *Annals of Association of American Geographers*, Vol. XXVII, pp. 23–43; R. Hartshorne, 'A New Map of the Manufacturing Belt in North America', *Economic Geography*, Vol. XII, 1936, pp. 45–53.

'units that present unique combinations of traits'[1] as 'socio-economic areas'. Each area 'tends to be fairly homogeneous internally, and to differ significantly from the areas that adjoin it'.[2] The system, claims Bogue, 'refines the principle of regionalism' and has the advantage of adhering to the 3,000 odd county boundaries. It has been checked and approved by local authorities. It provides four levels of homogeneity; and thus permits the assembly of a wide variety of population data from the census.

5. Planning and Development Regions[3]

Physical planning is a matter of 'designing a pattern of human works and constructions which will bear harmonious relations to the underlying resources'. Such planning cannot be done for the nation as a whole. 'The national area is too large and too lacking in homogeneity to be viewed from a single vantage point.' Many avenues of approach to planning have been developed for *ad hoc* purposes, in great variety —by groups interested in particular commodities and industries, or particular services (e.g. banking); by departments of the federal and State governments (e.g. administration of forest and range land and waterways); and by governmental agencies which perform scientific functions (e.g. the United States Geographical Survey). 'There is, therefore, a fundamental necessity for relating the various interests and their peculiar contributions into a uniform and integrated national programme', that is, the planner needs 'a sub-national unit of area, which will furnish him a wieldy and manageable region'. For this purpose the State is not a satisfactory unit. Very many problems, such as navigable waterways, are of an inter-state character, that is, they demand agreement between adjacent States rather than action by the federal government, which is very limited in sovereignty. Further, such problems as reafforestation and the development of hydro-electricity call for joint action by groups of States. Moreover, social and economic allegiances extend across State boundaries to form distinct socio-economic units based on history and present interests which demand recognition in questions of planning.

Many proposals have been put forward for a regional division of the United States which shall serve as a basis for the inter-State treatment of physical planning. These regions fall into five categories:

[1] D. J. Bogue, *Population of the United States*, Free Press, Glencoe, 1959, p. 77.
[2] *Ibid.*, p. 77.
[3] See Chapter by George Renner in *Our Natural Resources and their Conservation*, edited by A. E. Parkins and J. B. Whitaker, 1936. Also Galloway and associates, *Planning for America*, 1941. Quotations are from Renner's article. See also *Regional Factors in National Planning*, National Resources Committee, 1935.

arrangements involving groups of states (Fig. 111); the spheres of influence of the great metropolitan cities (Fig. 108); regions designed by federal bureaux for administrative convenience with easy access to a central administrative city; single-function areas (Fig. 112); and composite-function areas (Fig. 109). Each of the first four types of region has its particular uses. Renner in a general discussion of the problem concluded that:

'in order to have genuine regional planning, it must be based upon *a composite of factors and elements*, both physical and human. This type of region has been defined as an area characterized by general unity in its human ecology.

'A major geographic principle is that in an area where resources are roughly uniform throughout, there is permitted the development of a general socio-economic homogeneity. The basis for determining the lineaments of major regionalism within the nation is inherent in such a principle. Indeed, this has to a certain extent already emerged spontaneously, as is revealed by the common use of such terms as the Middle West, the South, the East, the Pacific Northwest, and other endemic regional designations. Such regions, if their outlines be sufficiently flexible, would seem to be fairly satisfactory sub-national divisions for decentralized national planning. Moreover, they possess the added virtues of being readily identifiable and of expressing already existing regional loyalty and consciousness to which planning can be harnessed.' [1]

This idea of 'spontaneous regionalism' has been re-echoed in the following words. 'When like thoughts and attitudes dominate entire groups of people, there emerges the dynamic force of public opinion or group thinking, which shapes and moulds the life of a region or a nation.' In a measure, these evolve from 'the human, economic, and physical surroundings'.[2]

More recently an American scholar, Max Lerner, has written as follows.

'By its nature the outlines of the region are elusive. The most frequent usage (no two lists will agree) is to speak of New England, the Middle-Atlantic Region, the Upper South, the Deep South, the South-west, the Mid-west, the Great Lakes Region, the Rocky Mountain Region,

[1] Renner, on 'National Regional Planning in Resource Use', in Parkins and Whitaker, *Our Natural Resources*, 1936.
[2] See Helen Strong, 'Regionalism: its Cultural Significance', *Economic Geography*, Vol. XII, 1936, pp. 392–410. This author then instances as such regions: Middle West, South, New England, Pacific Northwest, the West, California and the East. See also Max Lerner, *America as a Civilization*, 1957, Vol. I, pp. 182–206, with long bibliography.

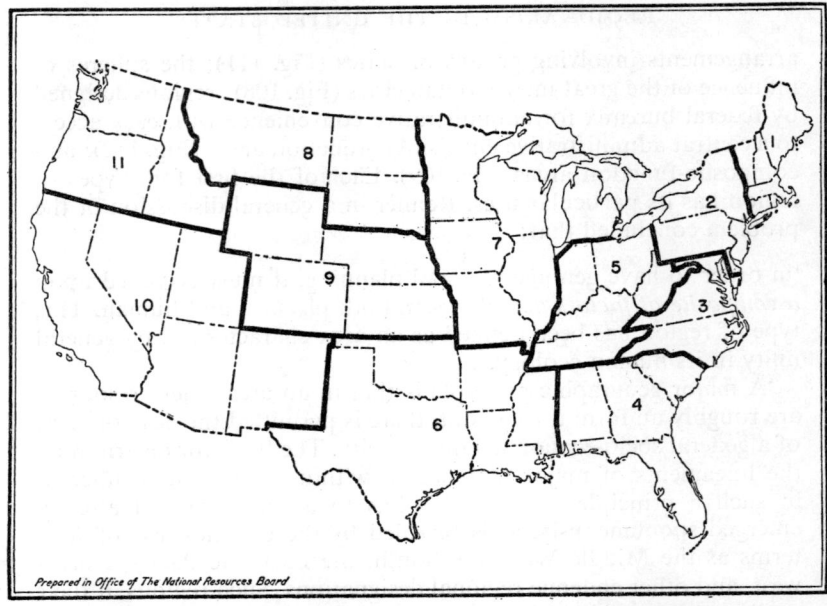

Fig. 111. United States: National Resources Board Planning Districts, based upon Group-of-States arrangements.

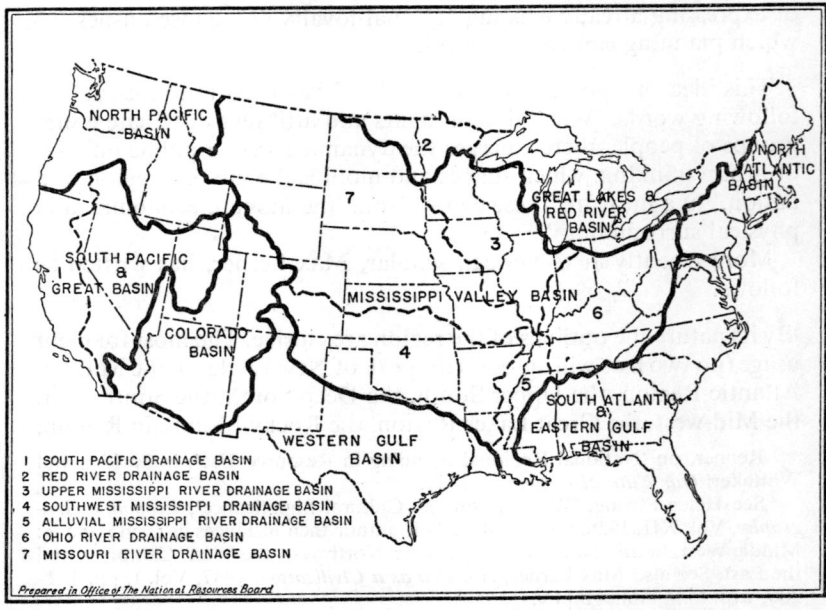

Fig. 112. United States: National Resources Board Water Resources Districts, based upon a single function.

the Far West, and the Pacific Northwest. These are at once geographic (by which the author means physical), economical, and cultural units. There are also agricultural groupings which cut across them: the type-farming regions such as the Cotton Belt, the Wheat Belt, the Range Livestock area, the Dairy area, the Western Special Crop area . . . the larger regional units are in turn broken into sub-regions. . . . The picturesque calendar of such sub-regions could stretch almost endlessly[1] . . . or a region is a cultural unit within a frame; in some areas the frame may be mountains or river basin or lakes, delta or bayou or desert; in others it may be the type of crop grown there; in still others the decisive element may be the enforced isolation or the uniformity of stock and tradition. The components may vary, but to form a region or sub-region there must be a roughly homogeneous physical environment and a roughly homogeneous economic unity which together serve as a frame for community living and a common history and consciousness . . . regional cultures are the carriers of American diversity.' [2]

Many writers have observed that it is not possible to define regions in advance of planning, for differing areas will be required for different purposes. Thus, regional planning headquarters will be established in those areas where there is a marked clustering of related resources and a marked consciousness of unity among the peoples. The boundaries of the region would not be fixed for all purposes, but would vary according to specific planning problems, though all would pivot on the same central capital centre. The boundaries would thus, in effect, be elastic.

A region for planning purposes within the framework of nation-wide planning in the United States, as stated in the report of a Special Committee to the National Resources Committee, should fulfil the following requirements:[3] It should be characterized by compactness and contiguity, by homogeneity, by 'unity, organic inter-relationship, and cohesion', by a major combination of resources (that is, it should be a natural economic unit), it should include whole problem areas and not partial areas, it should be a 'total areal pattern of culture and works', it should not cut across such patterns, it should possess regional identity as evidenced by popular usage and by a popular name (such as New England or the Middle West), and lastly, it should be of a fairly large size.

[1] Examples quoted are Blue Ridge country, Panhandle country, Ozarks, etc. See the volumes entitled *American Folkways*.
[2] Max Lerner, *America as a Civilization*, Vol. I, *The Basic Frame*, New York, 1957, p. 183.
[3] *Regional Factors in National Planning*, National Resources Committee, 1935, p. 157.

REGIONALISM AND THE CITY-REGION

The authors of this report to the National Resources Committee submitted a scheme of regions for nation-wide planning purposes. They considered every type of natural and administrative division of the country and discovered that very many of these regions coincided in their general extent and that they had a common core, although the boundaries were indeterminate and zonal. Using as a basis a great variety of criteria, twelve regions were established for 'composite planning purposes', and these were given a popular regional name, which however is devoid of political meaning. These regions are shown on Fig. 109.

The characteristics of these geographical regions may be illustrated by reference to two clearly defined major planning regions, namely, New England and the Pacific Northwest. In both these regions Regional Planning Commissions were established in 1934, in accordance with suggestions from the National Planning Board, with the object of co-ordinating the planning of interstate problems. They had purely advisory functions. The New England area covered the six States east of the Hudson river with an area of 62,000 square miles and a population of just over eight millions.

'It is the geographical region east of the Hudson valley. It is the historical region of the Yankee. It is the ethical region of the New England conscience and of Puritanism. It is an industrial region separate from all other industrial regions, a recreational region of rugged coast, tumbled mountains, crystal streams and lakes, sloping orchards, and white pine forests. Movements such as the one that culminated in the organization of the New England Council show that New England is not too large to have a consciousness of community aims.'[1]

There are, however, fundamental contrasts within this whole especially as between the north and the south, the latter in particular being overwhelmingly attracted to Boston and New York City.

Industrial southern New England is quite different from northern New England, and it has a close relation with the entire manufacturing region of the north-eastern States; part of Connecticut is definitely associated with the New York metropolitan area more than with New England; certain important land-use problem areas extend westward beyond the borders of Massachusetts and Vermont; the great northern recreational belt is functionally related to the whole North Atlantic seaboard city complex.[2]

[1] W. R. Greeley, 'Regional and City Planning in New England', in *New England's Prospect*, 1933, American Geographical Society, p. 406.
[2] *Regional Factors in National Planning*, p. 122.

REGIONALISM IN THE UNITED STATES

The Pacific Northwest, as the name indicates, lies in the extreme north-west of the United States on the Pacific slope, and its character as a physical and human unit is undoubted in both the scientific and popular senses, although the extent of the region from each point of view differs widely. The region finds varied definition. From the standpoint of regional planning the Pacific Northwest Commission defined it as including 'not only the Columbia Basin, but Puget Sound in north-western Washington, and that part of the Missouri Basin lying in western Montana, as well as the coastal areas fronting the Pacific in Oregon and Washington. All are inseparably linked economically and socially into one zone.'[1] This whole region has an area of 392,000 square miles and a population of three and a half millions (in 1960, over six millions).

The whole, however, while recognized by its authorities as a good planning unit, is geographically diverse, as well as being very large. It has three major divisions—the Pacific mountain and valley section, the Columbia Basin section (that is mainly agricultural), and (western) Montana, characterized by wheat farming and livestock ranching, with spots of irrigated agricultural land.

The coastal section is dominated by the metropolitan influence of Portland and Seattle and their neighbours, while eastern Montana looks towards the Twin Cities. There were also marked political differences, the coastal section voting Democratic, the 'Inland Empire', centred on Spokane, voting Republican, while Montana varied in its allegiance between the two major parties and had third-party leanings. There is, however, one social factor tending for regionality in the Pacific Northwest. This is the unusual homogeneity of the population of the region, which is primarily Anglo-Saxon.[2] Political alignments, however, as evidenced by Presidential elections, though formerly reflected in diverse sectional interests, have now largely disappeared.

The Pacific Northwest Commission, on behalf of the National Resources Committee, undertook in 1935 an investigation of the nature and degree of the homogeneity of the Northwest as a basis for the regional treatment of common planning problems. The basis of regional homogeneity was sought in tests of 'historical data relating to cultural habits and economic intercourse'.

'It has studied a few of these factors, such as the distribution of lumbering in the four States, the distribution of different types of agriculture . . ., the traffic density as shown by studies of motor

---

[1] *Pacific Northwest Regional Planning Commission, Progress Report*, February 1935, Portland, Oregon, p. 130, quoted in *Regional Factors in National Planning*, National Resources Committee, December 1935, p. 122.

[2] *Ibid.*, quoted in *Regional Factors in National Planning*, p. 123.

vehicle traffic . . ., the analysis of regional transportation facilities, and the correspondent bank relationships between cities and towns within the four States and with banking centres outside. The regional organization of the two great mail-order banks furnishes another clue to economic and commercial intercourse. Among possible culture tests of homogeneity, the study made use of available information concerning religious affiliation, newspaper distribution, and long-distance telephone messages between selected toll centres. It also studied . . . the votes cast on initiative and referendum measures in two elections separated by intervals of about twenty years. Lack of time and inaccessibility of other significant test data made it impossible to be sure of a precise boundary in Montana and in Idaho, but the net effect of the factors examined appears to be that Oregon and Washington, western Montana, and all of Idaho except the southeast counties made up a unit which for general planning purposes might rule and constitute the Pacific Northwest region.' [1]

'. . . The test of homogeneity for regional determination, from whatever angle we approach it, is in final analysis the behaviour of people. We need therefore to look for similarities of living habits and standards, similarities of knowledge and skills required to solve their economic difficulties (in which the conservation and utilization of natural resources loom very large), unity of religious outlooks, and expressions of feelings of regional unity. As incidental clues to some of these elements we shall look for physical (e.g. transportation) and institutional (e.g. banking) ties that act as canals for an intense social intercourse.' [2]

The Pacific Northwest, as thus defined, is an entity that is suited for many purposes of federal government. No central planning agency has been established, however, since the abolition of the Commission in the forties.

With the ending of the National Resources Planning Board in 1943, most of the State Planning Boards ceased to exist in their original form and new organizations became increasingly concerned in the fifties with 'development' rather than 'planning', that is to say, they became more concerned with specific problems relevant to areal economic development rather than with surveys of 'comprehensive' planning of land, use and activities, and organization. All the States now have agencies of this kind and fifteen have Development Credit Corporations that provide loans to public and private borrowers.

[1] *Regional Planning*, Part I—*Pacific Northwest*, National Resources Committee, May 1936, p. xii.
[2] *Ibid.* Staff Report—Section III, p. 100. See in particular R. F. Bessey, *Pacific Northwest Regional Planning: A Review*, Division of Power Resources, State of Washington, 1963.

So rapid has been this kind of trend that today there are over 5,000 area development groups of different kinds in the States. Metropolitan and urban expansion has greatly accelerated this development with the support of business and government operations.

The vogue of trying to define composite 'regions' seems to have died down in the last twenty years, but increasing attention has been given to their substance—nature resources and population, and the many-sided problems of taking care of both in particular regional situations.

Regional planning in the United States is currently applied to a variety of activities—the development of natural resources of river basins and other resource regions, such as the Tennessee Valley and the Columbia Basin; the guidance of the physical growth of city-regions; the management of the regional organization of special services such as highways, ports, transport, water, etc.; and plans directed to the economic development of special areas. Thus, in the words of Perloff:

'Regional planning and development activities—whether dealing with the orderly growth of a broad city-region, or with the multiple-purpose development and integrated management of a river-control system, or with the factors influencing the economic expansion of a depressed region—are by their very nature concerned with the interrelation of certain basic physical, economic, political, and social elements as they influence a broad range of private and public decisions.'[1]

American natural resources have been the subject of exhaustive enquiries, official and non-official, in recent years, and many of these must, of necessity, have a regional frame and be a source for regional reference. There are the three-volume report of the *Water Resources Policy Commission* (1950–51); the report of the Paley Commission on *Resources for Freedom*, 1952, in five volumes, and the Twentieth Century Fund volume on *America's Needs and Resources* by J. F. Dewhurst and associates, New York, 1956.

There have also been big developments in the planning of natural resources. The most spectacular is the growth of soil conservation districts. There are now 2,700 such small districts in the nation concerned with soil erosion and with soil and water conservation. Increasing attention is also being paid by these bodies to land-use planning. Perhaps the most striking development is that of river-basin planning, by the Army Corps of Engineers and the Bureau of Reclamation. The federal highway programme with its plan for

[1] H. S. Perloff, *Education for Planning*, Resources for the Future, Baltimore, 1957, p. 70.

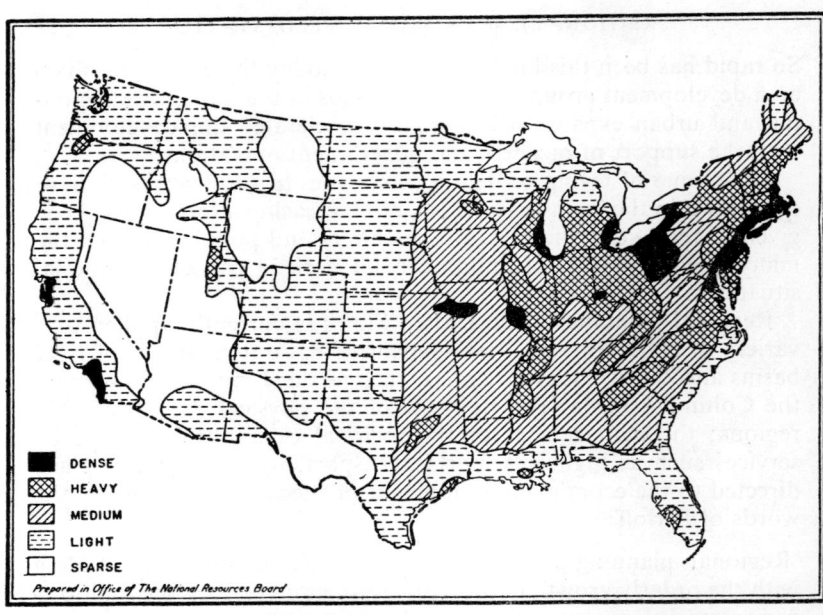

FIG. 113. United States: Population Regions (after U.S. Census).

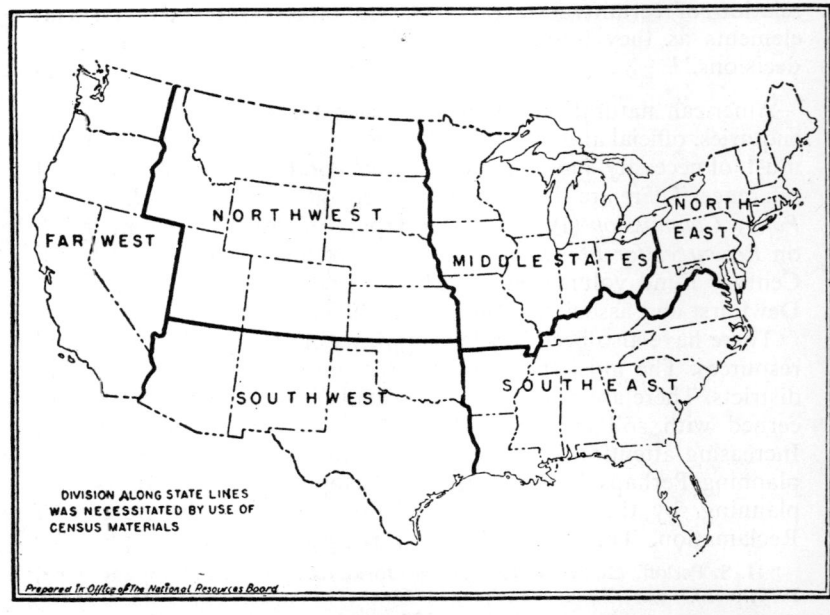

FIG. 114. United States: Socio-economic Regions (after Odum and Wooster).

41,000 miles of interstate super highways demands careful economic studies on regional lines. 'It is no exaggeration to say that never in our national history has a centrally conceived construction programme offered such a large opportunity for shaping directions of population and industrial growth.'[1]

6. Metropolitan Regionalism

The phenomenal impact of the metropolitan city on the countryside has been a dominant feature of the internal scene in the United States since the war. In order to emphasize the gravity and urgency of the 'urban explosion' in its varied aspects let us briefly enumerate some of its consequences.[2]

First, there is the impact of urban land uses—'scatteration' as some Americans like to call it—on agricultural land uses. Over one million acres of farm land has been eaten up yearly by urban land uses for several decades. There is also a loss to agriculture of nearly another million acres a year through soil erosion, afforestation, water-logging, and the like. Of 465 million acres of cropland only 72 millions are in what is described as Class I land and over one-half of this land is within reach of the urban areas. It has been argued that if the present levels of agricultural production and consumption continue, the nation, at this rate of loss, will produce by the mid-sixties no more food than will be required by the demands of its increased population. Some readjustment is obviously going to be essential. Will it be a decrease in production (and the disappearance of export surpluses) or increased production from a decreased area of cropland? There are those who are perturbed; there are others who are prepared to let economic trends take their natural course, through which the remaining agricultural land will be cultivated to bring higher yields—a general trend during recent decades.

Second, there is the question of water consumption that in some cities seems to be outrunning the existing supply. New Jersey, the most highly urbanized State in the Union, draws most of its water from wells. In the mid-fifties the State was using some 10 per cent. more than its long-term average yield and a sub-normal year could bring disaster. The kitchen taps of Atlantic City sometimes yield saline water, yet the people voted against taxation for a new storage reservoir. Cities must seek increasing supplies from new sources over greatly increased distances, and often involving bitter conflicts between cities and States.

[1] *Ibid.*, p. 89.
[2] On this general topic see in particular E. Higbee, *The Squeeze: Cities without Space*, New York, 1960, and *The Exploding Metropolis*, by the Editors of *Fortune*, New York, 1957. Most recent publication is Jean Gottmann's *Megalopolis*, Twentieth Century Fund, New York, 1962.

Third, there are sanitary problems, that arise especially where housing takes place without adequate cognizance of the physical conditions of the site, and especially when the pipe and disposal systems are in the hands of separate municipalities in one urban area. Septic tanks can absorb the sewage of plots of over one acre, but when houses are built on average suburban plots to say 60 by 135 feet, the gardens may become quickly waterlogged when the occupants first flush their toilets. Above all, there is the problem of widespread water pollution by the use of rivers as open sewers.

A fourth consequence of urban expansion is the steady decrease of the availability and accessibility of open space in and around the urban areas. Open space is needed to conserve water, to maintain special types of agriculture, to avoid flood hazards and land slips, to afford playing space, to form buffers against noise and nuisance, and above all for recreation. 'The demand for outdoor recreation is likely to increase tenfold in fifty years, simply in terms of the expected growth in population, income, leisure, and mobility.'[1] Much of this demand will be located in scenery and places far removed from the metropolitan cities. This is already evident over wide areas up to 50 and 75 miles from the cities, where there are cabins, and transformed farm-houses, on the shores of lakes and in the hills, motels along the highways, and extensive State and National Parks. 'If our present preserves are not rapidly expanded, overuse will create many wilderness slums by 1970.' In New York a plan has been formed to increase the permanent open space by 60,000 acres but right now this would involve a cost of two billion dollars. A remarkable report has recently been published on public outdoor recreation in California. It points out that the present recreational facilities are 'overused' by more than 30 per cent., with 60 per cent. of the recreation being 'water centred'. Thus, greater access is sorely needed. By 1980 the population of the State will have doubled and the people will have more leisure and more rapid transport. By 1980 it is calculated that 30 per cent. of the outdoor recreation will be spent within two miles of one's dwelling (day-use), 25 per cent. within 250 miles (overnight use), and 10 per cent. beyond 250 miles (overnight use). In terms of 'activity days', the demand will be four times greater than today. The State is thus threatened with an 'overwhelming deficiency' and overcrowding of recreational facilities. Therefore, 'the State should lead a bold programme to develop a comprehensive statewide landuse plan in which recreational needs are adequately recognized'.[2]

[1] Catherine Bauer Wurster in *Goal for Americans*, Report of the President's Commission on National Goals, 1960.
[2] *California Public Outdoor Recreation Plan*, 1960, 2 Vols., Documents Section, Printing Division, Sacramento.

A fifth consequence of urban expansion is the need for drastic revision of the boundaries of municipalities. A large number of independent municipalities lie around each large central city, and owing to expansion beyond the boundaries of the central city to marginal municipalities and small incorporated or even unincorporated areas, that do not have municipal equipment of their own, boundary revisions and the co-operation of municipalities are needed in the interests of economy and viable system of taxation, and for the financial maintenance of mass transit by train and bus.

Transport presents a sixth problem. Mass transit (rail and bus) carries large numbers of outside-commuters who are not required by taxation to support the system. It is suffering from the quite cataclysmic competition of the automobile that normally brings people to their work in the cities more quickly, and cheaper, and with greater comfort, than the train or bus. Most companies have suffered a tremendous loss of passenger traffic (to automobiles) in the fifties, and most of them are in the red. The provision of new services will involve tremendous financial outlay (and tax increases) for the regional groups of municipalities, that would be concerned, as in the proposed system for the Bay Area of San Francisco.[1]

A seventh consequence of urban expansion is the need for a new geographic base for taxation. Municipal taxation in the States depends almost entirely on land and buildings. Indirect taxation is small and irksome (e.g. retail sales tax). Industrial and commercial properties have much higher assessments than residential property. Expenditures, on the other hand, for maintenance, protection and public services, are greatest in the residential areas, notoriously so in the suburban areas. The latter have inadequate revenue from their residential properties to meet the costs of providing sewage, water, police and fire protection, and especially schools, that are needed much faster than they can be built. Hence the suburban municipalities must seek outside aid, either by bringing in industrial plants or by receiving financial help from outside, for they jealously resist absorption with a larger neighbouring city. There are municipalities in the metropolitan districts in which virtually the whole of the area is in industrial uses and the resident population numbers a mere few hundreds. There is an urgent need for larger areas of taxation and government, and more realistically related to the areas of the distribution of population and places of work.

---

[1] There is a vast literature on this topic. See Jean Labatut and Wheaton J. Lane, *Highways in our National Life*, Princeton, 1950; W. Owen, *The Metropolitan Transportation Problem*, Brookings Institution, Washington, 1956; and R. B. Mitchell and C. Rapkin, *Urban Traffic, A Function of Land Use*, Columbia University Press, New York, 1954.

Lastly, the central cities, confronted with the flight of people and their money to the suburbs, have suffered for several decades from the depreciation of land and property value and thus of tax revenue; from the steady deterioration of buildings; and from the virtual stoppage of building in the depression years and then during the war. Meanwhile, many northern cities, if present trends continue, will soon have large Negro majorities, as southerners move in and the Whites move out to the suburban peripheries.

All these are, of course, problems associated with modern cities in Europe as well as in the United States and Canada. The last ten years, however, have witnessed a new attack on these problems in the States, and a large share of the financial burden is being carried by the federal government. Slums are being cleared, though so far the rate of demolition and replacement for the lower-income brackets is distressingly slow. Blighted areas are being 'refurbished' and 'conserved'. Express highways are being built around, under, through, and over, the central cities, often at three or four levels. Skyscraper apartments and office buildings are being built with exteriors of aluminium, stainless steel, bronze and gold leaf. The building of colossal civic centres is in progress. Parking areas are appearing both above and below ground. But close to one-third of the homes in the country are still considered to be inadequate on current standards and the problem of rehousing their occupants, through federal aid (and this is the only solution), has scarcely been touched as yet.

Here are enormous tasks of planning and government that are becoming daily more complex since the process of growth is so alarmingly rapid. The essential problem for the immediate future, particularly in view of the great expansion of new highways (or 'freeways'), is to find effective ways and means of preventing urban sprawl. The States have constitutional powers for the acquisition of land for highway construction and for the purchase of development rights and rights of zoning in urban and rural areas, that would permit immediate withdrawal of land from uncontrolled development. There is also need, however, for a new rationale of land-use planning on a nation-wide scale. This should reach beyond the usual practice of city and regional planning, and probably operate within the framework of a few major planning regions, larger than the States and defined with due regard to the distribution of population. This will be a longer process and would call for greater federal powers and the education of public opinion on the issues at stake. Urban expansion is proceeding with such rapidity that immediate action on such lines is essential.

In conclusion, the problems of metropolitan government require further comment. They arise from the fragmentation and multiplicity of local municipalities and special districts of local government in the metropolitan urban areas. It is necessary to co-ordinate these districts and combine the municipalities so as to cope more effectively with the common problems of life and organization of the metropolitan community.[1]

As of January 1958 there were nearly 16,000 local government units in the 174 metropolitan areas, one-seventh of the total in the nation. One-half of these are school districts, and the balance are municipal areas and many districts for special services. The New York area had over 1,400 local units, the Chicago area nearly 1,000 units, and Philadelphia 700. These governmental areas are concerned with the provision of services such as education, water supply, sewage and garbage disposal, control of surface drainage, fire and police protection, transportation, and a large number of health and welfare activities. The patterns could be co-ordinated or enlarged so as to increase the efficiency of service and reduce the costs of taxation.

Every standard metropolitan district contains a large central city, and a considerable number of contiguous municipalities, that are small in area and population and often badly balanced in uses and tax resources. The following general comment about Chicago is equally true of every big urban area in the United States.

'All local services supported in whole or most part by real estate taxation are affected by the metropolitan land-use pattern, so that study of the services themselves is not likely to be adequate without some consideration of the effects of metropolitan growth and layout upon their financial base. A case in point. One district includes an industrial area and this has an assessed valuation of $200,000 per pupil. The other district was entirely residential (much of it related to the plants in the separate school district) and it is financially distressed with a valuation less than one-third that of its neighbour.'[2]

Various methods have been devised to readjust these governmental relationships in metropolitan areas. Annexation was frequent until the opening of this century. There are a few more recent examples of such procedures, as in Houston, Dallas, Atlanta, and San Antonio. These are in general concerned with the annexation of *unincorporated* areas that do not have their own governmental set-up. It is much more difficult for one municipality to absorb another without full consent of the area to be annexed. Unincorporated fringe areas often cannot be absorbed because of the annexation laws that differ from

[1] Coleman Woodbury, quoted in L. S. Lyon, *Governmental Problems in the Chicago Metropolitan Area*, p. 6. See also R. H. Connery and R. H. Leach, *The Federal Government and Metropolitan Areas*, Harvard University Press, 1960.
[2] Connery and Leach, *op. cit.*

State to State, though the legal matter could be simplified, as in Texas and Virginia, by means of special action of the State legislature. Consolidation involves the merger of the governments of the county with the central city. There are a few such instances—New Orleans, Boston, Philadelphia, New York, and Baton Rouge—but all these took place before 1900. The municipalities may federate so as to form a single metropolitan government. An outstanding example is Toronto, but this method has not yet met with success in the States.

Common action with regard to a specific function may be reached by intergovernmental contracts. This is the usual procedure in the United States. It is often effected by the transfer of functions to the county unit, but this is not the best unit area. Metropolitan special districts may be formed to serve a central city and its surroundings for special purposes—fire, street lighting, rural improvement, etc. Illinois and California lead in the number of such districts. The Port of New York Authority, that handles transport and terminal facilities, the Sanitary District of Chicago, and the sewage disposal and water supply metropolitan district of Boston, are examples of this kind of government.

All these problems of metropolitan organization have been present for a generation. They have become more urgent since the war through the 'urban explosion'. Current trends, that are occurring at an alarming rate, demand immediate action and the grass root procedure is very slow. It remains to be seen what the federal government can do to implement rapid and effective action.[1]

The whole field of regional planning and especially the problems associated with metropolitan growth have been the concern of many organizations in the last twenty years. Outstanding are the researches of the Committee on Economic Development, Resources for the Future Inc., and the Twentieth Century Fund. Furthermore, funds have been made available to University groups for particular enquiries. One of these, for example, is the second nine-volume survey of the New York Region, carried out by the Harvard Graduate School of Public Administration. University departments of city and regional planning, public administration and social studies are actively concerned in training personnel at the graduate level and in programmes of sponsored research.

Progress is slow, but there is a possibility, writes Perloff, that 'within the next generation a new structure of urban government and metropolitan planning will have evolved in the United States'.[2]

---

[1] Among many publications, in the form of inventories and programmes, both official and non-official, the reader will find it particularly interesting to read the Report of the President's Commission (appointed by Eisenhower) on National Goals, entitled *Goals for Americans*, published in 1960 as a paper-back by Prentice-Hall.   [2] H. S. Perloff, *op. cit.*, p. 85.

Chapter 18

REGIONALISM IN GERMANY

The problem of regionalism in Germany is far more complicated than in France and Britain, for it has been tied up with the need for the political reorganization of the Reich, in which the government of Prussia, with about two-thirds of the area and two-thirds of the population, was a dominant partner, until its abolition after World War II. The movement for the territorial reorganization of Germany assumed great prominence after World War I and received continuing attention from both official bodies and numerous private researchers between the two World Wars. Great advances have been made since 1945, but the problem is not yet finally resolved, though the government is legally committed to its solution. The problem has had four aspects—first, the dominance of Prussia over the federated states of the Reich; second, the heritage of complicated territorial boundaries that have no relation to the demands of contemporary government; third, the fact that there are broad geographical groupings in the cultural heritage and consciousness of the people; and fourth, the most important groupings in modern society are those concerned with the distribution, movements, activities, and common interests of the population. These conditions make it necessary to revise and rearrange political territories so as to bring boundaries into closer alignment with contemporary groupings and needs. It is the same situation as in other countries, but it clearly has individual features and problems.

1. The Problem of *Neugliederung*

Let us look at the problem as it appeared and was tackled in the twenties and thirties, and then turn to the post-1945 developments.

The term Regionalism is not used in Germany. Its equivalent is *Neugliederung*—a new territorial organization, with new political boundaries. The problem arose in the Weimar Republic as a matter of abolishing the giant governmental and territorial partner of

Prussia, and, of eliminating dwarf States and the inliers and outliers of political territory. In their place should be established a number of compact well-balanced States, including essentially the existing *Länder*, and the provinces of Prussia (with important modifications of boundaries and regrouping of territories) raised to the status of new *Länder*. It was generally agreed that such new *Länder* were needed, but there was continuing difference of opinion on what should be done about Prussia, and, how the new *Länder* should be defined.

The political pattern in 1919 was in essentials the same as established in 1871. Indeed, most of the political boundaries—the historical mosaic that is repeatedly grouped, as it were, from time to time—are derived from the Middle Ages. In 1933 there were seventeen *Länder*—formerly called Free States (*Frei Staaten*). The largest were the States of southern Germany—Bavaria, Württemberg, and Baden; the States of central Germany—Saxony, Thuringia, and Hesse; and all the Prussian provinces west of the Elbe—Saxony, Hesse-Nassau, Rhineland, Westphalia, and Hanover. Each of these corresponds with the type of new unit that was generally envisaged. This also applies to the Prussian provinces east of the Elbe—Brandenburg, Pomerania, East Prussia, and Silesia. Entirely different States were, however, the remnants of old historical units—Oldenburg, Brunswick, Anhalt, Waldeck (absorbed by Prussia in 1929), the two Lippe states, the two Mecklenburgs (united in 1934), and the cluster of Thuringian States united in 1920. Prussia had fourteen divisions, including the city of Berlin and the small outlying province of Hohenzollern in the heart of Württemberg. The average area of each of the remaining provinces was about 25,000 square kilometres with a population of 3·0 millions. The other States ranged from Bavaria with 78,000 square kilometres and 8·3 million inhabitants to Schaumburg-Lippe with 340 square kilometres and 54,000 inhabitants. Among them were also the free cities of Lübeck, Bremen, and Hamburg. These States and Provinces had many detached outlying pieces of territory situated in a State from whose local government they were independent, but with which they had the closest social and economic associations. Some of these small territories were states in themselves and long had the apparatus and authority of an independent government.

During the past hundred years Germany experienced a revolution in its economic structure. This, in effect, took place between 1870 and 1914. As a result, the geographical distribution of human activities and spatial relationships cuts right across the medieval frontiers which impose ridiculous and harmful restrictions on the efficiency of government. Thus, it is necessary that new political provinces be established, and that these provinces, in order to be effective units of government and administration, should be so defined as to combine a maximum of social and economic interest, although at the same time respecting, wherever possible, the existing political boundaries. Such was the problem. It came to the front of the programme of the National Assembly at Weimar in 1919 when abortive attempts were made to recast the major political divisions in accordance with the Weimar constitution. It was given much attention by government authorities and by scholars during the inter-war period. Theories and facts bearing on it have given rise to a large literature which has carried the scientific analysis of the patterns of geographical or spatial relationships much further than in any other country. In the early twenties general schemes for a new division of the Reich were put forward, without, however, an adequate basis of fact. In the following years numerous public authorities and scholars published elaborate investigations of the various aspects of the general problem and of particular regions.

Important regroupings of administrative areas were effected between 1919 and 1939. Under the Weimar regime, the most notable change was the formation of the new *Land* of Thuringia in 1920, from a number of scattered units. The Nazis also removed some of the old territorial anomalies which had been matters of bitter contention for many years. They created a single administrative authority at Hamburg, transferred Lübeck to Schleswig, and eliminated the many small outliers of territory between Lübeck and Hamburg and along the Mecklenburg border. They established a new framework of administrative regions for regional planning and party organization, following the principles suggested above. They standardized the administration throughout the Reich and standardized the status of the *Länder*, albeit by depriving them of their rights of democratic self-government.

2. Inter-war Proposals

The central question between the wars was: What shall be the basis of a new set of political units as component elements in the new Reich? The proposals of the various bodies adopted, in general, the existing political pattern, with the absorption into it of all the small territories. This, as we have just indicated, is not enough. Others sought a basis in the tribal areas of the old *Volksstämme* which show the regional differences in dialect, tradition, temperament, and folklore. Special investigations of particular areas were based on various criteria, sometimes with the deliberate aim of supporting a contention for territorial gain. Many schemes for such a division of the

Reich were made. The most effective units are to be found (subject, however, to a clearly defined policy as to area and population), not in historical units, nor in existing divisions, nor in cultural associations, but in the natural entities of modern activity, interests, and organization that are inherent in the structure of society. These afford the widest basis of assessment for measuring that homogeneity which is the essential basis for an effective political unit.

FIG. 115. Germany: Regions proposed by Preuss in 1918 (after Vogel).

Professor H. Preuss prepared a constitution in November 1918 for the new Weimar Republic. This was to be a federal State, with *Länder* of roughly equal size, with at least a million inhabitants. He envisaged sixteen States (Fig. 115)—Prussia (east and west), Silesia, Brandenburg, Lower Saxony, Upper Saxony, Hesse, Thuringia, Westphalia, Rhineland, Baden, Württemberg, Bavaria, Austria, Berlin, Vienna, and the Hansa cities of Hamburg, Bremen, and Lübeck. Preuss' scheme failed owing to the opposition of the existing State governments, notably that of Prussia, and of the National

Assembly in 1919. The question of a *Neugliederung* raised so many difficulties that the National Assembly shelved it. The root difficulty seems to have been that it was held, on the one hand, that the new central Reich government should displace the Prussian government, and the Prussian provinces should rank as the other *Länder*; while, on the other hand, it was argued that, in view of the international situation, the strength and unity of the Prussian government should be maintained at any price. The last view won, and Preuss' scheme for the new territorial organization of the Reich failed in its immediate purpose. The National Assembly, however, recommended the establishment of a Central Committee for the Territorial Organization of the Reich (*Zentralstelle für Gliederung des Reiches*) in 1920, but this body produced no tangible results and was abolished in 1929. The only important change it effected was the creation of Thuringia as a unified *Land* out of many small fragments by a *Reichsgesetz* in 1920.

Other schemes were put forward to remedy the defects of the constitution and the territorial organization. A conference of leading ministers from each *Land* was called by the Reich government in 1928 to discuss the problem. It declared that a new territorial organization was necessary, that the dualism of *Reich* and *Land* should be abolished, and that twenty-one *Länder*, roughly equal in area and population, should be established with the provinces of Prussia standing as equals with the old States. Another scheme was elaborated for the *Bund zur Erneuerung des Reiches*, founded in 1928, by the Reichschancellor, Dr. H. Luther (Fig. 116). This scheme differed fundamentally from that of Preuss in that Prussia was to remain as a single political unit (*Reichsland*), directly controlled by the Reich government. This new *Reichsland* was to consist of twelve existing provinces of Prussia (with Berlin as a separate province), together with Thuringia, Hesse, Mecklenburg (Schwerin and Strelitz), and the two Hansa cities of Hamburg and Bremen. Other small *Länder* were to be absorbed into the neighbouring Prussian provinces to form five new divisions. In addition, there were to be four provinces outside the *Reichsland*, with a greater measure of administrative independence—Saxony, Bavaria, Baden, and Württemberg.

The schemes of Preuss and Luther both adhered closely to the existing divisions, grouping some of them and abolishing all the outliers. They had the great advantage of adhering to the existing framework rather than elaborating an entirely new system with entirely new boundaries as some radical schemes suggested. Nevertheless, such schemes could not give adequate recognition in detail to the facts of the distribution of population and social and economic associations. Professor Walther Vogel[1] suggested in 1932, in summing up the spate of literature and discussion on the subject, that the existing political units be adhered to as closely as possible. He also urged that local studies be undertaken to examine the distribution of settlement, traffic movements, economic and social relations, and the historical development of the existing political divisions, in

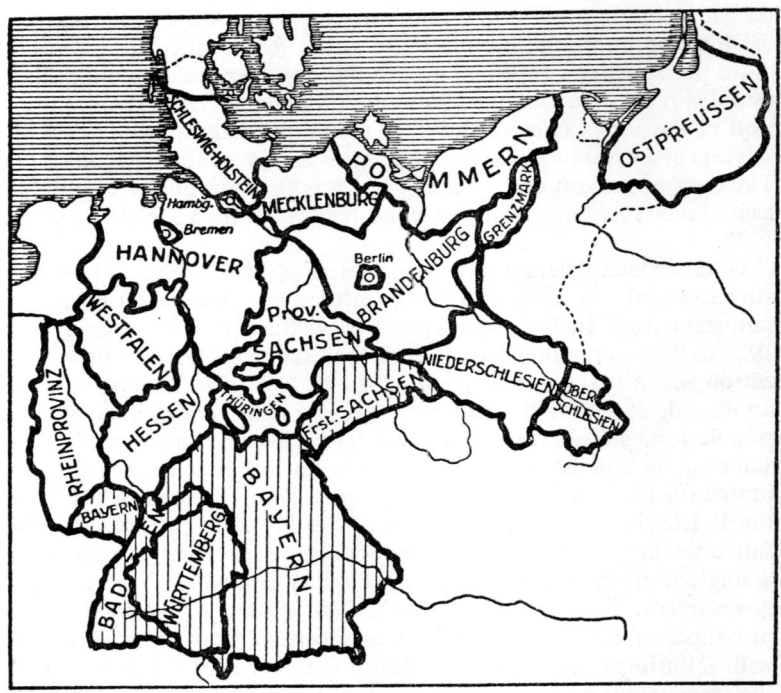

FIG. 116. Germany: Regions proposed by Luther in 1928 (after Vogel).

order to facilitate the definition of new provinces and the clear delineation of their boundaries. The new province, he also stipulated, should conform to a standard population rather than a standard area, and this not only so that the province should be adequately represented in the *Reichsrat*, but so that it would be able to lead a

[1] Walther Vogel, late professor of historical geography in the University of Berlin, made a special study of this problem in all its aspects in *Reichsgliederung und Reichsreform in Vergangenheit und Gegenwart* (1932). He was a friend of Preuss and took an important part in the proposals for the framing of the new politico-geographical pattern in 1919.

balanced economic and cultural life, that is, it should be able to support a University, technical schools, museums, libraries, theatres, concerts, etc., and, we would add, the complete apparatus of representative government. He also gave support to the view that Berlin, Hamburg, and Bremen should be constituent provinces.

There was a good deal of administrative decentralization as in other countries. The central Reich government established its own nation-wide organization for many *ad hoc* purposes independent of the *Länder*—partly because the latter vary so much in size, partly to short-circuit the governments of the *Länder* which might grow too powerful. This applied to finance, administration, social administration (unemployment insurance, etc.), control of waterways, education, and so on. This process, known as *Aushöhlung*, by establishing an independent regional system of Reich government, parallel to and independent of that of the *Länder*, undermined and weakened the authority of the latter, and was the cause of a great deal of friction. It also resulted in greater concentration of authority in Berlin. In the realm of taxation, '*Reich* and *Land* are like a married couple, when the husband earns the money, the wife pays it out, but they do not tell each other what the income is and what the money is spent for'.[1]

The Reich was divided into provinces for a great variety of purposes—by departments of the Reich government as noted above, by industrial concerns for the transaction of business or the distribution of supplies from central offices, and by trade and professional organizations. Although these provinces differed considerably and were naturally based on the existing political divisions, they often reflected a necessary regard for such considerations as community of economic interest and activities. One of the most significant groups was the *Wirtschaftskammer*, the regional chamber of commerce that was subordinate to the *Reichswirtschaftskammer*. Each of the seventeen provincial chambers had on it representatives of local industrial and trade interests for each *Bezirk* in the province, and it also cared for the interests of all employed persons. A related body was the Ministry of Labour (*Reichsarbeitsministerium*), which handled labour questions, such as unemployment and insurance, in each of its thirteen districts (*Landesarbeitsämter*). The organization established by the Nazi government for the settlement of labour disputes—the *Treuhänder der Arbeit*—also had a Reich-wide division into the following districts—East Prussia, Silesia, Brandenburg, Pomerania, Nordmark, Lower Saxony (*Niedersachsen*), Westphalia, Rhineland, Hesse, Central Germany (*Mitteldeutschland*), Saxony, Bavaria, south-west

[1] W. Vogel, *Reichsgliederung und Reichsreform in Vergangenheit und Gegenwart*, 1932, p. 97.

Germany, and Saar-Palatinate. These are important examples of the many divisions of the Reich adopted for purposes of Reich administration and for the care of economic interests. Another important sphere of regional organization was connected with regional planning (*Landesplanung*). Such organizations differed in origin from the above in that they were groupings of local government authorities formed, as in Berlin, for the purpose of fact-finding and making recommendations for joint problems of physical planning—or, more correctly, inter-town planning. As in other countries, these organizations were in the first place voluntary, with, however, one very important exception. They came into being entirely since World War I, although Dr. Robert Schmidt just before that war put forward the case for the formation of a single planning authority for the Ruhr industrial area. Such a body, known as the *Siedlungsverband Ruhrkohlenbezirk*, was established in 1921, with Dr. Schmidt as its first President, with full legal powers for dealing with traffic, housing, open spaces, and railway traffic for the region as a whole. The region extends as a belt from near Hamm in the east, across the Rhine westwards to the Belgian frontier. Voluntary regional planning organizations, without any legal authority to carry their proposals into effect, were established afterwards elsewhere in the Reich, and these usually had their centres in the great cities. Thus, to quote a few examples, a Greater Hamburg regional planning authority was formed in the twenties, covering the area within thirty kilometres of the city centre, and similar bodies were established around other great cities, such as Frankfurt and Cologne. Many of these authorities took as their geographical limits the boundaries of the political divisions, usually the *Regierungsbezirk*. Of special interest are the elaborate investigations and recommendations made by the *Mitteldeutschland* regional planning body for the future development of the brown-coalfield in the middle Elbe basin, an entirely new industrial area that overlaps the boundaries of Prussia, Saxony, Thuringia, Anhalt, and many small territorial outliers. All this development, as in Britain, was piecemeal and voluntary and without central co-ordination. The Nazis organized the whole of the Reich into regions, incorporating these planning authorities, for purposes of physical and economic and social planning.

It will be obvious that for statistical purposes, the State or *Land* and the Prussian Province, with their interlocking territories were inadequate for the appraisal of conditions in compact geographical areas. For this reason, for example, in addition to the existing political divisions, the German census has long used a set of economic units (*Wirtschaftsgebiete*), grouping together all the separate political territories in each unit. These were as follows: East Prussia,

Pomerania, Berlin–Brandenburg, Silesia, Saxony, Central Germany, Province Saxony, Anhalt, Thuringia, Bavaria together with the Palatinate, North Elbe (Hamburg and Schleswig-Holstein), Lower Saxony, including roughly the Province Hanover, and the *Länder* of Braunschweig, Oldenburg, Bremen, and Lippe, Rhineland-Westphalia, Hesse (Hesse-Nassau and the province of Hesse), and the south-west. Similar divisions are in use in West Germany today.

From this brief enumeration of regional divisions used for a variety of purposes one notices at once the recurrence of names and groupings that had no political existence. This is the kind of geographical grouping that is inherent in the organization of modern society, based upon the actual areas of modern regional associations. In East Germany, the *ad hoc* units consistently conformed to the Prussian provinces. Elsewhere, we may note in particular several groupings that do not appear on the political map. Central Germany or *Mitteldeutschland*, it will be noted, is the name usually given to the whole or parts of the *Länder* of Anhalt, Thuringia, and Province Saxony— the new brown-coal industrial area and the old industrial area of Saxony. Lower Saxony has its nucleus in the Province of Hanover and includes many small political divisions in and around it. The south-west usually includes the *Länder* of Württemberg and Baden. Rhine–Main includes the area around Frankfurt, comprising Hesse and Hesse–Nassau, with variations in its limits.

3. Investigation and Action in the Thirties

A vast amount of work has been done by both public and private authorities in Germany on the geographical structure of the regions of Germany. Public bodies have financed such investigations. Numerous bodies attached to the Universities encouraged research on all aspects of the regional problems. Comprehensive atlases for several of the regions are models of their kind and such work is now being continued in a magnificent atlas for each *Land* of the *Bund* of West Germany. There are several exhaustive and authoritative atlases for the Reich as a whole showing economic data—agriculture, industry, and commerce—in which respects Britain has only just made a start. Studies of regional aspects of physical, economic, and commercial problems are numerous in the publications of scientific societies.

Another aspect of this work covered the proposals actually put forward by individuals, based on various criteria, for the regional division of the Reich, that in their view, would be best suited to serve the needs of a regional reconstruction. Inter-war political reformers, as we have seen, aimed at the creation of regions that should be effective political and cultural units, but that should also, in the interests of expediency, fit as closely as possible with existing political units. These schemes in varying measure, fail to give adequate weight to the facts of regional economic activity and orientation. However, a good deal of work on these lines was undertaken. Thus, Erwin Scheu, professor of geography at Königsberg, thoroughly examined in 1927 the *innere Verflechtung* of the Reich (Fig. 117). He recognized twenty-two smaller regions (*Wirtschaftsbezirke*) and nine

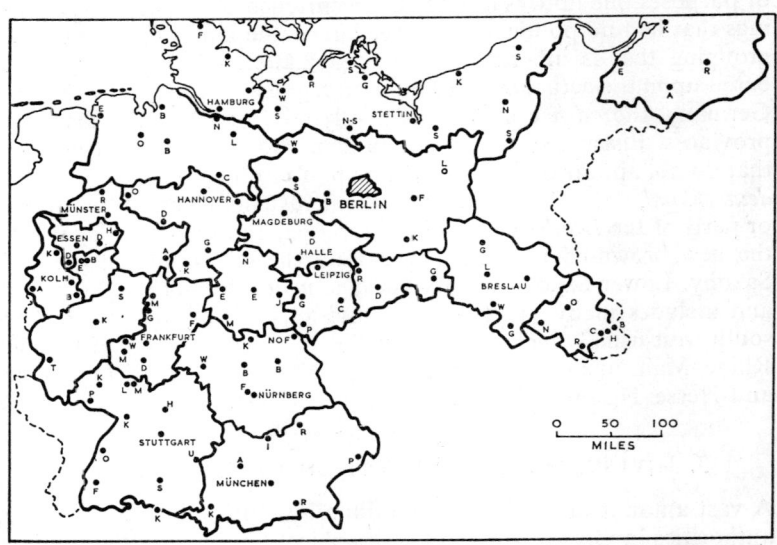

FIG. 117. Germany: Economic Regions in 1927 (after Scheu).

larger provinces (*Wirtschaftsprovinzen*), basing his study mainly on the facts of industrial and agricultural production, and commerce. The larger provinces are the Baltic province (Schleswig–Holstein, Mecklenburg, Pomerania, East Prussia), Lower Saxony, Berlin–Brandenburg, Silesia, Central Germany, Rhenish–Westphalia, Rhine–Main, South-west, and Bavaria. A. Weitzel, a public administrator of Frankfurt, made an investigation of the Rhine–Main region in 1928 in terms of the orbit of Frankfurt and, using this as a basis, suggested a division of the Reich into twelve regions (Fig. 118) as determined by 'the economic interests of the separate sections of the Reich, their geographical continuity, their social structure, and cultural unity'. Many other schemes were prepared—some taking account primarily of the historical units, others of cultural data, others of the sources and distribution of power as the basis of

REGIONALISM IN GERMANY

economic activity and orientation (Fig. 119), and still others on other assessments in an attempt to fit a particular point of view or to suit particular desiderata.[1]

The Nazis placed in the forefront of their programme in 1933 a co-ordinated plan of regional and national development. On 29 March 1935, a National Board (*Reichsstelle*) was created to regulate the land requirements of public bodies 'in a way that suits the needs

FIG. 118. Germany: Regions proposed by Weitzel in 1928 based on spheres of influence of chief cities (after Vogel).

of people and state'. On 26 June 1935, the title of National Planning Board (*Reichsstelle für Raumordnung*) was conferred on this body, and to it was entrusted the 'comprehensive co-ordinated planning of the whole Reich'. To facilitate this, the Reichsstelle was made responsible for the organization and control of all national and regional planning authorities.

A framework was established by the National Planning Board in February 1936 (Fig. 120). The Reich was divided into twenty-three planning regions (*Planungsräume*) which generally coincided with the

[1] It should be noted that such proposals appeared in great numbers in the twenties, when the whole problem, as raised by the first Weimar Assembly, was right to the fore. The Nazis discouraged the private publication of such proposals, but research continued and solutions were effected from the centre, dealing summarily with questions of heated controversy, e.g. Great Hamburg.

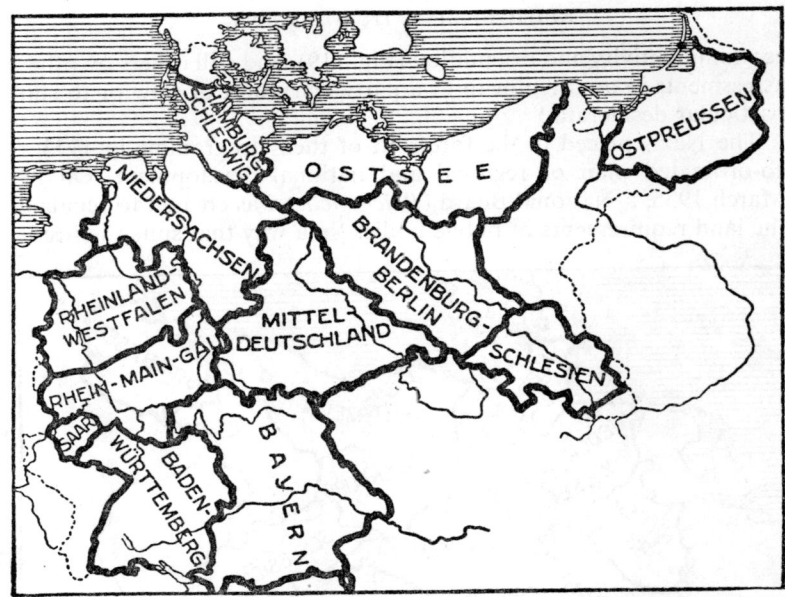

FIG. 119. Germany: Regions proposed by Baumann in 1928 on the basis of power distribution and railway traffic (after Vogel).

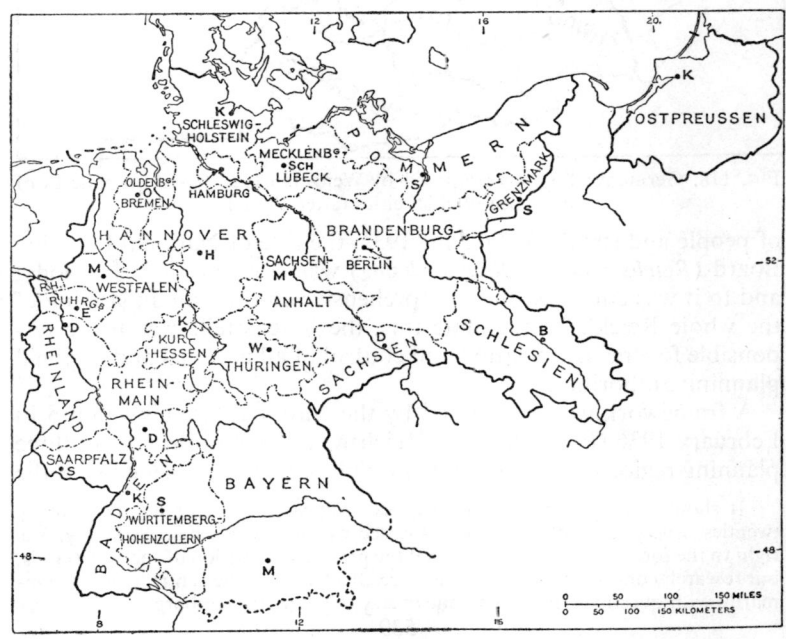

FIG. 120. Germany: Regional Planning Districts in 1936.

provinces of Prussia and the *Länder*. The Ruhr region (*Ruhrsiedlungsbezirk*), Berlin, and Hamburg were separate regions. In each region the chief planning authority was the supreme representative of the Reich (*Reichstatthalter*, or, in the provinces, *Oberpräsident*), who was directly responsible to the National Board. The main organization was the Regional Planning Federation (*Landesplanungsgemeinschaft*), a body with statutory and executive powers, on which were represented all facets of activity in the region—social, economic, political, administrative, and academic. This body was responsible for examining the conditions and needs of its region and for constructing a comprehensive regional plan. The actual work of planning lay in the hands of the Regional Planner. The Board also established a central body for the direction and co-ordination of planning research (*Reichsarbeitsgemeinschaft für. Raumforschung*). Groups were formed subordinate to this body in most Universities to co-ordinate the investigation of general conditions and specific problems of their regions.

Thus, to sum up. After 1871 the new Reich was a loose federation of States, each of which had a large measure of real self-government, though the federation was completely dominated by Prussia. After World War I, in spite of the strong movements for decentralization from Berlin and a large measure of autonomy free from the control of Berlin, the pendulum swung in the opposite direction. Thus, the Weimar National Assembly decreed virtually complete control of taxation by the Reich government, a most momentous decision, and established a Defence Ministry, and centralized all the State railway concerns as a single State organization (*Reichsbahngesellschaft*). The States or *Länder* as they were called in the Weimar Republic remained responsible for justice, education, police, and social welfare, but controlled virtually no taxation. In effect, the whole system of taxation was controlled by the Reich and the *Länder* received their finances from the pocket of the central Treasury.

This centralization became even more marked under the Nazi regime, for an avowed and much vaunted aim of Nazi domestic policy was to co-ordinate systems of law and government throughout the Reich, and to regroup the political divisions of the Reich within the new framework, though depriving them of every semblance of real self-government by reducing the status of the *Länder* to that of mere units of administration with a greatly swollen bureaucratic machine.

4. Post-war Developments

After the collapse of Germany in 1945 substantial changes in the government and political divisions took place. New *Länder* were established in the western Zones in 1946 and 1947. The changes were based on a regrouping of the existing areas, but they went far to solve the problems of a *Neugliederung*. Above all else, Prussia was completely eliminated, and in the place of its provinces there emerged the new *Länder* of Nordrhein–Westfalen, Niedersachsen, and Schleswig–Holstein, with Bremen and Hamburg remaining with the status of *Länder*. In addition, Hesse was created by the Americans in their Zone. Württemberg and Baden were temporarily divided between the American and French Zones of Occupation, but were rejoined to form one *Land* with the withdrawal of the Occupation Authorities; Bavaria remained intact, except for the loss of Rhineland territory to Hesse. The French created the new division of Rheinpfalz in their Zone and this remains as a *Land*, to the general dissatisfaction of the Germans, since it satisfies none of the essential criteria of a coherent political unit noted above. The Saarland was added in 1957. Berlin is *de facto* if not *de jure*, also a *Land*, thus making a total of eleven in all. It will be noted that the new *Länder*, especially in West Germany, broadly correspond to the units noticed above and that they contain all the 'inliers' and 'outliers'—though these still remain as lesser units in the administrative system of each *Land*. These are big steps indeed towards the solution of the problem of *Neugliederung*, but they are not enough. For the boundaries both of the *Länder* and of their subdivisions are in need of revision. And here we take up further progress by the *Bund* itself.

After World War II the federal principle was recognized and new *Länder* were formulated and in 1949 a new federal constitution based on these *Länder* came into being in West Germany. In East Germany five new *Länder* were formed from the pre-existing divisions, with modified boundaries in 1950. But in 1952 they were abolished and their place taken by fourteen districts that sought to eliminate regional independence and concentrate power and authority in the centre.

The last chance for reform in western Germany came in the summer of 1948 when an investigation was encouraged by the foreign ministers' conference in London. But the ministers' conference of the German *Länder* concentrated on the new constitution and paid no attention to the definition of the boundaries of the *Länder*. This matter, however, as embodied in Article 29 of the Basic Law, was to be pursued as an objective of the new constitution. The military government caused this resolution to be suspended and it was not until the recognition of full sovereignty on May 5th of 1955 that the law came into force. Only the union of Baden and Württemberg was effected in 1952 by means of a plebiscite.

Article 29 pertaining to the new territorial organization reads as follows: 'The area of the *Bund*, in consideration of its folk associations, historical and cultural ties, economic efficiency, and social co-

REGIONALISM IN GERMANY

hesion, is to be reorganized under federal law. The reorganization shall create States (*Länder*), which in size and capacity should be able effectively to carry out the functions allotted to them.'[1]

In order to carry out the instruction of the law, a federal committee was appointed in September 1949 and under its instruction work was initiated through the *Institut für Raumforschung und Raumordnung* in

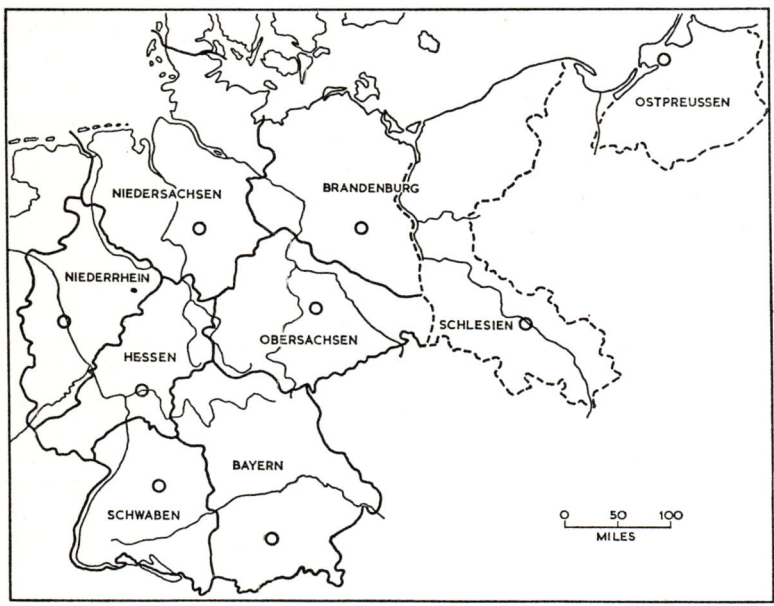

FIG. 121. Germany: Regions proposed by Münchheimer in 1949.

Bonn and the *Akademie für Raumforschung und Landesplanung* in Hanover. A research committee was appointed by the *Bundestag* in June 1951 to formulate a proposal for new *Länder*. Dr. H. Luther, who, it will be recalled, was a leader in this field after World War I, once again became its chairman. The official views of the *Länder* were solicited, but the strongly vested interests of the political parties made difficult an acceptable solution. Many voluminous official reports reveal viewpoints and proposals that are often at loggerheads on basic problems of areal definition and boundaries.

[1] 'Das Bundesgebiet ist unter Berücksichtigung der landsmannschaftlichen Verbundenheit, der geschichtlichen und kulturellen Zusammenhänge, der wirtschaftlichen Zweckmässigkeit und des sozialen Gefüges durch Bundesgesetz zu gliedern. Die Neugliederung soll Länder schaffen, die nach Grösse und Leistungsfähigkeit die ihnen obliegendend Aufgaben wirksam erfüllen können.'

543

The Luther committee published its reports in autumn of 1955.[1] Three points are made by a German commentator.[2]

First, such a reform must be undertaken for West Germany, but should not obstruct the way for a rational reorganization of the political framework for a reunited West and East Germany. The zonal boundary, however, is already established as an effective division between two differently organized societies. Difficulties would arise also from the fact that since 1952 East Germany has been territorially reorganized in a larger number of divisions that are at variance with the older established regional divisions, so that there would be problems eventually in reorganizing units—especially for example *Mitteldeutschland*—across the boundaries of the zonal frontier.

Second, the report holds that the present *Länder* have an identity and historical cohesion which fit with the requirements of effective government, and they should, in general, be retained, certainly with regard to their 'core areas', as the basis of the new framework. It does not advocate any radical revision as the Basic Law evidently foresees. One problem is the economic weakness of Schleswig-Holstein that would not be adequately compensated by union with Hamburg or through the establishment of a new northern State. Nordrhein and Westfalen (at present united) are considered as having strong enough identity and weight to be regarded as separate *Länder*. This, however, is not advisable, since they are so intimately associated through their common relationships with the Ruhr. Further, their territory should not be extended too much on the periphery in one direction or another since this would break their economic cohesion.

Third, there is one area in which there is difficulty in defining the predominant political associations. This is the area called by the Commission *Mittelwestdeutschland*—the hill and lowland country centred on Koblenz, Trier, and Kassel, which is diversified, in respect to its physique, historical and cultural development, and current economic and social structure. Here one does not find concordance between these conditions as required by the Basic Law. Existing *Länder* boundaries cut through the urban regions of Rhine–Main and Rhine–Neckar. The Rhine itself is an old-established political boundary that also cuts through these great urban agglomerations.[3]

[1] This is reported on by K. G. Faber, 'Die Neugliederung der Bundesrepublik Deutschland und die Landeskunde', *Berichte z. d. Landeskunde*. Bd. 16, Heft 2, 1956, pp. 194–211.
[2] Peter Schöller, *Länderreform und Landeskunde*, Westfälische Forschungen, Mitt. d. Provinzialinstitut f. Westf. Landes u. Volkskunde, 12 Band, 1959, pp. 73–97.
[3] See Gutachten, *Die Neugliederung des Bundesgebietes*, 1955, p. 46. See p. 551, below.

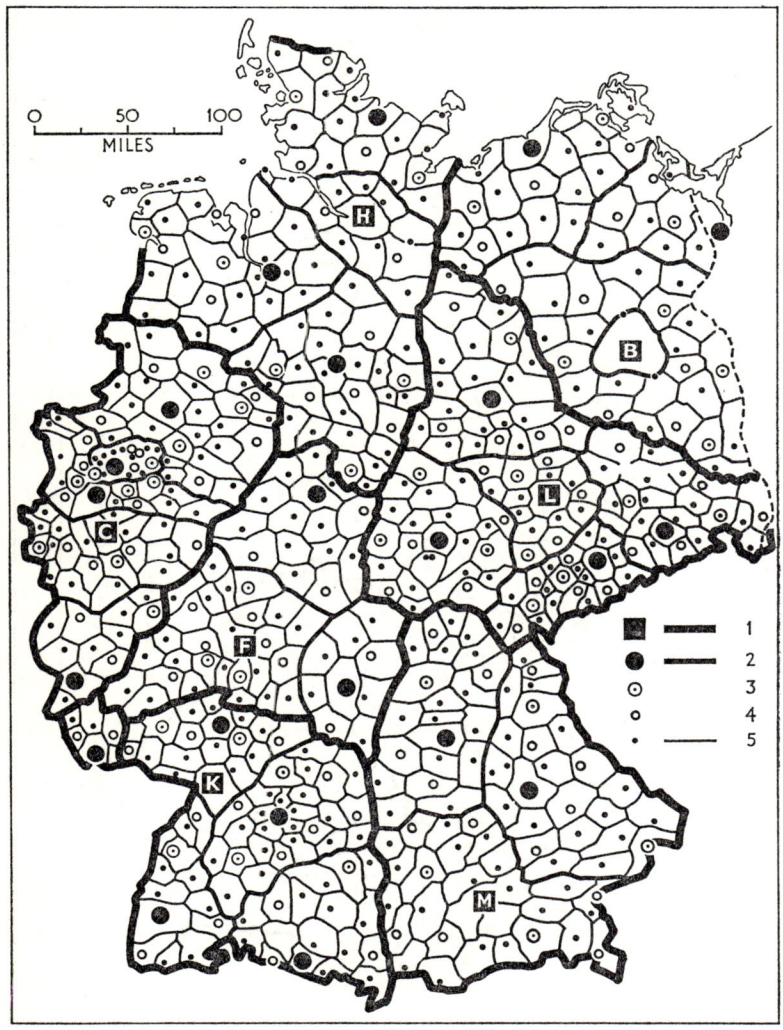

FIG. 122. Germany: Regions proposed by Christaller in 1949. Symbols indicate, in order, capitals of 1. *Region*; 2. *Land*; 3. *Provinz*; 4. *Gau*; and 5. *Kreis*.

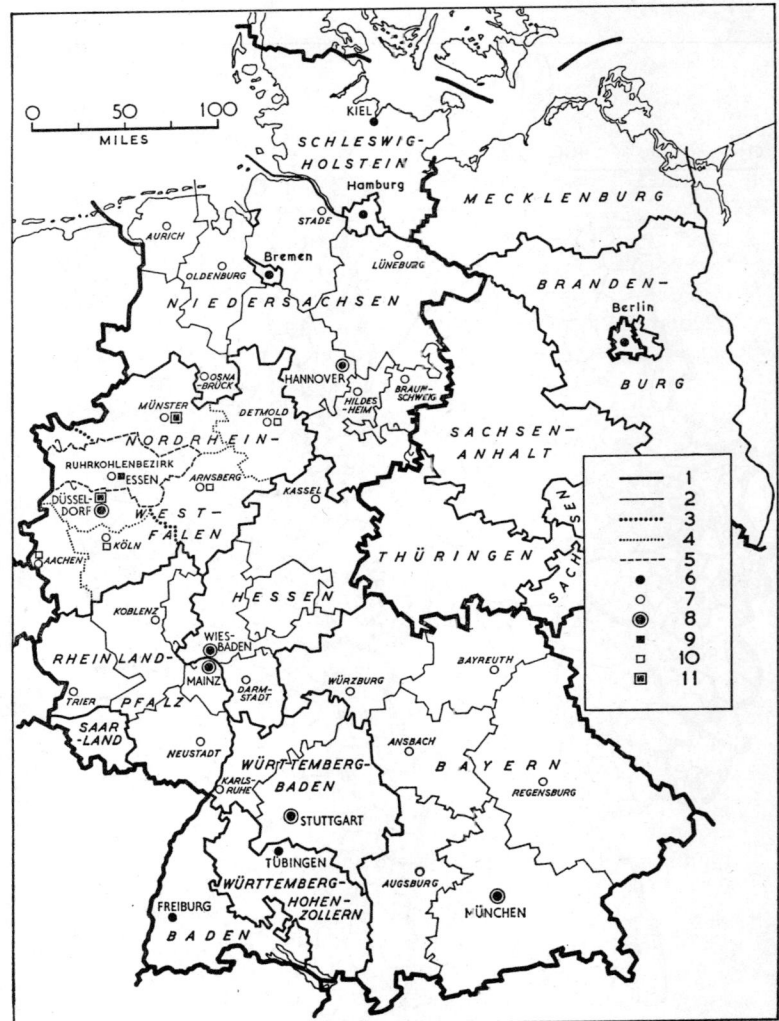

FIG. 123. West Germany: Regions of Planning Authorities. These are based on administrative regions, 1952 (after Institut für Raumforschung).

Regions: 1. Land. 2. Bezirk. 3. Rheinland and Westfalen. 4. Bezirke in Rheinland and Westfalen. 5. Ruhrkohlenbezirk. *Centres of Offices*: 6. Land. 7. Bezirk. 8. Offices of 6. and 7. in same town. 9. Land Rheinland–Westfalen and Ruhrsiedlungs–Verband. 10. Bezirk centres of Land Rheinland–Westfalen. 11. Offices of Land Rheinland–Westfalen and Bezirk in same town.

The public reception of the Luther commission's report was not encouraging. There was a general reluctance by public, press, and government, to accept its proposals. The first step has been taken, however, to implement the *Neugliederung* process. In April 1956, seven *Volksbegehren* were held in doubtful districts, provided that 10 per cent. of the eligible electorate turned out to vote. The results are shown on Fig. 124. Votes were registered for the re-establishment of the *Länder* of Oldenburg and of Schaumburg–Lippe, thus expressing the great strength of 'togetherness' and tradition in these areas, in spite of the fact that, in general, they are anachronistic as units of modern government. The districts of Koblenz and Trier, at present in Rheinland–Pfalz, voted for transfer to Nordrhein–Westfalen. The district of Montabaur voted for transfer from Rheinland–Pfalz to Hessen. Votes in the Pfalz as a whole were indeterminate, since less than the required 10 per cent. voted, the issue being transfer either to Bavaria or to Baden–Württemberg. In September 1956 a *Volksbegehrung* was held throughout Baden, and 15 per cent. voted for the re-establishment of a separate *Land*, separate from Württemberg. According to the Basic Law the *Neugliederung* should have been effected three years from 5 May 1955, when West Germany became a State. The three years is more than passed, no action has been taken and the decisions recorded above have not been acted on.

5. POST-WAR SITUATION

The task of redefining the *Länder* is still not carried out, but it is appropriate here to look at the criteria that the law calls for consideration—folk character, historical ties, cultural ties, and economic associations.

Further investigations have accumulated in the post-war years. Two individual studies have presented, once again, alternative solutions for new *Länder* divisions, one by W. Münchheimer[1] (Fig. 121) and the other by W. Christaller (Fig. 122). The latter is particularly interesting since it fits in with his theoretical approach as discussed in Chapter 3. We also have the published reports of the official Luther commission appointed by the *Bund* government. Special attention is also drawn to the very important work of the *Institut für Raumforschung* in Bad Godesberg and the *Akademie für Raumforschung* in Hanover. Studies have appeared in their monographs and in the pages of the periodical *Raumforschung und Raumordnung*. The Director, Dr. Erich Dittrich, has a group of papers printed in monograph form on

---

[1] W. Münchheimer, 'Worum geht es bei der Neugliederung Deutschlands?', *Frankfurter Geog. Hefte*, 1951. Contains a series of maps, including the proposals of Münchheimer and Christaller from which Figs. 121 and 122 are drawn.

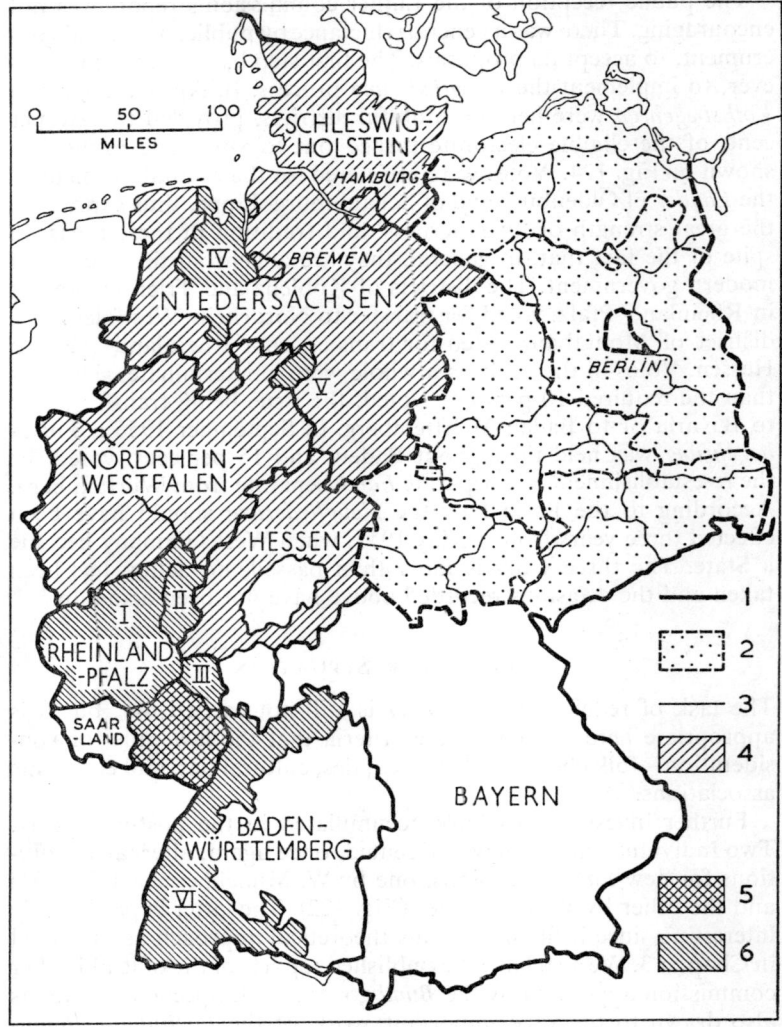

Fig. 124. West Germany: Changes in State areas as expressed by popular vote (after Schöller).

1. West Germany and the *Länder*. 2 and 3. East Germany and its divisions. 4. *Länder* established since World War II. 5. Pfalz. 6. Areas of the Vote in April, 1956: I Trier, II Koblenz, III Montabaur, IV Oldenburg, V Schaumburg-Lippe, VI Baden. The seventh area is the Pfalz.

the bases of areal planning in Germany (see below) and his periodical contains many articles dealing with actual problems of city and regional planning. The late Dr. K. Brüning of Hanover pursued studies for over thirty years, and is mainly responsible for the progress of the magnificent Planning Atlas of western Germany, that has appeared as a series of sheet maps to cover each of the *Länder*.

Let us first look at the changes in the economic geography of the post-war Germany.[1] The separation of West and East Germany by the Iron Curtain, the consequent shifts of traffic flows, the isolation of the districts near the Iron Curtain in West Germany, and the phenomenally rapid growth of the Rhineland provinces, all add new and unexpected dimensions to the problem of regional economic development and the reorganization of the political divisions.

Post-war changes have radically altered the geographical structure of the traffic of West Germany. Formerly the main traffic axes of western Europe crossed the Reich from west to east and from north to south. Moreover, there was an intimate relationship, and a dense net of traffic by rail and road, between the eastern section, especially the middle Elbe basin and Berlin, and western Germany, and especially with the Ruhr. Today, traffic stops at the Iron Curtain. The west–east flows by rail and road have dwindled to a trickle on the frontier. The Rhine axis (by rail, road, and water) today dominates the commercial structure of western Germany, with a less important axis from Munich through Nuremberg to Hanover and Hamburg.

A further dominant fact in the post-war situation in West Germany is what Dittrich has called the *West–Ost Gefäll*. This refers to the contrast between the densely populated and rapidly growing industrial western section in the Rhinelands, and the areas in the eastern section. The latter are faced with large numbers of refugees, and considerable underemployment, due to the severing of local connections and a generally isolated situation owing to the proximity of the Soviet border. Many of the refugees who crowded in the eastern section immediately after the war, have now moved west to find new jobs in the industrial areas of the west. Areas near to the 'curtain', especially in Bavaria, are economically handicapped by their 'backwater' location. The west–east axis from the Ruhr to Berlin is cut to the east of Braunschweig, but the latter, plus Salzgitter and Wolfsburg around it, is a growing new industrial area, which has rapidly recovered from the post-war distress, largely through the recruitment of refugee labour. The axis connecting the Ruhr and the industrial areas of Bielefeld, Hanover, and Braunschweig remains a major axis of the

[1] E. Dittrich, *Grundfragen deutscher Raumordnung, Mitt. aus dem Inst. f. Raumforschung*, Heft 21, Bad Godesberg, January 1955.

German economy, even though it is sharply severed at the Soviet border. The regional framework in West Germany shows, of course, essentially the same configuration as before the war. The Ruhr has even greater dominance. It is also the dominant focal area of the west European economy. It draws into its economic sphere essentially the whole of the industrial complex of the *Land* of Rhineland-Westphalia. Niedersachsen has a productive agricultural area in its centre that has long served as a feeder of Rhineland-Westphalia. It also has a range of important raw materials, though it also draws both coal and gas from the Ruhr. Osnabrück, Bielefeld, Hanover, Peine, and Braunschweig, with the iron and steel works of Salzgitter and the Volkswagen plant at Wolfsburg, are its main centres. Bremen stands as the outlet for Niedersachsen and also serves the Ruhr. It has its own shipbuilding industry and one of the largest automobile plants in the country. Hessen falls into two sections, the Kassel orbit and the Frankfurt orbit. The former has suffered from its location near the Iron Curtain. It is closely tied with Niedersachsen to the north. The Frankfurt–Mainz area is one of the great European seats of industry. It is a cluster of urban settlements and its linkages reach out into Rheinland–Pfalz, Baden, Württemberg, and Bavaria. Both Würzburg and Mannheim lie within its orbit, though it in turn has close economic ties with the Ruhr. Rheinland–Pfalz does not have close ties with the Ruhr and belongs to an outer circle of associations. Occupying a peripheral position to the Ruhr, it draws upon both the Aachen and Saar coal-fields. Schleswig–Holstein is basically agricultural and this is accentuated by the enormous influx of refugees and the closing down of the naval workshops in Kiel. Hamburg has lost its role as an outlet for central Europe, but it is still the main outlet for West Germany and has attracted a variety of new industries, especially just outside the boundaries of the city. Mannheim–Ludwigshafen has ties both with Rheinland–Pfalz and with Baden–Württemberg. South Germany is not so closely linked with the Ruhr. Indeed, in the past it has had closer ties with the Saar. The great variety of highly skilled metalworking and textile-working industries are especially typical of Württemberg, with its rapidly growing capital in Stuttgart and a large number of smaller towns and many industrial villages around it. Bavaria has an agricultural base, but there is a widely dispersed textile industry in the north (Hof being an outlier of the Saxon Thuringian area, centred on Plauen). Other industrial clusters are grouped around Nuremberg–Furth, Augsburg, and Munich.

Two great industrial axes in West Germany emerge from this picture, which embrace all the major urban areas. One extends from the Rhinelands to the Neckar lowland and thence through Augsburg to Munich. The second extends eastwards from the Ruhr through Bielefeld, Osnabrück, and Hanover to Braunschweig and through Helmstedt to the East German border.

The above comments clearly lay particular emphasis on the location of the great centres of population and industry. In this connection, therefore, we should once again emphasize, as have many German scholars, the tremendous importance of economic associations as determinants of general geographical cohesion. These embrace the extent of the urbanized areas; second, the extent of the major entities dependent upon economic interlinkage as is most clearly revealed by traffic flows; and third, the range of the commuting areas of the major seats of employment. These areas are shown in the group of maps in Chapter 12 (Section 7, pp. 370–87).

Finally, we turn to the historico-cultural spatial associations. Here we have reference to the dialects, religion, culture, and traditions, out of which emerges that feeling of cohesion or 'togetherness'. These historically based associations, in a country that retains so many interlocking and anachronistic political boundaries and divisions, are of great importance in deciding on new political units. The Luther Commission paid special attention to this aspect. One of the maps of the Commission is reproduced on Fig. 73 (pp. 379).

All these spatial or areal aspects must be precisely evaluated in order to arrive at a synthesis of them all in their relevance to the redefinition of political units. They will be found, when mapped, to coincide closely in some cases or to overlap more or less widely in others, in such a way that one may recognize core areas and peripheral areas—core areas in which all criteria occur together with a sharp gradient, peripheral areas in which some occur, some do not. Outer boundaries overlap considerably although there may be well-marked 'gradients' at a natural obstacle or at old-established political frontiers. Moreover, it should be noted that, again in relevance to the problems of defining political units, the definition of unique geographical areas cannot be based on the same criteria in all cases, since areas differ greatly in the nature of their areal associations and in the relative importance of such associations.

Several special problems arise. As noted on page 544, a main question lies in the grouping of 'West Central Germany', between Trier, and Siegen. This whole area lacks a dominant focus and lies between two major cultural and economic spheres—the north-west and the middle Rhinelands. The problem of the divided orientation of this area is illustrated by the case of the Westerwald Plateau in the Rhine Plateau east of Koblenz. It is thinly peopled, with a series of small towns on its periphery. The predominance of daily local associations of these towns (commuting and service) reveals that the Westerwald never had a definite focus in the past and so today lacks a dominant city centre. It also maintains its historic character as a frontier zone with a peripheral position between the regions to the north and south. North–south valleys traverse the southern part of the Westerwald, and the higher Ober– and Hohen–Westerwald to the north have traditionally served as a zone of separation between north and south. Regional associations in the area are, in fact, oriented predominantly in an east–west direction. The new boundary between the *Länder* to the north (Rheinland–Westfalen) and to the south (Hessen) is likely to run across it. Where shall it be placed? In order to answer this question, the orbits of the existing urban centres were analysed as in the Siegen area. The *Länder* boundary was then suggested in such a way as to follow as closely as possible its historic course, but adjusted so as to follow the borders of the urban orbits and cut as little as possible across the patterns of their local associations. The orbits of Trier and Koblenz to the west are markedly oriented towards the north. What shall be done with this whole area in a new political set-up? Nordrhein and Westfalen are dominantly associated with the Ruhr, and it would be unwise to enlarge them by further annexations to the south. It might well be a better solution to merge this area with the Rhine–Main nucleus of the *Land* of Hessen. Alternatively, the whole area of the Westerwald, together with the orbits of Koblenz and Trier on the west–east axis of the Moselle and Lahn valleys, could become a new *Land*. But this would range from Trier to Kassel and would certainly have to be subdivided. Moreover, this solution, we are told, would certainly not meet with the public support. The question remains under dispute.

We have briefly enumerated, once again, the most important sets of spatial associations which are needed for the assessment of regional associations in West Germany. It is notable that the recommendations of the Basic Law emphasize economic and historical associations, but there is no reference in the Luther report to the tremendous importance of the city centres in organizing the modern areas of human spatial associations. Nor is there any mention of the role of the diversity of relief of the lands upon which human movements in such large degree still depend. These are the varied geographical aspects of the problem and there are masses of published investigations and maps to draw upon. The need is for action, as is the case in regard to the same problem in other countries. It is for the government to decide on the method of arriving at the definition of new units and their boundaries. These must clearly depend on the number, size, and purposes of the new units. The location of boundaries and the allegiance of areas, especially in doubtful borderlands, must ultimately depend on the wishes of the people. Researches into spatial associations have been going on for forty years. Some changes have been made. Preliminary votes in certain districts have been taken since the war. But the government at Bonn has still not decided to take the nettle by the hand and finally effect a definitive solution to this problem.

Chapter 19

INTERNATIONAL ASPECTS OF REGIONALISM: CONCLUSION

It is important to realize the close relations that exist between the city-region and the State. 'There are', writes an American economist, 'all kinds of regions. But the regionalism that is of greatest importance is metropolitan. Here we have an area inhabited by producers and consumers who from a radius usually of over a hundred miles look to one big centre for marketing their products and serving their supplies', and this region 'has grown to be a potential rival of the State'.[1]

1. CITY-REGION AND STATE

The great city, as a centre of industry, commerce, culture, and administration, and often as a great political capital, has grown up in the past, and especially in the last hundred years, through access to a unified political and economic unit, the State, and through access to the international world-wide market. It may reach the status of a super-metropolitan city, a 'primate city' within its State—even though the State be itself small in area and population. Vienna and Constantinople, which functioned for centuries as the capitals of great States, the one the centre of the Austro-Hungarian Empire in the Danubian lands, the other the centre of the Turkish Empire in the Middle East and the Balkans, suffered by the disintegration of these empires and by the erection in the inter-war period of tariffs to prevent the free interchange of goods across the new frontiers. The fate of Vienna is well known. Its tributary area was cut down to the size of Austria from its established markets in Danubia. It still houses nearly two million inhabitants. The difficulty of feeding its people, let alone giving them employment, is a familiar story. 'The disrobing of Vienna and Constantinople are crimes against metro-

[1] N. S. B. Gras, 'Regionalism and Nationalism', *Foreign Affairs*, Vol. VII, April 1929, pp. 454–67.

politan regionalism which are bound to cost dear', wrote an economist in 1929.[1]
'Cities do not grow of themselves. Countrysides set them up to do tasks that must be performed in central places.'[2] Turning to the large and densely populated States for a standard of measure, it was found that there is one city with over 100,000 people for every one to one and a quarter million people. It is a fairly safe assumption that almost a million people in Europe and America are needed to support a city with over 100,000 inhabitants, remembering always that the proportion of big cities (as of the total urban population) to the total population of a country depends both on the economic structure of the country and upon the measure of its dependence upon outside markets for the service of its urban population. Modern big cities in the western world grew fastest in the short period of urban growth from 1870 to 1914. In Europe the changes of political frontiers in 1918 often cut them off from the countryside they had grown to serve. This applied not only to the lands encircling inland cities but also to the hinterlands of ports—the areas to and from which they distribute and collect supplies—with the result that a number of them were like centres severed from their limbs, suffering 'surgical shock', from which some have never recovered fully. The port of Danzig has traditionally served the Vistula basin, the heart of Poland, behind it. But during the nineteenth century—from the partition of Poland down to 1919—it was entirely severed from this hinterland, because it lay in the belt of German territory that extended through west Prussia to east Prussia, south of which lay the Russian province of Congress Poland. The German–Russian frontier was a complete economic and cultural barrier. Poland was a backwater in Russia, deliberately cut off from all communications across the German frontier. Danzig dwindled to a shadow of its former self, testimony to its greatness in the Middle Ages down to the end of the eighteenth century being its rows of great multi-storeyed warehouses on the waterfront. The Treaty of Versailles established the independence of Poland, but set up Danzig, an entirely German-speaking city, as a Free State, and thus made difficult the unrestricted use of Danzig as an outlet for the trade of Poland. The result was that Gdynia was established as a direct outlet on Polish soil. The two in effect serve as partners as sea-outlets for the trade of Poland.

The Baltic States suffered similarly.[3] Their chief cities developed

[1] Gras, *op. cit.*
[2] M. Jefferson, 'The Distribution of the World's City Folks' *Geographical Review*, Vol. XXI, 1931, pp. 446–65.
[3] E. van Cleef, 'East Baltic Ports and Boundaries with special reference to Königsberg', *Geographical Review*, Vol. XXV, 1945, pp. 157–72.

in the nineteenth century in the economic framework of Russia. After the creation of the new States, they were far too large to serve such small and predominantly agricultural countries. Riga, the chief port and city of Esthonia, had nearly 400,000 people in a State with just over one million. It grew to its disproportionate size as a port serving extensive areas in west Russia. 'There were three or four times the number of people in west Russia who used and needed Riga, if analogies mean anything, though the economic countryside of a great city is not easy to delineate or define.'[1] A small country is often not big enough to support a large city. Copenhagen, for instance, accounts alone for a fifth of the population of Denmark: it is as big as Sweden's three 100,000 cities put together, though Denmark has only half the population of Sweden. One is led to suspect that Copenhagen does indeed draw upon southern Sweden both as a source for its population and for its trade. Switzerland has four 100,000 cities, but no big dominant city, and the commercial capitals of other countries—especially Paris, Berlin, Milan, to say nothing of the ports of Genoa, Antwerp, and Marseille—carry out for Switzerland many of the functions that would normally go to the dominant capital city.

Still more remarkable instances of the separation of cities from their hinterlands have emerged, through the dismemberment of Germany. Hamburg has its main pre-war hinterland in the middle Elbe basin, from Magdeburg to Saxony, and Berlin depended upon this port for its trade overseas. The trade of Hamburg with these areas, by water, rail, and road, has been cut to a fraction of its pre-war volume by the barrier of the Iron Curtain. The most tragic case of all is the subdivision of Berlin, whereby West Berlin is not only separated from East Berlin, but the former is an island in the midst of Soviet-occupied German territory of Brandenburg, which it has served since its inception in the Middle Ages.

2. Frontier Zones

There is another aspect to this question of the city in relation to political frontiers. The city, or, to be more correct, the urban tract, has been rapidly expanding geographically and economically during the past fifty years. This expansion is effected by the spread of houses, roads, railways, canals; the movement of workers to and from factories; the movement of daily supplies of milk, vegetables, and meat (that is, perishable foodstuffs); the supply and control of public services in general (electricity, water supply, drainage, gas, telephones, and other piped services); and the interdependence of

[1] M. Jefferson, *op. cit.*

INTERNATIONAL ASPECTS OF REGIONALISM: CONCLUSION

factories on each other and on the warehouses, offices, and exchanges in the city centre. All these space-relations unite a large area around the city into an effective natural geographical unit whose borders are very wide and vague, but whose city centres are the meeting-place of more and more of these relations. If a political frontier cuts through such a grouping it is a potential source of danger to the efficient functioning and organization of the whole and of its parts, and certainly a cause of great expenditure of effort and money in the process of reorientation and reorganization. If existing *before* the modern development took place, a compromise may have been found and the friction entailed in the existence of a frontier may be limited to an absolute minimum in the daily round and organization of all aspects of the life of the area.

An example of the second type is the densely peopled industrial area in Flanders on the borders of northern France and Belgium. This great textile-producing area lies for the most part on the French side, with its capital and greatest city in Lille, and its commercial and industrial centre in the combined towns of Roubaix–Tourcoing. But the populous areas across the frontier in Belgium are akin to those on the French side in respect to their towns and countryside, in their economic activities and in their organization, and there is a great daily current of traffic and workers across the frontier.

The first kind of situation is illustrated by Upper Silesia.[1] This great coalfield lay, before 1919, almost entirely in German territory, and found its markets mainly in south-eastern Europe. From 1919 to 1945 it was mainly in Poland, with relatively small sectors of it in Germany and Czechoslovakia. Its markets have been, in large measure, oriented towards Poland, owing to the competition of the German industrial areas of the middle Elbe basin and the Ruhr. Its manufactured products now find their chief markets in east central Europe. Its unfavourable location, stretching across three States and in the extreme corners of two of them (Germany and Poland), its lack of first-class waterways to connect it with the North and Baltic Seas and its long distance from the eastern Alps, whence it draws almost all the iron ores for its iron and steel industries, make the problem of industrial development of Upper Silesia, since 1945, one of integration with the Soviet block. Just as serious, however, is the problem of the organization of this extensive, straggling, and expanding urban area—the kind of problem that comes under the heading of 'regional planning', that was here confounded and complicated by the existence of political frontiers between the wars. For efficiency of organization in all respects, Upper Silesia must function as a unit.

[1] N. J. G. Pounds, *The Upper Silesian Industrial Region*, Indiana University Publications, 1958, p. 147.

It is not necessary to go into the details of this particular problem since they have been examined often and thoroughly. One of the aims of the League of Nations solution in the twenties was to facilitate the free functioning and unity of organization of the whole area on both sides of the German–Polish frontier, which cut arbitrarily right through it. The League of Nations control ended in the late thirties and the frontier difficulties were accentuated by the advent of the Nazi regime and its anti-Polish policy. The Silesian urban area, whose industrial development is in its infancy, has big prospects as the only large coalfield between the Ruhr (excluding the lignite field of central Germany) and the Donetz. It presented to Poland between the wars a dual problem—that of access to raw materials (iron ore) and markets (iron and steel goods and coal)—and that of organizing the whole area as an economic and urban complex, which must, in the interests of efficiency, override any potential barriers raised by political frontiers which cross it. Since 1953 the whole area has been organized as a single planning unit within Poland.[1]

There are, of course, still other examples of disruptions of local relations and difficulties in spatial organization brought about by the existence of a political frontier. The most remarkable case since World War II is the boundary between East and West Germany. This Iron Curtain has not only severed economic and social contacts between the two portions of Germany, it has cut through a close network of west–east communications. Roads and railways now come to a dead end on both sides of the border and the movement of people and traffic is reduced to a minimum. This has cut off towns near the border from their natural and old-established hinterlands. It has given to the areas near the boundary in western Germany a remote, isolated location, since they lie right on the eastern edge of West Germany. This disadvantage is particularly marked in Bavaria, which, in any case, is a relatively backward area. The port of Hamburg before the war had developed for over a hundred years as the principal outlet for the imports and exports of the great industrial areas of the middle Elbe and for Berlin. Since 1945 it has been cut off from this natural hinterland (by river, canal, and road and rail) by the Iron Curtain and this traffic has remained a tiny fraction of the pre-war figure. The great industrial area of the middle Elbe grew up in the closest relationship with the Ruhr and the rest of western Germany, and these linkages have of necessity been disrupted and their markets have in large measure been reoriented.

There are many cases of similar situations on the borders of the States of America. Such are urbanized regions that lie astride State

[1] N. J. G. Pounds, *The Upper Silesian Industrial Region*, Indiana University Publications, 1958, p. 147.

INTERNATIONAL ASPECTS OF REGIONALISM: CONCLUSION

boundaries (e.g. the New York region), or States that have sectors remote from their centres of population which are more closely allied, socially and economically, with neighbouring States, e.g., Idaho.

3. THE CITY-REGION IN THE STATE

The city has emerged more and more in the last hundred years as the focus of the activities of the towns, villages, and countryside around it. Indeed, the growth of cities has proceeded so far that the really great city is too large to offer the best conditions for human living. Disintegration has already started through the operation of centrifugal forces, the shift of factories, institutions, houses, and people, out from the centre—although hitherto in a haphazard fashion without any attempt at a 'design for living'. It is to be hoped that the future will see the continuation of this redistribution of urban functions and buildings from the congested centres, so that the city settlement area, and, beyond it, the city trade area, will emerge more and more as the effective grouping of real social and economic life, ready to be adopted in principle as the unit of democratic activity and land planning and regional development.

There is, however, every indication in the post-war years that economic growth has taken place so rapidly that the play of economic forces has resulted in the accelerated concentration of industrial sites in existing large urban areas—London, Paris, Ruhr, Stuttgart, and the great cities of America. There has been some dispersion but far less than the continued concentration. As Gravier has pointed out in France, dwellings and public services for industrial workers cost three to five times as much as the workplace itself. Every time the problem of site arises, the entrepreneur is swayed by the mobility of industry rather than by the mobility of labour.[1] Factories can be erected and come into operation long before the dwellings of the workers can be erected. Decentralization is one of the primary objectives of all planning authorities. The small industrial town is a feature of large areas of Germany, France, and the Low Countries. But decentralization can go much further in the shape of new towns and extensions of existing towns. Even the New Towns in Britain represent a small fraction of all the houses built and industries established in the last twenty years.

The metropolitan region within the State is a rival of the component States, as in the U.S.A., and of the existing major political provinces (the direct descendants of the historical provinces) as in Britain (counties), France (*départements*), Italy (*compartimenti*), and of the *Länder* in Germany. Each of these political divisions is a

[1] J. F. Gravier, *Décentralisation et progrès technique*, p. 320.

unit within fixed political boundaries in respect of many aspects of social organization—such as government, administration and law—and, in the U.S.A., and Germany until recently, has enjoyed, in varying degree, the rights of a sovereign State. But, the circulation unit, clearly defined as to its great city centres and their environs, often vague as to its limits, is the effective *de facto* unit for many of the most vital aspects of modern life, and has emerged as the natural (unplanned) framework of many activities. This fact is revealed by population distribution, circulation flows, the distribution of economic activities and interests, flows of capital and investment, and the multifarious private and government organizations of the State. Such groupings, therefore, form the best units in which to handle many aspects of the scientific study of society, since they have more in common than any other groupings of similar size. It is for this reason that in recent studies of social and economic trends this type of grouping is emphasized as the real unit of modern life; and that in plans for reorganizing administrative units, from whatever point of view, the city and its region must be the basic and primary consideration.

M. Jean Labasse, whose work on Lyon has already been quoted, after pointing out the overwhelming importance of the metropolitan city in directing the work and organization of space, develops this argument from the case of Lyon and its wide field of influence. There are some nine cities of this order and their associated regions in France. The twenty-two regions adopted for planning purposes may be convenient for the collection and organization of materials, but they are certainly not properly adapted to a country like France in which extensive areas are rural and large urban agglomerations few in number and very widely spaced one from another. These nine regions are comparable with the eleven in Great Britain (the standard regions of the Board of Trade) and the nine *Länder* of West Germany (if one excludes the city-states of Bremen and Hamburg). This number will gladden the heart of Christaller, who regards nine as a fixed figure in his administrative system, and finds that in western Europe there are nine major socio-historical units which he takes as a springboard in his theoretical distribution of the capitals of Europe.

The fundamental importance of the major regional groupings in the life of modern society is especially relevant to the problem of Germany. We have shown that the pre-war Germany consisted of eleven major natural provinces with two smaller units.

In western Germany three of these major provinces lie astride the Rhine—Rhineland-Westphalia, Rhine–Main (or Hesse as it may alternatively be called), and the Southwest. The Ruhr cannot be severed from Cologne and its great brown-coal area, nor from the

INTERNATIONAL ASPECTS OF REGIONALISM: CONCLUSION

rest of north-western Germany. The Frankfurt–Mainz complex cannot be severed from the territories around it. The Southwest is a unit and, what is just as important, it has common interests and affiliations with the French provinces of Alsace and Lorraine, and with the Saar that are based not only upon linguistic and cultural ties, but also on their common interests in the navigation of the Rhine. A second fact of fundamental importance is the essential economic interdependence of these three Rhineland provinces with each other and with Alsace-Lorraine, Switzerland, Belgium, and Netherlands—each of which is comparable in area and population with the German provinces. This interdependence is based upon the interchange that is necessary between the coalfields of the Ruhr and Belgium and the vast iron-ore fields of French Lorraine. Since 1919, when Germany lost her Lorraine ores, which had been developed in the closest economic dependence with the Ruhr, the latter imported larger quantities of foreign ores up the Rhine and by rail and through Emden by canal. The iron and steel industries on the coalfields of the Ruhr and central Belgium need Lorraine ores. The iron and steel industries of Lorraine and the Saar need the coking coal of these areas, since those of the northern coalfield of France and imports are inadequate. Further, there is the common interest of western Germany, France, Switzerland, Belgium, and the Netherlands in the navigation of the Rhine and Moselle. Antwerp and Rotterdam are the chief ports for the whole of the Rhinelands, together with the river ports of Duisburg–Ruhrort, Mannheim–Ludwigshafen, and Strasbourg. The essential economic interdependence of all these lands is indisputable and finds expression in the dominance of this great area in the economic organization of the Common Market countries. (It is symbolized by the opening of the Moselle Canal in May 1964.)

4. Problems of Regional Economic Development

Discussion of the growth and expansion of urban areas inevitably impinges on the whole question of regional economic development that currently plays such an important part in national affairs. This involves the question of establishing a more effective balance of rural and urban populations as between one area and another. This means, in effect, improving the level of living of the farmer by the transfer of surplus cultivators to non-agricultural occupations. This involves the decentralization of industry and commerce from the large cities. It involves the localization of industry on new sites in smaller centres where additional occupations are needed to provide employment for the people of the countryside, so as to raise the

REGIONALISM AND THE CITY-REGION

general level of living. The last problem is particularly urgent in those large areas that are predominantly agricultural with large surpluses of unemployed and underemployed labour. These include the peripheral areas of Europe, such as Brittany, southern Italy, the Central Massif of France, the highlands of Scotland and the western districts of Ireland. They also include pockets of underdevelopment in the countries of western Europe, in the midst of areas that enjoy much higher levels of industrial and commercial activity and higher levels of living. Recent investigations have assisted in reasonably precise definition of these areas. The problem is how to organize the work and life of the better favoured and more densely peopled areas, and how to bring up the more backward areas by their bootstraps. One of the principal measures of ensuring the latter is to provide for the increased growth of new industries and services that will steadily increase as the level of economic development is increased. And this means increase of the population living in urban centres.

These problems, together with those of other aspects of spatial planning, are all involved in the scope of regional and national planning. Indeed, they are a primary concern in the international planning of the countries of the Common Market. This raises two questions. First, specifically what kinds of problems of development and urban growth are presented by different kinds of areas? And second, what is the use of the kinds of investigation discussed in this book for action in such problems, and how far are they being used in the work of planning authorities? Two examples will suffice.

The first is the case of the planning organization of the Netherlands and the kind of work it is doing in the field of regional economic development. It has a planning organization at the provincial level with teeth in it and in which geographers often play an outstanding part. The case in point is that of the southern province of the Netherlands, North Brabant. This is part of the poverty-stricken agricultural area of the sandy Campine. The province has an exceptionally high birth-rate (1949–50, 29·9 per 1,000, just about the highest in western Europe) and fifty years ago suffered from extreme poverty and agricultural underemployment. It was in order to draw on this reservoir of labour that Philips established their first electrical apparatus plant in Eindhoven in the 1880's and that other industries have been located in the smaller towns. Eindhoven has grown to have over 100,000 people and is virtually a Philips' town. Thousands of workers travel in daily to work from the surrounding countryside. The small towns on the edge of the Campine are also growing as industrial centres, and their labour is drawn from their local market areas. The province, however, is still faced with the prospect of an increase in its total population by one-third by 1970 and must, therefore, be provided with further job opportunities and improvements in its level of living. The provincial planners determined the exact location by *gemeenten* (parishes) of the 'depressed areas' that had: (1) the highest population increases and (2) the greatest agricultural underemployment. In these areas they selected lesser centres for further development of industry and service, so that each centre has a tributary area of about 6 km. free from the competition of the fields of other such centres. This is applied geography in action.

As one of the 'development areas' in the Netherlands, steps were taken by the government to improve its infra-structure (roads and industrial sites) and premiums were awarded to industrial entrepreneurs for the building of factories (25 per cent. of building costs). The provincial administration promoted the construction of industrial sites, the improvement of industrial facilities and the expansion of technical education. Since 1950 over one-half of the total increase of workers in the industries of the Netherlands took place in the south, including Brabant and Limburg. Most of this was concentrated in the towns on the edge and in the eastern and western districts of Brabant.

The second case is that of Württemberg. The particular problems of this *Land* are as follows. First, there is the extremely rapid growth of Stuttgart in the post-war years, far faster, as noted above, than is considered to be either economically or socially desirable. Second, the *Land* already has a widely dispersed industry in large and small towns in the countryside, through the deliberate policy of the *Land* government since the middle of the nineteenth century. The traditional industries are of the 'light' kind and are in general oriented towards the local skilled labour supply. This is today the classic area of the long-distance journey to work, that has grown as a normal feature of its socio-economic structure. Third, most of the *Gemeinden* have only a small proportion of agricultural workers and their dependent families, but even so, there is a large surplus of underemployed labour, owing to the minuteness of the holdings and the frequency with which they are subdivided (*Realteilung*) and scattered. There is also the lack of local alternative jobs. Finally, there are certain areas which are *predominantly* agricultural with very few small towns and with very little local industry, that are relatively far removed from places of employment in larger towns. This is the case in the districts of the extreme north-east, notably in the Hohenlohe Ebene area east and north-east of Heidelberg, east of the Odenwald. This counts as a depressed area in West Germany. There is need here for speeding up the location of new, and preferably small-scale, industries in small towns, and thereby continuing the old-established tradition of the *Land*. The mouth-organs of a famous firm are made in a large village that was once exclusively agricultural and is still surrounded by strip fields. The village has many new houses of workers within it, and farms are transformed to residences or shops placed between the original farmsteads. Textile- and metal-working industries (refrigerators, weighing machines, etc.) have grown in recent decades with remarkable speed on the edge of the Swabian Alb and given rise to new urban centres drawing on labour from the villages.

The planning authority of the *Land* has prepared a base map to serve the needs of development (1955). An outline plan has been prepared in which the principle of centrality is used in the definition of a hierarchy of socio-economic units to serve as a permanent basis of investigation and action. The map on Fig. 125 shows the composite division with the units demarcated by clearly defined boundaries that follow the boundaries of the *Gemeinden*. The smallest units, *Raumschaften* as they are called, have several central places. These units are grouped into larger units called Districts (e.g. Breisgau) and these again into Regions (*Landschaften*) (e.g. Oberrhein). These names are merely labels for the hierarchy of three orders of socio-economic units. They are based, first, on the designation of all central places, characterized according to their population; second, on the range of the urban fields of each centre; and, third, according to the nature of the economic structure of every *Gemeinde*, classed according to the percentage of their workers engaged in non-agricultural work. The urban fields have been determined by reference to every individual *Gemeinde*. Several socio-economic units are recognized on this base, so that each unit should have the same essential areal structure. The unit areas (*Raumschaften*) normally consist of one or several central places with a group of surrounding workers' *Gemeinden*, or workerpeasant *Gemeinden*, or peasant *Gemeinden*. On the original map the *Gemeinden* are shown in varying intensity of shade according to the degree of urbanization along the main routes so that there are brought out the main fields of influence and the direction of movements within the unit areas. The map reproduced here simply shows the three orders of division, based upon these very detailed analyses.

We are not concerned here with developing just how far these investigations have been carried out and applied. It is sufficient to show that these concepts of socio-economic structure, focused upon the notion of centre and field, have been used here, as in many other areas, as a basis of appraisal of the spatial structure of an area for purposes of diagnosing the needs of planning for future development. These are the units of spatial cohesion, the 'areas of common living' that are used for purposes of investigation and planning.

The spatial structure of populations and their variations have been investigated on a wider national basis in both Germany and France, the Netherlands, and Belgium. Studies have been undertaken by such organizations as the *Institut National de la Statistique et des Études Économiques* in France and by the *Institut für Raumforschung und*

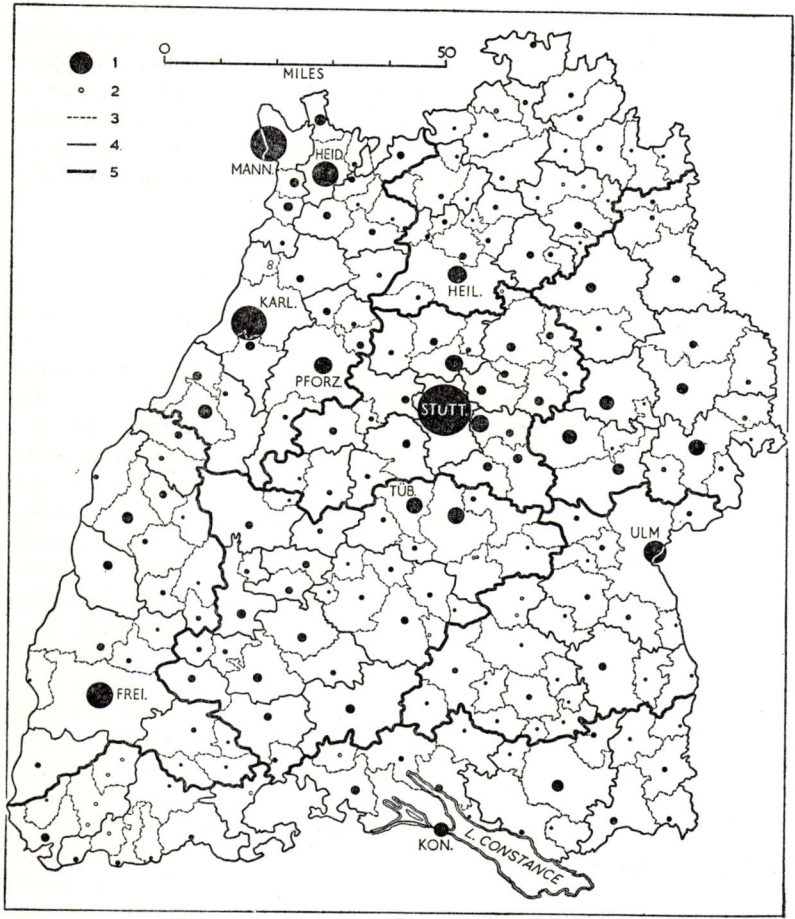

Fig. 125. Socio-economic Units in Baden-Württemberg
(after *Landesplanungsstelle*, Stuttgart).

1. Central places with size of circle proportional to population. 2. Several competitive *Gemeinden*, as a potential central place. 3. Boundaries of smallest units. 4. Boundaries of Regions and of 5. Provinces.

Raumordnung and the *Akademie für Raumforschung* of Hanover in Germany. These are concerned with the whole range of problems of the geographic structure of their respective countries. These problems include matters of regional planning, as well as locating and characterizing areas according to the level of their economic development. Attention to the underdeveloped areas of each of these countries has been particularly prominent in the post-war years and will increase as the Common Market Organization becomes more effective in the coming years. We repeat that the concepts of central place and urban field play a prominent part in the conceptual framework of these investigations. We have been dealing in this book with the structure of spatial systems and spatial arrangements of settlements. Such studies are finding widespread practical application to specific problems at the local, regional, or national levels.

5. THE CITY AND ITS REGION

A word may be said in conclusion concerning the planning of the city and its region.

Many large urban agglomerations continue to increase in size at a faster rate than the countries in which they are situated. During the next decades even more people will be withdrawn from agriculture and transferred to centralized occupations. While planners aim at decentralization and its variants, these objectives have been of no avail in checking the more rapid growth of the big cities. Efforts by their governments to check the growth of the regions of London and Paris have failed and hold out little prospect of being able to do so. South-eastern England is the fastest growing section of Britain. The population of the London region was 10 millions in 1938, 12·3 millions today and could reach 14·3 millions in twenty years. The same is true of Paris and a new twenty-year plan anticipates that the present population of the Paris region (three Departments) will reach 11 million by 1975 and possibly 16 million by A.D. 2,000. Evidently not much is expected of the governments' plans for decentralization.

We have emphasized the structure of the city, both as a built-up entity and in its regional relations. The city, in the fullest sense—and there are few cities that fill this ideal—will continue as the head of our civilization. It is, however, generally agreed that planning for the future should aim at reducing the size of the great urban agglomeration, while improving and making more widely accessible the amenities of city civilization in town and country alike. Decentralization of industry and population, in the sense of a widespread redistribution far from the direct influence of the great city, was only an incipient development in the inter-war years. It should more accurately be described as deconcentration, since the shifts took place merely to the margins of the built-up areas and tended to expand the area of the urban tract. War-time evacuation of factories and commercial and administrative concerns was, on the other hand, real decentralization, real dispersal. The planned balance of activities in new and expanding towns is best called 'recentralization'. However far decentralization may go in the future and the urban agglomeration be reduced in size, the city as the fount of civilization, provides the best it has to offer. And such a trend will inevitably tend to increase the reality of the extensive city-region through the interdependence of its parts and their relations with the chief cities.

This means that a new kind of symbiosis of country and town must be strived for and especially in those areas in which the urban way of life is making increasing impact on the activities and way of life of the countryside. The diminishing number of farmers must be effectively integrated with the city, land must be open to urban dwellers for recreation and retirement and yet preserved as to its amenities. Residential evasion must be directed, water supplies must be assured, travel facilities must be adequate, etc.

Some writers, like Mumford, seem to be particularly pessimistic about the future of our urbanized society. Others, like Gottmann, the student of Megalopolis on the Atlantic Seaboard of the States, and the Lloyd Rodwin and Kevin Lynch group in America, are more optimistic. In any case, the explosion of the city is rapidly taking place in America. Efforts are being made to stop it in Britain by Green Belts, but while there is doubt about the efficacy of this concept, there seems to be no clear idea as to how the urban expansion of the future should be shaped. Central cities are being transformed, since they are obsolescent, damaged, derelict, often overcrowded, and unhealthy. This situation is probably worst in the 'insensate industrial towns' in Britain, and any student or inhabitant of these areas must of necessity be pessimistic, so vast is the problem, so drab the environments. Large areas are derelict with tens of thousands of 'blighted' dwellings in every nineteenth-century city, but progress is slow. In Britain in particular promises are still being made (as thirty years ago) for an acceleration of the slum-clearing and housing programme, that is, in fact, far behind the tempo of development in Germany where in the next ten years the housing problem will be solved.

The central business district is changing rapidly on the Continent and especially in the United States. Frank Lloyd Wright used to envisage the city centre as a place for banking and prostitution, whereas the planners, such as Robert Moses in New York, are seeking to establish a seat of commerce and culture as the worthy focus of the vast population it serves. Such cities exist on the Continent, but at the present rate of progress, it will be many decades before such goals can be reached in the industrial metropolises of Britain. In any case, we have the curious paradox that this most highly urbanized people in the world is highly averse to the amenities and habits of living in cities.

Among the greatest problems of urban life are the betterment of the environment and indeed the provision and maintenance of services and amenities. This is a matter mainly of land ownership and costs. These we have noted in the previous pages. The costs of the provision of services—schools, libraries, utilities, police, fire protection, etc.—have to be set against the income derived by the municipal authority from its taxes (rates). The clearance of obsolescent properties and urban renewal costs make demands far beyond the capacity of single municipal authorities. Expenditures are continually increasing as urban areas extend and as the social facilities increase. Water shortage, stream pollution, overcrowded schools, inadequate roads, urban renewal, etc. confront all cities with problems that are insoluble under the existing organization of municipal government, without financial aid from outside—the national government or a 'regional government' of some kind—*Land* in Germany, *State* in the U.S.A.—or by the creation of large new units of government—the last still being matters of enquiry and dispute. Hundreds of municipalities and *ad hoc* areas make the need of co-ordination on these lines especially urgent. The problem is acute in the States, for example, where the municipalities are still largely dependent on their own resources for the provision of services. Regional governments as well as State assistance are urgently needed in all the great urbanized regions of the western world.

The major problem concerns the fact that the central cities are full up and large areas are obsolescent. But land values are so high in the free market that purchase by the city for redevelopment is prohibitive from its own resources. The rehousing of people who cannot be accommodated also requires proper legal and financial facilities for joint planning by municipal authorities on a wide regional basis. In British cities, calculations are made of how many of the inadequately housed population in a city can be accommodated and how many must go elsewhere. The 'overspill' must be arranged for by the provision of housing elsewhere by arrangement with another independent municipality. This leads to interminable wrangles with neighbouring local government authorities. Deliberate decentralization obviously lies beyond the powers of town and advisory regional-town planning authorities, and can be effected only through the guidance and authority of a body with nation-wide or regional powers.

6. The Viability of the Local Government Unit

The prevalence of the extended journey to work, from one municipality to another, raises formidable financial problems, in terms of the income and expenditure of the municipality. The journey to work means that communities find many and even most of their workers travelling daily to work to more or less distant centres and this raises many problems. One of these is the imbalance of income and expenditure in local communities with abnormal rates of increase or decrease of population. The increase of industrial employment is almost invariably accompanied by a much slower rate of increase of persons engaged in services. Abnormally rapid increase in population means an increased rate of capital outlay that is beyond the tax resources of the community. The rural unit that, in purely agricultural areas, is often experiencing a decrease in numbers, also has an inadequate tax base to provide for communal needs at increasing costs *per capita*. Cities grow so fast that they too are in the same position, beyond the reach of private capital or investment. Thus, the costs of condemnation and acquisition of land for re-development, exposed to the normal price behaviour on the open market, places insuperable strains on the financial resources of the city. This applies in particular to the demolition of slums and the rehousing of the displaced people, projects that cost vast sums of money but bring no corresponding profits. Thus, there arises the urgent need for the distribution of income and expenditure between town and country on a new geographic base, with available funds distributed according to needs (however defined). In Germany, for example, the principal source of income of the local authorities is from taxes on industry. But industry is still strongly attracted to urban centres and the bigger the centre the stronger the attraction. There are various ways of meeting this problem, on a national basis, or some kind of regional basis (in Germany on the basis of the *Länder* governments). One of the ways devised in Germany is by the so-called *Gewerbesteuerausgleich*. This sum is paid to the *Land* by the *Gemeinde* for every employee who lives outside the *Gemeinde*. The sum is paid to the *Gemeinde* in which the worker lives. This provides the latter with a certain income. The financial provision of a parent authority in Britain to another authority in whose area an overspill population is to be housed is another compromise. In Britain and Holland grants are made to each local authority according to its estimated needs or proportional to its population.

A second major problem is the tremendous increase of commuting traffic to the cities. This has been occasioned by the rapid re-establishment of industries in them, so that people have been employed far quicker than houses can be built, with an enormous leeway to be made up in the early fifties, through the devastation of wartime bombing. Many people are thus travelling long distances, one or two hours a day, to their work. In Stuttgart, the growth of commuting has put a great burden on the federal railways which need twice as much rolling stock as before the war to cope with the short-distance passenger traffic at minimum fares. The big increase in road traffic adds greatly to the financial burden in the *Land* in maintaining roads to and from the city. Rapid growth of industry has now exceeded the existing water supply. Thousands of commuters need houses urgently. These are the problems of rapid urban growth, that are to be found as the normal process of urban growth, but they have been particularly acute in Germany during the fifties. We should point out, however, that during the last five years West Germany as a whole has been building new dwellings at the rate of 500,000 per year. This means that within a period of ten years, West Germany will have solved, repeat solved, its housing problem. This surely should give Britons, with approximately the same size of population, food for thought, since the rate of building in this country we are told cannot, under any circumstances, be increased, because of the government's varied commitments, to more than 350,000 per year.

It is for these various reasons that measures are being taken in Europe to check the growth of the big cities by encouraging new and smaller plants to locate in the small towns in the country, so that they may draw on workers from shorter distances by bus and bicycle. To live in a village and travel up to one hour to one's work in one of several nearby smaller urban centres has developed as a normal part of the socio-economic structures of various parts of Germany, Belgium, and the Netherlands, and this trend is being encouraged as sound community planning. Yet the fact remains that while decentralization is generally considered to be socially desirable, the big city still continues to attract the employer, and no country in Europe or the United States has succeeded either in stopping the rapid growth of a big city, or in effectively changing the trend of localization from the big city to the small country town. In spite of all the efforts and controls exercised (some would say not effectively as the law would allow) this trend of continuing concentration has not been stopped. Maybe this must be accepted (before it is too late) and other planning principles devised. In other words, we should devise new economic and social objectives of land planning adapted to the natural trends towards the increasing growth and expansion of urban regions.

7. THE MONSTER-CITY AND THE NOTION OF MEGALOPOLIS

The name of megalopolis has been given prominence by the American philosopher, Lewis Mumford, and it has recently been used by Jean Gottmann to describe the chain of cities along the Atlantic Seaboard in America. Mumford identifies it with the character of bigness and concentration that results in the overgrown and oversized metropolis. It was in this sense that it was used by Patrick Geddes fifty years ago. Gottmann gives it a new slant by referring to a vast aggregation of sprawling cities as Megalopolis. In point of fact both aspects—the oversized and over-concentrated metropolis and the limitless uncontrolled spread of the urbanized area—are aspects of the same notion that were recognized by Geddes. This is one of the dominant and ever-growing features of our contemporary civilization.

The basic idea of a hierarchy of centres spatially organized round a common focus is evident in the historical interpretation of the city as developed by Geddes, Ebenezer Howard, Mumford, Gras, and others. Mumford, adopting the interpretation of Geddes, writes of the six stages in the growth of the city.[1] Eopolis is the village community, which emerged in the Neolithic era, and is still characteristic of pre-industrial agricultural societies. The Polis is 'an association of villages or blood-groups having a common site that lends itself to defence against depredation'. It begins with a common deity, defensive site, periodical assembly for trade, administration and worship, and the rise of handicrafts. Later, a community grows around this nucleus, self-governing and with its own institutions—temple, stadium, theatre, agora, market-place. This was characteristic of the Greek city and the medieval city in Europe, and of the cities and towns of other culture spheres that are not seriously affected by modern growth. Third, there emerges the Metropolis. 'Within the region one city emerges, from the less differentiated groups of villages and country towns.' This is the 'mother city' that is increasingly dependent on other areas for food and markets. Megalopolis is the 'beginning of the decline. The city under the influence of a capitalistic mythos concentrates upon bigness and power.' 'Triumph of mechanism', 'lust for power', and 'cultural aggrandizement', are among its hallmarks. Representatives have been Alexandria in the third century and Rome in the second century, Byzantium in the tenth century, Paris in the eighteenth century, and New York in the twentieth century. Tyrannopolis is marked by parasitism, imperialistic wars, starvation, and disease. (Geddes' Parasitopolis and Patholopolis.) Finally, comes the debacle of Necropolis, the city of

[1] Lewis Mumford, *The City in History*, New York, 1960, London, 1961.

the dead, marked by war, famine, and disease, and eventually by destruction—Babylon, Nineveh, Rome. The historic culture survives, if at all, in the provinces and the remote villages. This view of history postulates a sequence or cycle in the development of civilization that is shared by Spengler and Toynbee. But Mumford does not regard the final outcome of contemporary civilization as inevitable. He sees straws in the wind, and to propagate and convince is the purpose of his writings.

Megalopolitan civilization, argues Mumford, today simply means that urbanism is the dominant basis of life of the Industrial Society and is rapidly spreading to the other parts of the world. It is characterized by the growth of the vast formless agglomeration in whose heart are concentrated powers of life and death. Bigness, concentration, and sprawl, are completely out of scale with human values, both with regard to the size of the central city and the endless wilderness of low-density suburban sprawl. Megalopolitanism is growing through its own momentum faster than powers of public opinion can control it—cities get bigger, their urbanized areas more extensive and amoebic. It is marked by the vast accretion of power—economic, social, and political; by the growth over the last hundred years of a swollen bureaucracy—the service occupations alone now outnumber the manufacturing industries. Industry and commerce continue to accumulate in the urban areas. Growth takes place by private enterprise with little concern with social values. Cities spread and coalesce, with little control of the arrangement of land use on the basis of accepted values and action. Congestion goes apace, decongestion to the periphery adds to the chaos, and decentralization completely away from the big aggregate is negligible as a counterpart. The age-old function of the city as a cultural focus is dwarfed by bigness. It must be emphasized, however, that all these trends, deplored in 1938 by Mumford, have continued with even greater vigour in the United States, Great Britain, Germany, and elsewhere.

We are approaching Necropolis. Can our megalopolitan civilization survive? The chances are slim, but Mumford sees a way out. This lies in the fact that many thinkers are dedicating themselves to the problem. The challenge is to effect a programme of action against current trends. The views of Mumford in this respect are well known. He sees salvation by the reconstruction of the role of the historic metropolis. Any effort must go *against* the accepted trends of current urban growth, against the established patterns of metropolitan economy. It must work against population increase in larger cities, against multiplying the mechanical facilities for congestion, against the expansion of the continuous urban area, against unmanageable bigness and irrational 'greatness'. The proof that this alone will provide a relief from metropolitan difficulties, he writes, lies in the experience of the last twenty-five years.[1]

Attention on both sides of the Atlantic has long been drawn by philosophers to the breakdown of the traditional corporate life of the historic city—both as a whole and in its component parts—through the great growth of numbers, the separation of home from workplace, and the increasingly complex scale of economic organization and social service. Metropolitan life must find new local associations, which the individual and the family need as an inherent part of human make-up. Traditional ties of local interest and locality have been usurped by nation-wide associations. The former now cover trade and social associations of the modern state. The latter include the local ties with smaller beyond-the-family groups—of one's immediate neighbours or the district in which one lives. It is important that while connections of all kinds reduce personal dependence on local associations—be it church-going or shopping or club membership—the essential ties that remain are based especially on the children of the family, and it is understandable that the school and the school district remain as the keynotes of local community relations. And Europeans need to realize that the United States, with its very high post-war birth-rate, finds its urban life strongly oriented to the life and needs of the family as the basis of new neighbourhood relations. The primary geographical group is weakened since face-to-face relationships are diminished. But, as was said by John Dewey— 'Unless local community life can be restored, the public cannot adequately resolve its most urgent problem: to find and identify itself.' 'Democracy', he said, 'must begin at home and its home is the neighbourly community.' These are the new values that must be sought for. In concrete terms, they seem to lie in the provision of schools for the children, and in the physical separation of school districts by traffic arteries. Traffic islands, as they have been called, will serve as the framework for such community groups.[2]

The problem is, says Mumford, 'to overcome the barbarism of the submerged areas of the metropolis' through the medium of 'an appropriate social nucleus' to serve as a meeting point in its suburban areas as well as in its higher focal points. Hull House in Chicago and Toynbee Hall in London and the 'community centre' are seen as appropriate rallying points of this order. The vast megalopolitan mass should be replaced by self-contained urban

[1] Mumford, *Culture of Cities*, p. 296. Note that this was written in 1938, see *The City in History* for his latest views.
[2] See the interesting article by Morton and Lucia White on 'The American Intellectual Versus the American City', in *The Future Metropolis*, edited by Lloyd Rodwin, Constable, London, 1962.

communities, with a balanced occupational structure, adequate in size to support a healthy social life, controlled arrangement of land uses and surrounded by a guaranteed belt of green, sterilized from urban encroachment so as to prevent coalescence with other towns. The ideal size of such a town would be 30,000 to 50,000 people. This idea was first put forward by Ebenezer Howard and put into practice in England at Letchworth and Welwyn and in the United States at Radburn and the Green-Belt towns (a term that Mumford prefers to Garden City). It is now embodied in the New Towns in Britain, and other new centres are being built elsewhere on the Continent both as town and suburb. Then Mumford goes further, as did Howard, in envisaging a cluster of such towns that would form a 'social city' or 'regional city', focused upon a central 'mother city' that would provide them with the facilities of economy, culture, and leisure, that they are too small to provide, for, as Mumford never ceases to remind us, art and culture—religious, social, organizational, and recreational activities—are the most ancient and essential hallmarks of a real city. The central city would not have more than a million inhabitants and attention would be paid not only to the provision of economic functions, but also to museums, galleries, hospitals, concert halls, etc.

The ideas of the neighbourhood and the green belt are today basic to the practices of town planning in various countries, most of all in Great Britain. Since both ideas have come in for a good deal of criticism, especially in the United States, it should be made clear that they are an attempt to break away from the bigness and anonymity of modern urbanism. If there are errors, they lie in the planning practices and new ways must be tried. The far-flung English town with low-density houses, gardens, narrow roads, wide verges, and side-walks, give an empty and monotonous sprawl that does not favour social cohesion or personal convenience. These practices need to be superseded by others, aiming at a more compact unit, with a variety of dwelling types, and a more effective and accessible social nucleus. All these are variants working against the megalopolitan trend and in that sense are steps in the right direction.

It will be evident that many of these ideas reflect the actual spatial pattern of society that is inherent in the natural mode of growth before the advent of modern urbanism. They are not in any way novel. Mumford has emphasized in his works how the neighbourhood group through history has given to the town in the past a sense of human scale. This is one of the main themes we have emphasized in our study of the historical town in Europe.[1] Further, the ideal metropolitan arrangement with a family of dependent towns and

[1] *The West European City*, Routledge, London, Second Edition, 1961.

INTERNATIONAL ASPECTS OF REGIONALISM: CONCLUSION

villages emerged in Europe during the Middle Ages and is still to be found in large areas of western Europe in which excessive urban growth has not taken place. Small cities such as Dijon and many others in France—with about 100,000 inhabitants—or Würzburg or Bamberg in south Germany, are regional capitals in the fullest sense, and enjoy cultural attributes, embodied in centuries of regional associations, that are every bit as important as their economic functions—though less easy to measure.

We need to know then more of the size and spatial structure of urban communities; and of the nature, location, and size of the nuclei of neighbourhood groups; of the functions and trends and needs in central business districts; of the spatial distribution of towns and their relationships with each other; and the ways in which they do, in fact, form groups of towns focused upon outstanding regional or mother cities. We have not been greatly concerned in this book with the philosophical aspects of this problem. We have examined the actual character and determinants of the spatial structure of urban societies. Out of the actual conditions we can obtain better understanding of the current needs of urban society. But this cannot be done without sound social values, and elasticity and experiment in planning practices.

8. Conclusion

In conclusion, the aim of this book has been to indicate something of the pattern and fabric of those spatial associations in western Europe and the United States upon which planning and reconstruction should find its basic geographical foundation.

This whole field of study has now become of great importance as a basis for plans of reconstruction and regional development. Its investigation made a tardy appearance in Britain but has made much progress since the war. Elaborate social surveys between the wars neglected this aspect, with few exceptions, such as the survey of Merseyside. Civic and Regional Surveys were dominated by the idea of Place, Work, and Folk, which embraces all the relevant sciences on a footing of equality in a broad and invaluable philosophical concept, but failed, in the actual organization and prosecution of research in town or country, to canalize and direct investigation to specific problems in their spatial aspects with clearly defined central objectives. Nor, indeed, can it be expected that the architect or the professional planner or the highway engineer can possibly cover the whole field of scientific investigation that should be preliminary to the formulation of planning proposals for houses, open spaces, new towns, roads, and the like. There is, in other words, a very serious dearth of trained investigators in this whole field. The social sciences, particularly in the field of human ecology, have much leeway to make up. There is great need for what Max Lock has called 'civic diagnosis'. The same may be said of 'rural diagnosis', on the lines indicated by the survey prepared by Dr. Orwin and his collaborators and more recently by Dr. Bracey in his study of rural services in Wiltshire. Moreover, there is no clear-cut division between one problem and another, and between one discipline and another. The fusion of disciplines in the common pursuit of particular problems is a characteristic of the scientific approach in our time, and while the specialist has his own field and expertise he is constantly impinging on the fields of others. The study of modern society, on the same lines as the anthropologist studies primitive societies, needs institutes of research, attached to the Universities, with trained personnel, and working in close collaboration with the planners and builders, dedicated to what is, in effect, a virgin field of investigation. The advancement of applied geography and the rapid growth of 'regional science' and 'ekistics' are evidences of this kind of need in relation to land planning. The Universities in the United States are involved in this vast research process and planning authorities can draw upon well-trained University graduates. It is virtually impossible to find funds for a bona fide research project in the social sciences in Britain, but research on the scale with which it is demanded, as well as an adequate output of trained personnel, are absolutely impossible without post-graduate training. Resources are being deplorably wasted in the British Universities. We need to know much more of man's organization of space. Without diagnosis of these aspects of society by the social scientist and the careful mapping of his data whenever relevant, and without a body of theory of spatial distributions, the planner cannot provide for the optimum use of the land, the architect cannot build to suit the immediate and long-term needs of the people, and principles of planning, taking shape as the law of the land, can neither be worked out, nor put into effect, on a permanent and socially desirable basis.

INDEX

Aachen, 266, 344, 345, 347, 382
Abercrombie, Sir P., 439, 472, 492
Abercrombie Report, 411
Aberdeen, 400, 420, 422
Abrams, Charles, 41
Adams, Thomas, 439f
administration: as city function, 21f; and town distribution, 56ff
administrative units: natural, 4; optimum minimum for, 120f; origins, 60f; size, 63; *see also* local government
Agen, 101, 367, 453
agora, 21
agriculture, decline of, 26
Agriculture, Ministry of, 496
agro-industrial society, 232
agrotown, 111
Ahlmann, H. W., *et al.*, 152n
Aix-en-Provence, 350, 364, 451
Akademie für Raumforschung und Landesplanung, 543, 547, 565
Albany (N.Y.), 318
Albuquerque (New Mex.), 69, 290, 293
Alençon, 452
Alexander, J. W., 68, 69
Alexandersson, G., 68, 312
Alexandria, 571
Algeria, 63
Alleghany County Planning Commission, 509
Alps, 92, 265
Alsace, 90, 349, 366
Altenkirchen, 95
Amiens, 151, 366, 367, 451, 460
Amsterdam, 337, 347, 356, 440
Amtgerichtsort, 62
Amtsbezirke, 74
Amtsorte, 64, 74
Anderson, A. H., and Miller, C. J., 106
Andrews, R. B., 68, 171
Angers, 366, 367, 452, 453, 459
Angoulême, 453
Annecy, 260, 367
Antibes, 232
Antwerp, 337, 347, 561
area, natural/functional, 199ff; ecological studies, 201f; *see also* neighbourhood
Argentina, 64
Ariès, P., 453
Arnhem, 347
Arnold, J. H., and Montgomery, F., 253
Arras, 369, 451
arrondissements, 62, 453, 465
Asia, cities in, 21
assimilation, zone of, 222

Association for Regional Planning and Reconstruction, 479
Atlanta (Ga.), 290, 292, 293, 315, 316, 318, 326, 527
Atlantic City (N.J.), 523
atlases, German planning, 537, 549
Auburn, 304
Auch, 452
Augsburg, 208, 345, 550
Aurillac, 369
Aurousseau, M., 227
Aushöhlung, 535
Austria, 27, 30, 63, 337
authority, planning, 493, 494
Auvergne, 366
auxiliary centres, 92

Baden, 74
bailliages, 451, 453
Baltimore, 170, 287, 290, 315, 318, 321, 325
Bamberg, 575
Bank of America, 330
Bank of England, 417
banking: in England, 417; and Lyon, 258f
banlieue, grande, 232
Barathon, C., 450, 452
Bardet, Gaston, 45, 201f
Barlow Commission, 492, 499
Barnes, F. A., 415
Barnsley, 277, 397, 407
Barthelemy, J., 455
Basel, 76
basing points, 65, 326
Bastié, J., 148; and Brichler, M., 131, 148
Bates, Edwin, 332
Bath, 71
Batley, 503
Baton Rouge (La.), 528
Bavaria, 63, 74, 76, 90, 91, 345; centrality in, 92ff
Beaver, S. H., 168, 169
Bedford, 217
Belfast, 337
Belgium, 26, 27, 30, 64, 232, 357; commuting, 190, 357, 361f; population growth, 341f; urban agglomerations, 337, 338, 347
Bellet, M., 448
Benard, E., 239
Berliet, Marius, 261
Berlin, 16, 170, 250, 337, 380, 556
Berry, B. J. L., and Pred, A., 53, 58
Besançon, 365, 367, 369, 451, 460
Best, R. H., 174

577

INDEX

Bethune, 369
Béziers, 231, 365
Bezirk, 74
Bezirksämter, 74
Bezirksort, 212
Bielefeld, 345, 359, 380, 382, 549, 550, 551
Birkenhead, 406; *see also* Merseyside
Birmingham (Ala.), 293, 312, 315, 318, 327
Birmingham (England), 11, 16, 71, 79, 168, 180, 339, 356, 399, 403, 404, 410, 411, 412, 414, 420, 421, 422, 425, 488, 502; as business centre, 416, 418; population, 179; *see also* West Midlands
Black Forest, 92
Black Patch areas, 183
Blanchard, Raoul, 9, 10, 363
blight, urban, 185f
Bobek, H., 91, 229
Bogue, Donald, J., 10, 235f, 251, 288, 289, 313, 513, 514; and Kitagawa, E. M., 249
Bolton, 431
Bonn, 266, 344, 345
Borchert, J. R., 328
Bordeaux, 76, 349, 350, 364, 370, 451, 453, 459
Boston (Lincs.), 217
Boston (Mass.), 37, 41, 47, 167, 170, 287, 290, 299, 312, 315, 318, 320, 321f, 507, 528
Boudeville, J. R., 370
Boulogne, 369, 452
bourgade, 98, 100, 120
Bourges, 151, 366, 367, 451, 459
bourgs, 20, 99f, 465
Boustedt, O., 58, 93, 239, 240, 373
Bowman, I., 247
Bracey, H. E., 112, 120, 576
Bradford, 79, 405, 412, 422, 488; as business centre, 416, 417, 418; *see also* Leeds–Bradford; Yorkshire, West
Brandenburg, 80
Braunschweig, 344, 345, 356, 359, 549, 550, 551
Brazil, 64
Breda, 347
Bremen, 344, 373, 380, 550
Brighouse, 277
Brighton, 15, 397; University, 420
Bristol, 79, 192, 397, 422, 425; as business centre, 418; market area, 413ff
Britain, 29, 31, 32, 33, 64, 65, 251, 337, 338, 343; administrative divisions, 62, 119f, 467f; basic/non-basic ratio, 70; central business districts 221; commuting journeys, 357; drift to South, 403, 408; growth of conurbations, 402; local government areas, 486ff; major cities, regional functions, 412ff; number of divisions, for various purposes, 480; population density, 179; population growth, 398f; regional cities, 394ff; regionalism in, 467ff; retail trade, 71; shopping patterns, 215ff; typical urban institutions, 77; *see also* England; Scotland; names of towns
Brittany, 99, 365, 366

Brockport, 304
Brunhes, Jean, 450, 452, 453; and Deffontaines, P., 458
Brüning, K., 549
Brunner, E. de S.; and Kolb, J. H., 103, 105, 251, 253; and Lorge, I., 105
Brush, J. E., 107, 212; and Bracey, H. E., 115
Brussels, 337, 347, 362
Buchanan Report, 503
Buffalo (N.Y.), 290, 292, 304, 315, 318, 323
building forms, city, 22f
buildings, obsolescent, replacement, 33
Bund zur Erneuerung des Reiches, 533
Bunge, W., 58
Burgess, E. W., 125, 127, 131
burgs, 60
Burgundy, 366
Burnham plan (Chicago), 143
Bury St. Edmunds, 76
bus centres, 118
bus transport, growth, 190, 357, 401
business district, central, *see* central business district
Butte (Montana), 312
bye-laws, urban, 41
by-passes, 302
Byzantium, 571

Caen, 367, 369, 459
Calabria, 343
California, 34, 35
Cambridge, 419
Campania, 343
Campine, 562
Canada, 26, 27, 30
Cannes, 232
Canterbury, university, 420
cantons (France), 62, 63, 100, 456, 465
capital: natural, 8f; regional, 8ff, 67, 356, 479
capitale régionale, 98, 465
capitale secondaire, 367
capitalism, rent, 231
Cardiff, 16, 79, 397, 407, 422, 425; as business centre, 418; market area, 414
Carol, H., 212, 244ff
Carroll, J. Douglas, 189
Carr-Saunders, A. M., and Jones, D. C., 479
Carruthers, W. I., 217, 421, 425
Castle, I. M., and Gittus, E., 183
Cavan, Ruth S., 185
Census Bureau, U.S.A., 510
Census, standard regions (Britain), 482
central business districts, 220ff, 567; changes in, 297; growth of, in Britain, 410ff
centrality, 49, 73, 91
centralization, index of, 72
centre local, 98, 100
centres: city, use, 41f; English, classification, 421; —— second-order, 424f; —— service areas, 422f; hierarchy of, 52f, 72ff, 421f; higher- and lower-order, 113ff, 116; regional, 6, 312, 422
centrifugal and centripetal forces, 39, 165
Chabot, G., 238, 367f

578

INDEX

Chalons, 366, 452
Chambers of Commerce (France), regions, 448f, 464
Chambery, 260, 261, 262
Charleroi, 337, 347
Charles-Brun, J., 447, 456
Chartres, 101, 367
Chattanooga, 293
Cheekowaga (N.Y.), 304
chef-lieu, 8f; *communal*, 98
Chelmsford, 409
Chelsea, 41, 47
Chemnitz, 168, 356, 380
Chesterfield, 407
Chicago, 16, 37, 81, 83, 85, 126f, 167, 169f, 177, 179, 190, 222, 287, 292, 293, 295, 299, 312, 315, 318, 319, 323f, 507, 527; community areas, 142, 200; industrial plants, types, 178f; mode of growth, 131ff; Negro areas, 141, 185, 297; neighbourhood areas, 207; population changes, 136f, 138; social disorganization, 184f; urban area, 131
Chicago Regional Planning Association, 509
Chisholm, M., 247
Cholet, 350, 352
Chombart de Lauwe, P. H., 127, 145, 148
Christaller, W., 53, 58, 63, 74, 92, 120, 249, 388f, 545, 547, 560
churches, location, 211
Cincinnati, 69, 287, 292, 315, 318, 319, 325
cité, 20, 60
city (cities): basic and non-basic activities, 67ff; buildings and site, 22f; centres, change in nature, 37f; central zones, population changes, 296ff; characteristics of, 79; as container and magnet, 19; functional classification, 311ff; functions of, 21ff; hinterland-access, 236; history and meaning, 20; major, 79; metropolitan, 81, 235ff, 287, *see also* metropolis; modern change in function, 11f; national planning differences, 167f; organization, 23; regional associations, 228f; as regional focus, 7, 66, 228ff; relations with country, 230f; spatial structure, forces producing, 125; super- and primate, 13f; and surrounding land use, 246; Western Europe, hierarchy, 388ff; zones of, 163ff, 235
city-region: concept, 227ff; in Europe, 336ff; and location of industry, 249ff; relation to State, 554ff; and rural economy, 246-8; and socio-economic conditions, 251ff; structure, 233ff; zones of, 235
city settlement area, 236, 237f
city-state, 60
city trade area, *see* trade area
Civil Defence Regions, 470f, 479ff
civitas, 20, 59f, 451
Clark, Colin, 247
Cleef, E. van, 555
Clementel, M., 448
Clermont-Ferrand, 343, 350, 364, 459, 460.
Cleveland (O.), 167, 287, 292, 297, 315, 318, 319, 323

Clozier, R., 238
Clyde (N.Y.), 304
Clydebank, 407
Clyde-Forth area, 16, 400
Clydeside, 394, 396, 400, 402, 407, 503; *see also* Glasgow
coffin belt, 499
Colchester, University, 420
Cole, G. D. H., 470, 474, 475ff
Cologne, 11, 14, 16, 28, 76, 223, 265ff, 337, 363, 373, 380, 382, 385, 440, 441, 536; as business centre, 272; commuting traffic, 271; expansion, 268f; hinterland, 273; history, 265f; industries, 271; layout, 266ff; nodality, 271f; region, 269, 270; as supply centre, 272f
Colombia, 64
Colorado River Compact, 508
Columbus (O.), 318, 323
commerce: as city function, 22; location of, 212ff
Commissariat Général du Plan, 462
Common Market, 444, 561
communes, 63, 453, 465
community: areas, 206, 207; centres, 573f; rural, 104
comté, 451
Comte, Auguste, 447
concentration, intra-urban, 40f
concentric growth, 125ff
Connecticut, 300
Connery, R. H., and Leach, R. H., 527
Constantinople, 554
conurbations, 16, 237, 339; British, definition, 396
Copenhagen, 337, 556
Coppolani, J., 98, 100, 363, 367
Cork, 337
Costa Rica, 63
Côte d'Azur, 231
Cotton, J., 411
counties, British, 62, 467, 468, 469
countryside, spillover of city to, 162; *see also* overspill
county boroughs, 467
County of London Plan, 206, 492
court neighbourhoods, 208f
Covent Garden, 413f
Coventry, 397; University, 420
Craven, 469
Cressey, P. F., 141
Crewe, 399
criteria, diagnostic, of region, 6
Crowther, Sir Geoffrey, 504
Crowther report, 503
Crozier, 239
cultural centres, England, 419ff
Czechoslovakia, 64

Dallas (Texas), 292, 293, 315, 316, 318, 326f, 330, 527
Danelagh, 61
Dansereau, H. K., 301, 302
Danzig, 555
Darlington, 422
Dauphiné, 366
Davie, M. R., 127, 130, 199
Dawley, 495
decentralization, 44, 559, 566

579

INDEX

deconcentration, 43f
de Geer, Sten, 152, 319
delinquency, 183ff
Denmark, 30, 232, 337, 556
density, population: in cities, 179ff, 238, 239; control of, 41; minimum, for urbanized areas, 239
Denver (Colo.), 290, 292, 315, 318, 331
départements, 61, 62, 63, 101, 447f, 455
department stores, business area, 214
Derby, 337, 397, 399, 407; market area, 414
Des Moines (Iowa), 312
deterioration, 48; zones of, 42, 185, 221
Detmold, 380
Detroit, 37, 69, 292, 299, 315, 318, 319, 323, 324
Deutz, 268
development areas, 499, 500
Development Credit Corporations (U.S.A.), 520
Dewey, John, 573
Dewhurst, J. F., *et al.*, 521
Dewsbury, 405, 503
Dickinson, R. E., 89, 115, 250, 273, 358, 361, 362, 574
Dijon, 14, 365, 451, 460, 575
Dinkelsbühl, 90
dioceses, ecclesiastical, 60, 451
discard, zone of, 222
disorganization, social, areas of, 182ff
Dittrich, Erich, 547, 549
Dombes, 265
dominance, 47, 235f
Doncaster, 275, 277
Dortmund, 344, 380, 383
Douai, 451
Douglass, H. P., 211, 212
Drainage, Greater London, Report on, 470
Draper, Earle S., 508
Dresden, 380
Dublin, 337
Duisburg, 380, 383, 561
Duluth, 328
Duncan, Beverly, 139, 188, 189
Duncan, O, D., 7f, 66, 317, 329, 330
Dundee, 400, 420, 422
Durham, 492; University, 419
Düsseldorf, 16, 76, 266, 337, 373, 380, 382, 385, 441

East Anglia, 77, 115, 120, 469
East Dane county (Wis.), 104
Eastshore Freeway, 303
Economic Development, Committee on, 528
economic growth, rates of, 30
Edinburgh, 67, 72, 400, 420, 422; Greater, 16
Eindhoven, 250, 347, 363, 562
Elbe, middle, 536
electricity supply regions (England), 483, 484f
Ely, R. T., and Wehrwein, G. S., 247, 248, 253
employment, internal, 69
England, 61, 63, 233, 238; centrality in, 112ff; commuting areas, 425ff; country towns, 61; land uses, 174; regionalism in, 467ff; *see also* Britain; United Kingdom; names of specific towns
Eopolis, 571
Essen, 76, 380, 383
Europe, Western: access to cities, 352f; growth rates of metropolitan areas, 338; hierarchy of cities, 388ff; population changes, 342; urbanized areas, 339ff
European Economic Community, 445
exchange, zone of, 236
Exchanges, British, 416
Exeter, 71, 418, 492; University, 420
expansion, urban, limitations on, 496f
explosion, urban, 25, 33f, 43, 172, 505, 523; consequences in U.S.A., 523f
exurbia, 173

Faber, K. G., 544
Fabian Society, 470, 472
fallow, social, 231
Faris, R. F. L., and Dunham, H. W., 185
farmers, side-walk and suitcase, 110
farming conditions, and distance from city, 252f
Fawcett, C. B., 121, 237, 436, 470, 472, 475, 476, 484
Federal Highway Act (1956), 301
Federal Reserve districts, 315, 316
Federation of British Industries, 416
Fédération Régionaliste Française, 447
Fellman, J. D., 134
Fens, the, 469
Figheira, M., 448
finance, local, in Britain, 490f
financial centres, in U.S.A., 285
Finland, 64
Firey, W., 106, 173, 220; Firey, Loomis, C. P., and Beegle, J. A., 31, 32, 255, 256
Fisher, Sir Warren, 488
Flanders, 22, 100, 557
flats, multi-storeyed, 176
Flecken, 20
Flint (Mich.), 173
Florence, P. Sargant, 53n
Florida, 293
focal places, clusters of, 83
focus, city as, 49f
Foley, Donald L., 189
food marketing, in Britain, 411ff
Forest of Dean, 469
Forshaw, J. H., and Abercrombie, P., 206
Fort Worth (Texas), 292, 293, 315, 318, 326f
forum, 21
France, 26, 27, 30, 46, 233, 238, 239, 338, 343, 347f, 354, 356; administrative areas, 62, 64; centrality in, 98ff; city/country relations, 230f; conurbations, 16, 337; —— growth rates, 338, 339; industrial zones, 352; national plan, 252, 263; occupational changes, 28; planning regions, 462f; population changes, 349f; proposals for regions, 456ff; provinces, historical, 450ff; —— names, 61, 452; regional cities, 363ff; regionalism in, 438f, 447ff;

580

INDEX

regions, 8, 448ff; trade settlements, 22; *see also* names of towns and provinces
Frankfurt, 11, 76, 91, 337, 344, 359, 373, 380, 389, 536, 550; zones of influence, 376ff
Frazier, E. F., 185, 186
Freeman, O. W., and Martin, A. H., 332
Freeman, T. W., 396, 399, 400
freeways, 303
Freiburg-im-Breisgau, 14, 21, 37
friction of space, 38, 40, 163, 194
Friedmann, G., 230
fringe, urban, 165, 171ff, 237, 243f, 296
frontiers, political, and disruption, 555ff
fruit and vegetables, distribution, 413f
function, specialization of, by place, 12

Galloway, *et al.*, 514
Galpin, C. G., 103; and Kolb, J. H., 104
Galveston (Texas), 292, 293, 295, 327
Garden City Parkway, 303
Garrison, 58
gas supply regions, England, 485
Gascogne, 366
Gau, Gaustadt, 76
Gaul, 37, 60, 257
Gdynia, 555
Geddes, Sir Patrick, 5, 15ff, 28, 29, 237, 292, 339, 396, 404, 571; and Branford, V., 436ff
Gemeinden, 62, 80, 232, 240, 371ff, 564; types, 240, 371
généralités, 451
Genoa, 349
geographers, and region concept, 5
Geographical Association, 478
Geographical Distribution of Industrial Population, Commission on, 470
George, P., 27
Germany, 26, 27, 29, 30, 33, 37, 46, 61, 62, 64, 168, 190, 215, 232, 238, 239, 337, 338, 354, 356, 439, 560f; centrality in, 73ff; commuting movement, 357, 358ff; conurbations, 16; East, 544; economic regions, 538; functional structure of towns, 79ff; medieval towns, distribution, 22, 61, 88; metropolitan cities, 11; *Neugliederung*, 530; occupational structures, 371ff; planning, regional, 536; population, changes, 343f; —— density, 179; provinces, 379; regional cities, 370ff, 381; regionalism, 529ff; rehousing, 570; small town expansion, 23, 43; urbanized areas, 239ff, 345ff; village/town relations, 88ff; *see also* names of towns and provinces
Gewerbesteuerausgleich, 569
Ghent, 337
Gilbert, E. W., 479, 481, 485, 486
Gist and Halbert, 184, 185
Glasgow, 11, 262, 407, 412, 420, 422; Greater, 16; *see also* Clydeside
Glass, D. V., 183
Glass, Ruth, 202
Gloucester, 71
Godlund, Sven, 72, 233
Goodland, 110f
Gottmann, Jean, 31, 32, 292, 320, 340, 462, 523, 567, 571

gouvernements, 451
Gradmann, Robert, 88
Grand Rapids, 83
Gras, N. S. B., 10, 235, 287, 554, 555, 571
Grasse, 232
Gravier, J. F., 150, 350, 369, 450, 455, 465, 559
Great Britain, *see* Britain
Greater London Plan, 492, 493, 501
Greece, 63
Greeley, W. R., 518
Green, F. H. W., 278, 421
Green, Howard L., 321
Green, Howard W., 200
Green, L. P., 235, 428, 472, 486, 489, 490, 491
green belt, 176, 497, 498, 567, 574
green strips, 303
Greensboro, 293
Grenoble, 10, 14, 258, 260, 261, 339, 365, 367, 451, 460
grey areas, 164
grid plan, 167
Gropius, W., 411
Grossstadt, 244
group principle, planning on, 208f
growth, urban, theories of, 125ff
Guéret, 452
Gutachten, 544
Gutkind, E. A., 6
Guyeure, 366

Haarlem, 337
Hadow Committee, 470
Hagen, 385
Hager, J. M., 326
Hagerstrand, T., 58, 233
Hague, The, 298, 347
Haigh, R. M., 40; and McCrea, M. C., 38
Halifax, 274, 277, 405
Hallamshire, 469
Halle, 380
Hamburg, 76, 337, 344, 373, 380, 389, 440, 536, 550, 556, 558
hamlet, definition, 107
Hampstead Garden Suburb, 472
Hanover, 11, 337, 344, 345, 373, 380, 382, 549, 550, 551
Harlem (N.Y.), 185
Harris, C. D., 279, 311, 312; and Ullman, E. L., 129
Harris, G. Montague, 63
Harrogate, 71, 277, 399
Hart, Frazer, 312
Hartford, 318, 323
Hartshorne, R., 328, 513
Hartsough, M., 328
Haubner, K., 240
Hauser, M., 448
Hawley, Amos, 181, 228
health, economic, 34
Health Service, National, 489
Heidelberg, 337
Heilbronn, 344
Helmstedt, 551
Hennessy, Jean, 448, 458
Herbert Commission, 501
Hesse, 74, 76, 90
Hesse, P., 240

581

INDEX

Hettner, Alfred, 240
Higbee, E., 523
highway: as axis of expansion, 300ff; controls on land use, 302
Hilfszentralen, 92
Hinterland, 98, 235
Hoffer, C. R., 105
Holderness, 469
Holland, *see* Netherlands
home rule movement, 468
homogeneity, regional, 6
Hoover, E. M., 52; and Vernon, R., 195
Hospital Boards, regions, 484, 485
hotels, sites, 222
house, change of, 298f
housing: expansion of low-income, 299; provision of, 495f; sub-standard, 180
Houston (Texas), 292, 293, 295, 315, 318, 327, 527
Howard, Ebenezer, 495, 497, 571, 574
Hoyt, Homer, 69, 127f, 130, 171n, 186, 214
Huddersfield, 274, 276, 277, 278, 405
Hull, 70, 79, 180, 274, 275, 277, 397; market area, 413ff; University, 420
Hull House (Chicago), 573
Hungary, 354

implosion, urban, 39
India, 27, 443
Indianapolis, 83, 293, 318, 323, 324
industrial complexes, large, 45
industries/industry: and city development, 22; decline, in central cities, 299; dispersion from city, 250; interchange of, 66f; light and heavy, 177; location of, 65, 67, 176ff, 493f; —— city-region and, 249ff; manpower, 26, 27; small, placement of, 45f; suburbanization of, 32, 254f
innovations, spread of, 233
Inspecteurs, 462f
Institut National de la Statistique, 565
Institut für Raumforschung und Raumordnung, 543, 546, 547, 565
insurance business, 417
interchange, zone of, 236
interdependence, economic, 560f
International Urban Research Group, 336
interurbia, 32, 172, 300
Ipswich, 217, 422
Ireland, 64, 337, 468
Iron Curtain, and Germany, 558
Isard, W., 8, 58, 251; and Whitney, V. H., 234
Isenberg, Gerhard, 79, 81, 344
isotims, 248
Italy, 26, 27, 30, 64, 76, 338, 339, 343, 356, 439; medieval towns, 22; town–country relation, 231

Jacksonville, 293, 315, 318, 327
James, Henry, 298
Japan, 27, 238
Java, 63
Jefferson, Mark, 14, 49, 238, 319, 555, 556
Johannesburg, 235
Johnson, C. S., 141

Jonasson, O., 248
Jones, C. F., 513
Jones, D. Caradog, 183
Jones, J. H., 65f
journey to work, 186ff, 356, 569
Juillard, E., 230, 232
Jura, 265

Kansas, 110
Kansas City, 287, 290, 292, 293, 312, 315, 318, 319, 325, 329
Kant, E., 224
Karlsruhe, 91, 345
Kassel, 345, 380, 550
Keeble, L. B., 492, 494
Keele, University, 420
Keighley, 274
Kenya, 443
Kerngebiet, 373
Key, C. W., 489
Kiel, 345, 380
Kimball, S. T., 106
Kings Lynn, 496
Knoxville, 293, 319
Koblenz, 266, 380, 552
Kolb, J. H., 107; and Day, L. J., 106; and Marshall, D. G., 104
Kollmorgen, W. M., and Jenks, G. F., 109
Koomoos, Dr., 340
Krefeld, 382
Kreis, 63, 74, 76
Kreisstadt, 74, 76, 80
Kroeber, 6
Kuske, Bruno, 265, 273

Labasse, Jean, 257, 341, 464, 560
Labatut, J., and Lane, W. J., 525
labour, mobility of, 187f
labour market areas, 190
Lakes, Great (U.S.A.), 17
Lancashire, 15; central, coalfield, 397, 404; metropolitan, structure, 428ff; South-east conurbation, 396, 402, 404, 428ff, 489ff; *see also* Manchester
Lancashire Development Plan, 489
Lancaster, University, 420
land use, agricultural, circumburban, 246f
Länder, 62, 530, 533ff, 541ff
Landeshauptstädte, 91
Landeskommissariatsbezirk, 76
Landesmetropole, 244
Landesplanung, 536
Landkreis, 62
Landstadt, 76, 80
land use: in Britain, 174; of city fringe, 172; and movement requirements, 194; —— urban, 40, 126; —— controls on, 41
land values: and central business district, 221; and centrifugal drift, 182; and proximity to city, 255
Languedoc, 366; Bas, 230
Laon, 453
La Rochelle, 451, 459
Las Vegas, 290
Lawton, R., 425, 427, 428
Lazio, 67
Leamington, 422
Le Creusot, 28

INDEX

Leeds, 35, 71, 79, 141, 356, 405, 425, 488; as business centre, 418; market area, 414, 416
Leeds-Bradford, 273ff; as administrative centre, 275; areas of influence, 275ff; as business centre, 274, 418; as cultural centre, 275; *see also* Yorkshire, West; West Riding
Le Havre, 151
Leicester, 79, 397; market area, 414; University, 420
Leipzig, 337, 380
Le Mans, 151, 349, 366, 367
Lens, 369
Le Play, Frédéric, 447
Le Puy, 369
Lerner, Max, 515, 517
Letchworth, 495, 574
Leverkusen, 271
Liège, 28, 337, 347
Liepmann, K., 186f
Lievin, 369
Lilienthal, David, 510
Lille, 14, 168, 337, 349, 364, 451, 460, 557
Limburg (Dutch), 347, 361
Limoges, 364, 452, 453, 459, 460
Limousin, 366
Lindstrom, D. E., 106
linkage, of establishments, 194
Lisbon, 389
Little Rock (Ark.), 312
Liverpool, 15, 70, 79, 389, 406, 410, 411, 421, 422, 425, 488; as business centre, 418; market area, 413ff; population density, 179; social disorganization, 183f; *see also* Merseyside
Livingstone, 495
local government, reorganization, 4, 439, 440
Local Government Act (1958), 488
Local Government Boundary Commission, 486ff
Local Government Commission, 432
Lock, Max, 576
London, 41, 47, 70, 170, 179, 250, 262, 339, 356, 411, 422, 566; community structure, 206; early extension, 166; growth of business district, 410; market area, 412ff; population movements, 141; University, 419, 420
London, Greater, 15, 396, 402ff, 408ff; criteria of area, 403; employment in, 409; population density, 180; reorganization, 488f, 499ff; service centres, 217
London County Council, 492
Longwy, 349
Lorraine, 231, 349, 365, 366, 561
Los Angeles, 35, 85, 167, 190, 287, 292, 293, 295, 298, 303, 315, 318, 330, 331, 507
Los Angeles County Regional Planning Commission, 509
Lösch, A., 58
Louisville, 253, 315, 318, 325
Lübeck, 21, 37, 345
Ludwigshafen, 45, 91, 337, 344, 358, 359, 373, 550, 561; commuting pattern, 387
Luther, H., 533, 543

Luton, 409, 499
Lymm, 494, 496
Lynch, Kevin, 567
Lyon, 10, 14, 76, 162, 250, 257ff, 337, 339, 349, 350, 352, 356, 363, 364, 370, 451, 453, 460; as administrative centre, 262f; commuting traffic, 263, 265; financial interests, 262; industries, 261; modernization, 262; and rural economy, 264; services, 263f; telephone net, 260; as traffic centre, 259f
Lyon, L. S., 527

McCarty, H. H., 319, 323, 332
McKenzie, R. D., 10, 12, 13, 181, 182, 235
Mackinder, Sir Halford, 49, 501
Macon, 260, 453
Madison (Wis.), 69f
Magdeburg, 380
Mainz, 91, 344
Manchester, 11, 14, 15, 71, 79, 141, 168, 180, 216, 262, 275, 277, 356, 401, 404, 410, 411, 412, 488, 491; as business centre, 416, 418; commuting area, 426f; as cultural centre, 421; market area, 413ff; placing of overspill, 494; proposed reorganization, 502; replanning schemes, 472ff; *see also* Lancashire, South-east
Manchester Development Plan, 489
Manhattan, *see* New York
Mannheim, 76, 91, 337, 344, 373, 380, 550, 561
Mansfield, 407
manufacturing, small, and cities, 36
manufacturing belt, U.S.A., 319ff
Marches, 61
market areas, regional and local, 67
market towns, 20, 37, 60
Marktort, 76, 244
Marseille, 76, 337, 339, 349, 350, 364, 460
Marshall, D. G., 256
Martin, J., 255
Martin, R. C., 510
Massachusetts Division of Metropolitan Planning, 509
Massif Central, 99, 265, 364, 369
Mayer, H. M., 136, 143; and Kohn, 321
meat distribution, 412
Megalopolis, 17, 292, 320, 321, 341, 571f
Memphis, 315, 318, 327
merchants, and city development, 22
Merseyside, 396, 399, 402, 406, 412, 488; proposed County Council, 502; *see also* Liverpool
metropolis, 571; economic, 10f, 287; qualifications for title, 13, 242f
metropolitan area, standard, 241ff; definition, 306ff; distribution, 290f; growth of, 288f; populations, 333ff
—— distribution, changes, 296ff; rates of increase, 293, 333
Metropolitan Board of Works, 491, 492
Metropolitan Water Board, 491
Metz, 349, 364, 367, 369, 451, 460
Meynen, E., 269
Miami, 292, 293, 318f
Michigan, 106, 255, 292, 295, 507
Middlesbrough, 202, 276

583

INDEX

Midlands, West, *see* West Midlands
Midlandton, 16
Mid-Trent, 407
Milan, 14, 76, 262, 356, 389
milk distribution, 414f
Milk Marketing Board, 415
Miller, R., and Tivy, J., 420
Milwaukee, 44, 83, 292, 295, 315, 318, 319, 324
Milwaukee County Regional Planning Department, 509
Minneapolis, 212, 287, 292, 298, 312, 315, 318, 328f
Mitchell, R. B., and Rapkin, C., 193f, 525
Mittelstadt, 76
Mittelwestdeutschland, 544
'mixed uses', areas of, 48
Mönchen-Gladbach, 382
Monnet, Jean, 349
Montauban, 452
Montgomery (Ala.), 293, 312
Montluçon, 370
Montpellier, 231, 365, 452, 459
Montreal, 287
Morgan, A. H., 419
Mormons, 280
Moscow, 170
Moser, C. A., and Scott, W., 70
Moses, Robert, 567
motels, 33
Motherwell, 407
motor transport, effects of, 13, 170f, 285
Moulins, 451
movement: daily, increase, 34; intra-urban, 187ff
Mulhouse, 349
multiple nuclei growth theory, 128, 129f
Mumford, Lewis, 5, 19, 28, 37, 284, 567, 571ff
Münchheimer, W., 543, 547
Munich, 11, 14, 37, 76, 91, 262, 337, 344, 373, 380, 550, 551
municipalities, readjustment, in U.S.A., 527f
Münster, 14, 344, 383
Murphy, R. E., and Vance, J. E., 220ff

Nancy, 14, 76, 349, 364f, 369, 451, 460
Nantes, 364, 459, 460
Naples, 76
Nashville, 312, 318, 326
National Parks and Access to Countryside Act (1949), 493
National Resources Board (U.S.A.), 508, 516
National Resources Committee (U.S.A.), 510, 518
National (Resources) Planning Board (U.S.A.), 507f, 520
Nazis, and regionalism, 531, 539, 641
Neckar basin, 91
Necropolis, 571
Negroes: in Chicago, 141, 185; in New York, 185; influx into central cities, 297
neighbourhood, 104f, 201ff, 574; definitions, 204; local, 47; as planned unit, 203ff
Nelson, Howard J., 35, 312

Netherlands, 26, 27, 30, 64, 190, 232, 250, 337, 338, 341, 347f; commuting in, 361f; planning in, 562f
Neugliederung, 529, 533ff
Nevers, 452
Newcastle on Tyne, 71, 79, 274, 275, 406, 410, 411, 412, 422, 425; as business centre, 416, 418; market area, 413ff
Newcastle under Lyme, 418
New England Council, 508
New Haven (Conn.), 199
New Orleans, 287, 295, 315, 318, 327, 528
Newport News, 325
newspaper circulation areas, U.S.A., 315
new towns, 495, 496, 499, 574
New Towns Act (1946), 492
New York, 14, 69, 82, 85, 167, 169, 170, 179, 190, 287, 290, 303, 312, 315, 318, 320, 321f, 507, 528, 571; Greater, 16; journey to work in, 189; Metropolitan Region, 195; Negro areas, 185, 297; population movements, 141; regional plan, 509; sequent occupance, 195ff
New York Port Authority, 528
New York Throughway, 303f
New Zealand, 64
Nicaragua, 64
Nice, 232, 349, 364, 367, 460
Niedersachsen, 380
Nigeria, 443
Nîmes, 231, 365
nomadism, urban, 298
non-farm population, rural, 304, 305
Norfolk (Va.), 319, 325
Normandy, 366
Northeastern Illinois, Metropolitan Area Planning Commission, 143
Norway, 30
Norwich, 71, 79, 422, 425; as business centre, 418; University, 420
Nottingham, 79, 337, 356, 396, 397, 399, 407f, 422, 425; market area, 414, 416; University, 420
nuclei, city, in history, 39
Nuremberg, 89, 91, 337, 344, 356, 337, 380
Nuremberg-Fürth, 76, 91, 550

Oakland, *see* San Francisco
Oberämter, 74
occupance, sequent, 47
occupational structure, 25ff
Offenbach, 373
offices: control of location, 493; removal from central cities, 299
Ogden, 282, 283, 331
Oklahoma City, 318, 329f
Oldham, 15
Olsson, W. W., *see* William-Olsson
Omaha, 315, 318, 319, 324, 329
oppidum, 60
Orleans, 151, 366, 367, 451, 459
Orwin, C. S., 121, 576
Oshkosh, 69f
Oslo, 337
Osnabrück, 359, 382, 550, 551
Otremba, D. E., 249
Ouest, Région de l', 366
overspill, 496, 568; from London, 501

INDEX

Owen, W., 190, 525
Oxford, 492, 499

Pacific Northwest Commission, 519
pagi, 451
Palatinate, 359
Paraguay, 64
Paris, 168, 170, 179, 337, 339, 571; concentric zones, 146ff; domination of, 450; highway development, 151f; mode of growth, 131, 144ff; population changes, 145, 146, 350; regional plan for, 151; urban area, 131
Paris, Greater, 16, 239
Paris Region, 151, 440, 566
parishes, 468
Park Forest (Chicago), 208
Parlements, 451
Passfield, Lord, *see* Webb, S.
Patterson (N.J.), 67
Pau, 367, 451
pays, 451, 452
Pays d'état and *d'élection*, 451
Peabody (Mass.), 215
Peake, H. J. E., 120, 478
Peine, 550
Peoria, 293, 324
Pepler, G. L., 472
Perigueux, 101, 453
Perloff, H. S., 521
Perpignan, 367, 451
Perry, Clarence, 203, 206
Peru, 64
Pétain, P., 449f
Petri, F., *et al.*, 95
Peytral, Victor, 448
Philadelphia, 16, 167, 170, 190, 213, 287, 290, 315, 318, 320, 321, 507, 528
Philadelphia Tri-State District Regional Planning Federation, 509
Philbrick, A. K., 81ff, 312
Phoenix (Ariz.), 290, 292, 293, 319
Pick, Frank, 4f
Pittsburgh, 16, 37, 292, 299, 315, 318, 319, 323
planning: problems requiring, 443; regional, 436, 439ff, 493; State, in U.S.A., 507; town, 439ff
planning authorities, 492f
planning units, in U.S.A., 506
plant, obsolescence of, 298, 299
Plymouth, 79, 414, 416, 422, 425; as business centre, 418, 419; plan for, 492
Poitiers, 366, 367, 369, 451, 453, 459
Poland, 26, 64
polis, 59, 571
P.E.P., 79
Ponsard, 58
Pontefract, 277
population: distribution, 179ff; urban, definition, 288
Portland (Ore.), 293, 295, 315, 318, 332
Portsmouth (England), 397
Portsmouth (R.I.), 319
Portugal, 30
Potteries, 397, 418, 483
Pounds, N. J. G., 557, 558
Powell, A. G., 408, 409
power sources, effects of development, 29

Pratt, Edwin A., 61
Preuss, H., 532
Prevet, F., 448
Prewett, F. J., 412
product, national, growth of, 30
Proudfoot, Malcolm, 213
Provence, 366
Providence (R.I.), 323
province, in Britain, conception of, 476ff
Provinz, 62
Provinzstadt, 76
Prussia, 529f; administrative units, 62, 74, 76, 80
public-houses, location, 211
Pueblo, 290
Puerto Ricans, and New York, 297
pyramid, occupational, 65

Quinn, J. E., 184

Radburn, 574
radial plan, 168
railways: and city development, 168f; diminishing use, 192f
Rannells, John, 220
Rastorte, 89
Ratcliff, R. U., 40
Ratzel, F., 23
Raumschaften, 564
Reading, 409
Realteilung, 359
recentralization, 45, 567
Redditch, 495
Regierungsbezirk, 62, 63, 76
region: as intermediate area, 435f; metropolitan, spatial structure, 12; —— in U.S.A., 313ff; as social unit, 4ff; use of term, 3ff
Regional Commissioners, Civil Defence, 481
Regional Planning Commissions (U.S.A.), 508
Regional Planning Federation (Germany), 541
regional science, 58
regionalism: spontaneous, 515; urban, 3
Reichsarbeitsgemeinschaft für Raumforschung, 541
Reichsstelle, 539
Reichstadt, 76
Reichsteile, 76
Reims (Rheims), 151, 366, 460
Remscheid, 382
Renner, G. T., 443, 514, 515
Rennes, 349, 364, 365, 370, 451, 459, 460
Resources for the Future Inc., 528
retail trades, 71; location, 212f; new type centres, 214
revolutions, palaeotechnic and neotechnic, 29
Rheims, *see* Reims
Rhine, river, 265f, 268f, 544, 561
Rhineland, 76, 265, 272, 273, 344, 345, 382; commuting pattern, 383f
Rhodesia, 247
Rhuddlan, Statute of, 468
ribbon development, 32, 166, 292, 300
Richmond (Va.), 315, 318, 325, 326
Riga, 556

INDEX

Riom, 452
Ripon, 71
Riviera, French, 16, 349
roads, effects of development, 24, 31f
Roanne, 261
Robson, W. A., 470, 475
Rodwin, Lloyd, 567
Rognon, Étienne, 448
Rome (Italy), 440, 571
Rome (N.Y.), 292
Roper-Power, E. R., 204
Rorchert, J. R., and Adams, R. B., 328
Rotherham, 396, 397, 407, 488
Rotterdam, 337, 347, 561
Roubaix, 337, 349, 364, 557
Rouen, 151, 364, 451, 459, 460
Roy, Henri, 448
Ruhr region, 16, 45, 337, 339, 356, 359, 373, 382, 385, 536, 550; service areas, 385
Ruhr Regional Planning Federation, 441
Runcorn, 495
rural districts, 62, 63, 467
'rurban community', 103; centre, 120

Saar, 91
Saintes, 452
Saint-Étienne, 28, 168, 257, 258, 260, 261, 262, 349, 356, 367, 460
Saint-Germain, 150
St. Helens, 397, 404
St. Joseph, 329
St. Louis, 37, 212, 287, 290, 292, 297, 299, 312, 315, 318, 319, 325, 327
St. Louis Regional Planning Association, 509
St. Paul, 287, 292, 312, 315, 318, 328f
St. Petersburg, 319
Saint-Quentin, 151
Sale, 473
Salford, 412, 429, 473, 474, 491
Salt Lake City, 279ff, 315, 331; occupations, 279f; as traffic centre, 282f; tributary areas, 280ff
Salzgitter, 549, 550
San Antonio (Tex.), 318, 527
Sanders, W. Stephen, 470
Sanderson, Dwight, 104
San Diego (Cal.), 318f, 331
San Francisco, 37, 167, 190, 222, 223, 287, 292, 293, 295, 299, 303, 318, 330; commercial centres, 218ff
San Luis Obispo (Cal.), 330
Sardinia, 343
Saxony, 62
Schenectady, 304, 318
Scheu, Erwin, 538
Schlier, Otto, 378
Schmid, Calvin F., 212
Schmidt, Robert, 536
Schöller, P., 95, 96ff, 544
school, elementary, and neighbourhood, 206, 573
Scotland, 394, 400, 468; Universities, 419, 420
Scott Committee, 174f, 470, 472
Scranton, 67
Seattle, 44, 190, 287, 292, 293, 295, 315, 318, 332

sector growth, 127f
segregation, residential, 46f
Seine, *département*, 145
Sert, J. L., 227
service areas: suburban, 32; urban, 209ff
service centres, 7; towns as, 65ff
service institutions: grouping, 209ff; replanning, 211
services, location of, 51f, 65, 209ff
Sharp, Thomas, 492
Shaw, Clifford R., 184
Sheffield, 16, 79, 247, 275, 277, 337, 396, 397, 407, 422, 488; as business centre, 416, 418; market area, 414, 416
Sherman County (Kansas), 109f
shires, *see* counties
shopping centres: regional, in Britain, 216; rural-urban, 213f
Siegen, 95ff
Siegerland, 92, 95ff, 382
Silesia, Upper, 557f
silk industry, 258, 259
Simon, Sir Ernest D., 472, 473, 474
Simpson, E. S., 415
Sioux City, 329
Skelmersdale, 495
Skipton, 71
skyscrapers, 33, 163f, 221
slum clearance, 33, 401
slums, growth of, 299
Smailes, A. E., 77f, 421, 422; and Hartley, G., 217
Smith, Wilfred, 179
social unit, 4f
soil conservation districts, 521
Soissons, 452, 453
Solingen, 382
Sombart, W., 66
sous-capitale, 98
Southampton, 70, 79, 399, 416, 418; University, 420
Southend, 409
South Riding, 396
South Wales Plan, 493
Sozialbrache, 231
Spain, 26, 27, 63, 76, 439
special review areas, 488f
Spen Valley, 274
Spengler, O., 572
Spokane, 315, 331
sprawl, urban, 24, 25, 526
Stadt, 20, 74, 244
Städtchen, 74
Stadtregion, 240, 373
Stamford (Conn.), 297
standard of living, effects of rising, 31
star plan, of city lay-out, 167
State Planning Boards, U.S.A., 507
status areas, 41, 47
Steers, J. A., 175
Stephenson, F. and G., 204
Stewart, P. W., 252
Stockholm, 27, 44, 131, 170, 179, 201, 215, 224, 337; Greater, 152; land use, 153ff; method of growth, 152ff; new suburbs, 160; population distribution, 152, 153
Stockport, 429
Stoke on Trent, 418

INDEX

Strasbourg, 76, 91, 349, 352, 364, 451, 460, 561
Stretford, 429, 473
Strong, Helen M., 319, 513, 515
Stuttgart, 11, 76, 91, 337, 344, 356, 359, 373, 380, 550
sub-towns, 78
suburban area, of city, 13
suburbs, population growth, 36, 296ff
Sunderland, 406
super-city, 13, 14
supermarkets, 216
surveys, social, 120
Swansea, 16, 397, 407; market area, 414
Sweden, 27f, 30, 64, 73, 233; retail trade, 72
Switzerland, 30, 64, 90, 212, 232, 337, 556
symbiosis, town/country, 230f
Syracuse (N.Y.), 72, 292, 297, 304, 318

Tacoma, 292, 293, 295
Tampa, 293, 312, 319
taxation, municipal, 569; (U.S.A.), 525
Taylor, Eva G. R., 479, 480
Taylor, Griffith, 131
Teesmouth/Teesside, 397, 399
Tennessee Valley Authority, 3, 443, 507, 508, 509f
Texas, 17
Theodorson, G. A., 201, 255
Thionville, 349
Thomas, L. F., and Crisler, R. M., 313
Thrasher, F. M., 184
von Thünen, J. H., 246, 249
Thuringia, 531, 533
Tilburg, 347
Tokyo, 179
Toledo (O.), 318
Toronto, 131, 170, 441, 492, 528
Toul, 452
Toulon, 349
Toulouse, 350, 364, 370, 451, 459, 460
Tourcoing, 337, 349, 364, 557
tourism, increase, 33, 232, 301
Tours, 366, 367, 451, 453, 459
Towards a National Survey, 478
town(s): classification, 354f; definition, 20; distribution, factors affecting, 54ff; fully-fledged, 78; new, 44; shopping in, 215
Town and Country Planning, Ministry of, 492
town and country planning, regions, 485f
Town and Country Planning Act (1947), 176, 492
Town Development Act (1952), 493
Town Planning Acts, 472
Toynbee, A., 572
Toynbee Hall, 573
Trabantenstadt, 241
trade areas, 52ff; of city, 238; of metropolis, 13
trades and services, manpower, 26, 27
traffic, road: classification of data, 192; increasing density, 192ff
traffic analysis, 193
traffic islands, 207, 573
traffic routes, medieval German, 89
trait complex, 78

transport: and city functioning, 24; and city growth, 24f; inter-urban and intra-urban, 166, 170, 357; modern, effect on city, 12f; and town distribution, 55f
Trévoux, 452
Trewartha, G., 107
Trier, 380, 552
Troy (N.Y.), 318
Troyes, 151, 366, 452
Tucson, 290, 292, 293
Tulsa (Okla.), 330
Tunnard, C., 32, 300
Turkey, 27, 64
Twentieth Century Fund, 528
Twin Cities, *see* Minneapolis; St. Paul
Tylor, W. Russell, 204, 205
Tyneside, 16, 402, 406f, 502; Royal Commission on Local Government in, 470, 486
Tyrannopolis, 571
Tyrol, 90

Ullman, E. A., and Dacey, M. F., 69
Umland, 97, 235
underground transport, 170
Union Régionale Bretonne, 447
U.S.S.R., 3, 439
Unions, Poor Law, 62, 63
unit, social, *see* social unit
United Kingdom: national product, 30; occupations, 27; *see also* Britain; England
United States, 26, 27, 29, 30, 31, 33, 36, 41, 63, 65, 251ff; central business districts, 221ff; centrifugal drift, 181; city access, areas, 294, 295; city regions, 284ff; —— changing structure, 296ff; city traffic trends, 190f; conurbations, 16; functional centrality in, 81ff, 102ff; highway development, 301; inter-urban transport, 25; journey to work, 189f; local government reorganization, 103; metropolitan cities, 11, 14; —— regions, 313ff, 523ff; Middle West cities, 67; population, density, 179; —— distribution, 286, 522; —— growth, urban, 288ff; regionalism in, 439, 505ff; regional planning, 508ff; regions, agricultural, 510, 511; —— economic, 513f, 522; —— geographical, 510ff; —— manufacturing, 511; —— proposals for, 514f; —— urban, 290ff; retail trade, 71f; settlement, history, 285; State planning, 507f; urban/rural population, 284, 289; *see also* names of cities and States
units, social, hierarchy of, 202
universities: growth of, 31; English, 419f
Unwin, R., 497
urban districts, 467
urban institutions, typical, 77
urban regions, 15f; U.S.A., extent, 294, 295
urban/rural balance, improvement, 561
urban/rural distinction, loss of meaning, 44
urban/rural relations, 87ff
urban settlements, reasons for growth, 50
urban tract, 236, 238ff

587

INDEX

Urbanisme, Loi d', 461
urbanization, regional, 17, 290
urbanized area: definition, 239, 243; descriptions, 239ff
Urmston, 429
Uthwatt Committee, 470, 492
Utica (N.Y.), 292, 304
Utrecht, 337, 347

Valence, 260
Valenciennes, 452
Vällingby, 160
Vance, James, 218
Vance, R. B., and Smith, S., 316
Venezuela, 64
Vermont, 300
Vernon, R., 35, 298, 299
Versailles, 148, 150
Vidal de la Blache, P., 8, 363, 448, 456, 458f
Vienna, 223, 337, 554
village: definition, 107, 354; repopulation, 121; and town, interrelations, 87ff; urban, 79
villages-centres, 98
village-towns, 354
ville, 20
ville maîtresse, 98, 101, 367
villes-relais, 367
Vogel, Walther, 534, 535
Volksbegehren, 547
Vorortsbereich, 244

wage rates, and location of industry, 250
Wakefield, 277
Wales, administrative divisions, 468, 488
Wales, South, 337, 396, 397, 399, 407
Waleston, 16, 237, 396
Walker, Mabel L., 186
Wallasey, 406
Wallis, C. V., 327
Walworth County (Wisconsin), 103, 104
Ward, David, 134
Warntz, 58
Warrington, 431
Wasatch Oasis, 282
Washington, 290, 318f, 507
water consumption, U.S.A., 523
water transport, 24, 230
Watford, 216
Weald, the, 469
Webb, Sidney and Beatrice, 475
Wehrwein, G. S., 171
Weitzel, A., 538
Wells, H. G., 17, 292
Welwyn Garden City, 215, 495, 574
Weser Upland, 380, 382
Wesseling, 271
Wessex, 469, 479
West Central Germany, 551
West Dane County (Wis.), 104

Westergaard, J., 425
Westerwald, 380, 382, 551f
Westfalen, *see* Westphalia
West Midlands, conurbation, 396, 402, 404f; *see also* Birmingham
West Midlands Plan, 493
West-Ost Gefäll, 549
West Palm Beach, 293
Westphalia, 273, 345, 382; commuting pattern, 383f
West Riding, 16, 35, 71, 276, 277; *see also* Leeds–Bradford; Yorkshire, West
Wharfedale, 277
Wheeling, 323
White, M. and L., 573
Whyte, William H., 208
Wiesbaden, 91
Wigan, 397, 400, 431
Wilkes-Barre, 319
William-Olsson, W., 131, 152, 157, 209, 354
Wilmington, 321
Winston-Salem, 293
Wirtschaftsbezirke, 538
Wirtschaftsgebeiete, 536
Wirtschaftskammer, 535
Wirtschaftsprovinzen, 538
Wisconsin, 103ff, 115ff, 508
Wissink, G. A., 171
Wissler, 6
Wolfsburg, 45, 358, 549, 550; commuting pattern, 386
Woodbury, Coleman, 527
work, journey to, 186ff, 356ff
World's Metropolitan Areas, 243
Worringen, 269
Wright, A. J., 513
Wright, Frank Lloyd, 567
Wuppertal, 337, 373, 382
Wurster, C. B., 524
Württemberg, 46, 74, 90, 91, 250, 345, 358, 359, 375, 563ff; traffic flows, 375
Würzburg, 550, 575
Wythenshawe, 473, 494

York, 71, 274; University, 420
Yorkshire, South, 277; *see also* Sheffield; South Riding
Yorkshire Region, 275; marketing areas, 278
Yorkshire, West, conurbation, 396, 402, 405f, 412, 488, 502; *see also* West Riding; Leeds–Bradford
Youngstown, 323
Yugoslavia, 27, 64, 439

Zentralort, 58, 92
Zimmer, B. G., and Hawley, A. H., 255
zone du voisinage, 369
zoning laws, 41
Zurich, 44, 76, 91, 212, 244ff, ¶337
Zwergstädte, 90

The International Library of *Sociology*
and Social Reconstruction

Edited by W. J. H. SPROTT
Founded by KARL MANNHEIM

ROUTLEDGE & KEGAN PAUL
BROADWAY HOUSE, CARTER LANE, LONDON, E.C.4

CONTENTS

General Sociology	3	Sociology of Religion	9
Foreign Classics of Sociology	3	Sociology of Art and Literature	9
Social Structure	4	Sociology of Knowledge	9
Sociology and Politics	4	Urban Sociology	10
Foreign Affairs: Their Social, Political and Economic Foundations	5	Rural Sociology	10
		Sociology of Migration	11
Criminology	5	Sociology of Industry and Distribution	11
Social Psychology	6		
Sociology of the Family	7	Anthropology	12
The Social Services	7	Documentary	13
Sociology of Education	8	*Reports of the Institute of Community Studies*	14
Sociology of Culture	9		

PRINTED IN GREAT BRITAIN BY HEADLEY BROTHERS LTD
109 KINGSWAY LONDON WC2 AND ASHFORD KENT

International Library of Sociology

GENERAL SOCIOLOGY

Brown, Robert. Explanation in Social Science. *208 pp. 1963. (2nd Impression 1964.) 25s.*
Gibson, Quentin. The Logic of Social Enquiry. *240 pp. 1960. (2nd Impression 1963.) 24s.*
Goldschmidt, Professor Walter. Understanding Human Society. *272 pp. 1959. 21s.*
Homans, George C. Sentiments and Activities: Essays in Social Science. *336 pp. 1962. 32s.*
Jarvie, I. C. The Revolution in Anthropology. *Foreword by Ernest Gellner. 272 pp. 1964. 40s.*
Johnson, Harry M. Sociology: a Systematic Introduction. *Foreword by Robert K. Merton. 710 pp. 1961. (4th Impression 1964.) 42s.*
Mannheim, Karl. Essays on Sociology and Social Psychology. *Edited by Paul Kecskemeti. With Editorial Note by Adolph Lowe. 344 pp. 1953. 30s.*
 Systematic Sociology: An Introduction to the Study of Society. *Edited by J. S. Erös and Professor W. A. C. Stewart. 220 pp. 1957. (2nd Impression 1959.) 24s.*
Martindale, Don. The Nature and Types of Sociological Theory. *292 pp. 1961. (2nd Impression 1965.) 35s.*
Maus, Heinz. A Short History of Sociology. *234 pp. 1962. (2nd Impression 1965.) 28s.*
Myrdal, Gunnar. Value in Social Theory: A Collection of Essays on Methodology. *Edited by Paul Streeten. 332 pp. 1958. (2nd Impression 1962.) 32s.*
Ogburn, William F., and **Nimkoff, Meyer F.** A Handbook of Sociology. *Preface by Karl Mannheim. 656 pp. 46 figures. 38 tables. 5th edition (revised) 1964. 40s.*
Parsons, Talcott, and **Smelser, Neil J.** Economy and Society: A Study in the Integration of Economic and Social Theory. *362 pp. 1956. (3rd Impression 1964.) 35s.*
Rex, John. Key Problems of Sociological Theory. *220 pp. 1961. (3rd Impression 1965.) 25s.*
Stark, Werner. The Fundamental Forms of Social Thought. *280 pp. 1962. 32s.*

FOREIGN CLASSICS OF SOCIOLOGY

Durkheim, Emile. Suicide. A Study in Sociology. *Edited and with an Introduction by George Simpson. 404 pp. 1952. (2nd Impression 1963.) 30s.*
 Socialism and Saint-Simon. *Edited with an Introduction by Alvin W. Gouldner. Translated by Charlotte Sattler from the edition originally edited with an Introduction by Marcel Mauss. 286 pp. 1959. 28s.*
 Professional Ethics and Civic Morals. *Translated by Cornelia Brookfield. 288 pp. 1957. 30s.*
Gerth, H. H., and **Mills, C. Wright.** From Max Weber: Essays in Sociology. *502 pp. 1948. (5th Impression 1964.) 35s.*
Tönnies, Ferdinand. Community and Association. (*Gemeinschaft und Gesellschaft.*) *Translated and Supplemented by Charles P. Loomis. Foreword by Pitirim A. Sorokin. 334 pp. 1955. 28s.*

SOCIAL STRUCTURE

Andrzejewski, Stanislaw. Military Organization and Society. *With a Foreword by Professor A. R. Radcliffe-Brown. 226 pp. 1 folder. 1954. 21s.*

Cole, G. D. H. Studies in Class Structure. *220 pp. 1955. (3rd Impression 1964.) 21s.*

Coontz, Sydney H. Population Theories and the Economic Interpretation. *202 pp. 1957. (2nd Impression 1961.) 25s.*

Coser, Lewis. The Functions of Social Conflict. *204 pp. 1956. (2nd Impression 1965.) 18s.*

Glass, D. V. (Ed.). Social Mobility in Britain. *Contributions by J. Berent, T. Bottomore, R. C. Chambers, J. Floud, D. V. Glass, J. R. Hall, H. T. Himmelweit, R. K. Kelsall, F. M. Martin, C. A. Moser, R. Mukherjee, and W. Ziegel. 420 pp. 1954. (2nd Impression 1963.) 40s.*

Kelsall, R. K. Higher Civil Servants in Britain: From 1870 to the Present Day. *268 pp. 31 tables. 1955. 25s.*

Marsh, David C. The Changing Social Structure in England and Wales, 1871-1961. *288 pp. 2nd edition 1965. In preparation.*

Ossowski, Stanislaw. Class Structure in the Social Consciousness. *212 pp. 1963. 25s.*

SOCIOLOGY AND POLITICS

Barbu, Zevedei. Democracy and Dictatorship: Their Psychology and Patterns of Life. *300 pp. 1956. 28s.*

Crick, Bernard. The American Science of Politics: Its Origins and Conditions. *284 pp. 1959. 28s.*

Kornhauser, William. The Politics of Mass Society. *272 pp. 20 tables. 1960. (2nd Impression 1965.) 28s.*

Laidler, Harry W. Social-Economic Movements: An Historical and Comparative Survey of Socialism, Communism, Co-operation, Utopianism; and other Systems of Reform and Reconstruction. *864 pp. 16 plates. 1 figure. 1949. (3rd Impression 1960.) 50s.*

Mannheim, Karl. Freedom, Power and Democratic Planning. *Edited by Hans Gerth and Ernest K. Bramstedt. 424 pp. 1951. (2nd Impression 1965.) 35s.*

Mansur, Fatma. Process of Independence. *Foreword by A. H. Hanson. 208 pp. 1962. 25s.*

Martin, David A. Pacificism: an Historical and Sociological Study. *202 pp. 1965. 30s.*

Myrdal, Gunnar. The Political Element in the Development of Economic Theory. *Translated from the German by Paul Streeten. 282 pp. 1953. (4th Impression 1965.) 25s.*

Polanyi, Michael, F.R.S. The Logic of Liberty: Reflections and Rejoinders. *228 pp. 1951. 18s.*

Verney, Douglas V. The Analysis of Political Systems. *264 pp. 1959. (3rd Impression 1965.) 28s.*

Wootton, Graham. The Politics of Influence: British Ex-Servicemen, Cabinet Decisions and Cultural Changes, 1917 to 1957. *320 pp. 1963. 30s.*

FOREIGN AFFAIRS: THEIR SOCIAL, POLITICAL AND ECONOMIC FOUNDATIONS

Baer, Gabriel. Population and Society in the Arab East. *Translated by Hanna Szöke. 228 pp. 10 maps. 1964. 40s.*

Bonné, Alfred. The Economic Development of the Middle East: An Outline of Planned Reconstruction after the War. *192 pp. 58 tables. 1945. (3rd Impression 1953.) 16s.*

State and Economics in the Middle East: A Society in Transition. *482 pp. 2nd (revised) edition 1955. (2nd Impression 1960.) 40s.*

Studies in Economic Development: with special reference to Conditions in the Under-developed Areas of Western Asia and India. *322 pp. 84 tables. 2nd edition 1960. 32s.*

Mayer, J. P. Political Thought in France from the Revolution to the Fifth Republic. *164 pp. 3rd edition (revised) 1961. 16s.*

Schlesinger, Rudolf. Central European Democracy and its Background: Economic and Political Group Organization. *432 pp. 1953. 40s.*

Thomson, David Meyer E., and **Briggs, A.** Patterns of Peacemaking. *408 pp. 1945. 25s.*

Trouton, Ruth. Peasant Renaissance in Yugoslavia 1900-1950: A Study of the Development of Yugoslav Peasant Society as affected by Education. *370 pp. 1 map. 1952. 28s.*

CRIMINOLOGY

Ancel, Marc. Social Defence: A Modern Approach to Criminal Problems. *Foreword by Leon Radzinowicz. 240 pp. 1965. 32s.*

Cloward, Richard A., and **Ohlin, Lloyd E.** Delinquency and Opportunity: A Theory of Delinquent Gangs. *248 pp. 1961. 25s.*

Downes, David. The Delinquent Solution. A Study in Sub-cultural Theory. *304 pp. 1965. 42s.*

Dunlop, A. B., and **McCabe, S.** Young Men in Detention Centres. *192 pp. 1965. 28s.*

Friedländer, Dr. Kate. The Psycho-Analytical Approach to Juvenile Delinquency: Theory, Case Studies, Treatment. *320 pp. 1947. (5th Impression 1961.) 28s.*

Glueck, Sheldon and **Eleanor.** Family Environment and Delinquency. *With the statistical assistance of Rose W. Kneznek. 340 pp. 1962. 35s.*

Mannheim, Hermann. Group Problems in Crime and Punishment, and other Studies in Criminology and Criminal Law. *336 pp. 1955. 28s.*

Comparative Criminology: a Textbook. *Two volumes. 416 pp. and 360 pp. 1965. 42s. each.*

Morris, Terence. The Criminal Area: A Study in Social Ecology. *Foreword by Hermann Mannheim. 232 pp. 25 tables. 4 maps. 1957. 25s.*

Morris, Terence and **Pauline,** assisted by **Barbara Barer.** Pentonville: a Sociological Study of an English Prison. *416 pp. 16 plates. 1963. 50s.*

Spencer, John C. Crime and the Services. *Foreword by Hermann Mannheim. 336 pp. 1954. 28s.*

Trasler, Gordon. The Explanation of Criminality. *144 pp. 1962. 20s.*

SOCIAL PSYCHOLOGY

Barbu, Zevedei. Problems of Historical Psychology. *248 pp. 1960. 25s.*

Blackburn, Julian. Psychology and the Social Pattern. *184 pp. 1945. (7th Impression 1964.) 16s.*

Fleming, C. M. Adolescence: Its Social Psychology: With an Introduction to recent findings from the fields of Anthropology, Physiology, Medicine, Psychometrics and Sociometry. *271 pp. 2nd edition (revised) 1963. (2nd Impression 1964.) 25s.*

The Social Psychology of Education: An Introduction and Guide to Its Study. *136 pp. 2nd edition (revised) 1959. 11s.*

Fleming, C. M. (Ed.). Studies in the Social Psychology of Adolescence. *Contributions by J. E. Richardson, J. F. Forrester, J. K. Shukla and P. J. Higginbotham. Foreword by the editor. 292 pp. 29 figures. 13 tables. 5 folder tables. 1951. 23s.*

Halmos, Paul. Towards a Measure of Man: The Frontiers of Normal Adjustment. *276 pp. 1957. 28s.*

Homans, George C. The Human Group. *Foreword by Bernard DeVoto. Introduction by Robert K. Merton. 526 pp. 1951. (4th Impression 1965.) 35s.*

Social Behaviour: its Elementary Forms. *416 pp. 1961. 30s.*

Klein, Josephine. The Study of Groups. *226 pp. 31 figures. 5 tables. 1956. (4th Impression 1965.) 21s.*

Linton, Ralph. The Cultural Background of Personality. *132 pp. 1947. (5th Impression 1965.) 16s.*

Mayo, Elton. The Social Problems of an Industrial Civilization. With an appendix on the Political Problem. *180 pp. 1949. (4th Impression 1961.) 18s.*

Ridder, J. C. de. The Personality of the Urban African in South Africa. A Thematic Apperception Test Study. *196 pp. 12 plates. 1961. 25s.*

Rose, Arnold M. (Ed.). Mental Health and Mental Disorder: A Sociological Approach. *Chapters by 46 contributors. 654 pp. 1956. 45s.*

Human Behaviour and Social Processes: an Interactionist Approach. *Contributions by Arnold M. Ross, Ralph H. Turner, Anselm Strauss, Everett C. Hughes, E. Franklin Frazier, Howard S. Becker, et al. 696 pp. 1962. 60s.*

Smelser, Neil J. Theory of Collective Behaviour. *448 pp. 1962. 45s.*

Spinley, Dr. B. M. The Deprived and the Privileged: Personality Development in English Society. *232 pp. 1953. 20s.*

Wolfenstein, Martha. Disaster: A Psychological Essay. *264 pp. 1957. 23s.*

Young, Professor Kimball. Personality and Problems of Adjustment, *742 pp. 12 figures, 9 tables, 2nd edition (revised) 1952. (2nd Impression 1959.) 40s.*
Handbook of Social Psychology. *658 pp. 16 figures. 10 tables. 2nd edition (revised) 1957. (3rd Impression 1963.) 40s.*

SOCIOLOGY OF THE FAMILY

Banks, J. A. Prosperity and Parenthood: A study of Family Planning among the Victorian Middle Classes. *262 pp. 1954. (2nd Impression 1965.) 24s.*
Chapman, Dennis. The Home and Social Status. *336 pp. 8 plates. 3 figures. 117 tables. 1955. 35s.*
Klein, Josephine. Samples from English Cultures. *1965.*
  1. Three Preliminary Studies and Aspects of Adult Life in England. *447 pp. 50s.*
  2. Child-Rearing Practices and Index. *247 pp. 35s.*
Klein, Viola. Britain's Married Women Workers. *176 pp. 1965. 28s.*
Myrdal, Alva and **Klein, Viola.** Women's Two Roles: Home and Work. *238 pp. 27 tables. 1956. (2nd Impression 1962.) 25s.*
Parsons, Talcott and **Bales, Robert F.** Family: Socialization and Interaction Process. *In collaboration with James Olds, Morris Zelditch and Philip E. Slater. 456 pp. 50 figures and tables. 1956. (2nd Impression 1964.) 35s.*

THE SOCIAL SERVICES

Ashdown, Margaret and **Brown, S. Clement.** Social Service and Mental Health: An Essay on Psychiatric Social Workers. *280 pp. 1953. 21s.*
Hall, M. Penelope. The Social Services of Modern England. *416 pp. 6th edition (revised) 1963. (2nd Impression with a new Preface 1965.) 30s.*
Hall, M. P., and **Howes, I. V.** The Church in Social Work. A Study of Moral Welfare Work undertaken by the Church of England. *320 pp. 1965. 35s.*
Heywood, Jean S. Children in Care: the Development of the Service for the Deprived Child. *264 pp. 2nd edition (revised) 1965. 32s.*
An Introduction to teaching Casework Skills. *192 pp. 1964. 28s.*
Jones, Kathleen. Lunacy, Law and Conscience, 1744-1845: the Social History of the Care of the Insane. *268 pp. 1955. 25s.*
Mental Health and Social Policy, 1845-1959. *264 pp. 1960. 28s.*
Jones, Kathleen and **Sidebotham, Roy.** Mental Hospitals at Work. *220 pp. 1962. 30s.*
Kastell, Jean. Casework in Child Care. *Foreword by M. Brooke Willis. 320 pp. 1962. 35s.*
Rooff, Madeline. Voluntary Societies and Social Policy. *350 pp. 15 tables. 1957. 35s.*
Shenfield, B. E. Social Policies for Old Age: A Review of Social Provision for Old Age in Great Britain. *260 pp. 39 tables. 1957. 25s.*

Timms, Noel. Psychiatric Social Work in Great Britain (1939-1962). *280 pp. 1964. 32s.*
Social Casework: Principles and Practice. *256 pp. 1964, 25s.*
Trasler, Gordon. In Place of Parents: A Study in Foster Care. *272 pp. 1960. (2nd Impression 1965.) 30s.*
Young, A. F., and **Ashton, E. T.** British Social Work in the Nineteenth Century. *288 pp. 1956. (2nd Impression 1963.) 28s.*

SOCIOLOGY OF EDUCATION

Banks, Olive. Parity and Prestige in English Secondary Education: a Study in Educational Sociology. *272 pp. 1955. (2nd Impression 1963.) 28s.*
Bentwich, Joseph. Education in Israel. *224 pp. 8 pp. plates. 1965. 24s.*
Blyth, W. A. L. English Primary Education. A Sociological Description. *1965.*
  1. Schools. *232 pp. 30s.*
  2. Background. *168 pp. 25s.*
Collier, K. G. The Social Purposes of Education: Personal and Social Values in Education. *268 pp. 1959. (2nd Impression 1962.) 21s.*
Dale, R. R. and **Griffith, S.** Downstream: Failure in the Grammar School. *112 pp. 1965. 20s.*
Dore, R. P. Education in Tokugawa Japan. *356 pp. 9 pp. plates. 1965. 35s.*
Edmonds, E. L. The School Inspector. *Foreword by Sir William Alexander. 214 pp. 1962. 28s.*
Evans, K. M. Sociometry and Education. *158 pp. 1962. 18s.*
Foster, P. J. Education and Social Change in Ghana. *336 pp. 3 maps. 1965.*
Fraser, W. R. Education and Society in Modern France. *150 pp. 1963. 20s.*
Hans, Nicholas. New Trends in Education in the Eighteenth Century. *278 pp. 19 tables. 1951. (2nd Impression 1965.) 25s.*
Comparative Education: A Study of Educational Factors and Traditions. *360 pp. 3rd (revised) edition 1958. (4th Impression 1964.) 25s.*
Holmes, Brian. Problems in Education. A Comparative Approach. *336 pp. 1965. 32s.*
Mannheim, Karl and **Stewart, W. A. C.** An Introduction to the Sociology of Education. *208 pp. 1962. (2nd Impression 1965.) 21s.*
Musgrove, F. Youth and the Social Order. *176 pp. 1964. 21s.*
Ortega y Gasset, Jose. Mission of the University. *Translated with an Introduction by Howard Lee Nostrand. 88 pp. 1946. (3rd Impression 1963.) 15s.*
Ottaway, A. K. C. Education and Society: An Introduction to the Sociology of Education. *With an Introduction by W. O. Lester Smith. 212 pp. Second edition (revised). 1962. (3rd Impression 1965.) 21s.*
Peers, Robert. Adult Education: A Comparative Study. *398 pp. 2nd edition 1959. 35s.*
Pritchard, D. G. Education and the Handicapped: 1760 to 1960. *258 pp. 1963. 28s.*
Samuel, R. H., and **Thomas, R. Hinton.** Education and Society in Modern Germany. *212 pp. 1949. 16s.*

Simon, Brian and **Joan** (Eds.). Educational Psychology in the U.S.S.R. Introduction by Brian and Joan Simon. Translation by Joan Simon. Papers by D. N. Bogoiavlenski and N. A. Menchinskaia, D. B. Elkonin, E. A. Fleshner, Z. I. Kalmykova, G. S. Kostiuk, V. A. Krutetski, A. N. Leontiev, A. R. Luria, E. A. Milerian, R. G. Natadze, B. M. Teplov, L. S. Vygotski, L. V. Zankov. *296 pp. 1963. 40s.*

SOCIOLOGY OF CULTURE

Fromm, Erich. The Fear of Freedom. *286 pp. 1942. (8th Impression 1960.) 21s.*
The Sane Society. *400 pp. 1956. (3rd Impression 1963.) 28s.*

Mannheim, Karl. Diagnosis of Our Time: Wartime Essays of a Sociologist. *208 pp. 1943. (7th Impression 1962.) 21s.*
Essays on the Sociology of Culture. Edited by Ernst Mannheim in co-operation with Paul Kecskemeti. Editorial Note by Adolph Lowe. *280 pp. 1956. (2nd Impression 1962.) 28s.*

Weber, Alfred. Farewell to European History: or The Conquest of Nihilism. Translated from the German by R. F. C. Hull. *224 pp. 1947. 18s.*

SOCIOLOGY OF RELIGION

Argyle, Michael. Religious Behaviour. *224 pp. 8 figures. 41 tables. 1958. (2nd Impression 1965.) 25s.*

Knight Frank H., and **Merriam, Thornton W.** The Economic Order and Religion. *242 pp. 1947. 18s.*

Watt, W. Montgomery. Islam and the Integration of Society. *320 pp. 1961. (2nd Impression.) 32s.*

SOCIOLOGY OF ART AND LITERATURE

Beljame, Alexandre. Men of Letters and the English Public in the Eighteenth Century: 1660-1744, Dryden, Addison, Pope. Edited with an Introduction and Notes by Bonamy Dobree. Translated by E. O. Lorimer. *532 pp. 1948. 32s.*

Misch, Georg. A History of Autobiography in Antiquity. Translated by E. W. Dickes. 2 Volumes. *Vol. 1, 364 pp., Vol. 2, 372 pp. 1950. 45s. the set.*

Schucking, L. L. The Sociology of Literary Taste. *112 pp. 2nd edition, 1965. 18s.*

Silbermann, Alphons. The Sociology of Music. *224 pp. 1963. 28s.*

SOCIOLOGY OF KNOWLEDGE

Hodges, H. A. The Philosophy of Wilhelm Dilthey. *410 pp. 1952. 30s.*

Mannheim, Karl. Essays on the Sociology of Knowledge. Edited by Paul Kecskemeti. Editorial note by Adolph Lowe. *352 pp. 1952. (3rd Impression 1964.) 35s.*

International Library of Sociology

Schlesinger, Rudolf. Marx: His Time and Ours. *464 pp. 1950. (2nd Impression 1951.) 32s.*

Stark, W. America: Ideal and Reality. The United States of 1776 in Contemporary Philosophy. *136 pp. 1947. 12s.*

—The Sociology of Knowledge: An Essay in Aid of a Deeper Understanding of the History of Ideas. *384 pp. 1958. (2nd Impression 1960.) 36s.*

—Montesquieu: Pioneer of the Sociology of Knowledge. *244 pp. 1960. 25s.*

URBAN SOCIOLOGY

Anderson, Nels. The Urban Community: A World Perspective. *532 pp. 1960. 35s.*

Ashworth, William. The Genesis of Modern British Town Planning: A Study in Economic and Social History of the Nineteenth and Twentieth Centuries. *288 pp. 1954. (2nd Impression 1965.) 32s.*

Bracey, Howard. Neighbours: Neighbouring and Neighbourliness on New Estates and Subdivisions in England and the U.S.A. *220 pp. 1964. 28s.*

Cullingworth, J. B. Housing Needs and Planning Policy: A Restatement of the Problems of Housing Need and "Overspill" in England and Wales. *232 pp. 44 tables. 8 maps. 1960. 28s.*

Dickinson, Robert E. City and Region: A Geographical Interpretation. *608 pp. 125 figures. 1964. 60s.*

—The West European City: A Geographical Interpretation. *600 pp. 129 maps. 29 plates. 2nd edition 1962. (2nd Impression 1963.) 55s.*

Dore, R. P. City Life in Japan: A Study of a Tokyo Ward. *498 pp. 8 plates. 4 figures. 24 tables. 1958. (2nd Impression 1963.) 45s.*

Jennings, Hilda. Societies in the Making: a Study of Development and Redevelopment within a County Borough. *Foreword by D. A. Clark. 286 pp. 1962. 32s.*

Kerr, Madeline. The People of Ship Street, *240 pp. 1958. 23s.*

Mann, P. H. An Approach to Urban Sociology. *240 pp. 1965. 30s.*

Morris, R. N., and **Mogey, J.** The Sociology of Housing. Studies at Berinsfield. *232 pp. 4 pp. plates. 1965. 42s.*

Rosser, C., and **Harris, C.** The Family and Social Change. A Study of Family and Kinship in a South Wales Town. *352 pp. 8 maps. 1965. 45s.*

RURAL SOCIOLOGY

Bracey, H. E. English Rural Life: Village Activities, Organizations and Institutions. *302 pp. 1959. 30s.*

Infield, Henrik F. Co-operative Living in Palestine. *With a Foreword by General Sir Arthur Wauchope, G.C.B. 170 pp. 8 plates. 7 tables. 1946. 12s. 6d.*

Littlejohn, James. Westrigg: the Sociology of a Cheviot Parish. *172 pp. 5 figures. 1963. 25s.*

Saville, John. Rural Depopulation in England and Wales, 1851-1951. *Foreword by Leonard Elmhirst. 286 pp. 6 figures. 39 tables. 1 map. 1957. 28s. (Dartington Hall Studies in Rural Sociology.)*

Williams, W. M. The Country Craftsman: A Study of Some Rural Crafts and the Rural Industries Organization in England. *248 pp. 9 figures. 1958. 25s. (Dartington Hall Studies in Rural Sociology.)*
  The Sociology of an English Village: Gosforth. *272 pp. 12 figures. 13 tables. 1956. (3rd Impression 1964.) 25s.*

SOCIOLOGY OF MIGRATION

Eisenstadt, S. N. The Absorption of Immigrants: a Comparative Study based mainly on the Jewish Community in Palestine and the State of Israel. *288 pp. 1954. 28s.*

SOCIOLOGY OF INDUSTRY AND DISTRIBUTION

Anderson, Nels. Work and Leisure. *280 pp. 1961. 28s.*

Blau, Peter M., and Scott, W. Richard. Formal Organizations: a Comparative approach. *Introduction and Additional Bibliography by J. H. Smith. 328 pp. 1963. (2nd Impression 1964.) 28s.*

Jefferys, Margot, with the assistance of Winifred Moss. Mobility in the Labour Market: Employment Changes in Battersea and Dagenham. *Preface by Barbara Wootton. 186 pp. 51 tables. 1954. 15s.*

Levy, A. B. Private Corporations and Their Control. *Two Volumes. Vol. 1, 464 pp., Vol. 2, 432 pp. 1950. 80s. the set.*

Levy, Hermann. The Shops of Britain: A Study of Retail Distribution. *268 pp. 1948. (2nd Impression 1949.) 21s.*

Liepmann, Kate. The Journey to Work: Its Significance for Industrial and Community Life. *With a Foreword by A. M. Carr-Saunders. 230 pp. 40 tables. 3 folders. 1944. (2nd Impression 1945.) 18s.*
  Apprenticeship: An Enquiry into its Adequacy under Modern Conditions. *Foreword by H. D. Dickinson. 232 pp. 6 tables. 1960. (2nd Impression.) 23s.*

Millerson, Geoffrey. The Qualifying Associations: a Study in Professionalization. *320 pp. 1964. 42s.*

Smelser, Neil J. Social Change in the Industrial Revolution: An Application of Theory to the Lancashire Cotton Industry, 1770-1840. *468 pp. 12 figures. 14 tables. 1959. (2nd Impression 1960.) 40s.*

Williams, Gertrude. Recruitment to Skilled Trades. *240 pp. 1957. 23s.*

Young, A. F. Industrial Injuries Insurance: an Examination of British Policy. *192 pp. 1964. 30s.*

ANTHROPOLOGY
(*Demy 8vo.*)

Crook, David and Isabel. Revolution in a Chinese Village: Ten Mile Inn. *230 pp. 8 plates. 1 map. 1959. 21s.*
The First Years of Yangyi Commune. *288 pp. 12 plates. 1965. 42s.*

Dube, S. C. Indian Village. *Foreword by Morris Edward Opler. 276 pp. 4 plates. 1955. (5th Impression 1965.) 25s.*
India's Changing Villages: Human Factors in Community Development *260 pp. 8 plates. 1 map. 1958. (2nd Impression 1960.) 25s.*

Fei, Hsiao-Tung. Peasant Life in China: a Field Study of Country Life in the Yangtze Valley. *Foreword by Bronislaw Malinowski. 320 pp. 14 plates. 1939. (5th Impression 1962.) 30s.*

Firth, Raymond. Malay Fishermen. Their Peasant Economy. *420 pp. 17 pp. plates. 2nd edition (revised and enlarged 1965.) 55s.*

Gulliver, P. H. The Family Herds. A Study of two Pastoral Tribes in East Africa, The Jie and Turkana. *304 pp. 4 plates. 19 figures. 1955. 25s.*
Social Control in an African Society: a Study of the Arusha, Agricultural Masai of Northern Tanganyika. *320 pp. 8 plates. 10 figures. 1963. 35s.*

Hogbin, Ian. Transformation Scene. The Changing Culture of a New Guinea Village. *340 pp. 22 plates. 2 maps. 1951. 30s.*

Hsu, Francis L. K. Under the Ancestors' Shadow: Chinese Culture and Personality. *346 pp. 26 figures. 1949. 21s.*

Lowie, Professor Robert H. Social Organization. *494 pp. 1950. (3rd Impression 1962.) 35s.*

Maunier, René. The Sociology of Colonies: An Introduction to the Study of Race Contact. *Edited and translated by E. O. Lorimer. 2 Volumes. Vol. 1, 430 pp. Vol. 2, 356 pp. 1949. 70s. the set.*

Mayer, Adrian C. Caste and Kinship in Central India: A Village and its Region, *328 pp. 16 plates. 15 figures. 16 tables. 1960. (2nd Impression 1965.) 35s.*
Peasants in the Pacific: A Study of Fiji Indian Rural Society. *232 pp. 16 plates. 10 figures. 14 tables. 1961. 35s.*

Osborne, Harold. Indians of the Andes: Aymaras and Quechuas. *292 pp. 8 plates. 2 maps. 1952. 25s.*

Smith, Raymond T. The Negro Family in British Guiana: Family Structure and Social Status in the Villages. *With a Foreword by Meyer Fortes. 314 pp. 8 plates. 1 figure. 4 maps. 1956. (2nd Impression 1965.) 28s.*

DOCUMENTARY
(Demy 8vo.)

Meek, Dorothea L. (Ed.). Soviet Youth: Some Achievements and Problems. *Excerpts from the Soviet Press, translated by the editor. 280 pp. 1957. 28s.*

Schlesinger, Rudolf (Ed.). Changing Attitudes in Soviet Russia.
1. The Family in the U.S.S.R. *Documents and Readings, with an Introduction by the editor. 434 pp. 1949. 30s.*
2. The Nationalities Problem and Soviet Administration. Selected Readings on the Development of Soviet Nationalities Policies. *Introduced by the editor. Translated by W. W. Gottlieb. 324 pp. 1956. 30s.*

Reports of the Institute of Community Studies

(*Demy 8vo.*)

Cartwright, Ann. Human Relations and Hospital Care. *272 pp. 1964. 30s.*

Jackson, Brian. Streaming: an Education System in Miniature. *168 pp. 1964. 21s. Paper 10s.*

Jackson, Brian and **Marsden, Dennis.** Education and the Working Class: Some General Themes raised by a Study of 88 Working-class Children in a Northern Industrial City. *268 pp. 2 folders. 1962. (3rd Impression 1965.) 28s.*

Marris, Peter. Widows and their Families. *Foreword by Dr. John Bowlby. 184 pp. 18 tables. Statistical Summary. 1958. 18s.*

Family and Social Change in an African City. A Study of Rehousing in Lagos. *196 pp. 1 map. 4 plates. 53 tables. 1961. 25s.*

The Experience of Higher Education. *232 pp. 27 tables. 1964. 25s.*

Mills, Enid. Living with Mental Illness: a Study in East London. *Foreword by Morris Carstairs. 196 pp. 1962. 28s.*

Runciman, W. G. Relative Deprivation and Social Justice. *344 pp. 1966. 40s.*

Townsend, Peter. The Family Life of Old People: An Inquiry in East London. *Foreword by J. H. Sheldon. 300 pp. 3 figures. 63 tables. 1957. (2nd Impression 1961.) 30s.*

Willmott, Peter. The Evolution of a Community: a study of Dagenham after forty years. *168 pp. 2 maps. 1963. 21s.*

Willmott, Peter and **Young, Michael.** Family and Class in a London Suburb. *202 pp. 47 tables. 1960. (2nd Impression 1961.) 21s.*

Young, Michael. Innovation and Research in Education. *192 pp. 1965. 25s.*

Young, Michael and **Willmott, Peter.** Family and Kinship in East London. *Foreword by Richard M. Titmuss. 252 pp. 39 tables. 1957. (3rd Impression 1965.) 25s.*

The British Journal of Sociology. Edited by Terence P. Morris. Vol. 1, No. 1, March 1950 and Quarterly. Roy 8vo., £2 10s. p.a.; 12s. 6d. a number, post free.

All prices are net and subject to alteration without notice